Fundamentals of **Investing, The Financial System,** and **Financial Markets**

Custom Edition for
Florida State University

Taken from:

Fundamentals of Investing, Ninth Edition
by Lawrence J. Gitman and Michael D. Joehnk

Money, The Financial System, and the Economy, Fifth Edition
by R. Glenn Hubbard

Cover Art: *Pattern 9/Supply & Demand*, by Angela Sciaraffa.

Taken from:

Fundamentals of Investing, Ninth Edition
by Lawrence J. Gitman, and Michael D. Joehnk

Published by Addison-Wesley
A Pearson Education Company
Boston, Massachusetts 02116

Money, the Financial System, and the Economy, Fifth Edition
by R. Glenn Hubbard

Published by Addison-Wesley

This special edition published in cooperation with Pearson Custom Publishing.

Printed in the United States of America

10 9 8 7 6 5 4 3 2 1

ISBN 0-536-84445-3

2004160146

KK

Please visit our web site at www.pearsoncustom.com

PEARSON CUSTOM PUBLISHING
75 Arlington Street, Suite 300, Boston, MA 02116
A Pearson Education Company

Brief Contents

Part One: Fundamentals of Investing

Selections taken from:
Fundamentals of Investing, Ninth Edition
by Lawrence J. Gitman, and Michael D. Joehnk

Part Two: Money, the Financial System, and the Economy

Selections taken from:
Money, the Financial System, and the Economy, Fifth Edition
by R. Glenn Hubbard

Part One: Fundamentals of Investing

Taken from:
Fundamentals of Investing, Ninth Edition
by Lawrence J. Gitman, and Michael D. Joehnk

Contents: Fundamentals of Investing

CHAPTER 10 Fixed-Income Security 243

CHAPTER 13 Mutual Funds: Professionally Managed Portfolios 287

Fundamentals of Investing

CHAPTER 1

THE INVESTMENT ENVIRONMENT

CHAPTER 1

THE INVESTMENT ENVIRONMENT

Learning Goals

After studying this chapter, you should be able to:

LG 1 Understand the meaning of the term *investment* and the factors commonly used to differentiate among types of investments.

LG 2 Describe the investment process and types of investors.

LG 3 Discuss the principal types of investment vehicles.

LG 4 Describe the steps in investing, particularly establishing investment goals, and cite fundamental personal tax considerations.

LG 5 Discuss investing over the life cycle and investing in different economic environments.

LG 6 Understand the popular types of short-term investment vehicles.

In just a few years, the world of investments has moved to center stage in American life. Twenty years ago, the only exposure to investment news that most people had came in the form of a 10-second announcement on the evening news about the change in the Dow Jones Industrial Average that day. Today, more than half of all Americans own stocks, and many of them have been investing only since 1996. Finding information about investing has become easier than ever. Cable TV stations like CNNfn specialize in business and financial news, and network newscasters feature business news more prominently. You can't pass a newsstand without seeing headlines that scream, "Ten Stocks to Buy Now!" or "The Hottest Mutual Funds," as well as advice on how to change your investment strategies as current market conditions change. Besides the *Wall Street Journal*, you can subscribe to *Investors Business Daily*, *Barron's*, *Kiplinger's Personal Finance Magazine*, *Money*, *Smart Money*, and dozens of other publications that focus on investing.

The Internet has played a major role in opening the world of investing to individual investors. By giving them access to tools formerly restricted to investment professionals, it creates a more level playing field. The Internet also makes enormous amounts of information readily available and puts a way to trade securities just a few mouse clicks away. In short, technology makes investing much easier—and at the same time can increase the risks for inexperienced investors.

Regardless of whether you conduct transactions online or use a traditional broker, the same investment fundamentals presented in this textbook apply. Chapter 1 introduces the various types of investments, the investment process, key investment vehicles, the role of investment plans, and the importance of meeting liquidity needs. Becoming familiar with investment alternatives and developing realistic investment plans should greatly increase your chance of achieving financial success.

Investments and the Investment Process

LG 1 LG 2

Note: The Learning Goals shown at the beginning of the chapter are keyed to text discussions using these icons.

investment
any vehicle into which funds can be placed with the expectation that it will generate positive income and/or preserve or increase its value.

returns
the rewards from investing, received as current income and/or increased value.

Note: *Investing in Action* boxes, which appear in each chapter, describe real-life investing situations or elaborate on innovative investment vehicles. These high-interest boxes have been written with student readers in mind and contain Critical Thinking Questions for discussion.

You are probably already an investor. If you have money in a savings account, you already have at least one investment to your name. An **investment** is simply any vehicle into which funds can be placed with the expectation that it will generate positive income and/or preserve or increase its value. The rewards, or **returns,** from investing are received in two basic forms: current income and increased value. For example, money invested in a savings account provides current income in the form of periodic interest payments. A share of common stock purchased as an investment is expected to increase in value between the time it is purchased and the time it is sold. Historically, since 1926 the average annual return on a savings account was about 3%, whereas the average annual return on the common stock of large companies was about 12.2%. Of course, during the major market downturn driven by the collapse of the high-flying tech stocks and an economic slowdown that started in 2000 and ran until late 2002, the returns on nearly all investment vehicles were well below these long-term historical averages. (We'll look more carefully at historical returns in Chapter 4.)

Is cash placed in a simple (no-interest) checking account an investment? No, because it fails both tests of the definition. It does not provide added income, nor does its value increase. (In fact, if the money kept in a checking account is in excess of the amount needed to pay bills or if the interest rate is high, its value is likely to decrease, because it is eroded over time by inflation.)

Before we proceed, you might want to establish a baseline on your investing "know-how" by testing your Investment IQ using the instrument given in the *Investing in Action* box on page 4. Studying this textbook should allow you to improve your Investment IQ. We now begin our study of investments by looking at types of investments and at the structure of the investment process.

Types of Investments

When you invest, the organization in which you invest—whether it is a company or a government entity—offers you an expected future benefit in exchange for the current use of your funds. Organizations compete for the use of your funds. The one that will get your investment dollars is the one that offers a benefit you judge to be better than any competitor offers. But, different investors judge benefits differently. As a result, investments of every type are available, from "sure things" such as earning 1% interest on your bank savings account, to the possibility of tripling your money fast by investing in a newly issued biotech stock. The investments you choose will depend on your resources, your goals, and your personality. We can differentiate types of investments on the basis of a number of factors.

securities
investments that represent debt or ownership or the legal right to acquire or sell an ownership interest.

property
investments in real property or tangible personal property.

Securities or Property Investments that represent debt or ownership or the legal right to acquire or sell an ownership interest are called **securities.** The most common types of securities are stocks, bonds, and options. The focus of this book is primarily on securities, particularly common stocks.

Property, on the other hand, consists of investments in real property or tangible personal property. *Real property* is land, buildings, and that which is permanently affixed to the land. *Tangible personal property* includes items such as gold, artwork, antiques, and other collectibles.

INVESTING IN ACTION

TEST YOUR INVESTMENT IQ

How much do you know about investing? Take this investor literacy quiz, developed by *Money* magazine and the Vanguard Group to test the investment savvy of 1,500 mutual fund investors.

The average score (for the full 20-question quiz) was only 37%. But don't despair if you, too, don't score well. You'll learn the answers to these and many other questions from this book.

1. Which type of investment has offered the best protection against inflation over long periods of time?
   a. Money market funds and bank accounts.
   b. Government National Mortgage Association securities (also known as Ginnie Maes or GNMAs).
   c. Stocks.
   d. Corporate bonds.
2. Common stocks always provide higher returns than bonds or money market investments.
   a. True. b. False.
3. As an individual, the most you can contribute to an IRA each year is:
   a. $1,000. b. $2,000.
   c. $5,000. d. $10,000.
4. Interest earned by municipal bonds is exempt from federal income tax.
   a. True. b. False.
5. If interest rates declined, the price of a bond or bond fund generally would:
   a. Increase.
   b. Decrease.
   c. Stay about the same.
   d. It is impossible to predict.
6. If you own only U.S. stocks in your investment portfolio, you will reduce your overall risk by adding international stocks.
   a. True. b. False.
7. Which market benchmark or stock exchange is the best gauge of the performance of the entire U.S. stock market?
   a. S&P 500 Index.
   b. Wilshire 5000 Total Market Index.
   c. Dow Jones Industrial Average.
   d. Nasdaq Composite Index.
8. If you invest in a 401(k) plan at work, you are not eligible to contribute to an IRA.
   a. True. b. False.
9. From 1926 to 2002, the return on U.S. stocks has averaged:
   a. 5% per year.
   b. 12% per year.
   c. 19% per year.
   d. 28% per year.
10. Which of the following is not an attribute of mutual funds?
    a. Diversification.
    b. Professional management.
    c. Guaranteed return.
    d. None of the above.
11. If your investment returned 10% last year and inflation was 3%, your "real" (i.e., adjusted for inflation) return was:
    a. 3.3%. b. 7%.
    c. 13%. d. 30%.
12. A mutual fund that invests in government securities is guaranteed not to lose money.
    a. True. b. False.

Answers: 1 (c); 2 (b); 3 (b); 4 (a); 5 (a); 6 (a); 7 (b); 8 (b); 9 (b); 10 (c); 11 (b); 12 (b).

CRITICAL THINKING QUESTION How high is your investment IQ, as measured by the quiz? Make a note of your score so that you can impress yourself at the end of the course with how much you've learned.

Sources: Laura Lallos, "What's Your Investing IQ?" *Money,* August 2000, pp. 91–92; quiz downloaded from cgi.money.com/cgi-bin/money/polls/vanguard/vanguard.plx.

Note: Theinvestingportal.com is one of many sites that provide extensive links to other Web sites for investors. The links are organized by popular search terms and "best of the Web". You will find links to many of the other sites discussed in this chapter, as well as many others, at www.theinvestingportal.com.

direct investment
investment in which an investor directly acquires a claim on a security or property.

indirect investment
investment made in a *portfolio,* or collection of securities or properties.

portfolio
collection of securities or properties, typically constructed to meet one or more investment goals.

debt
funds lent in exchange for interest income and the promised repayment of the loan at a given future date.

equity
ongoing ownership in a business or property.

derivative securities
securities that are structured to exhibit characteristics similar to those of an underlying security or asset and that derive their value from the underlying security or asset.

risk
the chance that actual investment returns will differ from those expected.

speculation
the purchase of high-risk investment vehicles that offer highly uncertain returns and future value.

short-term investments
investments that typically mature within one year

long-term investments
investments with maturities of longer than a year or with no maturity at all.

Direct or Indirect A **direct investment** is one in which an investor directly acquires a claim on a security or property. If you buy a stock or bond in order to earn income or preserve value, you have made a direct investment.

An **indirect investment** is an investment made in a **portfolio,** or collection of securities or properties, typically constructed to meet one or more investment goals. For example, you may purchase a share of a *mutual fund.* This share gives you a claim on a fraction of the entire portfolio rather than on the security of a single firm.

Debt, Equity, or Derivative Securities Usually, an investment represents either a debt or an equity interest. **Debt** represents funds lent in exchange for interest income and the promised repayment of the loan at a given future date. When you buy a debt instrument like a *bond,* in effect you lend money to the issuer. The issuer agrees to pay you a stated rate of interest over a specified period of time, at the end of which the original sum will be returned.

Equity represents ongoing ownership in a business or property. An equity investment may be held as a security or by title to a specific property. The most popular type of equity security is *common stock.*

Derivative securities are neither debt nor equity. They derive their value from, and have characteristics similar to those of, an underlying security or asset. *Options* are an example: An investor essentially buys the opportunity to sell or buy another security or asset at a specified price during a given period of time. Options and other derivative security investments, though not so common as debt and equity investments, have grown rapidly in popularity in recent years.

Low- or High-Risk Investments are sometimes differentiated on the basis of risk. As used in finance, **risk** is the chance that actual investment returns will differ from those expected. Of course, the actual return depends on the amount of the investment that is recouped. The broader the range of possible values or returns associated with an investment, the greater its risk.

Investors are confronted with a continuum of investments that range from low to high risk. Although each type of investment vehicle has a basic risk characteristic, the actual level of risk depends on the specific vehicle. For example, stocks are generally believed to be more risky than bonds. However, it is not difficult to find high-risk bonds that are more risky than the stock of a financially sound firm such as IBM or McDonald's.

Low-risk investments are those considered safe with regard to the receipt of a positive return. *High-risk investments* are considered speculative: Their levels of return are highly uncertain. **Speculation** offers highly uncertain returns and future value, so it is high-risk investment. Because of this greater risk, the returns associated with speculation are expected to be greater. Both investment and speculation differ from gambling, which involves playing games of chance. In this book we will use the term *investment* for both investment and speculation.

Short- or Long-Term The life of an investment can be described as either short- or long-term. **Short-term investments** typically mature within one year. **Long-term investments** are those with longer maturities or, like common stock, with no maturity at all. It is not unusual to find investors matching the maturity of an investment to the period of time over which they wish to invest their funds.

Note: Discussions of international investing are highlighted by this icon.

domestic investments
debt, equity, and derivative securities of U.S.-based companies.

foreign investments
debt, equity, and derivative securities of foreign-based companies.

Domestic or Foreign As recently as 15 to 20 years ago, individuals invested almost exclusively in purely **domestic investments:** the debt, equity, and derivative securities of U.S.-based companies. Today, these same investors routinely also look for **foreign investments** (both direct and indirect) that might offer more attractive returns or lower risk than purely domestic investments. Information on foreign companies is now readily available, and it is now relatively easy to make foreign investments. As a result, many individuals now actively invest in foreign securities. All aspects of foreign investing are therefore routinely considered throughout this book.

The Structure of the Investment Process

financial institutions
organizations that channel the savings of governments, businesses, and individuals into loans or investments.

financial markets
forums in which suppliers and demanders of funds make financial transactions, often through intermediaries.

The investment process brings together *suppliers* of extra funds with *demanders* who need funds. Suppliers and demanders of funds are most often brought together through a financial institution or a financial market. (Occasionally, especially in property transactions, buyers and sellers deal directly with one another.) **Financial institutions** are organizations that channel the savings of governments, businesses, and individuals into loans or investments. Banks and insurance companies are financial institutions. **Financial markets** are forums in which suppliers and demanders of funds make financial transactions, often through intermediaries. They include securities, commodities, and foreign exchange markets.

The dominant financial market in the United States is the *securities market*. It includes stock markets, bond markets, and options markets. Similar markets exist in most major economies throughout the world. Their common feature is that the price of an investment vehicle at any point in time results from an equilibrium between the forces of supply and demand. As new information about returns and risk becomes available, the changes in supply and demand may result in a new equilibrium or *market price*. Financial markets streamline the process of bringing together suppliers and demanders of funds, and they allow transactions to be made quickly and at a fair price. They also publicize security prices.

Figure 1.1 diagrams the investment process. Note that the suppliers of funds may transfer their resources to the demanders through financial institutions, through financial markets, or in direct transactions. As the broken lines show, financial institutions can participate in financial markets as either suppliers or demanders of funds.

Note: Investor Facts offer interesting or entertaining tidbits of information.

INVESTOR FACTS

AMERICANS LOVE STOCKS—Even during the recent bear market, Americans continued to hold stocks. A recent survey showed that 52% of Americans now own stocks or stock mutual funds, compared to just 19% in 1983. Financial assets represent 42% of total assets. Stocks and mutual funds now account for about 34% of total household financial assets, up from 28% in 1995—and this figure does not include investments held in retirement accounts, which represent another 28% of financial assets.

Source: Ana M. Azicorbe, Arther B. Kennickell, and Kevin B. Moore, "Recent Changes in U.S. Family Finances: Results from the 1998 and 2001 Survey of Consumer Finances," *Federal Reserve Bulletin*, Board of Governors of the Federal Reserve System, Washington, D.C., January 2003, pp. 9, 15.

Participants in the Investment Process Government, business, and individuals are the three key participants in the investment process. Each may act as a supplier and a demander of funds. For the economy to grow and prosper, funds must be available to qualified individuals and to government and business. If individuals began suddenly hiding their excess funds under floorboards rather than putting them in financial institutions or investing them in the financial markets, then government, business, and individuals in need of funds would have difficulty obtaining them. As a result, government spending, business expansion, and consumer purchases would decline, and economic activity would slow.

Government All levels of government—federal, state, and local—require vast sums of money to finance long-term projects related to the construction of

FIGURE 1.1

The Investment Process

Note that financial institutions participate in the financial markets as well as transfer funds between suppliers and demanders. Although the arrows go only from suppliers to demanders, for some transactions (e.g., the sale of a bond), the principal amount borrowed by the demander from the supplier (the lender) is eventually returned.

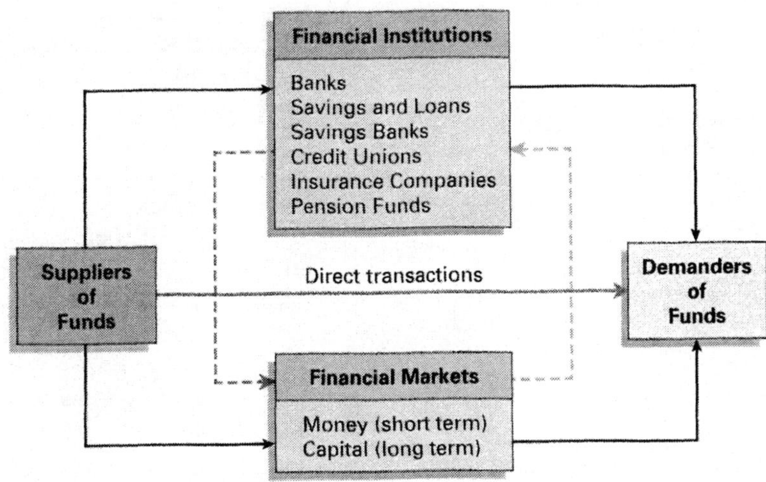

public facilities, such as schools, hospitals, public housing, and highways, and to meet operating needs—the money required to keep the government running. Occasionally, governments supply funds by making short-term investments to earn a positive return on temporarily idle funds. In general, though, government is a *net demander of funds*—it demands more funds than it supplies. The financial activities of governments, both as demanders and suppliers of funds, significantly affect the behavior of financial institutions and financial markets.

Business Most business firms require large sums of money to support operations. Like government, business has both long- and short-term financial needs. Businesses issue a wide variety of debt and equity securities to finance these needs. They also supply funds when they have excess cash. But like government, business firms in general are *net demanders of funds.*

Individuals You might be surprised to learn that the individual's role in the investment process is significant. Individuals frequently demand funds in the form of loans to finance the acquisition of property—typically automobiles and houses. Although the individual demand for funds seems great, individuals as a group are *net suppliers of funds:* They put more funds into the financial system than they take out.

Types of Investors When we refer to individuals in the investment process, we do so to differentiate households from government and business. We can further characterize the participation of individuals in the investment process in terms of who manages the funds. **Individual investors** manage their personal funds to achieve their financial goals. The individual investor usually concentrates on earning a return on idle funds, building a source of retirement income, and providing security for his or her family.

individual investors
investors who manage their own funds.

institutional investors
investment professionals who are paid to manage other people's money.

Individuals who lack the time or expertise to make investment decisions often employ **institutional investors**—investment professionals who are paid to manage other people's money. These professionals trade large volumes of securities for individuals, businesses, and governments. Sizable brokerage cost savings typically result from the large volumes traded. Institutional investors include financial institutions (banks, life insurance companies, mutual funds, and pension funds). Financial institutions invest large sums to earn a significant return for their customers. For example, a life insurance company invests its premium receipts to earn returns that will permit payments to policyholders or beneficiaries.

Both individual and institutional investors apply similar fundamental principles. However, institutional investors generally invest larger sums of money on behalf of others and therefore are often more sophisticated in investment knowledge and methods. The information presented in this textbook is aimed primarily at individual investors; it represents only the first step toward developing the expertise needed to qualify as an institutional investor.

HOT

Getting investment information is now only a few "mouse clicks" away. Everything from stock quotations, to news articles, to Wall Street research is on the Web. Many Web sites provide financial information tutorials.

InvestorGuide.com contains links to many of the Web's resources, and free investing guides. Check out [University] and follow some of the links to the educational information available for free. Also follow the [Links Directory] link to the list of other sites that you can link to from there. Some of the sites give comparisons between investment sites, helping you to choose the best sites for you.

www.investorguide.com

Note: Addresses of additional information sources that can be found on the Internet are interspersed throughout the chapters.

CONCEPTS IN REVIEW

1.1 Define the term *investment,* and explain why individuals invest.

1.2 Differentiate among the following types of investments, and cite an example of each: (a) securities and property investments; (b) direct and indirect investments; (c) debt, equity, and derivative securities; and (d) short-term and long-term investments.

1.3 Define the term *risk,* and explain how risk is used to differentiate among investments.

1.4 What are *foreign investments,* and what role do they play today for the individual investor?

1.5 Describe the structure of the overall investment process. Explain the role played by *financial institutions* and *financial markets.*

1.6 Classify the role of (a) government, (b) business, and (c) individuals as net suppliers or net demanders of funds.

1.7 Differentiate between *individual investors* and *institutional investors.*

Note: The Concepts in Review questions at the end of each text section encourage you, before you move on, to test your understanding of the material you've just read.

Investment Vehicles

LG 3

A wide variety of investment vehicles are available to individual investors. Vehicles differ in terms of maturities or lives, costs, return and risk characteristics, and tax considerations. We devote the bulk of this book—Chapters 6 through 16—to describing the characteristics, special features, returns and risks, and possible investment strategies that can be used with vehicles available to the individual investor. Here we will introduce these investment vehicles. Table 1.1 summarizes the information presented in this section.

TABLE 1.1 Overview of Investment Vehicles

Type	Description	Examples	Where Covered in This Book
Short-term vehicles	Savings instruments with lives of 1 year or less. Used to warehouse idle funds and to provide liquidity.	Deposit accounts Series EE savings bonds U.S. Treasury bills (T-bills) Certificates of deposit (CDs) Commercial paper Banker's acceptances Money market mutual funds	Ch. 1 Ch. 1 Ch. 1 Ch. 1 Ch. 1 Ch. 1 Ch. 1
Common stock	Equity investment vehicles that represent ownership in a corporation.		Chs. 6–9
Fixed-income securities	Investment vehicles that offer a fixed periodic return.	Bonds Preferred stock Convertible securities	Chs. 10, 11 Ch. 12 Ch. 12
Mutual funds	Companies that raise money from sale of shares and invest in and professionally manage a diversified portfolio of securities.		Ch. 13
Derivative securities	Securities that are neither debt nor equity but are structured to exhibit the characteristics of the underlying securities or assets from which they derive their value.	Options Futures	Ch. 15 Ch. 16
Other popular investment vehicles	Various other investment vehicles that are widely used by investors.	Real estate Tangibles Tax-advantaged investments	On text's Web site, www.aw-bc.com/gitman_joehnk

Short-Term Vehicles

short-term vehicles savings instruments that usually have lives of 1 year or less.

liquidity the ability of an investment to be converted into cash quickly and with little or no loss in value.

Short-term vehicles include savings instruments that usually have lives of 1 year or less. Short-term vehicles generally carry little or no risk. Often such instruments are used to "warehouse" idle funds and earn a return while long-term vehicles are being evaluated. They are also popular among conservative investors, who may use short-term vehicles as a primary investment outlet. Short-term vehicles also provide **liquidity.** That is, they can be converted into cash quickly and with little or no loss in value. Provision for liquidity is an important part of any financial plan. The role of short-term vehicles in financial planning and the key features of the most popular short-term vehicles are discussed later in this chapter.

Common Stock

common stock equity investment that represents ownership in a corporation; each share represents a fractional ownership interest in the firm.

Common stock is an equity investment that represents ownership in a corporation. Each share of common stock represents a fractional ownership interest in the firm. For example, one share of common stock in a corporation that has 10,000 shares outstanding would represent 1/10,000 ownership interest. Next to short-term vehicles and home ownership, common stock is the most popular form of investment vehicle. Today more than half of all U.S. families own some common stock.

dividends
periodic payments made by firms to their shareholders.

capital gains
the amount by which the sale price of an asset *exceeds* its original purchase price.

The return on investment in common stock comes from either of two sources: dividends or capital gains. **Dividends** are periodic payments made by the corporation to its shareholders from its current and past earnings. **Capital gains** result from selling the stock (or any asset) at a price that *exceeds* its original purchase price. For example, say you purchased a single share of One Tech Industries common stock for $40 per share. During the first year you owned it, you received $2.50 per share in cash dividends. At the end of the year, you sold the stock for $44 per share. If we ignore the costs associated with buying and selling the stock, you earned $2.50 in dividends and $4 in capital gains ($44 sale price—$40 purchase price). Since 1926, the average annual rate of return on common stocks of large firms has been about 12.2%, and the more risky common stocks of smaller firms have earned an average annual return of about 16.9%.

Fixed-Income Securities

fixed-income securities
investment vehicles that offer a fixed periodic return.

Fixed-income securities are investment vehicles that offer a fixed periodic return. Some forms offer contractually guaranteed returns. Others have specified, but not guaranteed, returns. Because of their fixed returns, fixed-income securities tend to be popular during periods of high interest rates, when investors seek to "lock in" high returns. The key forms of fixed-income securities are bonds, preferred stock, and convertible securities.

bonds
long-term debt instruments (IOUs), issued by corporations and governments, that offer a known interest return plus return of the bond's *face value* at maturity.

preferred stock
ownership interest in a corporation; has a stated dividend rate, payment of which is given preference over common stock dividends of the same firm.

convertible security
a fixed-income obligation (bond or preferred stock) with a feature permitting the investor to convert it into a specified number of shares of common stock.

Bonds **Bonds** are the long-term debt instruments (IOUs) issued by corporations and governments. A bondholder has a contractual right to receive a known interest return, plus return of the bond's *face value* (the stated value given on the certificate) at maturity (typically 20 to 40 years). If you purchased a $1,000 bond paying 9% interest in semiannual installments, you would expect to be paid $45 (9% × ½ year × $1,000) every 6 months. At maturity you would receive the $1,000 face value of the bond. An investor may be able to buy or sell a bond prior to maturity. Since 1926, the average annual rate of return on long-term corporate bonds has been about 6.2%, and the average annual return on less risky long-term government bonds has been about 5.8%.

Preferred Stock Like common stock, **preferred stock** represents an ownership interest in a corporation. Unlike common stock, preferred stock has a stated dividend rate. Payment of this dividend is given preference over common stock dividends of the same firm. Preferred stock has no maturity date. Investors typically purchase it for the dividends it pays, but it may also provide capital gains.

HOT

Successful investing can be surprisingly simple and straightforward. There are many baseline investing sites. Log on to SmartMoney.com. Scroll down the home page to Smart Money University and read the sections on Investing 101 and Strategic Investing that explain the fundamentals of stocks, bonds, and mutual funds.

www.smartmoney.com

Convertible Securities A **convertible security** is a special type of fixed-income obligation (bond or preferred stock). It has a feature permitting the investor to convert it into a specified number of shares of common stock. Convertible bonds and convertible preferreds provide the fixed-income benefit of a bond (interest) or preferred stock (dividends) while offering the price-appreciation (capital gain) potential of common stock.

INVESTOR FACTS

THE FEELING'S MUTUAL!—In mid-2003, the 8,200 mutual funds in the United States accounted for investment assets of more than $6.7 trillion. The 4,712 stock funds led the way with almost $3 trillion (44%) of the total, followed by 684 taxable money market funds with $1.9 trillion (28%).

Source: "Trends in Mutual Fund Investing, May 2003," Investment Company Institute, Washington, D.C., June 26, 2003, downloaded from www.ici.org.

Mutual Funds

A company that raises money from sale of its shares and invests in and professionally manages a diversified portfolio of securities is called a **mutual fund.** Investors in the fund own an interest in the fund's portfolio of securities. All mutual funds issue and repurchase shares of the fund at a price that reflects the value of the portfolio at the time the transaction is made. **Money market mutual funds** are mutual funds that invest solely in short-term investment vehicles.

mutual fund
a company that raises money from sale of its shares and invests in and professionally manages a diversified portfolio of securities.

money market mutual funds
mutual funds that invest solely in short-term investment vehicles.

Derivative Securities

As noted earlier, *derivative securities* derive their value from that of an underlying security or asset. They typically possess high levels of risk, because they usually have uncertain returns or unstable market values. But, because of their above-average risk, these vehicles also have high levels of expected return. The key derivative securities are options and futures.

Options **Options** are securities that give the investor an opportunity to sell or buy another security at a specified price over a given period of time. Most often, options are purchased to take advantage of an anticipated change in the price of common stock. However, the purchaser of an option is not guaranteed any return and could even lose the entire amount invested because the option does not become attractive enough to use. Aside from their speculative use, options are sometimes used to protect existing investment positions against losses. Three common types of options are *puts, calls,* and *warrants,* which we will discuss in detail in Chapter 15.

options
securities that give the investor an opportunity to sell or buy another security at a specified price over a given period of time.

Futures **Futures** are legally binding obligations stipulating that the sellers of such contracts will make delivery and the buyers of the contracts will take delivery of a specified commodity or financial instrument at some specific date, at a price agreed on at the time the contract is sold. Examples of commodities sold by contract include soybeans, pork bellies, platinum, and cocoa. Examples of financial futures are contracts for Japanese yen, U.S. Treasury securities, interest rates, and stock indexes. Trading in commodity and financial futures is generally a highly specialized, high-risk proposition.

futures
legally binding obligations stipulating that the sellers of such contracts will make delivery and the buyers of the contracts will take delivery of a specified commodity or financial instrument at some specific date, at a price agreed on at the time the contract is sold.

Other Popular Investment Vehicles

Various other investment vehicles are also used by investors. The most common are real estate, tangibles, and tax-advantaged investments.

Real estate consists of entities such as residential homes, raw land, and a variety of forms of income property, including warehouses, office and apartment buildings, and condominiums. The appeal of real estate investment is the potential returns in the form of rental income, tax write-offs, and capital gains. **Tangibles** are investment assets, other than real estate, that can be seen or touched. They include gold and other precious metals, gemstones, and collectibles such as coins, stamps, artwork, and antiques. These assets are purchased as investments in anticipation of price increases. Because the federal income tax rate for an individual can be as high as 35%, many investors look

real estate
entities such as residential homes, raw land, and income property.

tangibles
investment assets, other than real estate, that can be seen or touched.

tax-advantaged investments investment vehicles and strategies for legally reducing one's tax liability.

for **tax-advantaged investments.** These are investment vehicles and strategies for legally reducing one's tax liability. With them, investors find that their after-tax rates of return can be far higher than with conventional investments.

CONCEPTS IN REVIEW

1.8 What are *short-term vehicles?* How do they provide *liquidity?*

1.9 What is *common stock* and what are its two sources of potential return?

1.10 Briefly define and differentiate among the following investment vehicles. Which offer fixed returns? Which are derivative securities? Which offer professional investment management?

a. Bonds
b. Preferred stock
c. Convertible securities
d. Mutual funds
e. Options
f. Futures

Making Investment Plans

LG 4 LG 5

The process of investing can be carried out by following a logical progression of steps. It is important that your investment plans take into account the impact of taxes. Your plans also should be responsive to your stage in the life cycle and to the changing economic environment.

Steps in Investing

Investing can be conducted on a strictly intuitive basis or on the basis of plans carefully developed to achieve specific goals. Evidence favors the more logical approach that begins with establishing a set of overall financial goals and then developing and executing an investment program consistent with those goals. The following brief overview of the steps in investing provides a framework for discussion of the concepts, tools, and techniques presented throughout the book.

Step 1: Meeting Investment Prerequisites Before investing, you must make certain that the *necessities of life* are adequately provided for. This category includes funds for housing, food, transportation, taxes, and clothing. In addition, a pool of easily accessible funds should be established for meeting emergency cash needs. (Meeting liquidity needs is discussed later in this chapter.)

Another prerequisite is adequate protection against the losses that could result from death, illness or disability, damage to property, or a negligent act. Protection against such risks can be acquired through life, health, property, and liability insurance.

HOT

Detailed information on meeting life insurance needs is available on this text's Web site. Click on the Web chapter titled Tax-Advantaged Investments and then on Deferred Annuities.

www.aw-bc.com/gitman_joehnk

Step 2: Establishing Investment Goals Once you have satisfied the prerequisites and set clearly defined financial goals, the next step is to establish *investment goals.* **Investment goals** are the financial objectives you wish to achieve by investing. Clearly, your investment goals will determine the types of investments you will make. Common investment goals include:

investment goals the financial objectives that one wishes to achieve by investing.

1. *Accumulating Retirement Funds.* Accumulating funds for retirement is the *single most important reason for investing.* Too often, people tend to rely heavily on Social Security and employers for retirement funds. It is of the utmost importance to review the amounts that can realistically be expected from these sources. You can then decide, on the basis of your retirement goals, *whether they will be adequate to meet your needs.* If they are not, they must be supplemented through your own investment program. The earlier in life you assess your retirement needs, the greater your chance of accumulating sufficient funds to meet them.

2. *Enhancing Current Income.* Investments enhance current income by earning dividends or interest. Retirees frequently choose investments offering *high current income at low risk.* The idea of a retired person "clipping coupons"—collecting interest—from high-grade bonds is a fair description of what most senior citizens should be doing at that point in their lives.

3. *Saving for Major Expenditures.* Families often put aside money over the years to accumulate the funds needed to make major expenditures. The most common of these are the down payment on a home, education, vacation travel, and capital to start a business. The appropriate types of investment vehicles depend on the purpose and the amount of money needed. For purposes such as the down payment on a home or a child's education, for example, much less risk should be tolerated than for other goals. The attainment of such basic goals should not, if possible, be placed in jeopardy.

HOT

Tax-advantaged investments are discussed on the text's Web site. Click on the Web chapter titled Tax-Advantaged Investments.

www.aw-bc.com/gitman_joehnk

4. *Sheltering Income from Taxes.* Federal income tax law allows certain noncash charges to be deducted from specified sources of income. Such deductions reduce the amount of final taxable income. Obviously, if a person can avoid (or defer) paying taxes on the income from an investment, he or she will have more funds left for reinvestment.

Step 3: Adopting an Investment Plan Once your general goals have been established, you should adopt an **investment plan**—a written document describing how funds will be invested. A series of supporting investment goals can be developed for each long-term goal. For each goal, specify the target date for achieving it and the amount of tolerable risk.

investment plan
a written document describing how funds will be invested and specifying the target date for achieving each investment goal and the amount of tolerable risk.

Generally, the more important the financial objective, the lower the risk that should be assumed. Suppose, for example, one long-run goal is to accumulate $80,000 in cash by the end of 10 years. That goal could be spelled out as a plan to accumulate $80,000 in cash by investing in a portfolio evenly divided between low-risk and speculative stocks providing a total return of 10% per year. The more specific you can be in your statement of investment goals, the easier it will be to establish an investment plan consistent with your goals.

Step 4: Evaluating Investment Vehicles Once you have your investment goals and plan laid out, you will want to evaluate investment vehicles by assessing each vehicle's potential return and risk. This process typically involves *valuation,* the use of measures of return and risk to estimate the worth of an investment vehicle. (Chapter 4 offers a general discussion of the procedures for measuring these key dimensions of potential investments. Subsequent chapters focus on the valuation of specific vehicles.)

HOT

The *Investing in Action* box at the book's Web site describes the role of professional financial planners in helping their clients formulate investment goals and plans.

www.aw-bc.com/gitman_joehnk

Step 5: Selecting Suitable Investments You now gather additional information and use it to select specific investment vehicles consistent with your goals. The best investments may not be those that simply maximize return. Other factors, such as risk and tax considerations, may also be crucial. For example, to receive maximum annual dividends, you might purchase the common stock of a firm expected to pay high dividends. However, if the firm whose stock you purchased goes bankrupt, you could lose the money. The stock of a firm that pays lower dividends but with less risk of bankruptcy might have been a better choice. Careful selection of investment vehicles is essential to successful investing. Vehicles should be consistent with established goals and offer acceptable levels of return, risk, and value.

Step 6: Constructing a Diversified Portfolio Selecting suitable investments involves choosing vehicles that enable you to achieve investment goals and that optimize return, risk, and investment values. To do this, you will assemble an investment *portfolio* that meets one or more investment goals. For example, your portfolio might contain common stock, government bonds, and short-term investments. **Diversification** is the inclusion of a number of different investment vehicles in a portfolio to increase returns or reduce risk. By *diversifying* in this way, investors are able to earn higher returns or be exposed to less risk than if they limit their investments to just one or two vehicles. Diversification is the financial term for the age-old advice "Don't put all your eggs in one basket." (Chapter 5 includes discussions of diversification and other modern portfolio concepts.)

diversification
the inclusion of a number of different investment vehicles in a portfolio to increase returns or reduce risk.

Step 7: Managing the Portfolio Once you have constructed your portfolio, you should measure its actual behavior in relation to expected performance. If the investment results are not consistent with your objectives, you may need to take corrective action. Such action usually involves selling certain investments and using the proceeds to acquire other vehicles for the portfolio. *Portfolio management* involves monitoring the portfolio and restructuring it as dictated by the actual behavior of the investments. Many individual investors buy mutual funds to achieve diversification and receive the benefit of professional managements (see Chapter 13); others will construct and manage their own portfolios (see Chapter 14).

The *Investing in Action* box on page 15 summarizes some general tips for successful investing.

HOT

Financial planning is too important to leave to luck. The Web is extremely useful in helping investors establish their investment plans. The Wall Street City Web site has an interactive program that helps investors develop these plans. Visit the following address to learn more about planning and choose [Other Features] and then [Financial Planning].

www.wallstreetcity.com

Considering Personal Taxes

Besides developing plans for achieving your specific investment goals, it's important to consider the tax consequences associated with various investments. A knowledge of the tax laws can help you reduce taxes. By doing so, you increase the amount of after-tax dollars available for achieving your investment goals. Because tax laws are complicated and subject to frequent revision, we present only the key concepts and how they apply to popular investment transactions.

INVESTING IN ACTION

LESSONS FOR INVESTMENT SUCCESS

The stock market has taken investors on a roller-coaster ride in recent years. Even in such volatile times, however, some basic rules still apply. Becoming a successful investor takes time and effort; there are no sure-fire schemes for beating the market. Here are some tips to help you get started on the road to financial security.

- **Harness the power of compounding.** With compounding, time is your biggest ally. The longer you invest your money, the faster it will grow. If you earn a 9% annual return on your investment and reinvest your yearly earnings at the same rate for a 20-year period, your overall return is 460%, an average annual return of 23% (460%/20). Start now; waiting will cost you money. If you invest $2,000 per year for 10 years ($20,000 total) at 8% per year, in 35 years you'll have $198,422. But wait 10 years and invest $2,000 per year for 25 years at 8% per year, and your (considerably greater) $50,000 investment will be only $146,212 at the end of that same 35-year period. You can start small. Invest just $200 at 10% and you'll have almost $20,000 in 25 years. Make investing a habit now.
- **Don't wait for the "right" time to invest.** There isn't one! The "best" time to invest is now. You can always find a reason to put off taking the plunge: It's an election year, the market is too high, there's a crisis somewhere in the world. Studies show that it's more important to invest than to pick the right time. In the short run, market activity is unpredictable, even for the experts. Don't make excuses, like you are too busy, investing is too hard, or you can't possibly save enough for college or retirement. Investing is one of the best uses of your time. Rethink your priorities: Is it more important to go to the movies or to plan for your financial future? And don't be intimidated by the investment process. Set realistic goals, learn the basics, and start with simple investments that you understand. Once you gain control of your finances, your confidence will increase.
- **Diversify your portfolio.** Spreading your money among different types of investments is less risky than putting all your eggs in one investment basket. If some of your holdings go down, others go up, and vice versa. Diversify your portfolio by investing in several types of securities: short-term vehicles such as money market funds, intermediate-term bonds or bond funds, and, for the long-term, growth stocks or growth mutual funds. You should also have some international stocks or mutual funds. Don't concentrate too heavily in one industry or buy just one or two stocks. No one knows which sector will be hot tomorrow.
- **Monitor your investments.** Don't just buy securities and hold them forever. Review your portfolio monthly to check your progress against your goals. Weed out your poor performers and evaluate current holdings relative to other investment opportunities. Don't be too quick to unload a stock or mutual fund or to chase after that hot stock tip, though. Do your homework and be sure you have a good reason to buy or sell.

CRITICAL THINKING QUESTIONS Why is it important to start investing now? Why is it a good idea to diversify?

Sources: Jonathan Clements, "Don't Ignore Luck's Role in Stock Picks," *Wall Street Journal,* September 26, 2000, p. C1; Jonathan Clements, "Lessons from the School of Hard Knocks, *Wall Street Journal,* March 14, 2000, p. C1; "Money 101: Basics of Investing," *Money.com,* downloaded from money.cnn.com/pf/101; Peter Psaras, "Ten Tips for Successful Investing," *The Motley Fool,* September 13, 2000, downloaded from fool.com; Linda Stern, "Post-traumatic Investing," *San Diego Union-Tribune,* April 27, 2003, p. H3.

Basic Sources of Taxation The two major types of taxes are those levied by the federal government and those levied by state and local governments. The federal *income tax* is the major form of personal taxation. Federal rates currently range from 10 to 35% of taxable income.

State and local taxes vary from area to area. Some states have income taxes that range as high as 15% or more of income. Some cities, especially large East Coast cities, also have local income taxes that typically range between 1% and 5% of income. In addition to income taxes, state and local governments rely heavily on sales and property taxes, which vary from community to community, as a source of revenue.

Income taxes at the federal, state, and local levels have the greatest impact on security investments, whose returns are in the form of dividends, interest, and increases in value. Property taxes can have a sizable impact on real estate and other forms of property investment.

Types of Income The income of individuals is classified into one of *three basic categories* defined below.

1. *Active income* consists of everything from wages and salaries to bonuses, tips, pension income, and alimony. Active income is made up of income earned on the job as well as most other forms of *noninvestment* income.
2. *Portfolio income* is earnings generated from various types of investment holdings. This category of income covers most (but not all) types of investments, from savings accounts, stocks, bonds, and mutual funds to options and futures. For the most part, portfolio income consists of interest, dividends, and capital gains (the profit on the sale of an investment).
3. *Passive income* is a special category of income, composed chiefly of income derived from real estate, limited partnerships, and other forms of tax-advantaged investments.

The key feature of these categories is that they limit the amount of deductions (write-offs) that can be taken, particularly for portfolio and passive income. The amount of allowable deductions for portfolio and passive income is *limited to the amount of income derived from these two sources.* For example, if you had a total of $380 in portfolio income for the year, you could deduct no more than $380 in investment-related interest expense. For deduction purposes, the portfolio and passive income categories cannot be mixed or combined with each other or with active income. *Investment-related expenses can be used only to offset portfolio income,* and (with a few exceptions) *passive investment expenses can be used only to offset the income from passive investments.*

Note: Key financial topics offer opportunities for additional study to enhance learning. A PC icon appears next to topics covered in the tutorials that are featured at the book's Web site.

Ordinary Income Regardless of whether it's classified as active, portfolio, or passive, ordinary income is taxed at one of six rates: 10, 15, 25, 28, 33, or 35%. There is one structure of tax rates for taxpayers who file *individual* returns and another for those who file *joint* returns with a spouse. Table 1.2 shows the tax rates and income brackets for these two categories. Note that the rates are *progressive.* That is, taxpayers with taxable income above a specified amount are taxed at a higher rate.

TABLE 1.2 Tax Rates and Income Brackets for Individual and Joint Returns (2003)

Tax Rates	Taxable Income: Individual Returns	Taxable Income: Joint Returns
10%	$0 to $7,000	$0 to $14,000
15%	$7,001 to $28,400	$14,001 to $56,800
25%	$28,401 to $68,800	$56,801 to $114,650
28%	$68,801 to $143,500	$114,651 to $174,700
33%	$143,501 to $311,950	$174,701 to $311,950
35%	Over $311,950	Over $311,950

An example will demonstrate how ordinary income is taxed. Consider the Ellis sisters, Joni and Cara. Both are single. Joni's taxable income is $25,000. Cara's is $50,000. Using Table 1.2, we can calculate their taxes as follows:

Joni:
(0.10 × $7,000) + [0.15 × ($25,000 − $7,000)] = $700 + $2,700 = $3,400

Cara:
(0.10 × $7,000) + [0.15 × ($28,400 − $7,000)]
+ [0.25 × ($50,000 − $28,400)] = $700 + $3,210 + $5,400 = $ 9,310

The progressive nature of the federal income tax structure can be seen by the fact that although Cara's taxable income is twice that of Joni, her income tax is about 2.75 times Joni's.

Capital Gains and Losses A *capital asset* is property owned and used by the taxpayer for personal reasons, pleasure, or investment. The most common types are securities and real estate, including one's home. A *capital gain* represents the amount by which the proceeds from the sale of a capital asset *exceed* its original purchase price. Capital gains are taxed at two different rates depending on the holding period.

The capital gains tax rate is 15% if the asset is held for more than 12 months. This 15% capital gains tax rate assumes that you're in the 25%, 28%, 33%, or 35% tax bracket. If you're in the 10% or 15% tax bracket, then the capital gains tax rate on an asset held for more than 12 months is just 5%. If the asset is held for less than 12 months, then the amount of any capital gain realized is added to other sources of income, and the total is taxed at the rates given in Table 1.2.

For example, imagine that James McFail, a single person who has other taxable income totaling $75,000, sold 500 shares of stock at $12 per share. He originally purchased this stock at $10 per share. The total capital gain on this transaction was $1,000 [500 shares × ($12/share − $10/share)]. Thus James's taxable income would total $76,000, which puts him in the 28% tax bracket (see Table 1.2).

If the $1,000 capital gain resulted from an asset that was held for more than 12 months, and because James is in the 28% tax bracket, the capital gain would be taxed at the maximum rate of 15%. His total tax would be calculated as follows:

Ordinary income ($75,000)
(0.10 × $7,000) + [0.15 × ($28,400 − $7,000)]
+ [0.25 × ($68,800 − $28,400)] + [0.28 × ($75,000 − $68,800)]
= $700 + $3,210 + $10,100 + $1,736 = $15,746

Capital gain ($1,000)
(0.15 × $1,000) = 150

Total tax $15,896

James's total tax would be $15,896. Had his other taxable income been below $28,401 (i.e., in the 15% bracket), the $1,000 capital gain would have been taxed at 5% rather than 15%. Had James held the asset for less than 12 months, his $1,000 capital gain would have been taxed as ordinary income, which in James's case would result in a 28% rate.

Capital gains are appealing to investors because they are not taxed until actually realized. For example, if you own a stock originally purchased for $50 per share that at the end of the tax year has a market price of $60 per share, you have a "paper gain" of $10 per share. This *paper (unrealized) gain* is not taxable, because you still own the stock. *Only realized gains are taxed.* If you sold the stock for $60 per share during the tax year, you would have a realized—and therefore taxable—gain of $10 per share.

capital loss
the amount by which the proceeds from the sale of a capital asset are *less than* its original purchase price.

net losses
the amount by which capital losses exceed capital gains; up to $3,000 of net losses can be applied against ordinary income in any year.

A **capital loss** results when a capital asset is sold for *less than* its original purchase price. Before taxes are calculated, all gains and losses must be netted out. Up to $3,000 of **net losses** can be applied against ordinary income in any year. Losses that cannot be applied in the current year may be carried forward and used to offset future income, subject to certain conditions.

tax planning
the development of strategies that will defer and minimize an individual's level of taxes over the long run.

Investments and Taxes The opportunities created by the tax laws make tax planning important in the investment process. **Tax planning** involves looking at your earnings, both current and projected, and developing strategies that will defer and minimize the level of taxes. The tax plan should guide your investment activities so that over the long run you will achieve maximum after-tax returns for an acceptable level of risk. For example, the fact that capital gains are not taxed until actually realized allows you to defer tax payments on them as well as control the timing of these payments. However, investments that are likely to lead to capital gains income generally have higher risk than those that provide only current investment income. Therefore, the choice of investment vehicles cannot be made solely on the basis of the possible reduction of tax payments. The levels of both return and risk need to be viewed in light of their tax effects. *It is the after-tax return and associated risk that matter.*

Tax plans should also reflect the (1) form of returns—current income, capital gains, or tax-advantaged income—and (2) the timing of loss recognition and profit taking. One common strategy is to claim losses as soon as they occur and to delay profit taking. Such an approach allows you to benefit from the tax deductibility of a loss and to delay having to claim income from gains. Tax planning, which is usually done in coordination with an accountant, tax expert, or tax attorney, is most common among individuals with high levels of income ($200,000 or more annually). Yet sizable savings can result for investors with lower incomes as well.

HOT

The material on tax strategies and tax-advantaged investments available on this text's Web site provides more detailed information on this topic. Click on Chapter 18.

www.aw-bc.com/gitman_joehnk

Tax-Advantaged Retirement Vehicles The federal government over the years has established a number of types of retirement vehicles that can be used to either supplement an existing employer retirement plan or to provide self-directed retirement accounts for employed and self-employed individuals. Employer-sponsored plans include profit-sharing plans, thrift and savings plans, and 401(k) plans. These plans are often *voluntary* and allow employees to both increase the amount of money held for retirement and enjoy attractive tax deferral benefits. Individuals can also set up their own tax-sheltered retirement programs—for example, Keogh plans and SEP-IRAs for self-employed individuals. Individual retirement arrangements (IRAs), both deductible and nondeductible, and Roth IRAs, can be set up by just about anybody subject to certain qualifications. In general, these plans allow individuals to defer taxes, typically on both the contributions and the earnings on them, until some future date when retirement withdrawals take place. Because, as noted earlier, the single most important goal of investing is to accumulate retirement funds, the use of various tax-advantaged retirement vehicles allows the individual investor to supplement an employer-sponsored retirement plan and/or to develop his or her own plan under very favorable tax provisions. Although the details of the various tax-advantaged vehicles mentioned here are not covered in this text, the individual investor should take advantage of these vehicles when they are available and appropriate to achieving his or her investment goals.

Investing Over the Life Cycle

TAX BITE—If you invest just $2,000 per year in taxable accounts and investments for the next 30 years, make no withdrawals, and earn an 8% average compounded annual rate of return, you'll accumulate about $227,000—until you pay Uncle Sam his share. Then you will have only $180,240, assuming that an average federal income tax rate of 28% is applied to your earnings above the total investment of $60,000 ($2,000 × 30 years). Taxes will reduce your earnings from the investment by slightly more than one-fourth!

Investors tend to follow different investment philosophies as they move through different stages of the life cycle. Generally speaking, most investors tend to be more aggressive when they're young and more conservative as they grow older. Typically, investors move through the following investment stages.

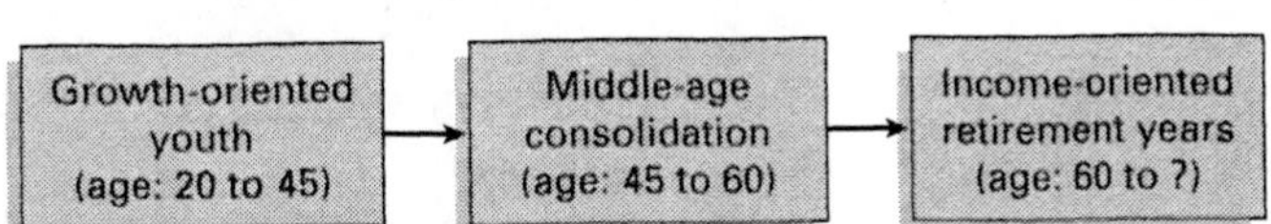

Most young investors, in their twenties and thirties, tend to prefer growth-oriented investments that stress *capital gains* rather than current income. Often young investors don't have much in the way of investable funds, so capital gains are viewed as the quickest (if not necessarily the surest) way to build capital. Young investors tend to favor growth-oriented and speculative vehicles, particularly high-risk common stocks, options, and futures.

As investors approach the middle-age consolidation stage of life (the mid-forties), family demands and responsibilities such as educational expenses and retirement contributions become more important. The whole portfolio goes through a transition to *higher-quality securities*. Low-risk growth and income stocks, high-grade bonds, preferred stocks, convertibles, and mutual funds are all widely used at this stage.

Finally, when investors approach their retirement years, preservation of capital and current income become the principal concerns. A secure, high level of income is paramount. Capital gains are viewed as merely a pleasant, occasional by-product of investing. The investment portfolio now becomes *highly conservative*. It consists of low-risk income stocks, high-yielding government bonds, quality corporate bonds, bank certificates of deposit (CDs), and other short-term vehicles. At this stage, investors reap the rewards of a lifetime of saving and investing.

Investing in Different Economic Environments

Despite the government's arsenal of weapons for moderating economic swings, numerous changes are sure to occur in the economy during your lifetime of investing. At all stages of the life cycle, your investment program must be flexible enough to allow you to recognize and react to changing economic conditions. The first rule of investing is to know *where* to put your money. The second is to know *when* to make your moves.

The first question is easier to deal with, because it involves matching the risk and return objectives of your investment plan with the available investment alternatives. For example, if you're a seasoned investor who can tolerate the risk, then speculative stocks may be right for you. If you're a novice who wants a fair return on your capital, perhaps you should consider a good growth-oriented mutual fund. Unfortunately, although stocks and growth funds may do well when the economy is expanding, they can turn out to be disasters at other times. This leads to the second, and more difficult, question: What effect do economic and market conditions have on investment returns?

The question of when to invest is difficult because it deals with *market timing*. The fact is that most economists and most professional money managers—not to mention most investors—cannot consistently predict the peaks and troughs in the economy or stock market. It's a lot easier to get a handle on the *current state* of the economy/market. That is, knowing whether the economy/market is in a state of expansion or decline is considerably different from being able to pinpoint when it's about to change course. Thus, for our purposes, we can define **market timing** as the process of identifying the current state of the economy/market and assessing the likelihood of its continuing on its present course.

market timing
the process of identifying the current state of the economy/market and assessing the likelihood of its continuing on its present course.

As an investor, it's best to confine your assessment of the economy to three distinct conditions: (1) a state of recovery or expansion, (2) a state of decline or recession, or (3) uncertainty as to the direction of its movement. These different stages are illustrated in Figure 1.2. It's easy to see when things are moving up (recovery/expansion) and when they're moving down (decline/recession). The difficulty comes with the peaks and troughs. At those points, you don't know whether the economy will continue in its current direction, up or down, or whether it will change direction. That is why these areas in the figure are shaded, depicting *uncertainty*. How you will respond to these conditions depends on the types of investment vehicles you hold (for example, stocks or bonds).

Stocks and the Business Cycle Common stocks and other equity-related securities (convertible securities, stock mutual funds, stock options, and stock index futures) are highly responsive to conditions in the economy. Economic conditions are described generically as the *business cycle*. The business cycle reflects the current status of a variety of economic variables, including GDP (gross domestic product), industrial production, personal disposable income, the unemployment rate, and more.

FIGURE 1.2

Different Stages of an Economic/Market Cycle

The economic/market cycle shows three different conditions: (1) a state of recovery/expansion, (2) a state of decline/recession, and (3) uncertainty as to the direction in which the economy/market is going to move (shown by the shaded areas).

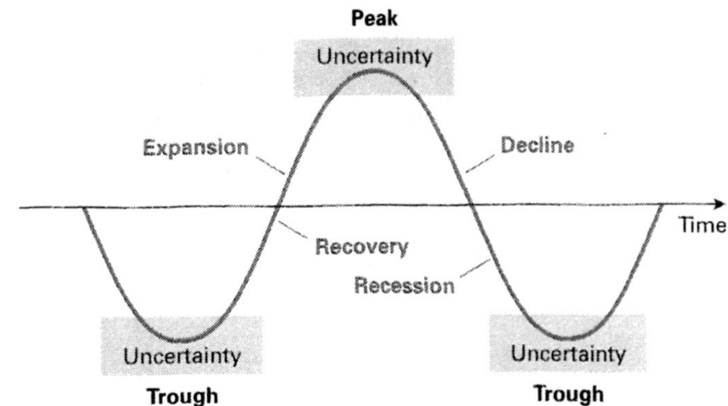

A strong economy is reflected in an expanding business cycle. When business is good and profits are up, stocks react by increasing in value and return. Growth-oriented and speculative stocks tend to do especially well in strong markets. To a lesser extent, so do low-risk and income-oriented stocks. In contrast, when economic activity is declining, the values and returns on common stocks tend to be off as well.

Bonds and Interest Rates Bonds and other forms of fixed-income securities (preferred stocks and bond funds) are highly sensitive to movements in interest rates. In fact, interest rates are the single most important variable in determining bond price behavior and returns to investors. Interest rates and bond prices move in opposite directions (as will be explained in Chapters 10 and 11). Therefore, rising interest rates are unfavorable for bonds already held in an investor's portfolio. Of course, high interest rates enhance the attractiveness of new bonds because these bonds must offer high returns to attract investors.

IN REVIEW

CONCEPTS

1.11 What should an investor first establish before developing and executing an investment program? Briefly describe each of the seven steps involved in investing.

1.12 What are four common investment goals?

1.13 Define and differentiate among the following. Explain how each is related to federal income taxes.

a. Active income
b. Portfolio and passive income
c. Capital gain
d. Capital loss
e. Tax planning
f. Tax-advantaged retirement vehicles

1.14 Describe the differing investment philosophies typically applied during each of the following stages of an investor's life cycle.

a. Youth (ages 20 to 45)
b. Middle age (ages 45 to 60)
c. Retirement years (age 60 on)

1.15 Describe the four stages of the economic/market cycle, and discuss the impact of this cycle on stock and bond investments.

Meeting Liquidity Needs: Investing in Short-Term Vehicles

LG 6

As discussed earlier, you should ensure that you have adequate liquidity. This provision is a prerequisite to implementing long-term investment goals. *Liquidity* is the ability to convert an investment into cash quickly and with little or no loss in value. A checking account is highly liquid. Stocks and bonds are not liquid, because there is no definite assurance that you will be able to quickly sell them at a price equal to or greater than their purchase price.

The Role of Short-Term Vehicles

Short-term vehicles are an important part of most savings and investment programs. They generate income—which can be quite high during periods of high interest rates. However, their primary function is to provide a pool of reserves that can be used for emergencies or simply to accumulate funds for some specific purpose. As a rule of thumb, financial planners often suggest that anywhere from 3 to 6 months' worth of after-tax income should be held in short-term vehicles to meet unexpected needs or to take advantage of attractive opportunities.

Investors usually hold short-term vehicles in their investment portfolios as a *temporary,* highly liquid investment until something better comes along. Some individuals choose to hold short-term vehicles because they simply are more comfortable with them. In fact, this approach has considerable merit during periods of economic and investment instability. Regardless of your motives for holding short-term vehicles, you should evaluate them in terms of their risk and return, just as you would longer-term investments.

Interest on Short-Term Investments Short-term investments earn interest in one of two ways. Some investments, such as savings accounts, pay a *stated rate of interest.* In this case, you can easily find the interest rate—it's the stated rate on the account.

discount basis
a method of earning interest on a security by purchasing it at a price below its redemption value; the difference is the interest earned.

Alternatively, interest is earned on short-term investments on a **discount basis.** This means that the security is purchased at a price below its redemption value, and the difference is the interest earned. U.S. Treasury bills (T-bills), for example, are issued on a discount basis.

Risk Characteristics Short-term investments are generally considered low in risk. Their primary risk results from the *loss of potential purchasing power* that occurs when the rate of return on these investments falls short of the inflation rate. This has often been the case with such vehicles as *passbook savings accounts,* the traditional bank savings accounts that generally pay a low rate of interest and have no minimum balance. Over long periods of time most other short-term investments have rates of return that are about equal to, or maybe slightly higher than, the average inflation rate.

HOT LINKS

A relatively simple formula can be applied when interest is earned on a discount basis in order to compare returns with vehicles earning a stated rate of interest. See this text's Web site for discussion of the formula.

www.aw-bc.com/gitman_joehnk

The *risk of default*—nonpayment—is virtually nonexistent with short-term investment vehicles. The principal reason is that the primary issuers of most short-term vehicles are highly reputable institutions, such as the U.S. Treasury, large banks, and major corporations. Deposits in commercial banks, savings and loans, savings banks, and credit unions also are insured for up to $100,000 per account by government agencies. Finally, because the value of short-term investments does not change much in response to changing interest rates, exposure to capital loss is correspondingly low.

Advantages and Disadvantages of Short-Term Investments As noted, the major advantages of short-term investments are their high liquidity and low risk. Most are available from local financial institutions and can be readily converted to cash with minimal inconvenience. Finally, because the returns on most short-term investments vary with inflation and market interest rates, investors can readily capture higher returns as rates move up. On the negative side, when interest rates go down, returns drop as well.

Although a decline in market rates has undesirable effects on most short-term vehicles, perhaps their biggest disadvantage is their relatively low return. Because these securities are generally so low in risk, you can expect the returns on short-term investments to average less than the returns on long-term investments.

Popular Short-Term Investment Vehicles

Over the past 30 years or so, the number of short-term investment vehicles being offered has greatly expanded. Investing in short-term securities is no longer the easy task it once was, when the decision for most people amounted to whether to place funds in a passbook savings account or in U.S. savings bonds. Today, even some checking accounts pay interest on idle balances. Along with the increase in investment alternatives has come greater sophistication in short-term investment management. Investors now know they can use short-term vehicles as secure investment outlets for the long haul or as a place to hold cash until they find a longer-term outlet for the funds.

A variety of short-term investment vehicles are available to the individual investor. Some are deposit-type accounts in which an investor can place money, earn a relatively low rate of interest, and conveniently withdraw funds at his or her discretion. The popular deposit-type accounts are summarized in Part A of Table 1.3 on page 24. Another group of short-term investment vehicles are those issued by the federal government. The more popular of those vehicles are summarized in Part B of Table 1.3. The final group of short-term vehicles are nongovernment issues, typically issued by a financial institution, a corporation, or a professional money manager. Some of the more popular nongovernment issues are summarized in Part C of Table 1.3.

Investment Suitability

Individual investors use short-term vehicles for both savings and investment. They use short-term vehicles to maintain a desired level of savings that will be readily available if the need arises—in essence, to provide *safety and security.* For this purpose, high yield is less important than safety, liquidity, and convenience. Passbook savings accounts, NOW accounts, and Series EE savings bonds are the most popular savings vehicles.

When short-term vehicles are used for *investment purposes*, yield is often just as important as liquidity. However, because the objective is different, the short-term vehicles tend to be used much more aggressively. Most investors will hold at least a part of their portfolio in short-term, highly liquid securities,

TABLE 1.3 Popular Short-Term Investment Vehicles

Part A. Deposit-Type Accounts

Type of Account	Brief Description	Minimum Balance	Interest Rate	Federal Insurance
Passbook savings account	Savings accounts offered by banks.* Used primarily for convenience or if investors lack sufficient funds to purchase other short-term vehicles.	Typically none	0.5%–4% depending on economy	Yes, up to $100,000 per deposit.
NOW (negotiated order of withdrawal) account	Bank checking account that pays interest on balances.	No legal minimum, but often set at $500 to $1,000	At or near passbook rates	Yes, up to $100,000 per deposit.
Money market deposit account (MMDA)	Bank deposit account with limited check-writing privileges.	No legal minimum, but often set at about $2,500	Typically slightly above passbook rate	Yes, up to $100,000 per deposit.
Asset management account	Deposit account at bank, brokerage house, mutual fund, or insurance company that combines checking, investing, and borrowing. Automatically "sweeps" excess balances into short-term investments and borrows to meet shortages.	Typically $5,000 to $20,000	Similar to MMDAs	Yes, up to $100,000 per deposit in banks. Varies in other institutions.

Part B. Federal Government Issues

Security	Issuer	Description	Initial Maturity	Risk and Return
Series EE savings bonds	U.S. Treasury	Savings bonds issued by the U.S. Treasury and sold at banks and through payroll deduction plans, in varying denominations, at 50% of face value; pay a variable rate of interest tied to U.S. Treasury security market yields and calculated every six months in May and November.	None	Lowest, virtually risk-free
Treasury bills	U.S. Treasury	Issued weekly at auction; sold at a discount; strong secondary market; exempt from local and state income taxes	91 and 182 days	Lowest, virtually risk-free

Part C. Nongovernment Issues

Security	Issuer	Description	Initial Maturity	Risk and Return
Certificates of deposit (CDs)	Commercial banks	Represent specific cash deposits in commercial banks; amounts and maturities tailored to investor needs	1 month to 3 years or more	Higher than U.S. Treasury issues and comparable to commercial paper
Commercial paper	Corporation with a high credit standing	Unsecured note of issuer; large denominations	3 to 270 days	Higher than U.S. Treasury issues and comparable to negotiable CDs
Banker's acceptances	Banks	Results from a bank guarantee of a business transaction; sold at discount from maturity value	30 to 180 days	About the same as negotiable CDs and commercial paper but higher than U.S. Treasury issues
Money market mutual funds	Professional portfolio management companies	Professionally managed portfolios of marketable securities; provide instant liquidity	None—depends on wishes of investor	Vary, but generally higher than U.S. Treasury issues and comparable to negotiable CDs and commercial paper

*The term *bank* refers to commercial banks, savings and loans (S&Ls), savings banks, and credit unions.

if for no other reason than to be able to act on unanticipated investment opportunities. Some investors, in fact, devote all or most of their portfolios to such securities.

One of the most common uses of short-term securities as investment vehicles is as temporary outlets. In that use, investors buy short-term vehicles either to warehouse funds until an attractive permanent investment can be found or to sit on the sidelines in times of unsettled or undesirable market conditions. For example, if you have just sold some stock but do not have a suitable long-term investment alternative, you might place the proceeds in a money fund until you find a longer-term use for them. Or if you feel that interest rates are about to rise sharply, you might sell your long-term bonds and use the proceeds to buy T-bills. The higher-yielding securities—like MMDAs, CDs, commercial paper, banker's acceptances, and money funds—are generally preferred for use as part of an investment program, as are asset management accounts at major brokerage firms.

To decide which securities are most appropriate for a particular situation, you need to consider such issue characteristics as availability, safety, liquidity, and yield. Though all the investments we have discussed satisfy the basic liquidity demand, they do so to varying degrees. A NOW account is unquestionably the most liquid of all. You can write as many checks on the account as you wish and for any amount. A certificate of deposit, on the other hand, is not so liquid, because early redemption involves an interest penalty. Table 1.4 summarizes the key characteristics of the short-term investments described in Table 1.3. The letter grade assigned for each characteristic reflects an estimate of the investment's quality in that area. For example, MMMFs rate only a B+ on liquidity, because withdrawals must usually be made in a minimum amount of $250 to $500. NOW accounts are somewhat better in this respect, because a

HOT LINKS

Get the latest Treasury securities data on 30-year bonds, 10-year notes, 5-year notes, and 13-week bills. Visit Yahoo! Finance, section U.S. Markets, [major U.S. Indices], to get the most current quote (last trade), the change from the previous trading day, the percent change, charts, news, and much more.

finance.yahoo.com

TABLE 1.4 A Scorecard for Short-Term Investment Vehicles

Savings or Investment Vehicle	Availability	Safety	Liquidity	Yield (Average Rate)*
Passbook savings account	A+	A+	A	D (0.6%)
NOW account	A–	A+	A+	F (0.5%)
Money market deposit account (MMDA)	B	A+	A	B– (0.7%)
Asset management account	B–	A	A+	B (1.0%)
Series EE savings bond	A+	A++	C–	B+ (2.6%)
U.S. Treasury bill (91-day)	B–	A++	A–	A– (0.9%)
Certificate of deposit (3-month, large denomination)	B	A+	C	A (1.1%)
Commercial paper (90-day)	B–	A–	C	A– (1.1%)
Banker's acceptance (90-day)	B–	A	B	A– (1.1%)
Money market mutual fund (MMMF)	B	A/A+	B+	A– (0.5%)

*The average rates reflect representative or typical rates that existed in early 2004.

withdrawal can be for any amount. Yields are self-explanatory. You should note, though, that if an investment scores lower on availability, safety, or liquidity, it will generally offer a higher yield.

CONCEPTS IN REVIEW

1.16 What makes an asset *liquid?* Why hold liquid assets? Would 100 shares of IBM stock be considered a liquid investment? Explain.

1.17 Explain the characteristics of short-term investments with respect to purchasing power and default risk.

1.18 Briefly describe the key features and differences among the following deposit accounts.

a. Passbook savings account
b. NOW account
c. Money market deposit account
d. Asset management account

1.19 Define, compare, and contrast the following short-term investments.

a. Series EE savings bonds
b. U.S. Treasury bills
c. Certificates of deposit
d. Commercial paper
e. Banker's acceptances
f. Money market mutual funds

Summary

Note: The end-of-chapter Summaries restate the chapter's Learning Goals and review the key points of information related to each goal.

Understand the meaning of the term *investment* and the factors commonly used to differentiate among types of investments. An investment is any vehicle into which funds can be placed with the expectation that they will generate positive income and/or that their value will be preserved or will increase. The returns from investing are received either as current income or as increased value.

Some investment vehicles are securities; others are forms of property. Some investments are made directly, others indirectly. An investment can be a debt, an equity, or a derivative security such as an option. It can possess risk ranging from very low to extremely high. An individual can invest in either short-term or long-term vehicles. Today, individual investors have ready access to both domestic and foreign investments.

LG 2

Describe the investment process and types of investors. The investment process is structured around financial institutions and financial markets that bring together suppliers and demanders of funds. The dominant financial market in the United States is the securities markets for stocks, bonds, and options. The participants in the investment process are government, business, and individuals. Of these groups, only individuals are net suppliers of funds. Investors can be either individual investors or institutional investors.

LG 3

Discuss the principal types of investment vehicles. A broad range of investment vehicles is available. Short-term vehicles have low risk. They are used to earn a return on temporarily idle funds, to serve as a primary investment outlet of conservative investors, and to provide liquidity. Common stocks offer dividends and capital gains. Fixed-income securities—bonds, preferred stock, and convertible securities—offer fixed periodic returns with some potential for gain in value. Mutual funds allow investors conveniently to buy or sell interests in a professionally managed, diversified portfolio of securities.

Derivative securities are high-risk, high-expected-return vehicles. The key derivatives are options and futures. Options offer the investor an opportunity to buy or sell another security at a specified price over a given period of time. Futures are contracts between a seller and a buyer for delivery of a specified commodity or financial instrument, at a specified future date, at an agreed-on price. Other popular investment vehicles include real estate, tangibles, and tax-advantaged investments.

LG 4 **Describe the steps in investing, particularly establishing investment goals, and cite fundamental personal tax considerations.** Investing is a process that should be driven by well-developed plans established to achieve specific goals. It involves a logical set of steps: meeting investment prerequisites, establishing investment goals, adopting an investment plan, evaluating investment vehicles, selecting suitable investments, constructing a diversified portfolio, and managing the portfolio. Investment goals determine the types of investments made. Common investment goals include accumulating retirement funds, enhancing current income, saving for major expenditures, and sheltering income from taxes.

The tax consequences associated with various investment vehicles and strategies must also be considered. The key dimensions are ordinary income, capital gains and losses, tax planning, and the use of tax-advantaged retirement vehicles.

LG 5 **Discuss investing over the life cycle and investing in different economic environments.** The investment vehicles selected are affected by the investor's stage in the life cycle and by economic cycles. Younger investors tend to prefer growth-oriented investments that stress capital gains. As they age investors move to higher-quality securities. As they approach retirement they become even more conservative. The stage of the economy—(1) recovery or expansion, (2) decline or recession, or (3) uncertainty as to the direction of its movement—both current and expected, also affects investment choice.

LG 6 **Understand the popular types of short-term investment vehicles.** Investment plans must ensure adequate liquidity. Liquidity needs can be met by investing in various short-term vehicles, which can earn interest at a stated rate or on a discount basis. They typically have low risk. Numerous short-term investment vehicles are available from banks, the government, and brokerage firms. Their suitability depends on the investor's attitude toward availability, safety, liquidity, and yield.

Putting Your Investment Know-How to the Test

The Chartered Financial Analyst® designation is globally recognized as the highest professional designation you can receive in the field of professional money management. The CFA® charter is awarded to those candidates who successfully pass a series of three exams, with each exam lasting six hours and covering a full range of investment topics. The CFA Program is administered by the Association for Investment Management and Research (AIMR®) in Charlottesville, Virginia. For more information about the CFA program go to: www.aimr.org.

Many CFA candidates turn to the Schweser Study Program for high-quality exam preparation. The Schweser Study Program was founded in 1990 by Dr. Carl Schweser, whose goal was to write study materials that were effective and easy to understand. The Schweser Institute™ offers certificate programs in critical areas of advanced financial education. For more information go to: www.schweser.com.

Starting with Chapter 2 of the text and for every chapter thereafter, you will find a series of CFA questions taken from the Level 1 exam program and of Schweser questions for the same level. The CFA questions have actually appeared on past exams or in AIMR study materials, and the Schweser questions have also been published in their study materials. You will also find sprinkled throughout some multiple-choice questions that mimic the CFA and Schweser study materials, as here in Chapter 1, where the concepts under study are basic and introductory in nature.

1. What represents an ownership share in a corporation?
   a. Fixed-income security
   b. Common stock
   c. Call option
   d. Commercial paper

2. Money market securities are characterized by
   a. A very short term to maturity.
   b. Low risk.
   c. High liquidity.
   d. All of the above.

3. An example of a portfolio investment is a
   a. Stock.
   b. Bond.
   c. Mutual fund.
   d. All of the above.

4. Tangible assets include
   a. Residential homes.
   b. Gold and other precious metals.
   c. Certificates of deposit.
   d. Stocks and bonds.

5. You purchased ABC stock at $52 per share. The stock paid $2 in dividends and is currently selling at $48 per share. Your total return includes
   a. $4 in capital loss and $2 in dividend income.
   b. $2 in capital loss.
   c. $4 in capital gain and $2 in dividend income.
   d. $4 in investment loss.

6. A particularly attractive feature of T-bills is that
   a. They are exempt from local and state income taxes.
   b. They can be purchased from the U.S. government directly.
   c. They are default free.
   d. All of the above.

7. Three-month T-bill auctions are conducted
   a. Daily.
   b. Weekly.
   c. Monthly.
   d. Quarterly.

8. Commercial paper is a short-term security issued to raise funds by
   a. The United States Treasury.
   b. Commercial banks.
   c. The Federal Reserve.
   d. Large corporations.

9. Short-term investment vehicles, ranked in order of liquidity, are
   a. Commercial paper, certificates of deposit, T-bills, and NOW accounts.
   b. NOW accounts, passbook savings, T-bills, and EE-series savings bonds.
   c. Banker's acceptances, money market deposit accounts, T-bills, and commercial paper.
   d. Money market mutual funds, EE-series savings bonds, passbook savings, and certificates of deposit.

10. Which of the activities mentioned below are *not* part of investment planning?
    a. Evaluating suitable investment vehicles
    b. Constructing a diversified portfolio
    c. Performing tax analysis and sheltering income from taxes
    d. Timing the market

Answers: 1. b; 2. d; 3. c; 4. b; 5. a; 6. d; 7. b; 8. d; 9. b; 10. d

Discussion Questions

LG 4 LG 5

Note: The Discussion Questions at the end of the chapter ask you to analyze and synthesize information presented in the chapter. These questions, like all other end-of-chapter assignment materials, are keyed to the chapter's learning goals.

Q1.1. Assume that you are 35 years old, are married with two young children, are renting a condo, and have an annual income of $90,000. Use the following questions to guide your preparation of a rough investment plan consistent with these facts.

a. What are your key investment goals?
b. How might personal taxes affect your investment plans? Use current tax rates to assess their impact.
c. How might your stage in the life cycle affect the types of risk you might take?

LG 6

Q1.2. What role, if any, will short-term vehicles play in your portfolio? Why? Complete the following table for the short-term investments listed. Find their yields in a current issue of the *Wall Street Journal,* and explain which, if any, you would include in your investment portfolio.

Savings or Investment Vehicle	Minimum Balance	Yield	Federal Insurance	Method and Ease of Withdrawing Funds
a. Passbook savings account	None		Yes	In person or through teller machines; very easy
b. NOW account				Unlimited check-writing privileges
c. Money market deposit account (MMDA)				
d. Asset management account				
e. Series EE savings bond	Virtually none			
f. U.S. Treasury bill				
g. Certificate of deposit (CD)				
h. Commercial paper				
i. Banker's acceptance				
j. Money market mutual fund (MMMF)				

Problems

LG 4 LG 5

Note: The Problems at the end of the chapter offer opportunities to perform calculations using the tools and techniques learned in the chapter. A Web icon appears next to problems that can be solved using the text's software accessible at its Web site: www.aw-bc.com/gitman_joehnk.

P1.1 Sonia Gomez, a 45-year-old widow, wishes to accumulate $250,000 over the next 15 years to supplement the retirement programs that are being funded by the federal government and her employer. She expects to earn an average annual return of about 8% by investing in a low-risk portfolio containing about 20% short-term securities, 30% common stock, and 50% bonds.

Sonia currently has $31,500 that at an 8% annual rate of return will grow to about $100,000 at the end of 15 years (found using time-value techniques that will be described in Chapter 4). Her financial adviser indicated that for every $1,000 Sonia wishes to accumulate at the end of 15 years, she will have to make an annual investment of $36.83. (This amount is also calculated on the basis of an 8% annual rate of return using the time-value techniques that are described in Chapter 4.) Sonia plans to accumulate needed funds by making equal, annual, end-of-year investments over the next 15 years.

a. How much money does Sonia need to accumulate by making equal, annual, end-of-year investments to reach her goal of $250,000?
b. How much must Sonia deposit annually to accumulate at the end of year 15 the sum calculated in part **a**?

LG 4

P1.2 During 2003, the Allens and the Zells both filed joint tax returns. The Allens' taxable income was $130,000, and the Zells had total taxable income of $65,000 for the tax year ended December 31, 2003.

a. Using the federal tax rates given in Table 1.2, calculate the taxes for both the Allens and the Zells.
b. Calculate and compare the ratio of the Allens' to the Zells' taxable income and the ratio of the Allens' to the Zells' taxes. What does this demonstrate about the federal income tax structure?

LG 4

P1.3 Robert Pang, a 53-year-old software engineer, and his wife, Jean, have $50,000 to invest. They will need the money at retirement in 10 years. They are considering two investments. The first is a utility company common stock that costs $50 per share and pays dividends of $2 per share per year (a 4% dividend yield). They do not expect the value of this stock to increase. The other investment under consideration is a highly rated corporate bond that currently sells at par in $1,000 increments, and pays annual interest at a rate of 5%, or $50 per $1,000 invested. After 10 years, these bonds will be repaid at par, or $1,000 per $1,000 invested. Assume that the Pangs keep the income from their investments, but do not reinvest it (they keep the cash under a mattress). They will, however, need to pay income taxes on their investment income. They will sell the stock after 10 years if they buy it. If they buy the bonds, they will get the amount they invested back in 10 years. The Pangs are in the 33% tax bracket.

a. How many shares of the stock can the Pangs buy?
b. How much will they receive each year in dividend income if they buy the stock, after taxes?
c. What is the total amount they would have from their original $50,000 if they purchased the stock and it all went as planned?
d. How much will they receive each year in interest if they purchase the bonds, after taxes?
e. What is the total amount they would have from their original $50,000 if they purchased the bonds and all went as planned?
f. Based only on your calculations and ignoring other risk factors, should they buy the stock or the bonds?

LG 4

P1.4 Mike and Linda Smith are a working couple. They will file a joint income tax return. This year, they have the following taxable income:

1. $125,000 from salary and wages (ordinary income).
2. $1,000 in interest income.
3. $3,000 in dividend income.
4. $2,000 in profit from a stock they purchased two years ago.
5. $2,000 in profit from a stock they purchased this year and sold this year.

Use the federal income tax rates given in Table 1.2 to work this problem.

a. How much will Mike and Linda pay in federal income taxes on 2 above?
b. How much will Mike and Linda pay in federal income taxes on 3 above?
c. How much will Mike and Linda pay in federal income taxes on 4 above?
d. How much will Mike and Linda pay in federal income taxes on 5 above?

See the text Web site (www.aw-bc.com/gitman_joehnk) for Web exercises that deal with *the investment environment*.

Case Problem 1.1

LG 1 LG 2 LG 3

Investments or Golf?

Note: Two Case Problems appear at the end of every chapter. They ask you to apply what you have learned in the chapter to a hypothetical investment situation.

Judd Read and Judi Todd, senior accounting majors at a large midwestern university, have been good friends since high school. Each has already found a job that will begin after graduation. Judd has accepted a position as an internal auditor in a medium-sized manufacturing firm. Judi will be working for one of the major public accounting firms. Each is looking forward to the challenge of a new career and to the prospect of achieving success both professionally and financially.

Judd and Judi are preparing to register for their final semester. Each has one free elective to select. Judd is considering taking a golf course offered by the physical education department, which he says will help him socialize in his business career. Judi is planning to take a basic investments course. Judi has been trying to convince Judd to take investments instead of golf. Judd believes he doesn't need to take investments, because he already knows what common stock is. He believes that whenever he has accumulated excess funds, he can invest in the stock of a company that is doing well. Judi argues that there is much more to it than simply choosing common stock. She feels that exposure to the field of investments would be more beneficial than learning how to play golf.

Questions

a. Explain to Judd the structure of the investment process and the economic importance of investing.

b. List and discuss the other types of investment vehicles with which Judd is apparently unfamiliar.

c. Assuming that Judd already gets plenty of exercise, what arguments would you give to convince Judd to take investments rather than golf?

Case Problem 1.2

LG 4 LG 5 LG 6

Preparing Carolyn Bowen's Investment Plan

Carolyn Bowen, who just turned 55, is a widow currently employed as a receptionist for the Xcon Corporation, where she has worked for the past 20 years. She is in good health, lives alone, and has two grown children. A few months ago, her husband died. Carolyn's husband left her with only their home and the proceeds from a $75,000 life insurance policy. After she paid medical and funeral expenses, $60,000 of the life insurance proceeds remained. In addition to the life insurance proceeds, Carolyn has $37,500 in a savings account, which she had secretly built over the past 10 years. Recognizing that she is within 10 years of retirement, Carolyn wishes to use her limited resources to develop an investment program that will allow her to live comfortably once she retires.

Carolyn is quite superstitious. After consulting with a number of psychics and studying her family tree, she feels certain she will not live past 80. She plans to retire at either 62 or 65, whichever will better allow her to meet her long-run financial goals. After talking with a number of knowledgeable individuals—including, of course, the psychics—Carolyn estimates that to live comfortably, she will need $45,000 per year, before taxes, once she retires. This amount will be required annually for each of 18 years if she retires at 62 or for each of 15 years if she retires at 65. As part of her financial plans, Carolyn intends to sell her home at retirement and rent an apartment. She has estimated that she will net $112,500 if she sells the house at 62 and $127,500 if she sells it at 65. Carolyn has no financial dependents and is not concerned about leaving a sizable estate to her heirs.

If Carolyn retires at age 62, she will receive from Social Security and an employer-sponsored pension plan a total of $1,359 per month ($16,308 annually); if she waits until age 65 to retire, her total retirement income will be $1,688 per month ($20,256 annually). For convenience, Carolyn has already decided that to convert all her assets at the time of retirement into a stream of annual income, she will at that time purchase an annuity by paying a single premium. The annuity will have a life just equal to the number of years remaining until her 80th birthday. Because Carolyn is uncertain as to the actual age at which she will retire, she obtained the following interest factors from her insurance agent to estimate the annual annuity benefit provided for a given purchase price.

Life of Annuity	Interest Factor
15 years	11.118
18 years	12.659

The yearly annuity benefit can be calculated by dividing the factors into the purchase price. Carolyn plans to place any funds currently available into a savings account paying 6% compounded annually until retirement. She does not expect to be able to save or invest any additional funds between now and retirement. To calculate the future value of her savings, she will need to multiply the amount of money currently available to her by one of the following factors, depending on the retirement age being considered.

Retirement Age	Time to Retirement	Future-Value Interest Factor
62	7 years	1.504
65	10 years	1.791

Questions

a. Assume that Carolyn places currently available funds in the savings account. Determine the amount of money Carolyn will have available at retirement once she sells her house if she retires at (1) age 62 and (2) age 65.

b. Using the results from question (a) and the interest factors given above, determine the level of annual income that will be provided to Carolyn through purchase of an annuity at (1) age 62 and (2) age 65.

c. With the results found in the preceding questions, determine the total annual retirement income Carolyn will have if she retires at (1) age 62 and (2) age 65.

d. From your findings, do you think Carolyn will be able to achieve her long-run financial goal by retiring at (1) age 62 or (2) age 65? Explain.

e. Evaluate Carolyn's investment plan in terms of her use of a savings account and an annuity rather than some other investment vehicles. Comment on the risk and return characteristics of her plan. What recommendations might you offer Carolyn? Be specific.

Excel with Spreadsheets

Note: Excel spreadsheet exercises at the end of each chapter will assist you in learning some useful applications of this tool in the personal investing process.

In the following chapters of this text, you will be asked to solve spreadsheet problems using Microsoft Excel®. While each person's skill and experience with Excel will vary, an assumption has been made that you understand the basics of Excel. This includes the entering of text and numbers, copying or moving a cell, moving and copying using "drag and drop," inserting and deleting rows and columns, and checking your spelling. The review in this chapter focuses on entering and editing data in the worksheet.

To complete the spreadsheet review, go to www.aw-bc.com/gitman_joehnk and go to "Student Resources." Click on "Spreadsheet Review." There you will be asked to create a spreadsheet and perform the following tasks.

Questions

a. Add and subtract data with a formula
b. Multiply and divide data with a formula
c. Total cells using the sum function and calculate an average
d. Use the average function
e. Copy a formula using the "drag and drop" method

CHAPTER 2

MARKETS AND TRANSACTIONS

CHAPTER 2

MARKETS AND TRANSACTIONS

LEARNING GOALS

After studying this chapter, you should be able to:

LG 1 Identify the basic types of securities markets and describe the IPO process.

LG 2 Explain the characteristics of organized securities exchanges.

LG 3 Understand the over-the-counter markets, including Nasdaq and alternative trading systems, and the general conditions of securities markets.

LG 4 Review the importance of global securities markets, their performance, and the investment procedures and risks associated with foreign investments.

LG 5 Discuss trading hours and the regulation of securities markets.

LG 6 Explain long purchases and the motives, procedures, and calculations involved in making margin transactions and short sales.

The market turmoil that rocked the global capital markets set the stage for major changes in the way U.S. securities markets and related financial institutions operate. Beset by scandals, from corporate wrongdoing to internal problems at the venerable New York Stock Exchange (NYSE), Wall Street's institutions are taking stock of how they operate and reassessing their own standards.

A few years ago Nasdaq, the pioneer of electronic trading systems that billed itself as "the market for the next 100 years," was grabbing market share from the NYSE. Its less stringent listing requirements and state-of-the-art technology made Nasdaq the preferred route for entrepreneurial companies to raise capital. Technology companies especially flocked to Nasdaq, and as their fortunes rose in the 1990s, so did Nasdaq's. When the technology bubble burst in 2000, contributing to the bear market that followed, Nasdaq was—not surprisingly—hit harder than the other exchanges. It retrenched, canceling its own initial public offering and curtailing the operations of Nasdaq Europe and other overseas ventures. Nevertheless, its automated matching system, which eliminates the middleman, remains popular with many customers.

The NYSE remains one of the few exchanges worldwide that is not wholly electronic. Criticized for its adherence to a traditional people-centered trading system, it managed to weather the bear market in better shape than its electronic counterparts. Even though its $0.078/share transaction fee is usually the lowest priced, high-speed electronic communications networks (ECNs) are coming close to that rate and beating it at times. Institutional investors are moving more of their trades from the exchange floor to ECNs such as Archipelago, Instinet, Posit, and the Internet-based Liquidnet. ECNs now handle about 15% of all NYSE trades.

The increasing competition among exchanges should benefit investors. It will promote better governance, encourage more innovation, and result in technological advances that improve the quality, fairness, and accuracy of securities transactions.

In this chapter, we will study the markets, the exchanges, the regulations, and the transactions that enable companies to raise money in the capital markets and institutions and individuals to invest in these companies.

Sources: Kim Clark, "Closing Bell for the NYSE?" *U.S. News & World Report*, June 9, 2003, p. 26; Mara Der Hovanesian, "The Big Board Risks Losing the Big Trades," *Business Week*, May 5, 2003, p. 40; Paula Dwyer and Amy Borrus, "Nasdaq, the Fight of Its Life," *Business Week*, August 11, 2003, p. 40; Gretchen Morgenson, "Is the Big Board Getting Creaky?" *The New York Times*, April 27, 2003, section 3, p. 1; and Andrei Postelni, "The Bull Market Hero at Bay," *Financial Times*, August 30, 2003, p. 13.

Securities Markets

Securities markets are forums that allow suppliers and demanders of *securities* to make financial transactions. They permit such transactions to be made quickly and at a fair price. In this section we will look at the various types of markets, their organization, and their general behavior.

LG 1 LG 2 LG 3

Types of Securities Markets

securities markets
forums that allow suppliers and demanders of *securities* to make financial transactions; they include both the *money market* and the *capital market.*

money market
market where *short-term* securities (with maturities less than one year) are bought and sold.

capital market
market in which *long-term* securities (with maturities greater than one year) such as stocks and bonds are bought and sold.

primary market
the market in which *new issues* of securities are sold to the public.

initial public offering (IPO)
the first public sale of a company's stock.

Securities and Exchange Commission (SEC)
federal agency that regulates securities offerings and markets.

public offering
the sale of a firm's securities to the general public.

rights offering
an offer of new shares of stock to existing stockholders on a pro rata basis.

private placement
the sale of new securities directly, without SEC registration, to selected groups of investors.

HOT

The SEC site, in addition to providing corporate documents such as annual reports, offers basic information and warnings to new investors.

www.sec.gov

Securities markets may be classified as either money markets or capital markets. The **money market** is the market where *short-term* securities (with maturities less than one year) are bought and sold. Investors turn to the **capital market** to make transactions involving *long-term* securities (with maturities greater than one year) such as stocks and bonds. In this book we will devote most of our attention to the capital market. There, investors can make stock, bond, mutual fund, options, and futures transactions. Capital markets can be classified as either *primary* or *secondary,* depending on whether securities are being sold initially by their issuing company or by intervening owners.

The Primary Market The market in which *new issues* of securities are sold to the public is the **primary market.** In the primary market, the issuer of the equity or debt securities receives the proceeds of sales. In 2003, only 79 companies offered their stock for sale in the primary market. This number compared miserably with the 452 companies that went public three years earlier. The main vehicle in the primary market is the **initial public offering (IPO),** the first public sale of a company's stock. The primary markets also provide a forum for the sale of new securities, called *seasoned new issues,* by companies that are already public.

Before offering its securities for public sale, the issuer must register them with and obtain approval from the **Securities and Exchange Commission (SEC).** This federal regulatory agency must confirm both the adequacy and the accuracy of the information provided to potential investors before a security is publicly offered for sale. In addition, the SEC regulates the securities markets.

To market its securities in the primary market, a firm has three choices. It may make (1) a **public offering,** in which the firm offers its securities for sale to the general public; (2) a **rights offering,** in which the firm offers new shares to existing stockholders on a pro rata basis; or (3) a **private placement,** in which the firm sells new securities directly, without SEC registration, to selected groups of investors such as insurance companies and pension funds.

Going Public: The IPO Process Most companies that go public are small, fast-growing companies that require additional capital to continue expanding. For example, credit and debit card processing company iPayment, Inc., raised almost $80 million when it went public in May 2003 at $16 per share. In addition, large companies may decide to spin off a unit into a separate public corporation. AT&T did this when it spun off its wireless operations into AT&T Wireless in April 2000, raising over $10 billion at $29.50 per share.

When a company decides to go public, it first must obtain the approval of its current shareholders, the investors who own its privately issued stock. Next, the company's auditors and lawyers must certify that all documents for the company are

Click on [IPOS] for current IPO news, a calendar of new issues, SEC filings, and more

cbs.marketwatch.com

legitimate. The company then finds an investment bank willing to *underwrite* the offering. This underwriter is responsible for promoting the stock and facilitating the sale of the company's IPO shares. The underwriter often brings in other investment banking firms as participants. We'll discuss the role of the investment banker in more detail in the next section.

The company files a registration statement with the SEC. One portion of the registration statement is called the **prospectus.** It describes the key aspects of the issue, the issuer, and its management and financial position. During the waiting period between the statement's filing and its approval, prospective investors can receive a preliminary prospectus. This preliminary version is called a **red herring,** because a notice printed in red on the front cover indicates the tentative nature of the offer. The cover of the preliminary prospectus describing the 2003 stock issue of Hewitt Associates, Inc., a leading global provider of human resources outsourcing and consulting services, is shown in Figure 2.1 (on page 38). Note the red herring printed vertically on its left edge.

prospectus
a portion of a security registration statement that describes the key aspects of the issue, the issuer, and its management and financial position.

red herring
a preliminary *prospectus* made available to prospective investors during the waiting period between the registration statement's filing with the SEC and its approval.

After the SEC approves the registration statement, the investment community can begin analyzing the company's prospects. However, from the time it files until at least one month after the IPO is complete, the company must observe a *quiet period,* during which there are restrictions on what company officials may say about the company. The purpose of the quiet period is to make sure that all potential investors have access to the same information about the company—that which is presented in the preliminary prospectus—and not to any unpublished data that might give them an unfair advantage.

The investment bankers and company executives promote the company's stock offering through a *road show,* a series of presentations to potential investors—typically institutional investors—around the country and sometimes overseas. In addition to providing investors with information about the new issue, road show sessions help the investment bankers gauge the demand for the offering and set an expected pricing range. After the underwriter sets terms and prices the issue, the SEC must approve the offering.

Table 2.1 (on page 39) shows, for each year between 1993 and 2002, the number of offerings, the average first-day return, and the gross proceeds of the given years' IPOs. Note the exceptionally high first-day returns and large number of offerings during 1999 and 2000 caused by the technology-stock-driven bull market that ended in late 2000. Since then, the number of offerings and the first-day returns have declined dramatically, consistent with the precipitous market decline that occurred in 2001 and 2002. During the boom of 1999 and 2000, it wasn't unusual for the price of an IPO to double on the first day. During that period many IPOs were underpriced, resulting in huge first-day gains. Some industry experts question whether the underwriters misjudge demand for an issue or set the price artificially low to please their institutional clients, who buy at the offering price and then resell the shares. Sometimes companies themselves support undervaluation so that their stock will generate excitement and additional investor interest when the price zooms upward on opening day.

Log on to individualinvestor.com and click [education], [how to read], [A Prospectus].

www.individualinvestor.com

The IPO markets haven't been particularly active in recent years. Their lack of activity has been a direct result of the weakness of the public equity markets. Investing in IPOs is risky business, particularly for individual investors who can't easily acquire shares at the offering

FIGURE 2.1

Cover of a Preliminary Prospectus for a Stock Issue

Some of the key factors related to the 2003 common stock issue by Hewitt Associates, Inc. are summarized on the cover of the prospectus. The type printed vertically on the left edge is normally red, which explains its name "red herring." (*Source:* Hewitt Associates, Inc., July 28, 2003, p. 1.)

The information in this preliminary prospectus is not complete and may be changed. These securities may not be sold until the registration statement filed with the Securities and Exchange Commission is effective. This preliminary prospectus is not an offer to sell nor does it seek an offer to buy these securities in any jurisdiction where the offer or sale is not permitted.

Subject to Completion. Dated July 28, 2003.

9,850,000 Shares

Hewitt

Class A Common Stock

All of the shares of common stock of Hewitt Associates, Inc. in the offering are being sold by the selling stockholders identified in this prospectus. We will not receive any of the proceeds from the sale of the shares. We have agreed to pay for the expenses of the offering.

Our class A common stock is quoted on the New York Stock Exchange under the symbol "HEW". The last reported sale price of class A common stock on July 25, 2003 was $26.79 per share.

See "Risk Factors" beginning on page 10 to read about factors you should consider before buying shares of class A common stock.

Neither the Securities and Exchange Commission nor any other regulatory body has approved or disapproved of these securities or passed upon the adequacy or accuracy of this prospectus. Any representation to the contrary is a criminal offense.

	Per Share	Total
Initial price to public	$	$
Underwriting discount	$	$
Proceeds to the selling stockholders	$	$

To the extent that the underwriters sell more than 9,850,000 shares of class A common stock, the underwriters have the option to purchase up to an additional 1,477,500 shares from the selling stockholders at the initial price to public less the underwriting discount.

The underwriters expect to deliver the shares against payment in New York, New York on , 2003.

Goldman, Sachs & Co.

Banc of America Securities LLC

Citigroup

JPMorgan

UBS Investment Bank

Wachovia Securities

Prospectus dated , 2003.

investment banker
financial intermediary that specializes in selling new security issues and advising firms with regard to major financial transactions.

underwriting
the role of the *investment banker* in bearing the risk of reselling, at a profit, the securities purchased from an issuing corporation at an agreed-on price.

price. Most of those shares go to institutional investors and brokerage firms' best clients. Although news stories may chronicle huge first-day gains, the stocks may not be good long-term investments.

The Investment Banker's Role Most public offerings are made with the assistance of an **investment banker.** The investment banker is a financial intermediary (such as Goldman, Sachs & Co. or Citigroup) that specializes in selling new security issues and advising firms with regard to major financial transactions. The main activity of the investment banker is **underwriting.** This process involves purchasing the security issue from the issuing corporation at an agreed-on price and bearing the risk of reselling it to the public at a profit.

TABLE 2.1 Annual IPO Data, 1993–2002

Year	Number of Offerings	Average First-Day Return (%)	Gross Proceeds ($ million)
1993	507	12.7	29,257
1994	416	9.7	18,300
1995	465	21.0	28,872
1996	666	16.5	42.479
1997	484	13.9	33,218
1998	319	20.0	35,112
1999	490	69.1	65,460
2000	385	55.4	65,677
2001	81	13.7	34,368
2002	73	8.3	22,954

Source: Jay R. Ritter, "Some Factoids About the 2002 IPO Market," downloaded from Web site (www.bearcba.ufl.edu/ritter/work_papers/IPOs2002.pdf), January 14, 2003, Table 5.

underwriting syndicate
a group formed by an investment banker to share the financial risk associated with *underwriting* new securities.

selling group
a large number of brokerage firms that join the originating investment banker(s); each accepts responsibility for selling a certain portion of a new security issue and is paid a commission on the securities it sells.

The investment banker also provides the issuer with advice about pricing and other important aspects of the issue.

In the case of very large security issues, the investment banker brings in other bankers as partners to form an **underwriting syndicate.** The syndicate shares the financial risk associated with buying the entire issue from the issuer and reselling the new securities to the public. The originating investment banker and the syndicate members put together a **selling group,** normally made up of themselves and a large number of brokerage firms. Each member of the selling group accepts the responsibility for selling a certain portion of the issue and is paid a commission on the securities it sells. The selling process for a large security issue is depicted in Figure 2.2.

FIGURE 2.2

The Selling Process for a Large Security Issue

The investment banker hired by the issuing corporation may form an underwriting syndicate. The underwriting syndicate buys the entire security issue from the issuing corporation at an agreed-on price. The underwriter then has the opportunity (and bears the risk) of reselling the issue to the public at a profit. Both the originating investment banker and the other syndicate members put together a selling group to sell the issue on a commission basis to investors.

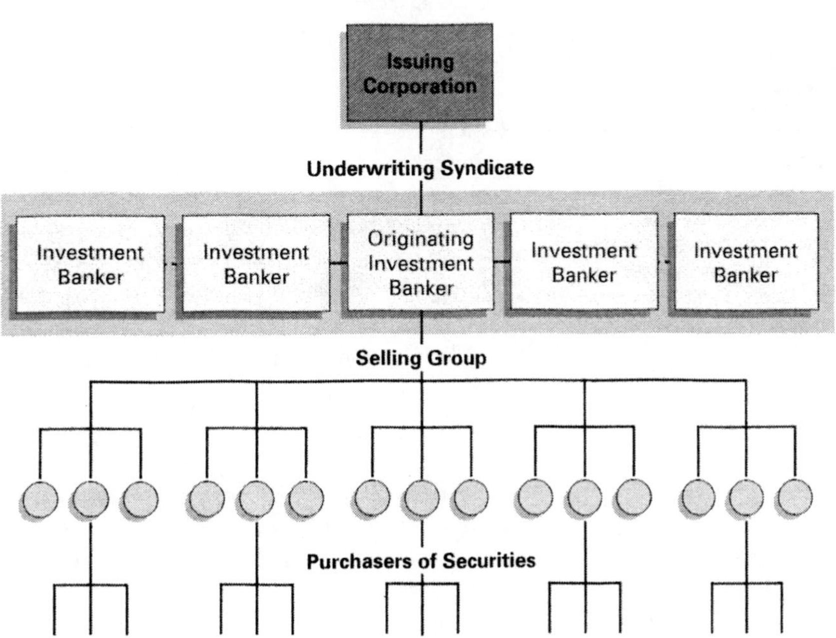

The relationships among the participants in this process can also be seen in the so-called *tombstone* for the July 2, 2003, common stock offering for White Electronic Designs shown in Figure 6.4 (on page 247). This layout of the announcement indicates the roles of the various participating firms. Isolated firm names or a larger typeface differentiates the underwriter and the underwriting syndicate from the selling group. (In the figure, the key participants in the offering are labeled in the margin at the right.)

Compensation for underwriting and selling services typically comes in the form of a discount on the sale price of the securities. For example, an investment banker may pay the issuing firm $24 per share for stock that will be sold for $26 per share. The investment banker may then sell the shares to members of the selling group for $25.25 per share. In this case, the original investment banker earns $1.25 per share ($25.25 sale price − $24 purchase price). The members of the selling group earn 75 cents for each share they sell ($26 sale price − $25.25 purchase price). Although some primary security offerings are directly placed by the issuer, the majority of new issues are sold through public offering via the mechanism just described.

HOT LINKS

Check out some leading investment banks, such as:

www.smithbarney.com,
www.gs.com, and
www.morganstanley.com

secondary market
the market in which securities are traded *after they have been issued.*

Secondary Markets The market in which securities are traded *after they have been issued* is the **secondary market,** or the *aftermarket*. The secondary market provides a way for owners of securities that are already issued to sell them to others. In the secondary market, unlike the primary market, the transaction does not involve the corporation that issued the securities. Instead, money and securities are exchanged between investors; the seller exchanges securities for cash paid by the buyer. The secondary market gives security purchasers *liquidity*. It also provides a mechanism for continuous pricing of securities to reflect their value at each point in time, on the basis of the best information then available.

organized securities exchanges
centralized institutions in which transactions are made in already outstanding securities.

over-the-counter (OTC) market
widely scattered telecommunications network through which transactions are made in both *initial public offerings (IPOs)* and securities that are already outstanding.

The secondary markets include the various organized securities exchanges and the over-the-counter market. **Organized securities exchanges** are centralized institutions that bring together the forces of supply and demand for securities that are already outstanding. These exchanges are *auction markets* in which the flow of buy and sell orders determines the price. The **over-the-counter (OTC) market,** on the other hand, is a widely scattered telecommunications network through which transactions are made in both *initial public offerings (IPOs)* and securities that are already outstanding. The OTC market is a *dealer market* that uses a quote system in which negotiation and dealer quotes determine the price. Because popular investment vehicles trade on the organized exchanges and in the over-the-counter market, individual investors are likely to make transactions in both of these markets.

Organized Securities Exchanges

Securities that trade on *organized securities exchanges* account for about 62% of the total *dollar volume* (about 46% of the total *share volume*) of domestic shares traded. Persons who are members of a given exchange (for example, the New York Stock Exchange on Wall Street) conduct all trading for that exchange in one place, under a broad set of rules. The best-known exchanges for stock and bond transactions are the New York Stock Exchange (NYSE) and

Go to the NYSE site and click on [Glossary] to find out the definition of a "growth stock," "American Depositary Receipt, ADR," and "S&P 500."

www.nyse.com

the American Stock Exchange (AMEX), both located in New York City. They account for approximately 90% and 4%, respectively, of the total annual dollar volume of shares traded on *organized* U.S. exchanges. Other domestic exchanges include *regional exchanges*, such as the Chicago Stock Exchange and the Pacific Exchange. Regional exchanges deal primarily in securities with regional or local appeal. Together, the regional exchanges account for about 6% of the annual dollar volume of shares traded on organized U.S. exchanges. In addition, foreign stock exchanges list and trade shares of firms in their own foreign markets. Separate domestic exchanges exist for options trading and for trading in futures. Here we will consider the basic structure, rules, and operations of each of these organized domestic securities exchanges. (We'll discuss foreign exchanges later.)

The New York Stock Exchange Most organized securities exchanges are modeled after the New York Stock Exchange (NYSE). It is the dominant organized exchange, often referred to as the "Big Board." To be a member, an individual or firm must own or lease a "seat" on the exchange. The word "seat" is used only figuratively, because its members trade securities standing up. The majority of seat holders are brokerage firms, and each typically owns more than one seat. The largest brokerage firm, Merrill Lynch, owns over 20 of the 1,366 seats on the NYSE.

Firms such as Merrill Lynch designate officers to occupy seats. Only such designated individuals can make transactions on the floor of the exchange. Although the majority of members make purchase and sale transactions on behalf of their customers, some members specialize in making transactions for other members or for their own account. There are two main types of floor brokers—commission brokers and independent brokers. *Commission brokers* execute orders for their firm's customers. An *independent broker* works for himself or herself and handles orders on a fee basis, typically for smaller brokerage firms or large firms that are too busy to handle their own orders.

Trading Activity Exchange members make all trades on the floor of the organized exchanges. The largest—the floor of the NYSE—is an area about the size of a football field. Its operation is typical of the various exchanges (though details vary). The NYSE floor has 20 trading posts. Certain stocks trade at each post. (Bonds and less active stocks are traded in an annex.) Around the perimeter are telephones and electronic equipment that transmit buy and sell orders from brokers' offices to the exchange floor and back again after members execute the orders.

All transactions on the floor of the exchange occur through an auction process. The goal is to fill all buy orders at the lowest price and to fill all sell orders at the highest price, with supply and demand determining the price. The actual auction takes place at the post where the particular security trades. Members interested in purchasing a given security publicly negotiate a transaction with members interested in selling that security. The job of the **specialist**—an exchange member who specializes in making transactions in one or more stocks—is to manage the auction process. The specialist buys or sells (at specified prices) to provide a continuous, fair, and orderly market in those securities assigned to her or him.

specialist
stock exchange member who specializes in making transactions in one or more stocks and manages the auction process.

Listing Policies To list its shares on an organized stock exchange, a firm must file an application and meet certain listing requirements. Currently, over 3,025 firms list their securities on the NYSE; they account for about 3,300 stocks (common and preferred) and 1,750 bond issues. Of these firms, almost 400 are non-U.S. corporations. Some firms have **dual listing,** or listings on more than one exchange.

dual listing
listing of a firm's shares on more than one exchange.

The New York Stock Exchange has the strictest listing requirements. To be listed on the NYSE, a firm must have at least 2,200 stockholders owning 100 or more shares and a minimum of 1.1 million shares of publicly held stock outstanding; aggregate pretax earnings of at least $6.5 million over the previous 3 years, with no loss in the previous 2 years; and a minimum market value of public shares of $100 million. A foreign company must have aggregate pretax earnings of at least $100 million over the previous 3 years, with at least $25 million in each of the previous 2 years. The firm also must pay a listing fee of between $150,000 and $250,000. Once the NYSE accepts a firm's securities for listing, the company must continue to meet SEC requirements for exchange-listed securities. Listed firms that fail to meet specified requirements may be *de-listed* from the exchange.

HOT LINKS

Read about index shares (Spiders and Diamonds), and also HOLDRS, at the AMEX Web site. Click on [ETFs] and browse the products. Be sure to look at some of the tear sheets for these shares. Do the same for the HOLDRS.

www.amex.com

The American Stock Exchange The American Stock Exchange (AMEX) is the second largest organized U.S. securities exchange in terms of number of listed companies. In terms of dollar volume of trading, the AMEX is actually smaller than the largest regional exchange—the Chicago. Its organization and its procedures are similar to those of the NYSE. Because its listing requirements are less stringent, many smaller and younger firms choose to list on the AMEX. In mid-1998 the AMEX merged with the National Association of Securities Dealers (NASD)—the backbone of the over-the-counter market—and, like the OTC, became a subsidiary of the NASD Market Holding Company. The AMEX has approximately 850 seats and about 800 listed stocks.

INVESTOR FACTS

TOTAL ACCESS OPTIONS—In October 2002, the American Stock Exchange took another step toward electronic options trading. In response to increasing demand from options traders, AMEX launched Total Access Options (TAO), an order entry system that routes orders electronically to all five U.S. options exchanges—even those of its rivals. Customers will now have the instantaneous electronic desktop option trading capability to send and receive orders through the Internet or private networks.

In recent years the AMEX has reinvented itself to focus on more specialized market instruments. Today about two-thirds of its daily volume comes from *exchange traded funds (ETFs)*, a security pioneered by AMEX about 10 years ago. These funds are baskets of securities that are designed to generally track an index of the broad stock or bond market, a stock industry sector, or an international stock, but trade like a single stock. Trading in stock options accounts for another large segment of the AMEX's business.

Regional Stock Exchanges Each of the regional exchanges typically lists the securities of 100–500 companies. As a group, these exchanges handle about 6% of the dollar volume of all shares traded on organized U.S. exchanges. The best-known regional exchanges are the Chicago, Pacific, Philadelphia, Boston, and Cincinnati exchanges. The Pacific Exchange's equity trading operations occur on the Archipelago Exchange, the first fully electronic national stock market in the United States. Most other regional exchanges are modeled after the NYSE, but their membership and listing requirements are considerably more lenient. Trading costs are also lower.

The majority of securities listed on regional exchanges are also listed on the NYSE or the AMEX. About 100 million NYSE shares pass through one of the regional exchanges on a typical trading day. This dual listing may enhance a security's trading activity. In addition, the *Intermarket Trading System (ITS)* links nine markets—five regional exchanges, the NYSE, the AMEX, the over-the-counter market, and the Chicago Board Options Exchange—through an electronic communications network that allows brokers and other traders to make transactions at the best prices.

Options Exchanges *Options* allow their holders to sell or to buy another security at a specified price over a given period of time. The dominant options exchange is the Chicago Board Options Exchange (CBOE). Options are also traded on the AMEX, the Pacific Exchange, the Philadelphia Stock Exchange, and the International Securities Exchange (ISE). Usually, an option to sell or buy a given security is listed on all five options exchanges. Options exchanges deal only in security options. Other types of options (not discussed in this text) result from private transactions made directly between sellers and buyers.

Futures Exchanges *Futures* are contracts that guarantee the delivery of a specified commodity or financial instrument at a specific future date at an agreed-on price. The dominant exchange for trading commodity and financial futures is the Chicago Board of Trade (CBT). There are a number of other futures exchanges, some of which specialize in certain commodities and financial instruments rather than handling the broad spectrum listed on the CBT. The largest of these exchanges are the New York Mercantile Exchange, the Chicago Mercantile Exchange, the Deutsche Terminboerse, the London International Financial Futures Exchange, the New York Coffee, Sugar & Cocoa Exchange, the New York Cotton Exchange, the Kansas City Board of Trade, and the Minneapolis Grain Exchange.

The Over-the-Counter Market

The *over-the-counter (OTC) market* is not a specific institution. It represents another way of trading securities. The OTC market is the result of an intangible relationship among sellers and purchasers of securities, who are linked by a telecommunications network. Nasdaq, the leading OTC market, accounts for about 38% of the total *dollar volume* (about 54% of the total *share volume*) of domestic shares traded, compared to approximately 56% for the NYSE, 2% for the AMEX, and 4% for regional exchanges. Instead of an auction system, the OTC market uses a quote system. This system relies on negotiation and dealer quotes to determine the prices at which securities trade in the OTC market. The actual process, which is described later, depends on the general activity of the security. Securities traded in this market are sometimes called *unlisted securities*.

About 35,000 stocks trade over the counter, as do most government and corporate bonds. The OTC market has three tiers. About 3,450 stocks have an active market in which transactions take place frequently, and another 3,600 trade on the OTC Bulletin Board. The rest are stocks of small, thinly traded companies. A majority of all corporate bonds, some of which are also listed on the NYSE, trade in the OTC market.

New Issues and Secondary Distributions To create a continuous market for unlisted securities, the OTC market also serves as a forum in which to sell both listed and unlisted *initial public offerings (IPOs)*. Subsequent transactions for listed securities then shift to the appropriate organized securities exchange;

secondary distributions
the public sales of large blocks of previously issued securities held by large investors.

unlisted securities continue to trade in the OTC market. **Secondary distributions**—the public sales of large blocks of previously issued securities held by large investors—are also made in the OTC market to minimize the potentially negative effects of such transactions on the price of listed securities. These transactions are forms of third- or fourth-market trades, which we will describe in a moment.

market makers
dealers who "make markets" by offering to buy or sell certain over-the-counter securities at stated prices.

Market Makers The market price of OTC securities results from a matching of supply and demand for securities by dealers known as **market makers.** Each market maker "makes markets" in certain securities by offering to buy or sell them at stated prices. Unlike the organized exchanges, where a *broker* brings together the buyer and seller of a security, the OTC market links a buyer or seller with a *market maker*. That is, the second party to an OTC transaction is always a market maker.

bid price
the highest price offered by a market maker to purchase a given security.

ask price
the lowest price at which a market maker is willing to sell a given security.

For example, a market maker in Raco Enterprises might offer to buy shares from investors at $29.50 and sell shares to other investors at $31. The **bid price** is the highest price the market maker offers to purchase a given security. The **ask price** is the lowest price at which the market maker is willing to sell a given security. Because more than one market maker frequently makes a market in a given security, they compete. Buyers and sellers attempt to find and negotiate the best price—lowest buy price or highest sell price—when making OTC market transactions. The market maker makes a profit from the spread between the bid price and the ask price.

Nasdaq (National Association of Securities Dealers Automated Quotation) system
an automated system that provides up-to-date bid and ask prices on certain selected, highly active OTC securities.

Nasdaq OTC market makers connect with the sellers and purchasers of securities through the **Nasdaq (National Association of Securities Dealers Automated Quotation) system.** Nasdaq is the first electronic communications network for securities trading. Its automated system provides up-to-date bid and ask prices on about 7,000 selected, highly active OTC securities. It enables buyers and sellers to locate one another easily. Not all OTC securities are listed on Nasdaq, however. To trade in securities not quoted on Nasdaq, buyers and sellers must find each other through references or through known market makers in the securities involved.

Nasdaq National Market
a list of national or international Nasdaq stocks that meet certain qualification standards of financial size, performance, and trading activity.

The Nasdaq Stock Market includes about 3,450 stocks divided into two groups. Included in the **Nasdaq National Market** are about 2,700 companies with a national or international shareholder base. These stocks meet certain qualification standards of financial size, performance, and trading activity. To list initially, companies must have significant net tangible assets or operating income, a minimum 1.1 million publicly held shares, at least 400 shareholders, and a minimum bid price of $5. Another 750 companies are part of the *Nasdaq SmallCap Market.* These companies too must also meet specified (but less stringent) requirements to list and trade their securities through Nasdaq's sophisticated electronic trading and surveillance system. Transactions in these two groups of stocks are reported quickly (immediately) and in detail similar to NYSE and AMEX trades in the financial press.

Alternative Trading Systems

third market
over-the-counter transactions made in securities listed on the NYSE, the AMEX, or one of the other organized exchanges.

Some individual and institutional traders now make direct transactions, without using brokers, securities exchanges, or Nasdaq, in the *third* and *fourth markets.* The **third market** consists of over-the-counter transactions made in securities listed on the NYSE, the AMEX, or one of the other organized exchanges. It allows large institutional investors, such as mutual funds, pension funds, and life insurance companies, to make large transactions at a reduced cost. These transactions are typically handled by firms or market makers that are not members of an organized securities exchange. Market makers charge lower commissions than the organized exchanges or Nasdaq would to bring together large buyers and sellers. Institutional investors are thus often able to realize sizable savings in brokerage commissions and to have minimal impact on the price of the transaction. Nasdaq also has third-market operations, called the Nasdaq InterMarket.

fourth market
transactions made directly between large institutional buyers and sellers of securities.

electronic communications networks (ECNs)
privately owned electronic trading networks that automatically match buy and sell orders that customers place electronically.

The **fourth market** consists of transactions made directly between large institutional buyers and sellers of securities. Unlike third-market transactions, fourth-market transactions bypass the market maker. The fourth market is a direct outgrowth of advanced computer technology. **Electronic communications networks** (ECNs) are at the heart of the fourth market. These privately owned electronic trading networks were formed in response to institutional investor frustration with the way organized exchanges handled large blocks of securities. Archipelago, Bloomberg Tradebook, Island, Instinet, and MarketXT are some of the many ECNs that handle these trades.

The ECNs' trading volume accounts for about a third of all Nasdaq transactions, as well as for an increasing share of New York Stock Exchange volume. They are most effective for high-volume, actively traded securities, and they play a key role in after-hours trading, discussed later in this chapter. They automatically match buy and sell orders that customers place electronically. If there is no immediate match, the ECN acts like a broker and posts its request on the Nasdaq under its own name. The trade will be executed if another trader is interested in making the transaction at the posted price.

ECNs can save customers money because they take only a transaction fee, either per share or based on order size. Money managers and institutions such as pension funds and mutual funds with large amounts of money to invest like ECNs for this reason. Many also use ECNs or trade directly with each other to find the best prices for their clients.

General Market Conditions: Bull or Bear

bull markets
favorable markets normally associated with rising prices, investor optimism, economic recovery, and government stimulus.

bear markets
unfavorable markets normally associated with falling prices, investor pessimism, economic slowdown, and government restraint.

Conditions in the securities markets are commonly classified as "bull" or "bear," depending on whether securities prices are rising or falling over time. Changing market conditions generally stem from changes in investor attitudes, changes in economic activity, and government actions aimed at stimulating or slowing down economic activity. **Bull markets** are favorable markets normally associated with rising prices, investor optimism, economic recovery, and government stimulus. **Bear markets** are unfavorable markets normally associated with falling prices, investor pessimism, economic slowdown, and government restraint. From 1990 through 2000, the stock market was bullish primarily as a result of low inflation, improving trade balances, shrinking budget deficits, and economic recovery. Unfortunately, from then until late 2003, the market was bearish due to the bursting of the technology stock bubble, the September 11, 2001, terrorist attacks, a crisis in corporate accounting, and the Iraq war. Beginning in late 2003, there were signs that the bear market was ending and an expectation of a more bullish market.

In general, investors experience higher (or positive) returns on common stock investments during a bull market. However, some securities are bullish in a bear market or bearish in a bull market. During bear markets, many investors invest in vehicles other than securities to obtain higher and less risky returns. Market conditions are difficult to predict and usually can be identified only after they exist. Sources of information that can be used to assess market conditions are described in Chapter 3 and are applied to the analysis and valuation of common stock price behavior in Chapters 7 through 9.

CONCEPTS IN REVIEW

2.1 Differentiate between each of the following pairs of terms:

a. *Money market* and *capital market*
b. *Primary market* and *secondary market*
c. *Organized securities* exchanges and *over-the-counter (OTC) market*

2.2 Briefly describe the *IPO* process and the role of the *investment banker* in underwriting a public offering. Differentiate among the terms *public offering, rights offering,* and *private placement.*

2.3 For each of the items in the left-hand column, select the most appropriate item in the right-hand column. Explain the relationship between the items matched.

a. AMEX	1. Trades unlisted securities
b. CBT	2. Futures exchange
c. NYSE	3. Options exchange
d. Boston Stock Exchange	4. Regional stock exchange
e. CBOE	5. Second largest organized U.S. exchange
f. OTC	6. Has the most stringent listing requirements

2.4 Explain how the *over-the-counter market* works. Be sure to mention *market makers, bid and ask prices, Nasdaq,* and the *Nasdaq National Market.* What role does this market play in initial public offerings (IPOs) and secondary distributions? What are the *third* and *fourth markets?*

2.5 Differentiate between a *bull market* and a *bear market.*

Globalization of Securities Markets

LG 4

diversification
the inclusion of a number of different investment vehicles in a portfolio to increase returns or reduce risk.

Today investors, issuers of securities, and securities firms look beyond the markets of their home countries to find the best returns, lowest costs, and best international business opportunities. The basic goal of most investors is to earn the highest return with the lowest risk. This outcome is achieved through **diversification**—the inclusion of a number of different investment vehicles in a portfolio to increase returns or reduce risk. The investor who includes foreign investments in a portfolio can greatly increase the potential for diversification by holding (1) a wider range of industries and securities, (2) securities traded in a larger number of markets, and (3) securities denominated in different currencies. The smaller and less diversified an investor's home market is, the greater the potential benefit from prudent international diversification. However, even investors from the United States and other highly developed markets can benefit from global diversification.

In short, globalization of the securities markets enables investors to seek out opportunities to profit from rapidly expanding economies throughout the world. Here we consider the growing importance of international markets, international investment performance, ways to invest in foreign securities, and the risks of investing internationally.

Growing Importance of International Markets

Securities exchanges now operate in over 100 countries worldwide. Both large (Tokyo) and small (Fiji), they are located not only in the major industrialized nations such as Japan, Great Britain, Canada, and Germany but also in emerging economies such as Brazil, Chile, India, South Korea, Malaysia, Mexico, Poland, Russia, and Thailand. The top four securities markets worldwide (based on dollar volume) are the New York, Nasdaq, London, and Tokyo stock exchanges. Other important foreign exchanges include Paris, Osaka, Toronto, Montreal, Sydney, Hong Kong, Zurich, and Taiwan.

This site provides links to many of the world's exchanges, including stocks and commodities.

www.libraries.rutgers.edu/rul/rr_gateway/research_guides/busi/stocks.shtml

The economic integration of the European Monetary Union (EMU), along with pressure from financial institutions that want an efficient process for trading shares across borders, is changing the European securities market environment. Instead of many small national exchanges, countries are banding together to create cross-border markets and compete more effectively in the pan-European equity-trading markets. The Paris, Amsterdam, and Brussels exchanges merged to form Euronext, and the Scandinavian markets formed Norex. Other stock exchanges are forming cooperative agreements—for example, Tokyo and Australia. The New York, Tokyo, Hong Kong, Australia, Mexico, Toronto, São Paulo, and Euronext exchanges are discussing the formation of a Global Equity Market (GEM). The exchanges would not merge but would form a 24-hour global market alliance, trading the stocks of selected large international companies via an electronic order-matching system. Nasdaq, with joint ventures in Japan, Hong Kong, Canada, and Australia, plans to expand into Latin America and the Middle East. As noted at the beginning of the chapter, these mergers and cooperative arrangements could be the first step toward a worldwide stock exchange.

INVESTOR FACTS

U.S. MARKET SHARE—Even though the U.S. securities markets lead the world in terms of market share, the U.S. accounts for about 36% of the more than 30,000 companies in the worldwide equity markets.

Bond markets, too, have become global, and more investors than ever before regularly purchase government and corporate fixed-income securities in foreign markets. The United States dominates the international government bond market, followed by Japan, Germany, and Great Britain.

This site presents country credit ratings.

www.institutionalinvestor.com/

International Investment Performance

A primary motive for investing overseas is the lure of high returns. In fact, only once since 1980 did the United States finish first among the major stock markets of the world in terms of the rate of increase in its stock price index. For example, in 2003, an overall good year after three years of declines, investors would have earned higher returns in many foreign markets. During that year the Dow Jones Global Index in U.S. dollars for Thailand increased 139%; for

Germany increased 61%; for France increased 39%; for Japan increased 38%; for Mexico increased 32%; for the Netherlands increased 25%; and for Finland increased 17%. By comparison, the U.S. stock price index increased about 28%. Of course, foreign securities markets tend to be more risky than U.S. markets. A market with high returns in one year may not do so well in the next.

Investors can compare activity on U.S. and foreign exchanges by following market indexes that track the performance of those exchanges. For instance, the Dow Jones averages and the Standard & Poor's indexes are popular measures of the U.S. markets, and indexes for more than 20 different stock markets are available. (We'll discuss indexes in more detail in Chapter 3.) The *Wall Street Journal* publishes daily reports on most major indexes, trading activity in selected stocks on major foreign exchanges, and currency exchange rates. Other financial publications also include regular reports. Also, the *Wall Street Journal*'s "World Stock Markets" in Section C frequently compares the performance of the U.S. exchanges with that of selected foreign markets.

Go to the Yahoo site and check the World Finance section for investment performance.

finance.yahoo.com/m2

Ways to Invest in Foreign Securities

Investors can make foreign security transactions either indirectly or directly. One form of *indirect* investment is purchasing shares of a U.S.-based multinational with substantial foreign operations. Many U.S.-based multinational firms, such as ExxonMobil, IBM, Citicorp, Dow Chemical, Coca-Cola, Colgate-Palmolive, and Hewlett-Packard, receive more than 50% of their revenues from overseas operations. By investing in the securities of such firms, an investor can achieve a degree of international diversification. Purchasing shares in a mutual fund that invests primarily in foreign securities is another way to invest indirectly. Investors can make both of these indirect foreign securities investment transactions in a conventional fashion through a stockbroker, as explained in Chapter 3 and in Chapter 13 (which is devoted to mutual funds).

HOT LINKS

For information about ADRs, check out ADR.com, a joint project by JPMorgan Chase Bank ("JPMorgan") and Thomson Financial.

adr.com

To make *direct* investments in foreign companies, investors have three options: They can purchase securities on foreign exchanges, buy securities of foreign companies that trade on U.S. exchanges, or buy *American depositary receipts (ADRs)*.

The first way—purchasing securities on foreign exchanges—involves additional risks because the securities do not trade in U.S. dollars. This approach is not for the timid or inexperienced investor.

Because each country's exchange has its own regulations and procedures, investors must cope with currency exchange (dollars to pesos, for example). They also must cope with different securities exchange rules, transaction procedures, accounting standards, tax laws, and with language barriers. Direct transactions are best handled either through brokers at major Wall Street firms with large international operations or through major banks, such as JPMorgan Chase and Citibank, that have special units to handle foreign securities transactions. Alternatively, investors can deal with foreign broker-dealers, but such an approach is more complicated and more risky.

The second form of direct investment is to buy the securities of foreign companies that trade on both organized and over-the-counter U.S. exchanges.

Yankee bonds
dollar-denominated debt securities issued by foreign governments or corporations and traded in U.S. securities markets.

American depositary receipts (ADRs)
dollar-denominated negotiable receipts for the stocks of foreign companies that are held in the vaults of banks in the companies' home countries.

Transactions in foreign securities that trade on U.S. exchanges are handled in the same way as exchange-traded domestic securities. These securities are issued by large, well-known foreign companies. Stocks of companies such as Alcan (Canada), Gucci (Netherlands), National Westminster Bank (U.K.), and Unilever (Netherlands) trade directly on U.S. exchanges. In addition, **Yankee bonds**, dollar-denominated debt securities issued by foreign governments or corporations and traded in U.S. securities markets, trade on organized exchanges and in the over-the-counter market in the United States.

Finally, foreign stocks also trade on U.S. exchanges in the form of **American depositary receipts (ADRs)**. These are dollar-denominated negotiable receipts for the stocks of foreign companies that are held in the vaults of banks in the companies' home countries. Today, about 2,300 ADRs representing more than 50 different home countries are traded on U.S. exchanges. About one-fourth of them are actively traded. Included are ADRs of well-known companies such as DaimlerChrysler, Hitachi, Nokia, Philips Electronics, Sony, and Volvo. ADRs, which trade in the same way as standard domestic securities, are further discussed in Chapter 6.

Risks of Investing Internationally

Investing abroad is not without pitfalls. In addition to the usual risks involved in making any security transaction, investors must consider the risks associated with doing business in a particular foreign country. Changes in trade policies, labor laws, and taxation may affect operating conditions for the country's firms. The government itself may not be stable. When making investments in foreign markets, you must track similar environmental factors in each foreign country. This is clearly more difficult than following your home market, because you are less familiar with the foreign economic and political environments and may be following several countries.

U.S. securities markets are generally viewed as highly regulated and reliable. Foreign markets, on the other hand, may lag substantially behind the United States in both operations and regulation. Some countries place various restrictions on foreign investment. In Korea and Taiwan, for example, mutual funds are the only way for foreigners to invest. Mexico has a two-tier market, with some securities restricted to foreigners. Some countries make it difficult for foreigners to get their funds out, and many impose taxes on dividends. For example, Swiss taxes are about 20% on dividends paid to foreigners. In addition, accounting standards vary from country to country. Differences in accounting practices can affect a company's apparent profitability, conceal other attractive assets (such as the hidden reserves and undervalued assets that are permitted in many countries), and fail to disclose other risks. As a result, it is difficult to compare the financial performances and positions of firms operating in different foreign countries. Other difficulties include illiquid markets and an inability to obtain reliable investment information because of a lack of reporting requirements.

Furthermore, international investing involves securities denominated in foreign currencies. Trading profits and losses are affected not only by a security's price changes but also by changes in currency exchange rates. The values of the world's major currencies fluctuate with respect to each other on a daily basis. The relationship between two currencies at a specified date is called the

currency exchange rate the relationship between two currencies on a specified date.

currency exchange rate. On May 12, 2003, the currency exchange rate for the European Monetary Union euro (€) and the U.S. dollar (US$) was expressed as follows:

US$ = € 0.8652   € = US$ 1.1558

On that day, you would have received 0.8652 euros for every $1. Conversely, each euro was worth $1.1558.

Changes in the value of a particular foreign currency with respect to the U.S. dollar—or any other currency—are called *appreciation* and *depreciation.* For example, on August 11, 2003, the euro/US$ exchange rate was 0.8802. In the 3 months since May 12, 2003, the European Monetary Union euro had *depreciated* relative to the dollar (and the dollar had *appreciated* relative to the euro). On August 11 it took more euros to buy $1 (0.8802 versus 0.8652), so each euro was worth less in dollar terms ($1.1361 versus $1.1558). Had the European Monetary Union euro instead *appreciated* (and the dollar *depreciated* relative to the euro), each euro would have been worth more in dollar terms.

currency exchange risk the risk caused by the varying exchange rates between the currencies of two countries.

Currency exchange risk is the risk caused by the varying exchange rates between the currencies of two countries. For example, assume that on May 12, 2003, you bought 100 shares of a French stock at 100 euros per share, held it for about 3 months, and then sold it for its original purchase price of 100 euros. The following table summarizes these transactions:

Date	Transaction	Number of Shares	Price in Euros	Value of Transaction Euros	Exchange Rate Euros/US$	Value in US$
5/12/03	Purchase	100	100	10,000	0.8652	$11,558.02
8/11/03	Sell	100	100	10,000	0.8802	$11,361.05

Although you realized the original purchase price in euros, in dollar terms the transaction resulted in a loss of $196.97 ($11,558.02 − $11,361.05). The value of the stock in dollars decreased because the European Monetary Union euro was worth less—had depreciated—relative to the dollar. Investors in foreign securities must be aware that the value of the foreign currency in relation to the dollar can have a profound effect on returns from foreign security transactions.

CONCEPTS IN REVIEW

2.6 Why is globalization of securities markets an important issue today? How have international investments performed in recent years?

2.7 Describe how foreign security investments can be made, both indirectly and directly.

2.8 Describe the risks of investing internationally, particularly *currency exchange risk.*

Trading Hours and Regulation of Securities Markets

LG 5

Understanding the structure of domestic and international securities markets is an important foundation for developing a sound investment program. Now let's look at market trading hours and the regulation of U.S. securities markets.

Trading Hours of Securities Markets

crossing markets
after-hours trading in stocks that involve filling buy and sell orders by matching identical sell and buy orders at the desired price.

The regular trading session for organized U.S. exchanges and Nasdaq runs from 9:30 A.M. to 4:00 P.M. Eastern time. However, trading is no longer limited to these hours. The exchanges, Nasdaq, and ECNs offer extended trading sessions before and after regular hours. Most of the after-hours markets are **crossing markets** in which orders are filled only if they can be matched; that is, buy and sell orders are filled only if they can be matched with identical opposing sell and buy orders at the desired price. These allow U.S. securities markets to compete more effectively with foreign securities markets, in which investors can execute trades when U.S. markets are closed. The NYSE has two short electronic-trading sessions that begin after the 4:00 P.M. closing bell. One session, from 4:15 to 5:00 P.M., trades stocks at that day's closing prices via a computer matching system. Transactions occur only if a match can be made and are handled on a first-come, first-served basis. The other session lasts from 4:00 to 5:15 P.M. and allows institutional investors to trade large blocks of stock valued at $1 million or more. Since their inception, the NYSE has experienced increased volume in both sessions.

Nasdaq began its own extended-hours electronic-trading session in January 1992. Its Nasdaq International Market Session runs from 3:30 A.M. (when the London Exchange opens) to 9:00 A.M. Eastern Time, half an hour before the start of regular trading sessions in U.S. markets. Because it lists NYSE stocks as well as other U.S. equities and has less stringent disclosure requirements than other markets, Nasdaq International attracts traders from both the New York and the London exchanges. In addition, Nasdaq has an extended-hours session from 4:00 to 6:30 P.M. Eastern time, as well as two SelectNet trading sessions, from 8:00 to 9:30 A.M. Eastern time and from 4:00 to 5:15 P.M. Eastern time. Regional exchanges have also moved to after-hours trading sessions.

Until 1999, only large institutional investors could trade after hours. Most of this trading was through ECNs like Instinet and Market XT, which facilitated fourth-market transactions in thousands of U.S. and European stocks. Now individual investors, too, can participate in after-hours trading activity. Many large brokerage firms, both traditional and online, offer after-hours trading services for their individual clients.

It appears that after-hours trading will continue to expand and approximate a 24-hour market in the not too distant future. Many believe that the next big bull market will likely stimulate the development of a true 24-hour market. At the same time, it is important to recognize that the term "after-hours trading" is becoming obsolete because of the ability to trade major stocks on a variety of exchanges around the globe. For example, the stock of DaimlerChrysler, a major global automobile manufacturer, is traded in identical form on 11 worldwide exchanges in Asia, Europe, and the Americas. Clearly, by working through these exchanges you can effectively trade DaimlerChrysler on a 24-hour basis. The *Investing in Action* box on page 52 discusses the pros and cons of extended trading hours.

INVESTING IN ACTION

Stock Around the Clock

Trading 24/7—the idea sounds great. Pick up the phone or go to your computer at any hour and buy or sell stocks and mutual funds. While such round-the-clock live trading is not yet a reality, individual investors can trade securities before and after the close of regular trading sessions. Most of the after-hours trading currently takes place in the 90-minute periods before the NYSE and Nasdaq open at 9:30 A.M. and after these markets close at 4 P.M.

What's the appeal of extended trading hours? Some investors don't have time to reflect on market news during the day. Investors in the Pacific time zone (3 hours behind New York) want a longer trading day; their regular trading day ends at 1 P.M. Pacific time. Others want to act on company news that is released after the markets close or during the business day of companies headquartered outside the United States. Online trading and ECNs have made after-hours sessions accessible to individual investors, who have joined their institutional counterparts in trading about 70 million shares after the markets close. Although this traffic represents less than 6% of the NYSE's daily trading volume, investors who understand how to use these extended hours can profit or at least reduce losses. "The after-hours market allows you to beat everyone to the punch," says Mike Prus of MGP Capital Management in Boston.

Because companies often wait until after the closing bell to announce important news, stock prices in after-hours trading can exhibit more volatility than those during regular trading sessions. Savvy investors can use this extra time to get in or out of a stock ahead of other investors. For example, on February 5, 2003, scientific instrument manufacturer Agilent Technologies announced just after the market closed that its financial situation had taken a turn for the worse. Investors who sold in that day's after-hours market got out of the issue before the stock dropped 25% the following day. Similarly, early on February 6, 2003, Ericsson, a Swedish telecommunications equipment company, named a new chief executive. Early session investors bought Ericsson at $6.71, versus $7.42 after the bell sounded.

While still risky, after-hours trading has become less so since its introduction in 2000 and with the advent of higher volume. Like Agilent, most corporations continue to make their announcements after normal trading hours. If you want to benefit from extended-day trading, here are some basics to prepare you to enter this new arena:

- Understand how your brokerage firm handles after-hours trades—hours and methods to place orders. Each firm has different rules and may require separate orders for these trades.
- Learn how stock prices react to different types of company news, economic announcements, changes to major indexes, and new trading rules.
- Most extended-day trading is in blue-chip, large-cap stocks, so follow the after-hours trading patterns of the most active lists.
- To protect investors, most brokerages require limit orders (discussed in detail in Chapter 3) for after-hours trades, so that investors can set their highest buy/lowest sell price.

Critical Thinking Question What risks should individual investors consider before engaging in after-hours trading?

Sources: Mara der Hovanesian, "The Market's Closed—Wake Up," *Business Week*, March 3, 2003, pp. 132–133; and James McNair, "Happy-Hours Trading," *San Diego Union-Tribune*, July 2, 2000, pp. I–1, I–6.

Regulation of Securities Markets

Securities laws protect investors and participants in the financial marketplace. A number of state and federal laws require that investors receive adequate and accurate disclosure of information. Such laws also regulate the activities of participants in the securities markets. State laws that control the sale of securities

TABLE 2.2 Important Federal Securities Laws

Act	Brief Description
Securities Act of 1933	Passed to ensure full disclosure of information about new security issues. Requires the issuer of a new security to file with the Securities and Exchange Commission (SEC) a registration statement containing information about the new issue. The firm cannot sell the security until the SEC approves the registration statement, which usually takes about 20 days. Approval of the registration statement by the SEC merely indicates that the facts presented in the statement appear to reflect the firm's true position.
Securities Exchange Act of 1934	Formally established the SEC as the agency in charge of administering federal securities laws. The act gave the SEC the power to regulate the organized exchanges and the OTC market; their members, brokers, and dealers; and the securities traded in these markets. Each of these participants must file reports with the SEC and periodically update them. The 1934 act has been amended several times over the years.
Maloney Act of 1938	An amendment to the Securities Exchange Act of 1934, it provided for the establishment of trade associations to self-regulate the securities industry. Only one such trade association, the National Association of Securities Dealers (NASD), has been formed. NASD members include nearly all of the nation's securities firms that do business with the public. The NASD, operating under SEC supervision, establishes standardized procedures for securities trading and ethical behavior, monitors and enforces compliance with these procedures, and serves as the industry spokesperson. Today, any securities firms that are not members of the NASD must agree to direct SEC supervision.
Investment Company Act of 1940	Established rules and regulations for investment companies and formally authorized the SEC to regulate their practices and procedures. It required the investment companies to register with the SEC and to fulfill certain disclosure requirements. An *investment company* obtains funds by selling its shares to numerous investors and uses the proceeds to purchase securities. The dominant type of investment company is the *mutual fund* (discussed in detail in Chapter 13). A 1970 amendment prohibits investment companies from paying excessive fees to their advisers and from charging excessive commissions to purchasers of company shares.
Investment Advisers Act of 1940	To protect investors, it requires *investment advisers*, persons hired by investors to advise them about security investments, to disclose all relevant information about their backgrounds, conflicts of interest, and so on, as well as about any investments they recommend. Advisers must register and file periodic reports with the SEC. A 1960 amendment extended the SEC's powers to permit inspection of the records of investment advisers and to revoke the registration of advisers who violate the act's provisions.
Securities Acts Amendments of 1975	Amendment to the securities acts that requires the SEC and the securities industry to develop a competitive national system for trading securities. First the SEC abolished fixed-commission schedules, thereby providing for negotiated commissions. (Commissions are discussed in more detail in Chapter 3.) Second it established the *Intermarket Trading System (ITS)*, an electronic communications network linking nine markets and trading over 4,000 eligible issues, that allows trades to be made across these markets wherever the network shows a better price for a given issue.
Insider Trading and Fraud Act of 1988	The economic prosperity and rapidly rising stock prices in the 1980s caused many speculators to operate without regard for the legality of their actions. Many of the illegal gains were achieved through *insider trading*, using *nonpublic* information to make profitable securities transactions. It is both illegal and unethical. The act established penalties for insider trading. Insiders include anyone who obtains nonpublic information, typically a company's directors, officers, major shareholders, bankers, investment bankers, accountants, or attorneys. To allow it to monitor insider trades, the SEC requires corporate insiders to file monthly reports detailing all transactions made in the company's stock. Recent legislation substantially increased the penalties for insider trading and gave the SEC greater power to investigate and prosecute claims of illegal insider-trading activity.
Sarbanes-Oxley Act of 2002	Passed to protect investors against corporate fraud, particularly accounting fraud. It created an oversight board to monitor the accounting industry, tightened audit regulations and controls, toughened penalties against executives who commit corporate fraud, strengthened accounting disclosure requirements and ethical guidelines for financial officers, established corporate board structure and membership guidelines, established guidelines for analyst conflicts of interest, and increased the SEC's authority and budgets for auditors and investigators. The act also mandated instant disclosure of stock sales by corporate executives.

within state borders are commonly called *blue sky laws* because they are intended to prevent investors from being sold nothing but "blue sky." These laws typically establish procedures for regulating both security issues and sellers of securities doing business within the state. Most states have a regulatory body, such as a state securities commission, that is charged with enforcing the related state statutes. The most important securities laws enacted by the federal government are listed (in chronological order) and briefly summarized in Table 2.2 on the previous page.

insider trading
the use of *nonpublic* information about a company to make profitable securities transactions.

ethics
standards of conduct or moral judgment.

The intent of all of these federal securities laws is to protect investors. Most of these laws were passed in response to observed damaging abuses by certain market participants. The two most recent laws are the *Insider Trading and Fraud Act of 1988*, aimed at stopping **insider trading,** the use of *nonpublic* information about a company to make profitable securities transactions, and the *Sarbanes-Oxley Act of 2002*, which focused on eliminating corporate fraud related to accounting and other information releases. Both of these acts heightened the public's awareness of **ethics**—standards of conduct or moral judgment—in business. The financial community is continuing to develop and enforce ethical standards that will motivate market participants to adhere to laws and regulations. Although it is difficult to enforce ethical standards, it appears that opportunities for abuses in the financial markets are being reduced, thereby providing a more level playing field for all investors.

IN REVIEW

CONCEPTS

2.9 How are after-hours trades typically handled? What role do ECNs play in after-hours trading?

2.10 Briefly describe the key requirements of the following federal securities laws:
a. Securities Act of 1933.
b. Securities Exchange Act of 1934.
c. Maloney Act of 1938.
d. Investment Company Act of 1940.
e. Investment Advisers Act of 1940.
f. Securities Acts Amendments of 1975.
g. Insider Trading and Fraud Act of 1988.
h. Sarbanes-Oxley Act of 2002.

Basic Types of Securities Transactions

LG 6

An investor can make a number of basic types of security transactions. Each type is available to those who meet certain requirements established by various government agencies as well as by brokerage firms. Although investors can use the various types of transactions in a number of ways to meet investment objectives, we describe only the most popular use of each transaction here, as we consider the long purchase, margin trading, and short selling.

long purchase
a transaction in which investors buy securities in the hope that they will increase in value and can be sold at a later date for profit.

Long Purchase

The **long purchase** is a transaction in which investors buy securities in the hope that they will increase in value and can be sold at a later date for profit. The object, then, is to *buy low and sell high*. A long purchase is the most common type of transaction. Because investors generally expect the price of a security to rise over the period of time they plan to hold it, their return comes from any dividends or interest received during the ownership period, *plus* the difference (capital gain or loss) between the price at which they sell the security and the price they paid to purchase it. This return, of course, is reduced by the transaction costs.

Ignoring any dividends (or interest) and transaction costs, we can illustrate the long purchase by a simple example. After studying various aspects of Varner Industries, you are convinced that its common stock, which currently sells for $20 per share, will increase in value over the next few years. On the basis of your analysis, you expect the stock price to rise to $30 per share within 2 years. You place an order and buy 100 shares of Varner for $20 per share. If the stock price rises to, say, $40 per share, you will profit from your long purchase. If it drops below $20 per share, you will experience a loss on the transaction. Obviously, one of the major motivating factors in making a long transaction is an expected rise in the price of the security.

margin trading
the use of borrowed funds to purchase securities; magnifies returns by reducing the amount of equity that the investor must put up.

Margin Trading

margin requirement
the minimum amount of equity that must be a margin investor's own funds; set by the Federal Reserve Board (the "Fed").

INVESTOR FACTS

GOOD NEWS: MARGIN DEBT IS RISING—Rising levels of debt usually are not a reason to cheer. But increasing margin debt levels during the first half of 2003 gave investors hope that the recovery might be starting at last. Higher margin debt means that there is more liquidity in the markets—a positive sign for the stock markets, which tend to track margin debt trends closely. In July 2003, margin debt reached almost $148.5 billion, up from a four-year low of $130.2 billion in September 2002. Margin debt peaked in March 2000, the start of the market slide, at $278.5 billion.

Sources: Robin Goldwyn Blumenthal, "Summertime, and the Buying on Margin Is Easy," *Barron's*, July 21, 2003, p. 13; and "Margin Debt Fell Slightly in July to $148.5," *Wall Street Journal*, August 22, 2003, downloaded from www.wsj.com.

Security purchases do not have to be made on a cash basis; investors can use borrowed funds instead. This activity is referred to as **margin trading.** It is used for one basic reason: to magnify returns. As peculiar as it may sound, the term *margin* refers to the amount of equity (stated as a percentage) in an investment, or the amount that is *not* borrowed. If an investor uses 75% margin, for example, it means that 75% of the investment position is being financed with the person's own funds and the balance (25%) with borrowed money. Brokers must approve margin purchases. The brokerage firm then lends the purchaser the needed funds and retains the purchased securities as collateral. It is important to recognize that margin purchasers must pay a specified rate of interest on the amount they borrow.

The Federal Reserve Board (the "Fed"), which governs our banking system, sets the **margin requirement,** specifying the minimum amount of equity that must be the margin investor's own funds. The margin requirement for stocks has been at 50% for some time. By raising and lowering the margin requirement, the Fed can depress or stimulate activity in the securities markets.

A simple example will help to clarify the basic margin transaction. Assume that you wish to purchase 70 shares of common stock, which is currently selling for $63.50 per share. With the prevailing margin requirement of 50%, you need put up only $2,222.50 in cash ($63.50 per share × 70 shares × 0.50). The remaining $2,222.50 will be lent to you by your brokerage firm. You will, of course, have to pay interest on the amount you borrow, plus the applicable brokerage fees. With the use of margin, investors can purchase more securities than they could afford on a strictly cash basis. In this way, investors can magnify their returns (as demonstrated in a later section).

Although margin trading can lead to increased returns, it also presents substantial risks. One of the biggest is that the issue may not perform as expected. If this occurs, no amount of margin trading can correct matters. Margin trading can only magnify returns, not produce them. And if the security's return is negative, margin trading magnifies the loss. Because the security being margined is always the ultimate source of return, choosing the right securities is critical to this trading strategy.

Essentials of Margin Trading Investors can use margin trading with most kinds of securities. It is regularly used, for example, with both common and preferred stocks, most types of bonds, mutual funds, options, warrants, and futures. It is not normally used with tax-exempt municipal bonds, because the interest paid on such margin loans is not deductible for income tax purposes. Since mid-1990, it has been possible to use margin on certain foreign stocks and bonds that meet prescribed criteria and appear on the Fed's "New List of Foreign Margin Stocks." For simplicity, we will use common stock as the vehicle in our discussion of margin trading.

financial leverage
the use of debt financing to magnify investment returns.

Magnified Profits and Losses With an investor's equity serving as a base, the idea of margin trading is to employ **financial leverage**—the use of debt financing to magnify investment returns. Here's is how it works: Suppose you have $5,000 to invest and are considering the purchase of 100 shares of stock at $50 per share. If you do not margin, you can buy outright 100 shares of the stock (ignoring brokerage commissions). If you margin the transaction—for example, at 50%—you can acquire the same $5,000 position with only $2,500 of your own money. This leaves you with $2,500 to use for other investments or to buy on margin another 100 shares of the same stock. Either way, by margining you will reap greater benefits from the stock's price appreciation.

HOT LINKS

Read about margin trading at:

www.sec.gov/investor/pubs/margin.htm

The concept of margin trading is more fully illustrated in Table 2.3. It shows an unmargined (100% equity) transaction, along with the same transaction using various margins. Remember that the margin rates (e.g., 65%)

TABLE 2.3 The Effect of Margin Trading on Security Returns

	Without Margin (100% Equity)	With Margins of 80%	65%	50%
Number of $50 shares purchased	100	100	100	100
Cost of investment	$5,000	$5,000	$5,000	$5,000
Less: borrowed money	0	1,000	1,750	2,500
Equity in investment	$5,000	$4,000	$3,250	$2,500
A. Investor's position if price rises by $30 to $80/share				
Value of stock	$8,000	$8,000	$8,000	$8,000
Less: cost of investment	5,000	5,000	5,000	5,000
Capital gain	$3,000	$3,000	$3,000	$3,000
Return on investor's equity (capital gain/ equity in investment)	(60%)	(75%)	(92.3%)	(120%)
B. Investor's position if price falls by $30 to $20/share				
Value of stock	$2,000	$2,000	$2,000	$2,000
Less: cost of investment	5,000	5,000	5,000	5,000
Capital loss	$3,000	$3,000	$3,000	$3,000
Return on investor's equity (capital loss/ equity in investment)*	(60%)	(75%)	(92.3%)	(120%)

*With a capital loss, return on investor's equity is *negative*.

indicate the investor's equity in the investment. When the investment is unmargined and the price of the stock goes up by $30 per share (see Table 2.3, part A), the investor enjoys a very respectable 60% rate of return. However, observe what happens when margin is used: The rate of return shoots up as high as 120%, depending on the amount of equity in the investment. This occurs because the gain is the same ($3,000) *regardless of how the investor finances the transaction*. Clearly, as the investor's equity in the investment *declines* (with lower margins), the rate of return *increases* accordingly.

Three facets of margin trading become obvious from the table: (1) The price of the stock will move in whatever way it is going to, regardless of how the position is financed. (2) The lower the amount of the investor's equity in the position, the *greater the rate of return* the investor will enjoy when the price of the security rises. (3) The *loss is also magnified* (by the same rate) when the price of the security falls (see Table 2.3, part B).

Note that Table 2.3 has an "Excel with Spreadsheets" icon. Throughout the text, tables with this icon indicate that they are available as spreadsheets on the Web site, www.aw-bc.com/gitman_joehnk. The use of electronic spreadsheets in finance and investments, as well as in all functional areas of business, is pervasive. Excel makes managing numeric information much easier through its ability to create worksheets, databases, and charts. We use spreadsheets from time to time through-out the text to demonstrate how the content has been constructed or calculated. As you know from Chapter 1, we include Excel spreadsheet exercises at the end of most chapters. By working these exercises, you should develop the ability to clearly set out and visualize the logic needed to solve investment problems.

Advantages and Disadvantages of Margin Trading A magnified return is the major advantage of margin trading. The size of the magnified return depends on both the price behavior of the security that is margined and the amount of margin used. Another, more modest benefit of margin trading is that it allows for greater diversification of security holdings, because investors can spread their capital over a larger number of investments.

The major disadvantage of margin trading, of course, is the potential for magnified losses if the price of the security falls. Another disadvantage is the cost of the margin loans themselves. A **margin loan** is the official vehicle through which the borrowed funds are made available in a margin transaction. All margin loans are made at a stated interest rate, which depends on prevailing market rates and the amount of money being borrowed. This rate is usually 1% to 3% above the **prime rate**—the lowest interest rate charged the best business borrowers. For large accounts, it may be at the prime rate. The loan cost, which investors pay, will increase daily, reducing the level of profits (or increasing losses) accordingly.

margin loan
vehicle through which borrowed funds are made available, at a stated interest rate, in a margin transaction.

prime rate
the lowest interest rate charged the best business borrowers.

Making Margin Transactions To execute a margin transaction, an investor must establish a **margin account** with a minimum of $2,000 in equity, in the form of either cash or securities. The broker will retain any securities purchased on margin as collateral for the loan.

margin account
a brokerage account for which margin trading is authorized.

The margin requirement established by the Federal Reserve Board sets the minimum amount of equity for margin transactions. Investors need not execute all margin transactions by using exactly the minimum amount of margin; they can use more than the minimum if they wish. Moreover, it is not unusual for brokerage firms and the major exchanges to establish their own margin

TABLE 2.4 Initial Margin Requirements for Various Types of Securities

Security	Minimum Initial Margin (Equity) Required
Listed common and preferred stock	50%
OTC stocks traded on Nasdaq National Market	50%
Convertible bonds	50%
Corporate bonds	30%
U.S. government bills, notes, and bonds	10% of principal
U.S. government agencies	24% of principal
Options	Option premium plus 20% of market value of underlying stock
Futures	2% to 10% of the value of the contract

requirements, which are more restrictive than those of the Federal Reserve. In addition, brokerage firms may have their own lists of especially volatile stocks for which the margin requirements are higher. There are basically two types of margin requirements: initial margin and maintenance margin.

initial margin
the minimum amount of equity that must be provided by a margin investor *at the time of purchase.*

restricted account
a margin account whose equity is less than the initial margin requirement; the investor may not make further margin purchases and must bring the margin back to the initial level when securities are sold.

maintenance margin
the absolute minimum amount of margin (equity) that an investor must maintain in the margin account at all times.

margin call
notification of the need to bring the equity of an account whose margin is below the maintenance level up above the maintenance margin level or to have enough margined holdings sold to reach this standard.

Initial Margin The minimum amount of equity that must be provided by the investor *at the time of purchase* is the **initial margin.** It prevents overtrading and excessive speculation. Generally, this is the margin requirement to which investors refer when discussing margin trading. All securities that can be margined have specific initial requirements, which the governing authorities can change at their discretion. Table 2.4 shows initial margin requirements for various types of securities. The more stable investment vehicles, such as U.S. government issues, generally have substantially lower margin requirements and therefore offer greater opportunities to magnify returns. OTC stocks traded on the Nasdaq National Market can be margined like listed securities; all other OTC stocks are considered to have no collateral value and therefore cannot be margined.

As long as the margin in an account remains at a level equal to or greater than prevailing initial requirements, the investor may use the account in any way he or she wants. However, if the value of the investor's holdings declines, the margin in his or her account will also drop. In this case, the investor will have what is known as a **restricted account,** one whose equity is less than the initial margin requirement. It does not mean that the investor must put up additional cash or equity. But as long as the account is restricted, the investor may not make further margin purchases and must bring the margin back to the initial level when securities are sold.

Maintenance Margin The absolute minimum amount of margin (equity) that an investor must maintain in the margin account at all times is the **maintenance margin.** When an insufficient amount of maintenance margin exists, an investor will receive a **margin call.** This call gives the investor a short period of time (perhaps 72 hours) to bring the equity up above the maintenance margin. If this doesn't happen, the broker is authorized to sell enough of the investor's margined holdings to bring the equity in the account up to this standard.

Margin investors can be in for a surprise if markets are volatile. When the Nasdaq stock market fell 14% in one day in early April 2000, brokerages made many more margin calls than usual. Investors rushed to sell shares, often at a loss, to cover their margin calls—only to watch the market bounce back a few days later.

The maintenance margin protects both the brokerage house and investors: Brokers avoid having to absorb excessive investor losses, and investors avoid being wiped out. The maintenance margin on equity securities is currently 25%. It rarely changes, although it is often set slightly higher by brokerage firms for the added protection of brokers and customers. For straight debt securities such as government bonds, there is no official maintenance margin except that set by the brokerage firms themselves.

The Basic Margin Formula The amount of margin is always measured in terms of its relative amount of equity, which is considered the investor's collateral. A simple formula can be used with all types of long purchases to determine the amount of margin in the transaction at any given point. Basically, only two pieces of information are required: (1) the prevailing market value of the securities being margined and (2) the **debit balance,** which is the amount of money being borrowed in the margin loan. Given this information, we can compute margin according to Equation 2.1.

debit balance
the amount of money being borrowed in a margin loan.

Equation 2.1

$$\text{Margin} = \frac{\text{Value of securities} - \text{Debit balance}}{\text{Value of securities}}$$

Equation 2.1a

$$= \frac{V - D}{V}$$

To illustrate the use of this formula, consider the following example. Assume you want to purchase 100 shares of stock at $40 per share at a time when the initial margin requirement is 70%. Because 70% of the transaction must be financed with equity, the (30%) balance can be financed with a margin loan. Therefore, you will borrow 0.30 × $4,000, or $1,200. This amount, of course, is the *debit balance*. The remainder ($4,000 − $1,200 = $2,800) represents your equity in the transaction. In other words, equity is represented by the numerator ($V - D$) in the margin formula.

What happens to the margin as the value of the security changes? If over time the price of the stock moves to $65, the margin is then

$$\text{Margin} = \frac{V - D}{V} = \frac{\$6{,}500 - \$1{,}200}{\$6{,}500} = 0.815 = \underline{\underline{81.5\%}}$$

Note that the margin (equity) in this investment position has risen from 70% to 81.5%. *When the price of the security goes up, the investor's margin also increases.*

On the other hand, *when the price of the security goes down, so does the amount of margin.* For instance, if the price of the stock in our illustration drops to $30 per share, the new margin is only 60% [($3,000 − $1,200) ÷ $3,000]. In that case, we would be dealing with a *restricted account,* because the margin level would have dropped below the prevailing initial margin of 70%.

Finally, note that although our discussion has been couched largely in terms of individual transactions, the same margin formula applies to margin accounts. The only difference is that we would be dealing with input that applies to the account as a whole—the value of all securities held in the account and the total amount of margin loans.

Return on Invested Capital When assessing the return on margin transactions, you must take into account the fact that you put up only part of the funds. Therefore, you are concerned with the *rate of return* earned on only the portion of the funds that you provided. Using both current income received from dividends or interest and total interest paid on the margin loan, we can apply Equation 2.2 to determine the return on invested capital from a margin transaction.

Equation 2.2

$$\text{Return on invested capital from a margin transaction} = \frac{\begin{array}{c}\text{Total}\\ \text{current}\\ \text{income}\\ \text{received}\end{array} - \begin{array}{c}\text{Total}\\ \text{interest}\\ \text{paid on}\\ \text{margin loan}\end{array} + \begin{array}{c}\text{Market}\\ \text{value of}\\ \text{securities}\\ \text{at sale}\end{array} - \begin{array}{c}\text{Market}\\ \text{value of}\\ \text{securities}\\ \text{at purchase}\end{array}}{\text{Amount of equity at purchase}}$$

This equation can be used to compute either the expected or the actual return from a margin transaction. To illustrate: Assume you want to buy 100 shares of stock at \$50 per share because you feel it will rise to \$75 within 6 months. The stock pays \$2 per share in annual dividends, and during your 6-month holding period you will be entitled to receive half of that amount, or \$1 per share. You are going to buy the stock with 50% margin and will pay 10% interest on the margin loan. Therefore, you are going to put up \$2,500 equity to buy \$5,000 worth of stock that you hope will increase to \$7,500 in 6 months. Because you will have a \$2,500 margin loan outstanding at 10% for 6 months, you will pay \$125 in total interest costs (\$2,500 × 0.10 × 6/12 = \$125). We can substitute this information into Equation 2.2 to find the expected return on invested capital from this margin transaction:

$$\text{Return on invested capital from a margin transaction} = \frac{\$100 - \$125 + \$7{,}500 - \$5{,}000}{\$2{,}500} = \frac{\$2{,}475}{\$2{,}500} = 0.99 = \underline{\underline{99\%}}$$

Keep in mind that the 99% figure represents the rate of return earned over a 6-month holding period. If you wanted to compare this rate of return to other investment opportunities, you could determine the transaction's annualized rate of return by multiplying by 2 (the number of 6-month periods in a year). This would amount to an annual rate of return of 198% (99% × 2 = 198%).

pyramiding
the technique of using paper profits in margin accounts to partly or fully finance the acquisition of additional securities.

Uses of Margin Trading Investors most often use margin trading in one of two ways. As we have seen, one of its uses is to magnify transaction returns. The other major margin tactic is called pyramiding, which takes the concept of magnified returns to its limits. **Pyramiding** uses the paper profits in margin accounts to partly or fully finance the acquisition of additional securities. This allows investors to make such transactions at margins below prevailing initial margin levels, and sometimes substantially so. In fact, with this technique it is even possible to buy securities with no new cash at all. Rather, they can all be financed entirely with margin loans. The reason is that the paper profits in the account lead to **excess margin**—more equity in the account than required. For instance, if a margin account holds $60,000 worth of securities and has a debit balance of $20,000, it is at a margin level of 66⅔% [($60,000 − $20,000) ÷ $60,000]. This account would hold a substantial amount of excess margin if the prevailing initial margin requirement were only 50%.

excess margin
more equity than is required in a margin account.

The principle of pyramiding is to use the excess margin in the account to purchase additional securities. The only constraint—and the key to pyramiding—is that when the additional securities are purchased, the investor's margin account must be at or above the prevailing required initial margin level. Remember that it is the *account,* not the individual transactions, that must meet the minimum standards. If the account has excess margin, the investor can use it to build up security holdings. Pyramiding can continue as long as there are additional paper profits in the margin account and as long as the margin level exceeds the initial requirement that prevails when purchases are made. The tactic is somewhat complex but is also profitable, especially because it minimizes the amount of new capital required in the investor's account.

In general, margin trading is simple, but it is also risky. Risk is primarily associated with potential price declines in the margined securities. A decline in prices can result in a *restricted account.* If prices fall enough to cause the actual margin to drop below the maintenance margin, the resulting margin call will force the investor to deposit additional equity into the account almost immediately. In addition, losses (resulting from the price decline) are magnified in a fashion similar to that demonstrated in Table 2.3, part B. Clearly, the chance of a margin call and the magnification of losses make margin trading more risky than nonmargined transactions. Margin should be used only by investors who fully understand its operation and appreciate its pitfalls. The *Ethics* box on page 62 discusses the perilous side of margin trading in the story of one man's financial ruin through buying on margin.

Short Selling

In most cases, investors buy stock hoping that the price will rise. What if an investor expects the price of a particular security to fall? By using short selling, the investor may be able to profit from falling security prices. (Until 1997 investors could use short selling to *protect* themselves from falling security prices, a strategy called *shorting-against-the-box.*) Almost any type of security can be "shorted": common and preferred stocks, all types of bonds, convertible securities, listed mutual funds, options, and warrants. In practice, though, the short-selling activities of most investors are limited almost exclusively to common stocks and to options.

HOT LINKS

This site discusses the pros and cons of short selling.

www.fool.com/duelingfools/2001/duelingfools01060600.htm

Essentials of Short Selling **Short selling** is generally defined as the practice of selling borrowed securities. Unusual as it may sound, selling borrowed securities is (in most cases) legal and quite common. Short sales start when securities that have been borrowed from a broker are sold in the marketplace. Later, when the price of the issue has declined, the short seller buys back the securities,

short selling
the sale of borrowed securities, their eventual repurchase by the short seller, and their return to the lender.

The Perils of Margin Trading

The downfall of Bernard Ebbers, CEO of the global telecommunications giant, WorldCom—a company he built from scratch—was about as spectacular as his meteoric rise to power. As a result of the biggest corporate bankruptcy in U.S. history, the former basketball coach, club bouncer, and Sunday school teacher emerged broke with a negative net worth approaching nine digits. However, what brought Ebbers down was less his greed and more his devotion and loyalty to the company: Ebbers simply owned too much of WorldCom stock that he bought on margin.

By investing his generous compensation and exercising the right to buy tens of millions of shares from his options package, Ebbers saw his holdings of company stock grow at a fast rate—much faster than he could afford. When his personal funds were insufficient, he would finance new purchases by using his existing holdings as collateral to borrow money, a practice known as *buying on margin*. This was not a problem as long as the stock of WorldCom was going up. In 1999, when its shares were trading close to $70, Ebbers' net worth—estimated to be $1.4 billion—put him on Forbes' list of richest Americans.

However, when WorldCom stock began its descent in 2000, Ebbers started receiving margin calls because the value of his initial collateral (WorldCom shares) was insufficient to maintain the loans from brokers that he had used to purchase additional shares. Because he could not meet tens of millions of dollars of margin calls, Ebbers faced difficult choices: either sell some of his vast holdings of stock and use the proceeds to pay the margin loans, or apply for personal loans to cover the calls. When WorldCom's board of directors learned about his margin calls, it rejected the first option on the grounds that the CEOs dumping of millions of WorldCom shares on the market would not only depress the price of the stock but also erode investor confidence in the company. Instead, the company granted Ebbers a low-interest loan for margin calls. However, as the bear market continued to unravel, prices of telecommunications companies took the hardest hit, and Ebbers faced new and bigger margin calls, which required new personal loans from the company. Borrowing money to cover margin calls may be a good idea if the stock recovers, but it may also result in financial ruin if the stock continues to fall.

In the end, WorldCom granted Ebbers $341 million in personal loans, the largest amount of money any publicly traded company has ever lent to one of its officers. WorldCom shares became worthless, and the company filed for Chapter 11 bankruptcy in July 2002 amidst allegation of accounting fraud. Although Ebbers so far has managed to escape federal indictments, he faces charges of violating state securities and tax laws associated with an $11 billion accounting fraud that brought WorldCom to its knees.

The policy of boards of directors regarding authorizing loans for senior executives raises important ethical questions. "A large loan to a senior executive epitomizes concerns about conflict of interest and breach of fiduciary duty," said former SEC enforcement official Seth Taube. The number of companies authorizing such loans has recently increased dramatically. In 2002, Congress addressed this issue by passing the Sarbanes-Oxley Act, which forbade companies from making such loans.

Critical Thinking Question Although it is legal to do so, in the wake of the WorldCom collapse, should executives be allowed to use margin accounts to trade the stocks of their companies?

Note: Ethics boxes, which appear in several chapters, focus on the ethical dimensions of particular situations and issues in the investments world. Each box includes a Critical Thinking Question for discussion.

which are then returned to the lender. A short seller must make an initial equity deposit with the broker, subject to rules similar to those for margin trading. The deposit plus the proceeds from sale of the borrowed shares assure the broker that sufficient funds are available to buy back the shorted securities at a later date, even if their price increases. Short sales, like margin transactions, require investors to work through a broker.

EXCEL with SPREADSHEETS

TABLE 2.5 The Mechanics of a Short Sale

Step 1—Short sale initiated:	
100 shares of borrowed stock are *sold* at $50/share:	
Proceeds from sale to investor	$5,000
Step 2—Short sale covered:	
Later, 100 shares of the stock are *purchased* at $30/share and returned to broker from whom stock was borrowed:	
Cost to investor	3,000
Net profit	$2,000

INVESTOR FACTS

SHORT INTEREST INDICATES?—Monitoring the short-selling levels can help you measure investor moods. Each month the *Wall Street Journal* reports the short interest, which reflects the number of shares that have not yet been repurchased to cover the short sales. A higher level tends to indicate a more pessimistic outlook and expectations of a downturn. For example, for the month ended August 15, 2003, the Nasdaq short interest fell 6% over the July level, while the NYSE level was 4.2% lower. These figures were in line with more positive investor attitudes resulting from stronger economic activity.

Source: Craig Karmin, "Short Interest Fell on Nasdaq in Latest Month," *Wall Street Journal*, August 27, 2003, p. B8.

Making Money When Prices Fall Making money when security prices fall is what short selling is all about. Like their colleagues in the rest of the investment world, short sellers are trying to make money by *buying low and selling high*. The only difference is that they reverse the investment process: *They start the transaction with a sale and end it with a purchase.*

Table 2.5 shows how a short sale works and how investors can profit from such transactions. (For simplicity, we ignore transaction costs.) The transaction results in a net profit of $2,000 as a result of an initial sale of 100 shares of stock at $50 per share (step 1) and subsequent covering (purchase) of the 100 shares for $30 per share (step 2). The amount of profit or loss generated in a short sale depends on the price at which the short seller can buy back the stock. Short sellers earn profit only when the proceeds from the sale of the stock are greater than the cost of buying it back.

Who Lends the Securities? Acting through their brokers, short sellers obtain securities from the brokerage firm or from other investors (brokers are the principal source of borrowed securities). As a service to their customers, they lend securities held in the brokers' portfolios or in *street name* accounts. It is important to recognize that when the brokerage firm lends street name securities, it is lending the short seller the securities of other investors. Individual investors typically do not pay fees to the broker for the privilege of borrowing the shares and, as a result, do not earn interest on the funds they leave on deposit with the broker.

Margin Requirements and Short Selling To make a short sale, the investor must make a deposit with the broker that is equal to the initial margin requirement (currently 50%) applied to the short sale proceeds. In addition, the broker retains the proceeds from the short sale. To demonstrate, assume that you sell short 100 shares of Smart, Inc., at $50 per share at a time when the initial margin requirement is 50% and the maintenance margin on short sales is 30%. The values in lines 1 through 4 under column A in Table 2.6 (on page 64) indicate that your broker would hold a total deposit of $7,500 on this transaction. Note in columns B and C that regardless of subsequent changes in Smart, Inc.'s stock price, your deposit with the broker would remain at $7,500 (line 4). By subtracting the cost of buying back the shorted stock at the given share price (line 5), your equity in the account under the current (column A) and two subsequent share prices (columns B and C) is shown in line 6. It can be seen that at the initial short sale price of $50 per share your equity would

TABLE 2.6 **Margin Positions on Short Sales**

Line	Item	A Initial Short Sale Price	B Subsequent Share Prices	C
1	Price per share	$50	$30	$70
2	Proceeds from initial short sale [(1) × 100sh]	$5,000		
3	Initial margin deposit [.50 × (2)]	2,500		
4	Total deposit with broker [(2) + (3)]	$7,500	$7,500	$7,500
5	Current cost of buying back stock [(1) × 100sh]	5,000	3,000	7,000
6	Account equity [(4) − (5)]	$2,500	$4,500	$ 500
7	Actual margin [(6) ÷ (5)]	50%	150%	7.14%
8	Maintenance margin position [(7) > 30%?]	OK	OK	Margin call*

*Investor must either deposit at least an additional $1,600 with the broker to bring the total deposit to $9,100 ($7,500 + $1,600), which would equal the current value of the 100 shares of $7,000 plus a 30% maintenance margin deposit of $2,100 (.30 × $7,000), or buy back the 100 shares of stock and return them to the broker.

equal $2,500 (column A); if the share price subsequently drops to $30, your equity would rise to $4,500 (column B); and if the share price subsequently rises to $70, your equity would fall to $500 (column C). Dividing these account equity values (line 6) by the then-current cost of buying back the stock (line 5), the actual margins at each share price are calculated in line 7. It can be seen that at the current $50 price the actual margin is 50%, whereas at the $30 share price it is 150%, and at the $70 share price it is 7.14%.

As noted in line 8, given the 30% maintenance margin requirement, your margin would be okay at the current price of $50 (column A) or lower (column B), but at the $70 share price the 7.14% actual margin would be below the 30% maintenance margin, thereby resulting in a margin call. In that case (or whenever the actual margin on a short sale falls below the maintenance margin), the investor must respond to the margin call either by depositing additional funds with the broker or by buying the stock and covering (i.e., closing out) the short position.

If you wished to maintain the short position when the share price has risen to $70, you would have to deposit an additional $1,600 with the broker, which would increase your total deposit to $9,100 ($7,500 + $1,600)—an amount equal to the $7,000 value of the shorted stock plus the 30% maintenance margin, or $2,100 (.30 × $7,000). Buying back the stock to cover the short position would cost $7,000, thereby resulting in the return of the $500 of equity in your account from your broker. Clearly, margin requirements tend to complicate the short sale transaction and the impact of an increase in the shorted stock's share price on required deposits with the broker.

Advantages and Disadvantages The major advantage of selling short is, of course, the chance to profit from a price decline. The key disadvantage of many short-sale transactions is that the investor faces limited return opportunities, along with high risk exposure. The price of a security can fall only so far (to a value of or near zero), yet there is really no limit to how far such securities can rise in price. (Remember, a short seller is hoping for a price decline; when a security goes up in price, a short seller loses.) For example, note in Table 2.5 that the stock in question cannot possibly fall by more than $50, yet who is to say how high its price can go?

A less serious disadvantage is that short sellers never earn dividend (or interest) income. In fact, short sellers owe the lender of the shorted security any dividends (or interest) paid while the transaction is outstanding. That is, if a dividend is paid during the course of a short-sale transaction, the short seller must pay an equal amount to the lender of the stock. (The mechanics of these payments are taken care of automatically by the short seller's broker.)

Uses of Short Selling Investors short sell primarily to seek speculative profits when they expect the price of a security to drop. Because the short seller is betting against the market, this approach is subject to a considerable amount of risk. The actual procedure works as demonstrated in Table 2.5. Note that had you been able to sell the stock at $50 per share and later repurchase it at $30 per share, you would have generated a profit of $2,000 (ignoring dividends and brokerage commissions). However, if the market had instead moved against you, all or most of your $5,000 investment could have been lost.

CONCEPTS IN REVIEW

2.11 What is a *long purchase?* What expectation underlies such a purchase? What is *margin trading,* and what is the key reason why it is sometimes used as part of a long purchase?

2.12 How does margin trading magnify profits and losses? What are the key advantages and disadvantages of margin trading?

2.13 Describe the procedures and regulations associated with margin trading. Be sure to explain *restricted accounts,* the *maintenance margin,* and the *margin call.* Define the term *debit balance,* and describe the common uses of margin trading.

2.14 What is the primary motive for *short selling?* Describe the basic short-sale procedure. Why must the short seller make an initial equity deposit?

2.15 What relevance do margin requirements have in the short-selling process? What would have to happen to experience a "margin call" on a short-sale transaction? What two actions could be used to remedy such a call?

2.16 Describe the key advantages and disadvantages of short selling. How are short sales used to earn speculative profits?

Summary

LG 1 **Identify the basic types of securities markets and describe the IPO process.** Short-term investment vehicles trade in the money market; longer-term securities, such as stocks and bonds, trade in the capital market. New security issues are sold in the primary market. Once securities are outstanding, investors buy and sell them in the secondary markets. The first public issue of a company's common stock is called an initial public offering (IPO). The company selects an investment banker to advise it and sell the securities. The lead investment banker may form a syndicate with other investment bankers and then create a selling group to sell the issue. The IPO process includes filing a registration statement with the Securities and Exchange Commission (SEC), getting SEC approval, promoting the offering to investors, pricing the issue, and selling the shares.

LG 2 **Explain the characteristics of organized securities exchanges.** The organized securities exchanges are auction markets. They include the New York Stock Exchange (NYSE), the American Stock Exchange (AMEX), regional stock exchanges, options exchanges, and futures exchanges. In these centralized markets, the forces of supply and demand determine prices. The organized exchanges act as secondary markets where existing securities trade.

LG 3 **Understand the over-the-counter markets, including Nasdaq and alternative trading systems, and the general conditions of securities markets.** The over-the-counter (OTC) market acts as a primary market in which initial public offerings are made. It also handles secondary trading in unlisted securities. It is a dealer market in which negotiation and market maker quotes, often obtained through its automated system, Nasdaq, determine price. Over-the-counter transactions in listed securities are made in the third market. Transactions directly between buyers and sellers are made in the fourth market. Electronic communications networks (ECNs) now offer an alternative to organized exchanges and Nasdaq. Market conditions are commonly classified as "bull" or "bear," depending on whether securities prices are generally rising or falling.

LG 4 **Review the importance of global securities markets, their performance, and the investment procedures and risks associated with foreign investments.** Today securities markets must be viewed globally. Securities exchanges operate in over 100 countries—both large and small. Foreign security investments can be made indirectly by buying shares of a U.S.-based multinational with substantial foreign operations or by purchasing shares of a mutual fund that invests primarily in foreign securities. Direct foreign investment can be achieved by purchasing securities on foreign exchanges, by buying securities of foreign companies that are traded on U.S. exchanges, or by buying American Depositary Receipts (ADRs). International investments can enhance returns, but they entail added risk, particularly currency exchange risk.

LG 5 **Discuss trading hours and the regulation of securities markets.** No longer are investors limited to trading securities during regular market hours (9:30 A.M. to 4:00 P.M., Eastern time). Pre- and post-market trading sessions are available to both individual and institutional investors. Most of these after-hours markets are crossing markets, in which orders are filled only if they can be matched. Trading activity during these sessions can be quite risky because of greater volatility and lack of centralized pricing data. The securities markets are regulated by the federal Securities and Exchange Commission (SEC) and by state commissions. The key federal laws regulating the securities industry are the Securities Act of 1933, the Securities Exchange Act of 1934, the Maloney Act of 1938, the Investment Company Act of 1940, the Investment Advisers Act of 1940, the Securities Acts Amendments of 1975, the Insider Trading and Fraud Act of 1988, and the Sarbanes-Oxley Act of 2002.

LG 6 **Explain long purchases and the motives, procedures, and calculations involved in making margin transactions and short sales.** Most investors make long purchases—buy low, sell high—in expectation of price increases. Many investors establish margin accounts to use borrowed funds to enhance their buying power. The Federal Reserve Board establishes the margin requirement—the minimum investor equity in a margin transaction, both initially and during the margin transaction. The return on invested capital in a margin transaction is magnified; positive returns *and* negative returns are larger than in a comparable unmargined transaction. Paper profits can be used to pyramid a margin account by investing its excess margin. The risks of margin trading are the chance of a restricted account or margin call and the consequences of magnification of losses due to price declines.

Short selling is used when a decline in security prices is anticipated. It involves selling securities, typically borrowed from the broker, with the expectation of earning a profit by repurchasing them at a lower price in the future. To execute a short sale, the investor must make an initial equity deposit with the broker, who also holds the initial sales proceeds. If the price of a shorted stock rises, the investor may receive a margin call from the broker, which can be remedied either by increasing the deposit with the broker or by buying back the stock to cover the short position. The major advantage of selling short is the chance to profit from a price decline. The disadvantages of selling short are that the return opportunities are limited in spite of the unlimited potential for loss, and that short sellers never earn dividend (or interest) income. Short selling is used primarily to seek speculative profits from an anticipated decline in share price.

Putting Your Investment Know-How to the Test

1. All of the following statements about primary and secondary markets are true *except:*
   a. A primary market is a market in which new securities are sold.
   b. A secondary market is a market in which existing securities are traded among investors.
   c. The primary market benefits from the liquidity provided by the secondary market.
   d. The proceeds from a sale in the secondary market go to the issuing firm, not the current owner of a security.

2. Direct trading of securities between two parties with no broker intermediary occurs in
   a. The "third market."
   b. The "fourth market."
   c. Over-the-counter trading.
   d. A listed exchange market.

3. Phil Barnes purchased land for $100,000, financing 80% of the purchase price at a rate of 10%. Six months later Barnes sold the property for $115,000. His annualized return on investment is *closest* to
   a. 15%.
   b. 30%.
   c. 55%.
   d. 110%.

4. One year ago, an investor purchased a 10-year $1,000 par value, 8% semiannual coupon bond. Now, one year later, interest rates remain unchanged at 8%. If the investor sells the bond today (immediately after receiving the second coupon payment and with no transaction costs), he will have a capital
   a. Gain of $80.
   b. Loss of $80.
   c. Gain of $0.
   d. Gain of $50.

5. The majority of initial public offerings of stocks go to
   a. Institutional investors.
   b. Day traders.
   c. Market makers and specialists.
   d. The company's current stockholders.

6. The main reason for investing abroad is to
   a. Reduce currency fluctuations.
   b. Diversify portfolios and reduce risks.
   c. Increase returns.
   d. Provide capital to multinational corporations.

7. There are approximately _______ stocks listed on the New York Exchange.
   a. 2,500 b. 1,900
   c. 4,500 d. 3,300

8. To maintain a fair and orderly market, stock exchange specialists in the United States are expected to
   a. Buy against the market when the market is definitely declining and are expected to sell against the market when the market is definitely rising.
   b. Buy against the market when the market is definitely declining but are not expected to sell against the market when the market is definitely rising.
   c. Sell against the market when the market is definitely rising but are not expected to buy against the market when the market is definitely declining.
   d. Neither buy nor sell against the market, regardless of market trends.

9. You purchased 100 shares of XYZ stock on margin for $50 per share. The initial margin is 50%. The stock pays no dividend. If you sell the stock at $40 per share your investment return would be
   a. −20%. b. −40%.
   c. −50%. d. 25%.

10. An investor buys a stock at $32 per share, using a 50% margin; she hopes to hold the stock for a year and then sell it for $37.50 per share. Assume the maintenance margin is 25%, the stock pays no dividends, and transaction and borrowing costs are zero. Given this information, calculate the expected rate of return on this margin transaction, **and** the price at which the investor will receive a margin call.

	Expected Rate of return	Margin Call Will Occur When Stock Hits a Price of:
a.	17.2%	$16.00
b.	22.9%	$21.33
c.	34.4%	$21.33
d.	34.4%	$38.40

Answers: 1. d; 2. b; 3. d; 4. c; 5. a; 6. b; 7. d; 8. a; 9. b; 10. c

Discussion Questions

LG 1

Q2.1 From 1990 to 2003, the average IPO rose 24% in its first day of trading. In 1999, 117 deals doubled in price on the first day, compared to only 39 in the previous 24 years combined. In 2001, 2002, and 2003, no deals doubled on the first day. What factors might contribute to the huge first-day returns on IPOs? Some critics of the current IPO system claim that underwriters may knowingly underprice an issue. Why might they do this? Why might issuing companies accept lower IPO prices? What impact do institutional investors have on IPO pricing?

LG 2 LG 3

Q2.2 Why do you think some large, well-known companies such as Cisco Systems, Intel, and Microsoft prefer to trade on the Nasdaq National Market rather than on a major organized exchange such as the NYSE (for which they easily meet the listing requirements)? Discuss the pros and cons of listing on a major organized exchange.

LG 2 LG 3 LG 4

Q2.3 On the basis of the current structure of the world's financial markets and your knowledge of the NYSE and OTC markets, describe the key features, functions, and problems that would be faced by a single global market (exchange) on which transactions can be made in all securities of all of the world's major companies. Discuss the likelihood of such a market developing.

LG 5

Q2.4 Critics of longer trading hours believe that expanded trading sessions turn the stock market into a casino and place the emphasis more on short-term gains than on long-term investment. Do you agree? Why or why not? Is it important to have a "breathing period" to reflect on the day's market activity? Why are smaller brokerages and ECNs, more than the NYSE and Nasdaq, pushing for longer trading hours?

LG 6

Q2.5 Describe how, if at all, conservative and aggressive investors might use each of the following types of transactions as part of their investment programs. Contrast these two types of investors in view of these preferences.

a. Long purchase
b. Margin trading
c. Short selling

Problems

LG 4

P2.1 The current exchange rate between the U.S. dollar and the Japanese yen is 116.915 (Yen/$). How many dollars would you get for 1,000 Japanese yen?

LG 4

P2.2 An investor recently sold some stock that was a Eurodollar investment for 20,000 euros. The U.S.$/euro exchange rate is currently 1.1. How many U.S. dollars will the investor receive?

LG 4

P2.3 In each of the following cases, calculate the price of one share of the foreign stock measured in United States dollars (US$).

a. A Belgian stock priced at 103.2 euros (€) when the exchange rate is .8595 €/US$.
b. A Swiss stock priced at 93.3 Swiss francs (Sf) when the exchange rate is 1.333 Sf/US$.
c. A Japanese stock priced at 1,350 yen (¥) when the exchange rate is 110 ¥/US$.

LG 4

P2.4 Lola Paretti purchased 50 shares of BMW, a German stock traded on the Frankfurt Exchange, for 64.5 euros (€) per share exactly 1 year ago, when the exchange rate was .78 €/US$. Today the stock is trading at 68.4 € per share, and the exchange rate is .86 €/US$.

a. Did the € *depreciate* or *appreciate* relative to the US$ during the past year? Explain.
b. How much in US$ did Lola pay for her 50 shares of BMW when she purchased them a year ago?
c. For how much in US$ can Lola sell her BMW shares today?
d. Ignoring brokerage fees and taxes, how much profit (or loss) in US$ will Lola realize on her BMW stock if she sells it today?

LG 4

P2.5 An investor believes that the U.S. dollar will rise in value relative to the Japanese yen. The same investor is considering two investments with identical risk and return characteristics: One is a Japanese yen investment and the other is a U.S. dollar investment. Should the investor purchase the Japanese yen investment?

LG 6

P2.6 Elmo Inc.'s stock is currently selling at $60 per share. For each of the following situations (ignoring brokerage commissions), calculate the gain or loss that Maureen Katz realizes if she makes a 100-share transaction.

a. She sells short and repurchases the borrowed shares at $70 per share.
b. She takes a long position and sells the stock at $75 per share.
c. She sells short and repurchases the borrowed shares at $45 per share.
d. She takes a long position and sells the stock at $60 per share.

LG 6

P2.7 Assume that an investor buys 100 shares of stock at $50 per share, putting up a 60% margin.

a. What is the debit balance in this transaction?
b. How much equity capital must the investor provide to make this margin transaction?

LG 6

P2.8 Assume that an investor buys 100 shares of stock at $50 per share, putting up a 60% margin. If the stock rises to $60 per share what is the investor's new margin position?

LG 6

Note: A PC icon appears next to problems and case questions that can be solved using the computation routines available at the book's Web site.

P2.9 Assume that an investor buys 100 shares of stock at $50 per share, putting up a 70% margin.

a. What is the *debit balance* in this transaction?
b. How much equity funds must the investor provide to make this margin transaction?
c. If the stock rises to $80 per share, what is the investor's new margin position?

LG 6

P2.10 Doug purchased 100 shares of Can'tWin.com for $50 per share, using as little of his own money as he could. His broker has a 50% initial margin requirement and a 30% maintenance margin requirement. The price of the stock falls to $30 per share. What does Doug need to do?

LG 6

P2.11 Jerri Kingston bought 100 shares of stock at $80 per share, using an *initial margin* of 60%. Given a *maintenance margin* of 25%, how far does the stock have to drop before Ms. Kingston faces a *margin call?* (Assume that there are no other securities in the margin account.)

LG 6

P2.12 An investor buys 200 shares of stock selling at $80 per share, using a margin of 60%. The stock pays annual dividends of $1 per share. A margin loan can be obtained at an annual interest cost of 8%. Determine what return on invested capital the investor will realize if the price of the stock increases to $104 within 6 months. What is the *annualized* rate of return on this transaction?

LG 6

P2.13 Marlene Bellamy purchased 300 shares of Writeline Communications stock at $55 per share, using the prevailing minimum *initial margin* requirement of 50%. She held the stock for exactly 4 months and sold it without any brokerage costs at the end of that period. During the 4-month holding period, the stock paid $1.50 per share in cash dividends. Marlene was charged 9% annual interest on the margin loan. The minimum *maintenance margin* was 25%.

a. Calculate the initial value of the transaction, the *debit balance,* and the equity position on Marlene's transaction.
b. For each of the following share prices, calculate the actual margin percentage, and indicate whether Marlene's margin account would have excess equity, would be restricted, or would be subject to a margin call.
   (1) $45
   (2) $70
   (3) $35

c. Calculate the dollar amount of (1) dividends received and (2) interest paid on the margin loan during the 4-month holding period.
d. Use each of the following sale prices at the end of the 4-month holding period to calculate Marlene's *annualized* rate of return on the Writeline Communications stock transaction.
   (1) $50
   (2) $60
   (3) $70

LG 6 P2.14 Not long ago, Dave Edwards bought 200 shares of Almost Anything Inc. at $45 per share; he bought the stock on margin of 60%. The stock is now trading at $60 per share, and the Federal Reserve has recently lowered *initial margin* requirements to 50%. Dave now wants to do a little *pyramiding* and buy another 300 shares of the stock. What is the minimum amount of equity that he'll have to put up in this transaction?

LG 6 P2.15 An investor short sells 100 shares of a stock for $20 per share. The initial margin is 50%. How much equity will be required in the account to complete this transaction?

LG 6 P2.16 An investor short sells 100 shares of a stock for $20 per share. The initial margin is 50%. Ignoring transaction costs, how much will be in the investor's account after this transaction if this is the only transaction the investor has undertaken and the investor has deposited only the required amount?

LG 6 P2.17 An investor short sells 100 shares of a stock for $20 per share. The initial margin is 50%, and the maintenance margin is 30%. The price of the stock falls to $12 per share. What is the margin, and will there be a margin call?

LG 6 P2.18 An investor short sells 100 shares of a stock for $20 per share. The initial margin is 50% and the maintenance margin is 30%. The price of the stock rises to $28 per share. What is the margin, and will there be a margin call?

LG 6 P2.19 Calculate the profit or loss per share realized on each of the following short-sale transactions.

Transaction	Stock Sold Short at Price/Share	Stock Purchased to Cover Short at Price/Share
A	$75	$83
B	30	24
C	18	15
D	27	32
E	53	45

LG 6 P2.20 Charlene Hickman expected the price of Bio International shares to drop in the near future in response to the expected failure of its new drug to pass FDA tests. As a result, she sold short 200 shares of Bio International at $27.50. How much would Charlene earn or lose on this transaction if she repurchased the 200 shares 4 months later at each of the following prices per share?
a. $24.75
b. $25.13
c. $31.25
d. $27.00

See the text Web site (www.aw-bc.com/gitman_joehnk) for Web exercises that deal with *markets and transactions*.

Case Problem 2.1 *Dara's Dilemma: What to Buy?*

LG 6

Dara Simmons, a 40-year-old financial analyst and divorced mother of two teenage children, considers herself a savvy investor. She has increased her investment portfolio considerably over the past 5 years. Although she has been fairly conservative with her investments, she now feels more confident in her investment knowledge and would like to branch out into some new areas that could bring higher returns. She has between $20,000 and $25,000 to invest.

Attracted to the hot market for technology stocks, Dara was interested in purchasing a tech IPO stock and identified "NewestHighTech.com," a company that makes sophisticated computer chips for wireless Internet connections, as a likely prospect. The 1-year-old company had received some favorable press when it got early-stage financing and again when its chip was accepted by a major cell phone manufacturer.

Dara also was considering an investment in 400 shares of Casinos International common stock, currently selling for $54 per share. After a discussion with a friend who is an economist with a major commercial bank, Dara believes that the long-running bull market is due to cool off and that economic activity will slow down. With the aid of her stockbroker, Dara researches Casinos International's current financial situation and finds that the future success of the company may hinge on the outcome of pending court proceedings on the firm's application to open a new floating casino on a nearby river. If the permit is granted, it seems likely that the firm's stock will experience a rapid increase in value, regardless of economic conditions. On the other hand, if the company fails to get the permit, the falling stock price will make it a good candidate for a short sale.

Dara felt that the following alternatives were open to her:

Alternative 1: Invest $20,000 in NewestHighTech.com when it goes public.

Alternative 2: Buy Casinos International now at $54 per share and follow the company closely.

Alternative 3: Sell Casinos short at $54 in anticipation that the company's fortunes will change for the worse.

Alternative 4: Wait to see what happens with the casino permit and then decide whether to buy or short the Casinos International stock.

Questions

a. Evaluate each of these alternatives. On the basis of the limited information presented, recommend the one you feel is best.

b. If Casinos International's stock price rises to $60, what will happen under alternatives 2 and 3? Evaluate the pros and cons of these outcomes.

c. If the stock price drops to $45, what will happen under alternatives 2 and 3? Evaluate the pros and cons of these outcomes.

Case Problem 2.2 *Ravi Dumar's High-Flying Margin Account*

Ravi Dumar is a stockbroker who lives with his wife, Sasha, and their five children in Milwaukee, Wisconsin. Ravi firmly believes that the only way to make money in the market is to follow an aggressive investment posture—for example, to use margin trading. In fact, Ravi himself has built a substantial margin account over the years. He currently holds $75,000 worth of stock in his margin account, though the *debit balance* in the account amounts to only $30,000. Recently, Ravi uncovered a stock that, on the basis of extensive analysis, he feels is about to take off. The stock, Running Shoes (RS), currently trades at $20 per share. Ravi feels it should soar to at least $50 within a year. RS pays no dividends, the prevailing *initial margin* requirement is 50%, and margin loans are now carrying an annual interest charge of 10%. Because Ravi feels so strongly about RS, he wants to do some *pyramiding* by using his margin account to purchase 1,000 shares of the stock.

Questions

a. Discuss the concept of pyramiding as it applies to this investment situation.

b. What is the present margin position (in percent) of Ravi's account?

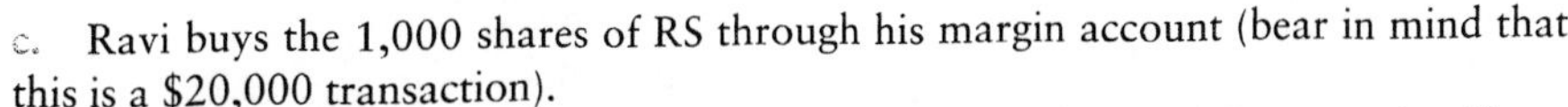

c. Ravi buys the 1,000 shares of RS through his margin account (bear in mind that this is a $20,000 transaction).

1. What will the margin position of the account be after the RS transaction if Ravi follows the prevailing initial margin (50%) and uses $10,000 of his money to buy the stock?
2. What if he uses only $2,500 equity and obtains a margin loan for the balance ($17,500)?
3. How do you explain the fact that the stock can be purchased with only 12.5% margin when the prevailing initial margin requirement is 50%?

d. Assume that Ravi buys 1,000 shares of RS stock at $20 per share with a minimum cash investment of $2,500 and that the stock does take off and its price rises to $40 per share in 1 year.

1. What is the *return on invested capital* for this transaction?
2. What return would Ravi have earned if he had bought the stock without margin—that is, if he had used all his own money?

e. What do you think of Ravi's idea to pyramid? What are the risks and rewards of this strategy?

Excel with Spreadsheets

You have just learned about the mechanics of margin trading and want to take advantage of the potential benefits of financial leverage. You have decided to open a margin account with your broker and to secure a margin loan. The specifics of the account are as follows:

- Initial margin requirement is 70%.
- Maintenance margin is 30%.
- You are informed that if the value of your account falls below the maintenance margin, your account will be subject to a margin call.

You have been following the price movements of a stock over the past year and believe that it is currently undervalued and that the price will rise in the near future. You feel that the opening of a margin account is a good investment strategy. You have decided to purchase three round lots (i.e., 100 shares per round lot) of the stock at its current price of $25 per share.

Create a spreadsheet similar to the spreadsheet for Table 2.3, which can be viewed at www.aw-bc.com/gitman_joehnk, to model and analyze the following market transactions.

Questions

a. Calculate the value of the investment in the stock as if you did not make use of margin trading. In other words, what is the value of the investment if it is funded by 100% cash equity?

b. Calculate the debit balance and the cash equity in the investment at the time of opening a margin account, adhering to the initial margin requirement.

c. If you use margin and the price of the stock rises by $15 to $40/share, calculate the capital gain earned and the return on investor's equity.

d. What is the current margin percentage based on question **b**?

e. If you use margin and the price of the stock falls by $15 to $10/share, calculate the capital loss and the respective return on investor's equity.

f. What is the new margin percentage based on question **e**, and what is the implication for you, the investor?

Fundamentals of Investing

CHAPTER 3

ONLINE INFORMATION AND INVESTING

CHAPTER 3

ONLINE INFORMATION AND INVESTING

LEARNING GOALS

After studying this chapter, you should be able to:

LG 1 Discuss the growth in online investing, including educational sites and investment tools, and the pros and cons of using the Internet as an investment tool.

LG 2 Identify the major types and sources of traditional and online investment information.

LG 3 Explain the characteristics, interpretation, and uses of the commonly cited stock and bond market averages and indexes.

LG 4 Review the roles of full-service, premium discount, and basic discount stockbrokers, including the services they provide, selection of a stockbroker, opening an account, and transaction basics.

LG 5 Describe the basic types of orders (market, limit, and stop-loss), online transactions, transaction costs, and the legal aspects of investor protection.

LG 6 Discuss the roles of investment advisers and investment clubs.

There are millions of Web pages devoted to stocks and investment strategies that put everything at your fingertips—literally—and most of it is free. Here are the basic steps to follow.

First, determine your investment objectives and do some initial research to identify your risk tolerance, investing style (value and growth are two of several styles), and other criteria such as your time horizon. Then visit financial portal sites such as those offered by Yahoo! (finance.yahoo.com), Morningstar.com (www.morningstar.com), and CNN/Money (money.cnn.com). They can help you familiarize yourself with stocks and what's happening currently in the markets. Explore Yahoo!, for example, and you will find current and historical company data and industry comparisons.

Because you love to dine out, you might decide to look for promising restaurant stocks. Stock screening tools at sites like Quicken (www.quicken.com) and Morningstar will narrow the field. For example, you might define search criteria such as a price/earnings (P/E) ratio of less than 35, a debt-equity ratio of less than 1.0, and above-average earnings growth. In a few seconds, you'll have a list of stocks that meet these parameters. Then, head to each company's Web site to find the latest annual report, press releases, and other material. The more detailed Securities and Exchange Commission (SEC) filings are available online as well at www.sec.gov and www.freeedgar.com. Find out what the securities analysts say. If your broker doesn't offer free research reports on your top picks, you can buy individual stock research reports at Yahoo! or Reuters Investor (www.investor.reuters.com). Now evaluate your finalists and make your decisions—that's all there is to it!

Well, it's not quite that easy! Nevertheless, the power of the Internet enables you to access information in minutes that in the past was either unavailable to the average investor or would take weeks to accumulate. In Chapter 3, you'll learn more about the many sources of investment information, both online and offline, as well as how to make transactions.

Sources: Adapted from Carol Marie Cropper, "So How Well Does the Net Trawl for Stocks?" *Business Week*, May 27, 2002, pp. 103–104; Selena Maranjian, "Researching Companies Online," *Motley Fool*, May 29, 2003, downloaded from www.fool.com; and Susan Scherreik, "How to Dig Deep with a Few Mouse Clicks," *Business Week*, May 27, 2002, p. 101.

Online Investing

LG 1

Today the Internet is a major force in the investing environment. It has opened the world of investing to individual investors, creating a more level playing field and providing access to tools formerly restricted to professionals. You can trade many types of securities online and also find a wealth of information. This information ranges from real-time stock price quotes to securities analysts' research reports and tools for investment analysis. The savings from online investing in terms of time and money are huge. Instead of wading through mounds of paper, investors can quickly sort through vast databases to find appropriate investments, monitor their current investments, and make securities transactions—all without leaving their computers.

This chapter introduces you to online investing, types and sources of investment information, and the basics of making securities transactions. We will continue discussing online investing in subsequent chapters focused on analysis and selection of various types of securities. In addition, throughout the book you will find descriptions of useful investing Web sites that will help you become a more proficient and confident investor.

Because new Web sites appear every day and existing ones change constantly, it's impossible to describe all the good ones. Our intent is to give you a sampling of Web sites that will introduce you to the wealth of investing information available on the Internet. You'll find plenty of good sources to help you stay current.

The Growth of Online Investing

Online investing's popularity continues to grow at a rapid pace. It is expected to increase from about 14.3 million Internet users investing online in 2000 to 32.4 million in 2004, a 127% increase over a 5-year period. About 25 million households manage over $1 trillion in assets online. It's easy to see why online investing attracts new investors: The Internet makes buying and selling securities convenient, relatively simple, inexpensive, and fast. In today's rapidly changing stock markets, it provides the most current information, updated continuously. Even if you prefer to use a human broker, the Internet provides an abundance of resources to help you become a more informed investor.

To successfully navigate the cyberinvesting universe, open your Web browser and explore the multitude of investing sites. These sites typically include a combination of resources for novice and sophisticated investors alike. For example, look at brokerage firm TD Waterhouse's homepage (www.tdwaterhouse.com), shown in Figure 3.1 (on page 78). With a few mouse clicks you can learn about TD Waterhouse's services, open an account, and begin trading. In addition, you will find the day's and week's market activity, price quotes, news, analysts' research reports, and more. You can learn about various aspects of investing, including products, and make banking transactions through the TD Waterhouse Bank.

All this information can be overwhelming and intimidating. It takes time and effort to use the Internet wisely. But the Internet itself helps you sort through the maze. Educational sites are a good place to start. Then you can check out the many investment tools. In the following section, we'll discuss how to use the Internet wisely to become a smarter investor.

FIGURE 3.1

Investment Resources at the TD Waterhouse Web Site

TD Waterhouse's Web site presents a wealth of investment resources. You can open an account, assess market activity, obtain news, access analysts' research, and more.
(*Source:* TD Waterhouse Investor Services, Inc., New York, www.tdwaterhouse.com.)

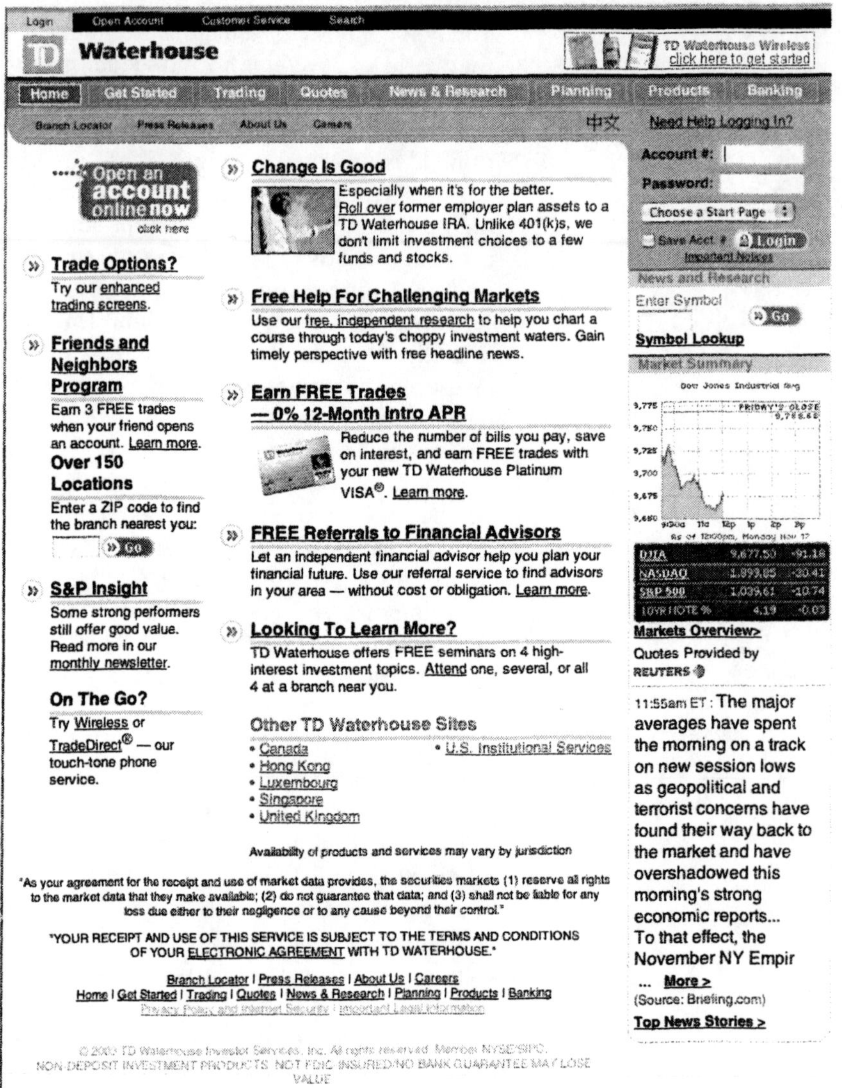

Investment Education Sites The Internet offers many tutorials, online classes, and articles to educate the novice investor. Even experienced investors will find sites that expand their investing knowledge. Although most investing-oriented Web sites and financial portals (described later) include many educational resources, here are a few good sites that feature investing fundamentals.

- *Investing Online Resource Center* (www.investingonline.org) is an educational site that provides a wealth of information for those getting started online as well as those already investing online. It includes an investment simulator that creates an online interactive learning experience that allows the user to "test drive" online trading.
- *Investor Guide.com* (www.investorguide.com) is a free educational site offering Investor Guide University, which is a collection of educational articles about investing and personal finance. In addition, the site pro-

vides access to quotes and charts, portfolio tracking software, research, news and commentary, and a glossary through Investor Words.com (www.investorwords.com).

- *The Motley Fool* (www.fool.com) has sections on investing basics, mutual fund investing, choosing a broker, and investment strategies and styles, as well as lively discussion boards and more.
- Investopedia (www.investopedia.com) is an educational site featuring tutorials on numerous basic and advanced investing and personal finance topics, a glossary of investing terms, and other useful investment aids.
- *WSJ.com* (www.wsj.com), a free site from the *Wall Street Journal,* is an excellent starting place to learn what the Internet can offer investors.
- Nasdaq (www.nasdaq.com) has an Education Initiatives section that provides links to a number of investment education resources.

Other good educational sites include leading personal finance magazines such as *Money* (money.cnn.com), *Kiplinger's Personal Finance Magazine* (www.kiplinger.com), and *Smart Money* (www.smartmoney.com).

Investment Tools Once you are familiar with investing basics, you can use the Internet to develop financial plans and set investment goals, find securities that meet your objectives, analyze potential investments, and organize your portfolio. Many of these tools, once used only by professional investment advisers, are free online. You'll find financial calculators and worksheets, screening and charting tools, and stock quotes and portfolio trackers at general financial sites (described in the later section on financial portals) and at the Web sites of larger brokerage firms. You can even set up a personal calendar that notifies you of forthcoming earnings announcements and can receive alerts when one of your stocks has hit a predetermined price target.

HOT LINKS

See NAIC, a not-for-profit organization site, for investment education of individuals and investment clubs.

www.better-investing.org

Planning Online calculators and worksheets help you find answers to your financial planning and investing questions. With them you can figure out how much to save each month for a particular goal, such as the down payment for your first home, a college education for your children, or retiring when you are 60. For example, the brokerage firm Fidelity (www.fidelity.com) has a wide selection of planning tools: life events, financial goals, retirement planning, estate planning, and college planning. It also makes a number of interactive tools and calculators available for use in investment planning, retirement, estate planing, college, tax, and annuity and life insurance. (Because not all calculators give the same answer, you may want to try out those at several sites.)

One of the best sites for financial calculators is FinanCenter.com (www.financenter.com). It includes over 140 calculators for financial planning, insurance, auto and home buying, and investing. Figure 3.2 (on page 80) lists, in question form, the 9 calculators specifically concerned with stocks. Other investment-related calculators focus on bonds, mutual funds, and retirement.

Screening With screening tools, you can quickly sort through huge databases of stocks, bonds, and mutual funds to find those that have specific characteristics. For stocks, you can specify low or high price/earnings ratios, small market

FIGURE 3.2 Financial Calculators Concerned with Stocks

At sites like FinanCenter, you'll find many calculators that can be used to solve specific problems. Below is the screen listing, in question form, of the 9 investment-related stock calculators available at FinanCenter. Input the variables for your situation, and the calculator will show you the selling price at which you will earn the desired return on your stock investment. (Source: FinanCenter, www.financenter.com/products/calculators/stock. Screenshot courtesy of FinanCenter. ©2003 FinanCenter)

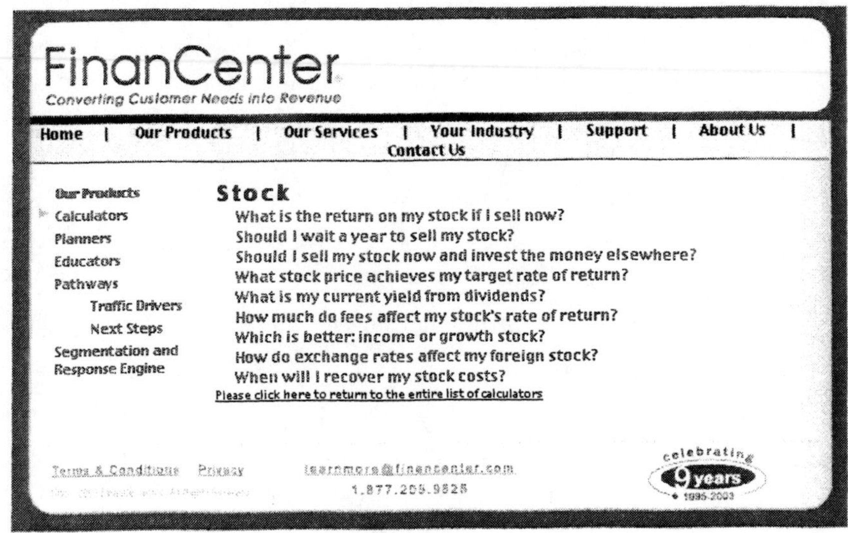

value, high dividend return, specific revenue growth, and/or a low debt-to-equity ratio. For bonds, you can specify a given industry, maturity date, or yield. For mutual funds, you might specify low minimum investment, a particular industry or geographical sector, and low fees. Each screening tool uses a different method to sort. You answer a series of questions to specify the type of stock or fund, performance criteria, cost parameters, and so on. Then you can do more research on the stocks, bonds, or mutual funds that meet your requirements.

Quicken.com (www.quicken.com/investments) provides online brokerage and has some of the best free tools. Figure 3.3 shows the opening page for Quicken's "Brokerage Stock Search" screen that lists searches based on the most popular investment strategies. The full search lets you select industry, valuation, growth rates, analyst estimates, financial strength, and similar qualities. Morningstar (www.morningstar.com) offers some free tools but charges $11.95 a month or $109 a year for its premium tools. Wall Street City (www.wallstreetcity.com) offers some of the best screening tools. You can check out the site's prebuilt search strategies free—for example, "stocks with reversal potential" and "strong stocks/recently weak." More experienced investors can subscribe to its Wall Street City Pro for $9.95 a month and gain access to its ProSearch screening tool, which allows the creation of customized stock screens with over 300 criteria.

Charting *Charting* is a technique that plots the performance of stocks over a specified time period, from months to decades and beyond. Looking at the

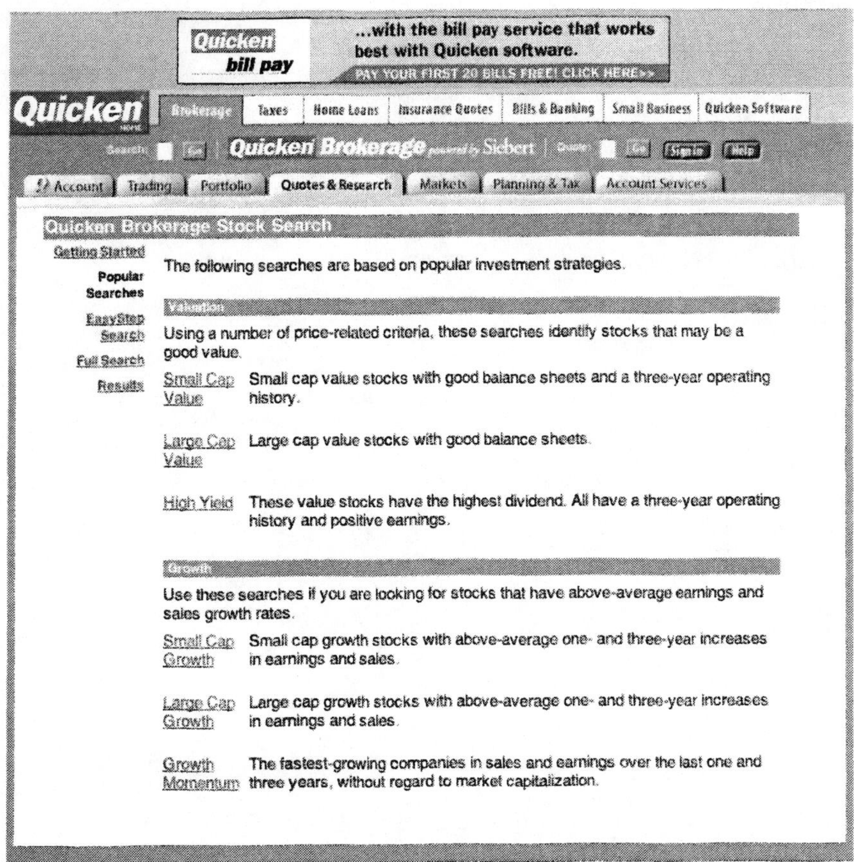

FIGURE 3.3

Quicken's Brokerage Stock Search Tool

Search for stocks based on popular investment strategies. The full search allows selection from a list of variables, such as industry, valuation, growth rates, analyst estimates, financial strength, and similar qualities. Quicken's stock screening tool will give you a list of stocks that meet your specifications. (*Source:* Quicken.com, www.quicken.com/investments/stocks/search/popular/. Screenshot courtesy of Intuit. Copyright ©2003 Intuit.)

1-year stock chart for Qualcomm (QCOM) in Figure 3.4 (on page 82), it's obvious that charting can be tedious and expensive. But by going online, today you can see the chart for a selected stock in just seconds. With another click you can compare one company's price performance to that of other stocks, industries, sectors, or market indexes, choosing the type of chart, time frame, and indicators. Several good sites are Barchart.com (www.barchart.com), BigCharts (bigcharts.marketwatch.com), and Stock Charts (www.stockcharts.com). All have free charting features; Barchart.com charges a monthly fee for advanced capabilities. Another popular free site that offers good charting capabilities is Silicon Investor (siliconinvestor.com).

Stock Quotes and Portfolio Tracking Almost every investment-oriented Web site includes stock quotation and portfolio tracking tools. Simply enter the stock symbol to get the price, either in real time or delayed several minutes.

FIGURE 3.4

Stock Chart for Qualcomm

Specify the company's time frame and frequency (e.g., daily, weekly), and BigCharts will in seconds perform the tedious process of charting the selected stock's price (in this case, the price of Qualcomm) over the specified time frame (in this case, the year ended November 17, 2003). (*Source:* BigCharts Inc. is a service of MarketWatch.com, Inc., 825 Battery Street, San Francisco, CA 94111. bigcharts.marketwatch.com.)

Once you create a portfolio of stocks in a portfolio tracker, the tracker automatically updates your portfolio's value every time you check. You can usually link to more detailed information about each stock. Many sites let you set up multiple portfolios. The features, quality, and ease of use of stock and portfolio trackers varies, so check several to find the one that best meets your needs. Quicken.com/investments, MSN Money Investing (moneycentral.msn.com/investor), and E*Trade (www.etrade.com) have portfolio trackers that are easy to set up and customize.

Pros and Cons of Using the Internet as an Investment Tool

The power of the Internet as an investing tool is alluring. "Do-it-yourself" investing is readily available to the average investor, even novices who have never before bought stock. However, online investing also carries risks. Trading on the Internet requires that investors exercise the same—and possibly more—caution than they would if they were getting information from and placing orders with a human broker. You don't have the safety net of a live broker suggesting that you rethink your trade. The ease of point-and-click investing can be the financial downfall of inexperienced investors. Drawn by stories of others who have made lots of money, many novice investors take the plunge before they acquire the necessary skills and knowledge—often with disastrous results.

Online or off, the basic rules for smart investing are the same. Know what you are buying, from whom, and at what level of risk. Be skeptical. If it sounds too good to be true, it probably is! Always do your own research; don't accept someone else's word that a security is a good buy. Perform your own analysis before you buy, using the skills you will develop in later chapters of this book.

Here is some additional advice:

- Don't let the speed and ease of making transactions blind you to the realities of online trading. More frequent trades mean high total transaction costs. Although some brokers advertise per-trade costs as low as $7, the average online transaction fee is higher (generally about $15 to $20). If you trade often, it will take longer to recoup your costs. Studies reveal that the more often you trade, the harder it is to beat the market. In addition, on short-term trades of less than one year, you'll pay taxes on profits at the higher, ordinary income tax rates, not the lower capital gains rate.
- Don't believe everything you read on the Internet. It's easy to be impressed with a screen full of data touting a stock's prospects or to act on a hot tip you find on a discussion board or in an online chat (more on this later). But what do you know about the person who posts the information? He or she could be a shill for a dealer, posing as an enthusiastic investor to push a stock. Stick to the sites of major brokerage firms, mutual funds, academic institutions, and well-known business and finance publications.
- If you get bitten by the online buying bug, don't be tempted to use margin debt to increase your stock holdings. You may instead be magnifying your losses, as noted in Chapter 2.

We will return to the subject of online investment fraud and scams and will discuss guidelines for online transactions in subsequent sections of this chapter.

CONCEPTS IN REVIEW

3.1 Discuss the impact of the Internet on the individual investor, and summarize the types of resources it provides.

3.2 Identify the four main types of online investment tools. How can they help you become a better investor?

3.3 What are some of the pros and cons of using the Internet to choose and manage your investments?

Types and Sources of Investment Information

LG 2

As you learned in Chapter 1, becoming a successful investor starts with developing investment plans and meeting your liquidity needs. Once you have done that, you can search for the right investments to implement your investment plan and monitor your progress toward achieving your goals. Whether you use the Internet or print sources, you should examine various kinds of investment information to formulate expectations of the risk–return behaviors of potential investments and to monitor them once they are acquired. This section describes the key types and sources of investment information; the following section focuses on market averages and indexes.

descriptive information
factual data on the past behavior of the economy, the market, the industry, the company, or a given investment vehicle.

analytical information
available current data in conjunction with projections and recommendations about potential investments.

Investment information can be either descriptive or analytical. **Descriptive information** presents factual data on the past behavior of the economy, the market, the industry, the company, or a given investment vehicle. **Analytical information** presents available current data in conjunction with projections and recommendations about potential investments. The sample page from *Value Line* included in Figure 3.5 provides both descriptive and analytical information on Wal-Mart Stores. Items that are primarily descriptive are marked with a D, analytical items with an A. Examples of descriptive information are the company's capital structure (7D) and monthly stock price ranges for the past 13 years (13D). Examples of analytical information are rank for timeliness (1A) and projected price range and associated annual total returns for the next 3 years (4A).

Some forms of investment information are free; others must be purchased individually or by annual subscription. You'll find free information on the Internet; in newspapers, in magazines, and at brokerage firms; and at public, university, and brokerage firm libraries. Alternatively, you can subscribe to free and paid services that provide periodic reports summarizing the investment outlook and recommending certain actions. Many Internet sites now offer free e-mail newsletters and alerts. You can even set up your own personalized home page at many financial Web sites so that stock quotes, portfolio tracking, current business news, and other information on stocks of interest to you appear whenever you visit the site. Other sites charge for premium content, such as brokerage research reports, whether in print or online form.

Although the Internet has increased the amount of free information, it may still make sense to pay for services that save you time and money by gathering material you need. But first consider the value of potential information: For example, paying $40 for information that increases your return by $27 would not be economically sound. The larger your investment portfolio, the easier it is to justify information purchases, because they are usually applicable to a number of investments.

Types of Information

Investment information can be divided into five types, each concerned with an important aspect of the investment process.

1. *Economic and current event information* includes background as well as forecast data related to economic, political, and social trends on a domestic as well as a global scale. Such information provides a basis for assessing the environment in which decisions are made.
2. *Industry and company information* includes background as well as forecast data on specific industries and companies. Investors use such information to assess the outlook in a given industry or a specific company. Because of its company orientation, it is most relevant to stock, bond, or options investments.
3. *Information on alternative investment vehicles* includes background and predictive data for securities other than stocks, bonds, and options, such as mutual funds and futures.

FIGURE 3.5 A Report Containing Descriptive and Analytical Information

Value Line's full-page report on Wal-Mart Stores from November 14, 2003, contains both descriptive (marked D) and analytical (marked A) information. (*Source:* Adapted from *The Value Line Investment Survey,* Ratings and Reports, November 14, 2003. ©Value Line Publishing, Inc., www.valueline.com. ©2003 Reproduced with the permission of Value Line Publishing, Inc.)

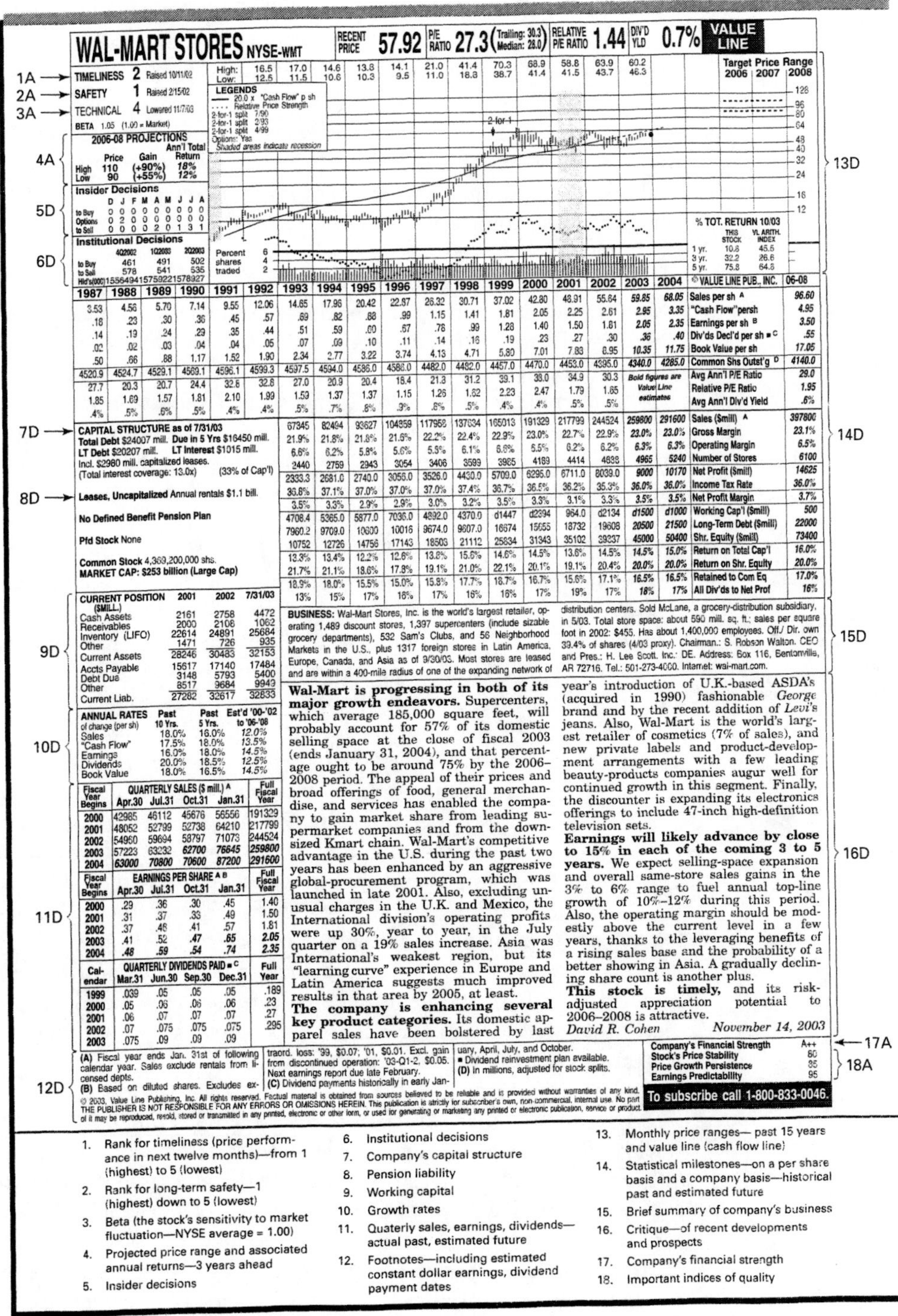

WAL-MART STORES NYSE-WMT | RECENT PRICE 57.92 | P/E RATIO 27.3 (Trailing: 30.3; Median: 28.0) | RELATIVE P/E RATIO 1.44 | DIV'D YLD 0.7% | VALUE LINE

1A → TIMELINESS 2 Raised 10/11/02
2A → SAFETY 1 Raised 2/15/02
3A → TECHNICAL 4 Lowered 11/7/03
BETA 1.05 (1.00 = Market)

High:	16.5	17.0	14.6	13.8	14.1	21.0	41.4	70.3	68.9	58.8	63.9	60.2
Low:	12.5	11.5	10.6	10.3	9.5	11.0	18.8	38.7	41.4	41.5	43.7	46.3

Target Price Range 2006 | 2007 | 2008

LEGENDS
— 20.0 x "Cash Flow" p sh
.... Relative Price Strength
2-for-1 split 7/90
2-for-1 split 2/93
2-for-1 split 4/99
Options: Yes
Shaded areas indicate recession

4A 2006-08 PROJECTIONS

	Price	Gain	Ann'l Total Return
High	110	(+90%)	18%
Low	90	(+55%)	12%

5D Insider Decisions

	D	J	F	M	A	M	J	J	A
to Buy	0	0	0	0	0	0	0	0	0
Options	0	2	0	0	0	0	0	0	0
to Sell	0	0	0	0	2	0	1	3	1

6D Institutional Decisions

	4Q2002	1Q2003	2Q2003
to Buy	461	491	502
to Sell	578	541	535
Hld's(000)	1556494	1575922	1578927

Percent shares traded 6 4 2

13D

% TOT. RETURN 10/03

	THIS STOCK	VL ARITH. INDEX
1 yr.	10.8	45.5
3 yr.	32.2	26.6
5 yr.	75.8	64.8

14D

1987	1988	1989	1990	1991	1992	1993	1994	1995	1996	1997	1998	1999	2000	2001	2002	2003	2004	© VALUE LINE PUB., INC.	06-08
3.53	4.56	5.70	7.14	9.55	12.06	14.65	17.96	20.42	22.87	26.32	30.71	37.02	42.80	48.91	55.64	59.85	68.05	Sales per sh A	96.60
.18	.23	.30	.36	.45	.57	.69	.82	.88	.99	1.15	1.41	1.81	2.05	2.25	2.61	2.95	3.35	"Cash Flow" per sh	4.95
.14	.19	.24	.29	.35	.44	.51	.59	.60	.67	.78	.99	1.28	1.40	1.50	1.81	2.05	2.35	Earnings per sh B	3.50
.02	.02	.03	.04	.04	.05	.07	.09	.10	.11	.14	.16	.19	.23	.27	.30	.36	.40	Div'ds Decl'd per sh ■ C	.55
.50	.66	.88	1.17	1.52	1.90	2.34	2.77	3.22	3.74	4.13	4.71	5.80	7.01	7.88	8.95	10.35	11.75	Book Value per sh	17.05
4520.9	4524.7	4529.1	4569.1	4596.1	4599.3	4597.5	4594.0	4586.0	4586.0	4482.0	4482.0	4457.0	4470.0	4453.0	4395.0	4340.0	4285.0	Common Shs Outst'g D	4140.0
27.7	20.3	20.7	24.4	32.6	32.8	27.0	20.9	20.4	18.4	21.3	31.2	39.1	38.0	34.9	30.3	Bold figures are		Avg Ann'l P/E Ratio	29.0
1.85	1.69	1.57	1.81	2.10	1.99	1.59	1.37	1.37	1.15	1.26	1.62	2.23	2.47	1.79	1.65	Value Line		Relative P/E Ratio	1.95
.4%	.5%	.6%	.5%	.4%	.4%	.5%	.7%	.8%	.9%	.8%	.5%	.4%	.4%	.5%	.5%	estimates		Avg Ann'l Div'd Yield	.6%

1993	1994	1995	1996	1997	1998	1999	2000	2001	2002	2003	2004		06-08
67345	82494	93627	104859	117958	137634	165013	191329	217799	244524	259800	291600	Sales ($mill) A	397800
21.9%	21.8%	21.8%	21.6%	22.2%	22.4%	22.9%	23.0%	22.7%	22.9%	23.0%	23.0%	Gross Margin	23.1%
6.6%	6.2%	5.8%	5.6%	5.5%	6.1%	6.6%	6.5%	6.2%	6.2%	6.3%	6.3%	Operating Margin	6.5%
2440	2759	2943	3054	3406	3599	3985	4189	4414	4688	4965	5240	Number of Stores	6100
2333.3	2681.0	2740.0	3056.0	3526.0	4430.0	5709.0	6295.0	6711.0	8039.0	9000	10170	Net Profit ($mill)	14625
36.8%	37.1%	37.0%	37.0%	37.0%	37.4%	36.7%	36.5%	36.2%	35.3%	36.0%	36.0%	Income Tax Rate	36.0%
3.5%	3.3%	2.9%	2.9%	3.0%	3.2%	3.5%	3.3%	3.1%	3.3%	3.5%	3.5%	Net Profit Margin	3.7%
4708.4	5365.0	5877.0	7036.0	4892.0	4370.0	d1447	d2394	964.0	d2134	d1500	d1000	Working Cap'l ($mill)	500
7960.2	9709.0	10600	10016	9674.0	9607.0	16674	15655	18732	19608	20500	21500	Long-Term Debt ($mill)	22000
10752	12726	14756	17143	18503	21112	25834	31343	35102	39337	45000	50400	Shr. Equity ($mill)	73400
13.3%	13.4%	12.2%	12.6%	13.8%	15.6%	14.6%	14.5%	13.6%	14.5%	14.5%	15.0%	Return on Total Cap'l	16.0%
21.7%	21.1%	18.0%	17.8%	19.1%	21.0%	22.1%	20.1%	19.1%	20.4%	20.0%	20.0%	Return on Shr. Equity	20.0%
18.9%	18.0%	15.5%	15.0%	15.8%	17.7%	18.7%	16.7%	15.6%	17.1%	16.5%	16.5%	Retained to Com Eq	17.0%
13%	15%	17%	16%	17%	16%	16%	17%	19%	17%	18%	17%	All Div'ds to Net Prof	16%

7D → **CAPITAL STRUCTURE as of 7/31/03**
Total Debt $24007 mill. **Due in 5 Yrs** $16450 mill.
LT Debt $20207 mill. **LT Interest** $1015 mill.
Incl. $2980 mill. capitalized leases.
(Total interest coverage: 13.0x) (33% of Cap'l)

8D → **Leases, Uncapitalized** Annual rentals $1.1 bill.

No Defined Benefit Pension Plan

Pfd Stock None

Common Stock 4,369,200,000 shs.
MARKET CAP: $253 billion (Large Cap)

9D

CURRENT POSITION ($MILL.)	2001	2002	7/31/03
Cash Assets	2161	2758	4472
Receivables	2000	2108	1062
Inventory (LIFO)	22614	24891	25684
Other	1471	726	935
Current Assets	28246	30483	32153
Accts Payable	15617	17140	17484
Debt Due	3148	5793	5400
Other	8517	9684	9949
Current Liab.	27282	32617	32833

10D

ANNUAL RATES of change (per sh)	Past 10 Yrs.	Past 5 Yrs.	Est'd '00-'02 to '06-'08
Sales	18.0%	16.0%	12.0%
"Cash Flow"	17.5%	18.0%	13.5%
Earnings	16.0%	18.0%	14.5%
Dividends	20.0%	18.5%	12.5%
Book Value	18.0%	16.5%	14.5%

11D

Fiscal Year Begins	QUARTERLY SALES ($ mill.) A Apr.30	Jul.31	Oct.31	Jan.31	Full Fiscal Year
2000	42985	46112	45676	56556	191329
2001	48052	52799	52738	64210	217799
2002	54960	59694	58797	71073	244524
2003	57223	63232	62700	76645	259800
2004	63000	70800	70600	87200	291600

Fiscal Year Begins	EARNINGS PER SHARE A B Apr.30	Jul.31	Oct.31	Jan.31	Full Fiscal Year
2000	.29	.36	.30	.45	1.40
2001	.31	.37	.33	.49	1.50
2002	.37	.46	.41	.57	1.81
2003	.41	.52	.47	.65	2.05
2004	.48	.59	.54	.74	2.35

Cal-endar	QUARTERLY DIVIDENDS PAID ■ C Mar.31	Jun.30	Sep.30	Dec.31	Full Year
1999	.039	.05	.05	.05	.189
2000	.05	.06	.06	.06	.23
2001	.06	.07	.07	.07	.27
2002	.07	.075	.075	.075	.295
2003	.075	.09	.09	.09	

15D **BUSINESS:** Wal-Mart Stores, Inc. is the world's largest retailer, operating 1,489 discount stores, 1,397 supercenters (include sizable grocery departments), 532 Sam's Clubs, and 56 Neighborhood Markets in the U.S., plus 1317 foreign stores in Latin America, Europe, Canada, and Asia as of 9/30/03. Most stores are leased and are within a 400-mile radius of one of the expanding network of distribution centers. Sold McLane, a grocery-distribution subsidiary, in 5/03. Total store space: about 590 mill. sq. ft.; sales per square foot in 2002: $455. Has about 1,400,000 employees. Off./Dir. own 33.4% of shares (4/03 proxy). Chairman.: S. Robson Walton. CEO and Pres.: H. Lee Scott. Inc.: DE. Address: Box 116, Bentonville, AR 72716. Tel.: 501-273-4000. Internet: wal-mart.com.

16D **Wal-Mart is progressing in both of its major growth endeavors.** Supercenters, which average 185,000 square feet, will probably account for 57% of its domestic selling space at the close of fiscal 2003 (ends January 31, 2004), and that percentage ought to be around 75% by the 2006–2008 period. The appeal of their prices and broad offerings of food, general merchandise, and services has enabled the company to gain market share from leading supermarket companies and from the downsized Kmart chain. Wal-Mart's competitive advantage in the U.S. during the past two years has been enhanced by an aggressive global-procurement program, which was launched in late 2001. Also, excluding unusual charges in the U.K. and Mexico, the International division's operating profits were up 30%, year to year, in the July quarter on a 19% sales increase. Asia was International's weakest region, but its "learning curve" experience in Europe and Latin America suggests much improved results in that area by 2005, at least.
The company is enhancing several key product categories. Its domestic apparel sales have been bolstered by last year's introduction of U.K.-based ASDA's (acquired in 1990) fashionable *George* brand and by the recent addition of *Levi's* jeans. Also, Wal-Mart is the world's largest retailer of cosmetics (7% of sales), and new private labels and product-development arrangements with a few leading beauty-products companies augur well for continued growth in this segment. Finally, the discounter is expanding its electronics offerings to include 47-inch high-definition television sets.
Earnings will likely advance by close to 15% in each of the coming 3 to 5 years. We expect selling-space expansion and overall same-store sales gains in the 3% to 6% range to fuel annual top-line growth of 10%–12% during this period. Also, the operating margin should be modestly above the current level in a few years, thanks to the leveraging benefits of a rising sales base and the probability of a better showing in Asia. A gradually declining share count is another plus.
This stock is timely, and its risk-adjusted appreciation potential to 2006–2008 is attractive.
David R. Cohen *November 14, 2003*

12D (A) Fiscal year ends Jan. 31st of following calendar year. Sales exclude rentals from licensed depts.
(B) Based on diluted shares. Excludes extraord. loss: '99, $0.07; '01, $0.01. Excl. gain from discontinued operation: '03-Q1-2, $0.05. Next earnings report due late February.
(C) Dividend payments historically in early January, April, July, and October.
■ Dividend reinvestment plan available.
(D) In millions, adjusted for stock splits.

Company's Financial Strength (17A)	A++
Stock's Price Stability	80
Price Growth Persistence	85
Earnings Predictability	95

18A

1. Rank for timeliness (price performance in next twelve months)—from 1 (highest) to 5 (lowest)
2. Rank for long-term safety—1 (highest) down to 5 (lowest)
3. Beta (the stock's sensitivity to market fluctuation—NYSE average = 1.00)
4. Projected price range and associated annual returns—3 years ahead
5. Insider decisions
6. Institutional decisions
7. Company's capital structure
8. Pension liability
9. Working capital
10. Growth rates
11. Quaterly sales, earnings, dividends—actual past, estimated future
12. Footnotes—including estimated constant dollar earnings, dividend payment dates
13. Monthly price ranges— past 15 years and value line (cash flow line)
14. Statistical milestones—on a per share basis and a company basis—historical past and estimated future
15. Brief summary of company's business
16. Critique—of recent developments and prospects
17. Company's financial strength
18. Important indices of quality

4. *Price information* includes current price quotations on certain investment vehicles, particularly securities. These quotations are commonly accompanied by statistics on the recent price behavior of the vehicle.
5. *Information on personal investment strategies* includes recommendations on investment strategies or specific purchase or sale actions. In general, this information tends to be educational or analytical rather than descriptive.

Sources of Information

A complete listing of the sources of each type of investment information is beyond the scope of this book. Our discussion focuses on the most common online and traditional sources of information on economic and current events, industries and companies, and prices, as well as other online sources.

Economic and Current Event Information Investors who are aware of current economic, political, and business events tend to make better investment decisions. Popular sources of economic and current event information include financial journals, general newspapers, institutional news, business periodicals, government publications, and special subscription services. These are available in print and online versions; often the online versions are free but may have limited content. Most offer free searchable article archives and charge a nominal fee for each article downloaded.

Wall Street Journal
a daily business newspaper, published regionally; the most popular source of financial news.

Financial Journals The ***Wall Street Journal*** is the most popular source of financial news. Published daily Monday through Friday in regional, European, and Asian editions, the *Journal* also has an online version called the *WSJ Online* (www.wsj.com), which is updated frequently throughout the day and on the weekends. In addition to giving daily price quotations on thousands of investment vehicles, it reports world, national, regional, and corporate news. The first page of the third section of the *Journal* usually contains a column called "Heard on the Street" that focuses on specific market and company events. In addition, a fourth section containing articles that address personal finance issues and topics is included in the Tuesday, Wednesday, and Thursday editions, and an Expanded version of that section, called "Weekend Journal," is included in Friday's edition. A print subscription to the *Wall Street Journal* costs \$189 annually, compared to \$79 per year for the online version; print subscribers pay \$39 to add the online edition. *WSJ Online* includes features such as quotes and news that provides stock and mutual fund charting, company profiles, financials, and analyst ratings; article searches; special online-only articles; and access to the Dow Jones article archives.

HOT

Federal Reserve Economic Data (FRED) has a historical database of economic and financial statistics.

www.research.stlouisfed.org/fred2/

Barron's
a weekly business newspaper; a popular source of financial news.

A second popular source of financial news is ***Barron's***, which is published weekly. *Barron's* generally offers lengthier articles on a variety of topics of interest to individual investors. Probably the most popular column in *Barron's* is "Up & Down Wall Street," which provides a critical and often humorous assessment of major developments affecting the stock market and business. *Barron's* also includes current price quotations and a summary of statistics on a range of investment vehicles. Subscribers to *WSJ Online* also have access to *Barron's* online edition (www.barrons.com) because both are published by Dow Jones & Company.

Investor's Business Daily is a third national business newspaper published Monday through Friday. It is similar to the *Wall Street Journal* but contains more detailed price and market data. Its Web site (www.investors.com) has limited free content. Another source of financial news is the *Financial Times* (www.ft.com), with U.S., U.K., European, and Asian editions.

General Newspapers Major metropolitan newspapers such as the *New York Times, Washington Post, Los Angeles Times,* and *Chicago Tribune* provide investors with a wealth of financial information in their print and online editions. Most major newspapers contain stock price quotations for major exchanges, price quotations on stocks of local interest, and a summary of the major stock market averages and indexes. Local newspapers are another convenient source of financial news. In most large cities, the daily newspaper devotes at least a few pages to financial and business news. Another popular source of financial news is *USA Today,* the national newspaper published daily Monday through Friday. It is available in print and online versions (usatoday.com). Each issue contains a "Money" section (Section B) devoted to business and personal financial news and to current security price quotations and summary statistics.

Institutional News The monthly economic letters of the nation's leading banks, such as Bank of America (based in Charlotte, North Carolina), Northern Trust (Chicago), and Wells Fargo (San Francisco), provide useful economic information. Wire services such as Dow Jones, Bloomberg Financial Services, AP (Associated Press), and UPI (United Press International) provide economic and business news feeds to brokerages, other financial institutions, and Web sites that subscribe to them. Bloomberg has its own comprehensive site (www.bloomberg.com). Business.com (www.business.com) offers industry-by-industry news, targeted business searches, and employment resources by industry. Web sites specializing in financial news include CNNMoney (money.cnn.com) and CBS MarketWatch (cbs.marketwatch.com).

Business Periodicals Business periodicals vary in scope. Some present general business and economic articles, others cover securities markets and related topics, and still others focus solely on specific industries. Regardless of the subject matter, most business periodicals present descriptive information, and some also include analytical information. They rarely offer recommendations.

The business sections of general-interest periodicals such as *Newsweek, Time,* and *U.S. News & World Report* cover business and economic news. Strictly business- and finance-oriented periodicals, including *Business Week, Fortune,* and *The Economist,* provide more in-depth articles. These magazines also have investing and personal finance articles.

Some financial periodicals specialize in securities and marketplace articles. The most basic, commonsense articles appear in *Forbes, Kiplinger's Personal Finance, Money, SmartMoney,* and *Worth*. *Forbes,* published every two weeks, is the most investment-oriented. *Kiplinger's Personal Finance, Money, SmartMoney,* and *Worth* are published monthly and contain articles on managing personal finances and on investments.

All these business and personal finance magazines have Web sites with free access to recent, if not all, content. Most include a number of other features. For example, *SmartMoney* has interactive investment tools, including a color-coded "Market Map 1000" that gives an aerial view of 1,000 U.S. and international stocks so that you can see which sectors and stocks are hot.

Government Publications A number of government agencies publish economic data and reports useful to investors. The annual *Economic Report of the President* (w3.access.gpo.gov/eop/) provides a broad view of the current and expected state of the economy. This document reviews and summarizes economic policy and conditions and includes data on important aspects of the economy. The *Federal Reserve Bulletin,* published monthly by the Board of Governors of the Federal Reserve System, and periodic reports published by each of the 12 Federal Reserve District Banks provide articles and data on various aspects of economic and business activity. (Visit www.federalreserve.gov to read many of these publications.) A useful Department of Commerce publication is the *Survey of Current Business* (www.bea.doc.gov/bea/pubs.htm). Published monthly, it includes indicators and data related to economic and business conditions. A good source of financial statement information on all manufacturers, broken down by industry and asset size, is the *Quarterly Financial Report for U.S. Manufacturing, Mining, and Trade Corporations* (www.census.gov/csd/qfr/view/qfr_mg.html), published by the Department of Commerce.

Special Subscription Services Investors who want additional insights into business and economic conditions can subscribe to special services. These reports include business and economic forecasts and give notice of new government policies, union plans and tactics, taxes, prices, wages, and so on. One popular service is the *Kiplinger Washington Letter,* a weekly publication that provides a wealth of economic information and analyses.

Industry and Company Information Of special interest to investors is information on particular industries and companies. Often, after choosing an industry in which to invest, an investor will want to analyze specific companies. A recent change in disclosure rules, discussed below, gives individual investors access to more company information than before. General business periodicals such as *Business Week, Forbes,* the *Wall Street Journal,* and *Fortune* carry articles on the activities of specific industries and individual companies. Trade publications such as *Chemical Week, American Banker, Computerworld, Industry Week, Oil and Gas Journal,* and *Public Utilities Fortnightly* provide more focused industry and company information. *Red Herring, PC Magazine, Business 2.0,* and *Fast Company* are magazines that can help you keep up with the high-tech world; all have good Web sites.

The Internet makes it easy to research specific industries and companies at the company's Web site, a publication's archive search, or database services such as the Dow Jones Publications Library. Company Web sites typically offer a wealth of information about the company, investor information—annual reports, filings, and financial releases, press releases, and more. Table 3.1 presents several free and subscription resources that emphasize industry and company information.

fair disclosure rule (Regulation FD)
rule requiring senior executives to disclose critical information simultaneously to investment professionals and the public via press releases or SEC filings.

Fair Disclosure Rules In August 2000, the SEC passed the **fair disclosure rule,** known as **Regulation FD,** a rule requiring senior executives to disclose

TABLE 3.1 Online Sources for Industry and Company Information

Web Site	Description	Cost
Hoover's Online (www.hoovers.com)	Reports and news on public and private companies with in-depth coverage of 21,000 of the world's top firms	$400 per year for individual accounts.
CNET (news.com.com)	One of the best sites for high-tech news, analysis, breaking news, great search capabilities, links.	Free.
Yahoo! Finance (finance.yahoo.com)	Provides information on companies from around the Web: stock quotes, news, investment ideas, research, financials, analyst ratings, insider trades, and more.	Free.
News Alert (www.newsalert.com)	Latest company news from various wire services. Searchable by industry or company. Good for earnings announcements and tech news.	Free.

critical information such as earnings forecasts and news of mergers and new products simultaneously to investment professionals and the public via press releases or SEC filings. Companies may limit contact with analysts if they are unsure whether the information requires a press release. However, Regulation FD does not apply to communications with journalists and securities ratings firms like Moody's Investor Service and Standard & Poor's. Violations of the rule carry injunctions and fines but are not considered fraud.

stockholders' (annual) report a report published yearly by a publicly held corporation; contains a wide range of information, including financial statements for the most recent period of operation.

Stockholders' Reports An excellent source of data on an individual firm is the **stockholders' report,** or **annual report,** published yearly by publicly held corporations. These reports contain a wide range of information, including financial statements for the most recent period of operation, along with summarized statements for several prior years. These reports are free and may be obtained from the companies themselves, from brokers, or downloaded from the company's Web site. A sample page from Wal-Mart Stores, Inc. 2003 stockholders' report is shown in Figure 3.6 (on page 90). Most companies now place their annual reports on their Web sites. Report Gallery (www.reportgallery.com) provides links to more than 2,000 company reports.

Form 10-K a statement that must be filed annually with the SEC by all firms having securities listed on an organized exchange or traded in the Nasdaq market.

In addition to the stockholders' report, many serious investors review a company's **Form 10-K.** This is a statement that firms with securities listed on an organized exchange or traded in the Nasdaq market must file annually with the SEC. Finding 10-K and other SEC filings is now a simple task, thanks to SEC/Edgar (Electronic Data Gathering and Analysis Retrieval), which has reports filed by all companies traded on a major exchange. You can read them free either at the SEC's Web site (www.sec.gov/edgar.shtml) or at EDGAR Online's FreeEdgar site (www.freeedgar.com).

Comparative Data Sources Sources of comparative data, typically broken down by industry and firm size, are a good tool for analyzing the financial condition of companies. Among these sources are Dun & Bradstreet's *Key Business Ratios,* Robert Morris and Associates' *Annual Statement Studies,* the *Quarterly Financial Report for U.S. Manufacturing, Mining, and Trade Corporations* (cited above), and the *Almanac of Business and Industrial*

FIGURE 3.6 **Pages from a Stockholders' Report**

The "Financial Highlights" on the right-hand page from the 2003 Annual Report of Wal-Mart Stores, Inc., quickly acquaints the investor with some key information on the firm's operations over the past year. The contents of the Annual Report are also shown. The actual Annual Report is available at Wal-Mart's Web site www.walmart.com. (*Source:* Wal-Mart Stores, Inc. 2003 Annual Report; Wal-Mart Stores, Inc., Investor Relations, 479-273-8446, Wal-Mart Stores, Inc., Bentonville, AR 72716-8611.)

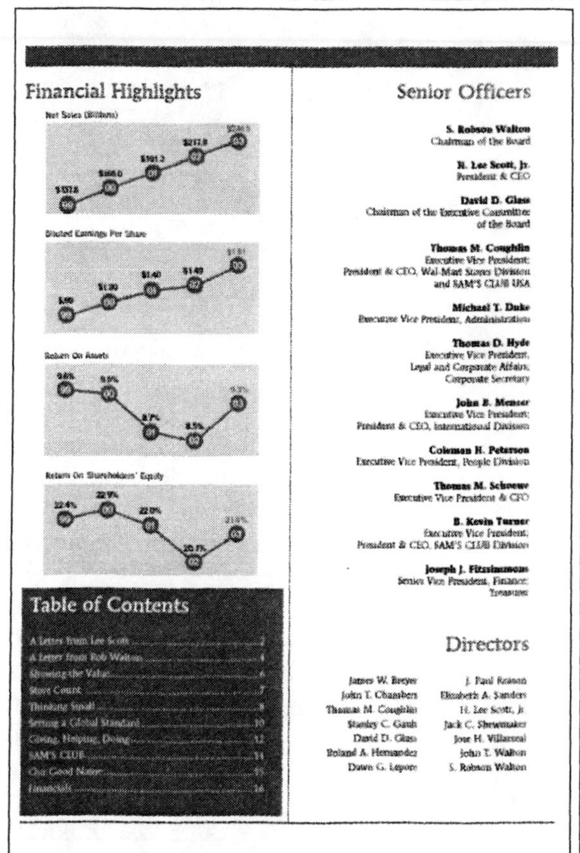

Financial Highlights

Net Sales (Billions)

Diluted Earnings Per Share

Return On Assets

Return On Shareholders' Equity

Table of Contents

Senior Officers

S. Robson Walton
Chairman of the Board

H. Lee Scott, Jr.
President & CEO

David D. Glass
Chairman of the Executive Committee of the Board

Thomas M. Coughlin
Executive Vice President; President & CEO, Wal-Mart Stores Division and SAM'S CLUB USA

Michael T. Duke
Executive Vice President, Administration

Thomas D. Hyde
Executive Vice President, Legal and Corporate Affairs, Corporate Secretary

John B. Menzer
Executive Vice President; President & CEO, International Division

Coleman H. Peterson
Executive Vice President, People Division

Thomas M. Schoewe
Executive Vice President & CFO

B. Kevin Turner
Executive Vice President; President & CEO, SAM'S CLUB Division

Joseph J. Fitzsimmons
Senior Vice President, Finance; Treasurer

Directors

James W. Breyer	J. Paul Reason
John T. Chambers	Elizabeth A. Sanders
Thomas M. Coughlin	H. Lee Scott, Jr.
Stanley C. Gault	Jack C. Shewmaker
David D. Glass	Jose H. Villarreal
Roland A. Hernandez	John T. Walton
Dawn G. Lepore	S. Robson Walton

Financial Ratios. These sources, which are typically available in public and university libraries, are a useful benchmark for evaluating a company's financial condition.

Subscription Services A variety of subscription services provide data on specific industries and companies. Today, many of these services are available on the Internet. Generally, a subscriber pays a basic fee to access the service's information and can purchase premium services for greater depth or range. The major subscription services provide both descriptive and analytical information, but they generally do not make recommendations. Most investors, rather than subscribing to these services, access them through their stockbrokers or a large public or university library. The Web sites for most services offer some free information and charge for the rest.

TABLE 3.2 Popular Offerings of the Major Subscription Services

Subscription Service/Offerings	Coverage	Frequency of Publication
Standard & Poor's Corporation (www.standardandpoors.com)		
Corporation Records	Detailed descriptions of publicly traded securities of over 12,000 public corporations.	Annually with updates throughout the year.
Stock Reports (sample shown in Figure 7.1, page 315)	Summary of financial history, current finances, and future prospects of about 5,000 companies.	Annually with updates throughout the year.
Stock Guide	Statistical data and analytical rankings of investment desirability for major stocks.	Monthly.
Bond Guide	Statistical data and analytical rankings of investment desirability of over 10,000 bonds.	Monthly.
The Outlook	Analytical articles with investment advice on the market, industries, and securities.	Weekly magazine.
Mergent (www.mergent.com)		
Mergent's Manuals	Eight reference manuals—*Bank and Finance, Industrial, International, Municipal and Government, OTC Industrial, OTC Unlisted, Public Utility,* and *Transportation*—with historical and current financial, organizational, and operational data on major firms.	Annually with monthly print updates (weekly online updates).
Handbook of Common Stocks	Common stock data.	Quarterly.
Dividend Record	Recent dividend announcements and payments.	Twice weekly, with annual summary.
Bond Record	Price and interest rate behavior of over 68,000 issues.	Monthly.
Value Line Investment Survey (www.valueline.com)		
Includes three reports:	A 40-page update listing about 1,700 of the most widely held stocks.	Weekly.
1. *Summary and Index*	Current ratings for each of the about 1,700 stocks.	
2. *Selection and Opinion*	A 12- to 16-page report featuring sample portfolios for different types of investors.	
3. *Ratings and Reports* (sample shown in Figure 3.5)	Full-page report including financial data, descriptions, analysis, and ratings for each of about 130 stocks.	

Standard & Poor's Corporation (S&P)
publisher of a large number of financial reports and services, including *Corporation Records* and *Stock Reports.*

Mergent
publisher of a variety of financial material, including *Mergent's Manuals.*

Value Line Investment Survey
one of the most popular subscription services used by individual investors; subscribers receive three basic reports weekly.

The dominant subscription services are those offered by Standard & Poor's, Mergent, and Value Line. Table 3.2 summarizes the most popular services of these companies. **Standard & Poor's Corporation** (S&P) (www.standardandpoors.com) offers a large number of different financial reports and services. Its Investing Web site, owned by *Business Week* (www.businessweek.com/investor), is geared toward individual investors. Although basic news and market commentary is free, *Business Week* subscribers obtain access to premium online services. **Mergent** (formerly Moody's Financial Information Services Division) (www.mergent.com) also publishes a variety of material, including its equity and bond portraits, corporate research, well-known reference manuals on eight industries, and numerous other products. The ***Value Line Investment Survey*** (www.valueline.com) is one of the most popular subscription services used by individual investors; it is available at most libraries and provides online access to additional services including data, graphing, portfolio tracking, and technical indicators.

Brokerage Reports Brokerage firms often make available to their clients reports from the various subscription services and research reports from their own securities analysts. They also provide clients with prospectuses for new security issues and *back-office research reports.* As noted in Chapter 2, a *prospectus* is a document that describes in detail the key aspects of the issue, the issuer, and its management and financial position. The cover of the preliminary prospectus describing the 2003 stock issue of Hewitt Associates, Inc., was shown in Figure 2.1 (on page 38). **Back-office research reports** include the brokerage firm's analyses of and recommendations on prospects for the securities markets, specific industries, or specific securities. Usually a brokerage firm publishes lists of securities classified by its research staff as either "buy," "hold," or "sell." Brokerage research reports are available on request at no cost to existing and potential clients.

back-office research reports
a brokerage firm's analyses of and recommendations on investment prospects; available on request at no cost to existing and potential clients or for purchase at some Web sites.

Securities analysts' reports are now available on the Web, either from brokerage sites or from sites that consolidate research from many brokerages. At Multex Investor (www.multexinvestor.com), a leading research site, over 1.5 million reports on companies and industries from over 700 brokerage and research firms cost from zero to $150 each. Investors can use Zacks's (www.zacks.com) Brokerage Research Report Service to find and purchase reports from 3,200 analysts on 7,500 companies for $10 to $150 per report or to read free brokerage report abstracts with earnings revisions and recommendations.

Investment Letters **Investment letters** are newsletters that provide, on a subscription basis, the analyses, conclusions, and recommendations of experts in securities investment. Some letters concentrate on specific types of securities; others are concerned solely with assessing the economy or securities markets. Among the more popular investment letters are *Blue Chip Advisor, Dick Davis Digest, The Dines Letter, Dow Theory Letters,* the *Growth Stock Outlook, Louis Rukeyser's Wall Street,* the *Prudent Speculator,* and *Zacks Advisor.* Most investment letters come out weekly or monthly and cost from $75 to $400 a year. Advertisements for many of these investment letters can be found in *Barron's* and in various business periodicals.

investment letters
newsletters that provide, on a subscription basis, the analyses, conclusions, and recommendations of experts in securities investment.

The *Hulbert Financial Digest* (cbs.marketwatch.com/hulbert) monitors the performance of investment letters. It is an excellent source of objective information on investment letters and a good place to check out those that interest you. Many investment letters now offer online subscriptions. Use a general search engine or Newsletter Access (www.newsletteraccess.com), a searchable database of newsletters that lists over 900 stock-investing newsletters!

Price Information Price information about various types of securities is contained in their **quotations,** which include current price data and statistics on recent price behavior. The Web makes it easy to find price quotes for actively traded securities, and many financially oriented sites include a stock price look-up feature or a stock ticker running across the screen, much like the ones that used to be found only in brokerage offices. The ticker consolidates and reports stock transactions made on the NYSE, AMEX, regional exchanges, and Nasdaq National Market as they occur. Cable TV subscribers in many areas can watch the ticker at the bottom of the screen on certain channels, including CNNfn, CNN Headline News, and MSNBC. The ticker symbols for some well-known companies are listed in Table 3.3.

quotations
price information about various types of securities, including current price data and statistics on recent price behavior.

TABLE 3.3 Symbols for Some Well-Known Companies

Company	Symbol	Company	Symbol
Amazon.com	AMZN	Microsoft	MSFT
Apple Computer	AAPL	Merrill Lynch	MER
AT&T	T	Nike	NKE
Cisco	CSCO	Oracle	ORCL
Dell	DELL	PepsiCo, Inc.	PEP
Eastman Kodak	EK	Reebok	RBK
ExxonMobil	XOM	Sears, Roebuck	S
Genentech	DNA	Starbucks	SBUX
General Electric	GE	Sun Microsystems	SUNW
Hewlett-Packard	HPQ	Texas Instruments	TXN
Intel	INTC	Time Warner	TWX
Int'l. Business Machines	IBM	United Parcel Service	UPS
Lucent Technologies	LU	Wal-Mart Stores	WMT
McDonald's Corporation	MCD	Yahoo!	YHOO

Investors can easily find the prior day's security price quotations in the published news media, both nonfinancial and financial. They also can find delayed or real-time quotations for free at numerous Web sites, including *financial portals* (described below), most business periodical Web sites, and brokerage sites. The Web sites for CNNfn and CNBC TV have real-time stock quotes, as do sites that subscribe to their news feed.

The major published source of security price quotations is the *Wall Street Journal*, which presents quotations for each previous business day's activities in all major markets. (We'll explain how to read and interpret actual price quotations in later chapters.)

Other Online Investment Information Sources Many other excellent Web sites provide information of all sorts to increase your investment skills and knowledge. Let's now look at financial portals, sites for bonds and mutual funds, international sites, and investment discussion forums. Table 3.4 (on page 94) lists some of the most popular financial portals, bond sites, and mutual fund sites. We'll look at online brokerage and investment adviser sites later in the chapter, and you'll find more specialized Web links in all chapters.

financial portals
supersites on the Web that bring together a wide range of investing features, such as real-time quotes, stock and mutual fund screens, portfolio trackers, news, research, and transaction capabilities, along with other personal finance features.

Financial Portals **Financial portals** are supersites that bring together a wide range of investing features, such as real-time quotes, stock and mutual fund screens, portfolio trackers, news, research, and transaction capabilities, along with other personal finance features. These sites want to be your investing home page. Some portals are general sites such as Yahoo! and Excite that offer a full range of investing features along with their other services, or they may be investing-oriented sites. You should check out several to see which best suits your needs, because their strengths and features vary greatly. Some portals, to motivate you to stay at their site, offer customization options so that your start page includes the data you want. Although finding one site where you can manage your investments is indeed appealing, you may not be able to find the

HOT LINKS

Superstar Investor provides descriptive summaries and more than 20,000 links to the best investing sites on the Internet. The Investsearch Directory guide for Online investing provides basic contact information for over 60,000 services and products of interest to investors and traders.

www.superstarinvestor.com
www.wallstreetdex.com

TABLE 3.4 Popular Investment Web Sites

The following Web sites are just a few of the thousands of sites that provide investing information. Unless otherwise mentioned, all are free.

Web Site	Description
Financial Portals	
America Online (proprietary portal)	Subscriber-only Personal Finance channel includes areas for business news, market and stock quotes, stocks, mutual funds, investment research, retirement, saving and planning, credit and debt, banking and loans, and more. Each area offers education, tools, and message boards. Ease of use is a big plus.
Excite (www.excite.com)	Offers an investing channel that provides news, market data, and research capabilities along with a variety of links for tracking stocks, portfolios, screening stocks, participating in conference calls, and obtaining SEC filings.
MSN MoneyCentral Investor (www.moneycentral.msn.com)	More editorial content than many sites; good research and interactive tools like Research Wizard; can consolidate accounts in portfolio tracker. (Many tools don't run on Macintosh.)
Motley Fool (www.fool.com)	Comprehensive and entertaining site with educational features, research, news, and message boards. Model portfolios cover a variety of investment strategies. Free but offers premium services such as Portfolio Trade Alerts for $25 a year.
Yahoo! Finance (http://finance.yahoo.com)	Simple design, content-rich; easy to find information quickly. Includes financial news, price quotes, portfolio trackers, bill paying, personalized home page, and a directory of other major sites.
Yodlee (www.yodlee.com)	Aggregation site that collects financial account data from banking, credit card, brokerage, mutual fund, mileage, and other sites. One-click access saves time and enables users to manage and interact with their accounts; offers e-mail accounts; easy to set up and track finances. Security issues concern potential users; few analytical tools.
Bond Sites	
Investing in Bonds (www.investinginbonds.com)	The Bond Market Association's Web site; good for novice investors. Investing guides, research reports, historical data, and links to other sites. Searchable database.
BondsOnline (www.bondsonline.com)	Comprehensive site for news, education, free research, ratings, and other bond information; strong emphasis on municipal bonds. Searchable database; Some charges for research.
CNNMoney Bonds & Rates (www.money.com/markets/bondcenter)	Individual investors can search for bond-related news, market data, and bond offerings.
Bureau of the Public Debt Online (www.publicdebt.treas.gov)	Run by U.S. Treasury Department; information about U.S. savings bonds and Treasury securities; can also buy Treasury securities online through Treasury Direct program.
Mutual Fund Sites	
Morningstar (www.morningstar.com)	Profiles of over 3,000 funds with ratings; screening tools, portfolio analysis and management; fund manager interviews, e-mail newsletters; educational sections. Advanced screening and analysis tools are $11.95 a month or $109 per year.
Mutual Fund Investor's Center (www.mfea.com)	Not-for-profit, easy-to-navigate site from the Mutual Fund Education Alliance with investor education, search feature, and links to profiles of funds, calculators for retirement, asset allocation, and college planning.
Fund Alarm (www.fundalarm.com)	Takes a different approach and identifies underperforming funds to help investors decide when to sell; alerts investors to fund manager changes. Lively commentary from the site founder, a CPA.
MAXfunds (www.maxfunds.com)	Offers several custom metrics and data points to help find the best funds and give investors tools other than past performance to choose funds. Covers more funds than any other on- or offline publication. MAXadvisor, a premium advisory service, costs $59.95 per year.
IndexFunds.com (www.indexfunds.com)	Comprehensive site covering only index funds.
Personal Fund (www.personalfund.com)	Especially popular for its fund cost calculator that shows the true cost of ownership, after fees, brokerage commissions, and taxes. Suggests lower-cost alternatives with similar investment objectives.

best of what you need at one portal. You'll want to explore several sites to find the ones that meet your needs. Table 3.4 includes a summary of the features of several popular financial portals.

Bond Sites Although many general investment sites include bond and mutual fund information, you can also visit sites that specialize in these investments. Because Internet bond-trading activity is fairly limited at the present time, there are fewer online resources for individuals. Some brokerage firms are starting to allow clients access to bond information that formerly was restricted to investment professionals. In addition to the sites listed in Table 3.4, other good sites for bond and interest rate information include Briefing.com (www.briefing.com) and WSJ.com (wsj.com).

The sites of the major bond ratings agencies—Moody's Investor Services (www.moodys.com), Standard & Poor's (www.standardandpoors.com), and Fitch (www.fitchibca.com)—provide ratings lists, recent ratings changes, and information about how they determine ratings.

Mutual Fund Sites With thousands of mutual funds, how do you find the ones that match your investment goals? The Internet makes this task much easier, offering many sites with screening tools and worksheets. Almost every major mutual fund family has its own Web site as well. Some allow visitors to hear interviews or participate in chats with fund managers. Fidelity (www.fidelity.com) is one of the most comprehensive sites, with educational articles, fund selection tools, fund profiles, and more. Portals and brokerage sites also offer these tools. Table 3.4 includes some independent mutual fund sites that are worth checking out.

HOT

FundAlarm is a great source of information on poorly performing funds. The site maintains a list of "3-alarm" funds that have underperformed their benchmarks for the past 12 months, 3 years, and 5 years.

www.fundalarm.com

International Sites The international reach of the Internet makes it a natural resource to help investors sort out the complexity of global investing, from country research to foreign currency exchange. Site-by-Site! International Investment Portal & Research Center (www.site-by-site.com/) is a comprehensive portal just for international investing. Free daily market data, news, economic insights, research, and analysis and commentary covering numerous countries and investment vehicles are among this site's features. For more localized coverage, check out Euroland European Investor (www.europeaninvestor.com), UK-Invest (www. uk-invest.com), LatinFocus (www.latin-focus.com), and similar sites for other countries and regions. J.P. Morgan's ADR site (www.adr.com) is a good place to research American depositary receipts and learn about their financial positions. For global business news, the *Financial Times* site (www.ft.com) gets high marks. CBS Marketwatch (cbs.marketwatch.com/news) has good technology and telecommunications news, as well as coverage of global markets.

Investment Discussion Forums Investors can exchange opinions about their favorite stocks and investing strategies at the *online discussion forums* (message boards and chat rooms) found at most major financial Web sites. However, remember that the key word here is opinion. You don't really know much about the qualifications of the person posting the information. *Always do your own research before acting on any hot tips!* The Motley Fool's (www.fool.com) boards are among the most popular, and Fool employees monitor the discussions. Message boards at Yahoo! Finance (http://messages.yahoo.com) are among the largest online, although many feel that the quality is not so good as at other sites. The Raging Bull (www.ragingbull.lycos.com) includes news along with its discussion groups. Technology investors flock to Silicon Investor (www.siliconinvestor.com), a portal site whose high-tech boards are considered among the best.

Avoiding Online Scams Just as the Internet increases the amount of information available to all investors, it also makes it easier for scam artists and others to spread false news and manipulate information. Anyone can sound like an investment expert online, posting stock tips with no underlying substance. As mentioned earlier, you may not know the identity of the person touting or panning a stock on the message boards. The person panning a stock could be a disgruntled former employee or a short seller. For example, the ousted former chief executive of San Diego's Avanir Pharmaceuticals posted negative remarks on stock message boards, adversely affecting share price. The company sued and won a court order prohibiting him from ever posting derogatory statements about the company on any Internet message boards.

In the fast-paced online environment, two types of scams turn up frequently: "pump-and-dump" schemes and get-rich-quick scams. In pump-and-dump schemes, promoters hype stocks, quickly send the prices sky-high, and then dump them at inflated prices. In get-rich-quick scams, promoters sell worthless investments to naïve buyers. One well-publicized pump-and-dump scheme demonstrates how easy it is to use the Internet to promote stocks. In September 2000, the SEC caught a 15-year-old boy who had made over $270,000 by promoting small-company stocks. The self-taught young investor would buy a block of a company's shares and then send out a barrage of false and/or misleading e-mail messages and message board postings singing the praises of that stock and the company's prospects. Once this misinformation pushed up the stock price, he sold and moved on to a new target company. His postings were so articulate that others at Silicon Investor's message boards thought he was a 40-year-old.

To crack down on cyber-fraud, in 1998 the SEC formed the Office of Internet Enforcement. Its staff members quickly investigate reports of suspected hoaxes and prosecute the offenders. Former SEC Chairman Arthur Levitt cautions investors to remember that the Internet is basically another way to send and receive information, one that has no controls for accuracy or truthfulness. The SEC Web site (www.sec.gov/investor/online/scams.htm) includes tips to avoid investment scams. Three key questions that investors should ask are:

- *Is the investment registered?* Check the SEC's EDGAR database (www.sec.gov/edgar.shtml) and with your state securities regulator (www.nasaa.org).
- *Who is making the sales pitch?* Make sure the seller is licensed in your state. Check with the NASD for any record of complaints or fraud.
- *Is it too good to be true?* Then it probably is. Just being on the Web doesn't mean it's legitimate.

Another place to check on online frauds is the "Online Fraud" link on the 123 Jump portal site (www.123jump.com) that provides links to recent news on online investment fraud.

CONCEPTS IN REVIEW

3.4 Differentiate between *descriptive information* and *analytical information.* How might one logically assess whether the acquisition of investment information or advice is economically justified?

3.5 What popular financial business periodicals would you use to follow the financial news? General news? Business news? Would you prefer to get your news from print sources or online, and why?

3.6 Briefly describe the types of information that the following resources provide.
a. Stockholders' report. b. Comparative data sources.
c. Standard & Poor's Corporation. d. Mergent.
e. *Value Line Investment Survey.*

3.7 How would you access each of the following types of information, and how would the content help you make investment decisions?
a. Prospectuses. b. Back-office research reports.
c. Investment letters. d. Price quotations.

3.8 Briefly describe several types of information that are especially well suited to being made available on the Internet. What are the differences between the online and print versions, and when would you use each?

Understanding Market Averages and Indexes

LG 3

The investment information we have discussed in this chapter helps investors understand when the economy is moving up or down and how individual investments have performed. Investors can use this and other information to formulate expectations about future investment performance. It is also important to know whether market behavior is favorable or unfavorable. The ability to interpret various market measures should help you to select and time investment actions.

A widely used way to assess the behavior of securities markets is to study the performance of market averages and indexes. These measures allow you conveniently to (1) gauge general market conditions, (2) compare your portfolio's performance to that of a large, diversified (market) portfolio, and (3) study market cycles, trends, and behaviors in order to forecast future market behavior. Here we discuss key measures of stock and bond market activity. In later chapters, we will discuss averages and indexes associated with other investment vehicles. Like price quotations, these measures of market performance are available at many Web sites.

averages
numbers used to measure the general behavior of stock prices by reflecting the arithmetic average price behavior of a representative group of stocks at a given point in time.

Stock Market Averages and Indexes

indexes
numbers used to measure the general behavior of stock prices by measuring the current price behavior of a representative group of stocks in relation to a base value set at an earlier point in time.

Stock market averages and indexes measure the general behavior of stock prices over time. Although the terms *average* and *index* tend to be used interchangeably when people discuss market behavior, technically they are different types of measures. **Averages** reflect the arithmetic average price behavior of a representative group of stocks at a given point in time. **Indexes** measure the current price behavior of a representative group of stocks in relation to a base value set at an earlier point in time.

FIGURE 3.7

Major Stock Market Averages and Indexes (August 25, 2003)

The "Major Stock Indexes" summarizes the key stock market averages and indexes. It includes statistics showing the change from the previous day, the 52-week change, and the year-to-date change. (*Source: Wall Street Journal,* August 26, 2003, p. C2. Reprinted by permission of the *Wall Street Journal.* ©Dow Jones & Company, Inc. All rights reserved.)

Major Stock Indexes

	DAILY					52-WEEK			YTD
Dow Jones Averages	HIGH	LOW	CLOSE	NET CHG	% CHG	HIGH	LOW	% CHG	% CHG
30 Industrials	9350.77	9280.94	9317.64	−31.23	−0.33	9428.90	7286.27	+ 4.47	+11.70
20 Transportations	2649.07	2624.08	2633.01	− 8.55	−0.32	2681.65	1942.19	+ 8.60	+13.99
15 Utilities	238.09	236.11	238.09	+ 1.79	+0.76	255.00	167.57	− 6.52	+10.65
65 Composite	2667.88	2651.33	2662.98	− 3.85	−0.14	2695.42	2033.44	+ 3.29	+12.13
Dow Jones Indexes									
US Total Market	233.91	232.51	233.79	− 0.09	−0.04	236.66	179.60	+ 6.12	+14.32
US Large-Cap	216.69	215.38	216.69	+ 0.20	+0.09	221.98	172.31	+ 2.96	+11.78
US Mid-Cap	273.84	271.74	272.91	− 0.91	−0.33	276.74	192.15	+14.19	+20.47
US Small-Cap	310.40	307.55	308.80	− 1.59	−0.51	314.87	209.81	+18.71	+25.03
US Growth	921.51	914.91	920.36	− 0.45	−0.05	926.66	687.99	+ 8.13	+18.69
US Value	1192.12	1185.39	1191.76	+ 0.48	+0.04	1235.14	938.11	+ 4.21	+10.30
Global Titans 50	162.65	162.00	162.46	− 0.20	−0.12	170.66	134.76	+ 1.19	+ 7.46
Asian Titans 50	94.69	93.62	93.87	− 0.81	−0.86	95.35	71.25	− 1.55	+13.77
DJ STOXX 50	2531.78	2507.89	2510.49	−20.66	−0.82	2852.49	1909.05	−10.12	+ 4.28
Nasdaq Stock Market									
Composite	1768.12	1752.12	1794.31	− 1.01	−0.06	1777.55	1114.11	+26.77	+32.11
Nasdaq 100	1307.85	1295.82	1306.64	+ 2.10	+0.16	1314.65	804.64	+28.51	+32.74
Biotech	715.81	708.89	712.61	− 2.32	−0.32	752.51	438.38	+35.54	+43.43
Computer	822.30	814.20	820.48	+ 0.74	+0.09	820.48	503.26	+24.59	+31.78
Telecommunications	150.18	148.08	150.11	+ 0.19	+0.13	160.42	81.43	+42.60	+37.98
Standard & Poor's Indexes									
500 Index	993.71	987.91	993.71	+ 0.65	+0.07	1011.66	776.76	+ 4.83	+12.94
MidCap 400	508.16	504.03	505.75	− 2.03	−0.40	514.00	372.88	+ 9.79	+17.67
SmallCap 600	238.77	237.00	238.19	− 0.58	−0.24	243.48	170.73	+14.60	+21.14
SuperComp 1500	220.59	219.36	220.58	+ 0.03	+0.01	223.12	171.10	+ 5.55	+13.60
New York Stock Exchange									
Composite	5594.93	5566.06	5585.64	− 9.29	−0.17	5722.85	4452.49	+ 3.66	+11.71
Industrials	654.95	651.84	654.68	− 0.20	−0.03	664.61	532.37	+ 3.38	+12.11
Finance	578.52	574.76	578.36	− 0.05	−0.01	599.39	437.72	+ 4.82	+13.30
Others									
Russell 2000	485.51	480.99	438.87	− 1.64	−0.34	494.82	327.04	+18.67	+26.31
Wilshire 5000	9613.36	9556.52	9588.68	−23.79	−0.25	9715.26	7342.84	+ 7.12	+14.93
Value Line	318.24	315.99	317.32	− 0.92	−0.29	322.47	219.50	+10.01	+20.21
Amex Composite	970.33	965.00	967.01	− 1.92	−0.20	977.57	771.88	+11.45	+17.30

Averages and indexes provide a convenient method of capturing the general mood of the market. They also can be compared at different points in time to assess the relative strength or weakness of the market. Current and recent values of the key averages and indexes are quoted daily in the financial news, in most local newspapers, and on many radio and television news programs. Figure 3.7, a version of which is published daily in the *Wall Street Journal,* provides a summary and statistics on the major stock market averages and indexes. Let's look at the key averages and indexes listed there.

Dow Jones Industrial Average (DJIA)
a stock market average made up of 30 high-quality stocks selected for total market value and broad public ownership and believed to reflect overall market activity.

The Dow Jones Averages Dow Jones & Company, publisher of the *Wall Street Journal,* prepares four stock averages. The most popular is the **Dow Jones Industrial Average (DJIA).** This average is made up of 30 stocks selected for total market value and broad public ownership. The group consists of high-quality stocks whose behaviors are believed to reflect overall market activity. The box at the bottom of Figure 3.8 lists the stocks currently included in the DJIA.

Occasionally, a merger, bankruptcy, or extreme lack of activity causes a change in the makeup of the average. Citicorp's merger with Travelers moved

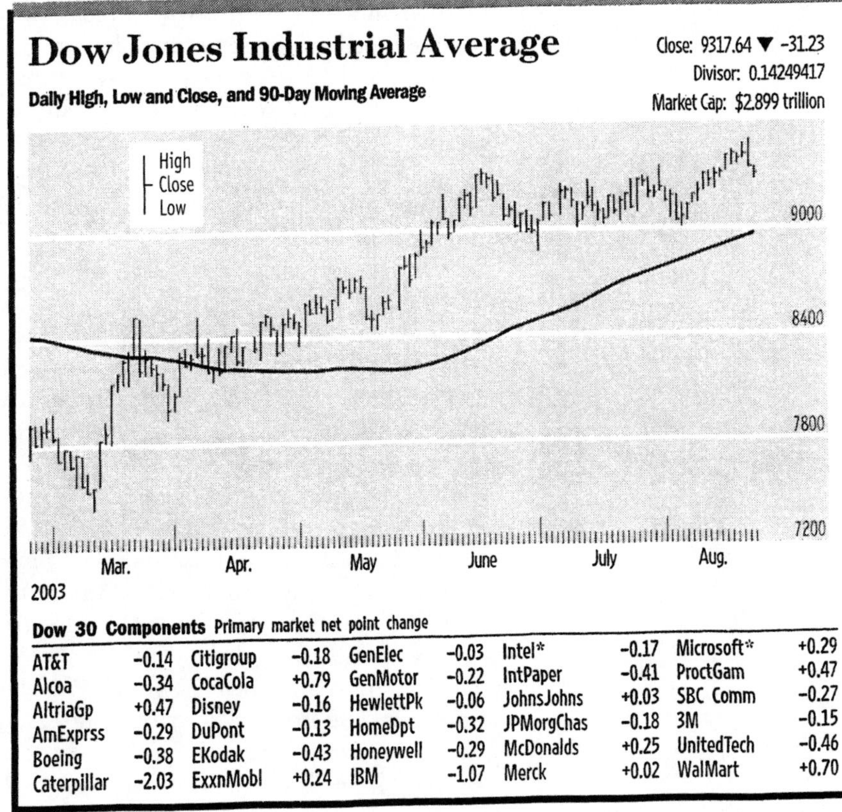

AT&T	−0.14	Citigroup	−0.18	GenElec	−0.03	Intel*	−0.17	Microsoft*	+0.29
Alcoa	−0.34	CocaCola	+0.79	GenMotor	−0.22	IntPaper	−0.41	ProctGam	+0.47
AltriaGp	+0.47	Disney	−0.16	HewlettPk	−0.06	JohnsJohns	+0.03	SBC Comm	−0.27
AmExprss	−0.29	DuPont	−0.13	HomeDpt	−0.32	JPMorgChas	−0.18	3M	−0.15
Boeing	−0.38	EKodak	−0.43	Honeywell	−0.29	McDonalds	+0.25	UnitedTech	−0.46
Caterpillar	−2.03	ExxnMobl	+0.24	IBM	−1.07	Merck	+0.02	WalMart	+0.70

FIGURE 3.8

The DJIA from February 26, 2003, to August 25, 2003

During this 6-month period, the stock market remained mildly bullish beginning in April and continuing through August. (*Source: Wall Street Journal*, August 26, 2003, p. C2. Reprinted by permission of the *Wall Street Journal*. © Dow Jones & Company, Inc. All rights reserved.)

it (Citigroup) to the DJIA. Changes to the 30 stocks also occur when Dow Jones believes that the average does not reflect the broader market. For example, in recent years technology companies such as Microsoft and Intel and financial services companies such as American Express replaced Allied Signal, Goodyear, and Union Carbide; Home Depot replaced Sears. When a new stock is added, the average is readjusted so that it continues to behave in a manner consistent with the immediate past.

The value of the DJIA is calculated each business day by substituting the *closing share prices* of each of the 30 stocks in the average into the following equation:

Equation 3.1

$$\text{DJIA} = \frac{\begin{array}{c}\text{Closing share price}\\ \text{of stock 1}\end{array} + \begin{array}{c}\text{Closing share price}\\ \text{of stock 2}\end{array} + \cdots + \begin{array}{c}\text{Closing share price}\\ \text{of stock 30}\end{array}}{\text{DJIA divisor}}$$

The value of the DJIA is merely the sum of the closing share prices of the 30 stocks included in it, divided by a "divisor." The purpose of the divisor is to adjust for any stock splits, company changes, or other events that have occurred over time. Without the divisor, whose calculation is very complex, the DJIA value would be totally distorted. The divisor makes it possible to use the DJIA to make time-series comparisons. On August 25, 2003, the sum of the closing prices of the 30 industrials was 1327.71, which, when divided by the divisor of 0.14249417, resulted in a DJIA value of 9317.64. The current divisor is included in the *Wall Street Journal* figure "Dow Jones Industrial Average" (printed in the upper-right corner, as seen in Figure 3.8).

Because the DJIA results from summing the prices of the 30 stocks, higher-priced stocks tend to affect the index more than do lower-priced stocks. For example, a 5% change in the price of a $50 stock (i.e., $2.50) has less impact on the index than a 5% change in a $100 stock (i.e., $5.00). In spite of this and other criticisms leveled at the DJIA, it remains the most widely cited stock market indicator.

The actual value of the DJIA is meaningful only when compared to earlier values. For example, the DJIA on August 25, 2003, closed at 9317. This value is meaningful only when compared to the previous day's closing value of 9349, a change of −0.33%. Many people mistakenly believe that one DJIA "point" equals $1 in the value of an average share. Actually, one point currently translates into about 0.47 cents in average share value. Figure 3.8 shows the DJIA over the 6-month period February 26, 2003, to August 25, 2003. During this 6-month period, the stock market remained mildly bullish, beginning in April and continuing through August. It started at about 7800 and dropped to about 7500 in mid-March. During the following 160 days, the market steadily increased to close at about 9320 at the end of August.

The three other Dow Jones averages are the transportation, utilities, and composite. The *Dow Jones Transportation Average* is based on 20 stocks, including railroads, airlines, freight forwarders, and mixed transportation companies. The *Dow Jones Utilities Average* is computed using 15 public utility stocks. The *Dow Jones 65 Stocks Composite Average* is made up of the 30 industrials, the 20 transportations, and the 15 utilities. Like the DJIA, each of the other Dow Jones averages is calculated using a divisor to allow for continuity of the average over time. The transportation, utilities, and 65-stocks composite are often cited in the financial news along with the DJIA, as shown in Figure 3.7.

Dow Jones also publishes numerous indexes as seen in the second section of Figure 3.7. The first one listed, the *Dow Jones U.S. Total Market Index*, is a market-weighted index. "Market-weighted" means that companies with large total market values have the most effect on the index's movement. The Dow Jones U.S. Total Market Index reflects 95% of the total market value for large-sized, medium-sized, and small-sized companies. The base value of the index is 100, which represents its value on June 30, 1997.

Standard & Poor's indexes true indexes that measure the current price of a group of stocks relative to a base (set in the 1941–1943 period) having an index value of 10.

Standard & Poor's Indexes Standard & Poor's Corporation, another leading financial publisher, publishes six major common stock indexes. One oft-cited S&P index is the 500-stock composite index. Unlike the Dow Jones averages, **Standard & Poor's indexes** are true indexes. They are calculated each business day by substituting the *closing market value of each stock* (closing price × number of shares outstanding) into the following equation:

Equation 3.2

$$\text{S\&P Index} = \frac{\begin{matrix}\text{Current closing} & & \text{Current closing} & & & & \text{Current closing} \\ \text{market value} & + & \text{market value} & + & \cdots & + & \text{market value} \\ \text{of stock 1} & & \text{of stock 2} & & & & \text{of last stock}\end{matrix}}{\begin{matrix}\text{Base period} & & \text{Base period} & & & & \text{Base period} \\ \text{closing market} & + & \text{closing market} & + & \cdots & + & \text{closing market} \\ \text{value of stock 1} & & \text{value of stock 2} & & & & \text{value of last stock}\end{matrix}} \times 10$$

The value of the S&P index is found by dividing the sum of the market values of all stocks included in the index by the market value of the stocks in the base period and then multiplying the resulting quotient by 10, the base value of the S&P indexes. Most S&P indexes are calculated in a similar fashion. The main differences lie in the stocks included in the index, the base period, and the base value of the index. For example, on August 25, 2003, the ratio of the closing market values of the S&P 500 composite stocks to the 1941–1943 base-period closing market values was 99.371, which, when multiplied by the base value of the S&P index of 10, results in an index value of 993.71 (as shown in Figure 3.7).

HOT

The Barra site contains the S&P/BARRA family of indexes. These include returns over various periods plus fundamental characteristics and sector weights for any date, back to the index inception.

www.barra.com/research

Certain of the S&P indexes contain many more shares than the Dow averages do, and all of them are based on *market values* rather than *share prices*. Therefore, many investors feel that the S&P indexes provide a more broad-based and representative measure of general market conditions than do the Dow averages. Although some technical computational problems exist with these indexes, they are widely used—frequently as a basis for estimating the "market return," an important concept that is introduced in Chapter 4.

Like the Dow averages, the S&P indexes are meaningful only when compared to values in other time periods or to the 1941–1943 base-period value of 10. For example, the August 25, 2003, value of the S&P 500 Stock Composite Index of 993.71 means that the market values of the stocks in the index increased by a factor of 99.371 (993.71 ÷ 10) since the 1941–1943 period. The August 25, 2003, market value of the stocks in the index was 1.28 times the lowest index value of 776.76 in the preceding 52-week period (993.71 ÷ 776.76), and hence represented an increase of 28%.

INVESTOR FACTS

ELECTION RETURNS—During election years, the stock market tends to rise substantially more than the average annual increase. Look at the market returns for U.S. presidential elections since 1976: In every year except 2000—a unique election in every way!—the market rose substantially more than the average.

Year and Election Winner	S&P 500 Return for the Year
2000–George W. Bush	−10.1%
1996–Bill Clinton	+16.0%
1992–Bill Clinton	+17.7%
1988–George H. W. Bush	+12.4%
1984–Ronald Reagan	+25.8%
1980–Ronald Reagan	+19.1%
1976–Jimmy Carter	+15.6%

The eight major common stock indexes published by Standard & Poor's are

- The *industrials index,* made up of the common stock of 400 industrial firms.
- The *transportation index,* which includes the stock of 20 transportation companies.
- The *utilities index,* made up of 40 public utility stocks.
- The *financials index,* which contains 40 financial stocks.
- The *composite index* (described above), which consists of the total of 500 stocks that make up the industrials, transportation, utilities, and financials indexes.
- The *MidCap index,* made up of the stocks of 400 medium-sized companies.
- The *SmallCap index,* made up of 600 small-sized companies.
- The *1500 SuperComp index,* which includes all stocks in the composite, MidCap, and SmallCap indexes.

Like the Dow averages and indexes, many of the S&P indexes are frequently quoted in the financial news, as shown in Figure 3.7.

Although the Dow Jones averages and S&P indexes tend to behave in a similar fashion over time, their day-to-day magnitude and even direction (up or down) can differ significantly because the Dows are averages and the S&Ps are indexes.

NYSE composite index
measure of the current price behavior of stocks listed on the NYSE, relative to a base of 5000 set at December 31, 2002.

AMEX composite index
measure of the current price behavior of all shares traded on the AMEX, relative to a base of 550 set at December 29, 1995.

Nasdaq Stock Market indexes
measures of current price behavior of securities sold OTC, relative to a base of 100 set at specified dates.

Value Line composite index
stock index that reflects the percentage changes in share price of about 1,700 stocks, relative to a base of 100 set at June 30, 1961.

Wilshire 5000 index
measure of the total dollar value (in billions of dollars) of more than 5,000 actively traded stocks, including all those on the NYSE and the AMEX in addition to active OTC stocks.

NYSE, AMEX, and Nasdaq Indexes Three indexes measure the daily results of the New York Stock Exchange (NYSE), the American Stock Exchange (AMEX), and the National Association of Securities Dealers Automated Quotation (Nasdaq) system. Each reflects the movement of stocks listed on its exchange. The **NYSE composite index** includes about 2,100 or so stocks listed on the "Big Board." The index's base of 5000 reflects the December 31, 2002, value of stocks listed on the NYSE. In addition to the composite index, the NYSE publishes indexes for industrials and finance subgroups. The behavior of the NYSE industrial index is normally similar to that of the DJIA and the S&P 500 indexes.

The **AMEX composite index** reflects the price of all shares traded on the American Stock Exchange, relative to a base of 550 set at December 29, 1995. Although it does not always closely follow the S&P and NYSE indexes, the AMEX index tends to move in the general direction they do.

The **Nasdaq Stock Market indexes** reflect over-the-counter market activity. The most comprehensive of the Nasdaq indexes is the *composite index,* which is calculated using the about 3,450 domestic common stocks traded on the Nasdaq system. It is based on a value of 100 set at February 5, 1971. Also important is the *Nasdaq 100,* which includes 100 of the largest domestic and international nonfinancial companies listed on Nasdaq. It is based on a value of 125, set on January 1, 1994. The other three commonly quoted Nasdaq indexes are the *biotech,* the *computer,* and the *telecommunications indexes.* Although their degrees of responsiveness may vary, the Nasdaq indexes tend to move in the same direction at the same time as the other major indexes.

Value Line Indexes Value Line publishes a number of stock indexes constructed by equally weighting the price of each stock included. This is accomplished by considering only the percentage changes in stock prices. This approach eliminates the effects of differing market price and total market value on the relative importance of each stock in the index. The **Value Line composite index** includes the about 1,700 stocks in the *Value Line Investment Survey* that are traded on the NYSE, AMEX, and OTC markets. The base of 100 reflects the stock prices on June 30, 1961. In addition to its composite index, Value Line publishes other specialized indexes.

Other Averages and Indexes A number of other indexes are available. The **Wilshire 5000 index,** published by Wilshire Associates, Inc., is reported daily in the *Wall Street Journal.* It represents the total dollar value (in billions of dollars) of more than 5,000 actively traded stocks, including all those on the NYSE and the AMEX in addition to active OTC stocks. Frank Russell Company, a pension advisory firm, publishes three primary indexes. The *Russell 1000* includes the 1,000 largest companies, the most widely quoted *Russell 2000* includes 2,000 small- to medium-sized companies, and the *Russell 3000* includes all 3,000 companies in the Russell 1000 and 2000.

In addition, the *Wall Street Journal* publishes a number of global and foreign stock market indexes summarized in the "International Stocks & Indexes" section, normally in Section C. Included are Dow Jones indexes for countries in the Americas, Latin America, Europe, South Africa, and the Asia-Pacific region that are based on a value of 100 set at December 31, 1991. More than 30 foreign stock market indexes and the Morgan Stanley Capital International (MSCI) Indexes are also given for major countries, including a

World Index and the *Europe/Australia/ Far East (EAFE MSCI) Index*. Each of the MSCI Indexes is calculated in local currencies and based on a value of 100 set at December 31, 1969. Like the purely domestic averages and indexes, these international averages and indexes measure the general price behavior of the stocks that are listed and traded in the given market. Useful comparisons of the market averages and indexes over time and across markets are often made to assess both trends and relative strengths of foreign markets throughout the world.

Bond Market Indicators

A number of indicators are available for assessing the general behavior of the bond markets. A "Bond Market Data Bank" that includes a wealth of return and price index data for various types of bonds and various domestic and foreign markets is published daily in the *Wall Street Journal*. However, there are fewer indicators of overall bond market behavior than of stock market behavior. The key measures of overall U.S. bond market behavior are bond yields, the Dow Jones Corporate Bond Index, and the New York Stock Exchange bond diary.

bond yield
summary measure of the total return an investor would receive on a bond if it were purchased at its current price and held to maturity; reported as an annual rate of return.

Bond Yields A **bond yield** is a summary measure of the total return an investor would receive on a bond if it were purchased at its current price and held to maturity. Bond yields are reported as annual rates of return. For example, a bond with a yield of 5.50% would provide its owner with a total return from periodic interest and capital gain (or loss) that would be equivalent to a 5.50% annual rate of earnings on the amount invested, if the bond were purchased at its current price and held to maturity.

Typically, bond yields are quoted for a group of bonds that are similar with respect to type and quality. For example, *Barron's* quotes the yields on the Dow Jones bond averages of 10 high-grade corporate bonds, 10 medium-grade corporate bonds, and a confidence index that is calculated as a ratio of the high-grade to medium-grade indexes. In addition, like the *Wall Street Journal,* it quotes numerous other bond indexes and yields, including those for Treasury and municipal bonds. Similar bond yield data are available from S&P, Moody's, and the Federal Reserve. Like stock market averages and indexes, bond yield data are especially useful when viewed over time.

Dow Jones Corporate Bond Index
mathematical averages of the *closing prices* for 96 bonds—32 industrial, 32 financial, and 32 utility/telecom.

Dow Jones Corporate Bond Index The **Dow Jones Corporate Bond Index** includes 96 bonds—32 industrial, 32 financial, and 32 utility/telecom bonds. It reflects the simple mathematical average of the *closing prices* for the bonds. It is based on a value of 100 set at December 31, 1996. The Index is published daily in the *Wall Street Journal* and summarized weekly in *Barron's*. A similar bond market index, prepared by investment banker Lehman Brothers, is also published daily in the *Wall Street Journal* and summarized weekly in *Barron's*.

NYSE Bond Diary The New York Stock Exchange is the dominant organized exchange on which bonds are traded. Thus certain summary statistics on daily bond-trading activity on the NYSE provide useful insight into the behavior of the bond markets in general. These statistics include the number of issues traded and the number that advanced, declined, remained unchanged, reached new highs, and reached new lows. For example, on August 22, 2003, 98 issues traded, 37 advanced, 47 declined, 14 remained unchanged, 3 achieved new highs, and 2 achieved new lows. Total sales volume was $5,911,000. The NYSE bond diary is published weekly, showing the past week's daily data, in *Barron's*.

IN REVIEW

CONCEPTS

3.9 Describe the basic philosophy and use of stock market averages and indexes. Explain how the behavior of an average or index can be used to classify general market conditions as bull or bear.

3.10 List each of the major averages or indexes prepared by (a) Dow Jones & Company and (b) Standard & Poor's Corporation. Indicate the number and source of the securities used in calculating each average or index.

3.11 Briefly describe the composition and general thrust of each of the following indexes.

a. NYSE composite index.
b. AMEX composite index.
c. Nasdaq Stock Market indexes.
d. Value Line composite index.
e. Wilshire 5000 index.

3.12 Discuss each of the following as they are related to assessing bond market behavior.

a. Bond yields.
b. Dow Jones Corporate Bond Index.
c. NYSE bond diary.

Making Securities Transactions

LG 4 LG 5

Now that you know how to find information to help you locate attractive security investments, you should understand how to make securities transactions. Whether you decide to start a self-directed online investment program or to use a traditional stockbroker, you must first open an account with a stockbroker to buy and sell securities. In this section we will look at the role stockbrokers play and how that role has changed with the growth in online investing. We will also explain the basic types of orders you can place, the procedures required to make regular and online securities transactions, the costs of investment transactions, and investor protection.

The Role of Stockbrokers

stockbrokers
individuals licensed by both the SEC and the securities exchanges to facilitate transactions between buyers and sellers of securities.

Stockbrokers—also called *account executives, investment executives,* and *financial consultants*—act as intermediaries between buyers and sellers of securities. They typically charge a commission to facilitate these securities transactions. Stockbrokers must be licensed by both the SEC and the securities exchanges on which they place orders and must follow the ethical guidelines of those bodies.

Although the procedure for executing orders on organized exchanges may differ from that in the OTC market, it starts the same way: An investor places an order with his or her stockbroker. The broker works for a brokerage firm that owns seats on the organized securities exchanges, and members of the securities exchange execute orders that the brokers in the firm's various sales offices transmit to them. For example, the largest U.S. brokerage firm, Merrill Lynch, transmits orders for listed securities from its offices in most major cities throughout the country to the main office of Merrill Lynch and then to the floor of the stock exchanges (NYSE and AMEX), where Merrill Lynch exchange members execute them. Confirmation of the order goes back to the broker placing the order, who relays it to the customer. This process can take a matter of seconds with the use of sophisticated telecommunications networks and Internet trading.

For an over-the-counter securities transaction, brokerage firms transmit orders to market makers, who are dealers in the OTC market specializing in that security. As we learned in Chapter 2, the Nasdaq system, along with the available information on who makes markets in certain securities, enables brokers to execute orders in OTC securities. Normally, OTC transactions are executed rapidly, because market makers maintain inventories of the securities in which they deal.

INVESTOR FACTS

TOO MUCH PAPERWORK— Wasn't the computer supposed to cut down on paperwork? Tell that to the stock brokerage firms and mutual fund companies that send you monthly and year-end statements, confirmations of buy and sell orders, newsletters, and so on. What can you throw away? Keep your most recent brokerage statements and the year-end documents (which you'll need to prepare your tax returns). Check over the monthly statements to make sure they're correct—and then toss them when the next month's statements arrive.

Brokerage Services The primary activity of stockbrokers is to execute clients' purchase and sale transactions at the best possible price. Brokerage firms will hold the client's security certificates for safekeeping; the securities kept by the firm in this manner are said to be held in **street name.** Because the brokerage house issues the securities in its own name and holds them in trust for the client (rather than issuing them in the client's name), the firm can transfer the securities at the time of sale without the client's signature. Street name is actually a common way of buying securities, because most investors do not want to be bothered with the handling and safekeeping of stock certificates. In such cases, the brokerage firm records the details of the client's transaction and keeps track of his or her investments through a series of bookkeeping entries. Dividends and notices received by the broker are forwarded to the client who owns the securities.

street name
security certificates issued in the brokerage firm's name but held in trust for its client, who actually owns them.

Stockbrokers also offer clients a variety of other services. For example, the brokerage firm normally provides free information about investments. Quite often, the firm has a research staff that periodically issues analyses of economic, market, industry, or company behavior and makes recommendations to buy, sell, or hold certain securities. As a client of a large brokerage firm, you can expect to receive regular bulletins on market activity and possibly a recommended investment list. You will also receive a statement describing your transactions for the month and showing commission and interest charges, dividends and interest received, and detailed listings of your current holdings.

Today, most brokerage firms will invest surplus cash left in a client's account in a money market mutual fund, allowing the client to earn a reasonable rate of interest on these balances. Such arrangements help the investor earn as much as possible on temporarily idle funds.

Types of Brokerage Firms Just a few years ago, there were three distinct types of brokerage firms: full-service, premium discount, and basic discount. No longer are the lines between these categories clear-cut. Most brokerage firms, even the most traditional ones, now offer online services. And many discount brokers now offer services, like research reports for clients, that were once available only from a full-service broker.

full-service broker
broker who, in addition to executing clients' transactions, provides them with a full array of brokerage services.

The traditional broker, or so-called **full-service broker,** in addition to executing clients' transactions, offers investors a full array of brokerage services: providing investment advice and information, holding securities in street name, offering online brokerage services, and extending margin loans. Investors who wish merely to make transactions and are not interested in taking advantage of other services should consider either a premium or basic discount broker.

premium discount broker
broker who charges low commissions to make transactions for customers but provides limited free research information and investment advice.

Premium discount brokers focus primarily on making transactions for customers. They charge low commissions and provide limited free research information and investment advice. The investor visits the broker's office, calls a toll-free number, or accesses the broker's Web site to initiate a transaction, and the discount broker confirms the transaction in person or by phone, e-mail, or regular mail. However, brokers like Charles Schwab, the first discount broker, now offer many of the same services that you'd find at a full-service broker. Other premium discounters are similar.

basic discount broker
typically a deep-discount broker through which investors can execute trades electronically online via a commercial service, on the Internet, or by phone. (Also called *online brokers* or *electronic brokers*.)

Basic discount brokers, also called *online brokers* or *electronic brokers,* are typically deep-discount brokers through which investors can execute trades electronically online via a commercial service, on the Internet, or by phone. The investor accesses the basic discounter's Web site to open an account, review the commission schedule, or see a demonstration of the available transactional services and procedures. Confirmation of online trades can take as little as 10 seconds, and most trades occur within 1 minute. Some firms, such as Ameritrade, E*Trade, and TD Waterhouse, operate primarily online, but also provide telephone and live broker backup in case there are problems with the Web site or the customer is away from his or her computer. In response to the rapid growth of online investors, particularly among affluent young investors who enjoy surfing the Web, most brokerage firms now offer online trading. These firms usually charge higher commissions when live broker assistance is required.

The rapidly growing volume of business done by both premium and basic discount brokers attests to their success. Today, many full-service brokers, banks, and savings institutions are making discount and online brokerage services available to their customers and depositors who wish to buy stocks, bonds, mutual funds, and other investment vehicles. Some of the major full-service, premium discount, and basic discount brokers are listed in Table 3.5.

TABLE 3.5 Major Full-Service, Premium Discount, and Basic Discount Brokers

Type of Broker		
Full-Service	Premium Discount	Basic Discount
A.G. Edwards	Charles Schwab	Ameritrade
Merrill Lynch	Fidelity Investments	Brown Co
Morgan Stanley	Quick & Reilly	E* Trade
Smith Barney	T. Rowe Price	Harris Direct
UBS Financial Services	USAA	Scottrade
Wells Fargo	Vanguard	TD Waterhouse

ETHICS IN INVESTING

Did Martha Stewart Cross the Line?

On June 4, 2003, the Securities and Exchange Commission filed securities fraud charges against Marth Stewart and her former stockbroker, Peter Bacanovic. According to the SEC, Martha Stewart committed illegal insider trading when she sold stock in a biotech company, ImClone Systems, Inc., on December 27, 2001, after receiving a tip from Bacanovic. The SEC also alleged that Stewart and Bacanovic created an alibi for her ImClone sales and attempted to obstruct justice during investigations into her trades. The homemaking queen, who has achieved financial success and celebrity status, has found herself tarred by a scandal, during which she resigned as Chairman and CEO of her company. In addition, the stock of her company dropped more than 20%, and her holdings took nearly a $200 million hit, wiping out more than a quarter of her net worth.

The government alleged that Bacanovic tipped off Stewart that two of his other clients, ImClone's CEO Samuel Waksal and Waksal's daughter, had just placed orders to sell all the ImClone stock they held in their Merrill Lynch accounts. Waksal, a long-time friend of Stewart, had secretly obtained information that the U.S. Food and Drug Administration (FDA) was about to reject ImClone's new key cancer product, Erbitux. Information about the Waksals' efforts to sell was confidential under Merrill Lynch policies, which prohibited employees from disclosing client transactions to third parties.

As a result of the tip, Stewart promptly sold all 3,928 shares of her ImClone stock, thus avoiding about $45,000 in losses. The very next day—December 28, 2001—ImClone announced that the FDA had rejected ImClone's application for Erbitux. By the close of the next trading day the price of ImClone stock dropped 16% to $46 per share. According to authorities, Stewart and Bacanovic fabricated an alibi for Stewart's trades, stating that she sold her ImClone stock because she and her broker had decided earlier that she would sell if the price fell below $60 per share. In addition, Stewart told the government that she did not recall anyone telling her that day that the Waksals were selling their ImClone stock.

It's for the courts to decide whether Martha Stewart broke the law. However, as Stephen M. Cutler, the SEC's Director of Enforcement, said, "It is fundamentally unfair for someone to have an edge on the market just because she has a stockbroker who is willing to break the rules and give her an illegal tip. It's worse still when the individual engaging in the insider trading is the Chairman and CEO of a public company."

Critical Thinking Question In light of the *Insider Trading and Fraud Act of 1988*, does Martha Stewart or any other investor have the right to sell stock every time a broker tells them to?

Selecting a Stockbroker If you decide to start your investing activities with the assistance of either a full-service or premium discount stockbroker, select the person you believe best understands your investment goals. Choosing a broker whose disposition toward investing is similar to yours is the best way to establish a solid working relationship. Your broker should also make you aware of investment possibilities that are consistent with your objectives and attitude toward risk.

You should also consider the cost and types of services available from the firm with which the broker is affiliated, to receive the best service at the lowest possible cost to you. The premium discount brokerage service is primarily transactional, and the basic discount brokerage service is *purely* transactional.

Contact with a broker, advice, and research assistance generally are available only at a higher price. Investors must weigh the added commissions they pay a full-service broker against the value of the advice they receive, because the amount of available advice is the only major difference among basic discount, premium discount, and full-service brokers.

Referrals from friends or business associates are a good way to begin your search for a stockbroker. Don't forget to consider the investing style and goals of the person making the recommendation. However, it is not important—and often not even advisable—to know your stockbroker personally. And in this age of online brokers, you may never meet your broker face to face! A strictly business relationship eliminates the possibility that social concerns will interfere with the achievement of your investment goals. This does not mean that your broker's sole interest should be commissions. Responsible brokers do not engage in **churning**—that is, causing excessive trading of their clients' accounts to increase commissions. Churning is both illegal and unethical under SEC and exchange rules. However, it is often difficult to prove. For an example of a stockbroker-client business relationship that may have crossed the line into illegal, see the *Ethics* box on page 107.

churning
an illegal and unethical practice engaged in by a broker to increase commissions by causing excessive trading of clients' accounts.

Opening an Account To open an account, the customer fills out various documents that establish a legal relationship between the customer and the brokerage firm. A signature card and a personal data card provide the information needed to identify the client's account. The stockbroker must also have a reasonable understanding of a client's personal financial situation to assess his or her investment goals—and to be sure that the client can pay for the securities purchased. The client also provides the broker with instructions regarding the transfer and custody of securities. Customers who wish to borrow money to make transactions must establish a margin account (described on page 109). If the customer is acting as a custodian, trustee, or executor or is a corporation, the brokerage firm will require additional documents. Today, all of this can be done online at most brokerage firms.

Investors may have accounts with more than one stockbroker. Many investors establish accounts at different types of firms to obtain the benefit and opinions of a diverse group of brokers and to reduce their overall cost of making purchase and sale transactions.

Next you must select the type of account best suited to your needs. We will briefly consider several of the more popular types.

Single or Joint A brokerage account may be either single or joint. Joint accounts are most common between husband and wife or parent and child. The account of a minor (a person younger than 18 years of age) is a **custodial account,** in which a parent or guardian must be part of all transactions. Regardless of the form of the account, the name(s) of the account holder(s) and an account number are used to identify it.

custodial account
the brokerage account of a minor; requires a parent or guardian to be part of all transactions.

Cash or Margin A **cash account,** the more common type, is one in which the customer can make only cash transactions. Customers can initiate cash transactions via phone or online and are given 3 business days in which to transmit the cash to the brokerage firm. The firm is likewise given 3 business days in which to deposit the proceeds from the sale of securities in the customer's cash account.

cash account
a brokerage account in which a customer can make only cash transactions.

margin account
a brokerage account in which the customer has been extended borrowing privileges by the brokerage firm.

A **margin account** is an account in which the brokerage firm extends borrowing privileges to a creditworthy customer. By leaving securities with the firm as collateral, the customer can borrow a prespecified proportion of the securities' purchase price. The brokerage firm will, of course, charge the customer a stated rate of interest on borrowings. (The mechanics of margin trading are covered in Chapter 2.)

wrap account
a brokerage account in which customers with large portfolios pay a flat annual fee that covers the cost of a money manager's services and the commissions on all trades. (Also called a *managed account*.)

Wrap The **wrap account** (also called a *managed account*) allows brokerage customers with large portfolios (generally $100,000 or more) to shift stock selection decisions conveniently to a professional money manager, either in-house or independent. In return for a flat annual fee equal to between 1% and 3% of the portfolio's total asset value, the brokerage firm helps the investor select a money manager, pays the manager's fee, and executes the money manager's trades. Initially the investor, broker, and/or manager discuss the client's overall goals. Wrap accounts are appealing for a number of reasons other than convenience. The annual fee in most cases covers commissions on all trades, virtually eliminating the chance of the broker churning the account. In addition, the broker monitors the manager's performance and provides the investor with detailed reports, typically quarterly.

odd lot
less than 100 shares of stock.

round lot
100-share units of stock or multiples thereof.

Odd-Lot or Round-Lot Transactions Investors can buy stock in either odd or round lots. An **odd lot** consists of less than 100 shares of a stock. A **round lot** is a 100-share unit or a multiple thereof. You would be dealing in an odd lot if you bought, say, 25 shares of stock but in round lots if you bought 200 shares. A trade of 225 shares would be a combination of an odd lot and two round lots.

Transactions in odd lots require either additional processing by the brokerage firm or the assistance of a specialist. For odd lots, an added fee—known as an *odd-lot differential*—is tacked on to the normal commission charge, driving up the costs of these small trades. Small investors in the early stages of their investment programs are primarily responsible for odd-lot transactions.

Basic Types of Orders

Investors can use different types of orders to make security transactions. The type placed normally depends on the investor's goals and expectations. The three basic types of orders are the market order, the limit order, and the stop-loss order.

market order
an order to buy or sell stock at the best price available when the order is placed.

Market Order An order to buy or sell stock at the best price available when the investor places the order is a **market order.** It is generally the quickest way to fill orders, because market orders are usually executed as soon as they reach the exchange floor or are received by the market maker. Because of the speed with which market orders are executed, the buyer or seller of a security can be sure that the price at which the order is transacted will be very close to the market price prevailing at the time the order was placed.

limit order
an order to buy at or below a specified price or to sell at or above a specified price.

Limit Order A **limit order** is an order to buy at or below a specified price or to sell at or above a specified price. When the investor places a limit order, the broker transmits it to a specialist dealing in the security. The specialist notes the number of shares and price of the limit order in his or her book and executes the order as soon as the specified market price (or better) exists. The specialist must first satisfy all other orders with precedence—similar orders received earlier, buy orders at a higher specified price, or sell orders at a lower specified price. Investors can place the limit order in one of the following forms:

1. A *fill-or-kill order,* which is canceled if not immediately executed.
2. A *day order,* which if not executed is automatically canceled at the end of the day.
3. A *good-'til-canceled (GTC) order,* which generally remains in effect for 6 months unless executed, canceled, or renewed.

Assume, for example, that you place a limit order to buy, at a limit price of $30, 100 shares of a stock currently selling at $30.50. Once the specialist clears all similar orders received before yours, and once the market price of the stock falls to $30 or less, he or she executes your order. It is possible, of course, that your order might expire (if it is not a GTC order) before the stock price drops to $30.

Although a limit order can be quite effective, it can also keep you from making a transaction. If, for instance, you wish to buy at $30 or less and the stock price moves from its current $30.50 price to $42 while you are waiting, you have missed the opportunity to make a profit of $11.50 per share ($42 − $30.50). If you had placed a *market order* to buy at the best available price ($30.50), the profit of $11.50 would have been yours. Limit orders for the sale of a stock are also disadvantageous when the stock price closely approaches, but does not attain, the minimum sale price limit before dropping substantially. Generally speaking, limit orders are most effective when the price of a stock fluctuates greatly, because there is then a better chance that the order will be executed.

stop-loss (stop) order
an order to sell a stock when its market price reaches or drops below a specified level; can also be used to buy stock when its market price reaches or rises above a specified level.

Stop-Loss Order When an investor places a **stop-loss order** or **stop order,** the broker tells the specialist to sell a stock when its market price reaches or drops below a specified level. Stop-loss orders are *suspended orders* placed on stocks; they are activated when and if the stock reaches a certain price. The stop-loss order is placed on the specialist's book and becomes active once the stock reaches the stop price. Like limit orders, stop-loss orders are typically day or GTC orders. When activated, the stop order becomes a *market order* to sell the security at the best price available. Thus it is possible for the actual price at which the sale is made to be well below the price at which the stop was initiated. Investors use these orders to protect themselves against the adverse effects of a rapid decline in share price.

For example, assume you own 100 shares of Ballard Industries, which is currently selling for $35 per share. Because you believe the stock price could decline rapidly at any time, you place a stop order to sell at $30. If the stock price does in fact drop to $30, the specialist will sell the 100 shares at the best price available at that time. If the market price declines to $28 by the time your stop-loss order comes up, you will receive less than $30 per share. Of course, if the market price stays above $30 per share, you will have lost nothing as a result of placing the order, because the stop order will never be initiated. Often investors raise the level of the stop as the price of the stock rises. Such action helps to lock in a higher profit when the price is increasing.

Investors can also place stop orders to buy a stock, although buy orders are far less common than sell orders. For example, an investor may place a stop order to buy 100 shares of MJ Enterprises, currently selling for $70 per share, once its price rises to, say, $75 (the stop price). These orders are commonly used either to limit losses on short sales (discussed in Chapter 2) or to buy a stock just as its price begins to rise.

To avoid the risk of the market moving against you when your stop order becomes a market order, you can place a *stop-limit order,* rather than a plain stop order. This is an order to buy or sell stock at a given price, or better, once a stipulated stop price has been met. For example, in the Ballard Industries example, had a stop-limit order been in effect, then when the market price of Ballard dropped to $30, the broker would have entered a limit order to sell your 100 shares at $30 a share or *better.* Thus you would have run no risk of getting less than $30 a share for your stock—unless the price of the stock kept right on falling. In that case, as is true for any limit order, you might miss the market altogether and end up with stock worth much less than $30. Even though the stop order to sell was triggered (at $30), the stock will not be sold, with a stop-limit order, if it keeps falling in price.

Online Transactions

The competition for your online business increases daily as more players enter an already crowded arena. Brokerage firms are encouraging customers to trade online and offering a variety of incentives to get their business, including free trades! However, low cost is not the only reason to choose a brokerage firm. As with any financial decision, you must consider your needs and find the firm that best matches them. One investor may want timely information, research, and quick, reliable trades from a full-service broker like Merrill Lynch or Smith Barney or a premium discounter like Charles Schwab or Quick & Reilly. Another, who is an active trader, will focus on cost and fast trades rather than research and so will sign up with a basic discounter like Ameritrade or Harris Direct. Ease of site navigation is a major factor in finding a basic discount broker to use in executing online transactions. Table 3.6 (on page 112) gives Smart Money's assessment of the features, services, and costs of a number of leading basic discount brokerage firms, all of which offer online trading of stocks. Some also offer online trading of bonds and mutual funds as well.

day trader
an investor who buys and sells stocks quickly throughout the day in hopes of making quick profits.

Day Trading For some investors, online stock trading is so compelling that they become day traders. The opposite of buy-and-hold investors with a long-term perspective, **day traders** buy and sell stocks quickly throughout the day. They hope that their stocks will continue to rise in value for the very short time they own them—sometimes just seconds or minutes—so they can make quick profits. Some also sell short, looking for small price decreases. True day traders do not own any stocks overnight—hence the term "day trader"—because they believe that the extreme risk of prices changing radically from day to day will lead to large losses. Day trading is not illegal or unethical, but it is highly risky. To compound their risk, day traders usually buy on margin to use leverage to earn higher profits. But as we saw in Chapter 2, margin trading also increases the risk of large losses.

TABLE 3.6 Smart Money's Assessment of the Features, Services, and Costs of Leading Basic Discount Brokerage Firms

Overall Rank	Broker	Notable Features	Minimum Opening Balance	Quality of service	Commissions and fees	Mutual Funds	Research Tools	Investment Products	Amenities	Commissions on Market Trades*	Average Phone Wait**	Trade* Execution Quality
1	TD Waterhouse www.tdwaterhouse.com	Widest range of products and services, and a strong showing on most every front.	None	6	7	1	2	1	2	$17.95	142	Good
2	Muriel Siebert www.siebertnet.com	Lots of research tools, plus no account fees.	None	5	8	8	1	2	3	$14.95	38	Good
3	Bidwell www.bidwell.com	Good customer service. Had the most-detailed account statements.	None	1	6	9	8[t]	3	11[t]	$12.75	16	Good
4	Scottrade www.scottrade.com	Few fees make it the cheapest broker, but the Web site is outdated.	$2,000	11	1	10	10	5	11[t]	$7.00	5	Good
5	Harris Direct www.harrisdirect.com	Wireless options galore. Cheap broker-assisted trades.	None	8	2	6	3	4	1	$20.00	59	Poor
6	BrownCo www.brownco.com	Easy-to-use online trading interface is a boon for active traders.	$15,000	3[t]	3	5	7	13	13	$5.00	47	Good
7	Firstrade www.firstrade.com	Cheap trades and great execution. But that's about it.	None	3[t]	4	11	13	10[t]	10	$6.95	22	Excellent
8	Ameritrade www.ameritrade.com	Least-detailed statements, but decent customer service.	$2,000	7	5	7	8[t]	9	7	$10.99	125	Excellent
9	E*Trade www.etrade.com	The highest fees of the bunch. At least the Web site is easy to navigate.	$1,000	10	10	13	5	6	8	$22.99	622	Poor
10	Wells Fargo www.wellsfargo.com	Great customer service; skimpy on the research.	$1,000	2	12	3	12	8	5[t]	$24.95	38	Excellent
11	Merrill Lynch Direct www.mldirect.com	Most expensive, with high trade commissions and lots of fees.	$2,000	9	13	2	4	10[t]	4	$29.95	143	Fair
12	Cititrade www.cititrade.com	Least-helpful phone and e-mail reps. One perk: low margin rates.	$2,000	12	9	12	6	10[t]	9	$24.95	85	Fair
13	Bank of America www.bankofamerica.com/investments	Frustrating site and poor customer service. No research reports.	None	13	11	4	11	7	5[t]	$24.95	161	Poor

t = Tie. *Trade costs are for 1,000 shares, with fees. **Phone wait is for customer service, in seconds. *Note:* Quality of service reflects customer service, trade execution, Web reliability.

Source: Anne Kadet and Eleanor Laise, "Basic Discount Brokers—Rankings," 2003 Broker Survey, *Smart Money,* August 5, 2003, p. 68, downloaded from smartmoney.com/brokers/index.cfm?story=2003-basic-table.

Because the Internet makes investment information and transactions accessible to the masses, day trading has grown in popularity. Day traders watch their computer screens continuously, trying to track numerous ticker quotes and price data to identify market trends. It's a very difficult task—essentially a very stressful, full-time job. Yet pitches for day trading make it seem like an easy route to quick riches. Quite the reverse is true. Day traders typically incur major financial losses when they start trading. Some never achieve profitability. Day traders also have high expenses for brokerage commissions, training, and computer equipment. They must earn sizable trading profits annually to break even on fees and commissions alone. The *Investing in Action* box on page 114 details an even darker side of day trading—how it can sometimes turn into compulsive investing.

Technical and Service Problems As the number of online investors increases, so do the problems that beset brokerage firms and their customers. During the past few years most brokerage firms have upgraded their systems to reduce the number of service outages. But the potential problems go beyond the brokerage sites. Once an investor places a trade at a firm's Web site, it goes through several other parties to be executed. Most online brokers don't have their own trading desks and have agreements with other trading firms to execute their orders on the *New York Stock Exchange* or *Nasdaq Stock Market*. Slowdowns at any point in the process can create problems confirming trades. Investors, thinking that their trades had not gone through, might place the order again—only to discover later that they have bought the same stock twice. Online investors who don't get immediate trade execution and confirmation use the telephone when they can't get through online or to solve other problems with their accounts, and they often face long waiting times on hold.

UP, UP, AND AWAY—Although online brokerage firms' share of trading volume on the NYSE and Nasdaq plummeted from 42% to about 12% during the 2000-2003 bear market, activity was again on the rise by mid-2003. Retail investors, who account for most of the online brokerages' customers, began buying stocks again fairly quickly. Not only did this trend bode well for these firms, but it also rejuvenated the markets in general. Because individual investors are usually among the last to respond to a market rally, analysts considered this a positive sign of renewed investor confidence.

Source: Bill Deener, "Online Trading Revival Bodes Well for Stocks," *San Diego Union-Tribune*, August 31, 2003, p. H8.

Tips for Successful Online Trades Successful online investors take additional precautions before submitting their orders. Here are some tips to protect yourself from common problems:

- *Know how to place and confirm your order before you begin trading.* This simple step can keep you from having problems later.
- *Verify the stock symbol of the security you wish to buy.* Two very different companies can have similar symbols. Some investors have bought the wrong stock because they didn't check before placing their order.
- *Use limit orders.* The order you see on your computer screen may not be the one you get. With a limit order, you avoid getting burned in fast-moving markets. Although limit orders cost more, they can save you thousands of dollars. For example, customers eager to get shares of a hot IPO stock placed market orders. Instead of buying the stock near the offering price of $9, some were shocked to find that their orders were filled at prices as high as $90 during the stock's first trading day. Investors who were aware of the price run-up tried to cancel orders but couldn't get through to brokers. Because of this, some brokers accept only limit orders for online IPO purchases on the first day of trading.
- *Don't ignore the online reminders that ask you to check and recheck.* It's easy to make a typo that adds an extra digit to a purchase amount.

INVESTING IN ACTION

Investment Junkies

When Howard, a young investor, watched his friends strike it rich, he stepped gingerly into the waters of online investing for himself. He made $4,000 in a matter of minutes on his first trade, and soon he was deep into *day trading*—the practice of buying and selling stocks very quickly to make a few cents profit. After he met with some success, Howard opened a margin account to leverage his profits. Before long he was a confirmed "investaholic." Not until the market tanked and he was deep in debt did reality hit home for Howard. "I never noticed the sunshine," said another compulsive investor. "All I did was watch CNBC and stare at my computer." Yet even after he stopped trading, he wistfully recalls the extreme euphoria: " I've never felt a high like that. Nothing can replace it."

These investment junkies were not alone. As long as the markets were up and paper profits climbed, the apparent ease of gaining quick riches lured many naive investors eager for quick profits. The speed and simplicity of point-and-click stock online trading led to more impulse buying, as well as a significant increase in the number of stock market gamblers. "It gives gamblers the quick fix and constant action they crave," comments Marvin Steinberg, psychologist and director of the Connecticut Council on Problem Gambling.

Investing as gambling? Hard to accept, but at one point stock traders represented about half the attendees at Gamblers Anonymous meetings. And because it's not uncommon for investment addicts to bet as much as $25,000 on one trade—whereas few gamblers would wager that much on one hand at the casino—the stock market can take them on a quick ride to bankruptcy.

As with other addictions, it's difficult to determine when you cross the line from making occasional impulse stock purchases to becoming a full-fledged investment junkie. According to the Council on Compulsive Gambling of New Jersey, problem gambling affects approximately 10% of investors. These investors can stop gambling after a big loss or intervention from family members. The 5% who cross into compulsive gambler territory have more trouble controlling their addiction.

Here are some warning signs to help you recognize a stock market gambling problem:

- Trading stocks to ease worries
- Becoming irritable when unable to trade
- Making increasingly speculative investments
- Borrowing to be able to invest more
- Experiencing euphoria when you hit it big and depression when you don't
- Needing to raise the amount you invest to feel the thrill

Critical Thinking Question How might online trading and market conditions contribute to an investor's gambling problem?

Sources: Steven T. Goldberg, "He Never Saw the Sun," *Kiplinger's Personal Finance Magazine*, August 2001, downloaded from www.kiplingerspersonalfinance.com; Ruth Simon and E. S. Browning, "Some Online Investors Can't Say No to Playing the Market," *Wall Street Journal*, August 4, 2000, pp. A1, A4; and Paul Sloan, "Can't Stop Checking Your Quotes?" *U.S. News & World Report*, July 10, 2000, p. 40.

- *Don't get carried away.* It's easy to churn your own account. In fact, new online investors trade about twice as much as they did before they went online. To control impulse trading, have a strategy and stick to it.
- *Open accounts with two brokers.* This protects you if your online brokerage's computer system crashes. It also gives you an alternative if one brokerage is blocked with heavy trading volume.

- *Double-check orders for accuracy.* Make sure each trade was completed according to your instructions. It's very easy to make typos or use the wrong stock symbol, so review the confirmation notice to verify that the right number of shares was bought or sold and that the price and commissions or fees are as quoted. Check your account for "unauthorized" trades.

Transaction Costs

Making transactions through brokers or market makers is considerably easier for investors than it would be to negotiate directly, trying to find someone who wants to buy that which they want to sell (or vice versa). To compensate the broker for executing the transaction, investors pay transaction costs, which are usually levied on both the purchase and the sale of securities. When making investment decisions, you must consider the structure and magnitude of transaction costs, because they affect returns.

fixed-commission schedules fixed brokerage commissions that typically apply to the small transactions usually made by individual investors.

negotiated commissions brokerage commissions agreed to by the client and the broker as a result of their negotiations; typically apply on large institutional transactions and to individual investors who maintain large accounts.

Since the passage of the *Securities Acts Amendments of 1975*, brokers have been permitted to charge whatever brokerage commissions they deem appropriate. Most firms have established **fixed-commission schedules** that apply to small transactions, the ones most often made by individual investors. On large institutional transactions, the client and broker may arrange a **negotiated commission**—commissions to which both parties agree. Negotiated commissions are also available to individual investors who maintain large accounts, typically above $50,000.

The commission structure varies with the type of security and the type of broker. We'll describe the basic commission structures for various types of securities in subsequent chapters. Because of the way brokerage firms charge commissions on stock trades, it is difficult to compare prices precisely. Traditional brokers generally charge on the basis of number of shares and the price of the stock at the time of the transaction. Internet brokers usually charge flat rates, often for transactions up to 1,000 shares, with additional fees for larger or more complicated orders. However, many traditional brokerage firms have reduced their commissions on broker-assisted trades and have instituted annual flat fees (on wrap accounts) set as a specified percentage of the value of the assets in the account. Unless you are a very active trader, you will probably be better off paying commissions on a per-transaction basis.

Obviously, premium and basic discount brokers charge substantially less than full-service brokers for the same transaction. However, most discounters charge a minimum fee to discourage small orders. For example, one basic discounter, Harris Direct, charges a minimum fee of about $20 but adds a surcharge of $25 for broker-assisted trades. The savings from the discounter are substantial: Depending on the size and type of transaction, premium and basic discount brokers can typically save investors between 30% and 80% of the commission charged by the full-service broker.

Securities Investor Protection Corporation (SIPC) a nonprofit membership corporation, authorized by the federal government, that insures each brokerage customer's account for up to $500,000, with claims for cash limited to $100,000 per customer.

Investor Protection: SIPC and Arbitration

Although most investment transactions take place safely, it is important for you to know what protection you have if things *don't* go smoothly. As a client, you are protected against the loss of the securities or cash held by your broker. The **Securities Investor Protection Corporation** (SIPC), a nonprofit membership corporation, was authorized by the *Securities Investor Protection Act of 1970* to protect customer accounts against the consequences of financial failure of the brokerage firm. The SIPC currently insures each customer's account for up to $500,000, with claims for cash limited to $100,000 per customer. Note that SIPC insurance does not guarantee that the investor will recover the dollar value of the securities; it guarantees only that the securities themselves will be returned. Some brokerage firms also insure certain customer accounts for amounts in excess of $500,000. Certainly, in light of the diversity and quality of services available among brokerage firms, this may be an additional service you should consider when you select a firm and an individual broker.

HOT LINKS

The Securities Investor Protection Corporation (SIPC) protects customers of broker-dealers registered with the U.S. Securities and Exchange Commission.

www.sipc.org

The SIPC provides protection in case your brokerage firm fails. But what happens if your broker gave you bad advice and, as a result, you lost a lot of money on an investment? Or what if you feel your broker is *churning* your account, the illegal but difficult-to-prove practice of causing excessive trading to increase commissions? In either case, the SIPC won't help. It's not intended to insure you against bad investment advice or churning. Instead, if you have a dispute with your broker, the first thing you should do is discuss the situation with the managing officer at the branch where you do business. If that doesn't do any good, then contact the firm's compliance officer and the securities regulator in your home state.

If you still don't get any satisfaction, you can use litigation (judicial methods in the courts) to resolve the dispute. Alternative dispute resolution processes that may avoid litigation include *mediation* and *arbitration.* **Mediation** is an informal, voluntary approach in which you and the broker agree to a mediator, who facilitates negotiations between the two of you to resolve the case. The mediator does not impose a solution on you and the broker. The NASD and securities-related organizations encourage investors to mediate disputes rather than arbitrate them, because mediation can reduce costs and time for both investors and brokers.

mediation
an informal, voluntary dispute resolution process in which a client and a broker agree to a mediator, who facilitates negotiations between them to resolve the case.

arbitration
a formal dispute resolution process in which a client and a broker present their argument before a panel, which then decides the case.

If mediation is not pursued or if it fails, you may have no choice but to take the case to **arbitration,** a formal process whereby you and your broker present the two sides of the argument before an arbitration panel. The panel then decides the case. Many brokerage firms require you to resolve disputes by *binding arbitration;* in this case, you don't have the option to sue. You must accept the arbitrator's decision, and in most cases you cannot go to court to review your case. Before you open an account, check whether the brokerage agreement contains a binding-arbitration clause.

Settling securities disputes through mediation or arbitration rather than litigation has advantages and disadvantages. Mediation and arbitration proceedings typically cost less and are resolved more quickly than litigation. Recent legislation has given many investors the option of using either securities industry panels or independent arbitration panels such as those sponsored by the American Arbitration Association (AAA). Independent panels are considered more sympathetic toward investors. In addition, only one of the three arbitrators on a panel can be connected with the securities industry. However, in 2003, in about 55% of the arbitration cases the client was awarded damages.

Probably the best thing you can do to avoid the need to mediate, arbitrate, or litigate with your broker is to select him or her carefully, understand the financial risks involved in the broker's recommendations, thoroughly evaluate the advice he or she offers, and continuously monitor the volume of transactions that he or she recommends and executes. Clearly, it is much less costly to choose the right broker initially than to incur later the financial and emotional costs of having chosen a bad one.

If you have a problem with an online trade, immediately file a written—not e-mail—complaint with the broker. Cite dates, times, and amounts of trades, and include all supporting documentation. File a copy with the NASD regulatory arm Web site (www.nasdr.com) and with your state securities regulator. If you can't resolve the problems with the broker, you can try mediation and then resort to arbitration, litigation being the last resort.

CONCEPTS IN REVIEW

3.13 Describe the types of services offered by brokerage firms, and discuss the criteria for selecting a suitable stockbroker.

3.14 Briefly differentiate among the following types of brokerage accounts:
a. Single or joint
b. Custodial
c. Cash
d. Margin
e. Wrap

3.15 Differentiate among *market orders, limit orders,* and *stop-loss orders.* What is the rationale for using a stop-loss order rather than a limit order?

3.16 Differentiate between the services and costs associated with *full-service, premium discount,* and *basic discount* brokers. Be sure to discuss online transactions.

3.17 What is *day trading,* and why is it risky? How can you avoid problems as an online trader?

3.18 In what two ways, based on the number of shares transacted, do brokers typically charge for executing transactions? How are online transaction fees structured relative to the degree of broker involvement?

3.19 What protection does the *Securities Investor Protection Corporation (SIPC)* provide securities investors? How are mediation and arbitration procedures used to settle disputes between investors and their brokers?

Investment Advisers and Investment Clubs

LG 6

Although financial information is available from numerous sources, many investors have neither the time nor the expertise to analyze it and make decisions on their own. Instead, they turn to an **investment adviser,** which is an individual or firm that provides investment advice, typically for a fee. Alternatively, some small investors join investment clubs. Here we will discuss using an investment adviser and then briefly cover the key aspects of investment clubs.

investment advisers
Individuals or firms that provide investment advice, typically for a fee.

Using an Investment Adviser

The "product" provided by an investment adviser ranges from broad, general advice to detailed, specific analyses and recommendations. The most general form of advice is a newsletter published by the adviser. These letters comment on the economy, current events, market behavior, and specific securities. Investment advisers also provide complete individualized investment evaluation, recommendation, and management services.

Regulation of Advisers As we noted in Chapter 2, the *Investment Advisers Act of 1940* ensures that investment advisers make full disclosure of information about their backgrounds, about conflicts of interest, and so on. The act requires professional advisers to register and file periodic reports with the SEC. A 1960 amendment permits the SEC to inspect the records of investment advisers and to revoke the registration of those who violate the act's provisions. However, financial planners, stockbrokers, bankers, lawyers, and accountants who provide investment advice in addition to their main professional activity are not regulated by the act. Many states have also passed similar legislation, requiring investment advisers to register and to abide by the guidelines established by the state law.

Be aware that the federal and state laws regulating the activities of professional investment advisers do not guarantee competence. Rather, they are intended to protect the investor against fraudulent and unethical practices. It is important to recognize that, at present, no law or regulatory body controls entrance into the field. Therefore, investment advisers range from highly informed professionals to totally incompetent amateurs. Advisers who possess a professional designation are usually preferred because they have completed academic courses in areas directly or peripherally related to the investment process. Such designations include CFA (Chartered Financial Analyst), CIMA (Certified Investment Management Analyst), CIC (Chartered Investment Counselor), CFP® (Certified Financial Planner), ChFC (Chartered Financial Consultant), CLU (Chartered Life Underwriter), and CPA (Certified Public Accountant).

Online Investment Advice You can also find financial advice online. Whether it's a retirement planning tool or advice on how to diversify your assets, automated financial advisers may be able to help you. If your needs are specific rather than comprehensive, you can find good advice at other sites. For example, T. Rowe Price has an excellent college planning section (www.troweprice.com/college). Financial Engines (www.financialengines.com), AdviceAmerica (www.adviceamerica.com), and DirectAdvice (www.directadvice.com) are among several independent advice sites that offer broader planning capabilities. Many mutual fund family Web sites have online financial advisers. For example, The Vanguard Group (www.vanguard.com) has a personal investors section that helps you choose funds for specific investment objectives, such as retirement or financing a college education.

The Cost and Use of Investment Advice Professional investment advice typically costs, annually, between 0.25% and 3% of the dollar amount of money being managed. For large portfolios, the fee is typically in the range of 0.25% to 0.75%. For small portfolios (less than $100,000), an annual fee ranging from 2% to 3% of the dollar amount of funds managed would not be unusual. These fees generally cover complete management of a client's money, excluding any purchase or sale commissions. The cost of periodic investment advice not provided as part of a subscription service could be based on a fixed-fee schedule or quoted as an hourly charge for consultation. Online advisers are much less expensive; they either are free or charge an annual fee.

Whether you choose a traditional investment advisory service or decide to try an online service, some are better than others. More expensive services do not necessarily provide better advice. It is best to study carefully the track record and overall reputation of an investment adviser before purchasing his or her services. Not only should the adviser have a good performance record, but he or she also should be responsive to the investor's personal goals.

How good is the advice from online advisers? It's very hard to judge. Their suggested plans are only as good as the input. Beginning investors may not have sufficient knowledge to make wise assumptions on future savings, tax, or inflation rates or to analyze results thoroughly. A good personal financial planner will ask lots of questions to assess your investing expertise and explain what you don't know. These early-stage automated tools may take too narrow a focus and not consider other parts of your investment portfolio. For many investors, online advisers lack what leads them to get help in the first place—the human touch. They want hand-holding, reassurance, and gentle nudging to follow through on their plans.

Investment Clubs

Another way to obtain investment advice and experience is to join an investment club. This route can be especially useful for those of moderate means who do not want to incur the cost of an investment adviser. An **investment club** is a legal partnership binding a group of investors (partners) to a specified organizational structure, operating procedures, and purpose. The goal of most clubs is to earn favorable long-term returns by making investments in vehicles of moderate risk.

investment club
a legal partnership through which a group of investors are bound to a specified organizational structure, operating procedures, and purpose, which is typically to earn favorable long-term returns from moderate-risk investments.

Individuals with similar goals usually form investment clubs to pool their knowledge and money to create a jointly owned and managed portfolio. Certain members are responsible for obtaining and analyzing data on a specific investment vehicle or strategy. At periodic meetings, the members present their findings and recommendations for discussion and further analysis by the membership. The group decides whether to pursue the proposed vehicle or strategy. Most clubs require members to make scheduled contributions to the club's treasury, thereby regularly increasing the pool of investable funds. Although most clubs concentrate on investments in stocks and bonds, some may concentrate on specialized investments such as options or futures.

Membership in an investment club provides an excellent way for the novice investor to learn the key aspects of portfolio construction and investment management, while (one hopes) earning a favorable return on his or her funds. In fact, many investment clubs regularly earn returns above the market and even above professional money managers. The reason? Investment clubs typically buy stocks for the long term, rather than trying to make the quick buck.

As you might expect, investment clubs have also joined the online investing movement. By tapping into the Internet, clubs are freed from geographical restrictions. Now investors around the world, many who have never met, can form a club and discuss investing strategies and stock picks just as easily as if they gathered in person. Finding a time or place to meet is no longer

HOT LINKS

A good source of information about investment clubs can be found at fool.com. Go to:

www.fool.com/InvestmentClub/InvestmentClubIntroduction.htm

an issue. Some clubs are formed by friends; others are strangers who have similar investing philosophies and may have met online. Online clubs conduct business via e-mail or set up a private Web site. Members of the *National Association of Investors Corporation (NAIC),* a not-for-profit organization, qualify for a site at Yahoo! that includes meeting rooms, investment tools, and other investment features. Other portals offer sites for nonmembers.

NAIC, which has over 325,000 individual and club investors and 28,000 regular and online investment clubs, publishes a variety of useful materials and also sponsors regional and national meetings. (To learn how to start an investment club, visit the NAIC Web site at www.better-investing.org. Or order an information package by calling the toll-free number 877-ASK-NAIC (877-275-6242) or writing NAIC, P.O. Box 220, Royal Oak, MI 48068.)

CONCEPTS IN REVIEW

3.20 Describe the services that professional investment advisers perform, the way in which they are regulated, online investment advisers, and the cost of investment advice.

3.21 What benefits does an *investment club* offer the small investor? Why do investment clubs regularly outperform the market and the pros? Would you prefer to join a regular or an online club, and why?

Summary

LG 1 **Discuss the growth in online investing, including educational sites and investment tools, and the pros and cons of using the Internet as an investment tool.** The Internet has empowered individual investors by providing information and tools formerly available only to investing professionals and by simplifying the investing process. The savings it provides in time and money are huge. Investors get the most current information, including real-time stock price quotes, market activity data, research reports, educational articles, and discussion forums. Tools such as financial planning calculators, stock-screening programs, charting, and stock quotes and portfolio tracking are free at many sites. Buying and selling securities online is convenient, relatively simple, inexpensive, and fast.

LG 2 **Identify the major types and sources of traditional and online investment information.** Investment information, descriptive or analytical, includes information about the economy and current events, industries and companies, and alternative investment vehicles, as well as price information and personal investment strategies. It can be obtained from financial journals, general newspapers, institutional news, business periodicals, government publications, special subscription services, stockholders' reports, comparative data sources, subscription services, brokerage reports, investment letters, price quotations, and electronic and online sources. Most print publications also have Web sites with access to all or part of their content. Financial portals bring together a variety of financial information online. Investors will also find specialized sites for bond, mutual fund, and international information, as well as discussion forums (message boards and chat rooms) that discuss individual securities and investment strategies. Because it is hard to know the qualifications of those who make postings on message boards, participants must do their own homework before acting on an online tip.

LG 3

Explain the characteristics, interpretation, and uses of the commonly cited stock and bond market averages and indexes. Investors commonly rely on stock market averages and indexes to stay abreast of market behavior. The most often cited are the Dow Jones averages, which include the Dow Jones Industrial Average (DJIA). Also widely followed are the Standard & Poor's indexes, the NYSE composite index, the AMEX composite index, the Nasdaq Stock Market indexes, and the Value Line indexes. Numerous other averages and indexes, including a number of global and foreign market indexes, are regularly reported in financial publications.

Bond market indicators are most often reported in terms of average bond yields and average prices. The Dow Jones Corporate Bond Index is among the most popular. A wealth of yield and price index data is also available for various types of bonds and various domestic and foreign markets. Both stock and bond market statistics are published daily in the *Wall Street Journal* and summarized weekly in *Barron's*.

LG 4

Review the roles of full-service, premium discount, and basic discount stockbrokers, including the services they provide, selection of a stockbroker, opening an account, and transaction basics. Stockbrokers facilitate transactions among buyers and sellers of securities, and they provide a variety of other client services. An investor should select a stockbroker who has a compatible disposition toward investing and whose firm offers the desired services at competitive costs. Today the distinctions among full-service, premium discount, and basic discount brokers is blurring. Most brokers now offer online trading capabilities, and many no-frills brokers are expanding their services to include research and advice. Investors can open a variety of types of brokerage accounts, such as single, joint, custodial, cash, margin, and wrap. An investor can make odd-lot transactions (less than 100 shares) or round-lot transactions (100 shares or multiples thereof). An added fee is typically charged on odd-lot transactions.

LG 5

Describe the basic types of orders (market, limit, and stop-loss), online transactions, transaction costs, and the legal aspects of investor protection. A market order is an order to buy or sell stock at the best price available. A limit order is an order to buy at a specified price or below or to sell at a specified price or above. Stop-loss orders become market orders as soon as the minimum sell price or the maximum buy price is hit. Limit and stop-loss orders can be placed as fill-or-kill orders, day orders, or good-'til-canceled (GTC) orders.

On small transactions, most brokers have fixed-commission schedules; on larger transactions, they will negotiate commissions. Commissions also vary by type of security and type of broker: full-service, premium discount, or basic discount. The Securities Investor Protection Corporation (SIPC) insures customers' accounts against the brokerage firm's failure. To avoid litigation, mediation and arbitration procedures are frequently employed to resolve disputes between investor and broker. These disputes typically concern the investor's belief that the broker either gave bad advice or churned the account.

LG 6

Discuss the roles of investment advisers and investment clubs. There are a variety of different types of investment advisers, who charge an annual fee ranging from 0.25% to 3% of the dollar amount being managed and are often regulated by federal and state law. Web sites that provide investment advice on topics such as retirement planning, asset diversification, and stock and mutual fund selection are now available as well. Investment clubs provide individual investors with investment advice and help them gain investing experience. Online clubs have members in various geographical areas and conduct business via e-mail or at a private Web site.

Putting Your Investment Know-How to the Test

1. Which *one* of the following statements regarding the Dow Jones Industrial Average (DJIA) is *false?*
   a. The DJIA is a price-weighted index.
   b. The DJIA consists of 30 blue-chip stocks.
   c. The DJIA is affected equally by changes in low- and high-priced stocks.
   d. The DJIA divisor needs to be adjusted for stock split.

2. An investor sold a stock short and is worried about rising prices. To protect himself from rising prices, the investor would place a
   a. Stop order to sell.
   b. Stop order to buy.
   c. Limit order to sell.
   d. Limit order to buy.

3. Which of the following statements about types of orders and market makers is *false?*
   a. Market orders are orders to buy and sell at the best price available.
   b. Limit orders are orders to buy or sell away from the current market price.
   c. A short sale is the sale of stock an investor does not own with the intent of buying it back later.
   d. A stop buy order is typically used to protect a short position in a security and is placed below the current market price.

4. In calculating the Standard & Poor's stock price indices, the adjustment for stock splits occurs
   a. By adjusting the divisor.
   b. Automatically, due to the manner in which the index is calculated.
   c. By adjusting the numerator.
   d. Quarterly, on the last trading day of each quarter.

5. If you want your buy order to be executed immediately, you will place a
   a. Limit fill-or-kill order at bid.
   b. Limit day order at bid.
   c. Market order.
   d. Stop-loss order.

6. Which of the following statements about a price-weighted index is *true?*
   a. The S&P's 500 Index Composite is an unweighted price index.
   b. The Dow Jones Industrial Average is an example of a price-weighted index.
   c. A price-weighted index assumes an equal dollar investment in each stock in the index.
   d. The main problem with a price-weighted index is that companies with greater market capitalization have more of an impact on the index than do companies with less market capitalization.

7. Initial margin requirements on stocks are set by
   a. The Securities and Exchange Commission.
   b. The New York Stock Exchange.
   c. The Federal Reserve.
   d. Brokerage houses.

8. Investors who do their own research and are interested in frequent trading of securities at the lowest possible cost should consider services of
   a. Basic discount brokers.
   b. Full-service brokers.
   c. Premium discount brokers.
   d. Investment advisors.

9. The XYZ stock trades at $30.15 bid and $30.20 ask. You want to protect your investment by placing a $30 stop-limit order. When the bid price suddenly drops to $29.90, your order
   a. Automatically executes at $30.
   b. Becomes a market order.
   c. May not execute since the bid price has dropped to less than $30.
   d. Becomes a stop-loss order.

10. Which of the following is *true* about day trading?
    a. It is allowed only in OTC-listed stocks.
    b. It is less risky than buy-and-hold investing because it usually does not involve overnight holding of securities.
    c. It usually involves trading on margin.
    d. It permits investors to buy and sell stocks on credit as long as they buy and sell stocks on the same day.

Answers: 1. c; 2. b; 3. d; 4. b; 5. c; 6. b; 7. c; 8. a; 9. c; 10. c

Discussion Questions

LG 2

Q3.1 Thomas Weisel, chief executive of a securities firm that bears his name, believes that individual investors already have too much information. "Many lose money by trading excessively on stray data," he says. Other industry professionals oppose the SEC's fair disclosure rule for the same reason. The Securities Industry Association's general counsel expressed concern that the rule will restrict rather than encourage the flow of information. Other securities professionals argue that individual investors aren't really capable of interpreting much of the information now available to them. Explain why you agree or disagree with these opinions.

LG 2

Q3.2 Innovative Internet-based bookseller Amazon.com has now expanded into other retail categories. Gather appropriate information from relevant sources to assess the following with an eye toward investing in Amazon.com.

a. Economic conditions and the key current events during the past 12 months.
b. Information on the status and growth (past and future) of the bookselling industry and specific information on Amazon.com and its major competitors.
c. Brokerage reports and analysts' recommendations with respect to Amazon.com.
d. A history of the past and recent dividends and price behavior of Amazon.com, which is traded on the Nasdaq National Market.
e. A recommendation with regard to the advisability of investing in Amazon.com.

LG 2 LG 6

Q3.3 Visit four financial portals or other financial information Web sites listed in Table 3.4. Compare them in terms of ease of use, investment information, investment tools, advisory services, and links to other services. Also catalog the costs, if any, of obtaining these services. Which would you recommend, and why?

LG 3

Q3.4 Gather and evaluate relevant market averages and indexes over the past 6 months to assess recent stock and bond market conditions. Describe the conditions in each of these markets. Using recent history, coupled with relevant economic and current event data, forecast near-term market conditions. On the basis of your assessment of market conditions, would you recommend investing in stocks, in bonds, or in neither at this time? Explain the reasoning underlying your recommendation.

LG 4

Q3.5 Prepare a checklist of questions and issues you would use when shopping for a stockbroker. Describe both the ideal broker and the ideal brokerage firm, given your investment goals and disposition. Discuss the pros and cons of using a full-service rather than a premium discount or basic discount broker. If you plan to trade online, what additional questions would you ask?

LG 4

Q3.6 Visit the sites of two brokerages listed in Table 3.6 or any others you know. After exploring the sites, compare them for ease of use, quality of information, availability of investing tools, reliability, other services, and any other criteria important to you. Summarize your findings and explain which you would choose if you were to open an account, and why.

LG 5

Q3.7 Describe how, if at all, a conservative and an aggressive investor might use each of the following types of orders as part of their investment programs. Contrast these two types of investors in view of these preferences.

a. Market.
b. Limit.
c. Stop-loss.

LG 5

Q3.8 Learn more about day trading at sites such as Edgetrade (www.edgetrade.com), Daytradingthemarkets.com (www.daytradingstocks.com), TrendVue (www.trendVUE.com), and The Rookie DayTrader (www.rookiedaytrader.com). On the basis of your research, summarize the way in which day trading works, some strategies for day traders, the risks, and the rewards. What type of person would make a good day trader?

LG 6

Q3.9 Differentiate between the financial advice you would receive from a traditional investment adviser and one of the new online planning and advice sites. Which would you personally prefer to use, and why? How could membership in an investment club serve as an alternative to a paid investment adviser?

Problems

LG 2

P3.1 Bill Shaffer estimates that if he does 10 hours of research using data that will cost $75, there is a good chance that he can improve his expected return on a $10,000, 1-year investment from 8% to 10%. Bill feels that he must earn at least $10 per hour on the time he devotes to his research.

a. Find the cost of Bill's research.
b. By how much (in dollars) will Bill's return increase as a result of the research?
c. On a strict economic basis, should Bill perform the proposed research?

LG 3

P3.2 Imagine that the Mini-Dow Average (MDA) is based on the closing prices of five stocks. The divisor used in the calculation of the MDA is currently 0.765. The closing prices for each of the five stocks in the MDA today and exactly a year ago, when the divisor was 0.790, are given in the accompanying table.

	Closing Stock Price	
Stock	Today	One Year Ago
Ace Computers	$ 65	$74
Coburn Motor Company	37	34
National Soap & Cosmetics	110	96
Ronto Foods	73	72
Wings Aircraft	96	87

a. Calculate the MDA today and that of a year ago.
b. Compare the values of the MDA calculated in part (a) and describe the apparent market behavior over the last year. Was it a bull or a bear market?

LG 3

P3.3 The SP-6 index (a fictitious index) is used by many investors to monitor the general behavior of the stock market. It has a base value set equal to 100 at January 1, 1970. In the accompanying table, the closing market values for each of the six stocks included in the index are given for three dates.

Stock	Closing Market Value of Stock June 30, 2005 (Thousands)	January 1, 2005 (Thousands)	January 1, 1970 (Thousands)
1	$ 430	$ 460	$240
2	1,150	1,120	630
3	980	990	450
4	360	420	150
5	650	700	320
6	290	320	80

a. Calculate the value of the SP-6 index on both January 1, 2005, and June 30, 2005, using the data presented here.
b. Compare the values of the SP-6 index calculated in part (a) and relate them to the base index value. Would you describe the general market condition during the 6-month period January 1 to June 30, 2005, as a bull or a bear market?

LG 3

P3.4 Carla Sanchez wishes to develop an average or index that can be used to measure the general behavior of stock prices over time. She has decided to include six closely followed, high-quality stocks in the average or index. She plans to use August 15, 1978, her birthday, as the base and is interested in measuring the value of the average or index on August 15, 2002, and August 15, 2005. She has found the closing prices for each of the six stocks, A through F, at each of the three dates and has calculated a divisor that can be used to adjust for any stock splits, company changes, and so on that have occurred since the base year, which has a divisor equal to 1.00.

Stock	Closing Stock Price August 15, 2005	August 15, 2002	August 15, 1978
A	$46	$40	$50
B	37	36	10
C	20	23	7
D	59	61	26
E	82	70	45
F	32	30	32
Divisor	0.70	0.72	1.00

Note: The number of shares of each stock outstanding has remained unchanged at each of the three dates. Therefore, the closing stock prices will behave identically to the closing market values.

a. Using the data given in the table, calculate the market average, using the same methodology used to calculate the Dow averages, at each of the three dates—the 15th of August 1978, 2002, and 2005.
b. Using the data given in the table and assuming a base index value of 10 on August 15, 1978, calculate the market index, using the same methodology used to calculate the S&P indexes, at each of the three dates.
c. Use your findings in parts **a** and **b** to describe the general market condition—bull or bear—that existed between August 15, 2002, and August 15, 2005.
d. Calculate the percentage changes in the average and index values between August 15, 2002, and August 15, 2005. Why do they differ?

LG 5

P3.5 Al Cromwell places a *market order* to buy a round lot of Thomas, Inc., common stock, which is traded on the NYSE and is currently quoted at $50 per share. Ignoring brokerage commissions, how much money would Cromwell probably have to pay? If he had placed a market order to sell, how much money will he probably receive? Explain.

LG 5 P3.6 Imagine that you have placed a *limit order* to buy 100 shares of Sallisaw Tool at a price of $38, though the stock is currently selling for $41. Discuss the consequences, if any, of each of the following.

a. The stock price drops to $39 per share 2 months before cancellation of the limit order.
b. The stock price drops to $38 per share.
c. The minimum stock price achieved before cancellation of the limit order was $38.50. When the limit order was canceled, the stock was selling for $47.50 per share.

LG 5 P3.7 If you place a *stop-loss order* to sell at $23 on a stock currently selling for $26.50 per share, what is likely to be the minimum loss you will experience on 50 shares if the stock price rapidly declines to $20.50 per share? Explain. What if you had placed a *stop-limit order* to sell at $23, and the stock price tumbled to $20.50?

LG 5 P3.8 You sell 100 shares of a stock short for $40 per share. You want to limit your loss on this transaction to no more than $500. What order should you place?

LG 5 P3.9 You have been researching a stock that you like, which is currently trading at $50 per share. You would like to buy the stock if it were a little less expensive—say, $47 per share. You believe that the stock price will go to $70 by year-end, and then level off or decline. You decide to place a limit order to buy 100 shares of the stock at $47, and a limit order to sell it at $70. It turns out that you were right about the direction of the stock price, and it goes straight to $75. What is your current position?

LG 5 P3.10 You own 500 shares of Ups&Downs, Inc., stock. It is currently priced at $50. You are going on vacation, and you realize that the company will be reporting earnings while you are away. To protect yourself against a rapid drop in the price, you place a limit order to sell 500 shares at $40. It turns out the earnings report was not so good, and the stock price fell to $30 right after the announcement. It did, however, bounce back, and by the end of the day it was back to $42. What happened in your account?

LG 5 P3.11 You have $5,000 in a 50% margin account. You have been following a stock that you think you want to buy. The stock is priced at $52. You decide that if the stock falls to $50, you would like to buy it. You place a limit order to buy 300 shares at $50. The stock falls to $50. What happens?

See the text Web site (www.aw-bc.com/gitman_joehnk) for Web exercises that deal with *online information and investing*.

Case Problem 3.1 *The Perezes' Good Fortune*

LG 2 LG 4 LG 6

Angel and Marie Perez own a small pool hall located in southern New Jersey. They enjoy running the business, which they have owned for nearly 3 years. Angel, a retired professional pool shooter, saved for nearly 10 years to buy this business, which he and his wife own free and clear. The income from the pool hall is adequate to allow Angel, Marie, and their two children, Mary (age 10) and José (age 4), to live comfortably.

Although he lacks formal education beyond the tenth grade, Angel has become an avid reader. He enjoys reading about current events and personal finance, particularly investing. He especially likes *Money* magazine, from which he has gained numerous ideas for better managing the family's finances. Because of the long hours required to run the business, Angel can devote 3 to 4 hours a day (on the job) to reading.

Recently, Angel and Marie were notified that Marie's uncle had died and left them a portfolio of stocks and bonds with a current market value of $300,000. They were elated to learn of their good fortune but decided it would be best not to change their lifestyle as a result of this inheritance. Instead, they want their newfound wealth to provide for their children's college education as well as their own retirement. They decided that, like their uncle, they would keep these funds invested in stocks and bonds. Angel felt that in view of this, he needed to acquaint himself with the securities currently in the portfolio. He knew that to manage the portfolio himself, he would have to stay abreast of the securities markets as well as the economy in general. He also realized that he would need to follow each security in the portfolio and continuously evaluate possible alternative securities that could be substituted as conditions warranted. Because Angel had plenty of time in which to follow the market, he strongly believed that with proper information, he could manage the portfolio. Given the amount of money involved, Angel was not too concerned with the information costs; rather, he wanted the best information he could get at a reasonable price.

Questions

a. Explain what role the *Wall Street Journal* and/or *Barron's* might play in meeting Angel's needs. What other general sources of economic and current event information would you recommend to Angel? Explain.

b. How might Angel be able to use the services of Standard & Poor's Corporation, Mergent, and the *Value Line Investment Survey* to learn about the securities in the portfolio? Indicate which, if any, of these services you would recommend, and why.

c. Recommend some specific online investment information sources and tools to help Angel and Marie manage their investments.

d. Explain to Angel the need to find a good stockbroker and the role the stockbroker could play in providing information and advice. Should he consider hiring a financial adviser to manage the portfolio?

e. Give Angel a summary prescription for obtaining information and advice that will help to ensure the preservation and growth of the family's newfound wealth.

Case Problem 3.2 *Peter and Deborah's Choices of Brokers and Advisers*

LG 4 LG 5 LG 6

Peter Chang and Deborah Barry, friends who work for a large software company, decided to leave the relative security of their employer and join the staff of OnlineSpeed Inc., a 2-year-old company working on new broadband technology for fast Internet access. Peter will be a vice president for new-product development; Deborah will be treasurer. Although they are excited about the potential their new jobs offer, they recognize the need to consider the financial implications of the move. Of immediate concern are their 401(k) retirement plans. On leaving their current employer, each of them will receive a lump-sum settlement of about $75,000 that they must roll over into self-directed, tax-deferred retirement accounts. The friends met over lunch to discuss their options for investing these funds.

Peter is 30 years old and single, with a bachelor's degree in computer science. He rents an apartment and would like to buy a condominium fairly soon but is in no rush. For now, he is happy using his money on the luxuries of life. He considers himself a bit of a risk taker and has dabbled in the stock market from time to time, using his technology expertise to invest in software and Internet companies. Deborah's undergraduate degree was in English, followed by an M.B.A. in finance. She is 32, is married, and hopes to start a family very soon. Her husband is a physician in private practice.

Peter is very computer-savvy and likes to pick stocks on the basis of his own Internet research. Although Deborah's finance background gives her a solid understanding of investing fundamentals, she is more conservative and has thus far stayed with blue-chip stocks and mutual funds. Among the topics that come up during their lunchtime conversation are stockbrokers and financial planners. Peter is leaning toward a bare-bones basic discount broker with low cost per online trade that is offering free trades for a limited time. Deborah is also cost-conscious but warns Peter that the low costs can be deceptive if you have to pay for other services or find yourself trading more often. She also thinks Peter is too focused on the technology sector and encourages him to seek financial advice to balance his portfolio. They agree to research a number of brokerage firms and investment advisers and meet again to compare notes.

Questions

a. Research at least four different full-service, premium discount, and basic discount stock brokerage firms, and compare the services and costs. What brokers would suit Peter's needs best, and why? What brokers would suit Deborah's needs best, and why? What are some key questions each should ask when interviewing potential brokers?

b. What factors should Peter and Deborah consider before deciding to use a particular broker? Compare the pros and cons of getting the personal attention of a full-service broker with the services provided by the discount brokers.

c. Do you think that a broker that assists in making transactions and focuses on personal attention would be a good choice for either Peter or Deborah?

d. Peter mentioned to Deborah that he had read an article about *day trading* and wanted to try it. What would you advise Peter about the risks and rewards of this strategy?

e. Prepare a brief overview of the traditional and online sources of investment advice that could help Peter and Deborah create suitable portfolios. Which type of adviser would you recommend for Peter? For Deborah? Explain your reasoning.

Excel with Spreadsheets

Peter Tanaka is interested in starting a stock portfolio. He has heard many financial reporters talk about the Dow Jones Industrial Average (DJIA) as being a proxy for the overall stock market. From visiting various online investment sites, Peter is able to track the variability in the Dow. Peter would like to develop an average or index that will measure the price performance of his selected portfolio over time. He has decided to create a price-weighted index, similar to the Dow where the stocks are held in proportion to their share prices. He wishes to form an index based on the following ten high quality stocks and has designated October 13, 1971, as the base year. The number of shares outstanding has remained constant over the time period 1971 through 2005. The implication is that the closing stock prices will behave just like the closing market values. Given the data below, create a spreadsheet to model and analyze the use of an index.

	Prices		
Stocks	10/13/2005	10/13/2001	10/13/1971
A	45	50	55
B	12	9	15
C	37	37	37
D	65	66	67
E	36	42	48
F	26	35	43
G	75	68	59
H	35	38	30
I	67	74	81
J	84	88	92

Questions

a. The divisor is 1.00 on October 13, 1971, .75 on October 13, 2001, and .85 on October 13, 2005. Using this information and the data supplied above, calculate the market average, using the same methodology used to calculate the Dow averages, on each of the three dates—the 13th of October 1971, 2001, and 2005.

b. The DJIA is the most widely cited stock market indicator, yet there are criticisms of the model. One criticism is that the higher-priced securities in the portfolio will impact the Dow more than the relatively lower-priced stocks. Assume that Stock J increases by 10%. Recalculate the market averages on each of the three dates.

c. Next, assume Stock J is back to its original level and Stock B increases by 10%. Recalculate the market averages on each of the three dates. Compare your findings in all three scenarios. Do you find support for the criticism of the Dow? Explain.

CHAPTER 4

RETURN AND RISK

CHAPTER 4

RETURN AND RISK

LEARNING GOALS

After studying this chapter, you should be able to:

LG 1 Review the concept of return, its components, the forces that affect the investor's level of return, and historical returns.

LG 2 Discuss the time value of money and the calculations involved in finding the future value of various types of cash flows.

LG 3 Explain the concept of present value, the procedures for calculating present values, and the use of present value in determining whether an investment is satisfactory.

LG 4 Describe real, risk-free, and required returns and the computation and application of holding period return, yield (internal rate of return), and growth rates.

LG 5 Discuss the key sources of risk and how they might affect potential investment vehicles.

LG 6 Understand the risk of a single asset, risk assessment, and the steps that combine return and risk.

When you go shopping for a stereo system, you go to the store, consult a catalog, or visit a Web site to examine the merchandise. When you invest in the stock of a company, you may be familiar with its products, but this information tells only part of the story. Suppose you are considering buying the stock of ChevronTexaco, a major global energy company. A visit to the company's Web site, www.chevrontexaco.com, would tell you that the company was on the upswing, with the first half of fiscal year 2003 (June 30, 2003) showing huge gains over the same period in 2002. For this 6-month period, revenues were up 30%, net income was up 218%, and earnings per share were up 210%. The company also reduced its debt from its December 31, 2002, levels and raised its dividend for the sixteenth consecutive year.

This promising picture might increase your desire to buy the stock. But before placing that buy order, you should investigate the risks associated with the stock by searching the business press and online investment sites for articles and investment research about ChevronTexaco. Your research would tell you that the higher 2003 revenues reflected product price increases, while the healthy jump in net income arose in part because 2002 earnings were low due to expenses of the Chevron–Texaco merger. The energy industry has risks specific to it, such as the potential for failure of costly exploration efforts. ChevronTexaco's presence in more than 180 countries exposes it to additional external risk. For example, a political coup in a country where ChevronTexaco has refineries or pipelines could disrupt operations. Changes in legislation in foreign countries could affect taxation. Currency exchange risk is another key factor for ChevronTexaco.

To use this information wisely, you need to understand the concepts of return and risk, which lie at the heart of any investment decision. In this chapter we'll explain which factors affect the level of investment return and consider how to assess the different types of risk.

Sources: "ChevronTexaco," Yahoo! Finance, downloaded from http://finance.yahoo.com, accessed September 29, 2003; "ChevronTexaco Reports Second Quarter Net Income of $1.6 Billion," ChevronTexaco Corporation press release, August 1, 2003, downloaded from the ChevronTexaco Web site, www.chevrontexaco.com.

The Concept of Return

LG 1

Investors are motivated to invest in a given vehicle by its expected return. The **return** is the level of profit from an investment—that is, the reward for investing. Suppose you have $1,000 in an insured savings account paying 5% annual interest, and a business associate asks you to lend her that much money. If you lend her the money for 1 year, at the end of which she pays you back, your return will depend on the amount of interest you charge. If you make an interest-free loan, your return will be zero. If you charge 5% interest, your return will be $50 (0.05 × $1,000). Because you are already earning a safe 5% on the $1,000, it seems clear that to equal that return you should charge your associate a minimum of 5% interest.

return
the level of profit from an investment—that is, the reward for investing.

Some investment vehicles guarantee a return; others do not. The return earned on $1,000 deposited in an insured savings account at a large bank can be viewed as certain. The return earned on a $1,000 loan to your business associate might be less certain. What is your return if she runs into financial difficulty? If she can repay you only $850, your return will be minus $150 ($850 − $1,000), or minus 15% (−$150 ÷ $1,000). Thus the size of the expected return is one important factor in choosing a suitable investment.

INVESTOR FACTS

DIVIDENDS MATTER—Don't overlook dividends when considering stock returns! According to Standard & Poor's, dividends account for 42% of the S&P 500's total return since 1926. Without dividends, the S&P returned on average only 6.3% annually, compared to 10.2% with dividends. In addition, dividend payers tended to be less volatile than non-dividend payers.

Source: Bob Bobala, "Get Paid to Invest," *Motley Fool*, August 28, 2003, downloaded from www.fool.com.

Components of Return

The return on an investment may come from more than one source. The most common source is periodic payments, such as dividends or interest. The other source of return is appreciation in value, the gain from selling an investment vehicle for more than its original purchase price. We call these two sources of return *current income* and *capital gains* (or *capital losses*), respectively.

Current Income Current income may take the form of dividends from stocks, interest received on bonds, or dividends received from mutual funds. To be considered income, it must be in the form of cash or be readily convertible into cash. For our purposes, **current income** is usually cash or near-cash that is periodically received as a result of owning an investment.

current income
usually cash or near-cash that is periodically received as a result of owning an investment.

Using the data in Table 4.1 (on page 134), we can calculate the current income from investments A and B, both purchased for $1,000, over a 1-year period of ownership. Investment A would provide current income of $80, investment B $120. Solely on the basis of the current income received over the 1-year period, investment B seems preferable.

Capital Gains (or Losses) The second dimension of return is concerned with the change, if any, in the market value of an investment. As noted in Chapter 1, the amount by which the proceeds from the sale of an investment exceed its original purchase price is called a *capital gain*. If an investment is sold for less than its original purchase price, a *capital loss* results.

We can calculate the capital gain or loss of the investments as shown in Table 4.1. For investment A, a capital gain of $100 ($1,100 sale price − $1,000 purchase price) is realized over the 1-year period. For investment B, a $40 capital loss results ($960 sale price − $1,000 purchase price).

Combining the capital gain (or loss) with the current income (calculated in the preceding section) gives the **total return** on each investment over the 1-year ownership period as shown in Table 4.2 (on page 134). In terms of the total return earned on the $1,000 investment over the 1-year period, investment A is superior to investment B.

total return
the sum of the current income and the capital gain (or loss) earned on an investment over a specified period of time.

TABLE 4.1 Profiles of Two Investments

	Investment A	Investment B
Purchase price (beginning of year)	$1,000	$1,000
Cash received		
1st quarter	$ 10	$ 0
2nd quarter	20	0
3rd quarter	20	0
4th quarter	30	120
Total current income (for year)	$ 80	$ 120
Sale price (end of year)	$1,100	$ 960

TABLE 4.2 Total Returns of Two Investments

Return	Investment A	Investment B
Current income	$ 80	$120
Capital gain (loss)	100	(40)
Total return	$180	$ 80

INVESTOR FACTS

WHAT A DIFFERENCE 9 MONTHS MAKES—Don't get too caught up in historical rates of return. Given the stock market's current volatility, they may not be a good predictor of future returns. For example, based on data through September 26, 2003, the 3-year return for the business/online services industry was −0.14%. Change the time horizon to 1 year, however, and the return soars to more than 158%, while for 3 months it's only 16%. Clearly, neither the 3-year nor the 1-year return is a good indicator of future performance for this industry.

Source: "Stock Returns," *Morningstar.com*, September 28, 2003, downloaded from www.morningstar.com.

The use of *percentage returns* is generally preferred to the use of dollar returns. Percentages allow direct comparison of different sizes and types of investments. Investment A earned an 18% return ($180 ÷ $1,000), whereas B yielded only an 8% return ($80 ÷ $1,000). At this point investment A appears preferable, but differences in risk might cause some investors to prefer B. (We will see why later in this chapter.)

Why Return Is Important

Return is a key variable in the investment decision: It allows us to compare the actual or expected gains of various investments with the levels of return we need. For example, you would be satisfied with an investment that earns 12% if you needed it to earn only 10%. You would not be satisfied with a 10% return if you needed a 14% return. Return can be measured historically, or it can be used to formulate future expectations.

Historical Performance Although most people recognize that future performance is not guaranteed by past performance, they would agree that past data often provide a meaningful basis for future expectations. A common practice in the investment world is to look closely at the historical performance of a given vehicle when formulating expectations about its future.

Interest rates and other measures of financial return are most often cited on an annual basis. Evaluation of past investment returns is typically done on the same basis. Consider the data for a hypothetical investment presented in Table 4.3. Two aspects of these data are important. First, we can determine the

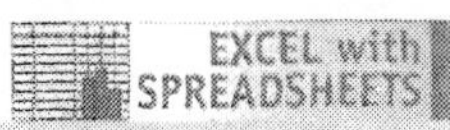

TABLE 4.3 Historical Investment Data for a Hypothetical Investment

		Market Value (Price)			Total Return	
Year	(1) Income	(2) Beginning of Year	(3) End of Year	(4) (3) − (2) Capital Gain	(5) (1) + (4) ($)	(6) (5) ÷ (2) (%)*
1996	$4.00	$100	$ 95	−$ 5.00	−$ 1.00	− 1.00%
1997	3.00	95	99	4.00	7.00	7.37
1998	4.00	99	105	6.00	10.00	10.10
1999	5.00	105	115	10.00	15.00	14.29
2000	5.00	115	125	10.00	15.00	13.04
2001	3.00	125	120	− 5.00	− 2.00	− 1.60
2002	3.00	120	122	2.00	5.00	4.17
2003	4.00	122	130	8.00	12.00	9.84
2004	5.00	130	140	10.00	15.00	11.54
2005	5.00	140	155	15.00	20.00	14.29
Average	$4.10			$ 5.50	$ 9.60	8.20%

*Percent return on beginning-of-year market value of investment.

average level of return generated by this investment over the past 10 years. Second, we can analyze the trend in this return. As a percentage, the average total return (column 6) over the past 10 years was 8.20%. Looking at the yearly returns, we can see that after the negative return in 1996, 4 years of positive and generally increasing returns occurred before the negative return was repeated in 2001. From 2002 through 2005, positive and increasing returns were again realized.

expected return
the return an investor thinks an investment will earn in the future.

Expected Return In the final analysis, it's the future that matters when we make investment decisions. Therefore, **expected return** is a vital measure of performance. It's what you think the investment will earn in the future that determines what you should be willing to pay for it.

To demonstrate, let's return to the data in Table 4.3. Looking at the historical return figures in the table, an investor would note the increasing trend in returns from 2002 through 2005. But to project future returns, we need insights into the investment's prospects. If the trend in returns seems likely to continue, an expected return in the range of 12% to 15% for 2006 or 2007 would seem reasonable. On the other hand, if future prospects seem poor, or if the investment is subject to cycles, an expected return of 8% to 9% may be a more reasonable estimate. Over the past 10 years, the investment's returns have cycled from a poor year (1996 and 2001) to 4 years of increasing returns (1997–2000 and 2002–2005). We might therefore expect low returns in 2006 to be followed by increasing returns in the 2007–2010 period.

Level of Return

The level of return achieved or expected from an investment will depend on a variety of factors. The key factors are internal characteristics and external forces.

Internal Characteristics Certain characteristics of an investment affect its level of return. Examples include the type of investment vehicle, the quality of management, how the investment is financed, and the customer base of the issuer. For example, the common stock of a large, well-managed, completely equity-financed plastics manufacturer whose major customer is IBM would be expected to provide a level of return different from that of a small, poorly managed, largely debt-financed clothing manufacturer whose customers are small specialty stores. As we will see in later chapters, assessing internal factors and their impact on return is one important step in analyzing potential investments.

External Forces External forces such as Federal Reserve actions, shortages, war, price controls, and political events may also affect the level of return. None of these are under the control of the issuer of the investment vehicle. Investment vehicles are affected differently by these forces. It is not unusual to find two vehicles with similar internal characteristics offering significantly different returns. As a result of the same external force, the expected return from one vehicle may increase, while that of another decreases. Likewise, the economies of various countries respond to external forces in different ways.

inflation
a period of generally rising prices.

deflation
a period of generally declining prices.

Another external force is the *general level of price changes,* either up—**inflation**—or down—**deflation.** Inflation tends to have a positive impact on investment vehicles such as real estate, and a negative impact on vehicles such as stocks and fixed-income securities. Rising interest rates, which normally accompany increasing rates of inflation, can significantly affect returns. The actions, if any, the federal government takes to control inflation can increase, decrease, or have no effect on investment returns. Furthermore, the return on each type of investment vehicle exhibits its own unique response to inflation. The *Investing in Action* box on page 137 looks at the returns in the stock market in recent years, and considers whether such returns are likely to continue and what to do if they do not.

Historical Returns

Investment returns vary both over time and between different types of investments. By averaging historical returns over a long period of time, it is possible to eliminate the impact of various types of risk. This enables the investor to focus on the differences in return that are attributable primarily to the types of investment. Table 4.4 shows the average annual rates of return for a number of

TABLE 4.4 Historical Returns for Popular Security Investments (1926–2002)

Investment	Average Annual Return
Large-company stocks	12.2%
Small-company stocks	16.9
Long-term corporate bonds	6.2
Long-term government bonds	5.8
U.S. Treasury bills	3.8
Inflation	3.1%

Source: Stocks, Bonds, Bills, and Inflation, 2003 Yearbook (Chicago: Ibbotson Associates, Inc., 2002), p. 33.

INVESTING IN ACTION

MANY HAPPY RETURNS . . . MAYBE

Until 2000, it was fairly easy to make money in the stock market. From April 1991 through December 2000, the economy continued to expand—for a record 117 months, compared to an average expansion of 35 months. Even novice investors have enjoyed stellar returns. For example, during the period 1990–1999 the average annual return on the S&P 500 stocks was 18.2%, and it climbed to a whopping 28.4% from 1995 through 1999. That return is considerably higher than the 1926–2002 average annual return of 12.2% per year, compared with 6.2% for long-term bonds over the same period. According to Jeremy Siegel, finance professor at the University of Pennsylvania's Wharton School, stocks outperformed bonds and cash in 80% of the 10-year periods dating back to 1802, when the first data became available.

Yet investors who started buying stocks during the past few years got a rude wake-up call in 2000, when the markets turned from bull to bear. No longer could they expect average returns of 15% to 30% and ignore the market's brief bear-like periods, saying, "It's just a minor correction. Stocks will bounce back." From 1998 to 2003, annual returns averaged a mere 1.7%; for the period January 1, 2000, to June 30, 2003, returns slid to −4.7% (based on the Dow Jones Industrial Average). Bond yields also tumbled to a four-decade low. If this kind of bear market coincides with your retirement, you could find yourself unable to afford the lifestyle you envisioned.

Many experts, including Warren Buffet and Wharton's Siegel, believe that lower returns will be the norm for at least the next decade as investors who saw their portfolios dwindle in the recent bear market hesitate to buy stocks again. Even with annual returns in the 5% to 7% range, however, stocks offer the best growth picture for the long term, outpacing bonds or cash after taking inflation into account. "That math isn't bad, but it is bad for people who expected long-term returns based on looking in the rear-view mirror," comments Buffett.

What can you do to ride out the market's twists and turns? Plan to invest for the long term, because you can't predict stock market gains in advance. They come in sudden clumps—a big month or two, followed by flat or down months. If you try to time the market, by selling when a price drop scares you and buying when prices are rising, you won't benefit from the market's successful long-term record. Focus on what share prices will be in the future, using analysis techniques like the ones we describe in Part Three of this book, not what they were 3 years ago. Invest as much as you can now, and let compounding work in your favor. Don't be dazzled by companies with rapid revenue growth but not profits. Finally, diversify your portfolio among asset classes (more on this in Chapter 5).

CRITICAL THINKING QUESTIONS What has history taught us about the stock market? What should you do to ride out the market's twists and turns?

Sources: Jeff Brown, "Even a Good January Doesn't Guarantee You Solid Returns This Year," *Knight Ridder Tribune News Service*, January 6, 2003, downloaded from ProQuest, proquest.umi.com; Jonathan Clements, "Why Baby Boomers Shouldn't Root for a Quick Stock-Market Rebound," *Wall Street Journal*, March 26, 2003, p. D.1; Terence Flanagan, "Buffett Tells Investors to Be Realistic About Stock Returns," *Washington Post*, May 4, 2003, p. A.7; and Kathy Kristof, "Bull Run Shouldn't Lead Expectations Astray," *Dallas Morning News*, May 5, 2000, p. 5H.

popular security investments (and inflation) over the 77-year period January 1, 1926, through December 31, 2002. Each rate represents the average annual rate of return an investor would have realized had he or she purchased the investment on January 1, 1926, and sold it on December 31, 2002. You can see that significant differences exist between the average annual rates of return realized on the various types of stocks, bonds, and bills shown. Later in this chapter, we will see how these differences in return can be linked to differences in the risk of each of these investments.

CONCEPTS IN REVIEW

4.1 Explain what is meant by the *return* on an investment. Differentiate between the two components of return—current income and capital gains (or losses).

4.2 What role do historical performance data play in estimating the expected return from a given investment? Discuss the key factors affecting investment returns—internal characteristics and external forces.

The Time Value of Money*

LG 2 LG 3

time value of money
the fact that as long as an opportunity exists to earn interest, the value of money is affected by the point in time when the money is received.

Imagine that at age 25 you begin making annual cash deposits of $1,000 into a savings account that pays 5% annual interest. After 40 years, at age 65, you will have made deposits totaling $40,000 (40 years × $1,000 per year). Assuming you made no withdrawals, what do you think your account balance will be—$50,000? $75,000? $100,000? The answer is none of the above. Your $40,000 will have grown to nearly $121,000! Why? Because the time value of money allows the deposits to earn interest, and that interest also earns interest over the 40 years. **Time value of money** refers to the fact that as long as an opportunity exists to earn interest, the value of money is affected by the point in time when the money is received.

As a general rule, *the sooner you receive a return on a given investment, the better.* For example, two investments each requiring a $1,000 outlay and each expected to return $100 interest over a 2-year holding period are *not necessarily* equally desirable. If the first investment returns $100 at the end of the first year and the second investment returns the $100 at the end of the second year, the first investment is preferable (assuming that the base value of each remains at $1,000). Investment 1 is preferable because the $100 interest it earns could be *reinvested to earn more interest* while the $100 in interest from investment 2 is still accruing at the end of the first year. You should not fail to consider time value concepts when making investment decisions.

Interest: The Basic Return to Savers

interest
the "rent" paid by a borrower for use of the lender's money.

A savings account at a bank is one of the most basic forms of investment. The saver receives interest in exchange for placing idle funds in an account. **Interest** can be viewed as the "rent" paid by a borrower for use of the lender's money. The saver will experience neither a capital gain nor a capital loss, because the value of the investment (the initial deposit) will change only by the amount of interest earned. For the saver, the interest earned over a given time frame is that period's current income.

simple interest
interest paid only on the initial deposit for the amount of time it is held.

Simple Interest The income paid on investment vehicles that pay interest (such as CDs and bonds) is most often calculated using **simple interest:** Interest

* This section presents the fundamental concepts and techniques of time value of money. Those already familiar with these important ideas may wish to skip this discussion and continue at the heading "Determining a Satisfactory Investment" on page 149.

is paid only on the initial deposit for the amount of time it is held. For example, if you held a \$100 initial deposit in an account paying 6% interest for 1½ years, you would earn \$9 in interest (1½ × 0.06 × \$100) over this period. Had you withdrawn \$50 at the end of half a year, the total interest earned over the 1½ years would be \$6. You would earn \$3 interest on \$100 for the first half-year (½ × 0.06 × \$100) and \$3 interest on \$50 for the next full year (1 × 0.06 × \$50).

true rate of interest (return)
the actual rate of interest earned.

When an investment earns simple interest, the stated rate of interest is the **true rate of interest** (or **return**). This is the actual rate of interest earned. In the foregoing example, the true rate of interest is 6%. Because the interest rate reflects the rate at which current income is earned regardless of the size of the deposit, it is a useful measure of current income.

compound interest
interest paid not only on the initial deposit but also on any interest accumulated from one period to the next.

Compound Interest **Compound interest** is interest paid not only on the initial deposit but also on any interest accumulated from one period to the next. This is the method typically used by savings institutions. When interest is compounded annually over a single year, compound and simple interest calculations provide similar results. In such a case, the stated interest rate and the true interest rate are equal.

The data in Table 4.5 illustrate compound interest. In this case, the interest earned each year is left on deposit rather than withdrawn. The \$50 of interest earned on the \$1,000 initial deposit during 2004 becomes part of the beginning (initial) balance on which interest is paid in 2005, and so on. *Note that simple interest is used in the compounding process;* that is, interest is paid only on the initial balance held during the given time period.

When an investment earns compound interest, the stated and true interest rates are equal only when interest is compounded annually. In general, *the more frequently interest is compounded at a stated rate, the higher the true rate of interest.* The interest calculations for the deposit data in Table 4.5, assuming that interest is compounded semiannually (twice a year), are shown in Table 4.6 (on page 140). The interest for each 6-month period is found by multiplying the beginning (initial) balance for the 6 months by half of the stated 5% interest rate (see column 3 of Table 4.6). You can see that larger returns are associated with more frequent compounding: Compare the end-of-2006 account balance at 5% compounded annually with the end-of-2006 account balance at 5% compounded semiannually. The semiannual compounding results in a higher balance (\$1,879.19 versus \$1,876.88). Clearly, with semiannual compounding, the true rate of interest is greater than the 5%

EXCEL with SPREADSHEETS

TABLE 4.5 **Savings Account Balance Data (5% interest compounded annually)**

Date	(1) Deposit (Withdrawal)	(2) Beginning Account Balance	(3) 0.05 × (2) Interest for Year	(4) (2) + (3) Ending Account Balance
1/1/04	\$1,000	\$1,000.00	\$50.00	\$1,050.00
1/1/05	(300)	750.00	37.50	787.50
1/1/06	1,000	1,787.50	89.38	1,876.88

TABLE 4.6 Savings Account Balance Data (5% interest compounded semiannually)

Date	(1) Deposit (Withdrawal)	(2) Beginning Account Balance	(3) 0.05 × 1/2 × (2) Interest for 6 Months	(4) (2) + (3) Ending Account Balance
1/1/04	$1,000	$1,000.00	$25.00	$1,025.00
7/1/04		1,025.00	25.63	1,050.63
1/1/05	(300)	750.63	18.77	769.40
7/1/05		769.40	19.24	788.64
1/1/06	1,000	1,788.64	44.72	1,833.36
7/1/06		1,833.36	45.83	1,879.19

TABLE 4.7 True Rate of Interest for Various Compounding Frequencies (5% stated rate of interest)

Compounding Frequency	True Rate of Interest	Compounding Frequency	True Rate of Interest
Annually	5.000%	Monthly	5.120%
Semiannually	5.063	Weekly	5.125
Quarterly	5.094	Continuously	5.127

annually compounded rate. The true rates of interest associated with a 5% stated rate and various compounding frequencies are shown in Table 4.7.

continuous compounding interest calculation in which interest is compounded over the smallest possible interval of time.

Continuous compounding calculates interest by compounding over the smallest possible interval of time. It results in the maximum true rate of interest that can be achieved with a given stated rate of interest. Table 4.7 shows that the more frequently interest is compounded, the higher the true rate of interest. Because of the impact that differences in compounding frequencies have on return, you should evaluate the true rate of interest associated with various alternatives before making a deposit.

Computational Aids for Use in Time Value Calculations

Time-consuming calculations are often involved in adjusting for the time value of money. Although you should understand the concepts and mathematics underlying these calculations, the application of time value techniques can be streamlined. We will demonstrate the use of financial tables, hand-held financial calculators, and computers and spreadsheets as computational aids.

Financial Tables Financial tables include various interest factors that simplify time value calculations. The values in these tables are easily developed from formulas, with various degrees of rounding. The tables are typically indexed by the interest rate (in columns) and the number of periods (in rows). Figure 4.1 shows this general layout. The interest factor at a 20% interest rate for 10 years would be found at the intersection of the 20% column and the 10-period row, as shown by the dark blue box. A full set of the four basic financial tables is included in Appendix A at the end of the book. These tables are described more fully later in this chapter.

FIGURE 4.1

Financial Tables

Layout and use of a financial table

	Interest Rate					↓		
Period	1%	2%	...	10%	...	**20%**	...	50%
1			...		...	⋮	...	
2			...		...	⋮	...	
3			...		...	⋮	...	
⋮	⋮	⋮	...	⋮	...	⋮	...	⋮
→ **10**	...	...	...	...	...	**X.XXX**	...	...
⋮	⋮	⋮	...	⋮	...	⋮	...	⋮
20			...		...		...	
⋮	⋮	⋮	...	⋮	...	⋮	...	⋮
50			...		...		...	

Financial Calculators Financial calculators also can be used for time value computations. Generally, *financial calculators* include numerous preprogrammed financial routines. In this and later chapters, we show the keystrokes for various financial computations.

We focus primarily on the keys pictured and defined in Figure 4.2. We typically use four of the five keys in the left column, plus the compute (CPT) key. One of the four keys represents the unknown value being calculated. (Occasionally, all five of the keys are used, with one representing the unknown value.) The keystrokes on some of the more sophisticated calculators are menu-driven: After you select the appropriate routine, the calculator prompts you to input each value; on these calculators, a compute key is not needed to obtain a solution. Regardless, any calculator with the basic time value functions can be used in lieu of financial tables. The keystrokes for other financial calculators are explained in the reference guides that accompany them.

HOT

The Time Value software Web site contains several financial calculators—home financing, investment, lease, personal finance, and retirement. To calculate time values on investments, go to Time Value software and then to Investment Calculators. As with any tool, we recommend that you exercise good judgment before relying on the results.

www.timevalue.com/toolinfo.htm

Once you understand the basic underlying concepts, you probably will want to use a calculator to streamline routine financial calculations. With a little practice, you can increase both the speed and the accuracy of your financial computations. Note that because of a calculator's greater precision, slight differences are likely to exist between values calculated by using financial

FIGURE 4.2

Calculator Keys

Important financial keys on the typical calculator

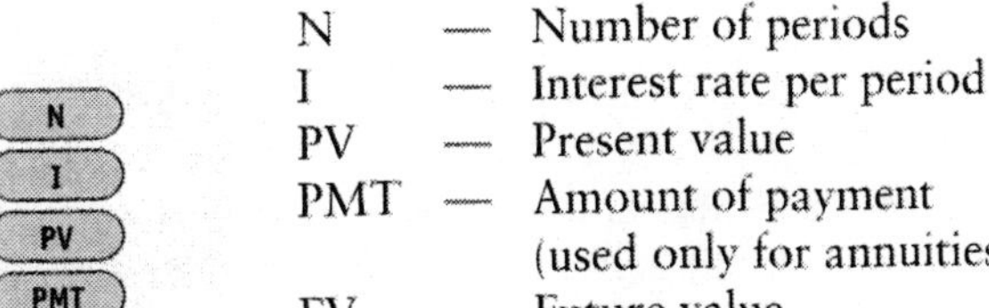

N — Number of periods
I — Interest rate per period
PV — Present value
PMT — Amount of payment (used only for annuities)
FV — Future value
CPT — Compute key used to initiate financial calculation once all values are input

tables and those found with a financial calculator. Remember that *conceptual understanding of the material is the objective*. An ability to solve problems with the aid of a calculator does not necessarily reflect such an understanding, so don't just settle for answers. Work with the material until you are sure you also understand the concepts.

Computers and Spreadsheets Like financial calculators, computers and spreadsheets have built-in routines that simplify time value calculations. We provide in the text a number of spreadsheet solutions that identify the cell entries for calculating time values. The value for each variable is entered in a cell in the spreadsheet, and the calculation is programmed using an equation that links the individual cells. If values of the variables are changed, the solution automatically changes as a result of the equation linking the cells. In the spreadsheet solutions in this book, the equation that determines the calculation is shown at the bottom of the spreadsheet.

The ability to use spreadsheets has become a prime skill for today's investors. As the saying goes, "Get aboard the bandwagon, or get run over." The spreadsheet solutions we present in this book will help you climb up onto that bandwagon!

Future Value: An Extension of Compounding

future value
the amount to which a current deposit will grow over a period of time when it is placed in an account paying compound interest.

Future value is the amount to which a current deposit will grow over a period of time when it is placed in an account paying compound interest. Consider a deposit of $1,000 that is earning 8% (0.08 in decimal form) compounded annually. The following calculation yields the future value of this deposit at the end of 1 year.

Equation 4.1

$$\text{Future value at end of year 1} = \$1{,}000 \times (1 + 0.08) = \underline{\underline{\$1{,}080}}$$

If the money were left on deposit for another year, 8% interest would be paid on the account balance of $1,080. Thus, at the end of the second year, there would be $1,166.40 in the account. This amount would represent the beginning-of-year balance of $1,080 plus 8% of the $1,080 ($86.40) in interest. The future value at the end of the second year would be calculated as follows.

Equation 4.2

$$\text{Future value at end of year 2} = \$1{,}080 \times (1 + 0.08) = \underline{\underline{\$1{,}166.40}}$$

To find the future value of the $1,000 at the end of year *n*, the procedure illustrated above would be repeated *n* times. Future values can be determined either mathematically or by using a financial table, financial calculator, or a computer and spreadsheet. Here we demonstrate use of a table of future-value interest factors, use of a calculator, and use of an Excel spreadsheet.

TABLE USE The factors in Appendix A, Table A.1 represent the amount to which an initial $1 deposit would grow for various periods (typically years) and interest rates. For example, a dollar deposited in an account paying 8%

interest and left there for 2 years would accumulate to $1.166. Using the future-value interest factor for 8% and 2 years (1.166), we can find the future value of an investment that can earn 8% over 2 years: We would *multiply* the amount invested by the appropriate interest factor. In the case of $1,000 left on deposit for 2 years at 8%, the resulting future value is $1,166 (1.166 × $1,000). This agrees (except for a slight rounding difference) with the value calculated in Equation 4.2.

A few points with respect to Appendix A, Table A.1, Future-Value Interest Factors for One Dollar, should be emphasized.

1. The values in the table represent factors for determining the future value of one dollar at the *end* of the given year.
2. As the interest rate increases for any given year, the future-value interest factor also increases. The higher the interest rate, the greater the future value.
3. For a given interest rate, the future value of a dollar increases with the passage of time.
4. The future-value interest factor is always greater than 1. Only if the interest rate were zero would this factor equal 1, and the future value would therefore equal the initial deposit.

INVESTOR FACTS

TIME IS ON YOUR SIDE—It's never too early to begin saving for retirement, even if it seems a long way off. The power of compounding—which Albert Einstein once called the "eighth wonder of the world"—will multiply your funds considerably. If you began today and socked away $2,000 per year for just the next 8 years into an account that earned 10% per year and left those funds on deposit until the end of 40 years, that $16,000 would grow to more than $480,000. You can wait, but it will cost you. Time is your biggest investment ally.

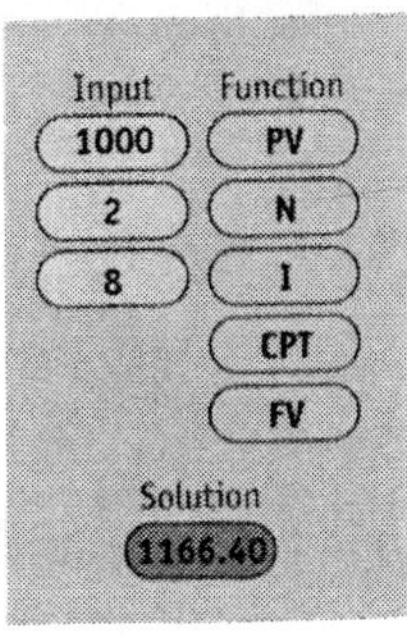

Calculator Use* A financial calculator can be used to calculate the future value directly.** First punch in $1,000 and depress **PV**; next punch in 2 and depress **N**; then punch in 8 and depress **I**.† Finally, to calculate the future value, depress **CPT** and then **FV**. The future value of $1,166.40 should appear on the calculator display as shown in the art at the left. On many calculators, this value will be preceded by a minus sign (−1166.40). *If a minus sign appears on your calculator, ignore it here as well as in all other "Calculator Use" illustrations in this text.*‡

The calculator is more accurate than the future value factors, which have been rounded to the nearest 0.001. Therefore, a slight difference will frequently exist between the values found by these alternative methods. In this case, there is a $.40 difference. Clearly, the improved accuracy and ease of

* Many calculators allow the user to set the number of payments per year. Most of these calculators are preset for monthly payments—12 payments per year. Because we work primarily with annual payments—one payment per year—it is important *to be sure that your calculator is set for one payment per year*. And although most calculators are preset to recognize that all payments occur at the end of the period, it is important *to make sure that your calculator is correctly set on the END mode*. Consult the reference guide that accompanies your calculator for instructions for setting these values.

** To avoid including previous data in current calculations, *always clear all registers of your calculator before inputting values and making each computation.*

† The known values *can be punched into the calculator in any order*. The order specified in this as well as other demonstrations of calculator use included in this text merely reflects convenience and personal preference.

‡ The calculator differentiates inflows from outflows with a negative sign. For example, in the problem just demonstrated, the $1,000 present value (PV), because it was keyed as a positive number (1000) is considered an inflow or deposit. Therefore, the calculated future value (FV) of −1166.40 is preceded by a minus sign to show that it is the resulting outflow or withdrawal. Had the $1,000 present value been keyed in as a negative number (−1000), the future value of $1166.40 would have been displayed as a positive number (1166.40). Simply stated, *present value* (PV) *and future value* (FV) *cash flows will have opposite signs.*

calculation tend to favor the use of the calculator. (*Note:* In future examples of calculator use, we will use only a display similar to that shown on the previous page. If you need a reminder of the procedure involved, come back and review the preceding paragraph.)

SPREADSHEET USE The future value of the single amount also can be calculated as shown on the following Excel spreadsheet.

	A	B
1	FUTURE VALUE OF A SINGLE AMOUNT	
2	Present value	$1,000
3	Interest rate, pct per year compounded annually	8%
4	Number of years	2
5	Future value	$1,166.40

Entry in Cell B5 is =FV(B3,B4,0,–B2,0).
The minus sign appears before B2 because the present value is an outflow (i.e., the initial deposit).

Future Value of an Annuity

annuity
a stream of equal cash flows that occur at equal intervals over time.

ordinary annuity
an annuity for which the cash flows occur at the *end* of each period.

An **annuity** is a stream of equal cash flows that occur at equal intervals over time. Receiving $1,000 per year at the end of each of the next 8 years is an example of an annuity. The cash flows can be *inflows* of returns earned from an investment or *outflows* of funds invested (deposited) to earn future returns.

Investors are sometimes interested in finding the future value of an annuity. Their concern is typically with what's called an **ordinary annuity**—one for which the cash flows occur at the *end* of each period. Here we can simplify our calculations by using either tables of the factors for an annuity, a financial calculator, or an Excel spreadsheet. (A complete set of these tables is included in Appendix A, Table A.2.)

TABLE USE The factors in Appendix A, Table A.2 represent the amount to which annual end-of-year deposits of $1 would grow for various periods (years) and interest rates. For example, a dollar deposited at the end of each year for 8 years into an account paying 6% interest would accumulate to $9.897. Using the future-value interest factor for an 8-year annuity earning 6% (9.897), we can find the future value of this cash flow: We would *multiply* the annual investment by the appropriate interest factor. In the case of $1,000 deposited at the end of each year for 8 years at 6%, the resulting future value is $9,897 (9.897 × $1,000).

Input	Function
1000	PMT
8	N
6	I
	CPT
	FV

Solution
9897.47

CALCULATOR USE When a financial calculator is used to find the future value of an annuity, the annual deposit is input using the **PMT** key (rather than the **PV** key, which was used to find the future value of a single deposit). Use of the **PMT** key tells the calculator that a stream of **N** (the number of years input) end-of-year deposits in the amount of **PMT** dollars represents the deposit stream.

Using the calculator inputs shown at the left, we find the future value of the $1,000, 8-year ordinary annuity earning a 6% annual rate of interest to be $9,897.47. This is a slightly more precise answer than that found by using the table.

SPREADSHEET USE The future value of the ordinary annuity also can be calculated as shown on the following Excel spreadsheet.

	A	B
1	**FUTURE VALUE OF AN ORDINARY ANNUITY**	
2	Annual payment	$1,000
3	Annual rate of interest, compounded annually	6%
4	Number of years	8
5	Future value of an ordinary annuity	$9,897.47
	Entry in Cell B5 is =FV(B3,B4,–B2) The minus sign appears before B2 because the annual payment is a cash outflow.	

Present Value: An Extension of Future Value

present value
the *value today* of a sum to be received at some future date; the inverse of future value.

discount rate
the annual rate of return that could be earned currently on a similar investment; used when finding present value; also called *opportunity cost*.

Present value is the inverse of future value. That is, rather than measuring the value of a present amount at some future date, **present value** expresses the *current value of a future sum.* By applying present-value techniques, we can calculate the *value today* of a sum to be received at some future date.

When determining the present value of a future sum, we are answering the basic question, "How much would have to be deposited today into an account paying *i*% interest in order to equal a specified sum to be received so many years in the future?" The applicable interest rate when we are finding present value is commonly called the **discount rate** (or *opportunity cost*). It represents the annual rate of return that could be earned currently on a similar investment.

The basic present-value calculation is best illustrated using a simple example. Imagine that you are offered an opportunity that will provide you, 1 year from today, with exactly $1,000. If you could earn 8% on similar types of investments, how much is the most you would pay for this opportunity? In other words, what is the present value of $1,000 to be received 1 year from now, discounted at 8%? Letting *x* equal the present value, we can use Equation 4.3 to describe this situation.

Equation 4.3

$$x \times (1 + 0.08) = \$1{,}000$$

Solving Equation 4.3 for *x*, we get:

Equation 4.4

$$x = \frac{\$1{,}000}{(1 + 0.08)} = \underline{\underline{\$925.93}}$$

Thus the present value of $1,000 to be received 1 year from now, discounted at 8%, is $925.93. In other words, $925.93 deposited today into an account paying 8% interest will accumulate to $1,000 in 1 year. To check this conclusion, *multiply* the future-value interest factor for 8% and 1 year, or 1.080 (from Appendix A, Table A.1), by $925.93. The result is a future value of $1,000 (1.080 × $925.93).

The calculations involved in finding the present value of sums to be received in the distant future are more complex than those for a 1-year investment. Here we use either tables of present-value interest factors to simplify these calculations, a financial calculator, or an Excel spreadsheet. (A complete set of these tables is included in Appendix A, Table A.3.)

TABLE USE The factors in Appendix A, Table A.3 represent the present value of \$1 associated with various combinations of periods (years) and discount (interest) rates. For example, the present value of \$1 to be received 1 year from now discounted at 8% is \$0.926. Using this factor (0.926), we can find the present value of \$1,000 to be received 1 year from now at an 8% discount rate by *multiplying* it by \$1,000. The resulting present value of \$926 (0.926 × \$1,000) agrees (except for a slight rounding difference) with the value calculated in Equation 4.4.

Another example may help clarify the use of present-value tables. The present value of \$500 to be received 7 years from now, discounted at 6%, is calculated as follows:

$$\text{Present value} = 0.665 \times \$500 = \underline{\underline{\$332.50}}$$

The 0.665 represents the present-value interest factor from Appendix A, Table A.3 for 7 years discounted at 6%.

A few points with respect to Appendix A, Table A.3, Present-Value Interest Factors for One Dollar, should be emphasized.

1. The present-value interest factor for a single sum is always less than 1. Only if the discount rate were zero would this factor equal 1.
2. The higher the discount rate for a given year, the smaller the present-value interest factor. In other words, the greater your opportunity cost, the less you have to invest today in order to have a given amount in the future.
3. The further in the future a sum is to be received, the less it is worth at present.
4. At a discount rate of 0%, the present-value interest factor always equals 1. Therefore, in such a case the future value of a sum equals its present value.

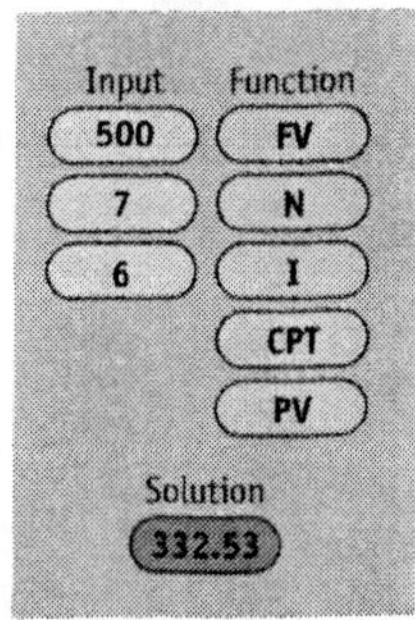

CALCULATOR USE Using the financial calculator inputs shown at the left, we find the present value of \$500 to be received 7 years from now, discounted at 6%, to be \$332.53. This value is slightly more precise than that found using the table, but for our purposes the difference is insignificant.

SPREADSHEET USE The present value of the single future amount also can be calculated as shown on the following Excel spreadsheet.

	A	B
1	PRESENT VALUE OF A SINGLE FUTURE AMOUNT	
2	Future value	\$500
3	Interest rate, pct per year compounded annually	6%
4	Number of years	7
5	Present value	\$332.53
	Entry in Cell B5 is =–PV(B3,B4,0,B2). The minus sign appears before PV to change the present value to a positive amount.	

The Present Value of a Stream of Returns

In the preceding paragraphs we illustrated the technique for finding the present value of a single sum to be received at some future date. Because the returns from a given investment are likely to be received at various future dates rather than as a single lump sum, we also need to be able to find the present value of a *stream of returns*. A stream of returns can be viewed as a package of single-sum returns; it may be classified as a mixed stream or an annuity. A **mixed stream** of returns is one that exhibits no special pattern. As noted earlier, an *annuity* is a stream of equal periodic returns. Table 4.8 shows the end-of-year returns illustrating each of these types of patterns. To find the present value of each of these streams (measured at the *beginning* of 2005), we must calculate the total of the present values of the individual annual returns. Because shortcuts can be used for an annuity, calculation of the present value of each type of return stream is illustrated separately.

mixed stream
a stream of returns that, unlike an annuity, exhibits no special pattern.

Present Value of a Mixed Stream To find the present value of the mixed stream of returns given in Table 4.8, we must find and then total the present values of the individual returns. Assuming a 9% discount rate, we can streamline the calculation of the present value of the mixed stream using financial tables, a financial calculator, or an Excel spreadsheet.

TABLE USE Table A.3 in Appendix A can be used to find the appropriate present-value interest factors for each of the 5 years of the mixed stream's life at the 9% discount rate. Table 4.9 (on page 148) demonstrates the use of these factors, shown in column 2, with the corresponding year's return, shown in column 1, to calculate the present value of each year's return, shown in column 3. The total of the present values of the returns for each of the 5 years is found by summing column 3. The resulting present value of $187.77 represents the amount today (*beginning* of 2005) that, invested at 9%, would provide the same returns as those shown in column 1 of Table 4.9.

CALCULATOR USE You can use a financial calculator to find the present value of each individual return, as demonstrated on page 146. You then sum the present values to get the present value of the stream. However, most financial calculators have a function that allows you to punch in *all returns* (typically referred to as *cash flows*), specify the discount rate, and then directly calculate the present value of the entire return stream. Because calculators provide solutions

EXCEL with SPREADSHEETS

TABLE 4.8 Mixed and Annuity Return Streams

End of Year	Returns	
	Mixed Stream	Annuity
2005	$30	$50
2006	40	50
2007	50	50
2008	60	50
2009	70	50

EXCEL with SPREADSHEETS

TABLE 4.9 Mixed-Stream Present-Value Calculation

End of Year	(1) Return	(2) 9% Present-Value Interest Factor	(3) (1) × (2) Present Value
2005	$30	.917	$ 27.51
2006	40	.842	33.68
2007	50	.772	38.60
2008	60	.708	42.48
2009	70	.650	45.50
		Present value of stream	$187.77

Note: Column 1 values are from Table 4.8. Column 2 values are from Appendix A, Table A.3, for a 9% discount rate and 1 through 5 periods (years).

more precise than those based on rounded table factors, the present value of the mixed stream of returns in Table 4.8, found using a calculator, will be close to, but not precisely equal to, the $187.77 (see Table 4.9).

SPREADSHEET USE The present value of the mixed stream of returns also can be calculated as shown on the following Excel spreadsheet.

	A	B
1	PRESENT VALUE OF A MIXED STREAM OF RETURNS	
2	Discount Rate, pct/year	9%
3	Year	Year-End Return
4	1	$30
5	2	$40
6	3	$50
7	4	$60
8	5	$70
9	Present value	$187.80
	Entry in Cell B9 is =NPV(B2,B4:B8).	

Investing about $188 would provide exactly a 9% return.

Present Value of an Annuity The present value of an annuity can be found in the same way as the present value of a mixed stream. Fortunately, however, there are simpler approaches. Here we simplify our calculations by using either tables of these factors for an annuity, a financial calculator, or an Excel spreadsheet. (A complete set of these tables is included in Appendix A, Table A.4.)

TABLE USE The factors in Appendix A, Table A.4 represent the present value of a $1 annuity for various periods (years) and discount (interest) rates. For example, the present value of $1 to be received at the end of each year for the next 5 years discounted at 9% is $3.890. Using the present-value interest factor for a 5-year annuity discounted at 9% (3.890), we can find the present value of the $50, 5-year annuity (given in Table 4.8) at a 9% discount rate: We *multiply* the annual return by the appropriate interest factor. The resulting present value is $194.50 (3.890 × $50).

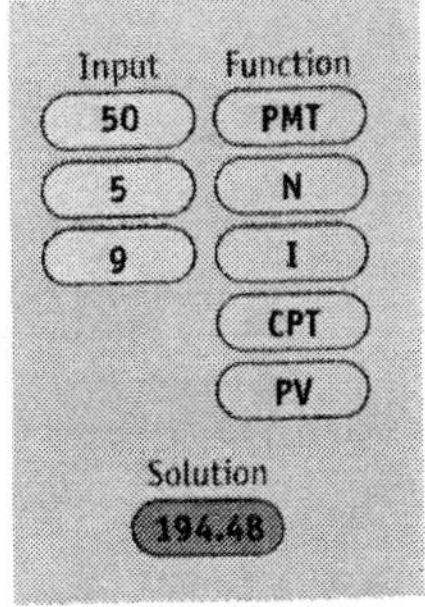

Calculator Use Using the calculator inputs shown at the left, we find the present value of the $50, 5-year ordinary annuity of returns, discounted at a 9% annual rate, to be $194.48. (*Note:* Because the return stream is an annuity, the annual return is input using the **PMT** key rather than the **FV** key, which was used for finding the present value of a single return.) The value obtained with the calculator is slightly more accurate than the answer found using the table.

Spreadsheet Use The present value of the annuity of returns also can be calculated as shown on the following Excel spreadsheet.

	A	B
1	PRESENT VALUE OF ANNUITY RETURNS	
2	Annual return	$50
3	Annual discount rate, compounded annually	9%
4	Number of years	5
5	Present value of an ordinary annuity	$194.48

Entry in Cell B5 is =PV(B3,B4,–B2).
The minus sign appears before B2 because
the annual return is a cash outflow.

Determining a Satisfactory Investment

satisfactory investment
an investment whose present value of benefits (discounted at the appropriate rate) *equals* or *exceeds* the present value of its costs.

Time value of money techniques can be used to determine an acceptable investment. Ignoring risk at this point, a **satisfactory investment** would be one for which the present value of benefits (discounted at the appropriate rate) *equals* or *exceeds* the present value of its costs. Because the cost of the investment would be incurred initially (at time zero), the cost and its present value are viewed as one and the same. The three possible benefit–cost relationships and their interpretations follow:

1. If the present value of the benefits *just equals the cost,* you would earn a rate of return equal to the discount rate.
2. If the present value of benefits *exceeds the cost,* you would earn a rate of return greater than the discount rate.
3. If the present value of benefits is *less than the cost,* you would earn a rate of return less than the discount rate.

You would prefer only those investments for which the present value of benefits equals or exceeds its cost—situations 1 and 2. In these cases, the rate of return would be equal to or greater than the discount rate.

The information in Table 4.10 (on page 150) demonstrates the application of present value to investment decision making using a financial table. (*Note:* A financial calculator or an Excel spreadsheet could have been used, as described earlier, to find the present value of this mixed-stream investment.)

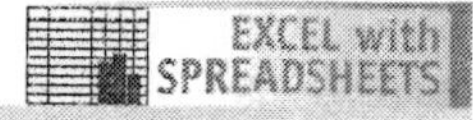

TABLE 4.10 Present Value Applied to an Investment

End of Year	(1) Return	(2) 8% Present-Value Interest Factor*	(3) (1) × (2) Present Value
2005	$ 90	.926	$ 83.34
2006	100	.857	85.70
2007	110	.794	87.34
2008	120	.735	88.20
2009	100	.681	68.10
2010	100	.630	63.00
2011	1,200	.583	699.60
		Present value of returns	$1,175.28

* Column 2 values are from Appendix A, Table A.3, for an 8% discount rate and 1 through 7 periods (years).

Assuming an 8% discount rate, we can see that the present value (at the beginning of 2005) of the returns (benefits) to be received over the assumed 7-year period (year-end 2005 through year-end 2011) is $1,175.28. If the cost of the investment (beginning of 2005) were any amount less than or equal to the $1,175.28 present value, it would be acceptable. At that cost, a rate of return equal to at least 8% would be earned. At a cost above the $1,175.28 present value, the investment would not be acceptable. At that cost, the rate of return would be less than 8%. Clearly, in that case it would be preferable to find an alternative investment with a present value of benefits that equals or exceeds its cost.

CONCEPTS IN REVIEW

4.3 What is the *time value of money?* Explain why an investor should be able to earn a positive return.

4.4 Define, discuss, and contrast the following terms.

a. Interest
b. Simple interest
c. Compound interest
d. True rate of interest (or return)

4.5 When interest is compounded more frequently than annually at a stated rate, what happens to the *true rate of interest?* Under what condition would the stated and true rates of interest be equal? What is *continuous compounding?*

4.6 Describe, compare, and contrast the concepts of *future value* and *present value.* Explain the role of the *discount rate* in calculating present value.

4.7 What is an *annuity?* How can calculation of the future value of an annuity be simplified? What about the present value of an annuity?

4.8 What is a *mixed stream* of returns? Describe the procedure used to find the present value of such a stream.

4.9 What is a *satisfactory investment?* When the present value of benefits exceeds the cost of an investment, what is true of the rate of return earned by the investor relative to the discount rate?

Measuring Return

LG 4

Thus far, we have discussed the concept of return in terms of its two components (current income and capital gains) and the key factors that affect the level of return (internal characteristics and external forces). These discussions intentionally oversimplified the computations involved in determining the historical or expected return. To compare returns from different investment vehicles, we need to incorporate time value of money concepts that explicitly consider differences in the timing of investment income and capital gains. We must also be able to place a current value on future benefits. Here we will look at several measures that enable us to compare alternative investment vehicles. First, we must define and consider the relationships among various rates of return.

Real, Risk-Free, and Required Returns

required return
the rate of return an investor must earn on an investment to be fully compensated for its risk.

Rational investors will choose investments that fully compensate them for the risk involved. The greater the risk, the greater the return required by investors. The return that fully compensates for an investment's risk is called the **required return.** To better understand required returns, it is helpful to consider their makeup. The required return on any investment *j* consists of three basic components: the real rate of return, an expected inflation premium, and a risk premium, as noted in Equation 4.5.

Equation 4.5

$$\text{Required return on investment } j = \text{Real rate of return} + \text{Expected inflation premium} + \text{Risk premium for investment } j$$

Equation 4.5a

$$r_j = r^* + IP + RP_j$$

real rate of return
the rate of return that could be earned in a perfect world where all outcomes are known and certain—where there is no risk.

expected inflation premium
the average rate of inflation expected in the future.

risk-free rate
the rate of return that can be earned on a risk-free investment; the sum of the real rate of return and the expected inflation premium.

The **real rate of return** is the rate of return that could be earned in a perfect world where all outcomes were known and certain—where there is no risk. In such a world, the real rate of return would create an equilibrium between the supply of savings and the demand for funds. The real rate of return changes with changing economic conditions, tastes, and preferences. Historically, it has been relatively stable and in the range of 0.5% to 2%. For convenience, we'll assume a real rate of return of 2%.

The **expected inflation premium** represents the average rate of inflation expected in the future. By adding the expected inflation premium to the real rate of return, we get the **risk-free rate.** This is the rate of return that can be earned on a risk-free investment, most commonly a 3-month U.S. Treasury bill. The formula for this rate is shown in Equation 4.6.

Equation 4.6

$$\text{Risk-free rate} = \text{Real rate of return} + \text{Expected inflation premium}$$

Equation 4.6a

$$R_F = r^* + IP$$

To demonstrate, a real rate of return of 2% and an expected inflation premium of 4% would result in a risk-free rate of return of 6%.

risk premium
a return premium that reflects the issue and issuer characteristics associated with a given investment vehicle.

The required return can be found by adding to the risk-free rate a **risk premium**, which varies depending on specific issue and issuer characteristics. *Issue characteristics* are the type of vehicle (stock, bond, etc.), its maturity (2 years, 5 years, infinity, etc.), and its features (voting/nonvoting, callable/noncallable, etc.). *Issuer characteristics* are industry and company factors such as the line of business and financial condition of the issuer. Together, the issue and issuer factors cause investors to require a risk premium above the risk-free rate.

Substituting the risk-free rate, R_F, from Equation 4.6a, into Equation 4.5a for the first two terms to the right of the equals signs ($r^* + IP$), we get Equation 4.7.

Equation 4.7

$$\text{Required return on investment } j = \text{Risk-free rate} + \text{Risk premium for investment } j$$

Equation 4.7a

$$r_j = R_F + RP_j$$

For example, if the required return on IBM common stock is 11% when the risk-free rate is 6%, investors require a 5% risk premium (11% − 6%) as compensation for the risk associated with common stock (the issue) and IBM (the issuer). Later in Chapter 5, we will explore further the relationship between the risk premium and required returns.

Next, we consider the specifics of return measurement.

Holding Period Return

The return to a *saver* is the amount of interest earned on a given deposit. Of course, the amount "invested" in a savings account is not subject to change in value, as is the amount invested in stocks, bonds, and mutual funds. Because we are concerned with a broad range of investment vehicles, we need a measure of return that captures both periodic benefits and changes in value. One such measure is *holding period return.*

holding period
the period of time over which one wishes to measure the return on an investment vehicle.

The **holding period** is the period of time over which one wishes to measure the return on an investment vehicle. When comparing returns, be sure to use holding periods of the same length. For example, comparing the return on a stock over the 6-month period ended December 31, 2004, with the return on a bond over the 1-year period ended June 30, 2004, could result in a poor investment decision. To avoid this problem, be sure you define the holding period. It is often best to annualize the holding period and use that as a standard. And when comparing the returns from alternative investment vehicles, you should use similar periods in time.

realized return
current income actually received by an investor during a given period.

Understanding Return Components Earlier in this chapter we identified the two components of investment return: current income and capital gains (or losses). The portion of current income received by the investor during the period is a **realized return.** Most but not all current income is realized. (Accrued interest on taxable zero-coupon bonds is treated as current income for tax purposes but is not a realized return until the bond is sold or matures.) Capital gains returns, on the other hand, are realized only when the investment vehicle is actually sold at the end of the holding period. Until the vehicle is sold, the capital gain is merely a **paper return.**

paper return
a return that has been achieved but not yet realized by an investor during a given period.

For example, the capital gain return on an investment that increases in market value from $50 to $70 during a year is $20. For that capital gain to be realized, you would have to have sold the investment for $70 at the end of that year. An investor who purchased the same investment but plans to hold it for another 3 years would also have experienced the $20 capital gain return during the year specified, but he or she *would not have realized the gain in terms of cash flow.* However, *even if the capital gains return is not realized during the period over which the total return is measured, it must be included in the return calculation.*

A second point to recognize about returns is that both the current income and the capital gains component can have a negative value. Occasionally, an investment may have negative current income. That is, you may be required to pay out cash to meet certain obligations. This situation is most likely to occur in various types of property investments. For example, assume you have purchased an apartment complex and the rental income is inadequate to meet the payments associated with its operation. In such a case, you would have to pay the deficit in operating costs, and that payment would represent negative current income. A capital loss can occur on *any* investment vehicle: Stocks, bonds, mutual funds, options, futures, real estate, and gold can all decline in market value over a given holding period.

holding period return (HPR)
the total return earned from holding an investment for a specified holding period (*usually 1 year or less*).

Computing the Holding Period Return (HPR) The **holding period return (HPR)** is the total return earned from holding an investment for a specified period of time (the holding period). The HPR is customarily used with holding periods of *1 year or less.* (We'll explain why later.) It represents the sum of current income and capital gains (or losses) achieved over the holding period, divided by the beginning investment value (market price). The equation for HPR is

Equation 4.8

$$\text{Holding period return} = \frac{\text{Current income during period} + \text{Capital gain (or loss) during period}}{\text{Beginning investment value}}$$

Equation 4.8a

$$HPR = \frac{C + CG}{V_0}$$

where

Equation 4.9

$$\text{Capital gain (or loss) during period} = \text{Ending investment value} - \text{Beginning investment value}$$

Equation 4.9a

$$CG = V_n - V_0$$

The HPR equation provides a convenient method for either measuring the total return realized or estimating the total return expected. For example, Table 4.11 (on page 154) summarizes the key financial variables for four investment vehicles over the past year. The total current income and capital

TABLE 4.11 **Key Financial Variables for Four Investment Vehicles**

	Investment Vehicle			
	Savings Account	Common Stock	Bond	Futures Contract
Cash received				
1st quarter	$15	$10	$ 0	$0
2nd quarter	15	10	70	0
3rd quarter	15	10	0	0
4th quarter	15	15	70	0
(1) Total current income	$60	$45	$140	$0
Investment value				
End-of-year	$1,000	$2,200	$ 970	$3,300
(2) Beginning-of-year	1,000	2,000	1,000	3,000
(3) Capital gain (loss)	$ 0	$ 200	($ 30)	$ 300
(4) Total return [(1) + (3)]	$ 60	$ 245	$ 110	$ 300
(5) Holding period return [(4) ÷ (2)]	6.00%	12.25%	11.00%	10.00%

gain or loss during the holding period are given in the lines labeled (1) and (3), respectively. The total return over the year is calculated, as shown in line (4), by adding these two sources of return. Dividing the total return value [line (4)] by the beginning-of-year investment value [line (2)], we find the holding period return, given in line (5). Over the 1-year holding period the common stock had the highest HPR (12.25%). The savings account had the lowest (6%).

As these calculations show, all we need to find the HPR is beginning- and end-of-period investment values, along with the value of current income received by the investor during the period. Note that if the current income and capital gain (or loss) values in lines (1) and (3) of Table 4.11 had been drawn from a 6-month rather than a 1-year period, the HPR values calculated in line 18 would have been *the same.*

Holding period return can be negative or positive. HPRs can be calculated with Equation 4.8 using either historical data (as in the preceding example) or forecast data.

Using the HPR in Investment Decisions The holding period return is easy to use in making investment decisions. Because it considers both current income and capital gains relative to the beginning investment value, it tends to overcome any problems that might be associated with comparing investments of different size. If we look only at the total returns calculated for each of the four investments in Table 4.11 [line (4)], the futures contract investment appears best, because it has the highest total return. However, the futures contract investment would require the largest dollar outlay ($3,000). The holding period return offers a *relative comparison,* by dividing the total return by the amount of the investment. Comparing HPRs [line (5)], we find the investment alternative with the *highest return per invested dollar* to be the common stock's HPR of 12.25%. Because the return per invested dollar reflects the efficiency of the investment, the HPR provides a logical method for evaluating and comparing investment returns, particularly for holding periods of 1 year or less.

Yield: The Internal Rate of Return

An alternative way to define a satisfactory investment is in terms of the compound annual rate of return it earns. Why do we need an alternative to the HPR? Because *HPR fails to consider the time value of money.* Although the holding period return is useful with investments held for 1 year or less, it is generally inappropriate for longer holding periods. Sophisticated investors typically do not use HPR when the time period is greater than 1 year. Instead, they use a present-value-based measure, called **yield** (or **internal rate of return**), to determine the compound annual rate of return earned on investments held for longer than 1 year. Yield can also be defined as the discount rate that produces a present value of benefits just equal to its cost.

yield (internal rate of return) the compound annual rate of return earned by a long-term investment; the discount rate that produces a present value of the investment's benefits that just equals its cost.

Once you know the yield you can decide whether an investment is acceptable. If the yield on an investment *is equal to or greater than the required return,* then the investment is acceptable. An investment with a yield *below the required return* is unacceptable; it will not compensate you adequately for the risk involved.

The yield on an investment providing a single future cash flow is relatively easy to calculate. The yield on an investment providing a stream of future cash flows generally involves more time-consuming calculations. Many hand-held financial calculators and Excel spreadsheets are available for simplifying these calculations.

Yield for a Single Cash Flow Some investments, such as U.S. savings bonds, stocks paying no dividends, zero-coupon bonds, and futures contracts, are purchased by paying a fixed amount up front. The investor expects them to provide *no periodic income,* but to provide a single—and, the investor hopes, a large—future cash flow at maturity or when the investment is sold. The yield on investments expected to provide a single future cash flow can be estimated using financial tables, a financial calculator, or an Excel spreadsheet.

Table Use Assume you wish to find the yield on an investment costing $1,000 today that you expect will be worth $1,400 at the end of a 5-year holding period. We can find the yield on this investment by solving for the discount rate that causes the present value of the $1,400 to be received 5 years from now to equal the initial investment of $1,000.

The first step involves dividing the present value ($1,000) by the future value ($1,400), which results in a value of 0.714. The second step is to find in the table of present-value interest factors the 5-year factor that is closest to 0.714. Referring to the present-value table (Appendix A, Table A.3), we find that for 5 years the factor closest to 0.714 is 0.713, which occurs at a 7% discount rate. Therefore, the yield on this investment is about 7%. If you require a 6% return, this investment is acceptable (7% expected return ≥ 6% required return).

Input	Function
1000	PV
-1400	FV
5	N
	CPT
	I

Solution
6.96

Calculator Use Using a financial calculator to find the yield for the investment described above, we can treat the earliest value as a present value, **PV**, and the latest value as a future value, **FV**. (*Note:* Most calculators require *either* the **PV** or the **FV** value to be input as a negative number to calculate an unknown yield.) Using the inputs shown at the left, we find the yield to be 6.96%. This is consistent with, but more precise than, the value found using Appendix A, Table A.3.

SPREADSHEET USE The yield for the single cash flow also can be calculated as shown on the following Excel spreadsheet.

	A	B
1	YIELD FOR A SINGLE CASH FLOW	
2	Point in Time	Cash Flow
3	Future	$1,400
4	Present	$1,000
5	Number of Years	5
6	Yield	6.96%

Entry in Cell B6 is
= Rate((B5),0,–B4,B3,0).
The minus sign appears before B4
because the present investment
is treated as a cash outflow.

Yield for a Stream of Income Investment vehicles such as income-oriented stock and bonds typically provide the investor with a *stream of income.* The yield (or internal rate of return) for a stream of income (returns) is generally more difficult to estimate. The most accurate approach is based on searching for the discount rate that produces a present value of income just equal to the cost of the investment. It can be applied using financial tables, a financial calculator, or an Excel spreadsheet.

TABLE USE If we use the investment in Table 4.10 and assume that its cost is $1,100, we find that the yield must be greater than 8%. At an 8% discount rate, the present value of income (calculated in column 3 of Table 4.10) is greater than the cost ($1,175.28 versus $1,100). The present values at 9% and

EXCEL with SPREADSHEETS

TABLE 4.12 Yield Calculation for an $1,100 Investment

Year	(1) Income	(2) 9% Present-Value Interest Factor	(3) (1) × (2) Present Value at 9%	(4) 10% Present-Value Interest Factor	(5) (1) × (4) Present Value at 10%
2005	$ 90	.917	$ 82.53	.909	$ 81.81
2006	100	.842	84.20	.826	82.60
2007	110	.772	84.92	.751	82.61
2008	120	.708	84.96	.683	81.96
2009	100	.650	65.00	.621	62.10
2010	100	.596	59.60	.564	56.40
2011	1,200	.547	656.40	.513	615.60
	Present value of income		$1,117.61		$1,063.08

INVESTOR FACTS

STAY THE COURSE—Don't give in to the temptation to buy and sell as market returns fluctuate. After the boom years of the late 1990s, the markets were down for the 3-year period 2000–2003. Yet if 10 years ago you had bought a portfolio containing a diversified group of stocks and left it alone, it would have earned an average return of 9% per year, for a total gain, with compounding, of 142%. Resisting the temptation to time the market can certainly pay off!

Source: Jeff Brown, "Even a Good January Doesn't Guarantee You Solid Returns This Year," *Knight Ridder Tribune News Service*, January 6, 2003, downloaded from Proquest, proquest.umi.com.

10% discount rates are calculated in Table 4.12. If we look at the present values of income calculated at the 9% and 10% rates, we see that the yield on the investment must be somewhere between 9% and 10%. At 9% the present value ($1,117.61) is too high. At 10% the present value ($1,063.08) is too low. The discount rate that causes the present value of income to be closer to the $1,100 cost is 9%, because it is only $17.61 away from $1,100. Thus, if you require an 8% return, the investment is clearly acceptable.

CALCULATOR USE A financial calculator can be used to find the yield (or *internal rate of return*) on an investment that will produce a stream of income. This procedure typically involves punching in the cost of the investment (typically referred to as the *cash outflow* at time zero) and all of the income expected each period (typically referred to as the *cash inflow* at in year *x*) and then directly calculating the yield (typically referred to as the *internal rate of return, IRR*). Because calculators provide solutions that are more precise than those based on rounded table factors, the yield of 9.32% found for the investment in Table 4.10 using a financial calculator (keystrokes not shown) is close to, but not equal to, the 9% value estimated above using Table 4.12.

SPREADSHEET USE The yield for a stream of income also can be calculated as shown on the following Excel spreadsheet.

	A	B
1	YIELD FOR A STREAM OF INCOME	
2	Year	Cash Flow
3	2011	$1,200
4	2010	$100
5	2009	$100
6	2008	$120
7	2007	$110
8	2006	$100
9	2005	$90
10	Yield	9.32%

Entry in Cell B10 is
=RATE((A3–A9),0,B9,–B3,0).
The expression A3–A9 in the entry calculates the number of years of growth.
The minus sign appears before B3 because the investment in 2011 is treated as a cash outflow.

Interest on Interest: The Critical Assumption The critical assumption underlying the use of yield as a return measure is an ability to earn a return equal to the yield on *all income* received during the holding period. This concept can best be illustrated with a simple example. Suppose you buy a $1,000 U.S. Treasury bond that pays 8% annual interest ($80) over its 20-year maturity. Each year you receive $80, and at maturity the $1,000 in principal is repaid. There is no loss of capital, no default; all payments are made right on time. But you must be able to reinvest the $80 annual interest receipts in order to earn 8% on this investment.

FIGURE 4.3

Earning Interest on Interest

If you invested in a $1,000, 20-year bond with an 8% coupon, you would have only $2,600 at the end of 20 years if you did not reinvest the $80 annual interest receipts—only about a 5% rate of return. If you reinvested the interest at the 8% interest rate, you would have $4,661 at the end of 20 years—an 8% rate of return. To achieve the calculated yield of 8%, you must therefore be able to earn interest on interest at that rate.

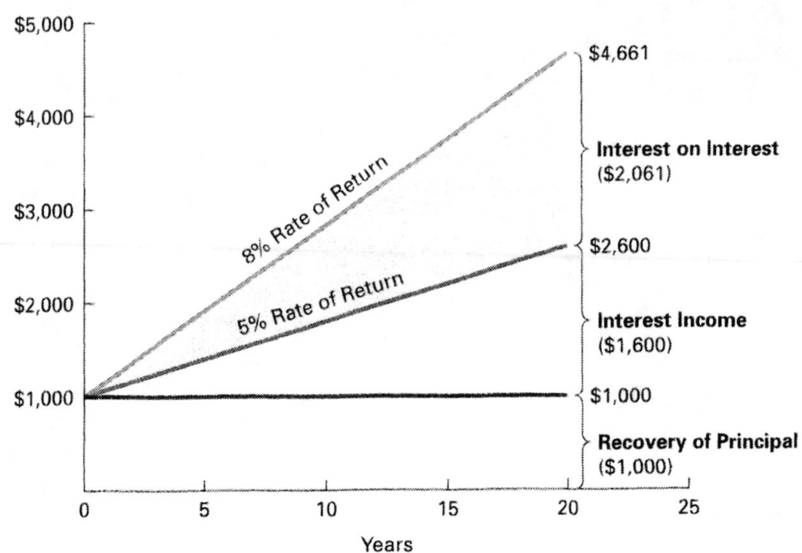

Figure 4.3 shows the elements of return on this investment to demonstrate the point. If you don't *reinvest* the interest income of $80 per year, you'll end up on the 5% line. You'll have $2,600—the $1,000 principal plus $1,600 interest income ($80/year × 20 years)—at the end of 20 years. (The yield on a single cash flow of $1,000 today that will be worth $2,600 in 20 years is about 5%.) To move to the 8% line, you have to earn 8% on the annual interest receipts. If you do, you'll have $4,661—the $1,000 principal plus the $3,661 future value of the 20-year $80 annuity of interest receipts invested at 8% [$80/year × 45.762 (the 8%, 20-year factor from Appendix A, Table A.2)]—at the end of 20 years. (The yield on a single cash flow of $1,000 today that will be worth $4,661 in 20 years is 8%.) The future value of the investment would be $2,061 greater ($4,661 − $2,600) with interest on interest than without reinvestment of the interest receipts.

It should be clear to you that if you start out with an 8% investment, *you have to earn that same rate of return when reinvesting your income.* The rate of return you start with is the required, or minimum, **reinvestment rate**—the rate of return earned on interest or other income received over the relevant investment horizon. By putting your current income to work at this rate, you'll earn the rate of return you set out to. If you fail to do so, your return will decline accordingly. Even though a bond was used in this illustration, the same principle applies to any other type of investment vehicle.

reinvestment rate
the rate of return earned on interest or other income received from an investment over its investment horizon.

The earning of interest on interest is what the market refers to as a **fully compounded rate of return.** It's an important concept: You can't start reaping the full potential from your investments until you start earning a fully compounded rate of return on them.

fully compounded rate of return
the rate of return that includes interest earned on interest.

Interest on interest is a particularly important element of return for investment programs that involve a lot of current income. You have to reinvest current income. (With capital gains, the investment vehicle itself is automatically doing the reinvesting.) It follows, therefore, that for investment programs that

TABLE 4.13 Dividends Per Share

Year	Year Number	Dividends per Share	Year	Year Number	Dividends per Share
1996	0	$2.45	2001	5	$3.15
1997	1	2.60	2002	6	3.20
1998	2	2.80	2003	7	3.20
1999	3	3.00	2004	8	3.40
2000	4	3.20	2005	9	3.50

lean toward income-oriented securities, the continued reinvestment of income plays an important role in investment success.

Finding Growth Rates

rate of growth
the compound annual rate of change in the value of a stream of income.

In addition to finding compound annual rates of return, we frequently need to find the **rate of growth.** This is the compound annual rate of change in the value of a stream of income, particularly dividends or earnings. Here we use an example to demonstrate a simple technique for estimating growth rates using a financial table, a financial calculator, or an Excel spreadsheet.

TABLE USE Imagine that you wish to find the rate of growth for the dividends given in Table 4.13. The year numbers in the table show that 1996 is viewed as the base year (year 0); the subsequent years, 1997–2005, are considered years 1 through 9, respectively. Although 10 years of data are presented in Table 4.13, they represent only 9 years of growth, because the value for the earliest year must be viewed as the initial value at time zero.

To find the growth rate, we first divide the dividend for the earliest year (1996) by the dividend for the latest year (2005). The resulting quotient is 0.700 ($2.45 ÷ $3.50). It represents the value of the present-value interest factor for 9 years. To estimate the compound annual dividend growth rate, we find the discount rate in Appendix A, Table A.3 associated with the factor closest to 0.700 for 9 years. Looking across year 9 in Table A.3 shows that the factor for 4% is 0.703—very close to the 0.700 value. Therefore, the growth rate of the dividends in Table 4.13 is approximately 4%.

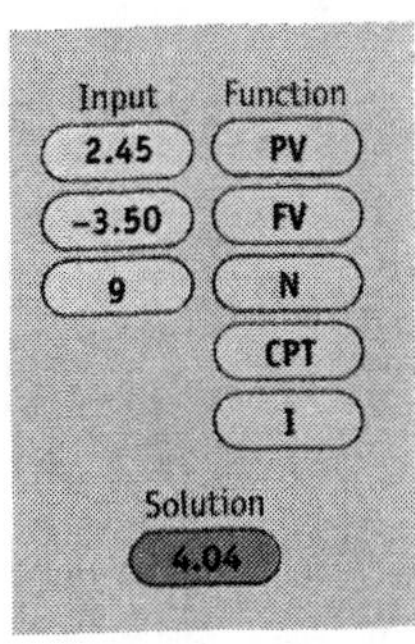

CALCULATOR USE Using a financial calculator to find the growth rate for the dividend stream shown in Table 4.13, we treat the earliest (1996) value as a present value, **PV**, and the latest (2005) value as a future value, **FV**. (*Note:* Most calculators require *either* the **PV** or the **FV** value to be input as a negative number to calculate an unknown growth rate.) As noted above, although 10 years of dividends are shown in Table 4.13, there are only 9 years of growth (**N** = 9) because the earliest year (1996) must be defined as the base year (year 0). Using the inputs shown at the left, we calculate the growth rate to be 4.04%. This rate is consistent with, but more precise than, the value found using the financial tables.

SPREADSHEET USE The growth rate for a dividend stream can also be calculated as shown on the Excel spreadsheet on page 160.

	A	B
1	GROWTH RATE FOR A DIVIDEND STREAM	
2	Year	Dividend/share
3	2005	$3.50
4	2004	$3.40
5	2003	$3.20
6	2002	$3.20
7	2001	$3.15
8	2000	$3.20
9	1999	$3.00
10	1998	$2.80
11	1997	$2.60
12	1996	$2.45
13	Annual growth rate	4.04%

Entry in Cell B13 is
=RATE((A3–A12),0,–B12,B3,0).
The expression A3–A12 in the entry
calculates the number of years of growth.
The minus sign appears before B12 because
the investment in 1996
is treated as a cash outflow.

The use of growth rates, which are often an important input to the common stock valuation process, is explored in greater detail in Chapter 8.

IN REVIEW

CONCEPTS

4.10 Define the following terms and explain how they are used to find the risk-free rate of return and the required rate of return for a given investment.

a. *Real rate of return.*
b. *Expected inflation premium.*
c. *Risk premium* for a given investment.

4.11 What is meant by the *holding period,* and why it is advisable to use holding periods of equal length when comparing alternative investment vehicles? Define the *holding period return (HPR),* and explain for what length holding periods it is typically used.

4.12 Define *yield* (or *internal rate of return*). When is it appropriate to use yield rather than the HPR to measure the return on an investment?

4.13 Explain why you must earn 10% on *all* income received from an investment during its holding period in order for its yield actually to equal the 10% value you've calculated.

4.14 Explain how either the present value (of benefits versus cost) or the yield measure can be used to find a *satisfactory investment.* Given the following data, indicate which, if any, of these investments is acceptable. Explain your findings.

	Investment		
	A	B	C
Cost	$200	$160	$500
Appropriate	7%	10%	9%
Present value of benefits	—	$150	—
Yield	8%	—	8%

Risk: The Other Side of the Coin

LG 5 LG 6

risk
the chance that the actual return from an investment may differ from what is expected.

risk-return tradeoff
the relationship between risk and return, in which investments with more risk should provide higher returns, and vice versa.

Thus far, our primary concern in this chapter has been return. However, we cannot consider return without also looking at risk. Expanding a bit on its definition in Chapter 1, **risk** is the chance that the actual return from an investment may differ from what is expected.

The risk associated with a given investment is directly related to its expected return. In general, the broader the range of possible returns, the greater the investment's risk, and vice versa. Put another way, riskier investments should provide higher levels of return. Otherwise, what incentive is there for an investor to risk his or her capital? In general, investors attempt to minimize risk for a given level of return or to maximize return for a given level of risk. This relationship between risk and return is called the **risk-return tradeoff.** It is introduced here and will be discussed in greater detail in Chapter 5. Here we begin by examining the key sources of risk. We then consider the measurement and assessment of risk: the risk of a single asset, the assessment of risk associated with a potential investment, and the steps by which return and risk can be combined in the decision process.

Sources of Risk

The risk associated with a given investment vehicle may result from a combination of possible sources. A prudent investor considers how the major sources of risk might affect potential investment vehicles. The combined impact of the presence of any of the sources of risk, discussed below, in a given investment vehicle would be reflected in its *risk premium*. As discussed earlier in the chapter and shown in Equation 4.7, the required return on an investment can be found by adding its risk premium to the risk-free rate. This premium in a broad sense results from the sources of risk, which derive from characteristics of both the issue (e.g., stock, bond) and issuer (e.g., voting/nonvoting, callable/noncallable). Of course, as discussed in Chapter 2, *currency exchange risk* is another source of risk that should also be considered when investing internationally.

business risk
the degree of uncertainty associated with an investment's earnings and the investment's ability to pay the returns owed investors.

Business Risk In general, **business risk** is the degree of uncertainty associated with an investment's earnings and the investment's ability to pay the returns (interest, principal, dividends) owed investors. For example, business owners may receive no return if the firm's earnings are not adequate to meet obligations. Debtholders, on the other hand, are likely to receive some (but not necessarily all) of the amount owed them, because of the preferential treatment legally accorded to debt.

Much of the business risk associated with a given investment vehicle is related to its kind of business. For example, the amount of business risk in a public utility common stock differs from the amount in the common stock of a high-fashion clothing manufacturer or an Internet start-up. Generally, investments in similar kinds of firms have similar business risk, although differences in management, costs, and location can cause varying levels of risk.

HOT LINKS

See an example where shareholders allegedly bore more risk than top executives in the *Ethics* box for Chapter 4 on the book's Web site at

www.aw-bc.com/gitman_joehnk

Financial Risk The degree of uncertainty of payment attributable to the mix of debt and equity used to finance a business is

financial risk
the degree of uncertainty of payment attributable to the mix of debt and equity used to finance a business; the larger the proportion of debt financing, the greater this risk.

purchasing power risk
the chance that changing price levels (inflation or deflation) will adversely affect investment returns.

interest rate risk
the chance that changes in interest rates will adversely affect a security's value.

financial risk. The larger the proportion of debt used to finance a firm, the greater its financial risk. Debt financing obligates the firm to make interest payments as well as to repay the debt, thus increasing risk. Inability to meet obligations associated with the use of debt could result in business failure and in losses for bondholders as well as stockholders and owners.

Purchasing Power Risk The chance that changing price levels (inflation or deflation) will adversely affect investment returns is **purchasing power risk.** Specifically, this risk is the chance that generally rising prices (inflation) will reduce *purchasing power* (the amount of a given commodity that can be purchased with a dollar). For example, if last year a dollar would buy three candy bars and today it can buy only two because candy bars now cost 50 cents each, the purchasing power of your dollar has decreased. In periods of declining price levels (deflation), the purchasing power of the dollar increases.

In general, investments whose values move with general price levels have low purchasing power risk and are most profitable during periods of rising prices. Those that provide fixed returns have high purchasing power risk, and they are most profitable during periods of low inflation or declining price levels. The returns on stocks of durable-goods manufacturers, for example, tend to move with the general price level, whereas returns from deposit accounts and bonds do not.

Interest Rate Risk Securities are especially affected by interest rate risk. This is particularly true for those securities that offer purchasers a fixed periodic return. **Interest rate risk** is the chance that changes in interest rates will adversely affect a security's value. The interest rate changes themselves result from changes in the general relationship between the supply of and the demand for money.

As interest rates change, the prices of many securities fluctuate: They typically decrease with increasing interest rates, and they increase with decreasing interest rates. As we will see in greater detail in Chapters 10, 11, and 12, the prices of fixed-income securities (bonds and preferred stock) drop when interest rates rise. They thus provide purchasers with the same rate of return that would be available at prevailing rates. The opposite occurs when interest rates fall: The return on a fixed-income security is adjusted downward to a competitive level by an upward adjustment in its market price.

A second, more subtle aspect of interest rate risk is associated with reinvestment of income. As noted in our earlier discussion of interest on interest, only if you can earn the initial rate of return on income received from an investment can you achieve a *fully compounded rate of return* equal to the initial rate of return. In other words, if a bond pays 8% annual interest, you must be able to earn 8% on the interest received during the bond's holding period in order to earn a fully compounded 8% rate of return over that period. This same aspect of interest rate risk applies to reinvestment of the proceeds received from an investment at its maturity or sale.

A final aspect of interest rate risk is related to investing in short-term securities such as U.S. Treasury bills and certificates of deposit (discussed in Chapter 1). Investors face the risk that when short-term securities mature, their proceeds may have to be invested in lower-yielding, new short-term securities. By initially making a long-term investment, you can lock in a return for a period of years, rather than face the risk of declines in short-term interest rates. Clearly, when interest rates are declining, the returns from a strategy of investing in short-term securities are adversely affected. On the other hand, interest rate increases have a positive impact on such a strategy. The chance that interest rates will decline is therefore the interest rate risk of a short-term security investment strategy.

Most investment vehicles are subject to interest rate risk. Although fixed-income securities are most directly affected by interest rate movements, they also affect other long-term vehicles such as common stock and mutual funds. *Generally, the higher the interest rate, the lower the value of an investment vehicle, and vice versa.*

liquidity risk
the risk of not being able to liquidate an investment conveniently and at a reasonable price.

Liquidity Risk The risk of not being able to liquidate an investment conveniently and at a reasonable price is called **liquidity risk.** The liquidity of a given investment vehicle is an important consideration. In general, investment vehicles traded in *thin markets,* where demand and supply are small, tend to be less liquid than those traded in *broad markets.*

One can generally sell an investment vehicle merely by significantly cutting its price. However, to be liquid, an investment must be easily sold *at a reasonable price.* For example, a security recently purchased for $1,000 would not be viewed as highly liquid if it could be quickly sold only at a greatly reduced price, such as $500. Vehicles such as stocks and bonds of major companies listed on the New York Stock Exchange are generally highly liquid; others, such as the stock of a small company in a declining industry, are not.

tax risk
the chance that Congress will make unfavorable changes in tax laws, driving down the after-tax returns and market values of certain investments.

Tax Risk The chance that Congress will make unfavorable changes in tax laws is known as **tax risk.** The greater the chance that such changes will drive down the after-tax returns and market values of certain investments, the greater the tax risk. Undesirable changes in tax laws include elimination of tax exemptions, limitation of deductions, and increases in tax rates.

In recent years, Congress has passed numerous changes in tax laws. One of the most significant was the *Tax Reform Act of 1986*, which contained provisions that reduced the attractiveness of many investment vehicles, particularly real estate and other tax shelters. More recently, the *Jobs and Growth Tax Relief Reconciliation Act of 2003* reduced tax rates, taxes on dividends, and taxes on capital gains. Clearly, this change benefits investors and does not represent the unfavorable consequences of tax risk.

Though virtually all investments are vulnerable to increases in tax rates, certain tax-advantaged investments, such as municipal and other bonds, real estate, and natural resources, generally have greater tax risk.

market risk
risk of decline in investment returns because of market factors independent of the given investment.

Market Risk **Market risk** is the risk that investment returns will decline because of market factors independent of the given investment. Examples include political, economic, and social events, as well as changes in investor tastes and preferences. Market risk actually embodies a number of different risks: purchasing power risk, interest rate risk, and tax risk.

The impact of market factors on investment returns is not uniform. Both the degree and the direction of change in return differ among investment vehicles. For example, legislation placing restrictive import quotas on Japanese goods may result in a significant increase in the value (and therefore the return) of domestic automobile and electronics stocks. Essentially, market risk is reflected in the *price volatility* of a security—the more volatile the price of a security, the greater its perceived market risk.

event risk
risk that comes from an unexpected event that has a significant and usually immediate effect on the underlying value of an investment.

Event Risk **Event risk** occurs when something happens to a company that has a sudden and substantial impact on its financial condition. Event risk goes beyond business and financial risk. It does not necessarily mean the company or market is doing poorly. Instead, it involves an unexpected event that has a significant and usually immediate effect on the underlying value of an investment. An example of event risk is the August 2000 offer by Bridgestone/Firestone to replace 6.5 million tires, mainly on Ford light trucks and SUVs, based on 46 deaths and more than 300 incidents involving Firestone tires that were alleged to have shredded on the highway. The stock of Bridgestone Corporation—the Japanese parent company of Bridgestone/Firestone—was quickly and negatively affected. It dropped by about 20% on the Tokyo Exchange during the two days immediately following the announcement.

Event risk can take many forms and can affect all types of investment vehicles. Fortunately, its impact tends to be isolated in most cases. For instance, the stocks of only a small number of companies were directly affected by Bridgestone/Firestone's offer to replace tires.

Risk of a Single Asset

Most people have at some time in their lives asked themselves how risky some anticipated course of action is. In such cases, the answer is usually a subjective judgment, such as "not very" or "quite." Such a judgment may or may not help in decision making. In finance, we are able to quantify the measurement of risk, which improves comparisons between investments and enhances decision making.

The risk or variability of both single assets and portfolios of assets can be measured statistically. Here we focus solely on the risk of single assets. We first consider standard deviation, which is an absolute measure of risk. Then we consider the coefficient of variation, a relative measure of risk. We will consider the risk and return of portfolios of assets in Chapter 5.

standard deviation, s
a statistic used to measure the dispersion (variation) of returns around an asset's average or expected return.

Standard Deviation: An Absolute Measure of Risk The most common single indicator of an asset's risk is the **standard deviation, s.** It measures the dispersion (variation) of returns around an asset's average or expected return. The formula is

Equation 4.10

$$\text{Standard deviation} = \sqrt{\frac{\sum_{j=1}^{n}\left(\begin{matrix}\text{Return for}\\ \text{outcome } j\end{matrix} - \begin{matrix}\text{Average or}\\ \text{expected return}\end{matrix}\right)^2}{\begin{matrix}\text{Total number}\\ \text{of outcomes}\end{matrix} - 1}}$$

Equation 4.10a

$$s = \sqrt{\frac{\sum_{j=1}^{n}(r_j - \bar{r})^2}{n-1}}$$

Consider two competing investments—A and B—described in Table 4.14. Note that both investments earned an average return of 15% over the 6-year period shown. Reviewing the returns shown for each investment in light of

TABLE 4.14 Returns on Investments A and B

	Rate of Return (r_j)	
Year (j)	Investment A	Investment B
2000	15.6%	8.4%
2001	12.7	12.9
2002	15.3	19.6
2003	16.2	17.5
2004	16.5	10.3
2005	13.7	21.3
Average ($\bar{r}$)	15.0%	15.0%

their 15% averages, we can see that the returns for investment B vary more from this average than do the returns for investment A.

The standard deviation provides a quantitative tool for comparing investment risk. Table 4.15 on page 166 demonstrates the calculation of the standard deviations, s_A and s_B, for investments A and B, respectively. Evaluating the calculations, we can see that the standard deviation of 1.49% for the returns on investment A is, as expected, considerably below the standard deviation of 5.24% for investment B. The greater absolute dispersion of investment B's return, reflected in its larger standard deviation, indicates that B is the more risky investment. Of course, these values are absolute measures based on *historical* data. There is no assurance that the risks of these two investments will remain the same in the future.

coefficient of variation, *CV*
a statistic used to measure the *relative* dispersion of an asset's returns; it is useful in comparing the risk of assets with differing average or expected returns.

Coefficient of Variation: A Relative Measure of Risk The **coefficient of variation, *CV*,** is a measure of the *relative* dispersion of an asset's returns. It is useful in comparing the risk of assets with differing average or expected returns. Equation 4.11 gives the formula for the coefficient of variation.

Equation 4.11

$$\text{Coefficient of variation} = \frac{\text{Standard deviation}}{\text{Average or expected return}}$$

Equation 4.11a

$$CV = \frac{s}{\bar{r}}$$

As was the case for the standard deviation, the higher the coefficient of variation, the greater the risk.

We can substitute into Equation 4.11a the standard deviation values (from Table 4.15) and the average returns (from Table 4.14) for investments A and B. We get a coefficient of variation for A of 0.099 (1.49% ÷ 15%) and for B of 0.349 (5.24% ÷ 15%). Investment B has the higher coefficient of variation and, as expected, has more relative risk than investment A. Because both investments have the same average return, the coefficient of variation in this case has not provided any more information than the standard deviation.

The real utility of the coefficient of variation is in comparing investments that have *different* expected returns. For example, assume you want to select the less risky of two alternative investments—X and Y. The average return, the

EXCEL with SPREADSHEETS

TABLE 4.15 **Calculation of Standard Deviations of Returns for Investments A and B**

Investment A

Year (j)	(1) Return, r_j	(2) Average Return, $\bar{r}$	(3) (1) − (2) $r_j - \bar{r}$	(4) $(3)^2$ $(r_j - \bar{r})^2$
2000	15.6%	15.0%	.6%	0.36%
2001	12.7	15.0	−2.3	5.29
2002	15.3	15.0	.3	0.09
2003	16.2	15.0	1.2	1.44
2004	16.5	15.0	1.5	2.25
2005	13.7	15.0	−1.3	1.69

$$\sum_{j=1}^{6}(r_j - \bar{r})^2 = 11.12$$

$$s_A = \sqrt{\frac{\sum_{j=1}^{6}(r_j - \bar{r})^2}{n-1}} = \sqrt{\frac{11.12}{6-1}} = \sqrt{2.224} = \underline{\underline{1.49\%}}$$

Investment B

Year (j)	(1) Return, r_j	(2) Average Return, $\bar{r}$	(3) (1) − (2) $r_j - \bar{r}$	(4) $(3)^2$ $(r_j - \bar{r})^2$
2000	8.4%	15.0%	−6.6%	43.56%
2001	12.9	15.0	−2.1	4.41
2002	19.6	15.0	4.6	21.16
2003	17.5	15.0	2.5	6.25
2004	10.3	15.0	−4.7	22.09
2005	21.3	15.0	6.3	39.69

$$\sum_{j=1}^{6}(r_j - \bar{r})^2 = 137.16$$

$$s_B = \sqrt{\frac{\sum_{j=1}^{6}(r_j - \bar{r})^2}{n-1}} = \sqrt{\frac{137.16}{6-1}} = \sqrt{27.432} = \underline{\underline{5.24\%}}$$

standard deviation, and the coefficient of variation for each of these investments are as follows.

Statistics	Investment X	Investment Y
(1) Average return	12%	20%
(2) Standard deviation	9%*	10%
(3) Coefficient of variation [(2) ÷ (1)]	0.75	0.50*

*Preferred investment using the given risk measure.

If you compared the investments solely on the basis of their standard deviations, you would prefer investment X. It has a lower standard deviation than investment Y (9% versus 10%). But by comparing the coefficients of variation, you can see that you would be making a mistake in choosing X over Y. The *relative* dispersion, or risk, of the investments, as reflected in the coefficient of variation, is lower for Y than for X (0.50 versus 0.75). Clearly, the coefficient of variation considers the relative size, or average return, of each investment.

TABLE 4.16 Historical Returns, Standard Deviations, and Coefficients of Variation for Popular Security Investments (1926–2002)

Investment	Average Annual Return	Standard Deviation	Coefficient of Variation*
Large-company stocks	12.2%	20.5%	1.68
Small-company stocks	16.9	33.2	1.96
Long-term corporate bonds	6.2	8.7	1.40
Long-term government bonds	5.8	9.4	1.62
U.S. Treasury bills	3.8	3.2	0.84
Inflation	3.1%	4.4%	1.42

*Calculated by dividing the standard deviation by the average annual return.

Source: Stocks, Bonds, Bills, and Inflation, 2003 Yearbook (Chicago: Ibbotson Associates, Inc., 2002), p. 33.

Historical Returns and Risk We can now use the standard deviation and coefficient of variation as a measure of risk to assess the historical (1926–2002) investment return data in Table 4.4. Table 4.16 repeats the historical returns and shows the standard deviations and coefficients of variation associated with each of them. A close relationship can be seen between the investment returns and the standard deviations and coefficients of variation: Investments with higher return have higher standard deviations and coefficients of variation. Because higher standard deviations and coefficients of variation are associated with greater risk, the historical data confirm the existence of a positive relationship between risk and return. That relationship reflects the fact that market participants require higher returns as compensation for greater risk. The historical data in Table 4.16 clearly show that during the 1926–2002 period investors were rewarded with higher returns on higher-risk investments.

HOT LINKS

Visit the Securities Industry Association site's Investing Essentials section. While there, click on [understanding risk], [understanding return], and [risk and return].

www.siainvestor.org/categories/investingessentials/ie_intro.htm

Assessing Risk

Techniques for quantifying the risk of a given investment vehicle are quite useful. However, they will be of little use if you are unaware of your feelings toward risk. The individual investor typically tends to seek answers to these questions: "Is the amount of perceived risk worth taking to get the expected return?" "Can I get a higher return for the same level of risk or a lower risk for the same level of return?" A look at the general risk-return characteristics of alternative investment vehicles and at the question of an acceptable level of risk will help shed light on how to evaluate risk.

Risk-Return Characteristics of Alternative Investment Vehicles A wide variety of risk-return behaviors are associated with each type of investment vehicle. Some common stocks offer low returns and low risk. Others offer high returns and high risk. In general, ignoring differences in maturity, the risk-return characteristics of the major investment vehicles are as shown in Figure 4.4 (on page 168). Of course, a broad range of risk-return behaviors exists for specific investments of each type. In other words, once you have selected the appropriate type of vehicle, you must still decide which specific security to acquire.

FIGURE 4.4

Risk-Return Tradeoffs for Various Investment Vehicles

A risk-return tradeoff exists such that for a higher risk one expects a higher return, and vice versa. In general, ignoring differences in maturity, low-risk/low-return investment vehicles include U.S. government securities and deposit accounts. High-risk/high-return vehicles include real estate and other tangible investments, options, and futures.

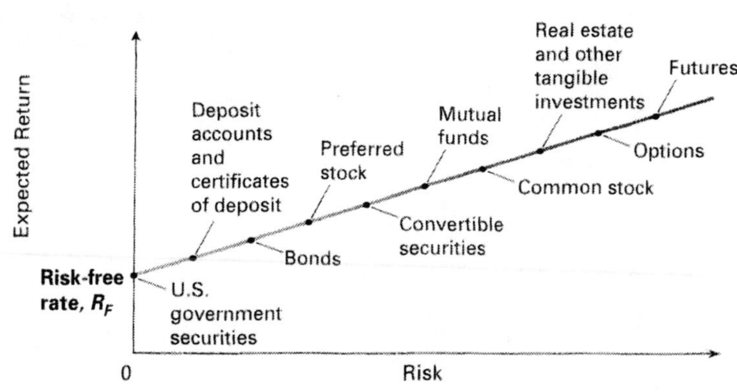

risk-indifferent
describes an investor who does not require a change in return as compensation for greater risk.

risk-averse
describes an investor who requires greater return in exchange for greater risk.

risk-seeking
describes an investor who will accept a lower return in exchange for greater risk.

An Acceptable Level of Risk The three basic risk preferences (risk-indifferent, risk-averse, and risk-seeking) are depicted graphically in Figure 4.5.

- For the **risk-indifferent** investor, the required return does not change as risk goes from x_1 to x_2. In essence, no change in return would be required for the increase in risk.
- For the **risk-averse** investor, the required return increases for an increase in risk. Because they shy away from risk, these investors require higher expected returns to compensate them for taking greater risk.
- For the **risk-seeking** investor, the required return decreases for an increase in risk. Theoretically, because they enjoy risk, these investors are willing to give up some return to take more risk.

Most investors are risk-averse: For a given increase in risk, they require an increase in return. This risk-averse behavior is also depicted in Figure 4.4.

Of course, the amount of return required by each investor for a given increase in risk differs depending on the investor's degree of risk aversion (reflected in the slope of the line). Investors generally tend to be conservative when accepting risk. The more aggressive an investor you are (the farther to

FIGURE 4.5

Risk Preferences

The risk-indifferent investor requires no change in return for a given increase in risk. The risk-averse investor requires an increase in return for a given risk increase. The risk-seeking investor gives up some return for more risk. The majority of investors are risk-averse.

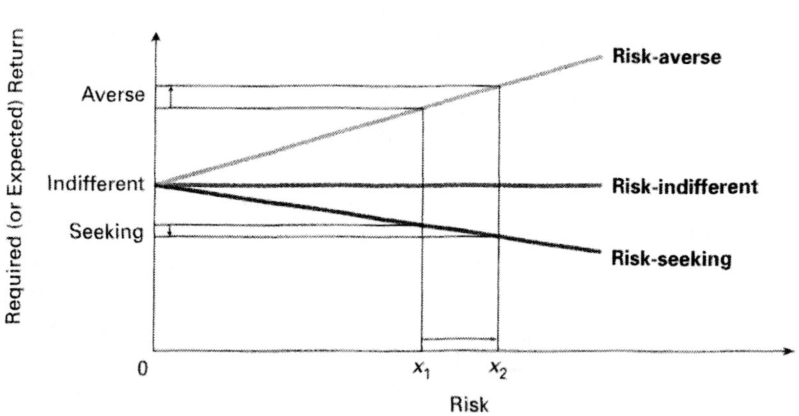

INVESTING IN ACTION

WHAT'S YOUR RISK TOLERANCE?

During the strong bull market of the 1990s and early 2000s, it seemed that investors couldn't lose. Even when the market took a nosedive, they rushed to buy at lower prices and assumed that their stocks would go up again. The lure of easy money pushed the idea of risk into the background for many investors, who assumed higher levels of risk without stopping to consider their personal risk tolerance. The rise of online, do-it-yourself investing also contributed to this new attitude toward risk.

The key to risk taking is to determine your personal level of risk tolerance—how comfortable you feel with the volatility of your investments. Understanding your risk tolerance will prevent you from taking on more risk than you can handle and will reduce the likelihood that you will panic and abandon your plan in midstream.

The following quiz can help you evaluate your personal capacity for risk. After you've taken it, you may want to check out a few other risk tolerance quizzes at these sites: Investor Education Fund's Risk quizzes, www.investored.ca/en/interactive/games_quizzes_risk.htm; MSN's Money Central, moneycentral.msn.com/articles/invest/prepare/risktol.asp; and Rutgers Cooperative Extension, www.rce.rutgers.edu/money/riskquiz/default.asp. With this information in hand, you can build a portfolio that will let you sleep better at night.

What is Your Investment Risk Tolerance?

1. Which best describes your feelings about investing?
   a. "Better safe than sorry."
   b. "Moderation in all things."
   c. "Nothing ventured, nothing gained."
2. Which is the most important to you as an investor?
   a. Steady income
   b. Steady income and growth
   c. Rapid price appreciation
3. You won! Which prize would you select?
   a. $4,000 in cash
   b. A 50% chance to win $10,000
   c. A 20% chance to win $100,000
4. The stocks in your retirement account have dropped 20% since last quarter. The market experts are optimistic. What would you do?
   a. Transfer out of stocks to avoid losing more.
   b. Stay in stocks and wait for them to come back.
   c. Shift more money into stocks. If they made sense before, they're a bargain now.
5. The stocks in your retirement account have suddenly gone up 20%. You have no more information. What would you do?
   a. Transfer out of stocks and lock in my gains.
   b. Stay in stocks, hoping for more gains.
   c. Transfer more money into stocks. They might go higher.
6. Would you borrow money to take advantage of a good investment opportunity?
   a. Never b. Maybe c. Yes
7. How would you characterize yourself as an investor?
   a. Conservative
   b. Moderate risk taker
   c. Aggressive

How to determine your score:

Each (a) answer is worth 1 point. Each (b) is worth 2 points. Each (c) is worth 3 points. Add them up to find your total score.

7-11 points: a conservative investor
12-16 points: a moderate risk taker
17-21 points: an aggressive investor

CRITICAL THINKING QUESTION Judging by your quiz results, what is your personal tolerance for investment risk? Using the graph in Figure 4.4, determine what investment vehicles might be appropriate for your level of risk tolerance.

Sources: Maria Crawford Scott, "Life-Cycle Investing: Investment Decisions and Your Personal Investment Profile" *AAII Journal*, March 1993, pp. 16–19; Ann Perry, "Putting Stock in the Market," *San Diego Union-Tribune*, July 18, 1993, pp. 11–12; and Jeff D. Opdyke, "Bumpy Market Reminds Investors to Assess Their Risk Tolerance," *Wall Street Journal*, July 14, 2002, pp. C1, C11.

the right you operate on the risk-averse line), the greater your tolerance for risk, and the greater your required return. To get a feel for your own risk-taking orientation, read the *Investing in Action* box on page 169.

Steps in the Decision Process: Combining Return and Risk

When you are deciding among alternative investments, you should take the following steps to combine return and risk.

1. Using historical or projected return data, estimate the expected return over a given holding period. Use yield (or present-value) techniques to make sure you give the time value of money adequate consideration.
2. Using historical or projected return data, assess the risk associated with the investment. Subjective risk assessment, use of the standard deviation or coefficient of variation of returns, and use of more sophisticated measures, such as beta (developed in Chapter 5), are the primary approaches available to individual investors.
3. Evaluate the risk-return behavior of each alternative investment to make sure that the return expected is reasonable given the level of risk. If other vehicles with lower levels of risk provide equal or greater returns, the investment is not acceptable.
4. Select the investment vehicles that offer the highest returns associated with the level of risk you are willing to take. As long as you get the highest return for your acceptable level of risk, you have made a "good investment."

Probably the most difficult step in this process is assessing risk. Aside from return and risk considerations, other factors, such as portfolio considerations, taxes, and liquidity, affect the investment decision. We will develop portfolio concepts in Chapter 5 and, in later chapters, will look at all of these factors as they are related to specific investment vehicles.

IN REVIEW

CONCEPTS

4.15 Define *risk.* Explain what we mean by the *risk-return tradeoff.* What happens to the required return as risk increases? Explain.

4.16 Define and briefly discuss each of the following sources of risk.

a. Business risk
b. Financial risk
c. Purchasing power risk
d. Interest rate risk
e. Liquidity risk
f. Tax risk
g. Market risk
h. Event risk

4.17 Briefly describe each of the following measures of risk or variability, and explain their similarity. Under what circumstances is each preferred when comparing the risk of competing investments?

a. Standard deviation
b. Coefficient of variation

4.18 Differentiate among the three basic risk preferences: *risk-indifferent, risk-averse,* and *risk-seeking.* Which of these behaviors best describes most investors?

4.19 Describe the steps involved in the investment decision process. Be sure to mention how returns and risks can be evaluated together to determine acceptable investments.

Summary

LG 1 **Review the concept of return, its components, the forces that affect the investor's level of return, and historical returns.** Return is the reward for investing. The total return provided by an investment includes current income and capital gains (or losses). Return is commonly calculated on a historical basis and then used to project expected returns. The level of return depends on internal characteristics and external forces, which include the general level of price changes. Significant differences exist between the average annual rates of return realized over time on various types of security investments.

LG 2 **Discuss the time value of money and the calculations involved in finding the future value of various types of cash flows.** Because investors have opportunities to earn interest on their funds, money has a time value. Interest can be applied using either simple interest or compound interest. The more frequently interest is compounded at a stated rate, the higher the true rate of interest. Financial tables, financial calculators, and computers and spreadsheets can be used to streamline time-value calculations. The future value of a present sum or an annuity can be found using compound interest concepts.

LG 3 **Explain the concept of present value, the procedures for calculating present values, and the use of present value in determining whether an investment is satisfactory.** The present value of a future sum is the amount that would have to be deposited today, into an account earning interest at a given rate, to accumulate the specified future sum. The present value of streams of future returns can be found by adding the present values of the individual returns. When the stream is an annuity, its present value can be more simply calculated. A satisfactory investment is one for which the present value of its benefits equals or exceeds the present value of its costs.

LG 4 **Describe real, risk-free, and required returns and the computation and application of holding period return, yield (internal rate of return), and growth rates.** The required return on an investment is the rate of return an investor must earn to be fully compensated for the investment's risk. It represents the sum of the real rate of return and the expected inflation premium (which together represent the risk-free rate), plus the risk premium for the investment. The risk premium varies depending on issue and issuer characteristics. The holding period return (HPR) is the return earned over a specified period of time. It is frequently used to compare returns earned in periods of 1 year or less.

Yield or internal rate of return is the compound annual rate of return earned on investments held for more than 1 year. If the yield is greater than or equal to the required return, the investment is acceptable. Implicit in the use of yield is an ability to earn a return equal to the calculated yield on all income received from the investment during the holding period. Present-value techniques can be used to find a rate of growth, which is the compound annual rate of change in the value of a stream of income, particularly dividends or earnings.

LG 5 **Discuss the key sources of risk and how they might affect potential investment vehicles.** Risk is the chance that the actual return from an investment will differ from what is expected. The total risk associated with a given investment vehicle may result from a combination of sources: business, financial, purchasing power, interest rate, liquidity, tax, market, and event risk. These risks typically have varying effects on different types of investment vehicles. The combined impact of any of the sources of risk in a given investment vehicle would be reflected in its risk premium.

LG 6 **Understand the risk of a single asset, risk assessment, and the steps that combine return and risk.** The risk of both single assets and portfolios of assets can be measured statistically on an absolute basis by the standard deviation and on a relative basis by the coefficient of variation. There is a tradeoff between risk and return. Historical return and risk data for popular security investments confirm that investors require higher returns as compensation for greater risk. Generally, each type of investment vehicle displays certain risk-return characteristics. Most investors are risk-averse: In exchange for a given increase in risk, they require an increase in return. The investment decision involves estimating the return and risk of each alternative and then selecting those investments that offer the highest returns for the level of risk the investor is willing to take.

Putting Your Investment Know-How to the Test

1. An investment of $231 will increase in value to $268 in 3 years. The annual compound growth rate in this case is closest to
   a. 3.0%. b. 4.0%.
   c. 5.0%. d. 6.0%.

2. What is the value in 5 years of $100 invested today at an interest rate of 8% per year, compounded quarterly?
   a. $144.50 b. $146.02
   c. $148.02 d. $148.59

3. All of the following statements about various types of risk are true *except*
   a. Business risk is the uncertainty of income flows caused by the nature of a firm's business.
   b. Financial risk is the uncertainty introduced by the method by which the firm finances its investments.
   c. Exchange rate risk is the uncertainty of returns caused by the possibility of a major change in the political or economic environment of a country.
   d. Liquidity risk is the uncertainty introduced by the secondary market for an investment.

4. An investor will receive a 5-year annuity of $2,500 per year. She will not receive the first payment until 3 years from today. If the annual rate is 8%, the present value of this annuity is *closest* to
   a. $8,105. b. $8,224.
   c. $8,558. d. $9,982.

5. An investor has a portfolio with a market value of $50,000 at the end of May. The market value of the portfolio is $48,700 at the end of June. The holding-period yield on the investor's portfolio for June is closest to
   a. −1.30%. b. −2.60%.
   c. −2.63%. d. −2.67%.

6. An investor holds a portfolio consisting of one share of each of the following stocks:

Stock	Price at the Beginning of the Year	Price at the End of the Year	Cash Dividend During the Year
A	$10	$20	$0
B	$50	$60	$1
C	$100	$110	$4

   For the 1-year holding period, the portfolio return as a weighted investment is *closest* to
   a. 15.79%. b. 18.42%.
   c. 18.75%. d. 21.88%.

7. Rob Monroe buys a $150,000 house and puts $30,000 down. He finances the house with a 30-year, fixed-rate loan. The rate on the mortgage loan is a 2% spread above the yield on a 6%, 10-year Treasury bond. The monthly mortgage payment is *closest* to
   a. $333. b. $881.
   c. $966. d. $996.

8. Which of the following is the *least likely* to affect the required rate of return on an investment?
   a. Real risk free rate.
   b. Asset risk premium.
   c. Expected rate of inflation.
   d. Investor's composite propensity to consume.

9. A bank lends a company $2,000,000 to be repaid in three year-end installments. If the bank charges 9% interest, the annual installment payment will be *closest* to
   a. $666,667. b. $724,871.
   c. $726,667. d. $790,110.

10. An individual deposits $1,500 today and $1,500 one year from today into an interest-earning account. The deposits earn 12% compounded annually. The total amount in the account 2 years from today is closest to
   a. $3,180. b. $3,360.
   c. $3,382. d. $3,562.

Answers: 1. c; 2. d; 3. c; 4. d; 5. b; 6. d; 7. b; 8. d; 9. d; 10. d

Discussion Questions

LG 1

Q4.1 Choose a publicly traded company that has been listed on a major exchange or in the over-the-counter market for at least 5 years. Use any data source of your choice to find the annual cash dividend, if any, paid by the company in each of the past 5 calendar years. Also find the closing price of the stock at the end of each of the preceding 6 years.

a. Calculate the return for each of the five 1-year periods.
b. Graph the returns on a set of year (x-axis)-return (y-axis) axes.
c. On the basis of the graph in part **b**, estimate the return for the coming year, and explain your answer.

LG 2 LG 3

Q4.2 Estimate the amount of cash you will need each year over the next 20 years to live at the standard you desire. Also estimate the rate of return you can reasonably expect to earn annually, on average, during that 20-year period by investing in a common stock portfolio similar to the S&P 500.

a. How large a single lump sum would you need today to provide the annual cash required to allow you to live at the desired standard over the next 20 years? (*Hint:* Be sure to use the appropriate discount rate.)
b. Would the lump sum calculated in part **a** be larger or smaller if you could earn a higher return during the 20-year period? Explain.
c. If you had the lump sum calculated in part **a** but decided to delay your planned retirement in 20 years for another 3 years, how much extra cash would you have accumulated over the 3-year period if you could invest it to earn a 7% annual rate of return?

LG 4

Q4.3 Access appropriate estimates of the expected inflation rate over the next year, and the current yield on one-year risk-free securities (the yield on these securities is referred to as the *nominal* rate of interest). Use the data to estimate the current risk-free *real* rate of interest.

LG 4 LG 5 LG 6

Q4.4 Choose three NYSE-listed stocks and maintain a record of their dividend payments, if any, and closing prices each week over the next 6 weeks.

a. At the end of the 6-week period, calculate the 1-week holding period returns (HPRs) for each stock for each of the 6 weeks.
b. For each stock, average the six weekly HPRs calculated in part **a** and compare them.
c. Use the averages you computed in part **b** and compute the standard deviation of the six HPRs for each stock. Discuss the stocks' relative risk and return behavior. Did the stocks with the highest risk earn the greatest return?

Problems

LG 1

P4.1 How much would an investor earn on a stock purchased 1 year ago for $63 if it paid an annual cash dividend of $3.75 and had just been sold for $67.50? Would the investor have experienced a capital gain? Explain.

LG 1

P4.2 An investor buys a bond for $10,000. The bond pays $300 interest every 6 months. After 18 months, the investor sells the bond for $9,500. Describe the types of income and/or loss the investor had.

LG 1

P4.3 Assuming you purchased a share of stock for $50 one year ago, sold it today for $60, and during the year received three dividend payments totaling $2.70, calculate the following.

a. Current income.
b. Capital gain (or loss).
c. Total return
   (1) In dollars.
   (2) As a percentage of the initial investment.

LG 1

P4.4 Assume you purchased a bond for $9,500. The bond pays $300 interest every 6 months. You sell the bond after 18 months for $10,000. Calculate the following:

a. Current income.
b. Capital gain or loss.
c. Total return in dollars and as a percentage of the original investment.

LG 1

P4.5 Consider the historical data given in the accompanying table.

a. Calculate the total return (in dollars) for each year.
b. Indicate the level of return you would expect in 2006 and in 2007.
c. Comment on your forecast.

		Market Value (Price)	
Year	Income	Beginning	Ending
2001	$1.00	$30.00	$32.50
2002	1.20	32.50	35.00
2003	1.30	35.00	33.00
2004	1.60	33.00	40.00
2005	1.75	40.00	45.00

LG 1

P4.6 Refer to the table in Problem 4.5. What is the total return in dollars and as a percentage of your original investment if you purchased 100 shares of the investment at the beginning of 2001 and sold it at the end of 2003?

LG 2

P4.7 For each of the savings account transactions in the accompanying table, calculate the following.

a. End-of-year account balance. (Assume that the account balance at December 31, 2004, is zero.)
b. Annual interest, using 6% simple interest and assuming all interest is withdrawn from the account as it is earned.
c. True rate of interest, and compare it to the stated rate of interest. Discuss your finding.

Date	Deposit (Withdrawal)	Date	Deposit (Withdrawal)
1/1/05	$5,000	1/1/07	$2,000
1/1/06	(4,000)	1/1/08	3,000

LG 2

P4.8 Using the appropriate table of interest factors found in Appendix A or a financial calculator, calculate the following.

a. The future value of a $300 deposit left in an account paying 7% annual interest for 12 years.
b. The future value at the end of 6 years of an $800 *annual* end-of-year deposit into an account paying 7% annual interest.

LG 2

P4.9 For each of the following initial investment amounts, calculate the future value at the end of the given investment period if interest is compounded annually at the specified rate of return over the given investment period.

Investment	Investment Amount	Rate of Return	Investment Period
A	$ 200	5%	20 years
B	4,500	8	7
C	10,000	9	10
D	25,000	10	12
E	37,000	11	5

LG 2

P4.10 Using the appropriate table of interest factors found in Appendix A or a financial calculator, calculate the future value in 2 years of $10,000 invested today in an account that pays a stated annual interest rate of 12%, compounded monthly.

LG 2

P4.11 For each of the following annual deposits into an account paying the stated annual interest rate over the specified deposit period, calculate the future value of the *annuity* at the end of the given deposit period.

Deposit	Amount of Annual Deposit	Interest Rate	Deposit Period
A	$ 2,500	8%	10 years
B	500	12	6
C	1,000	20	5
D	12,000	6	8
E	4,000	14	30

LG 2

P4.12 If you deposit $1,000 into an account at the end of each of the next 5 years, and the account pays an annual interest rate of 6%, how much will be in the account after 5 years?

LG 2

P4.13 If you could earn 9% on similar-risk investments, what is the least you would accept at the end of a 6-year period, given the following amounts and timing of your investment?

a. Invest $5,000 as a lump sum today.
b. Invest $2,000 at the end of *each* of the next 5 years.
c. Invest a lump sum of $3,000 today and $1,000 at the end of *each* of the next 5 years.
d. Invest $900 at the end of years 1, 3, and 5.

LG 3

P4.14 For each of the following investments, calculate the present value of the future sum, using the specified discount rate and assuming the sum will be received at the end of the given year.

Investment	Future Sum	Discount Rate	End of Year
A	$ 7,000	12%	4
B	28,000	8	20
C	10,000	14	12
D	150,000	11	6
E	45,000	20	8

LG 3

P4.15 A Florida state savings bond can be converted to $1,000 at maturity 8 years from purchase. If the state bonds are to be competitive with U.S. savings bonds, which pay 6% interest compounded annually, at what price will the state's bonds sell, assuming they make no cash payments prior to maturity?

LG 3

P4.16 Referring to Problem 4.15 above, at what price would the bond sell if U.S. savings bonds were paying 8% interest compounded annually? Compare your answer to your answer to the preceding problem.

LG 3

P4.17 How much should you be willing to pay for a lump sum of $10,000 5 years from now if you can earn 3% every 6 months on other similar investments?

LG 3

P4.18 Find the present value of each of the following streams of income, assuming a 12% discount rate.

A		B		C	
End of Year	Income	End of Year	Income	End of Year	Income
1	$2,200	1	$10,000	1-5	$10,000/yr
2	3,000	2-5	5,000/yr	6-10	8,000/yr
3	4,000	6	7,000		
4	6,000				
5	8,000				

LG 3

P4.19 Consider the streams of income given in the following table.

a. Find the present value of each income stream, using a 15% discount rate.
b. Compare the calculated present values and discuss them in light of the fact that the undiscounted total income amounts to $10,000 in each case.

End of Year	Income Stream A	Income Stream B
1	$ 4,000	$ 1,000
2	3,000	2,000
3	2,000	3,000
4	1,000	4,000
Total	$10,000	$10,000

LG 3

P4.20 For each of the investments below, calculate the present value of the *annual* end-of-year returns at the specified discount rate over the given period.

Investment	Annual Returns	Discount Rate	Period
A	$ 1,200	7%	3 years
B	5,500	12	15
C	700	20	9
D	14,000	5	7
E	2,200	10	5

LG 3

P4.21 Congratulations! You have won the lottery! Would you rather have $1 million at the end of each of the next 20 years or $15 million today? (Assume an 8% discount rate.)

LG 3

P4.22 Using the appropriate table of interest factors found in Appendix A, a financial calculator, or an Excel spreadsheet, calculate the following.

a. The present value of $500 to be received 4 years from now, using an 11% discount rate.

b. The present value of the following end-of-year income streams, using a 9% discount rate and assuming it is now the beginning of 2006.

End of Year	Income Stream A	Income Stream B
2006	$80	$140
2007	80	120
2008	80	100
2009	80	80
2010	80	60
2011	80	40
2012	80	20

LG 2 LG 3

P4.23 Terri Allessandro has an opportunity to make any of the following investments. The purchase price, the amount of its lump-sum future value, and its year of receipt are given below for each investment. Terri can earn a 10% rate of return on investments similar to those currently under consideration. Evaluate each investment to determine whether it is satisfactory, and make an investment recommendation to Terri.

Investment	Purchase Price	Future Value	Year of Receipt
A	$18,000	$30,000	5
B	600	3,000	20
C	3,500	10,000	10
D	1,000	15,000	40

LG 2 LG 3

P4.24 Kent Weitz wishes to assess whether the following two investments are satisfactory. Use his required return (discount rate) of 17% to evaluate each investment. Make an investment recommendation to Kent.

	Investment	
	A	B
Purchase price	$13,000	$8,500
End of Year	Income Stream	
1	$ 2,500	$4,000
2	3,500	3,500
3	4,500	3,000
4	5,000	1,000
5	5,500	,500

LG 3

P4.25 You purchased a car using some cash and borrowing $15,000 (the present value) for fifty months at 12% per year. Calculate the monthly payment (annuity).

LG 3

P4.26 Referring to Problem 4.25 above, assume you have made 10 payments. What is the balance (present value) of your loan?

LG 4

P4.27 Given a real rate of interest of 3%, an expected inflation premium of 5%, and risk premiums for investments A and B of 3% and 5% respectively, find the following.

a. The risk-free rate of return R_F

b. The required returns for investments A and B.

LG 4

P4.28 The risk free rate is 7%, and expected inflation is 4.5%. If inflation expectations change such that future expected inflation rises to 5.5%, what will the new risk-free rate be?

LG 4

P4.29 Calculate the holding period return (HPR) for the following two investment alternatives. Which, if any, of the return components is likely not to be realized if you continue to hold each of the investments beyond 1 year? Which vehicle would you prefer, assuming they are of equal risk? Explain.

	Investment Vehicle	
	X	Y
Cash received		
1st quarter	$ 1.00	$ 0
2nd quarter	1.20	0
3rd quarter	0	0
4th quarter	2.30	2.00
Investment value		
End of year	$29.00	$56.00
Beginning of year	30.00	50.00

LG 4

P4.30 You are considering two investment alternatives. The first is a stock that pays quarterly dividends of $0.50 per share, is trading at $25 per share, and you expect to sell the stock in six months for $27. The second is a stock that pays quarterly dividends of $0.60 per share, is trading at $27 per share, and you expect to sell the stock in one year for $30. Which stock will provide the better annualized holding period return?

LG 4

P4.31 You are considering purchasing a bond that pays annual interest of $50 per $1,000 of par value. The bond matures in one year, when you will collect the par value and the interest payment. If you can purchase this bond for $950, what is the holding period return?

LG 4

P4.32 Assume you invest $5,000 today in an investment vehicle that promises to return $9,000 in exactly 10 years.

a. Use the present-value technique to estimate the yield on this investment.
b. If a minimum return of 9% is required, would you recommend this investment?

LG 4

P4.33 You invest $7,000 in stock and receive $65, $70, $70, and $65 in dividends over the following 4 years. At the end of the four years, you sell the stock for $7,900. What was the yield on this investment?

LG 4

P4.34 Your friend asks you to invest $10,000 in a business venture. Based on your estimates, you would receive nothing for four years, at the end of year five you would receive interest on the investment compounded annually at 8%, and at the end of year six you would receive $14,500. If your estimates are correct, what would be the yield on this investment?

LG 4

P4.35 Use the appropriate present-value interest factor table, a financial calculator, or an Excel spreadsheet to estimate the yield for each of the following investments.

Investment	Initial Investment	Future Value	End of Year
A	$ 1,000	$ 1,200	5
B	10,000	20,000	7
C	,400	2,000	20
D	3,000	4,000	6
E	5,500	25,000	30

LG 4

P4.36 Rosemary Santos must earn a return of 10% on an investment that requires an initial outlay of $2,500 and promises to return $6,000 in 8 years.

a. Use present-value techniques to estimate the yield on this investment.
b. On the basis of your finding in part a, should Rosemary make the proposed investment? Explain.

LG 4

P4.37 Use the appropriate present-value interest factors, a financial calculator, or an Excel spreadsheet to estimate the yield for each of the following two investments.

	Investment A	Investment B
Initial Investment	$8,500	$9,500
End of Year	**Income**	
1	$2,500	$2,000
2	2,500	2,500
3	2,500	3,000
4	2,500	3,500
5	2,500	4,000

LG 4

P4.38 Elliott Dumack must earn a minimum rate of return of 11% to be adequately compensated for the risk of the following investment.

Initial Investment	$14,000
End of year	Income
1	$ 6,000
2	3,000
3	5,000
4	2,000
5	1,000

a. Use present-value techniques to estimate the yield on this investment.
b. On the basis of your finding in part **a**, should Elliott make the proposed investment? Explain.

LG 4

P4.39 Assume the investment that generates income stream B in Problem 4.22 can be purchased at the beginning of 2006 for $1,000 and sold at the end of 2012 for $1,200. Estimate the yield for this investment. If a minimum return of 9% is required, would you recommend this investment? Explain.

LG 4

P4.40 For each of the following streams of dividends, estimate the compound annual rate of growth between the earliest year for which a value is given and 2005.

	Dividend Stream		
Year	A	B	C
1996		$1.50	
1997		1.55	
1998		1.61	
1999		1.68	$2.50
2000		1.76	2.60
2001	$5.00	1.85	2.65
2002	5.60	1.95	2.65
2003	6.40	2.06	2.80
2004	7.20	2.17	2.85
2005	8.00	2.28	2.90

LG 4

P4.41 A company paid dividends of $1.00 per share in 1997, and just announced that it will pay $2.21 in 2004. Estimate the compound annual growth rate of the dividends.

LG 4

P4.42 A company reported net income in 2000 of $350 million. In 2004, the company expects net income to be $441.7 million. Estimate the annual compound growth rate of net income.

LG 6

P4.43 The historical returns for two investments—A and B—are summarized in the table below for the period 2001 to 2005. Use the data to answer the questions that follow.

	Investment	
	A	B
Year	Rate of Return	
2001	19%	8%
2002	1	10
2003	10	12
2004	26	14
2005	4	16
Average	12%	12%

a. On the basis of a review of the return data, which investment appears to be more risky? Why?

b. Calculate the standard deviation and the coefficient of variation for each investment's returns.
c. On the basis of your calculations in part **b**, which investment is more risky? Compare this conclusion to your observation in part **a**.
d. Does the coefficient of variation provide better risk comparison than the standard deviation in the case? Why or why not?

LG 6

P4.44 Referring to Problem 4.43, if one investment's required return is 12% and the other is 14%, which one is 14%

See the text Web site (www.aw-bc.com/gitman_joehnk) for Web exercises that deal with *return and risk.*

Case Problem 4.1 *Solomon's Decision*

LG 2 LG 3 LG 4

Dave Solomon, a 23-year-old mathematics teacher at Xavier High School, recently received a tax refund of $1,100. Because Dave didn't need this money for his current living expenses, he decided to make a long-term investment. After surveying a number of alternative investments costing no more than $1,100, Dave isolated two that seemed most suitable to his needs.

Each of the investments cost $1,050 and was expected to provide income over a 10-year period. Investment A provided a relatively certain stream of income. Dave was a little less certain of the income provided by investment B. From his search for suitable alternatives, Dave found that the appropriate discount rate for a relatively certain investment was 12%. Because he felt a bit uncomfortable with an investment like B, he estimated that such an investment would have to provide a return at least 4% *higher* than investment A. Although Dave planned to reinvest funds returned from the investments in other vehicles providing similar returns, he wished to keep the extra $50 ($1,100 − $1,050) invested for the full 10 years in a savings account paying 5% interest compounded annually.

As he makes his investment decision, Dave has asked for your help in answering the questions that follow the expected return data for these investments.

	Expected Returns			Expected Returns	
Year	A	B	Year	A	B
2006	$150	$100	2011	$ 150	$350
2007	150	150	2012	150	300
2008	150	200	2013	150	250
2009	150	250	2014	150	200
2010	150	300	2015	1,150	150

Questions

a. Assuming that investments A and B are equally risky and using the 12% discount rate, apply the present-value technique to assess the acceptability of each investment and to determine the preferred investment. Explain your findings.

b. Recognizing that investment B is more risky than investment A, reassess the two alternatives, adding the 4% risk premium to the 12% discount rate for investment A and therefore applying a 16% discount rate to investment B. Compare your findings relative to acceptability and preference to those found for question **a**.

c. From your findings in questions **a** and **b**, indicate whether the yield for investment A is above or below 12% and whether that for investment B is above or below 16%. Explain.

d. Use the present-value technique to estimate the yield on each investment. Compare your findings and contrast them with your response to question **c**.

e. From the information given, which, if either, of the two investments would you recommend that Dave make? Explain your answer.

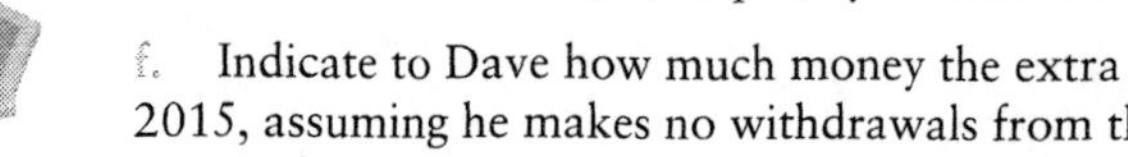

f. Indicate to Dave how much money the extra $50 will have grown to by the end of 2015, assuming he makes no withdrawals from the savings account.

Case Problem 4.2 *The Risk-Return Tradeoff: Molly O'Rourke's Stock Purchase Decision*

LG 4 LG 5 LG 6

Over the past 10 years, Molly O'Rourke has slowly built a diversified portfolio of common stock. Currently her portfolio includes 20 different common stock issues and has a total market value of $82,500.

Molly is at present considering the addition of 50 shares of one of two common stock issues—X or Y. To assess the return and risk of each of these issues, she has gathered dividend income and share price data for both over each of the last 10 years (1996 through 2005). Molly's investigation of the outlook for these issues suggests that each will, on average, tend to behave in the future just as it has in the past. She therefore believes that the expected return can be estimated by finding the average holding period return (HPR) over the past 10 years for each of the stocks. The historical dividend income and stock price data collected by Molly are given in the accompanying table.

	Stock X			Stock Y		
		Share Price			Share Price	
Year	Dividend Income	Beginning	Ending	Dividend Income	Beginning	Ending
1996	$1.00	$20.00	$22.00	$1.50	$20.00	$20.00
1997	1.50	22.00	21.00	1.60	20.00	20.00
1998	1.40	21.00	24.00	1.70	20.00	21.00
1999	1.70	24.00	22.00	1.80	21.00	21.00
2000	1.90	22.00	23.00	1.90	21.00	22.00
2001	1.60	23.00	26.00	2.00	22.00	23.00
2002	1.70	26.00	25.00	2.10	23.00	23.00
2003	2.00	25.00	24.00	2.20	23.00	24.00
2004	2.10	24.00	27.00	2.30	24.00	25.00
2005	2.20	27.00	30.00	2.40	25.00	25.00

Questions

a. Determine the holding period return (HPR) for each stock in each of the preceding 10 years. Find the expected return for each stock, using the approach specified by Molly.

b. Use the HPRs and expected return calculated in question a to find both the standard deviation and the coefficient of variation of the HPRs for each stock over the 10-year period 1996 to 2005.

c. Use your findings to evaluate and discuss the return and risk associated with stocks X and Y. Which stock seems preferable? Explain.

d. Ignoring her existing portfolio, what recommendations would you give Molly with regard to stocks *X* and *Y*?

Excel with Spreadsheets

From her Investment Analysis class, Laura has been given an assignment to evaluate several securities on a risk-return tradeoff basis. The specific securities to be researched are International Business Machines, Helmerich & Payne, Inc., and the S&P 500 Index. The respective ticker symbols for the stocks are IBM and HP. She finds the following (assumed) data on the securities in question. It is as follows:

Year	2000	2001	2002	2003	2004	2005
Price_{IBM}	\$ 49.38	\$ 91.63	\$112.25	\$112.00	\$107.89	\$ 92.68
Dividend_{IBM}	\$ .40	\$ .44	\$ .48	\$ .52	\$ .56	\$ .64
Price_{HP}	\$ 25.56	\$ 17.56	\$ 23.50	\$ 47.81	\$ 30.40	\$ 27.93
Dividend_{HP}	\$ .28	\$ .28	\$ .28	\$ .30	\$ .30	\$ .32
$\text{Value}_{S\&P}$	980.3	1,279.6	1,394.6	1,366.0	1,130.2	1,121.8

Note: The value of the S&P 500 Index includes dividends.

Questions

Part One

a. Use the given data that Laura has found on the three securities and create a spreadsheet to calculate the holding period return (HPR) for each year and the average return over a 5-year period. Specifically, the HPR will be based upon five unique periods of 1 year (i.e., 2000 to 2001, 2001 to 2002, 2002 to 2003, 2003 to 2004, 2004 to 2005). Use the following formula:

$$\text{HPR} = [C + (V_n - V_o)] / V_o$$

Where

C = current income during period
V_n = ending investment value
V_o = beginning investment value

Part Two

Create a spreadsheet similar to the spreadsheet for Table 4.15, which can be viewed at www.aw-bc.com/gitman_joehnk, in order to evaluate the risk-return tradeoff.

b. Calculate the standard deviations of the returns for IBM, HP, and the S&P 500 Index.

c. Calculate the coefficients of variation for IBM, HP, and the S&P 500 Index.

d. What industries are associated with IBM and HP?

e. Based on your answer in **d** and your results for the average return and the standard deviation and coefficient of variation, what conclusions can Laura make about investing in either IBM or HP?

Fundamentals of Investing

CHAPTER 6

COMMON STOCKS

CHAPTER 6

COMMON STOCKS

LEARNING GOALS

After studying this chapter, you should be able to:

LG 1 Explain the investment appeal of common stocks and why individuals like to invest in them.

LG 2 Describe stock returns from a historical perspective and understand how current returns measure up to historical standards of performance.

LG 3 Discuss the basic features of common stocks, including issue characteristics, stock quotations, and transaction costs.

LG 4 Understand the different kinds of common stock values.

LG 5 Discuss common stock dividends, types of dividends, and dividend reinvestment plans.

LG 6 Describe various types of common stocks, including foreign stocks, and note how stocks can be used as investment vehicles.

Bear or bull market? Lately, it's been hard to tell! One day the headlines proclaim, "Dow Industrials Surge." The next day, investors may read, "Stocks, Bonds Slip Back on Fed Move." Other articles discuss "Is the Rally Real?", as some analysts say "yes" while others call recent events a mere correction.

Take, for example, two seasoned mutual fund managers: Walter McCormick and John Rutledge. In March 2003, McCormick believed that the upward trend in the major market averages marked the beginning of a rally and pushed his firm to buy more stocks. Rutledge, in contrast, advised caution: "I am not sure we have seen the bottom; I think we could see new, lower lows."

The irony: Both fund managers work at Evergreen Investments. Their differing views were by no means unusual. "Do we have lots of positive economic reports signaling improvement? So far, no," said Clare Zempel, chief investment strategist at Robert W. Baird, a Milwaukee firm. "But I think the odds are extremely high . . . that this postwar rebound is sustainable." Through late summer 2003, McCormick and Zempel appeared to be right. In fact, both blue-chip stocks and technology issues hit new highs in August. Rutledge benefited from the gains—even as he held firm to his conviction that a decline was imminent—but saw his fund returns lag considerably behind those of his peers (his return from January 1 to August 22, 2003, was about 18%, compared to the category-average of 37.5%). McCormick's performance of 13.7% was just above his peer-group average, 13.4%.

How do you choose stocks during such confusing times? In boom times, it looked easy: Almost everything went up. During the bear market, investors wondered if they should still buy stocks. Regardless of market conditions, investors who place their money at risk must learn how to gather, analyze, and interpret information about each company they consider and the industry in which it operates. This chapter introduces you to common stocks and the key concepts and principles of investing in these complex but potentially rewarding securities.

Sources: E. S. Browning, "Dow Industrials Surge a Record 499.19," *The Wall Street Journal*, March 17, 2000, p. C1; E. S. Browning, "Experts Duel Over Fate of Bellwether Rally," *The Wall Street Journal*, June 16, 2003, pp. C1, C3; "Fund Returns," *Morningstar.com*, August 23, 2003, downloaded from www.morningstar.com; and James M. Pethokoukis, "Is the Rally Real?" *Newsweek*, July 7, 2003, pp. 16–17.

What Stocks Have to Offer

LG 1 LG 2

residual owners
owners/stockholders of a firm, who are entitled to dividend income and a prorated share of the firm's earnings only after all other obligations have been met.

The basic investment attribute of common stocks is that they enable investors to participate in the profits of the firm. Every shareholder is a part owner of the firm and, as such, is entitled to a piece of the firm's profits. This claim on income is not without limitations, however, because common stockholders are really the **residual owners** of the company. That is, they are entitled to dividend income and a share of the company's earnings only after all other corporate obligations have been met. Equally important, as residual owners, holders of common stock have no guarantee that they will ever receive any return on their investment. The challenge, of course, is to find stocks that will provide the kind of return you're looking for. That's no easy task, as there are literally thousands of actively traded stocks to choose from.

The Appeal of Common Stocks

Even in spite of the recent (2000–2002) bear market, common stocks remain a popular form of investing, used by literally millions of individual investors. They are popular, in part, because they offer investors the opportunity to tailor their investment programs to meet individual needs and preferences. Given the size and diversity of the stock market, it's safe to say that no matter what the investment objective, there are common stocks to fit the bill. For people living off their investment holdings, stocks provide a way of earning a steady stream of current income (from the dividends they produce). For investors less concerned about current income, common stocks can serve as the basis for long-run accumulation of wealth. With this strategy, stocks are used very much like a savings account: Investors buy stock for the long haul as a way to earn not only dividends but also a steady flow of capital gains. These investors recognize that stocks have a tendency to go up in price over time, and they simply position themselves to take advantage of that fact. Indeed, it is this potential for capital gains that is the real draw for most investors. Whereas dividends can provide a steady stream of income, the big returns—under normal, long-term market conditions—come from capital gains. And few securities can match common stocks when it comes to capital gains.

INVESTOR FACTS

THE LUMBERING BEAR—Bear markets occur when stock prices are falling. But not all falling markets end up as bears. A drop of *5% or more* in one of the major market indexes, like the Dow Jones Industrial Average (DJIA), is called a **routine decline**. Such declines are considered "routine" since they typically occur several times a year. A **correction** is a drop of *10% or more* in an index. A correction occurred in mid-summer 1998, when the DJIA plunged 19.3%. The term **bear market** is reserved for severe market declines of *20% or more*. Bear markets usually occur every 3 to 4 years, although the 1990s were totally bear-free. That all changed in 2000, however, when the market embarked on a 3-year bear run, making it one of the worst bear markets in the last 75 years and only the fourth time in the 108-year history of the DJIA that the index fell 3 years in a row.

Putting Stock Price Behavior in Perspective

Given the underlying nature of common stocks, when the market is strong, investors can generally expect to benefit from steady price appreciation. A good example is the performance that took place in 1999, when the market, as measured by the Dow Jones Industrial Average (DJIA), went up by more than 25%. Unfortunately, when markets falter, so do investor returns. Just look what happened over the 3-year period from early 2000 through late 2002, when the market (again, as measured by the DJIA) fell some 38%. Excluding dividends, that means a $100,000 investment would have declined in value to a little over $60,000. That hurts!

Make no mistake about it: The market does have its bad days, and sometimes those bad days seem to go on for months. Even though it may not always appear to be so, those bad days *really are the exception rather than the rule*. That was certainly the case over the 54-year period from 1950 through mid-2003, when the Dow went down (for the year) just 16 times. That's less than 30% of the time; the other 70% the market was up—anywhere from 2% on the year to more than 40%! True, there is some risk and price volatility (even in good markets), but that's the price you pay for all the upside potential. Consider, for example, the behavior of the market from 1982 through early 2000. Starting in August 1982, when the Dow stood at 777, this market saw the DJIA climb nearly 11,000 points to a high of 11,723, reached in January 2000. This turned out to be one of the longest bull markets in history, as the DJIA grew (over 18 years) at an average annual rate of nearly 17%. Yet, even in this market, there were some off days, and even a few off years. But, clearly, they were the exception rather than the rule.

From Stock Prices to Stock Returns

Our discussion so far has centered on *stock prices*, but what are even more important to investors are *stock returns*, which take into account not only price behavior but also dividend income. Table 6.1 uses the DJIA to show annual market returns over the 54-year period from 1950 to 2003. In addition to total returns, the table breaks market performance down into the two basic sources of return: dividends and capital gains. These figures, of course, reflect

TABLE 6.1 Annual Returns in the Stock Market, 1950–2003 (returns based on performance of the DJIA)

Year	Rate of Return from Dividends	Rate of Return from Capital Gains	Total Rate of Return	Year	Rate of Return from Dividends	Rate of Return from Capital Gains	Total Rate of Return
2003	2.20%	8.72%	10.92%	1976	4.12%	17.86%	21.98%
2002	2.27	−16.76	−14.49	1975	4.39	38.32	42.71
2001	1.81	−7.10	−5.29	1974	6.12	−27.57	−21.45
2000	1.61	−6.18	−4.58	1973	4.15	−16.58	−12.43
1999	1.47	25.22	26.69	1972	3.16	14.58	17.74
1998	1.65	16.10	17.75	1971	3.47	6.11	9.58
1997	1.72	22.64	24.36	1970	3.76	4.82	8.58
1996	2.03	26.01	28.04	1969	4.24	−15.19	−10.95
1995	2.27	33.45	35.72	1968	3.32	4.27	7.59
1994	2.75	2.14	4.89	1967	3.33	15.20	18.53
1993	2.65	13.72	16.37	1966	4.06	−18.94	−14.88
1992	3.05	4.17	7.22	1965	2.95	10.88	13.83
1991	3.00	20.32	23.32	1964	3.57	14.57	18.14
1990	3.94	−4.34	−0.40	1963	3.07	17.00	20.07
1989	3.74	26.96	30.70	1962	3.57	−10.81	−7.24
1988	3.67	11.85	15.52	1961	3.11	18.71	21.82
1987	3.67	2.26	5.93	1960	3.47	−9.34	−5.87
1986	3.54	22.58	26.12	1959	3.05	16.40	19.45
1985	4.01	27.66	31.67	1958	3.43	33.96	37.39
1984	5.00	−3.74	1.26	1957	4.96	−12.77	−7.81
1983	4.47	20.27	24.74	1956	4.60	2.27	6.87
1982	5.17	19.60	24.77	1955	4.42	20.77	25.19
1981	6.42	−9.23	−2.81	1954	4.32	43.96	48.28
1980	5.64	14.93	20.57	1953	5.73	−3.77	1.96
1979	6.08	4.19	10.27	1952	5.29	8.42	13.71
1978	6.03	−3.15	2.88	1951	6.07	14.37	20.44
1977	5.51	−17.27	−11.76	1950	6.85	17.63	24.48

Note: Total return figures are based on both dividend income *and* capital gains (or losses); all figures are compiled from DJIA performance information, as obtained from *Barron's* and the *Wall Street Journal;* 2003 figures are through the second quarter (June 30) of the year.

HOT LINKS

Stockcharts.com gives you the Nasdaq New Highs-New Lows Line ($NAHL). You can scroll down to the bottom of the chart to interpret the chart by clicking on Chart School.

www.stockcharts.com/gallery?$NAHL

the *general behavior of the market as a whole*, not necessarily that of *individual stocks*. Think of them as the return behavior on a well-balanced portfolio of common stocks.

The numbers show a market that, over the past 54 years, has provided annual returns ranging from a low of −21.45% (in 1974) to a high of +48.28% (in 1954). Breaking down the returns into dividends and capital gains reveals, not surprisingly, that the big returns (or losses) come from capital gains. Overall, as Table 6.2 shows, *stocks have provided average returns of around 11% over the 50-year period from 1953–2002*. But as can be seen in the table, the 1980s and 90s definitely were not average, especially not the last half of the nineties. Indeed, while the first 5 years of the decade produced below-average returns of "only" 10% per year, the second half turned in annual returns of over 26%. That all changed in 2000, however, when a bear market took hold, and the return on the Dow fell to a *minus* 4.3%. Factor that decline into the most recent 5-year holding period and you can see (in Table 6.2) what happened—from 1998 through mid-2003, the average annual return on the DJIA amounted to a measly 1.7%.

Keep in mind that the numbers here represent market performance; *individual* stocks can and often do perform quite differently. But at least the averages give us a benchmark against which we can assess current stock returns and our own expectations. For example, if a return of 10% to 12% can be considered a good long-term estimate for stocks, then *sustained* returns of 15% to 18% should definitely be viewed as extraordinary. (These higher returns are possible, of course, but to get them, investors must either take on more risk or hope for a continuation of the nineties bull market.) Likewise, long-run stock returns of only 6% to 8% should probably be viewed as substandard. If that's the best you think you can do, then you may want to consider sticking with bonds or CDs, where you'll earn almost as much, but with less risk.

TABLE 6.2 Holding Period Returns in the Stock Market 1950-2003

Holding Periods	Average Annual Returns	Cumulative Returns	Amount to Which $10,000 Will Grow
5(+) years: 1998–2003	1.7%	8.6%	$ 10,859
3(+) years: 2000–2003	*−4.3*	*−14.3*	*8,572*
5 years: 1995–1999	26.4	222.4	32,238
5 years: 1990–1994	10.0	60.7	16,075
10 years: 1993–2002	11.8	204.0	30,399
15 years: 1988–2002	12.8	504.6	60,465
25 years: 1978–2002	13.2	2,128.4	222,841
50 years: 1953–2002	10.7	15,806.9	1,590,690
The 1990s: 1990–1999	18.3	438.9	53,897
The 1980s: 1980–1989	17.2	390.5	49,049
The 1970s: 1970–1979	5.3	67.9	16,792
The 1960s: 1960–1969	5.2	66.0	16,602
The 1950s: 1950–1959	18.0	421.7	52,171

Note: Average annual return figures are fully compounded returns and assume that all dividend income and capital gains are automatically reinvested. All figures compiled from DJIA performance information, as obtained from *Barron's* and the *Wall Street Journal*; 2003 data through the second quarter.

INVESTING IN ACTION

ANATOMY OF A MARKET MELTDOWN

It seemed like the bull market that would never end. Between August 1982 and January 2000, the Dow Jones Industrial Average (DJIA) rose an average of 17% per year. When the U.S. economy really took off in 1995, the stock markets of the late 1990s carried investors on a wild ride. Share prices moved sharply upward as the DJIA broke through successive 1,000-point barriers, peaking at 11,723 on January 14, 2000. Annual returns from 1995 to 1999 averaged about 26%. Technology stocks led the way, and investors cheered as on paper at least they made impressive gains—even as Alan Greenspan, chairman of the Federal Reserve Board, cautioned against the "irrational exuberance" in the markets.

Throughout the 5-year run-up, naysayers warned that the market euphoria couldn't last forever. Each year investors wondered when the bull market would stumble, and each year it continued to surge ahead, spurred on by a strong economy and a relatively peaceful world situation. Excited investors bought stock in technology and Internet companies, many only a year or two old with no track records, products, or profits. Novices and pros alike ignored warning signs along the way. "In the '90s, the public got sucked into that vortex of speculation where they thought that 'this time is different' and that we would never have another recession," commented Ned Riley, chief investment strategist at State Street Global Advisors in Boston.

The year 2000 began with the DJIA and Nasdaq Composite reaching all-time highs in January and March, respectively. The Federal Reserve increased the money supply to guard against possible year-2000 computer problems, which contributed to the still-growing tech bubble. When the market peaked, tech stocks accounted for more than 40% of the S&P 500's value. But under Wall Street's slick surface were rumblings that all was not well. In March 2000, the Fed raised interest rates to curb inflation, and businesses reported decreasing investment in technology.

In the weeks that followed, the Nasdaq Composite lost 33% of its value. Dot-com sensations suffered; Yahoo!, for example, lost 40% of its market value in just 3 weeks. But blue chips held firm, leading market strategists to speculate whether the decline was a warning sign or another brief setback. Money continued to flow into stocks as a rebound followed each sharp drop. This up-and-down pattern continued for the next 3 years. For example, the DJIA took a record 499.19-point (4.9%) leap in mid-March 2000, but then resumed its downward spiral.

In the same way that tech stocks had led the market to new heights, so they pulled it down when the dot-com bubble burst. A comeback in spring and summer 2000 drew investors back to tech mainstays, but bad news such as lower sales at Dell Computer and the antitrust suit against Microsoft soon made investors reconsider their tech stock positions. By year-end 2000, shares of Oracle and Cisco had dropped 40%, and Intel's stock price had plunged 60%.

Once again the blue chips rallied, and the DJIA ended the year down just 8% from its high, although the more tech-heavy S&P 500 was down 14% and the Nasdaq had declined by 51%. Investors began to abandon tech companies that offered promises rather than earnings, turning to sectors that seemed safer—for example, financial institutions and utilities. One exciting new area was energy, where natural gas trading companies like Enron and Dynegy were revitalizing the utility industry.

The first of a series of Federal Reserve interest rate cuts in January 2001 sent the markets soaring. Subsequent cuts did little to stimulate the economy, however, and the country entered into a recession. Unable to revive sales, companies cut costs to keep earnings from falling farther. A spring rally was again short-lived; even blue chips provided no safe haven for investors. The markets continued to bounce investors around through the summer months.

On September 11, 2001, the financial markets suffered another blow—a physical one—as terrorists struck the World Trade Center towers in the heart of New York's financial district. A stunned United States and world went into shock. The markets closed for about a week, amid great uncertainty and insecurity. When they reopened, the Dow dropped another 14%. By September 2001, investors had lost more than $6 trillion since the January 2000 market peak.

To bolster the financial markets, the Fed again poured money into the system, sparking a rally

continued on next page

INVESTING IN ACTION

continued from previous page

that amazed everyone in light of the shocking terrorist attacks. The Nasdaq jumped 45% between September 2001 and January 2002, and the DJIA and S&P 500 were also up considerably. Was the market finally going to turn bullish again?

Investors had little time to savor the latest rebound, however. The battered markets soon faced a very different setback: corporate scandals that severely undermined investor confidence. The first to erupt involved Enron, the new-breed energy company. Under its glittering façade Enron was manipulating accounting rules to create the illusion of growth and enhance its financial statements. As Enron's financial games and phantom earnings became public knowledge in late 2001, its financial house of cards tumbled down. Along with it came the demise of Arthur Andersen, its once prestigious auditor. In addition, several other financial institutions found themselves under investigation for their involvement in Enron's off-balance-sheet deals.

Alarmed at how Enron had obscured financial information in its published financial reports, investors began to question the reliability of corporate financial reporting in general. Before long executives from Adelphia, Qwest, Tyco, WorldCom, Xerox, and other companies joined the rogue's gallery of corporate financial wrongdoers. A crackdown on stock analyst malfeasance by New York State's attorney general further damaged investor confidence. Money drained out of the equity markets and into bonds and other investment vehicles.

Matters went downhill from there, as the DJIA slid to 7,286 on October 9, 2002—a 38% decline. Likewise, the S&P 500 and Nasdaq, with their larger numbers of technology stocks, dropped 49% and 77% from their peaks, respectively.

What or who is to blame for this bear market, which ranks among the worst in market history? Fingers now point in many directions, as events unrelated to fiscal or monetary policy—among them the September 11 and subsequent terrorist threats, corporate scandals, and the war in Iraq—joined with the more traditional causes to create a sense of financial insecurity that weakened investor faith in the financial system. From 1999 through 2002, the DJIA closed lower at year end—the first time since 1941 it had declined in three successive years. The total return on investment for stocks in the DJIA plummeted from 27.2% in 1999 to –15% in 2002. Every sector, including the most solid blue chips, suffered greatly from the weakened economy, corporate scandals, and lower earnings. About 70% of stocks on major exchanges closed down for the year. Jaded investors looked to companies that paid dividends, not those promising astronomical growth rates.

In March 2003, after a few more false starts, the markets appeared to be moving steadily upward. By mid-September, the DJIA was up 16% for the year, while the S&P 500 posted an 18% gain and the Nasdaq composite saw growth of 39%. As noted in the chapter opener, however, experts remained divided on whether the bear market was over or the rebound represented a short-lived correction.

While investor mania is nothing new—in the seventeenth century, for example, Dutch investors speculated on tulips, not tech stocks—the recent boom-and-bust cycle has implications for important shifts in the workings of the economy and the capital markets. The stock market's meteoric rise brought individual investors, many of whom previously shunned equities as too risky, into the picture. Everyone wanted a piece of the tech stock action, as young companies went public to much acclaim; VA Linux Systems, for example, saw its share price rise an unbelievable 698% on its first day of trading. Have investors now learned their lessons, and realize that they should look for a solid track record and not empty promises? Only time will tell.

Critical Thinking Question Describe the major factors that contributed to the 2000 market meltdown. What steps can you take to protect yourself in the future?

Sources: Ken Brown, "Company Blowups Abound, Rebounds Rare," *The Wall Street Journal*, January 2, 2003, p. R2; E. S. Browning, "Investors Seek Ray of Hope," *The Wall Street Journal*, January 2, 2003, p. R1; E. S. Browning, "Stocks, Bonds Slip on Fed Move," *The Wall Street Journal*, June 26, 2003, p. C1; E. S. Browning and Ianthe Jeanne Dugan, "Aftermath of a Market Mania," *The Wall Street Journal*, December 16, 2002, pp. C1, C13; James M. Pethokoukis, "Is the Rally Real?" *Newsweek*, July 7, 2003, pp. 16–17; "2001 Investment Scoreboard," *The Wall Street Journal*, January 2, 2002, p. R2; "2002 Investment Scoreboard," *The Wall Street Journal*, January 2, 2003, p. R2; and Penelope Wang, Amy Feldman, Jon Birger, and Aravind Adiga, "How Bad Is It?" *Money*, September 2002, p. 78.

The Dow, the S&P, and the Nasdaq

Most of our discussion in this chapter has been in terms of the DJIA, in large part because the Dow is such a widely followed measure of market performance. However, the DJIA is just one measure of market behavior, and it doesn't always tell the whole story. Two other closely followed market indexes are the S&P (Standard & Poor's) 500 and the Nasdaq Composite.

The problem with the Dow is that it captures the performance of a small, very select group of (just 30) large-cap stocks. Thus, it does not always reflect what's happening in the broad market. In contrast, the *S&P 500* tracks the performance of 500 of the very biggest and most important firms in the market and as such, is felt to be far more representative of market behavior. The *Nasdaq Composite*, on the other hand, tracks the behavior of many of this country's *tech stocks*, from the very largest, like Microsoft and Intel, to most of the newest (and much smaller) dot-com firms.

Comparative Performance of the Three Market Measures To see how these market measures performed in the 1990s and beyond (through mid-2003), take a look at Figure 6.1. The upper panel shows the DJIA relative to the S&P 500, and the lower panel shows the Dow relative to the Nasdaq Composite. Starting with the upper panel, we can see very similar performances for the DJIA and S&P 500 at least through 1999. But the S&P was much harder hit by the bear market and, as a result, a noticeable gap between these two measures started to appear in early 2000, and it grew wider over time. The net result was a sharply lower return for the S&P 500. Indeed, as seen in Table 6.3 (on page 242), there was about a 1½-point spread in comparative returns over the full 13½-year period, from 1990 through mid-2003. The Dow ended up with an average annual return of 11.77%, while the S&P turned in a 10.20% return.

While you would expect some similarity in the behavior of the Dow and the S&P (after all, both track the performance of large-cap stocks), you wouldn't expect the same performance when you match the Dow with the Nasdaq Composite—and you don't get it. But look at the lower panel of Figure 6.1: There's probably more similarity between the two measures than you'd expect—especially in the first 5 or 6 years. Indeed, note in Table 6.3 that in the first half of the decade, the DJIA and the Nasdaq Composite had almost the same average annual returns (10.26% for the Dow versus 10.58% for the Nasdaq). In fact, these two measures tracked one another fairly closely through 1997. Then, in 1998, they went their separate ways. High-tech stocks and the Nasdaq moved up sharply, while large-cap "old economy" stocks continued up at a far more modest pace. Thus, by the end of the decade, whereas the Dow had a very respectable 10-year return of 18.35%, the Nasdaq registered an incredible 24.50% rate of return (see Table 6.3). But then along came the bear—and the Nasdaq Composite was hammered. In a little more than a year, the huge positive spread between the Nasdaq and the Dow totally disappeared, and suddenly it was the Nasdaq trailing the Dow. As a result, over the full 13½-year period ending mid-2003, the DJIA actually beat the Nasdaq Composite by almost two full percentage points.

Bulls, Bubbles, and Bears The bull market that began in August 1982 continued on through the 1980s and into the early 1990s. Except for the length of this market, it didn't appear to be out of the ordinary in any other way—at

FIGURE 6.1 **Thirteen Years of the Dow, the S&P, and the Nasdaq (1990 to 2002, *plus the first half of 2003*)**

Here's how the DJIA performed relative to the S&P 500 (top) and the Nasdaq Composite (bottom) in the 1990s, through mid-2003. As it turns out, the Dow held its own against not only the S&P 500, but also the tech-heavy Nasdaq Composite.

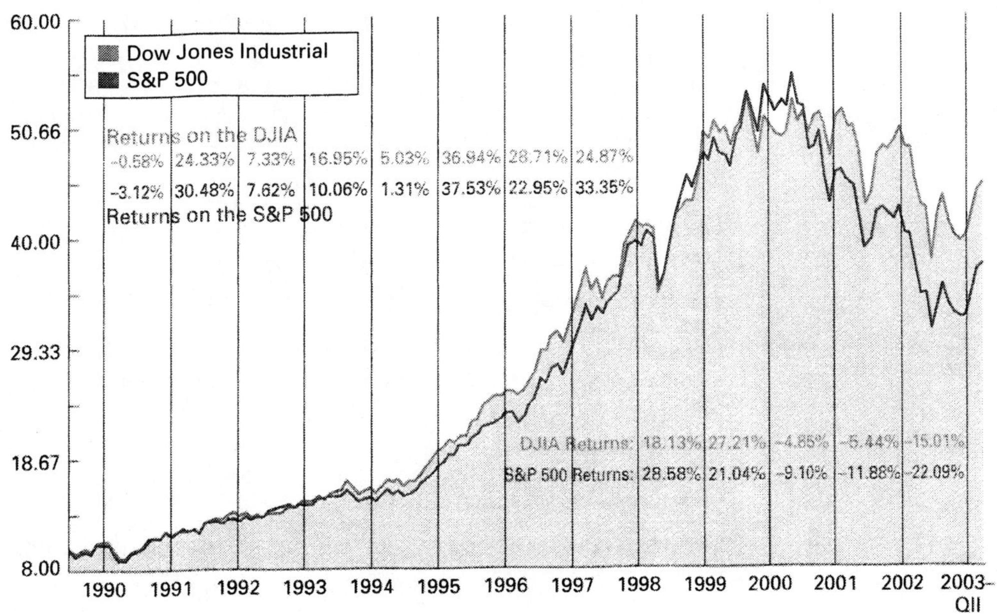

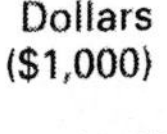

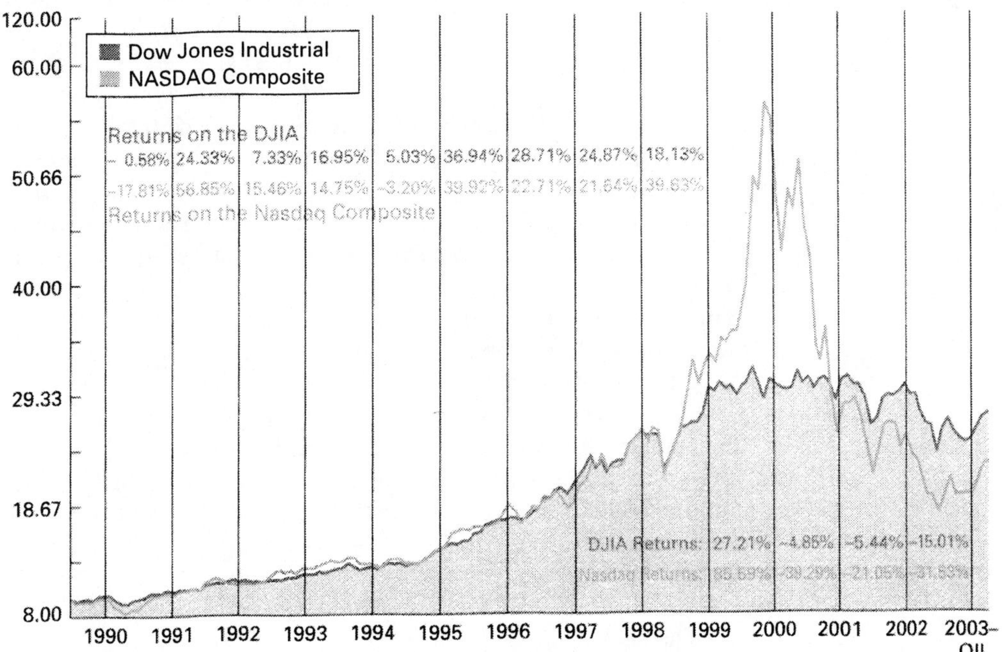

TABLE 6.3 **Comparative Returns on the Dow, the S&P, and the Nasdaq**

Holding Periods and Return Measures	DJIA	S&P 500	Nasdaq Composite
Full 13½-Year Period: 1990 to Mid-2003			
• Average annual returns	11.77%	10.20%	9.88%
• Cumulative returns	349.28%	271.22%	256.82%
• Amount to which $10,000 will grow	$44,928	$37,122	$35,682
3½-Year Period: 2000 to Mid-2003			
• Average annual returns	−5.07%	−9.79%	−23.10%
• Cumulative returns	−16.64%	−30.26%	−60.12%
• Amount to which $10,000 will grow	$8,336	$6,974	$3,988
The Decade of the '90s: 1990–1999			
• Average annual returns	18.35%	18.20%	24.50%
• Cumulative returns	438.97%	432.33%	794.75%
• Amount to which $10,000 will grow	$53,897	$53,233	$89,475
Last Half of the Decade: 1995–1999			
• Average annual returns	27.03%	28.54%	40.71%
• Cumulative returns	230.75%	250.91%	441.16%
• Amount to which $10,000 will grow	$33,075	$35,091	$54,116
First Half of the Decade: 1990–1994			
• Average annual returns	10.26%	8.69%	10.58%
• Cumulative returns	62.96%	51.70%	65.34%
• Amount to which $10,000 will grow	$16,296	$15,170	$16,534

Note: Average annual return figures are fully compounded and assume that all dividends and capital gains are reinvested.

Source: Morningstar Principia Pro, June 2003.

least through the first half of the nineties. Indeed, the average rate of growth in share prices through 1994 was just 12 percent. But then in 1995, 1996, and 1997, things began to heat up, and the average rate of growth in share prices jumped to more than 27%. And by 1998, the *tech stock bubble* was in full bloom. This is readily apparent in Figure 6.2, which tracks the behavior of the DJIA and the Nasdaq Composite over the 10-year period ending mid-2003.

As can be seen, in August 1998, the tech-heavy Nasdaq Composite began to skyrocket, and over the next 18 months, went up an incredible 240%. Outright speculation was in firm control of the market—price/earnings multiples (a widely used measure of market sentiment) went through the roof. In fact, it really didn't seem to matter whether companies were generating earnings or not. These kinds of details, we were told, were no longer important; the only thing that seemed to matter was whether the stock had a technology or Internet connection. That, of course, all came to a screeching halt in early 2000. The three major market indexes—The DJIA, the Nasdaq Composite, and the S&P 500—all peaked in early 2000: the Dow at 11,722.98, the Nasdaq at 5,048.62, and the S&P at 1,527.46. Over the course of the next 32 months, through September 2002, these market measures performed as follows:

- The Dow fell 38%.
- The S&P dropped 49%.
- The Nasdaq fell 77%

FIGURE 6.2 Bulls, Bubbles, and Bears

One of the greatest bull markets in history began on August 12, 1982, with the Dow at 777. It continued on through the 1980s and into the 1990s. But in late 1998, the bull turned into a bubble that lasted for about 18 months before it burst in early 2000, at which time the market went from a bubble to a full-fledged bear. (*Source:* Morningstar, Inc.)

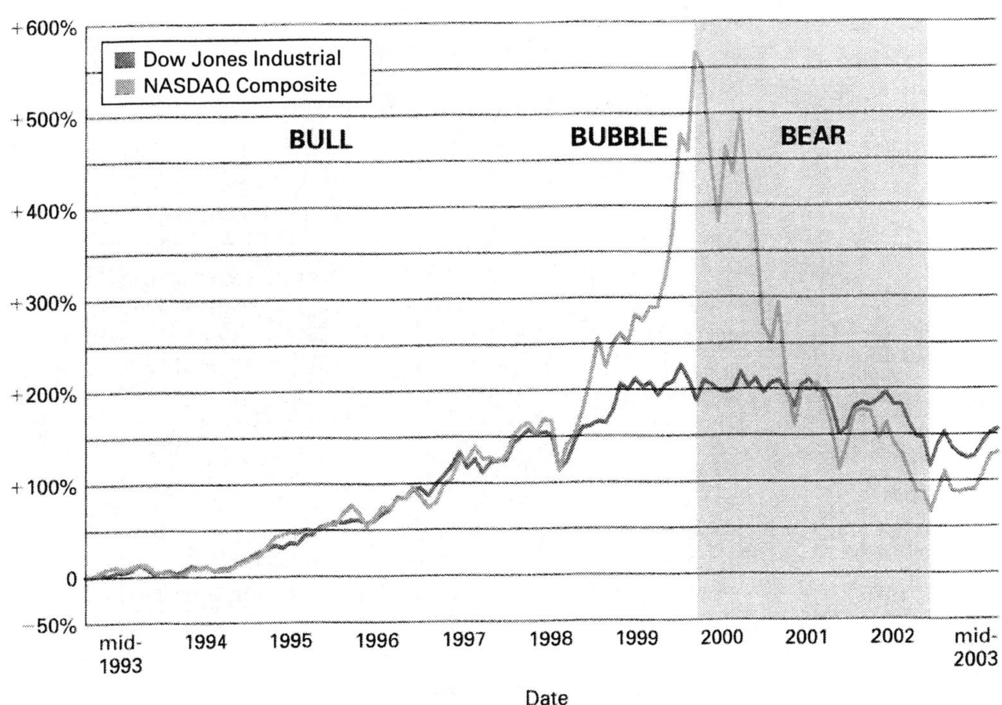

This period turned out to be one of the worst bear markets in recent history and clearly had a devastating effect on investor returns. All of the excesses that had built up over the last half of the 1990s were eliminated in a little more than 2½ years. But as the accompanying *Investing in Action* box (on pages 238–239) explains, this market was dealing with more than just old-fashioned speculation; it also had to cope with the September 11, 2001, terrorist attack on the United States, war, and various scandals, not to mention a weak economy.

The Pros and Cons of Stock Ownership

HOT LINKS

Based on broad stock market indexes such as the S&P 500, over long periods of time common stocks have outpaced inflation. Read about outpacing inflation at:

www.putnaminv.com
Click on "Individual Investor" "Education" "Outpacing Inflation"

Investors own stocks for all sorts of reasons: They like the potential for capital gains that stocks offer, or their current income, or perhaps the high degree of market liquidity. But as with any investment vehicle, there is a good side to these securities and a bad side.

The Advantages of Stock Ownership Certainly one reason stocks are so appealing to investors is the substantial return opportunities they offer. As we just saw, stocks generally provide attractive, highly competitive returns over the long haul. Indeed, common stock returns compare very favorably to other investment outlets such as long-term corporate bonds and U.S. Treasury securities. For example, over the period from 1950 through 2003, high-grade corporate bonds averaged annual returns of around 6%—*about half that of common stocks.* Although long-term bonds sometimes outperform stocks on a year-by-year basis (as they did in the early to mid-1980s and again in 2001–2003, when interest rates were in a free fall), the opposite is true far more often than not; that is, stocks outperform bonds, and usually by a wide margin. Because stocks can be counted on over most periods to provide returns that exceed annual inflation rates, they make ideal inflation hedges. Indeed, over the long run, as long as inflation rates remain at reasonably low levels of 3% to 4%, stocks are likely to continue to produce attractive inflation-adjusted returns.

Stocks offer other benefits as well: They are easy to buy and sell, and the transaction costs are modest. Moreover, price and market information is widely disseminated in the news and financial media. A final advantage is that the unit cost of a share of common stock is usually within the reach of most individual investors. Unlike bonds, which normally carry minimum denominations of at least $1,000, and some mutual funds that have fairly hefty minimum investments, common stocks don't have such minimums. Instead, most stocks today are priced at less than $50 or $60 a share—and any number of shares, no matter how few, can be bought or sold.

The Disadvantages There are also some disadvantages to common stock ownership, with risk being perhaps the most significant. Stocks are subject to various types of risk, including business and financial risk, purchasing power risk, market risk, and event risk. All of these can adversely affect a stock's earnings and dividends, its price appreciation, and, of course, the rate of return earned by an investor. Even the best of stocks possess elements of risk that are difficult to overcome, because company earnings are subject to many factors, including government control and regulation, foreign competition,

FIGURE 6.3

The Current Income of Stocks and Bonds

Clearly, the level of current income (dividends) paid to stockholders falls far short of the amount of interest income paid to bondholders. Note also that even though interest rates had fallen to 40-year lows by 2003, the dividend yield on stocks was still less than half the coupon yield on bonds.

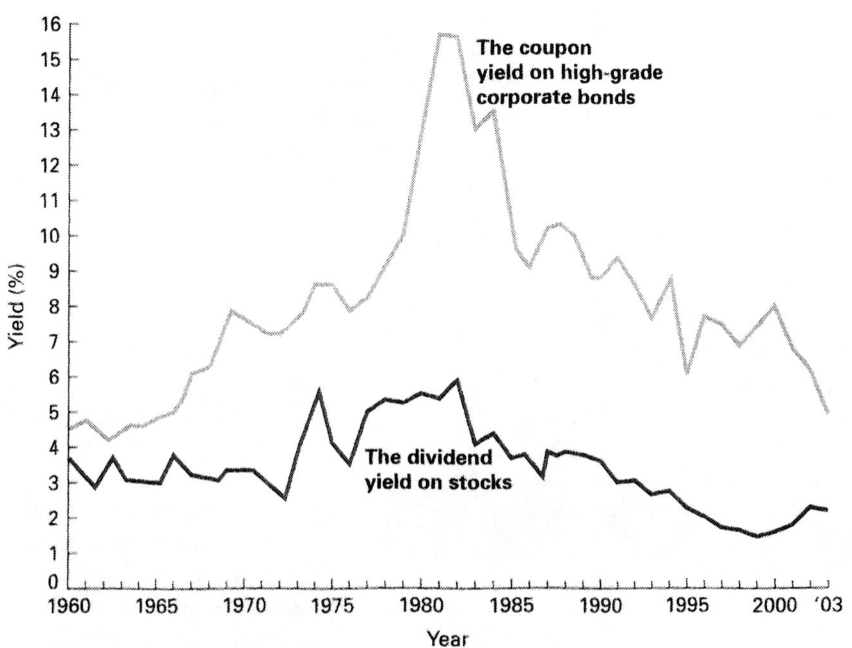

and the state of the economy. Because such factors affect sales and profits, they also affect the price behavior of the stock and possibly even dividends. All of this leads to another disadvantage: The earnings and general performance of stocks are subject to wide swings, so it is difficult to value common stocks and consistently select top performers. The selection process is complex because so many elements go into formulating expectations of stock performance. In other words, not only is the future outcome of the company and its stock uncertain, but the evaluation and selection process itself is far from perfect.

A final disadvantage of stocks is the sacrifice in current income. Several types of investments—bonds, for instance—pay higher levels of current income and do so with much greater certainty. Figure 6.3 compares the dividend yield on common stocks with the coupon yield on high-grade corporate bonds. It shows the degree of sacrifice common stock investors make in terms of current income. Clearly, even though the yield gap has narrowed a great deal in the past few years, common stocks still have a long way to go before they catch up with the *current income levels* available from bonds and most other types of fixed-income securities.

CONCEPTS IN REVIEW

6.1 What is a *common stock*? What is meant by the statement that holders of common stock are the *residual owners* of the firm?

6.2 What are two or three of the major investment attributes of common stocks?

6.3 Briefly describe the behavior of the U.S. stock market over the past 10 to 15 years, paying special attention to market behavior since the mid-1990s. Contrast the market's performance over the 1990s as measured by the DJIA with its performance as measured by the S&P 500 and by the Nasdaq Composite.

6.4 How important are dividends as a source of return? What about capital gains? Which is more important to total return? Which causes wider swings in total return?

6.5 What are some of the advantages *and* disadvantages of owning common stock? What are the major types of risk to which stockholders are exposed?

Basic Characteristics of Common Stock

LG 3 LG 4

Each share of common stock represents equity (ownership) in a company. It's this equity position that explains why common stocks are often referred to as *equity securities* or **equity capital.** Every share entitles the holder to an equal ownership position and participation in the corporation's earnings and dividends, an equal vote, and an equal voice in management. Together, the common stockholders own the company. The more shares an investor owns, the bigger his or her ownership position. Common stock has no maturity date—it remains outstanding indefinitely.

equity capital
evidence of ownership position in a firm, in the form of shares of common stock.

Common Stock as a Corporate Security

All corporations "issue" common stock of one type or another. But the shares of many, if not most, corporations are never traded, because the firms either are too small or are family controlled. The stocks of interest to us in this book

publicly traded issues
shares of stock that are readily available to the general public and are bought and sold in the open market.

are **publicly traded issues**—the shares that are readily available to the general public and which are bought and sold in the open market. The firms issuing such shares range from giants like AT&T and Microsoft to much smaller regional or local firms. The market for publicly traded stocks is enormous: The value of all actively traded listed and OTC stocks in mid-2003 was nearly $10 trillion.

public offering
an offering to sell to the investing public a set number of shares of a firm's stock at a specified price.

rights offering
an offering of a new issue of stock to existing stockholders, who may purchase new shares in proportion to their current ownership position.

Issuing New Shares Shares of common stock can be issued in several different ways. The most widely used procedure today is the **public offering.** In using this procedure, the corporation offers the investing public a certain number of shares of its stock at a certain price. Figure 6.4 shows an announcement for such an offering. Note in this case that *White Electronic Designs* is offering 5,175,000 shares of stock at a price of $10 per share, providing this Nasdaq-traded company with some $50 million in new capital.

New shares of stock can also be issued using what is known as a **rights offering.** In a rights offering, existing stockholders are given the first opportunity to buy the new issue. In essence, a stock right gives a shareholder the right (but not the obligation) to purchase new shares of the company's stock in proportion to his or her current ownership position. For instance, if a stockholder currently owns 1% of a firm's stock and the firm issues 10,000 additional shares, the rights offering will give that stockholder the opportunity to purchase 1% (100 shares) of the new issue. If the investor doesn't want to use the rights, he or she can sell them to someone who does. The net result of a rights offering is the same as that of a public offering: The firm ends up with more equity in its capital structure, and the number of shares outstanding increases.

stock spin-off
conversion of one of a firm's subsidiaries to a stand-alone company by distribution of stock in that new company to existing shareholders.

Stock Spin-Offs Perhaps one of the most creative ways of bringing a new issue to the market is through a **stock spin-off.** Basically, a spin-off occurs when a company gets rid of one of its subsidiaries or divisions. For example, Ralston Purina did this when it spun off its Energizer subsidiary. The company doesn't just sell the subsidiary to some other firm. Rather, it creates a new stand-alone company and then distributes stock in that company to its existing stockholders. Thus every Ralston Purina shareholder received a certain (prorated) number of shares in the newly created, and now publicly traded, Energizer company. There have been hundreds of stock spin-offs in the last 10 to 15 years. Some of the more notable ones were the spin-off of Coach (the designer bag company) by Sara Lee, Carmax by Circuit City in February 2002, the spin-off of debit-card processor Global Payments from NDCHealth, and the Edwards Lifesciences spin-off by Baxter International. Normally, companies execute stock spin-offs if they believe the subsidiary is no longer a good fit, or if they feel they've become too diversified and want to focus on their core products. The good news is such spin-offs often work very well for investors, too.

stock split
a maneuver in which a company increases the number of shares outstanding by exchanging a specified number of new shares of stock for each outstanding share.

HOT LINKS

Get the latest information on stock splits at:

biz.yahoo.com/c/s.html

Stock Splits Companies can also increase the number of shares outstanding by executing a **stock split.** In declaring a split, a firm merely announces that it will increase the number of shares outstanding by exchanging a specified number of new shares for each outstanding share of stock. For example, in a 2-for-1 stock split, two new shares of stock are exchanged for each old share. In a 3-for-2 split, three new shares are exchanged for every two old shares outstanding. Thus, a stockholder who owned 200 shares of stock before a 2-for-1

FIGURE 6.4 An Announcement of a New Stock Issue

This announcement indicates that the company—White Electronic Designs—is issuing over 5 million shares of stock at a price of $10 per share. For this manufacturer of specialty microelectronic memory products, the new issue will mean some $50,000,000 in new capital. (*Source: Wall Street Journal*, August 14, 2003.)

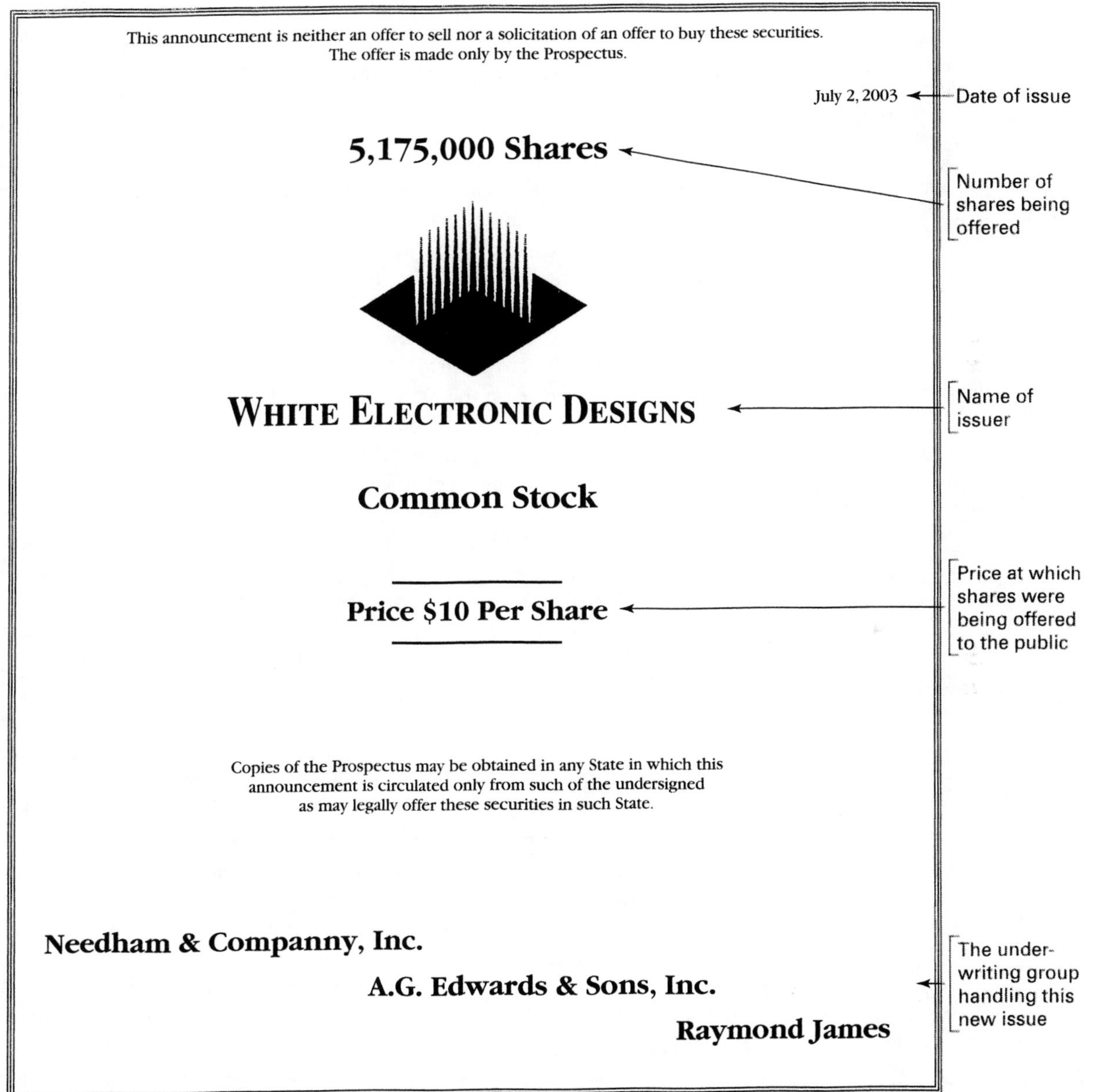
This announcement is neither an offer to sell nor a solicitation of an offer to buy these securities. The offer is made only by the Prospectus.

July 2, 2003

5,175,000 Shares

WHITE ELECTRONIC DESIGNS

Common Stock

Price $10 Per Share

Copies of the Prospectus may be obtained in any State in which this announcement is circulated only from such of the undersigned as may legally offer these securities in such State.

Needham & Companny, Inc.

A.G. Edwards & Sons, Inc.

Raymond James

split becomes the owner of 400 shares; the same investor would hold 300 shares if there had been a 3-for-2 split.

Stock splits are used when a firm wants to enhance its stock's trading appeal by lowering its market price. Normally, the firm gets the desired result: The price of the stock tends to fall in close relation to the terms of the split (unless the stock split is accompanied by a big increase in the level of dividends).

REDISCOVERING THE REVERSE STOCK SPLIT—The recent meltdown in the market has led to some incredibly low share prices. But companies don't like to see their stocks sell at bargain basement prices. So what do they do? One tactic is to improve profits and other fundamentals. A far easier way is to use a *reverse stock split*. This sleight of hand is guaranteed to raise share prices, but it won't change the overall value of the company or its fundamentals. In a normal stock split, you turn in 1 share of stock and get, say, 4 back; so the price of the stock *drops* from, say, $100 to $25 per share. A reverse stock split works in the opposite way: You turn in 4 shares and get 1 back, so the price of the stock goes *up* from, say, $5 to $20 per share. With so many stocks selling at such low prices, some market observers feel we're going to see a lot of these.

Source: Adapted from "Less Is Not More" by Michelle Deblasi, *Bloomberg Personal Finance*, July/August 2002, pp. 23–25.

For example, using the ratio of the number of old shares to new, we can expect a $100 stock to trade at or close to $50 a share after a 2-for-1 split. Specifically, we divide the original price per share by the ratio of new shares to old. That same $100 stock would trade at about $67 after a 3-for-2 split—that is, $\$100 \div 3/2 = \$100 \div 1.5 = \$67$. (A variation of the stock split, known as a stock dividend, will be discussed later in this chapter.)

Treasury Stock Instead of increasing the number of outstanding shares, corporations sometimes find it desirable to *reduce* the number of shares in the hands of the investing public by buying back their own stock. Generally speaking, firms repurchase their own stock when they view it as undervalued in the marketplace. When that happens, the company's own stock becomes an attractive investment candidate. Those firms that can afford to do so will purchase their stock in the open market by becoming investors, like any other individual or institution. When these shares are acquired, they become known as **treasury stock.** Technically, treasury stocks are simply shares of stock that have been issued and subsequently repurchased by the issuing firm. Treasury stocks are kept by the corporation and can be used at a later date for any number of reasons. For example, they could be used for mergers and acquisitions, to meet employee stock option plans, or as a means of paying stock dividends. Or the shares can simply be held in treasury for an indefinite time.

The impact of these share repurchases—or *buybacks*, as they're sometimes called—is not clear. Generally, the feeling is that if the buyback is substantial (involving a significant number of shares), the stockholder's equity position and claim on income will increase. This result is likely to benefit stockholders to the extent that such action has a positive effect on the market price of the stock. However, it has also been suggested that buybacks are often used merely as a way to prop up the price of an overvalued stock.

treasury stock
shares of stock that have been sold and subsequently repurchased by the issuing firm.

classified common stock
common stock issued by a company in different classes, each of which offers different privileges and benefits to its holders.

Classified Common Stock For the most part, all the stockholders in a corporation enjoy the same benefits of ownership. Occasionally, however, a company will *issue different classes of common stock*, each of which entitles holders to different privileges and benefits. These issues are known as **classified common stock.** Hundreds of publicly traded firms have created such stock classes. Though issued by the same company, each class of common stock is different and has its own value.

Classified common stock is customarily used to denote either different voting rights or different dividend obligations. For instance, class A could designate nonvoting shares, and class B would carry normal voting rights. Or the class A stock would receive no dividends, and class B would receive regular cash dividends. Notable for its use of classified stock is Ford Motor Company, which has two classes of stock outstanding. Ford's class A stock is owned by the investing public, and class B stock is owned by the Ford family and their trusts or corporations. The two classes of stock share equally in the dividends. But class A stock has one vote per share, whereas the voting rights of the class B stock are structured to give the Ford family a 40% absolute control of the company. Similar types of classified stock are used at the Washington Post, Dillards Department Stores, Dow Jones & Co., Nike, and Berkshire Hathaway. Regardless of the specifics, whenever there is more than one class of common stock outstanding, investors should take the time to determine the privileges, benefits, and limitations of each class.

Buying and Selling Stocks

Whether buying or selling stocks, you should become familiar with how stocks are quoted and with the costs of executing common stock transactions. Certainly, keeping track of *current prices* is an essential element in the buy-and-sell decisions of investors. They are the link in the decision process that lets investors decide when to buy or sell a stock; they also help investors monitor the market performance of their security holdings. Similarly, *transaction costs* are important because of the impact they can have on investment returns. Indeed, the costs of executing stock transactions can sometimes consume most (or all) of the profits from an investment. These costs should not be taken lightly.

Reading the Quotes Investors in the stock market have come to rely on a highly efficient information system that quickly disseminates market prices to the public. The stock quotes that appear daily in the financial press are a vital part of that information system. To see how price quotations work and what they mean, consider the quotes that appear daily (Monday through Friday) in the *Wall Street Journal*. As we'll see, these quotes give not only the most recent price of each stock but also a great deal of additional information.

Some NYSE stock quotes are presented in Figure 6.5 (on page 250)—let's use the Disney quotations for purposes of illustration. These quotes were published in the *Wall Street Journal* on Tuesday, July 8, 2003, and describe the trading activity that occurred the day before, which in this case was Monday, July 7. A glance at the quotations shows that stocks, like most other securities, are quoted in dollars and cents. In addition to stock prices, a typical stock quote conveys an array of other information, including

- The stock's year-to-date change in price—see the first column ("YTD % CHG"); note that Disney stock has gone up a whopping 26.2% since the first of the year. The next two columns, labeled "Hi" and "Lo," show the highest and lowest prices at which the stock sold during the past 52 weeks—you can see that Disney has traded between $21.55 and $13.48 a share during the preceding 52-week period.
- Listed to the right of the company's name is its *stock symbol*; Disney goes by the three-letter abbreviation **DIS**. These symbols are the abbreviations used to identify specific companies; every common stock (and mutual fund) has a unique three- to five-letter symbol that distinguishes it from any other security and is used to execute market trades.
- The figure listed after the stock symbol is the annual cash dividend paid on each share of stock, which for Disney was 21 cents. This is followed by the stock's dividend yield (1.0% for Disney) and its price/earnings (P/E) ratio, which amounted to 39 times earnings for Disney.
- The daily share volume follows the P/E ratio. The sales numbers are listed in lots of 100 shares, so the figure 66186 means that 6,618,600 shares of Disney stock were traded on July 7.
- The next entry, the "Close" column, contains the closing (final) price, $20.58, at which the stock sold on the day in question.
- Finally, as the last ("Net Change") column shows, Disney closed up 51 cents. This means the stock closed $0.51 higher than the day before (which in this case was Thursday, July 3, when it closed at $20.07).

FIGURE 6.5 Stock Quotations

This figure shows the quotations for a small sample of stocks traded on the NYSE, providing a summary of the transactions that occurred on one day. (*Source: Wall Street Journal*, July 8, 2003.)

YTD % CHG	52-WEEK HI	52-WEEK LO	STOCK (SYM)	DIV	YLD %	PE	VOL 100s	CLOSE	NET CHG
16.4	13.86	7.75	♣DnbryRes DNR		...	12	2530	13.15	-0.29
19.9	15.69	8.95	Dept56 DFS		...	7	741	15.47	0.31
-3.3	10.11	5.21	DescSA ADS DES	.56e	8.6	...	25	6.53	0.14
45.7	72.23	35.26	DtscheBK DB	1.53e	2.3	...	540	66.18	0.60
18.8	15.64	8.10	♣DtscheTel ADS DT		...	...	5203	15.09	0.09
35.1	29.62	17.25	DevDivRlty DDR	1.64	5.5	24	2779	29.70	0.32
47.9	26.38	12.10	DeVry DV		...	26	2205	24.57	0.72
-0.5	53	37.55	Diageo ADS DEO	1.69e	3.9	...	7071	43.59	-1.21
4.9	47.64	30	DiagnstPdt DP	.24	.6	24	1208	40.50	-0.05
-3.0	22.45	17.12	DialCp DL	.16	.8	29	4377	19.75	0.14
-5.7	28.70	17.30	DmndOffshr DO	.50	2.4	cc	16969	20.60	-0.93
99.4	38.83	12.15	DicksSprtgGds DKS n		...	20	3509	38.28	0.99
10.6	45.90	30.30	Diebold DBD	.68	1.5	25	4706	45.60	1.00
-13.2	28.14	12.32	Dillards DDS	.16	1.2	11	5716	13.76	0.09
21.7	7.50	5.35	♣Dimon DMN	.30	4.1	12	1050	7.30	0.18
26.2	21.55	13.48	Disney DIS	.21	1.0	39	66186	20.58	0.51
8.9	27.48	23.70	Disney 6.875Corts KVJ n	1.72	6.3	...	14	27.18	0.23
27.0	13.05	7.50	Dist&Srv ADS DYS	.21e	1.7	...	540	12.70	-0.20
211.2	**11.40**	**2.70**	**djOrthopedics DJO**		...	**dd**	**1703**	**11.70**	**0.69**
58.4	19.95	9.50	DlrGenl DG	.14	.7	23	13925	18.93	0.27
-7.1	26.60	14.35	♣DlrThrfty DTG		...	14	575	19.65	0.15
24.9	27.30	17.55	DomResBlkWar DOM	2.56e	9.5	...	196	27.05	-0.01
15.5	66.15	35.40	♣DominRes D	2.58	4.1	13	8587	63.43	-0.19
11.0	55	36.77	♣Domin un	4.38	8.1	...	95	53.90	-0.07
8.8	11.73	8.60	Domtar DTC	.17fg	...	...	840	10.95	-0.07
27.8	45.68	29.91	♣Donaldson DCI	.36	.8	22	924	46.01	0.57
23.2	28.40	16.94	Donnelly DNY	1.00	3.7	24	5762	26.83	0.78

Year-to-date changes in price, in percentages

High and low prices for previous 52 weeks

Company name and stock symbol

Annual dividends per share for past 12 months

Dividend yield (dividends as percent of share price)

Price/earnings ratio: $\left(\frac{\text{market price}}{\text{earnings per share}}\right)$

Share volume, in hundreds

Closing (final) price for the day—this is also the price used to compute dividend yield and the P/E ratio

Net change in price from previous day

The same basic quotation system is used for *some* OTC stocks. Actually, for quotation purposes, OTC stocks are divided into two groups: Nasdaq National Market issues and other OTC stocks. The National Market stocks are those of major, actively traded companies; *they are quoted just like NYSE issues.* Other OTC stocks (i.e., Nasdaq Small Cap issues) and AMEX stocks are quoted in a highly abbreviated form that includes only stock name, symbol, volume, closing price, and price change.

Transaction Costs As explained in Chapter 3, common stock can be bought and sold in round or odd lots. A *round lot* is 100 shares of stock or multiples thereof. An *odd lot* is a transaction involving less than 100 shares. For example, the sale of 400 shares of stock would be a round-lot transaction, whereas the sale of 75 shares would be an odd-lot transaction. Trading 250 shares of stock would involve a combination of two round lots and an odd lot.

An investor incurs certain transaction costs when buying or selling stock. In addition to some modest transfer fees and taxes paid by the *seller*, the major cost is the brokerage fee paid—by both *buyer and seller*—at the time of the transaction. As a rule, brokerage fees amount to 1% to 5% of most transactions. But they can go much higher, particularly for very small trades. Higher fees are connected with the purchase or sale of odd lots, which requires a specialist known as an *odd-lot dealer*. This usually results in an *odd-lot differential* of 10 to 25 cents per share, which is tacked on to the normal commission charge, driving up the costs of these small trades. Indeed, the relatively high cost of an odd-lot trade makes it better to deal in round lots whenever possible.

Common Stock Values

The worth of a share of common stock can be described in a number of ways. Terms such as *par value*, *book value*, *market value*, and *investment value* are all found in the financial media. Each designates some accounting, investment, or monetary attribute of a stock.

par value
the stated, or face, value of a stock.

Par Value The term **par value** refers to the stated, or face, value of a stock. Except for accounting purposes, it is relatively useless. In many ways, par value is a throwback to the early days of corporate law, when it was used as a basis for assessing the extent of a stockholder's legal liability. Because the term has little or no significance for investors, many stocks today are issued as no-par or low-par stocks. That is, they may have par values of only a penny or two.

book value
the amount of stockholders' equity in a firm; equals the amount of the firm's assets minus the firm's liabilities and preferred stock.

Book Value **Book value,** another accounting measure, represents the amount of stockholders' equity in the firm. As we will see in the next chapter, it is commonly used in stock valuation. Book value indicates the amount of stockholder funds used to finance the firm. It is calculated by subtracting the firm's liabilities and preferred stock from its assets. Let's assume that a corporation has $10 million in assets, owes $5 million in various forms of short- and long-term debt, and has $1 million worth of preferred stock outstanding. The book value of this firm would be $4 million.

Book value can be converted to a per-share basis—*book value per share*—by dividing it by the number of common shares outstanding. For example, if the firm just described has 100,000 shares of common stock outstanding, then its book value per share is $40. As a rule, most stocks have market prices that are well above their book values.

market value
the prevailing market price of a security.

Market Value **Market value** is one of the easiest stock values to determine. It is simply *the prevailing market price of an issue*. In essence, market value indicates how the market participants as a whole have assessed the worth of a share of stock. By multiplying the market price of the stock by the number of shares outstanding, we can also find the market value of the firm itself—or what is known as the firm's *market capitalization*. For example, if a firm has 1 million shares outstanding and its stock trades at $50 per share, the company has a market value (or "market cap") of $50 million. For obvious reasons, the market value of a share of stock is generally of considerable importance to stockholders.

investment value
the amount that investors believe a security should be trading for, or what they think it's worth.

Investment Value **Investment value** is probably the most important measure for a stockholder. It indicates the worth investors place on the stock—in effect, what they think the stock *should* be trading for. Determining a security's investment value is a complex process based on expectations of the return and risk characteristics of a stock. Any stock has two potential sources of return: annual dividend payments and the capital gains that arise from appreciation in market price. In establishing investment value, investors try to determine how much money they will make from these two sources. They then use those estimates as the basis for formulating the return potential of the stock. At the same time, they try to assess the amount of risk to which they will be exposed by holding the stock. Such return and risk information helps them place an investment value on the stock. This value represents the *maximum* price an investor should be willing to pay for the issue. Investment value is the major topic in Chapter 8.

IN REVIEW

CONCEPTS

6.6 What is a *stock split?* How does a stock split affect the market value of a share of stock? Do you think it would make any difference (in price behavior) if the company also changed the dividend rate on the stock? Explain.

6.7 What is a *stock spin-off?* In very general terms, explain how a stock spin-off works. Are these spin-offs of any value to investors? Explain.

6.8 Define and differentiate between the following pairs of terms.
a. *Treasury stock* versus *classified stock.*
b. *Round lot* versus *odd lot.*
c. *Par value* versus *market value.*
d. *Book value* versus *investment value.*

6.9 What is an *odd-lot differential* and what effect does it have on the cost of buying and selling stocks? How can you avoid odd-lot differentials? Which of the following transactions would involve an odd-lot differential?
a. Buy 90 shares of stock.
b. Sell 200 shares of stock.
c. Sell 125 shares of stock.

Common Stock Dividends

LG 5

In 2002, U.S. corporations paid out more than $400 billion in dividends. Yet, in spite of these numbers, dividends still don't get much respect. Many investors, particularly younger ones, often put very little value on dividends. To a large extent, that's because capital gains provide a much bigger source of return than dividends—at least over the long haul. But things are beginning to change. The protracted bear market of 2000–2002 revealed in a very painful fashion just how uncertain capital gains can be and, indeed, that all those potential profits can at times turn into substantial capital losses. At least with dividends, the cash flow is far more certain; plus, dividends provide a nice cushion when the market stumbles (or falls flat on its face). Moreover, recent changes in the (federal) tax laws put dividends on the same plane as capital gains, as both are now taxed at the same (maximum 15%) tax rate. Thus, capital gains are no longer taxed at more attractive rates, making dividends just as attractive and perhaps even more so, as they're far less risky. Let's now take a closer look at this important source of income.

INVESTOR FACTS

ANOTHER WAY THAT DIVIDENDS PAY—From the market peak in the spring of 2000 through mid-2003, the 100 highest yielding stocks in the S&P 500 were *up 2 percent.* That may not sound like a big deal, until you compare it to the 143 S&P stocks that don't pay any dividends at all—they were *down a whopping 28 percent.* It's still another reason that you have to love those dividends (at least in "soft" markets).

The Dividend Decision

By paying out dividends, typically on a quarterly basis, companies share with their stockholders some of the profits they've earned. Actually, the question of how much to pay in dividends is decided by a firm's board of directors. The directors evaluate the firm's operating results and financial condition to determine whether dividends should be paid and, if so, in what amount. If the directors decide to pay dividends, they also establish several important payment dates. In this section we'll look at the corporate and market factors that go into the dividend decision. Then we'll briefly examine some of the key payment dates.

Corporate Versus Market Factors When the board of directors assembles for its regular dividend meeting, it weighs a variety of factors in making the decision to pay out dividends. First, the board looks at the firm's earnings. Even though a company does not have to show a profit to pay dividends, profits are still considered a vital link in the dividend decision. With common stocks, the annual earnings of a firm are usually measured and reported in terms of **earnings per share (EPS)**. Basically, EPS translates aggregate corporate profits into profits on a per-share basis. It provides a convenient measure of the amount of earnings available to stockholders. Earnings per share is found by using the following formula:

earnings per share (EPS) the amount of annual earnings available to common stockholders, as stated on a per-share basis.

Equation 6.1

$$\text{EPS} = \frac{\begin{array}{c}\text{Net profit}\\\text{after taxes}\end{array} - \text{Preferred dividends}}{\begin{array}{c}\text{Number of shares of}\\\text{common stock outstanding}\end{array}}$$

For example, if a firm reports a net profit of \$1.25 million, pays \$250,000 in dividends to preferred stockholders, and has 500,000 shares of common stock outstanding, it has an EPS of \$2—that is, (\$1,250,000 − \$250,000)/500,000). Note in Equation 6.1 that preferred dividends are subtracted from profits, since they must be paid before any funds can be made available to common stockholders.

While assessing profits, the board also looks at the firm's growth prospects. It is very likely some of the firm's present earnings will be needed for investment purposes and to help finance expected growth. In addition, the board will take a close look at the firm's cash position. Depending on the company and the firm's current dividend rate, the payment of dividends can take up a large amount of cash, so board members will want to make sure plenty of this precious resource is available. Finally, the board will want to make sure that it is meeting all legal and contractual constraints. For example, the firm may be subject to a loan agreement that legally limits the amount of dividends it can pay.

After looking at internal matters, the board will consider certain market effects and responses. Most investors feel that if a company is going to retain earnings rather than pay them out in dividends, it should exhibit proportionately higher growth and profit levels. The market's message is clear: If the firm is investing the money wisely and at a high rate of return, fine; otherwise, pay a larger portion of earnings out in the form of dividends. Moreover, to the extent that different types of investors tend to be attracted to different types of firms, the board must make every effort to meet the dividend expectations of its shareholders. For example, income-oriented investors are attracted to firms that generally pay high dividends. Failure to meet those expectations can lead to disastrous results—a sell-off of the firm's stock—in the marketplace. Finally, the board cannot ignore the fact that investors today are placing a much higher value on dividends. Indeed, after being mothballed for the past decade or so, dividends definitely are now back in style.

HOT LINKS

Boards of directors have come under scrutiny in recent years. For some insight on this issue, see the *Ethics* box for Chapter 6 on the book's Web site at

www.aw-bc.com/gitman_joehnk

Some Important Dates Let's assume the directors decide to declare a dividend. Once that's done, they must indicate the date of payment and other important dates associated with the dividend. Normally, the directors issue a statement to the press indicating their dividend decision, along with the pertinent dividend payment dates. These statements are widely quoted in the financial media. Typical of such releases are the dividend news captions depicted in Figure 6.6.

date of record
the date on which an investor must be a registered shareholder to be entitled to receive a dividend.

payment date
the actual date on which the company will mail dividend checks to shareholders (also known as the *payable date*).

Three dates are particularly important to the stockholder: date of record, ex-dividend date, and payment date. The *date of record* is the date on which the investor must be a registered shareholder of the firm to be entitled to a dividend. All investors who are official stockholders as of the close of business on that date will receive the dividends that have just been declared. These stockholders are often referred to as *holders of record*. The **payment date,** also set by the board of directors, generally follows the date of record by a week or two. It is the actual date on which the company will mail dividend checks to holders of record. (Note that in the dividend news reported in Figure 6.6, this date is called the *payable date*.)

ex-dividend date
three business days up to the date of record; determines whether one is an official shareholder and thus eligible to receive a declared dividend.

Because of the time needed to make bookkeeping entries after a stock is traded, the stock will sell without the dividend (ex-dividend) for three business days up to and including the date of record. The **ex-dividend date** will dictate whether you were an official shareholder and therefore eligible to receive the declared dividend. If you sell a stock *on or after* the ex-dividend date, you receive the dividend—the reason is that the buyer of the stock (the *new* shareholder) will not have held the stock on the date of record. Instead, you (the seller) will still be the holder of record. Just the opposite will occur if you sell the stock *before* the ex-dividend date. In this case, the new shareholder (the buyer of the stock) will receive the dividend because he or she will be the holder of record.

To see how this works, consider the following sequence of events. On June 3, the board of directors of Cash Cow, Inc., declares a quarterly dividend of 50 cents a share to holders of record on June 18. Checks will be mailed on the payment date, June 30. The calendar on the next page shows these various dividend dates. In this case, if you bought 200 shares of the stock on June 15, you'd receive a check in the mail sometime after June 30 in the amount of $100.

FIGURE 6.6

Important Dates and Data About Dividends

The dividend actions of corporations are big news in the financial community. This news release, taken from the *Wall Street Journal*, provides timely information about cash and stock dividends, as well as stocks that have gone ex-dividend. (*Source: Wall Street Journal*, July 9, 2003.)

Corporate Dividend News

Procter & Gamble Co.

CINCINNATI—**Procter & Gamble** Co.'s board declared an 11% increase in the quarterly dividend of its common stock and Series A ESOP convertible preferred stock.

The consumer-products company raised the dividend on both classes of stock to 45.5 cents from 41 cents, payable Aug. 15 to holders of record on July 18.

In 4 p.m. composite trading yesterday on the New York Stock Exchange, P&G was at $90.10, off 69 cents.

Dividends Reported July 8

COMPANY	PERIOD	AMT	PAYABLE DATE	RECORD DATE
REGULAR				
Bank of New York	Q	.19	7-31-03	7-18
Cummins Inc	Q	.30	9-02-03	8-15
FirstBncp MIPS pfB	M	.173958	7-31-03	7-29
FirstBncp pfC	M	.154167	7-31-03	7-29
FirstBncp pfD	M	.151042	7-31-03	7-29
Golden Enterprises	Q	.0313	7-30-03	7-18
Kerr-McGee Corp	Q	.45	10-01-03	9-05
Liberty Homes A	Q	.07	8-15-03	7-28
Liberty Homes B	Q	.07	8-15-03	7-28
Lone Star Stkhse	Q	.165	7-28-03	7-14
Oriental Fin'l A	M	.148438	7-30-03	7-15
Paccar Inc	Q	.22	9-05-03	8-18
PFS Bancorp	Q	.075	7-25-03	7-15
Puget Energy Inc	Q	.25	8-15-03	7-18
Puget Sound 7.45%	Q	.465625	10-01-03	9-12
SBI Capital Tr pf	Q	.58125	7-31-03	7-15
Summit Sec S-3 pf	M	.006458	8-20-03	8-05
Weyerhaeuser Co	Q	.40	9-02-03	8-01
IRREGULAR				
Metropol Mtg E-7pf	M	.007917	8-20-03	8-05
Popular pfA	-	.132812	7-31-03	7-15
Western United pfA	M	.007083	8-20-03	8-05
FUNDS, REITS, INVESTMENT COS, LPS				
Anthracite Cap pf	-	.410156	7-31-03	7-15
Century Realty Tr	Q	.12	8-18-03	7-25
Colonial Intmk Inc	M	.054	8-01-03	7-15
Colonial InvGr Mun	M	.0575	8-01-03	7-15
Hatteras Inco Secs	M	.065	7-31-03	7-17
ML RegBk Hldrs	-	.0432	7-28-03	7-11
Insured MuniInco	M	.07	7-31-03	7-17
Invest GrdMuniInco	M	.08	7-31-03	7-17
NCE PetrofdTr	M	b.18	7-31-03	7-17
NCE PetrofdTr	M	b.18	8-29-03	8-15
NCE PetrofdTr	M	b.18	9-30-03	9-16
Pfd Inco Fd	M	.0915	7-31-03	7-24
Pfd Inco Oppy Fd	M	.073	7-31-03	7-24
Prudential RE A	-	.073	7-11-03	7-10
Prudential RE B	-	.052	7-11-03	7-10
Sabine Royalty Tr	M	r.20257	7-29-03	7-15
Scudder Intmdt Gvt	M	.03	7-31-03	7-17
Scudder Multi-Mkt	M	.0615	7-31-03	7-17
Scudder Muni Inco	M	.065	7-31-03	7-17
Scudder Strat Inco	M	.09	7-31-03	7-17
Scudder Strat Muni	M	.0725	7-31-03	7-17
Seligman Qlty Muni	M	.066	7-28-03	7-17
Seligman Sel Muni	M	.0575	7-28-03	7-17
Templeton China	A	h.1162	7-28-03	7-18
STOCKS				
GreenPoint Fin'l		s	8-20-03	8-08
s-3-for-2 stock split.				
Synergx Systems		s	r7-25-03	7-18
s-2-for-1 stock split.				
r-Revised to include payable date.				
FOREIGN				
ICICI Bank ADS	-	t.324	-	8-05

INCREASED

COMPANY	PERIOD	AMOUNTS NEW	AMOUNTS OLD	PAYABLE DATE	RECORD DATE
Bank Mutual Corp	Q	.11	.10	9-03-03	8-20
GreenPoint Fin'l	Q	.36	.3125	8-20-03	8-08
Procter & Gamble	Q	.455	.41	8-15-03	7-18
Smith (A.O.) Corp	Q	.15	.14	8-15-03	7-31
Weis Markets	Q	.28	.27	8-22-03	8-08

EXTRA

COMPANY	PERIOD	AMT	PAYABLE DATE	RECORD DATE
FrprtMcMrnC&GclD	Q	m2.2645	8-01-03	7-15

m-Represents fifth mandatory partial redemption.

A-Annual. M-Monthly. Q-Quarterly. S-Semi-annual.

b-Payable in Canadian funds. c-Corrected. h-From Income. k-From capital gains. r-Revised. t-Approximate U.S. dollar amount per American Depositary Receipt/Share before adjustment for foreign taxes.

Stocks Ex-Dividend July 10

COMPANY	AMOUNT	COMPANY	AMOUNT
ABM Industries Inc	.095	Neubrgr Brm RE Inc	.115
AES TrIII 6.75pf	.84375	Neubrgr Brm RltyIn	.1125
Amer AnnGrpl TOPrS	.578125	OGE Energy Capl pf	.523438
AmerFinl TOprS	.570312	Pep Boys	.0675
BankOneCapVI7.2%pf	.45	MerLynDepPrfTRUpS	.95625
BellS Cp Corts7.12	.89	MerLynDep 8.15%P+	.379201
BremerCapTr 9%pf	.5625	MerLyDep8.5%TRUCs	1.0625
Citigp 7% Trups	.4375	MerLynP+PhilMorls	.753819
FstUn Corts7.5	.9375	Provident Fin'l nt	.52344
FW Capl 9 3/8%pf	.234375	RPM Int'l	.13
Glacier WaterTr pf	.18875	Rotonics Mfg	.05
GBWCapTr1 10% TrupsA.	.25	Sadia S/A ADS	t.7515
HartfordLfCaplpfA	.45	Safeco Corts8.375	1.046876
Hartford Lf TrupsB	.476562	Safeco II Corts8.7	1.0875
Europe 2001 HOLDRs	t.020702	Safeco Corts8.75	1.09375
Int'l Game Tech	.075	Safeco Corts8.072	1.009
LehmnCorts Safeco	1.09375	Shelbourne PropII	6.75
LehmnCorts6%BellSt	.691667	St Paul Capl 7.6%	.475
LehmnCorts Altria	.46875	TECO Energy un	.59375
LehmnCorts HSBC	.633681	Universal Corp	.36
LehmnCorts JPM1-1A	.98125	US Home&Grdn 9.4%	.1958
LehmnCorts1-7KeyCp	1.09375		
LehmnCorts 7.2%JPM	.90		
MerLyn STRIDES BAC	.701		

t-Approximate U.S. dollar amount per American Depositary Receipt/Share before adjustment for foreign taxes.

On the other hand, if you purchased the stock on June 16, the *seller* of the stock would receive the check, because he or she will be recognized as the holder of record, not you.

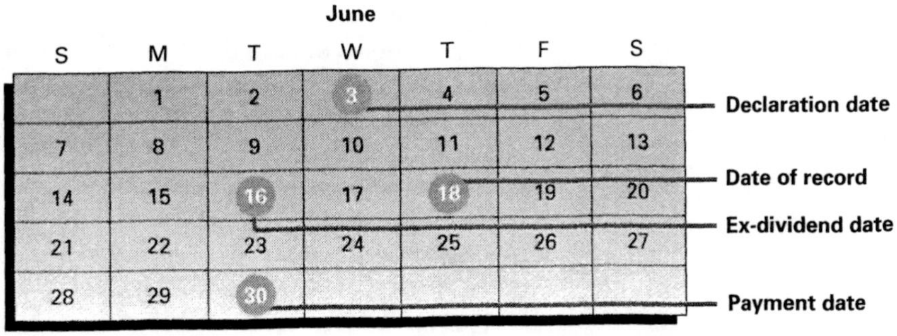

June

S	M	T	W	T	F	S
	1	2	3	4	5	6
7	8	9	10	11	12	13
14	15	16	17	18	19	20
21	22	23	24	25	26	27
28	29	30				

Declaration date

Date of record

Ex-dividend date

Payment date

Types of Dividends

cash dividend
payment of a dividend in the form of cash.

stock dividend
payment of a dividend in the form of additional shares of stock.

Normally, companies pay dividends in the form of cash, though sometimes they do so by issuing additional shares of stock. The first type of distribution is known as a **cash dividend**; the second is called a **stock dividend.** Occasionally, dividends are paid in still other forms, such as a *stock spin-off* (discussed earlier in this chapter) or perhaps even samples of the company's products. But dividends in the form of either cash or stock remain by far the most popular, so let's take a closer look at them.

Cash Dividends More firms pay *cash dividends* than any other type of dividend. A nice by-product of cash dividends is that *they tend to increase over time, as companies' earnings grow.* In fact, for companies that pay cash dividends, the average annual increase in dividends is around 3% to 5%. That's down considerably from the rate of growth that existed 15 or 20 years ago, but at least it is starting to go back up again. This trend represents good news for investors, because *a steadily increasing stream of dividends tends to shore up stock returns in soft markets.*

dividend yield
a measure that relates dividends to share price and puts common stock dividends on a relative (percentage) rather than absolute (dollar) basis.

A convenient way of assessing the amount of dividends received is to measure the stock's **dividend yield.** Basically, this is a measure of dividends on a relative (percentage) basis, rather than on an absolute (dollar) basis. Dividend yield, in effect, indicates the rate of current income earned on the investment dollar. It is computed as follows:

Equation 6.2

$$\text{Dividend yield} = \frac{\text{Annual dividends received per share}}{\text{Current market price of the stock}}$$

Thus, a company that annually pays $2 per share in dividends to its stockholders, and whose stock is trading at $40, has a dividend yield of 5%.

dividend payout ratio
the portion of earnings per share (EPS) that a firm pays out as dividends.

To put dividend yield into perspective, it is helpful to look at a company's **dividend payout ratio.** The payout ratio describes that portion of earnings per share (EPS) that is paid out as dividends. It is computed as follows:

Equation 6.3

$$\text{Dividend payout ratio} = \frac{\text{Dividends per share}}{\text{Earnings per share}}$$

A company would have a payout ratio of 50% if it had earnings of $4 a share and paid annual dividends of $2 a share. Although stockholders like to receive dividends, they normally do not like to see payout ratios over 60% to 70%. Payout ratios that high are difficult to maintain and may lead the company into trouble.

The appeal of cash dividends took a giant leap forward in 2003, when the federal tax code was changed so as to reduce the tax on dividends. Prior to this time, cash dividends were taxed as ordinary income, meaning they could be taxed at rates as high as 39%. For that reason, many investors viewed cash dividends as a highly unattractive source of income, especially since capital gains (when realized) were taxed at much lower preferential rates. Now, *both dividends and capital gains are taxed at the same low, preferential rate* (of 15% or less). That, of course, makes dividend-paying stocks far more attractive, even to investors in higher tax brackets. Other things being equal, the tax change should have a positive effect on the price behavior of dividend-paying stocks and, in turn, motivate companies either to begin paying dividends or to increase their dividend payout rate.

Stock Dividends Occasionally, a firm may declare a *stock dividend*. A stock dividend simply means that the dividend is paid in additional shares of stock. For instance, if the board declares a 10% stock dividend, each shareholder receives 1 new share of stock for each 10 shares currently owned.

Although they seem to satisfy some investors, *stock dividends really have no value*, because they represent the receipt of something already owned. The market responds to such dividends by adjusting share prices according to the terms of the stock dividend. Thus, in the example above, a 10% stock dividend normally leads to a decline of around 10% in the stock's share price. The market value of your shareholdings after a stock dividend, therefore, is likely to be the same as it was before the stock dividend. For example, if you owned 200 shares of stock that were trading at $100 per share, the total market value of your investment would be $20,000. After a 10% stock dividend, you'd own 220 shares of stock (i.e., 200 shares × 1.10), but they'd be trading at around $90 or $91 per share. Thus, you'd own more shares but they would be trading at lower prices, so the total market value of your investment would remain about the same. There is, however, one bright spot in all this: Unlike cash dividends, stock dividends are not taxed until the stocks are actually sold.

Dividend Reinvestment Plans

dividend reinvestment plans (DRIPs)
plans in which shareholders have cash dividends automatically reinvested into additional shares of the firm's common stock.

Want to have your cake and eat it too? When it comes to dividends, there is a way to do just that. You can participate in a **dividend reinvestment plan (DRIP)**. In these corporate-sponsored programs, shareholders can have their cash dividends automatically reinvested into additional shares of the company's common stock. (Similar reinvestment programs are offered by mutual funds, which we'll discuss in Chapter 13, and by some brokerage houses, such as Merrill Lynch and Fidelity.) The basic investment philosophy is that *if the company is good enough to invest in, it's good enough to reinvest in*. As Table 6.4 (on page 258) demonstrates, such an approach can have a tremendous impact on your investment position over time.

HOT LINKS

Use the directory of online resources about dividend reinvestment plans (DRIPs) and direct purchase of stocks at

www.stock1.com

Today more than 1,000 companies (including most major corporations) offer dividend reinvestment plans. Each one provides investors with a convenient and inexpensive way to accumulate capital. Stocks in most DRIPs are acquired free of any brokerage commissions, and most plans allow *partial participation*. That is, participants may specify a portion of their shares for dividend reinvestment and receive cash dividends on the rest. Some plans even sell stocks to their DRIP investors at below-market prices—often at discounts of 3% to 5%. In addition, most plans will credit fractional shares to the investor's account, and many will even allow investors to buy additional shares of the company's stock. For example, once enrolled in the General Mills plan, investors can purchase up to $3,000 worth of the company's stock each quarter, free of commissions.

Shareholders can join dividend reinvestment plans by simply sending a completed authorization form to the company. (Generally, it takes about 30 to 45 days for all the paperwork to be processed.) Once you're in, the number of

TABLE 6.4 **Cash or Reinvested Dividends?**

Situation: You buy 100 shares of stock at $25 a share (total investment $2,500); the stock currently pays $1 a share in annual dividends. The price of the stock increases at 8% per year; dividends grow at 5% per year.

Investment Period	Number of Shares Held	Market Value of Stock Holdings	Total Cash Dividends Received
		Take Dividends in Cash	
5 years	100	$ 3,672	$ 552
10 years	100	5,397	1,258
15 years	100	7,930	2,158
20 years	100	11,652	3,307
		Full Participation in Dividend Reinvestment Plan (100% of cash dividends reinvested)	
5 years	115.59	$ 4,245	$ 0
10 years	135.66	7,322	0
15 years	155.92	12,364	0
20 years	176.00	20,508	0

shares you hold will begin to accumulate with each dividend date. There is a catch, however: Even though these dividends take the form of additional shares of stock, you must still pay taxes on them *as though they were cash dividends*. Don't confuse these dividends with stock dividends—*reinvested dividends are treated as taxable income in the year they're received*, just as though they had been received in cash. But at least with the new preferential tax rate, even this feature is much less of a burden than it used to be.

IN REVIEW

CONCEPTS

6.10 Briefly explain how the dividend decision is made. What corporate and market factors are important in deciding whether, and in what amount, to pay dividends?

6.11 Why is the *ex-dividend date* important to stockholders? If a stock is sold on the ex-dividend date, who receives the dividend—the buyer or the seller? Explain.

6.12 What is the difference between a *cash dividend* and a *stock dividend?* Which would be more valuable to you? How does a stock dividend compare to a stock split? Is a 200% stock dividend the same as a 2-for-1 stock split? Explain.

6.13 What are *dividend reinvestment plans*, and what benefits do they offer to investors? Are there any disadvantages?

Types and Uses of Common Stock

LG 6

Common stocks appeal to investors because they offer the potential for everything from current income and stability of capital to attractive capital gains. The market contains a wide range of stocks, from the most conservative to the highly speculative. Generally, the kinds of stocks that investors seek will depend on their investment objectives and investment programs. We will examine several of the more popular types of common stocks here, as well as the various ways such securities can be used in different types of investment programs.

Types of Stocks

As an investor, one of the things you'll want to understand is the market system used to classify common stock. That's because a stock's general classification reflects not only its fundamental source of return but also the quality of the company's earnings, the issue's susceptibility to market risks, the nature and stability of its earnings and dividends, and even its susceptibility to adverse economic conditions. Such insight is useful in selecting stocks that will best fit your overall investment objectives. Among the many different types of stocks, the following are the most common: blue chips, income stocks, growth stocks, tech stocks, speculative stocks, cyclical stocks, defensive stocks, mid-cap stocks, and small-cap stocks. We will now look at each of these to see what they are and how they might be used.

HOT

At this site, you can choose stocks by company size and type, and access growth and return rates. Lists show stock prices, quotes, and ratios.

screen.yahoo.com/stocks.html

Blue-Chip Stocks Blue chips are the cream of the common stock crop. They are stocks that are unsurpassed in quality and have a long and stable record of earnings and dividends. **Blue-chip stocks** are issued by large, well-established firms that have impeccable financial credentials. These companies hold important, often leading positions in their industries and frequently set the standards by which other firms are measured.

blue-chip stocks
financially strong, high-quality stocks with long and stable records of earnings and dividends.

Not all blue chips are alike, however. Some provide consistently high dividend yields; others are more growth oriented. Good examples of blue-chip growth stocks are Wal-Mart, Proctor & Gamble, Microsoft, United Parcel Service, Pfizer, and 3M Company. (Some basic operating and market information about 3M's stock, as obtained from the introductory part of a typical *S&P Stock Report*, is shown in Figure 6.7.) Examples of high-yielding blue chips include such companies as Eastman Kodak, General Motors, ChevronTexaco, SBC Communications, and Kimberly-Clark.

FIGURE 6.7

A Blue-Chip Stock

(*Source:* Standard & Poor's *Stock Reports*, July 12, 2003.)

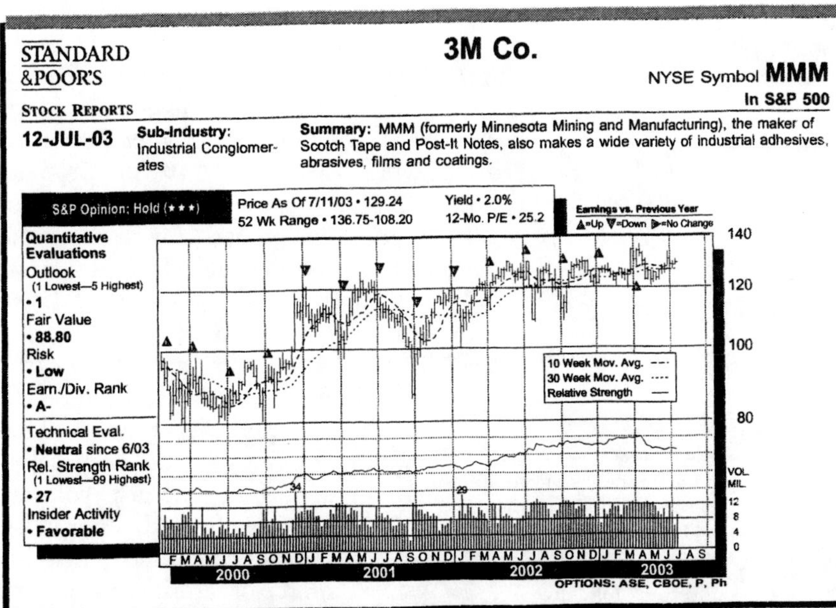

While blue-chip stocks (like most equity securities) are not immune from bear markets, they do nonetheless provide the potential for relatively attractive long-term returns. As such, they tend to appeal to investors who are looking for quality investment outlets that offer decent dividend yields and respectable growth potential. They're often used for long-term investment purposes and, because of their relatively low risk, as a way of obtaining modest but dependable rates of return.

income stocks
stocks with long and sustained records of paying higher-than-average dividends.

Income Stocks Some stocks are appealing simply because of the dividends they pay. This is the case with **income stocks.** These are issues that have a long and sustained record of regularly paying higher-than-average dividends. Income stocks are ideal for those who seek a relatively safe and high level of current income from their investment capital. But there's more: Holders of income stocks (unlike bonds and preferred stocks) can expect the dividends they receive to increase regularly over time. Thus, a company that paid, say, \$1.00 a share in dividends in 1990 would be paying almost \$1.50 a share in 2003, if dividends had been growing at just 3% per year. That's a big jump in dividends, and it's something that can have a definite impact on total return.

The major disadvantage of income stocks is that some of them may be paying high dividends because of limited growth potential. Indeed, it's not unusual for income securities to exhibit only low or modest rates of growth in earnings. This does not mean that such firms are unprofitable or lack future prospects. Quite the contrary: Most firms whose shares qualify as income stocks are highly profitable organizations with excellent future prospects. A number of income stocks are among the giants of U.S. industry, and many are also classified as quality blue chips. Many public utilities, such as FPL Group, Scana, DTE Energy, Dominion Resources, and Southern Company, are in this group. Also in this group are telecommunications stocks, such as Verizon and Alltel, and selected industrial and financial issues, such as Conagra Foods, Pitney Bowes, R. R. Donnelley, Bank of America, and AmSouth Bancorp. By their very nature, income stocks are not exposed to a great deal of business and market risk. They are, however, subject to a fair amount of interest rate risk.

growth stocks
stocks that experience high rates of growth in operations and earnings.

Growth Stocks Shares that have experienced, and are expected to continue experiencing, consistently high rates of growth in operations and earnings are known as **growth stocks.** A good growth stock might exhibit a *sustained* rate of growth in earnings of 15% to 18% per year over a period when common stocks, on average, are experiencing growth rates of only 6% to 8%. Generally speaking, established growth companies combine steady earnings growth with high returns on equity. They also have high operating margins and plenty of cash flow to service their debt. Lowe's, Boston Scientific, Progressive Corporation, Harley-Davidson, Starbucks, and Kohls (shown in Figure 6.8) are all prime examples of growth stocks. As this list suggests, some growth stocks also rate as blue chips and provide quality growth, whereas others represent higher levels of speculation.

HOT LINKS

To read about characteristics of growth and value companies and their performance in recent years, go to:

www.putnam.com
Click on "Individual Investor" "Education" "Value and Growth"

Growth stocks normally pay little or nothing in the way of dividends, so their payout ratios seldom exceed 10% to 15% of earnings. Instead, all or most of the profits are reinvested in the company and used to help finance rapid growth. Thus the major source of return to investors is price appreciation—and that can have both a good side and a bad side. That is, with growth

FIGURE 6.8

A Growth Stock

(*Source:* Standard & Poor's *Stock Reports*, July 12, 2003.)

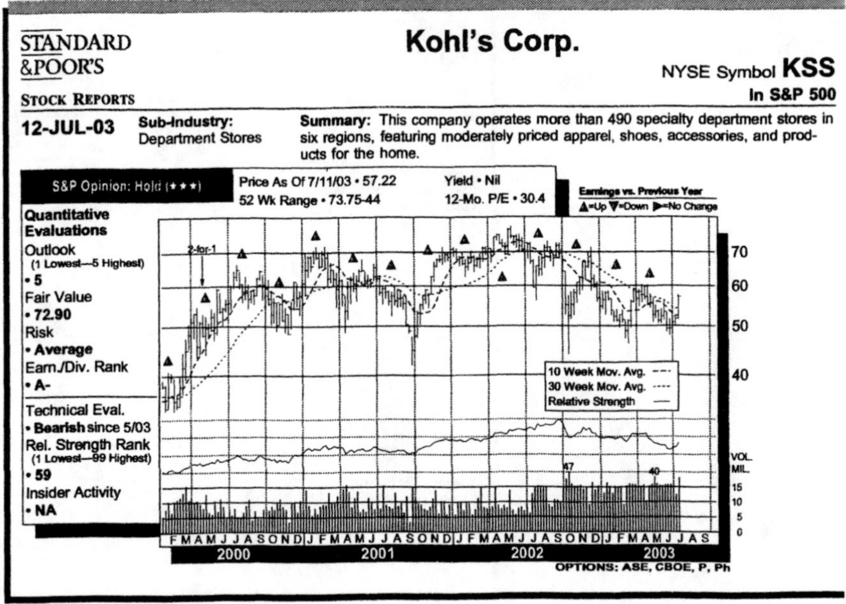

stocks, when the markets are good, these stocks are hot, but when the markets turn down, so do these stocks, often in a big way. Growth shares generally appeal to investors who are looking for attractive capital gains rather than dividends and who are willing to assume a higher element of risk.

tech stocks
stocks that represent the technology sector of the market.

Tech Stocks Over the past 15 years or so, *tech stocks* have become such a dominant force in the market (both positive and negative) that they deserve to be put in a class all their own. **Tech stocks** basically represent the technology sector of the market and include companies that produce or provide everything from computers, semiconductors, data storage, computer software, and computer hardware to peripherals, Internet services, content providers, networking, and wireless communications. These companies provide the high-tech equipment, networking systems, and online services to all lines of businesses, education, health care, communications, governmental agencies, and the home. Some of these stocks are listed on the NYSE and AMEX, though the vast majority are traded on the Nasdaq.

These stocks, in fact, dominate the Nasdaq market and, as such, the Nasdaq Composite Index and other Nasdaq measures of market performance. They were the ones that were hammered especially hard during the market fall of 2000–2002, when the tech-heavy Nasdaq Composite fell nearly 80%. Indeed, the value of many tech stocks fell to just pennies a share, as literally hundreds of these firms simply went out of business. The strongest did survive, however, and some even thrived.

These stocks would probably fall into either the *growth stock* category (see above) or the *speculative stock* class (see page 262), although some of them are legitimate *blue chips*. Tech stocks today may, indeed, offer the potential for attractive (and, in some cases, phenomenal) returns. But they also involve considerable risk, and are probably most suitable for the more risk-tolerant investor. Included in the tech-stock category you'll find some big

FIGURE 6.9

A Tech Stock

(*Source:* Standard & Poor's *Stock Reports*, November 1, 2003.)

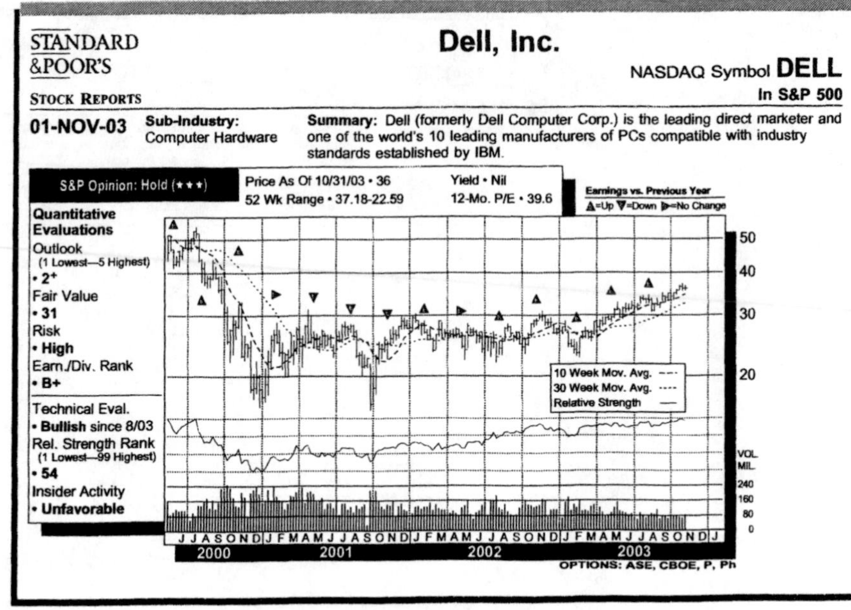

names, like Microsoft, Cisco Systems, Applied Materials, Qualcomm, and Dell (see Figure 6.9). You'll also find many not-so-big names, like BEA Systems, NVIDIA, KLA-Tencor, American Tower, Invitrogen, and Rambus.

speculative stocks
stocks that offer the potential for substantial price appreciation, usually because of some special situation, such as new management or the introduction of a promising new product.

Speculative Stocks Shares that lack sustained records of success but still offer the potential for substantial price appreciation are known as **speculative stocks.** Perhaps investors' hopes are spurred by a new management team that has taken over a troubled company or by the introduction of a promising new product. Other times, it's the hint that some new information, discovery, or production technique will favorably affect the growth prospects of the firm. Speculative stocks are a special breed of securities, and they enjoy a wide following, particularly when the market is bullish.

Generally speaking, the earnings of speculative stocks are uncertain and highly unstable. These stocks are subject to wide swings in price, and they usually pay little or nothing in dividends. On the plus side, speculative stocks such as P. F. Chang's China Bistro, Quicksilver, K-Swiss, Idexx Labs, Serena Software, and Dollar General offer attractive growth prospects and the chance to "hit it big" in the market. To be successful, however, an investor has to identify the big-money winners before the rest of the market does. Speculative stocks are highly risky; they require not only a strong stomach but also a considerable amount of investor know-how. They are used to seek capital gains, and investors will often aggressively trade in and out of these securities as the situation demands.

cyclical stocks
stocks whose earnings and overall market performance are closely linked to the general state of the economy.

Cyclical Stocks **Cyclical stocks** are issued by companies whose earnings are closely linked to the general level of business activity. They tend to reflect the general state of the economy and to move up and down with the business cycle. Companies that serve markets tied to capital equipment spending by business, or to consumer spending for big-ticket, durable items like houses and cars, typically head the list of cyclical stocks. Examples include Alcoa, Caterpillar, Genuine Parts, Maytag Corporation, Rohm & Haas, and Timken.

Cyclical stocks generally do well when the economy is moving ahead, but they tend to do *especially well* when the country is in the early stages of economic recovery. They are, however, perhaps best avoided when the economy begins to weaken. Cyclical stocks are probably most suitable for investors who are willing to trade in and out of these issues as the economic outlook dictates and who can tolerate the accompanying exposure to risk.

defensive stocks
stocks that tend to hold their own, and even do well, when the economy starts to falter.

Defensive Stocks Sometimes it is possible to find stocks whose prices remain stable or even increase when general economic activity is tapering off. These securities are known as **defensive stocks.** They tend to be less affected than the average issue by downswings in the business cycle. Defensive stocks include the shares of many public utilities, as well as industrial and consumer goods companies that produce or market such staples as beverages, foods, and drugs. An excellent example of a defensive stock is Bandag. This recession-resistant company is the world's leading manufacturer of rubber used to retread tires. Other examples are Checkpoint Systems, a manufacturer of antitheft clothing security clips, and WD-40, the maker of that famous all-purpose lubricant. Defensive shares are commonly used by more aggressive investors, who tend to "park" their funds temporarily in defensive stocks while the economy remains soft, or until the investment atmosphere improves.

Mid-Cap Stocks As explained earlier, a stock's size is based on its market value—or, more commonly, on what is known as its *market capitalization* (the market price of the stock times the number of shares outstanding). Generally speaking, the U.S. stock market can be broken into three segments, as measured by a stock's market "cap":

Small-cap	less than \$1 billion
Mid-cap	\$1 billion to \$4 or \$5 billion
Large-cap	more than \$4 or \$5 billion

The large-cap stocks are the real biggies—the Wal-Marts, GMs, and Microsofts of the investment world. Although there are far fewer large-cap stocks than any other size, these companies account for about 80% to 90% of the total market value of all U.S. equities. But as the saying goes, bigger isn't necessarily better. Nowhere is that statement more accurate than in the stock market. Indeed, both the small-cap and mid-cap segments of the market tend to hold their own, or even to outperform large stocks over time.

mid-cap stocks
medium-sized stocks, generally with market values of less than \$4 or \$5 billion but more than \$1 billion.

Mid-cap stocks are a special breed, and offer investors some attractive return opportunities. They provide much of the sizzle of small-stock returns, without as much price volatility. (We'll look at small-cap stocks soon.) At the same time, because mid-caps are fairly good-sized companies and many of them have been around for a long time, they offer some of the safety of the big, established stocks. Among the ranks of the mid-caps are such well-known companies as Wendy's International, Barnes & Noble, Petsmart (see Figure 6.10 on page 264), Outback Steakhouse, Lennar, and Cheesecake Factory. Although these securities offer a nice alternative to large stocks without the uncertainties of small-caps, they probably are most appropriate for investors who are willing to tolerate a bit more risk and price volatility.

FIGURE 6.10

A Mid-Cap Stock

(*Source:* Standard & Poor's *Stock Reports*, July 12, 2003.)

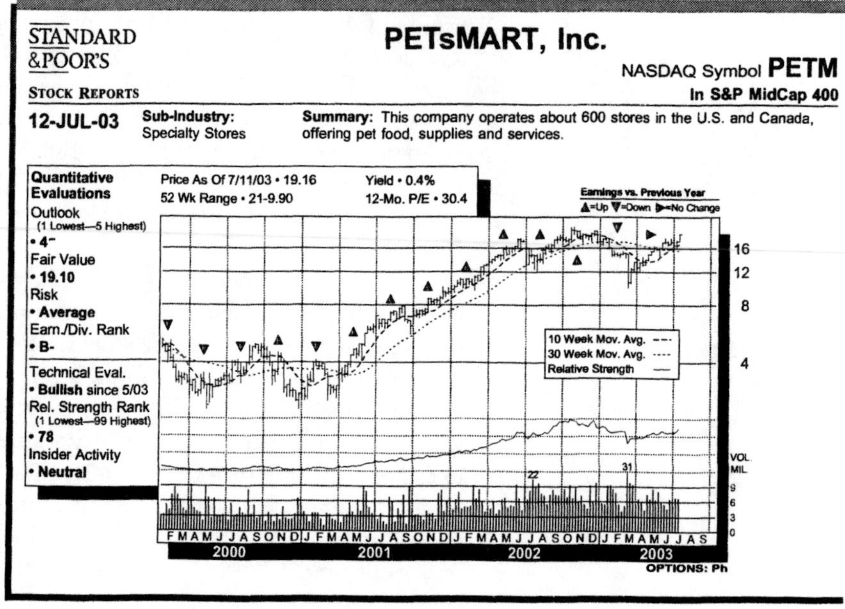

One type of mid-cap stock of particular interest is the so-called *baby blue chip*. Also known as "baby blues," these companies have all the characteristics of a regular blue chip *except size*. Like their larger counterparts, baby blues have rock-solid balance sheets, only modest levels of debt, and long histories of steady profit growth. Baby blues normally pay a modest level of dividends, but like most mid-caps, they tend to emphasize growth. Thus they're considered ideal for investors seeking quality long-term growth. Some well-known baby blues are Tootsie Roll, Reynolds & Reynolds, Hormel Foods, and Pall Corporation.

small-cap stocks
stocks that generally have market values of less than $1 billion but can offer above-average returns.

Small-Cap Stocks Some investors consider small companies to be in a class by themselves in terms of attractive return opportunities. And in many cases, this has turned out to be true. Known as **small-cap stocks,** these companies generally have annual revenues of less than $250 million. But because of their size, spurts of growth can have dramatic effects on their earnings and stock prices. Churchill Downs (where the Kentucky Derby is run), Green Mountain Power, Hancock Fabrics, Hot Topic, JoAnn Stores, and Sonic Corporation (see Figure 6.11) are some better-known small-cap stocks.

Although some small-caps (like Sonic) are solid companies with equally solid financials, that's not the case with most of them. Indeed, because many of these companies are so small, they don't have a lot of stock outstanding, and their shares are not widely traded. In addition, small-company stocks have a tendency to be "here today and gone tomorrow." Although some of these stocks may hold the potential for high returns, investors should also be aware of the very high risk exposure that comes with many of them.

A special category of small-cap stocks is the so-called *initial public offering (IPO)*. Most IPOs are small, relatively new companies that are going public for the first time. (Prior to their public offering, these stocks were pri-

FIGURE 6.11

A Small-Cap Stock

(Source: Standard & Poor's *Stock Reports,* July 12, 2003.)

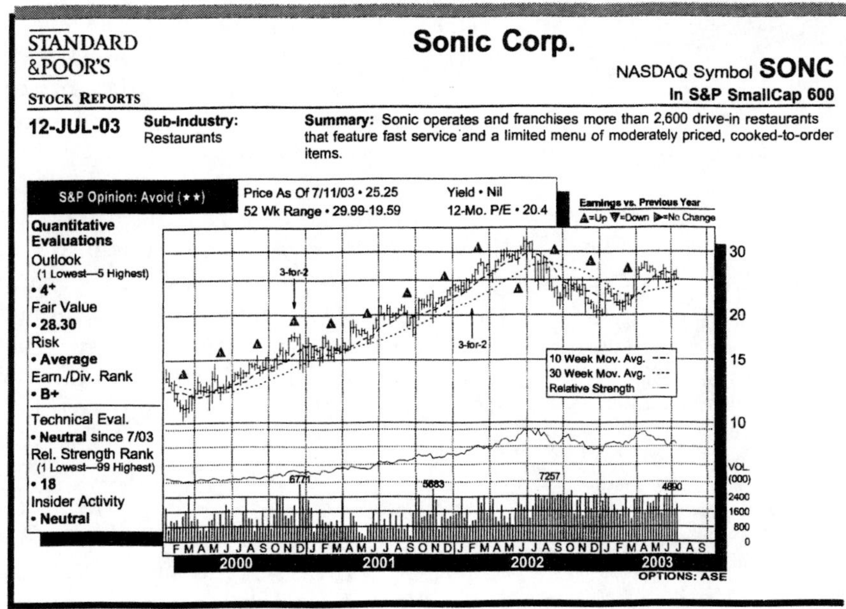

vately held and not publicly traded.) Like other small-company stocks, IPOs are attractive because of the substantial capital gains that investors can earn. Of course, there's a catch: To stand a chance of buying some of the better, more attractive IPOs, you need to be either an active trader or a preferred client of the broker. Otherwise, the only IPOs you're likely to hear of will be the ones these guys don't want. Without a doubt, IPOs are high-risk investments, with the odds stacked against the investor. Because there's no market record to rely on, these stocks should be used only by investors who know what to look for in a company and who can tolerate substantial exposure to risk.

Investing in Foreign Stocks

One of the most dramatic changes to occur in our financial markets in the 1980s and '90s was the trend toward globalization. Indeed, globalization became the buzzword of the 1990s, and nowhere was that more evident than in the world equity markets. Consider, for example, that in 1970 the U.S. stock market accounted for fully *two-thirds of the world market.* In essence, our stock market was twice as big as all the rest of the world's stock markets *combined.* That's no longer true: By 2002, the U.S. share of the world equity market had dropped to less than 50%.

Today the world equity markets are dominated by just six countries, which together account for about 80% of the total market. The United States, by far, has the biggest equity market, which in mid-2003 had a total market value of $10 *trillion.* In a distant second place was Japan (at about one-third the size of the U.S. market), closely followed by the United Kingdom. Rounding out the list were Germany, France and Canada. In addition to these six, another dozen or so markets are also regarded as major world players.

INVESTOR FACTS

A BAD DAY ON THE NIKKEI— On February 1, 2002, Japan's most popular stock index, the Nikkei 225, closed below the DJIA for the first time since 1957. On that Friday, the Nikkei closed at 9,791.43, while the Dow finished at 9,907.26. So, what's the big deal?

Just this: On the final day of trading in 1989, the Nikkei closed at its all-time high of 38,915.87; in contrast, the DJIA finished the year at 2,753.20. A little over 12 years later, that 36,000-point differential totally disappeared! Over that period, while the Dow went *up* some 7,150 points (a 260% increase), the Nikkei went *down* more than 29,000 points (for a 75% decline).

Source: "Tokyo Stock Market Passes Dubious Milestone," *Wall Street Journal,*" February 4, 2002, pp. C1–2.

Among the markets in this second tier are Switzerland, Australia, Italy, the Netherlands, Hong Kong, Spain, and Singapore. Finally, some relatively small, emerging markets—South Korea, Mexico, Malaysia, Portugal, Thailand, and Russia—are beginning to make their presence felt. Clearly, the landscape has changed a lot in the last 20 years, and there's every reason to believe that even more changes lie ahead.

Comparative Returns The United States dominates the world equity markets in terms of sheer size, as well as in the number of listed companies (over 10,000 of them). But that still leaves unanswered a very important question: How has the U.S. equity market performed in comparison to the rest of the world's major stock markets? The answer: not too well, unfortunately. Table 6.5 summarizes total annual returns (in U.S. dollars) for the 23-year period from 1980 through 2002, for eight of the world's largest equity markets. Note that the United States finished first only once (in 1982). Even so, in the decade of the 1990s, and through 2002, because the U.S. market consistently finished near the top (in every year but 1993), it turned in the best overall performance, closely followed by Switzerland. Also, observe in the table that the United States was not the only one to suffer losses over the 3-year period 2000–2002. Indeed the negative returns showed up across the board, with some countries—like Germany, Japan, and France—suffering much deeper losses. Keep in mind that the returns shown in Table 6.5 *are in U.S. dollars.* But as the *Investing in Action* box on pages 268–269 reveals, a good deal of the performance of non-U.S. markets is due to the behavior of *currency exchange rates* and not the markets themselves. Indeed, the U.S. stock market is one of the strongest and best performing in the world! Still, the fact remains that when both markets and currencies are combined, some very rewarding opportunities are available to U.S. investors who are willing to invest in foreign securities.

Going Global: Direct Investments Basically, there are two ways to invest in foreign stocks: through direct investments or through ADRs. (We'll discuss a third way—international mutual funds—in Chapter 13.) Without a doubt, the most adventuresome way is to *buy shares directly in foreign markets*. Investing directly is *not* for the uninitiated, however. For you have to know what you're doing and be prepared to tolerate a good deal of market risk. Although most major U.S. brokerage houses are set up to accommodate investors interested in buying foreign securities, there are still many logistical problems to be faced. To begin with, you have to cope with currency fluctuations and changing foreign exchange rates, as these can have a dramatic impact on your returns. But that's just the start: You also have to deal with different regulatory and accounting standards. The fact is that most foreign markets, even the bigger ones, are not as closely regulated as U.S. exchanges. Investors in foreign markets, therefore, may have to put up with insider trading and other practices that can cause wild swings in market prices. Finally, there are the obvious language barriers, tax problems, and general "red tape" that all too often plague international transactions. There's no doubt that the returns from direct foreign investments can be substantial, but so can the obstacles placed in your way.

HOT LINKS

Visit the CNN financial network to find out which country's stock market has registered the highest percentage change and which registered the lowest percentage change from the previous trading day. Can you cite the reasons why?

money.cnn.com/markets/world_markets.html

TABLE 6.5 Comparative Annual Returns in the World's Major Equity Markets, 1980–2002

	Annual Total Returns (in U.S. dollars)								
	Australia	Canada	France	Germany	Japan	Switzerland	United Kingdom	United States	Rank*
2002	−0.3%	−12.8%	−20.8%	−32.9%	−10.1%	−10.0%	−15.2%	−14.5%	5th
2001	2.6	−20.0	−22.0	−21.9	−29.2	−21.0	−14.0	−5.3	2nd
2000	−9.1	5.6	−4.1	−15.3	−28.1	6.4	−11.5	−4.6	4th
1999	18.7	54.4	29.7	20.5	61.8	−6.6	12.4	26.7	4th
1998	7.1	−5.7	42.1	29.9	5.2	24.0	17.8	17.8	4th
1997	−9.5	13.3	12.4	25.0	−23.6	44.8	22.6	24.4	3rd
1996	17.7	29.0	21.6	14.0	−15.3	2.8	27.2	28.0	2nd
1995	12.5	19.1	14.8	17.0	0.9	45.0	21.3	35.7	2nd
1994	1.4	−5.1	−7.3	3.1	21.4	30.0	−4.4	4.9	3rd
1993	33.4	17.4	19.6	34.8	23.9	41.7	19.0	16.4	8th
1992	−6.1	−4.6	5.2	−2.1	−26.0	26.0	14.0	7.2	3rd
1991	35.8	12.1	18.6	8.7	9.0	16.8	16.0	23.3	2nd
1990	−16.2	−12.2	−13.3	−8.8	−35.9	−5.1	10.4	−0.4	2nd
1989	10.8	25.2	37.6	48.2	2.3	28.0	23.1	30.7	3rd
1988	38.2	17.9	37.1	19.8	35.4	5.8	4.1	15.5	6th
1987	9.5	14.8	−13.9	−24.6	41.0	−9.2	35.2	5.9	5th
1986	45.0	10.8	79.9	36.4	101.2	34.7	27.7	26.1	7th
1985	21.1	16.2	84.2	138.1	44.0	109.2	53.4	31.7	6th
1984	−12.4	−7.1	4.8	−5.2	17.2	−11.1	5.3	1.2	4th
1983	55.2	32.4	33.2	23.9	24.8	19.9	17.3	24.7	5th
1982	−22.2	2.6	−4.2	10.5	−0.6	2.9	9.0	24.8	1st
1981	−23.8	−10.1	−28.5	−10.3	15.7	−9.5	−10.2	−2.8	2nd
1980	54.7	21.6	−2.0	−10.7	30.4	−7.8	42.0	20.6	5th
	Average Annual Returns Over Extended Holding Periods								
5 years									
1998–2002	3.4%	1.4%	1.7%	−7.0%	−4.9%	−2.6%	−3.1%	2.9%	
1995–1999	8.8	20.5	23.7	21.2	2.1	20.1	20.2	26.4	
1990–1994	7.6	0.9	3.7	6.2	−4.9	20.8	10.7	9.9	
Decades									
1993–2002	7.5%	8.0%	7.1%	5.2%	−2.5%	11.2%	7.1%	11.8%	
1990s	8.6	9.8	13.5	12.8	−0.7	17.4	14.2	17.9	
1980s	13.9	11.6	17.6	16.3	28.6	12.2	19.3	17.2	
23 years									
1980–2002	9.2%	7.5%	10.7%	8.9%	7.2%	12.6%	12.7%	13.8%	

Note: Total return = coupon income + capital gain (or loss) + profit (or loss) from changes in currency exchange rates.

*"Rank" shows how U.S. returns ranked among the listed major markets (e.g., in 2002, the United States ranked fifth out of the eight markets listed in the table).

Source: International returns obtained from Morgan Stanley Capital International; U.S. returns based on DJIA.

Going Global with ADRs Fortunately, there is an easier way to invest in foreign stocks, and that is to buy *American Depositary Receipts (ADRs)*, or *American Depositary Shares (ADSs)* as they're sometimes called. As we saw in Chapter 2, ADRs are negotiable instruments, with each ADR representing a specific number of shares in a specific foreign company. (The number of shares can range from a fraction of a share to 20 shares or more.) ADRs are great for investors who want foreign stocks but don't want the hassles that often come with them. That's because American Depositary receipts are bought and sold

INVESTING IN ACTION

In International Investing, Currencies Can Make or Break You

Investing overseas can pay off in many ways: It offers not only attractive return opportunities, but also attractive portfolio diversification properties. Capitalism is spreading like wildfire around the globe, and the economic expansion in many developing areas dwarfs U.S. growth. Accounting practices have improved, as many foreign companies realize that they must make extensive financial disclosures—beyond their normal comfort levels—if they want to attract U.S. investors. In addition, investing overseas can help to diversify and strengthen a portfolio. You may have to look overseas to find industry leaders, and foreign markets may rise when the U.S. market stalls.

Even with these advantages and global opportunities, it's still difficult to believe that an investor in international stocks can consistently outperform one who invests only in U.S. stocks. But take a look at the accompanying graph: *When measured in U.S. dollars,* foreign stocks (as represented by the EAFE index) actually outperformed American equities between 1985 and 1996. What these numbers don't reveal, however, is the impact of a weakening U.S. dollar. To see how currencies can affect international returns, take another look at the behavior of the EAFE, but this time in *local currencies.* From 1990 to mid-2003, the returns on foreign stocks lagged far behind the returns on U.S. equities. Indeed, for the total period 1985 through mid-2003, *if you exclude the currency factor, U.S. stocks outperformed their overseas counterparts by a wide margin.* For example, in the 10-year period ending June 30, 2003, the average annual total return for the Standard & Poor's 500 was approximately 10% per year, compared to just 3% for the EAFE in local currencies. Let's examine what this means for you as an investor.

A favorable currency movement for a U.S. investor in a foreign market is a *weakening* dollar. Money that is invested outside the domestic market is converted to a local currency and later converted back to dollars. If the dollar weakens between the time the investor buys and sells the stock, the local currency buys more dollars at the time of the sale. Such was the case during the first half of 2003, for example, as the dollar depreciated against the euro, boosting returns to investors in European equities.

In contrast, a *strengthening* dollar is bad news for U.S. investors buying overseas securities, because the local currency later buys fewer dollars. In the mid-1990s and again from 1997 to late 2002, the U.S. dollar strengthened against most currencies. To see the implications wrought by a stronger dollar, consider the Australian market: Over the 5-year period ending December 31, 2002, this market produced average returns of approximately 6.5% per year, when measured in Aussie dollars. When measured in U.S. dollars, however, the Australian market produced average annual returns of less than 3.5%. Why the big difference in returns? Just one reason: *changing currency exchange rates!* In other words, as the U.S. dollar strengthened relative to the Australian dollar, returns to U.S. investors declined. Under these conditions, U.S. investors

continued on next page

on U.S. markets just like stocks in U.S. companies. Their prices are quoted in U.S. dollars, not British pounds, Japanese yen, or euros. Furthermore, dividends are paid in dollars. Although there are about 400 foreign companies *whose shares are directly listed on U.S. exchanges* (over 200 of which are Canadian), most foreign companies are traded in this country as ADRs. Indeed, shares of about 1,000 companies, from more than 40 countries, are traded as ADRs on the NYSE, AMEX, and Nasdaq/OTC markets.

To see how ADRs are structured, take a look at Cadbury Schweppes, the British food and household products firm, whose ADRs are traded on the

INVESTING IN ACTION

continued from previous page

may have been in an appreciating market, but they were in a depreciating currency.

The fact is, when measured in local currencies, not many stock markets consistently outperform the U.S. markets, even in down years, like 2001–2002; it usually takes a weak dollar to achieve that goal. Even so, most of those markets that did outperform the U.S. market—among them, South Africa, Indonesia, South Korea, and Malaysia—carried significant risks beyond currency risk, such as political unrest and stability of their governments, that don't worry investors in U.S. stocks.

Critical Thinking Question Explain why a strengthening dollar erodes returns from non-U.S. investments. Is the dollar currently weak or strong, and what does this mean for investors?

Sources: Frederick Balfour, "Where to Strike as the Dollar Droops," *Business Week*, June 30, 2003, pp. 104–105; Craig Karmin, "A Year for Most Overseas Investors to Forget," *The Wall Street Journal*, January 3, 2003, pp. R16, R17; Julia Lichtblau, "Global Stocks: Make the World Your Oyster Again," *Business Week*, July 2, 2001, downloaded from www.businessweek.com; and "MSCI Index Returns," Morgan Stanley Capital International, downloaded from www.mscidata.com.

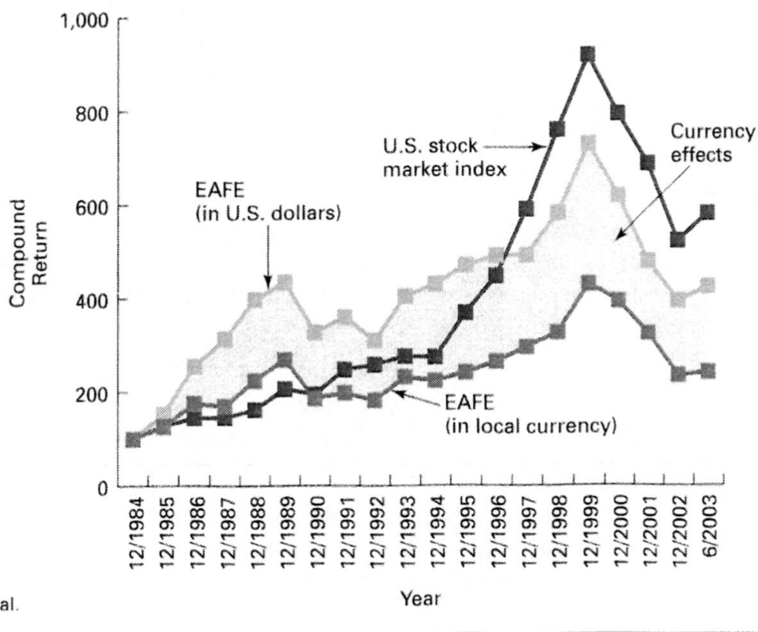

Source: Data from Morgan Stanley Capital International.

NYSE. Each Cadbury ADR represents ownership of four shares of Cadbury stock. These shares are held in a custodial account by a U.S. bank (or its foreign correspondent), which receives dividends, pays any foreign withholding taxes, and then converts the net proceeds to U.S. dollars, which it passes on to investors. Other foreign stocks that can be purchased as ADRs include Sony (a Japanese stock), Ericsson Telephone (from Sweden), Nokia (Finland), Vodafone Airtouch (U.K.), Royal Dutch Petroleum (Netherlands), Nestle's (Switzerland), Shanghai Petro-chemicals (China), Elan Corporation (Ireland), and Grupo Televisa (Mexico). You can even buy ADRs on Russian companies, such as Vimpel-Communications, a Moscow-based cellular phone company whose shares trade (as ADRs) on the NYSE.

Putting Global Returns in Perspective Whether you buy foreign stocks directly or through ADRs, the whole process of global investing is a bit more complex and more risky than domestic investing. The reason: when investing globally, *you have to pick both the right stock and the right market.* Basically, foreign stocks are valued much the same way as U.S. stocks. Indeed, the same variables that drive U.S. share prices (earnings, dividends, and so on) also drive stock values in foreign markets. On top of this, each market reacts to its own set of economic forces (inflation, interest rates, level of economic activity), which set the tone of the market. At any given time, therefore, some markets are performing better than others. The challenge facing global investors is to be in the right market at the right time. As with U.S. stocks, foreign shares produce the same two basic sources of returns: dividends and capital gains (or losses).

But with global investing, there is a third variable—*currency exchange rates*—that plays an important role in defining returns to U.S. investors. In particular, as the U.S. dollar weakens or strengthens relative to a foreign currency, the returns to U.S. investors from foreign stocks increase or decrease accordingly. In a global context, total return to U.S. investors in foreign securities is defined as follows:

Equation 6.4

$$\underset{\text{(in U.S. dollars)}}{\text{Total return}} = \underset{\text{(dividends)}}{\text{Current income}} + \underset{\text{(or losses)}}{\text{Current gains}} \pm \underset{\text{exchange rates}}{\text{Changes in currency}}$$

Because current income and capital gains are in the "local currency" (the currency in which the foreign stock is denominated, such as the euro or the Japanese yen), we can shorten the total return formula to:

Equation 6.5

$$\begin{array}{c}\text{Total return}\\\text{(in U.S. dollars)}\end{array} = \begin{array}{c}\text{Returns from current}\\\text{income and capital gains}\\\text{(in local currency)}\end{array} \pm \begin{array}{c}\text{Returns from}\\\text{changes in currency}\\\text{exchange rates}\end{array}$$

Thus, the two basic components of total return are *those generated by the stocks themselves* (dividends plus change in share prices) and *those derived from movements in currency exchange rates.*

Measuring Global Returns Employing the same two basic components noted in Equation 6.5, above, we can compute total return in U.S. dollars by using the following holding period return (HPR) formula, as modified for changes in currency exchange rates.

Equation 6.6

$$\begin{array}{c}\text{Total return}\\\text{(in U.S. dollars)}\end{array} = \left[\frac{\begin{array}{c}\text{Ending value of}\\\text{stock in foreign}\\\text{currency}\end{array} + \begin{array}{c}\text{Amount of dividends}\\\text{received in}\\\text{foreign currency}\end{array}}{\begin{array}{c}\text{Beginning value of stock}\\\text{in foreign currency}\end{array}} \times \frac{\begin{array}{c}\text{Exchange rate}\\\text{at end of}\\\text{holding period}\end{array}}{\begin{array}{c}\text{Exchange rate}\\\text{at beginning of}\\\text{holding period}\end{array}}\right] - 1.00$$

In Equation 6.6, the "exchange rate" represents the *value of the foreign currency in U.S. dollars*—that is, how much one unit of the foreign currency is worth in U.S. money.

This modified HPR formula is best used over investment periods of one year or less. Also, because it is assumed that dividends are received at the same exchange rate as the ending price of the stock, this equation provides only an approximate (though fairly close) measure of return. Essentially, the first component of Equation 6.6 provides returns on the stock in local currency, and the second element accounts for the impact of changes in currency exchange rates.

To see how this formula works, consider a U.S. investor who buys several hundred shares of Gucci, the luxury goods company that trades on the Amsterdam Stock Exchange. Since the Netherlands is part of the European Common Market, its currency is the *euro*. Now, assume the investor paid a price *per share* of 90.48 euros for the stock, at a time when the exchange rate between the U.S. dollar and the euro (U.S. \$/€) was \$0.945, meaning a euro was worth almost 95 (U.S.) cents. The stock paid *annual* dividends of 5 euros per share. Twelve months later, the stock was trading at 94.00 euros, when the U.S. \$/€ exchange rate was \$1.083. Clearly, the stock went up in price and so did the euro, so the investor must have done all right. To find out just what kind of return this investment generated (in U.S. dollars), we'll have to use Equation 6.6.

$$\begin{aligned}\text{Total return (in U.S. dollars)} &= \left[\frac{94.00 + 5.00}{90.48} \times \frac{\$1.083}{\$0.945}\right] - 1.00 \\ &= [1.0942 \times 1.1460] - 1.00 \\ &= [1.2540] - 1.00 \\ &= \underline{\underline{25.4\%}}\end{aligned}$$

With a return of 25.4%, the investor obviously did quite well. However, *most of this return was due to currency movements, not to the behavior of the stock*. Look at just the first part of the equation, which shows the return (in local currency) *earned on the stock* from dividends and capital gains: 1.0942 – 1.00 = 9.42%. Thus, the stock itself produced a return of less than 9½%. All the rest of the return—about 16% (i.e., 25.40 – 9.42)—came from the change in currency values. In this case, the value of the U.S. dollar went down relative to the euro and thus added to the return.

Currency Exchange Rates As we've just seen, exchange rates can have a dramatic impact on investor returns. They can convert mediocre returns or even losses into very attractive returns—and vice versa. Only one thing determines whether the so-called *currency effect* is going to be positive or negative: the behavior of the U.S. dollar relative to the currency in which the security is denominated. In essence, *a stronger dollar has a negative impact on total returns to U.S. investors, and a weaker dollar has a positive impact*. Thus, other things being equal, the best time to be in foreign securities is when the dollar is *falling*.

Of course, the greater the amount of fluctuation in the currency exchange rate, the greater the impact on total returns. The challenge facing global investors is to find not only the best-performing foreign stock(s) but also the best-performing foreign currencies. You want the *value of both the foreign stock and the foreign currency to go up over your investment horizon*. And note that this rule applies *both* to direct investment in foreign stocks and to the purchase of ADRs. (Even though ADRs are denominated in dollars, their quoted prices vary with ongoing changes in currency exchange rates.)

Alternative Investment Strategies

Basically, common stocks can be used (1) as a "storehouse" of value, (2) as a way to accumulate capital, and (3) as a source of income. Storage of value is important to all investors, as nobody likes to lose money. However, some investors are more concerned about it than others and, therefore, rank safety of principal as their most important stock selection criteria. These investors are more quality-conscious and tend to gravitate toward blue chips and other nonspeculative shares. Accumulation of capital, in contrast, is generally an important goal to those with long-term investment horizons. These investors use the capital gains and/or dividends that stocks provide to build up their wealth. Some use growth stocks for this purpose, others do it with income shares, and still others use a little of both. Finally, some investors use stocks as a source of income. To them, a dependable flow of dividends is essential. High-yielding, good-quality income shares are usually the preferred investment vehicle for these people.

Individual investors can use various *investment strategies* to reach their investment goals. These include buy-and-hold, current income, quality long-term growth, aggressive stock management, and speculation and short-term trading. The first three strategies appeal to investors who consider storage of value important. Depending on the temperament of the investor and the time he or she has to devote to an investment program, any of the strategies might be used to accumulate capital. In contrast, the current-income strategy is the logical choice for those using stocks as a source of income.

Buy-and-Hold Buy-and-hold is the most basic of all investment strategies, and is certainly one of the most conservative. The objective is to place money in a secure investment outlet (safety of principal is vital) and watch it grow over time. In this strategy, investors select high-quality stocks that offer attractive current income and/or capital gains and hold them for extended periods—perhaps as long as 10 to 15 years. This strategy is often used to finance future retirement plans, to meet the educational needs of children, or simply to accumulate capital over the long haul. Generally, investors pick out a few good stocks and then invest in them on a regular basis for long periods of time—until either the investment climate or corporate conditions change dramatically.

Buy-and-hold investors regularly add fresh capital to their portfolios (many treat them like savings plans). Most also plow the income from annual dividends back into the portfolio and reinvest in additional shares (often through dividend reinvestment plans). Long popular with so-called *value-oriented investors*, this approach is used by quality-conscious individuals who are looking for competitive returns over the long haul.

Current Income Some investors use common stocks to seek high levels of current income. Common stocks are desirable for this purpose not so much for their high dividend yields but because their *dividend levels tend to increase over time*. In this strategy, safety of principal and stability of income are vital, while capital gains are of secondary importance. Quality income shares are the obvious medium of choice for this strategy. Some investors adopt it simply as a way of earning high (and relatively safe) returns on their investment capital. More often, however, the current-income strategy is used by those who are trying to supplement their income. Indeed, many of these investors plan to use the added income for consumption purposes, such as a retired couple supplementing their retirement benefits with income from stocks.

Quality Long-Term Growth This strategy is *less conservative* than either of the first two in that it *seeks capital gains as the primary source of return*. A fair amount of trading takes place with this approach. Most of the trading is confined to *quality growth stocks* (including some of the better tech stocks, as well as baby blues and other mid-caps) that offer attractive growth prospects and the chance for considerable price appreciation. A number of growth stocks also pay dividends, which many growth-oriented investors consider *an added source of return*. But even so, this strategy still emphasizes capital gains as the principal way to earn big returns. The approach involves a greater element of risk, because of its heavy reliance on capital gains. Therefore, a good deal of diversification is often used. Long-term accumulation of capital is the most common reason for using this approach, but compared to the buy-and-hold tactic, the investor aggressively seeks a bigger payoff by doing considerably more trading and assuming more market risk.

A variation of this investment strategy combines quality long-term growth with high income. This is the so-called *total-return approach* to investing. Though solidly anchored in long-term growth, this approach also considers dividend income as a source of return that should be sought after, rather than relegated to an after-thought or treated as merely a pleasant by-product. In essence, with the total return approach, investors seek attractive long-term returns from *both* dividend income *and* capital gains. These investors hold both income stocks and growth stocks in their portfolios. Or they may hold stocks that provide both dividends and capital gains. In the latter case, the investor doesn't necessarily look for high-yielding stocks, but rather for stocks that offer the potential for *high rates of growth in their dividend streams*. Like their counterparts who employ current-income or quality long-term growth strategies, total-return investors are very concerned about quality. Indeed, about the only thing that separates these investors from current-income and quality long-term growth investors is that to them, what matters is not so much the *source of return* as *the amount of return*. For this reason, total-return investors seek the most attractive returns wherever they can find them—be it from a growing stream of dividends or from appreciation in the price of a stock.

Aggressive Stock Management Aggressive stock management also uses quality issues but seeks attractive rates of return through a fully managed portfolio. Such a portfolio would be one in which the investor aggressively trades in and out of stocks to achieve eye-catching returns, primarily from capital gains. Blue chips, growth stocks, big-name tech stocks, mid-caps, and cyclical issues are the primary investment vehicles. More aggressive investors might even consider small-cap stocks, including some of the more speculative tech stocks, foreign shares, and ADRs.

This approach is similar to the quality long-term growth strategy. However, it involves considerably more trading, and the investment horizon is generally much shorter. For example, rather than waiting 2 or 3 years for a stock to move, an aggressive stock trader would go after the same investment payoff in 6 months to a year. Timing security transactions and turning investment capital over fairly rapidly are both key elements of this strategy. These investors try to stay fully invested in stocks when the market is bullish. When it weakens, they shift to a more defensive posture by putting a big chunk of their money into defensive stocks or even into cash and other short-term debt instruments. This strategy has substantial risks. It also places real demands on the individual's time and investment skills. But the rewards can be equally substantial.

Speculation and Short-Term Trading Speculation and short-term trading characterize the least conservative of all investment strategies. The sole objective of this strategy is capital gains. And the shorter the time in which the objective can be achieved, the better. Although such investors confine most of their attention to speculative or small-cap stocks and tech stocks, they are not averse to using foreign shares (especially those in so-called *emerging markets*) or other forms of common stock if they offer attractive short-term opportunities. Many speculators feel that information about the industry or company is less important than market psychology or the general tone of the market. It is a process of constantly switching from one position to another as new opportunities unfold. Because the strategy involves so much risk, many transactions yield little or no profit, or even substantial losses. The hope is, of course, that when one does hit, it will be in a big way, and returns will be more than sufficient to offset losses. This strategy obviously requires considerable knowledge and time. Perhaps most important, it also requires the psychological and financial fortitude to withstand the shock of financial losses.

CONCEPTS IN REVIEW

6.14 Define and briefly discuss the investment merits of each of the following.

a. *Blue chips.*
b. *Income stocks.*
c. *Mid-cap stocks.*
d. *American Depositary Receipts.*
e. *IPOs.*
f. *Tech stocks.*

6.15 Why do most income stocks offer only limited capital gains potential? Does this mean the outlook for continued profitability is also limited? Explain.

6.16 With all the securities available in this country, why would a U.S. investor want to buy foreign stocks? Briefly describe the two ways in which a U.S. investor can buy stocks in a foreign company. As a U.S. investor, which approach would you prefer? Explain.

6.17 Which *investment approach (or approaches)* do you feel would be most appropriate for a quality-conscious investor? What kind of investment approach do you think you'd be most comfortable with? Explain.

Summary

LG 1 **Explain the investment appeal of common stocks and why individuals like to invest in them.** Common stocks have long been a popular investment vehicle, largely because of the attractive return opportunities they provide. From current income to capital gains, there are common stocks available to fit just about any investment need.

LG 2 **Describe stock returns from a historical perspective and understand how current returns measure up to historical standards of performance.** Stock returns consist of both dividends and capital gains, though price appreciation is the key component. Over the long haul, stocks have provided investors with annual returns of around 10% to 12%. The decade of the 1990s was especially rewarding, as stocks generated returns of anywhere from around 20% (on the Dow and S&P 500) to nearly 30% in the tech-heavy Nasdaq market. That situation changed in early 2000, when one of the biggest bull markets in history came to an abrupt end. In fact, the next 3 years, from 2000 through late 2002, saw the DJIA fall some 35% and the S&P 500 nearly 50%. But that was nothing compared to the Nasdaq, which fell an eye-popping 77% from its all-time high.

LG 3 **Discuss the basic features of common stocks, including issue characteristics, stock quotations, and transaction costs.** Common stocks are a form of equity capital and, as such, each share represents partial ownership of a company. Publicly traded stock can be issued via a public offering or through a rights offering to existing stockholders. Companies can also increase the number of shares outstanding through a stock split. To reduce the number of shares of stock in circulation, companies can buy back shares, which are then held as treasury stock. Occasionally, a company issues different classes of common stock, known as classified common stock.

LG 4 **Understand the different kinds of common stock values.** There are several ways to calculate the value of a share of stock. Book value represents accounting value. Market and investment values, which are most important to investors, represent what the stock is or should be worth.

LG 5 **Discuss common stock dividends, types of dividends, and dividend reinvestment plans.** Companies often share their profits by paying out cash dividends to stockholders. Such actions are normally taken only after carefully considering a variety of corporate and market factors. Sometimes companies declare stock dividends rather than, or in addition to, cash dividends. Many firms that pay cash dividends have dividend reinvestment plans, through which shareholders can have cash dividends automatically reinvested in the company's stock.

LG 6 **Describe various types of common stocks, including foreign stocks, and note how stocks can be used as investment vehicles.** The type of stock selected depends on an investor's needs and preferences. In today's market, investors can choose blue chips, income stocks, growth stocks, tech stocks, speculative issues, cyclicals, defensive shares, mid-cap stocks, small-cap stocks, and initial public offerings. In addition, U.S. investors can buy the common stocks of foreign companies either directly on foreign exchanges or on U.S. markets as American Depositary Receipts (ADRs). Generally speaking, common stocks can be used as a storehouse of value, as a way to accumulate capital, and as a source of income. Different investment strategies (buy-and-hold, current income, quality long-term growth, aggressive stock management, and speculation and short-term trading) can be followed to achieve these objectives.

Putting Your Investment Know-How to the Test

1. A Japanese investor buys stock in a New Zealand company for 70 New Zealand dollars (NZD), holds it for a year, and then sells the stock for 65 NZD. The stock paid a 2 NZD dividend. During the year, the NZD appreciated 6% relative to the yen. The investor's approximate yen return over the investment holding period is
   a. Equal to – 4.3%.
   b. Less than – 4.3% because of the currency appreciation.
   c. Greater than – 4.3%, because each NZD bought more yen over the period.
   d. Greater than – 4.3%, because each NZD bought fewer yen over the period.

2. The holding period return on a stock is equal to
   a. The capital gain during the period plus the inflation rate.
   b. The capital gain during the period plus the dividend yield.
   c. The current yield plus the dividend yield.
   d. The dividend yield plus the risk premium.

3. Growth stocks usually exhibit
   a. High dividend yields.
   b. Low price-to-book ratios.
   c. High P/E ratios.
   d. None of the above.

4. A firm's earnings per share increased from \$4 to \$6, its dividends increased from \$3.00 to 3.60, and its share price increased \$40 to \$50. Based upon this information, we can say that:
   a. the firm increased the number of shares outstanding.
   b. the stock's P/E ration has increased.
   c. the company's dividend payout ratio has decreased.
   d. the company's market capitalization has decreased.

5. The worth of a share of common stock for a stockholder can be best described as its
   a. Market value.
   b. Par value.
   c. Book value.
   d. Investment value.

6. The main reason for investing in stocks is
   a. They are easy to buy and sell.
   b. They have outperformed inflation in the long run.
   c. They provide superior returns compared to many other investment vehicles.
   d. All of the above.

7. Which of the following is true about various types of stocks?
   a. Income stocks have a record of consistent above-average earnings growth.
   b. Cyclical stocks provide superior returns during recessions.
   c. Small-cap stocks often have a lot of price volatility.
   d. Most defensive stocks are related to the aerospace and defense sectors.

8. You are considering purchasing shares of ABC company. You expect to collect \$2 in dividends and sell the stock for \$40 a year from now. What is the maximum price you would pay for a share of ABC today if you wanted to earn a 15% return?
   a. \$34.78
   b. \$36.52
   c. \$37.50
   d. \$46.00

9. Provided below and on the next page is information about the financial structure of AXZ Enterprises. (All information is for the fiscal year just ended).

   Number of common shares at the beginning of the year: 5,000,000
   Common stock dividend declared on July 1: 20%
   Net (after-tax) income: \$2,500,000

Dividend paid on common stock for the year: $1,100,000
Preferred dividends for the year: $300,000

Given this information, the company's EPS is closest to
a. $0.40. b. $0.50.
c. $0.30. d. $0.24.

10. Assuming that the common stock of AXZ currently trades at $10, its dividend yield is
a. 2.50%. b. 2.00%.
c. 2.20%. d. 2.55%.

Answers: 1. c; 2. b; 3. c; 4. c; 5. d; 6. d; 7. c; 8. b; 9. a; 10. b

Discussion Questions

LG 2

Q6.1 Look at the record of stock returns in Tables 6.1 and 6.2, particularly the return performance during the 1970s, 1980s, 1990s, and 2000–2003.

a. How would you compare the returns during the 1970s with those produced in the 1980s? How would you characterize market returns in the 1990s? Is there anything that stands out about this market? How does it compare with the market that existed from early 2000 through mid-2003?
b. Now look at Figure 6.2 and Table 6.3. On the basis of the information in these exhibits, how would you describe the market's performance during the 1990s and through the first half of 2003?
c. Considering the average annual returns that have been generated over holding periods of 5 years or more, what rate of return do you feel is typical for the stock market in general? Is it unreasonable to expect this kind of return, on average, in the future? Explain.

LG 3

Q6.2 Assume that the following quote for the Alpha Beta Corporation (a NYSE stock) was obtained from the Thursday, April 10, issue of the *Wall Street Journal.*

+6.8	254.00	150.50	AlphaBet	ALF	6.00	3.1	15	755	189.12	−3.88

Given this information, answer the following questions.

a. On what day did the trading activity occur?
b. At what price did the stock sell at the end of the day on Wednesday, April 9?
c. How much (in percentage terms) has the price of this stock gone up or down since the first of the year?
d. What is the firm's price/earnings ratio? What does that indicate?
e. What is the last price at which the stock traded on the date quoted?
f. How large a dividend is expected in the current year?
g. What are the highest and lowest prices at which the stock traded during the latest 52-week period?
h. How many shares of stock were traded on the day quoted?
i. How much, if any, of a change in price took place between the day quoted and the immediately preceding day? At what price did the stock close on the immediately preceding day?

LG 4

Q6.3 Listed below are three pairs of stocks. Look at each pair and select the security you would like to own, given that you want to *select the one that's worth more money.* Then, *after* you make all three of your selections, use the *Wall Street Journal* or some other source to find the latest market value of the two securities in each pair.

a. 50 shares of Berkshire Hathaway (stock symbol BRKA) or 150 shares of Coca-Cola (stock symbol KO). (Both are listed on the NYSE.)

b. 100 shares of WD-40 (symbol WDFC—a Nasdaq National Market issue) or 100 shares of Nike (symbol NKE—a NYSE stock).
c. 150 shares of Wal-Mart (symbol WMT) or 50 shares of Sears (symbol S). (Both are listed on the NYSE.)

How many times did you pick the one that was worth more money? Did the price of any of these stocks surprise you? If so, which one(s)? Does the price of a stock represent its value? Explain.

LG 6

Q6.4 Assume that a wealthy individual comes to you looking for some investment advice. She is in her early forties and has $250,000 to put into stocks. She wants to build up as much capital as she can over a 15-year period and is willing to tolerate a "fair amount" of risk.

a. What types of stocks do you think would be most suitable for this investor? Come up with at least three different types of stocks, and briefly explain the rationale for each.
b. Would your recommendations change if you were dealing with a smaller amount of money—say, $50,000? What if the investor were more risk-averse? Explain.

LG 6

Q6.5 Identify and briefly describe the three sources of return to U.S. investors in foreign stocks. How important are currency exchange rates? With regard to currency exchange rates, when is the best time to be in foreign securities?

a. Listed below are exchange rates (for the beginning and end of a hypothetical 1-year investment horizon) for three currencies: the British pound (B£), Australian dollar (A$), and Mexican peso (Mp).

	Currency Exchange Rates at	
Currency	Beginning of Investment Horizon	End of One-Year Investment Horizon
British pound (B£)	1.55 U.S.$ per B£	1.75 U.S.$ per B£
Australian dollar (A$)	1.35 A$ per U.S.$	1.25 A$ per U.S.$
Mexican peso (Mp)	0.10 U.S.$ per Mp	0.08 U.S.$ per Mp

From the perspective of a U.S. investor holding a foreign (British, Australian, or Mexican) stock, which of the above changes in currency exchange rates would have a positive effect on returns (in U.S. dollars)? Which would have a negative effect?

b. ADRs are denominated in U.S. dollars. Are their returns affected by currency exchange rates? Explain.

LG 6

Q6.6 Briefly define each of the following types of investment programs, and note the kinds of stock (blue chips, speculative stocks, etc.) that would best fit with each.

a. A buy-and-hold strategy.
b. A current-income portfolio.
c. Long-term total return.
d. Aggressive stock management.

Problems

LG 3

P6.1 An investor owns some stock in General Refrigeration & Cooling. The stock recently underwent a 5-for-2 stock split. If the stock was trading at $50 per share just before the split, how much is each share most likely selling for after the split? If the investor owned 200 shares of the stock before the split, how many shares would she own afterward?

LG 3

P6.2 An investor deposits $20,000 in a new brokerage account. The investor buys 1,000 shares of Tipco stock for $19 per share. Two weeks later, the investor sells the Tipco stock for $20 per share. When the investor receives his brokerage account statement, he sees that there is a balance of $20,900 in his account:

Item	Number	Price per Share	Total Transaction	Account Balance
1. Deposit			$20,000	$20,000
2. Tipco purchase	1,000 shares	$19	($19,000)	$20,000
3. Tipco sale	1,000 shares	$20	$20,000	$21,000
4.				
5. Balance				$20,900

What belongs in item 4 on this statement?

LG 4

P6.3 The Kracked Pottery Company has total assets of $2.5 million, total short- and long-term debt of $1.8 million, and $200,000 worth of 8% preferred stock outstanding. What is the firm's total book value? What would its book value per share be if the firm had 50,000 shares of common stock outstanding?

LG 4

P6.4 Lots ov' Profit, Inc., is trading at $25 per share. There are 250 million shares outstanding. What is the market capitalization of this company?

LG 5

P6.5 The MedTech Company recently reported net profits after taxes of $15.8 million. It has 2.5 million shares of common stock outstanding and pays preferred dividends of $1 million per year.

a. Compute the firm's earnings per share (EPS).
b. Assuming that the stock currently trades at $60 per share, determine what the firm's dividend yield would be if it paid $2 per share to common stockholders.
c. What would the firm's dividend payout ratio be if it paid $2 per share in dividends?

LG 5

P6.6 On January 1, 2002, an investor bought 200 shares of Gottahavit, Inc., for $50 per share. On January 3, 2003, the investor sold the stock for $55 per share. The stock paid a quarterly dividend of $0.25 per share. How much (in $) did the investor earn on this investment, and, assuming the investor is in the 33% tax bracket, how much will she pay in income taxes on this transaction?

LG 4 LG 5

P6.7 Consider the following information about Truly Good Coffee, Inc.

Total assets	$240 million
Total debt	$115 million
Preferred stock	$25 million
Common stockholders' equity	$100 million
Net profits after taxes	$22.5 million
Number of preferred stock outstanding	1 million shares
Number of common stock outstanding	10 million shares
Preferred dividends paid	$2/share
Common dividends paid	$0.75/share
Market price of the preferred stock	$30.75/share
Market price of the common stock	$25.00/share

Use the information above to find the following.

a. The company's book value.
b. Its book value per share.
c. The stock's earnings per share (EPS).
d. The dividend payout ratio.

e. The dividend yield on the common stock.
f. The dividend yield on the preferred stock.

LG 5

P6.8 East Coast Utilities is currently trading at $28 per share. The company pays a quarterly dividend of $0.28 per share. What is the dividend yield?

LG 5

P.6.9 West Coast Utilities had net profit of $900 million. It has 900 million shares outstanding, and paid annual dividends of $0.90 per share. What is the dividend payout ratio?

LG 5

P6.10 Collin Smythies owns 200 shares of Consolidated Glue. The company's board of directors recently declared a cash dividend of 50 cents a share payable April 18 (a Wednesday) to shareholders of record on March 22 (a Thursday).

a. How much in dividends, if any, will Collin receive if he *sells* his stock on March 20?
b. Assume Collin decides to hold on to the stock rather than sell it. If he belongs to the company's dividend reinvestment plan, how many new shares of stock will he receive if the stock is currently trading at $40 and the plan offers a 5% discount on the share price of the stock? (Assume that all of Collin's dividends are diverted to the plan.) Will Collin have to pay any taxes on these dividends, given that he is taking them in stock rather than cash?

LG 5

P6.11 Southern Cities Trucking Company has the following 5-year record of earnings per share.

Year	EPS
2000	$1.40
2001	2.10
2002	1.00
2003	3.25
2004	0.80

Which of the following procedures would produce the greater amount of dividends to stockholders over this 5-year period?

a. Paying out dividends at a fixed ratio of 40% of EPS.
b. Paying out dividends at a fixed rate of $1 per share.

LG 4 LG 5

P6.12 Using the resources available at your campus or public library, or on the Internet, select any three common stocks you like, and determine the latest book value per share, earnings per share, dividend payout ratio, and dividend yield for each. (Show all your calculations.)

LG 4 LG 5

P6.13 In January 2000, an investor purchased 800 shares of Engulf & Devour, a rapidly growing high-tech conglomerate. Over the 5-year period from 2000 through 2004, the stock turned in the following dividend and share price performance.

Year	Share Price at Beginning of Year	Dividends Paid During Year	Share Price at End of Year
2000	$42.50*	$0.82	$ 54.00
2001	54.00	1.28	74.25
2002	74.25	1.64	81.00
2003	81.00	1.91	91.25
2004	91.25	2.30	128.75

*Investor purchased stock in 2000 at this price.

On the basis of this information, find the annual holding period returns for 2000 through 2004. (*Hint:* See Chapter 4 for the HPR formula.)

LG 6

P6.14 George Robbins considers himself to be an aggressive investor. At the present time, he's thinking about investing in some foreign securities. In particular, he's looking at two stocks: (1) Siemens AG, the big German electronics firm, and (2) Swisscom AG, the Swiss telecommunications company.

Siemens, which trades on the Frankfurt Exchange, is currently priced at 53.25 euros per share. It pays annual dividends of 1.5 euros per share. Robbins expects the stock to climb to 60.00 euros per share over the next 12 months. The current exchange rate is 0.9025 €/U.S. $, but that's expected to rise to 1.015 €/U.S. $.

The other company, Swisscom, trades on the Zurich Exchange and is currently priced at 715 Swiss francs (Sf) per share. The stock pays annual dividends of 15 Sf per share. Its share price is expected to go up to 760 Sf within a year. At current exchange rates, one Sf is worth $0.75 U.S., but that's expected to go to $0.85 by the end of the 1-year holding period.

a. *Ignoring the currency effect*, which of the two stocks promises the higher total return (in its local currency)? Based on this information, which of the two stocks looks like the better investment?
b. Which of the two stocks has the better total return *in U.S. dollars*? Did currency exchange rates affect their returns in any way? Do you still want to stick with the same stock you selected in part (a)? Explain.

LG 6

P6.15 Bob buys $25,000 of UH-OH Corporation stock. Unfortunately, a major newspaper reveals the very next day that the company is being investigated for accounting fraud, and the stock price falls by 50%. What is the percentage increase now required for Bob to get back to $25,000 of value?

LG 6

P6.16 The euro is currently trading at a ratio of 1.02 relative to the dollar. You expect this to change such that the euro will be trading at 0.8941 to the dollar in 6 months.

a. If you are correct, what currency transaction would you execute to profit from this move?
b. If you had $10,000 and you executed the transaction, how much would you make before taxes, assuming your prediction was correct?

See the text Web site (www.aw-bc.com/gitman_joehnk) for Web exercises that deal with *common stocks*.

Case Problem 6.1 *Sara Decides to Take the Plunge*

LG 1 LG 6

Sara Thomas is a child psychologist who has built up a thriving practice in her hometown of Boise, Idaho. Over the past several years she has been able to accumulate a substantial sum of money. She has worked long and hard to be successful, but she never imagined anything like this. Success has not spoiled Sara. Still single, she keeps to her old circle of friends. One of her closest friends is Terry Jenkins, who happens to be a stockbroker, and who acts as Sara's financial adviser.

Not long ago, Sara attended a seminar on investing in the stock market and since then she's been doing some reading about the market. She has concluded that keeping all of her money in low-yielding savings accounts doesn't make any sense. As a result, Sara has decided to move part of her money to stocks. One evening, Sara told Terry about her decision and explained that she had found several stocks that she thought looked "sort of interesting." She described them as follows:

- *North Atlantic Swim Suit Company.* This highly speculative stock pays no dividends. Although the earnings of NASS have been a bit erratic, Sara feels that its growth prospects have never been brighter—"what with more people than ever going to the beaches the way they are these days," she says.

- *Town and Country Computer.* This is a long-established computer firm that pays a modest dividend yield (of about 1½%). It is considered a quality growth stock. From one of the stock reports she read, Sara understands that T&C offers excellent long-term growth and capital gains potential.

- *Southeastern Public Utility Company.* This income stock pays a dividend yield of around 5%. Although it's a solid company, it has limited growth prospects because of its location.

- *International Gold Mines, Inc.* This stock has performed quite well in the past, especially when inflation has become a problem. Sara feels that if it can do so well in inflationary times, it will do even better in a strong economy. Unfortunately, the stock has experienced wide price swings in the past. It pays almost no dividends.

Questions

a. What do you think of the idea of Sara keeping "substantial sums" of money in savings accounts? Would common stocks make better investments for her than savings accounts? Explain.

b. What is your opinion of the four stocks Sara has described? Do you think they are suitable for her investment needs? Explain.

c. What kind of common stock investment program would you recommend for Sara? What investment objectives do you think she should set for herself, and how can common stocks help her achieve her goals?

Case Problem 6.2 *Wally Wonders Whether There's a Place for Dividends*

LG 5 LG 6

Wally Wilson is a commercial artist who makes a good living by doing freelance work—mostly layouts and illustrations for local ad agencies and major institutional clients (such as large department stores). Wally has been investing in the stock market for some time, buying mostly high-quality growth stocks as a way to achieve long-term growth and capital appreciation. He feels that with the limited time he has to devote to his security holdings, high-quality issues are his best bet. He has become a bit perplexed lately with the market, disturbed that some of his growth stocks aren't doing even as well as many good-grade income shares. He therefore decides to have a chat with his broker, Al Fried.

During the course of their conversation, it becomes clear that both Al and Wally are thinking along the same lines. Al points out that dividend yields on income shares are indeed way up and that, because of the state of the economy, the outlook for growth stocks is not particularly bright. He suggests that Wally seriously consider putting some of his money into income shares to capture the high dividend yields that are available. After all, as Al says, "the bottom line is not so much where the payoff comes from as how much it amounts to!" They then talk about a high-yield public utility stock, Hydro-Electric Light and Power. Al digs up some forecast information about Hydro-Electric and presents it to Wally for his consideration:

Year	Expected EPS	Expected Dividend Payout Ratio
2004	$3.25	40%
2005	3.40	40
2006	3.90	45
2007	4.40	45
2008	5.00	45

The stock currently trades at $60 per share. Al thinks that within 5 years it should be trading at around $75 to $80 a share. Wally realizes that to buy the Hydro-Electric stock, he will have to sell his holdings of CapCo Industries—a highly regarded growth stock that Wally is disenchanted with because of recent substandard performance.

Questions

a. How would you describe Wally's present investment program? How do you think it fits him and his investment objectives?

b. Consider the Hydro-Electric stock.
   1. Determine the amount of annual dividends Hydro-Electric can be expected to pay over the years 2004 to 2008.
   2. Compute the total dollar return that Wally will make from Hydro-Electric if he invests $6,000 in the stock and all the dividend and price expectations are realized.
   3. If Wally participates in the company's dividend reinvestment plan, how many shares of stock will he have by the end of 2008? What will they be worth if the stock trades at $80 on December 31, 2008? Assume that the stock can be purchased through the dividend reinvestment plan at a net price of $50 a share in 2004, $55 in 2005, $60 in 2006, $65 in 2007, and $70 in 2008. Use fractional shares, to two decimals, in your computations. Also, assume that, as in part (b), Wally starts with 100 shares of stock and all dividend expectations are realized.

c. Would Wally be going to a different investment strategy if he decided to buy shares in Hydro-Electric? If the switch is made, how would you describe his new investment program? What do you think of this new approach? Is it likely to lead to more trading on Wally's behalf? If so, can you reconcile that with the limited amount of time he has to devote to his portfolio?

Excel with Spreadsheets

Efficient information that quickly disseminates market prices is imperative for investors in the stock market. A major component of the information system is the stock quote that appears daily in the financial press.

You found the following stock quote (on page 284) for City National Corporation (CYN) in the January 12, 2004 edition of the *Wall Street Journal*. Refer to Figure 6.5 "Stock Quotations" for an explanation of the array of information related to the listed stock. Given the respective quote, create a spreadsheet to answer the following questions concerning the common stock investment.

	A	B	C	D	E	F	G	H	I	J	K	L
1				New York Stock Exchange Composite Transactions								
2		YTD	52	WEEKS				YLD		VOL		NET
3		%CHG	HI	LO	STOCK (SYM)		DIV	%	PE	100S	LAST	CHG
4	[1]	−0.03	64.49	38.7	CityNtl CYN		1.117	18%	16.16	4887	?	−1.89
5												
6												
7												
8												

Questions

a. What was the closing price for this stock yesterday?

b. How many round lots of stock were traded yesterday? How many individual stocks does that translate into?

c. What are the current earnings per share (EPS) for this stock based on the data presented?

d. What is the current net income for this stock? (*Hint*: You must find out the number of shares outstanding.) Using the Internet, follow these steps:

- Go to www.moneycentral.msn.com.
- Place "CYN" in quote box and click "Go."
- Look on the left side for "Financial Results."
- Click on "Statements."
- Choose "Balance Sheet" from the pull-down financial statement menu and "annual" from the view box pull-down menu.
- At the bottom of the statement, look for "Total Common Shares Outstanding."

e. Calculate the dividend payout ratio for City National.

CHAPTER 10

FIXED-INCOME SECURITIES

CHAPTER 10

FIXED-INCOME SECURITIES

LEARNING GOALS

After studying this chapter, you should be able to:

LG 1 Explain the basic investment attributes of bonds and their use as investment vehicles.

LG 2 Describe the essential features of a bond and distinguish among different types of call, refunding, and sinking-fund provisions.

LG 3 Describe the relationship between bond prices and yields, and explain why some bonds are more volatile than others.

LG 4 Identify the different types of bonds and the kinds of investment objectives these securities can fulfill.

LG 5 Discuss the global nature of the bond market and the difference between dollar-denominated and non-dollar-denominated foreign bonds.

LG 6 Describe the role that bond ratings play in the market and the quotation system used with various types of bonds.

How do you get to be a highly regarded passenger airline in less than 3 years—and profitable in 1? If you are JetBlue Airlines, you begin with lots of start-up funding to become the best-capitalized new airline in history. Then, you fly only new Airbus A320 aircraft, luxuriously outfitted with all-leather seats and up to 24 channels of DirecTV programming for every customer. Add low fares, focus on the highest-quality customer service, and you have the ingredients for success. By fall 2003, just 3½ years after its February 2000 inaugural flight, JetBlue was serving 23 airports nationwide and adding new cites and flights as demand for its services continued to grow.

JetBlue has more than 47 Airbuses in service and more on order, as well as orders for smaller Embraer 190 aircraft to be delivered starting in 2005. Acquiring and maintaining this airline fleet is expensive; the company's annual capital expenditures in recent years have been in the range of $450 million to $540 million. Making these and future capital expenditures for aircraft and facilities is critical to JetBlue's continued success.

Like most companies in capital-intensive industries, JetBlue funds its growth by using a combination of equity (it went public in April 2002) and long-term debt. Its June 30, 2003, balance sheet showed $758.30 million in long-term debt, up from about $291 million on December 31, 2001. The company's overall financial strength makes it possible to issue long-term debt at competitive rates. For example, its floating-rate equipment notes due through 2014 carried a 3.5% weighted average rate. As of June 30, 2003, JetBlue's long-term debt to equity ratio was 1.58, compared to the industry average of about 2.15, and its interest coverage was 6.44 times—a healthy cushion.

Before you invest in any fixed-income debt securities, whether issued by JetBlue or any other company, you'll want to consider credit quality, interest rates, maturity, and other factors. Chapters 10 and 11 will provide the background you need to make wise choices in the bond market.

Sources: "JetBlue Airways to Accelerate Fleet Growth with Two Additional Airbus Orders in 2003," Company Press Release, February 10, 2003, downloaded from www.jetblue.com; material at JetBlue Web site, www.jetblue.com; and "JetBlue Airways Corp., finance.yahoo.com.

Why Invest in Bonds?

LG 1

bonds
negotiable, publicly traded long-term debt securities, whereby the issuer agrees to pay a fixed amount of interest over a specified period of time and to repay a fixed amount of principal at maturity.

In contrast to stocks, *bonds are liabilities*—they are nothing more than publicly traded IOUs where the bondholders are actually *lending money* to the issuer. Technically, **bonds** can be described as negotiable, publicly traded, long-term debt securities. They are issued in various denominations, by a variety of borrowing organizations, including the U.S. Treasury, agencies of the U.S. government, state and local governments, and corporations. Bonds are often referred to as *fixed-income securities* because the debt-service obligations of the issuers are fixed. That is, the issuing organization agrees to pay a fixed amount of interest periodically and to repay a fixed amount of principal at maturity.

Like many other types of investment vehicles, bonds provide investors with two kinds of income: (1) They provide a generous amount of current income, and (2) given the right market environment, they can also be used to generate substantial amounts of capital gains. The current income, of course, is derived from the interest payments received over the life of the issue. Capital gains, in contrast, are earned whenever market interest rates fall. A basic trading rule in the bond market is that *interest rates and bond prices move in opposite directions*. When interest rates rise, bond prices fall. When rates drop, bond prices move up. Thus, it is possible to buy bonds at one price and to sell them later at a higher price. Of course, it is also possible to incur a capital loss, should market rates move against you. Taken together, the current income and capital gains earned from bonds can lead to attractive returns.

Bonds are also a versatile investment outlet. They can be used conservatively by those who seek high current income, or they can be used aggressively by those who go after capital gains. Although bonds have long been considered attractive investments for those seeking current income, it wasn't until the late 1960s and the advent of volatile interest rates that they also became recognized for their capital gains potential and as trading vehicles. Investors found that, given the relation of bond prices to interest rates, the number of profitable trading opportunities increased substantially as wider and more frequent swings in interest rates began to occur.

In addition, certain types of bonds can be used for tax shelter: Municipal obligations are perhaps the best known in this regard. But as we'll see later in this chapter, Treasury and certain federal agency issues also offer some tax advantages. Finally, because of the general high quality of many bond issues, they can also be used for the preservation and long-term accumulation of capital. For with quality issues, not only do investors have a high degree of assurance that they'll get their money back at maturity, but the stream of interest income is also highly dependable.

Putting Bond Market Performance in Perspective

The bond market is driven by interest rates. In fact, *the behavior of interest rates is the single most important force in the bond market*. Interest rates determine not only the amount of current income investors will receive but also the amount of capital gains (or losses) bondholders will incur. It's not surprising, therefore, that bond market participants follow interest rates closely and that bond market performance is often portrayed in terms of market interest rates.

FIGURE 10.1

The Behavior of Interest Rates Over Time—1961–2003

From an era of relative stability, bond interest rates rose dramatically and became highly volatile. The net result was that bond yields not only became competitive with the returns offered by other securities but also provided investors with attractive capital gains opportunities. (2003 yields through the second quarter, June 2003.)

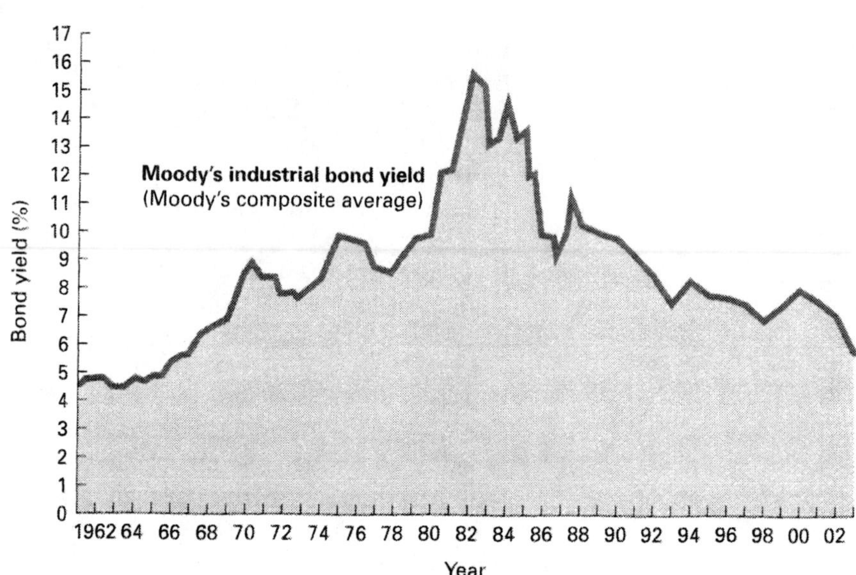

Figure 10.1 provides a look at bond interest rates over the 43-year period from 1961 through 2003. It shows that from a state of relative stability, interest rates rose steadily in the latter half of the 1960s. Over the course of the next 15 years, the rates paid on high-grade bonds nearly tripled. Indeed, interest rates rose from the 4% to 5% range in the early 1960s to over 16% by 1981. But then rates dropped sharply. By 1986 they were back to the single-digit range once again. Thus, after a protracted bear market, bonds abruptly reversed course, and the strongest bull market on record occurred from 1982 through early 1987. (The bond market is considered *bearish* when market interest rates are high or rising, *bullish* when rates are low or falling.) Even though interest rates did move back up for a short time in 1987–1988, they quickly retreated and by 2002–2003, had fallen to levels not seen in nearly 40 years (since the early 1960s). Indeed, by early 2003, long-term Treasury bonds were yielding *a little over 4%*.

Historical Returns As with stocks, *total returns* in the bond market are made up of both current income and capital gains (or losses). Tables 10.1 and 10.2 (on pages 417 and 418) provide an overview of (total) returns in the bond market—on an annual basis and for various investment horizons—over the 43-year period from 1961 through the second quarter of 2003. Take a look at Table 10.1, which lists *year-end market yields* and total *annual returns* for high-grade corporate bonds. Note how bond returns started to slip in 1965, as market yields began to climb. In fact, from 1965 to 1981, there were no fewer than 8 years when average returns were negative—which is highly unusual for the bond market. In contrast, look what happened over the 20-year period from 1982 through 2002, when rates were in a general state of decline: There were only 3 years of negative returns (in 1987, 1994, and 1999), whereas double-digit returns (of 10.7% to 43.8%) occurred in no fewer than 12 of the 20 years.

TABLE 10.1 **Historical Annual Yields and Returns in the Bond Market, 1961–2003***
(Yields and returns based on performance of high-grade corporate bonds)

Year	Year-End Bond Yields*	Total Rates of Return**	Year	Year-End Bond Yields*	Total Rates of Return**
2003*	5.25%	10.61%	1981	14.98%	−0.96%
2002	6.48	11.95	1980	13.15	−2.62
2001	7.08	12.16	1979	10.87	−4.18
2000	7.62	9.18	1978	9.32	−0.07
1999	7.05	−5.76	1977	8.50	1.71
1998	6.53	9.16	1976	8.14	18.65
1997	7.16	13.46	1975	8.97	14.64
1996	7.43	2.20	1974	8.89	−3.06
1995	6.86	27.94	1973	7.79	1.14
1994	8.64	−5.76	1972	7.41	7.26
1993	7.31	13.64	1971	6.48	11.01
1992	8.34	9.34	1970	6.85	18.37
1991	8.58	20.98	1969	7.83	−8.09
1990	9.61	6.48	1968	6.62	2.57
1989	9.18	15.29	1967	6.30	−4.95
1988	9.81	10.49	1966	5.55	0.20
1987	10.33	−1.47	1965	4.79	−0.46
1986	9.02	18.71	1964	4.46	4.77
1985	10.63	27.99	1963	4.46	2.19
1984	12.05	16.39	1962	4.34	7.95
1983	12.76	4.70	1961	4.56	4.82
1982	11.55	43.80			

*Year-end bond yields are for Aa-rated corporate bonds; 2003 yields and returns through the second quarter (June) 2003.
**Total return figures are based on interest income as well as capital gains (or losses).
Sources: Annual yields derived from year-end Moody's and S&P bond yields on Aa- (AA-) rated corporate issues. Total return figures (for 1961–1985) from Ibbotson and Sinquefield, *Stocks, Bonds, Bills, and Inflation: Historical Returns*. Total returns for 1986 through the second quarter of 2003 obtained from *the Lehman Bros. Long-Term Corporate Bond* database.

Table 10.2 contains return performance over various holding periods of 5 to 43 years. These figures demonstrate the type of long-term returns possible from bonds and show that *average annual returns of around 8% to 10% on high-grade issues are not out of the question.* Although such performance may lag behind that of stocks (which it should, *over the long run*, in light of the reduced exposure to risk), it really isn't that bad, especially from the perspective of risk-adjusted rate of return. The big question facing bond investors, however, is what kind of returns will they be able to produce over the next 10 to 12 years? The 1980s and 1990s, through 2002–2003, were very good for bond investors. *But that market was driven by falling interest rates, which in turn produced hefty capital gains and outsize returns.* Whether market interest rates will (or even can) continue on that path is doubtful. Most market observers, in fact, caution against expecting abnormally high rates of return over the next decade or so.

Bonds Versus Stocks Although bonds definitely have their good points (low risk, high levels of current income, and desirable diversification properties), they also have a significant downside: their *comparative* returns. The fact is, *relative* to stocks, there's a big give-up in returns—which, of course, is the price you pay for the even bigger reduction in risk! But just because there's a deficit

TABLE 10.2 **Holding Period Returns in the Bond Market: 1961–2003***

Holding Period	Average Annual Returns*	Cumulative Total Returns	Amount to Which a $10,000 Investment Will Grow Over the Holding Period
5(+) years: 1998–2003*	8.42%	55.98%	$15,598
5 years: 1993–97	9.70	58.88	15,888
10 years: 1993–2002	8.40	124.04	22,404
15 years: 1988–2002	9.72	301.98	40,198
25 years: 1978–2002	9.50	866.84	96,684
42(+) years: 1961–2003*	7.28	1,881.74	198,174
The 1990s: 1990–99	8.7%	130.2%	$23,020
The 1980s: 1980–89	13.0	240.2	34,022
The 1970s: 1970–79	6.2	83.1	18,305
The 1960s: 1960–69	1.7	18.1	11,809

*Average annual return figures are fully compounded returns and are based on interest income as well as capital gains (or losses). 2003 data through the second quarter (June).

Sources: Total return figures (1961–85) from Ibbotson and Sinquefield, *Stocks, Bonds, and Inflation: Historical Returns.* Total return data for 1986 through the second quarter of 2003 from *Lehman Bros. Long-Term Corporate Bond* series.

INVESTOR FACTS

IT WAS GREAT WHILE IT LASTED!—It went on for two decades and was one of the most remarkable runs in market history. No, we're not talking about stocks; we're talking about bonds! From the early 1980s through mid-2003, bond prices climbed as interest rates fell. Indeed, over the 22 years that ended in December 2002, the Lehman Bros. Aggregate Bond Index generated a fully compounded return of 10.4% per year, while the S&P 500 earned 12.2% annually. Sure, stocks still outperformed bonds, but by less than two percentage points. All things considered, that's a highly competitive return, and especially so when you factor in comparative levels of risk—i.e., as measured by their standard deviations, bonds had less than half the return variability of stocks.

in long-term returns, doesn't mean that bonds are always the underachievers. Consider, for example, what's happened over the past 20 years or so: Starting in the 1980s, fixed-income securities held their own against stocks and continued to do so through the early 1990s, only to fall far behind for the rest of the decade. But then along came a nasty bear market in stocks (2000–2002) and the impact was nothing short of spectacular. The net result of all this can be seen in Figure 10.2, which tracks the comparative returns of stocks (via the S&P 500) and bonds (using the Lehman Bros. Long Bond Index) over the 1990s and through mid-2003. As can be seen, for the first half of the period, bonds held up very well, pretty much matching the returns in the stock market. But things started to change in 1995, as stock returns shot up, while bond returns began to level off. Thus, for the decade as a whole (1990–1999), bonds produced average annual returns of 8.7%, whereas stocks turned in average returns of 18.2%. That difference meant that a $10,000 investment in bonds would have led to a terminal value of some $23,000, compared to more than $53,000 for stocks.

That's a high opportunity cost to pay for holding bonds, and it prompted some market observers to question whether bonds should have *any place at all* in an investment portfolio. They reasoned that if interest rates had, in fact, bottomed out, then bonds wouldn't have much to offer, other than relatively low returns. But the market experts overlooked one tiny detail: It wasn't bonds that would prove to be the problem, it was stocks! As can be seen in Figure 10.2, the bear market had a devastating effect on stocks. So much so, in fact, that by mid-2003 the differential returns between stocks and bonds had all but evaporated. Indeed, over the period from January 1990 through June 2003, stocks outperformed bonds by only half a percentage point (10.2% versus 9.7%). The bottom line was a terminal value of slightly over $37,000 for stocks, compared to nearly $35,000 for bonds.

FIGURE 10.2 **Comparative Performance of Stocks and Bonds in the 1990s and Through Mid-2003**

This graph shows what happened to $10,000 invested in bonds over the 13½-year period from January 1990 to June 2003, versus the same amount invested in stocks. Clearly, while stocks held a commanding lead through early 2000, the ensuing bear market erased virtually all of that advantage. As a result, stocks and bonds ended the period at almost the same ending (or "terminal") values. (*Source: Morningstar Principia Pro for Mutual Funds*, release date June 30, 2003.)

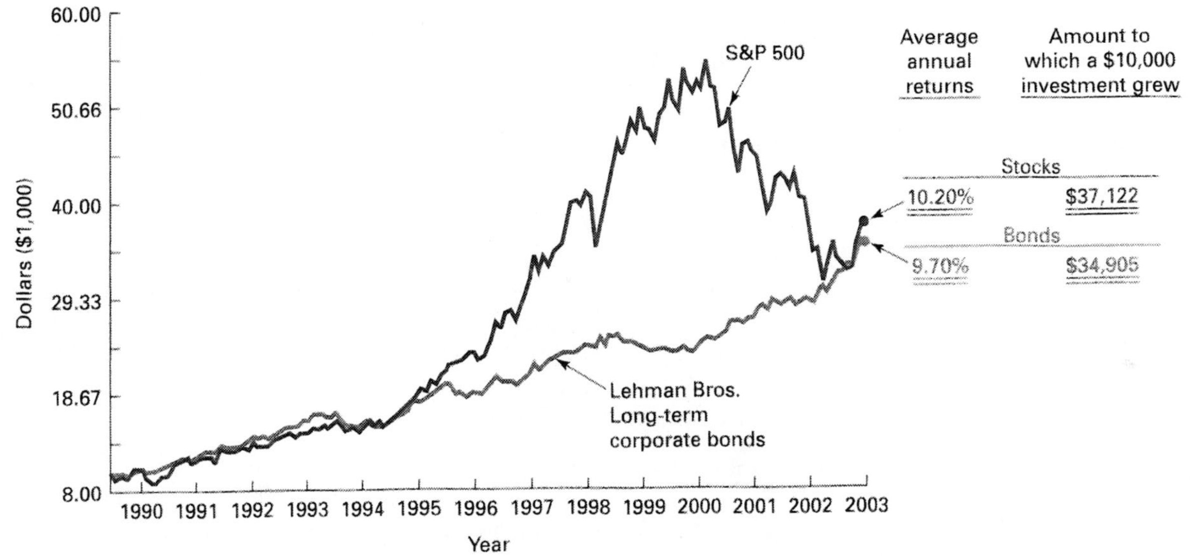

Note: Performance figures and graphs are based on fully compounded rates of return and include reinvested current income (dividends and interest) as well as capital gains (or losses); taxes have been ignored in all calculations.

HOT LINKS

For information on bond investment considerations, go to the Bond Market Association's site whose address is shown below. Click on [Bond Basics]: Key bond investment considerations.

www.investinginbonds.com

Most investors would agree that's a very low price to pay for *the level of stability that bonds bring to a portfolio*. The fact is, bond returns are far more stable than stock returns, plus they possess *excellent portfolio diversification properties*. Thus, except for the most aggressive of investors, bonds have a lot to contribute from a portfolio perspective. Indeed, as a general rule, adding bonds to a portfolio will, *up to a point*, have a much greater impact on lowering risk than on return. Face it: you don't buy bonds for their high returns (except when you think interest rates are heading down). Rather, you buy them for their current income and/or for the stability they bring to your portfolio. And that's still true, even today.

Exposure to Risk

Like any other type of investment vehicle, fixed-income securities should be viewed in terms of their risk and return. Generally speaking, bonds are exposed to five major types of risks: interest rate risk, purchasing power risk, business/financial risk, liquidity risk, and call risk.

- **Interest Rate Risk.** Interest rate risk is the number one source of risk to fixed-income investors, *because it's the major cause of price volatility in* *the bond market*. For bonds, interest rate risk translates into market risk: The behavior of interest rates, in general, affects *all* bonds and cuts across *all* sectors of the market, even the U.S. Treasury market. When market interest rates rise, bond prices fall, and vice versa. And as interest rates become more volatile, so do bond prices.

- **Purchasing Power Risk.** Purchasing power risk accompanies inflation. During periods of mild inflation, bonds do pretty well, because their returns tend to outstrip inflation rates. Purchasing power risk really heats up, though, when inflation takes off, as it did in the late 1970s; when that happens, bond yields start to lag behind inflation rates. The reason: Even though market yields are rising with inflation, your return is locked in by the fixed coupon rate on your bond.
- **Business/Financial Risk.** This is basically the risk that the *issuer will default on interest and/or principal payments*. Also known as *credit risk*, business/financial risk has to do with the quality and financial integrity of the issuer. The stronger the issuer, the less business/financial risk there is to worry about. This risk doesn't even exist for some securities (e.g., U.S. Treasuries). For others, such as corporate and municipal bonds, it's a very important consideration.
- **Liquidity Risk.** Liquidity risk is the risk that a bond will be difficult to unload, at a reasonable price, if you want to sell it. In certain sectors of the market, this is a far bigger problem than investors realize. For even though the U.S. bond market is enormous, much of the activity occurs in the primary/new-issue market. Therefore, with the exception of the Treasury market and a good deal of the agency market, relatively little trading is done in the secondary markets, particularly with corporates and municipals. And where there's little trading, there's lots of liquidity risk. So, if liquidity is important to you, steer clear of thinly traded bonds.
- **Call Risk.** Call risk, or *prepayment risk*, is the risk that a bond will be "called" (retired) long before its scheduled maturity date. Issuers are often given the opportunity to prepay their bonds, and they do so by calling them in for prepayment. (We'll examine call features later in this chapter.) When issuers call their bonds, the bondholders end up getting cashed out of the deal and have to find another place for their investment funds—and there's the problem. Because bonds are nearly always called for prepayment after interest rates have taken a big fall, comparable investment vehicles just aren't available. Thus you have to replace a high-yielding bond with a much lower-yielding issue. From the bondholder's perspective, a called bond means not only a disruption in cash flow but also a sharply reduced rate of return.

The returns on bonds are, of course, related to risk—other things being equal, the more risk embedded in a bond, the greater the expected return. But with bonds, the amount and types of risks involved depends, in large part, on the type of bond (i.e., its issue characteristics). For example, as we'll see later in the chapter, there's more interest rate risk with a long bond than a short bond. In addition, it's sometimes difficult to compare the risk exposure of one bond to another, because the bonds typically have different issue characteristics. That is, one issue could have *more* interest rate and call risks, but *less* credit and liquidity risks than another issue. These different degrees of risk exposure often get buried in the net differential returns. We'll examine the various features that affect a bond's risk exposure, like maturity, coupon, call features, and agency ratings, as we work our way through this chapter.

CONCEPTS IN REVIEW

10.1 What appeal do bonds hold for individual investors? Give several reasons why bonds make attractive investment outlets.

10.2 How would you describe the behavior of market interest rates and bond returns over the last 30–40 years? Do swings in market interest rates have any bearing on bond returns? Explain.

10.3 Identify and briefly describe the five types of risk to which bonds are exposed. What is the most important source of risk for bonds in general? Explain.

Essential Features of a Bond

LG 2 LG 3

A *bond* is a negotiable, long-term debt instrument that carries certain obligations (including the payment of interest and the repayment of principal) on the part of the issuer. Because bondholders are only lending money to the issuer, they are not entitled to any of the rights and privileges that go along with an ownership position. But bondholders, as well as bond issuers, do have a number of well-defined rights and privileges that together help define the essential features of a bond. We'll now take a look at some of these features. As you will see, when it comes to bonds, it's especially important to know what you're getting into, *for many seemingly insignificant features (like a bond's coupon or maturity) can have dramatic effects on its price behavior and investment return*. This is especially true in periods of low interest rates, because knowing what to buy and when to buy can mean the difference between earning a mediocre return and earning a highly competitive one.

Bond Interest and Principal

In the absence of any trading, a bond investor's return is limited to fixed interest and principal payments. That's because bonds involve *a fixed claim on the issuer's income* (as defined by the size of the periodic interest payments) and *a fixed claim on the assets of the issuer* (equal to the repayment of principal at maturity). As a rule, bonds pay interest every 6 months. There are exceptions, however; some issues carry interest payment intervals as short as a month, and a few as long as a year. The amount of interest due is a function of the **coupon**, which defines the annual interest income that will be paid by the issuer to the bondholder. For instance, a $1,000 bond with an 8% coupon pays $80 in interest annually—generally in the form of two $40 semiannual payments. The coupon return on a bond is often defined in terms of its **current yield**, which is a measure of the amount of annual interest income that a bond produces relative to its prevailing market price. It is found by dividing annual coupon income by the market price of the bond. For example, if an 8% bond

coupon
feature on a bond that defines the amount of annual interest income.

current yield
measure of the annual interest income a bond provides relative to its current market price.

is currently priced in the market at $875, then it would have a current yield of 9.14%: ($1,000 × .08)/$875 = $80/$875 = .0914. We'll look at this bond valuation measure in more detail in Chapter 11.

principal
on a bond, the amount of capital that must be repaid at maturity.

The **principal** amount of a bond, also known as an issue's *par value*, specifies the amount of capital that must be repaid at maturity. For example, there is $1,000 of principal in a $1,000 bond. Of course, debt securities regularly trade at market prices that differ from their principal (par) values. This occurs whenever an issue's coupon differs from the prevailing market rate of interest. That is, the price of the issue changes inversely with interest rates until its yield is compatible with the prevailing market yield. Such behavior explains why a 7% issue will carry a market price of only $825 in a 9% market. The drop in price from its par value of $1,000 is necessary to raise the yield on this bond from 7% to 9%. In essence, the new, higher yield is produced in part from annual coupons and in part from capital gains, as the price of the issue moves from $825 back to $1,000 at maturity.

Maturity Date

maturity date
the date on which a bond matures and the principal must be repaid.

Unlike common stock, all debt securities have limited lives and will expire on a given date in the future, the issue's **maturity date.** Whereas interest payments are made semiannually over the life of the issue, principal is repaid only at maturity—or possibly before, in the case of callable issues. The maturity date on a bond is fixed (and never changes). It not only defines the life of a new issue but also denotes the amount of time remaining for older, outstanding bonds. Such a life span is known as an issue's *term to maturity.* For example, a new issue may come out as a 25-year bond, but 5 years later, it will have only 20 years remaining to maturity.

term bond
a bond that has a single, fairly lengthy maturity date.

serial bond
a bond that has a series of different maturity dates.

note
a debt security originally issued with a maturity of from 2 to 10 years.

Two types of bonds can be distinguished on the basis of maturity: term and serial issues. A **term bond** has a single, fairly lengthy maturity date and is the most common type of issue. A **serial bond,** in contrast, has a series of different maturity dates, perhaps as many as 15 or 20, within a single issue. For example, a 20-year term bond issued in 2004 has a single maturity date of 2024, but that same issue as a serial bond might have 20 annual maturity dates that extend from 2004 through 2024. At each of these annual maturity dates, a certain portion of the issue would come due and be paid off. Maturity is also used to distinguish a *note* from a *bond.* That is, a debt security that's originally issued with a maturity of 2 to 10 years is known as a **note,** whereas a *bond* technically has an initial term to maturity of more than 10 years. In practice, notes are often issued with maturities of 5 to 7 years, whereas bonds normally carry maturities of 20 to 30 years or more.

Principles of Bond Price Behavior

The price of a bond is a function of its coupon, its maturity, and the movement of market interest rates. The relationship of bond prices to market interest rates is captured in Figure 10.3. Basically, the graph reinforces the *inverse relationship* that exists between bond prices and market rates: *Lower* rates lead to *higher* bond prices.

premium bond
a bond with a market value in excess of par; occurs when interest rates drop below the coupon rate.

Figure 10.3 also shows the difference between premium and discount bonds. A **premium bond** is one that sells for more than its par value. A premium results whenever market interest rates drop below the bond's coupon rate.

FIGURE 10.3 The Price Behavior of a Bond

A bond will sell at its par value so long as the prevailing market interest rate remains the same as the bond's coupon—in this case, 10%. However, when the market rates drop, bond prices move up. When rates rise, bond prices move down. As a bond approaches its maturity, the price of the issue moves toward its par value, regardless of the level of prevailing interest rates.

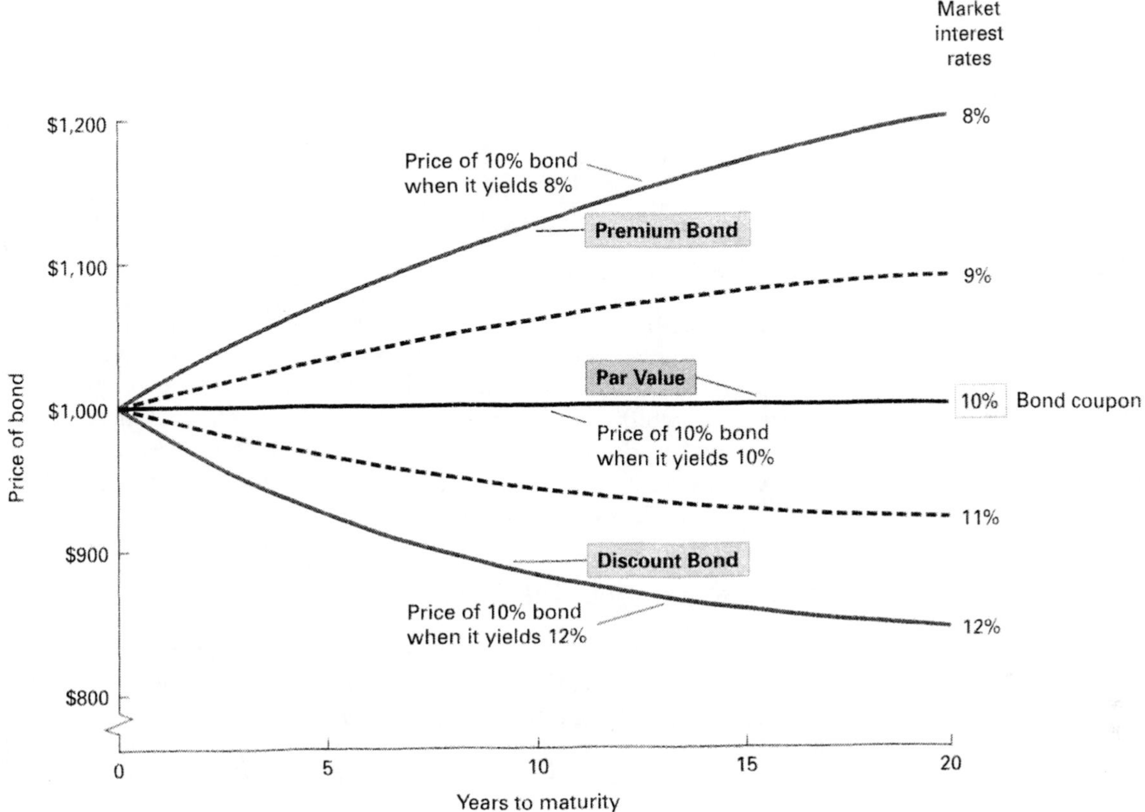

discount bond
a bond with a market value lower than par; occurs when market rates are greater than the coupon rate.

A **discount bond,** in contrast, sells for less than par. The discount is the result of market rates being greater than the issue's coupon rate. Thus, the 10% bond in Figure 10.3 trades at a premium when market rates are at 8%, but at a discount when rates are at 12%.

When a bond is first issued, it is usually sold to the public at a price that equals or is very close to its par value. Likewise, when the bond matures—some 15, 20, or 30 years later—it will once again be priced at its par value. What happens to the price of the bond in between is of considerable interest to most bond investors. And in this regard, we know that the extent to which bond prices move depends not only on the *direction* of change in interest rates but also on the *magnitude* of such change: The greater the moves in interest rates, the greater the swings in bond prices.

However, bond price volatility also varies according to an issue's coupon and maturity. That is, bonds with *lower coupons* and/or *longer maturities* have *lots of price volatility* and are more responsive to changes in market interest rates. (Note in Figure 10.3 that for a given change in interest rates—e.g., from 10% to 8%—the largest change in price occurs when the bond has the greatest number of years to maturity.) Therefore, if a *decline* in interest rates is anticipated, you should seek lower coupons and longer maturities (to maximize capital gains). When interest rates move *up*, you should do just the opposite: seek high coupons with short maturities. This choice will minimize price variation and act to preserve as much capital as possible.

Actually, of the two variables, the *maturity* of an issue has the greater impact on price volatility. For example, look what happens to the price of an 8% bond when market interest rates rise by 1, 2, or 3 percentage points:

	Change in the Price of an 8% Bond When Interest Rates Rise by:		
Bond Maturity	1 Percentage Point	2 Percentage Points	3 Percentage Points
5 years	−4.0%	−7.7%	−11.2%
25 years	−9.9%	−18.2%	−25.3%

For purposes of this illustration, we assume the changes in interest rate occur "instantaneously," so the maturities remain fixed, at 5 or 25 years. Given the computed price changes, it's clear that the shorter (5-year) bond offers a lot more price stability. Such behavior is universal with all fixed-income securities, and is very important. It means that if you want to reduce your exposure to capital loss or, more to the point, to lower the price volatility in your bond holdings, then just *shorten your maturities*.

Call Features—Let the Buyer Beware!

Consider the following situation: You've just made an investment in a high-yielding, 25-year bond. Now all you have to do is sit back and let the cash flow in, right? Well, perhaps. Certainly, that will happen for the first several years. But, if market interest rates drop, it's also likely that you'll receive a notice from the issuer that the bond is being *called*. This means that the issue is being retired before its maturity date. There's really nothing you can do but turn in the bond and invest your money elsewhere. It's all perfectly legal because every bond is issued with a **call feature**, which stipulates whether and under what conditions a bond can be called in for retirement prior to maturity.

call feature
feature that specifies whether and under what conditions the issuer can retire a bond prior to maturity.

Basically, there are three types of call features:

1. A bond can be *freely callable*, which means the issuer can prematurely retire the bond at any time.
2. A bond can be *noncallable*, which means the issuer is prohibited from retiring the bond prior to maturity.
3. The issue could carry a *deferred call*, which means the issue cannot be called until after a certain length of time has passed from the date of issue. In essence, the issue is noncallable during the deferment period and then becomes freely callable thereafter.

Obviously, in our illustration above, either the high-yielding bond was issued as freely callable or it became freely callable with the end of its call deferment period.

Call features are placed on bonds *for the benefit of the issuers*. They're used most often to replace an issue with one that carries a lower coupon, and the issuer benefits by the reduction in annual interest cost. Thus, when market interest rates undergo a sharp decline, bond issuers retire their high-yielding bonds (by calling them in) and replace them with lower-yielding obligations. *The net result is that the investor is left with a much lower rate of return than anticipated.*

call premium
the amount added to a bond's par value and paid to investors when a bond is retired prematurely.

call price
the price the issuer must pay to retire a bond prematurely; equal to par value plus the call premium.

In a half-hearted attempt to compensate investors who find their bonds called out from under them, a **call premium** is tacked onto a bond and paid to investors, along with the issue's par value, when the bond is called. The sum of the par value plus call premium represents the issue's **call price.** This is the amount the issuer must pay to retire the bond prematurely. As a general rule, call premiums usually equal about 8 to 12 months' interest at the earliest date of call and then become progressively smaller as the issue nears maturity. Using this rule, the initial call price of a 9% bond could be as high as $1,090, where $90 represents the call premium.

refunding provisions
provisions that prohibit the premature retirement of an issue from the proceeds of a lower-coupon refunding bond.

In addition to call features, some bonds may carry **refunding provisions.** These are much like call features except that they prohibit just one thing: the premature retirement of an issue from the proceeds of a lower-coupon bond. For example, a bond could come out as freely callable but *nonrefundable* for 5 years. In this case, the bond would probably be sold by brokers as a *deferred refunding issue*, with little or nothing said about its call feature. The distinction is important, however, as it means that a nonrefunding or deferred refunding issue *can still be called and prematurely retired for any reason other than refunding*. Thus, an investor could face a call on a high-yielding nonrefundable issue so long as the issuer has the cash to retire the bond prematurely.

Sinking Funds

sinking fund
a provision that stipulates the amount of principal that will be retired annually over the life of a bond.

Another provision that's important to investors is the **sinking fund,** which stipulates how a bond will be paid off over time. This provision applies only to term bonds, of course, because serial issues already have a predetermined method of repayment. Not all (term) bonds have sinking-fund requirements, but for those that do, a sinking fund specifies the annual repayment schedule that will be used to pay off the issue. It indicates how much principal will be retired each year. Sinking-fund requirements generally begin 1 to 5 years after the date of issue and continue annually thereafter until all or most of the issue is paid off. Any amount not repaid (which might equal 10% to 25% of the issue) would then be retired with a single "balloon" payment at maturity. Unlike a call or refunding provision, the issuer generally does not have to pay a call premium with sinking-fund calls. Instead, the bonds are normally called at par for sinking-fund purposes.

There's another difference between sinking-fund provisions and call or refunding features. That is, whereas a call or refunding provision gives the issuer the *right* to retire a bond prematurely, a sinking-fund provision *obligates* the issuer to pay off the bond systematically over time. The issuer has no choice. It must make sinking-fund payments in a prompt and timely fashion or run the risk of being in default.

Secured or Unsecured Debt

senior bonds
secured debt obligations, backed by a legal claim on specific property of the issuer.

A single issuer may have a number of different bonds outstanding at any given point in time. In addition to coupon and maturity, one bond can be differentiated from another by the type of collateral behind the issue. Issues can be either junior or senior. **Senior bonds** are secured obligations, which are backed

mortgage bonds
senior bonds secured by real estate.

collateral trust bonds
senior bonds backed by securities owned by the issuer but held in trust by a third party.

equipment trust certificates
senior bonds secured by specific pieces of equipment; popular with transportation companies such as airlines.

first and refunding bonds
bonds secured in part with both first and second mortgages.

junior bonds
debt obligations backed only by the promise of the issuer to pay interest and principal on a timely basis.

debenture
an unsecured (junior) bond.

subordinated debentures
unsecured bonds whose claim is secondary to other debentures.

income bonds
unsecured bonds requiring that interest be paid only after a specified amount of income is earned.

by a legal claim on some specific property of the issuer. Such issues would include **mortgage bonds,** which are secured by real estate; **collateral trust bonds,** which are backed by financial assets owned by the issuer but held in trust by a third party; **equipment trust certificates,** which are secured by specific pieces of equipment (e.g., boxcars and airplanes) and are popular with railroads and airlines; and **first and refunding bonds,** which are basically a combination of first mortgage and junior lien bonds (i.e., the bonds are secured in part by a first mortgage on some of the issuer's property and in part by second or third mortgages on other properties). (Note that first and refunding bonds are *less secure* than, and should *not* be confused with, straight first-mortgage bonds.)

Junior bonds, on the other hand, are backed only by the promise of the issuer to pay interest and principal on a timely basis. There are several classes of unsecured bonds, the most popular of which is known as a **debenture.** For example, a major company, like Hewlett-Packard, could issue, say, $500 million worth of 20-year debenture bonds. Being a debenture, the bond would be totally unsecured, meaning there is no collateral backing up the obligation, other than the good name of the issuer. In the final analysis, it's the quality of the issuer that matters. And for that reason, highly regarded firms have no trouble selling *billion-dollar issues*, and at highly competitive rates. It's done all the time.

Subordinated debentures can also be found in the market. These issues have a claim on income secondary to other debenture bonds. **Income bonds,** the most junior of all bonds, are unsecured debts requiring that interest be paid only after a certain amount of income is earned. With these bonds, there is no legally binding requirement to meet interest payments on a timely or regular basis so long as a specified amount of income has not been earned. These issues are similar in many respects to *revenue bonds* found in the municipal market.

CONCEPTS IN REVIEW

10.4 Can issue characteristics (such as coupon and call features) affect the yield and price behavior of bonds? Explain.

10.5 What is the difference between a *call feature* and a *sinking-fund provision?* Briefly describe the three different types of call features. Can a bond be freely callable but nonrefundable?

10.6 What is the difference between a *premium bond* and a *discount bond?* What three attributes are most important in determining an issue's price volatility?

The Market for Debt Securities

LG 4 LG 5

Thus far, our discussion has dealt with basic bond features. We now shift attention to a review of the market in which these securities are traded. To begin with, the bond market is chiefly over-the-counter in nature, as listed bonds represent only a small portion of total outstanding obligations. In addition, this market is far more stable than the stock market. Indeed, although interest rates—and therefore bond prices—do move up and down over time, when bond price activity is measured on a daily basis, it is *remarkably stable*.

There are two other things that stand out about the bond market: It's big, and it has been growing rapidly. From a $250 billion market in 1950, it has grown to the point where, in 2002, the amount of bonds outstanding in this country exceeded *$17 trillion!* That makes the bond market about 75% bigger than the U.S. stock market.

Here's what the U.S. bond market looked like in 2002:

	Amount Outstanding ($ in trillions)
U.S. Treasury securities	$2.2
Agency securities	2.1
Municipal bonds	1.5
Corporate bonds	5.2
Mortgage-backed securities	2.9
Foreign issues and Eurodollar bonds	3.3
Total	$17.2

Source: "Size & Structure of the World Bond Market: 2002," Merrill Lynch.

The growth in this market has also been remarkable, as it has more than doubled in size since 1992. That translates into a compound rate of growth of nearly 9% a year. Domestic issues alone (*excluding* foreign issues and Eurodollar bonds) account for $13.9 trillion, or 81% of the total U.S. market. Let's now take a look at the various segments of the market.

Major Market Segments

There are bonds available in today's market to meet almost any investment objective and to suit just about any type of investor. As a matter of convenience, the bond market is normally separated into four major segments, according to type of issuer: Treasury, agency, municipal, and corporate. As we shall see, each sector has developed its own features, as well as its own trading characteristics.

Treasury Bonds "Treasuries" (or "governments," as they are sometimes called) are a dominant force in the fixed-income market. If not the most popular type of bond, they certainly are the best known. In addition to T-bills (a popular short-term debt security), the U.S. Treasury issues notes and bonds. It also issues *inflation-indexed securities*, which are the newest type of Treasury debt, introduced in January 1997. All Treasury obligations are of the highest quality because they are all backed by the "full faith and credit" of the U.S. government. This backing, along with their liquidity, makes them very popular with individual and institutional investors both here and abroad. Indeed, Treasury securities are traded in all the major markets of the world, from New York to London to Sydney and Tokyo.

Treasury notes
U.S. Treasury debt securities that are issued with maturities of 2 to 10 years or less.

Treasury bonds
U.S. Treasury securities that are issued with 20- and 30-year maturities.

Treasury notes are issued with maturities of 2, 3, 5, and 10 years, whereas **Treasury bonds** carry 20- and 30-year maturities. (Note that while the Treasury is authorized to issue these securities, *the last time it issued 20-year bonds was in January 1986 and the last 30-year bond was issued in August 2001*. Even so, many of these bonds are still outstanding and actively traded in the secondary market.) The Treasury issues its securities at regularly scheduled auctions, the results of which are widely reported by the financial media (see Figure 10.4 on page 428). The Treasury establishes the initial yields and coupons on the securities it issues in this auction process.

FIGURE 10.4 **The Reported Results of a Treasury Note Auction**

Treasury auctions are closely followed by the financial media; here, the results of a 3-year Treasury note auction are reported. These auctions are highly competitive. The number of bids submitted generally far exceeds the size of the issue, so the spread between the highest and lowest bids is quite small—sometimes as small at 2 basis points, or 2/100 of 1%. (*Source:* Department of the Treasury—Bureau of Public Debt, and *Wall Street Journal*, August 6, 2003.)

AUCTION RESULTS

Here are the results of yesterday's Treasury auction of 3-year notes. All bids are awarded at a single price at the market-clearing yield. Rates are determined by the difference between that price and the face value.

3-YEAR NOTES

Applications	$31,575,013,000	The amount of bids submitted.
Accepted bids	$24,000,053,000	Size of the issue—the dollar amount of accepted bids.
Bids at market-clearing yield accepted	65.84%	
Accepted noncompetitively	$278,013,000	The amount of noncompetitive bids submitted (and accepted).
" Foreign noncompetitively	$0	
Auction price (Rate)	99.865 (2.422%)	The average price and yield (rate) on the issue.
Interest rate	2.375%	The coupon that the issue will carry, which is set after the auction.
CUSIP number	912828BF6	

The notes are dated August 15, 2003 and mature August 15, 2006.

All Treasury notes (and bonds) are sold in $1,000 denominations. Interest income from these securities is subject to normal federal income tax but *is exempt from state and local taxes*. The Treasury today issues only *noncallable* securities. The last time the U.S. Treasury issued callable debt was in 1984. Until then, most Treasury bonds carried long-term call deferments, under which the bonds became freely callable during the last 5 years of the issue's life. There are still some deferred-call Treasuries outstanding; they're easy to identify because the deferred-call features are a specific part of the bond listing system. For example, a 10% issue of 2005–2010 signifies that this Treasury bond has a maturity date of 2010 and a deferred-call feature that extends through 2005.

Treasury inflation-indexed obligations (TIPS)
a type of Treasury security that provides protection against inflation by adjusting investor returns for the annual rate of inflation.

Inflation-Protection Securities As noted above, the newest form of Treasury security is the **Treasury inflation-indexed obligation.** Also known as **TIPS**, which stands for "Treasury inflation-protection securities," they are issued as notes (with 10-year maturities) and, until 2001, as bonds (with 30-year maturities). They offer investors the opportunity to stay ahead of inflation by periodically adjusting their returns for any inflation that has occurred. That is, if inflation is running at an annual rate of, say, 3%, then at the end of the year, the par (maturity) value of the bond will increase by 3%. (Actually, the adjustments to par value are done every 6 months.) Thus the par value of a

INVESTING IN ACTION

Some Tips on TIPS

Bondholders look at inflation like Superman looks at kryptonite. Superman weakens when faced with the dreaded substance and would die if exposed to it for long. Bondholders weaken when inflation heats up because it causes bond prices to buckle and fixed payments to lose their purchasing power. Some people have the mistaken impression that they can't lose money investing in Treasury bonds. But they can because bond prices fall in an inflationary environment. So that investors can buy its bonds without fearing inflation, in 1997 Uncle Sam created TIPS, Treasury inflation-protected securities.

Here's how TIPS work: The government issues a 10-year bond with a $1,000 face value that pays, say, 3% interest—and that rate stays fixed for the life of the issue. But if the consumer price index rises, so does the face amount of the bond. For example, because the CPI rose 2.4% in 2002, the new face amount was adjusted up to $1,000 × 1.024 = $1,024. Therefore, in 2003, the annual interest payment was $30.72 (3% of $1,024). When the TIPS mature in 10 years, the investor gets the inflation-adjusted face value at that time, which could be as much as $2,000 if inflation really takes off. A lot can change over a decade, but inflation looks pretty tame these days. As one professional investor puts it, buying TIPS now is like buying flood insurance during a drought. TIPS also protect you if deflation occurs. The bond's value will not fall below its initial face value (of $1,000).

Unlike the case with conventional fixed-income securities, the investor doesn't have to worry about the Treasury bond's value plummeting if inflation heats up. Take a look at what happens to a conventional Treasury bond if inflation begins to rise sharply. If the bond's coupon is, say, 5%, investors get 5% per year, or $50, no matter what happens to the level of prices. In 10 years, that $1,000 principal will certainly have less purchasing power than it does today. It might be able to buy just $700 worth of goods. In addition, rising inflation generally means rising interest rates. In the marketplace, conventional bond prices fall when interest rates rise. Therefore, an investor who wishes to sell a conventional bond prior to maturity is likely to take a loss if interest rates are higher than when the bond was purchased.

TIPS protect investors from such erosion in bond prices. TIPS are not so great, however, if inflation stays dormant, because the investors are getting only 3% on their money. (In fact, the coupon for the July 2003 10 year TIPS was just 1⅞%, compared to 4.25% for a regular 10 year Treasury note issued in August 2003.)

There's one other downside to TIPS: taxes. Investors have to pay a tax on the increasing face value of their bonds—$34 in the first year in the foregoing example. That may not seem like much, but the government doesn't actually pay out the increase in the bond's face value until maturity. Thus you end up paying taxes on income you've earned but don't have in hand. For that reason, TIPS probably make the most sense for individual retirement accounts (IRAs) and other tax-deferred retirement accounts. You can buy TIPS directly from the U.S. Treasury using Treasury Direct or from a broker. Several mutual fund companies now offer funds that buy only TIPS.

TIPS are also a good idea for investors who want to allocate a portion of their assets to income-generating securities and don't want to worry that inflation will erode their value. But the tradeoff for that protection is significant: loss of about half the income.

Critical Thinking Questions Why would investors be interested in TIPS? Why would the U.S. Treasury issue such a security? What are the advantages and disadvantages of this security from the investor's point of view?

Sources: Robert Barker, "A Bond Anybody Can Love," *Business Week*, June 19, 2000, p. 260; Iris L. Blasi and Frank Byrt, "TIPS Are Finally Getting Respect," The *Wall Street Journal*, July 11, 2002, p. D.9; James Grant, "An Inflation Tip," *Forbes*, October 30, 2000, p. 402; and "Treasury Inflation Protected Securities: What You Should Know," *InvestinginBonds.com*, downloaded from www.investinginbonds.com, accessed September 30, 2003.

$1,000 bond will grow to $1,030 at the end of the first year. If the 3% inflation rate continues for the second year, the par value will once again increase, this time from $1,030 to $1,061 ($1,030 × 1.03). Unfortunately, the coupons on these securities are set very low, because they're meant to provide investors with so-called *real (inflation-adjusted) returns*. Thus one of these bonds might carry a coupon of only 3.5% at a time when regular T-bonds are paying, say, 6.5% or 7%. But there's an advantage even to this: *Even though the coupon rates are fixed for the life of the issue, the actual size of the coupon payment will increase over time as the par value on the bond goes up*. For investors who are concerned about inflation protection, these securities may be just the ticket. But as the accompanying *Investing in Action* box on page 427 suggests, TIPS are a lot more complex than the traditional Treasury bond.

agency bonds
debt securities issued by various agencies and organizations of the U.S. government.

Agency Bonds **Agency bonds** are debt securities issued by various agencies and organizations of the U.S. government, such as the Federal Home Loan Bank, the Federal Farm Credit Systems, the Small Business Administration, the Student Loan Marketing Association, and the Federal National Mortgage Association. Though these securities are the closest things to Treasuries, they are not obligations of the U.S. Treasury and technically should not be considered the same as Treasury bonds. Even so, *they are very high-quality securities that have almost no risk of default*. In spite of the similar default risk exposure, however, these securities usually provide yields that are comfortably above the market rates for Treasuries. Thus they offer investors a way to increase returns with little or no real difference in risk.

There are basically two types of agency issues: government-sponsored and federal agencies. Although there are only six government-sponsored organizations, the number of federal agencies exceeds two dozen. To overcome some of the problems in the marketing of many relatively small federal agency securities, Congress established the Federal Financing Bank to consolidate the financing activities of all federal agencies. (As a rule, the generic term *agency* is used to denote both government-sponsored and federal agency obligations.)

Selected characteristics of some of the more popular agency bonds are presented in Table 10.3. As the list of issuers shows, most of the government agencies that exist today were created to support either agriculture or housing. Although agency issues are not direct liabilities of the U.S. government, a few of them actually do carry government guarantees and therefore represent the full faith and credit of the U.S. Treasury. But even those issues that do not carry such guarantees are highly regarded in the marketplace. Because they are all viewed as *moral obligations* of the U.S. government, it's highly unlikely that Congress would ever allow one of them to default. Also, like Treasury securities, agency issues are normally noncallable or carry lengthy call deferment features. One final point: Since 1986 *all new agency (and Treasury) securities* have been issued in *book entry form*. This means that no certificate of ownership is issued to the buyer of the bonds. Rather, the buyer receives a "confirmation" of the transaction, and his or her name is entered in a computerized logbook, where it remains as long as the security is owned.

HOT LINKS

To access a database of corporate, agency, and municipal bond offerings, go to

www.investinginbonds.com

municipal bonds
debt securities issued by states, counties, cities, and other political subdivisions; most of these bonds are tax-exempt (free of federal income tax on interest income).

Municipal Bonds **Municipal bonds** are the issues of states, counties, cities, and other political subdivisions (such as school districts and water and sewer districts). This is a $1.5 trillion market today, and it's the only segment of the

TABLE 10.3 Characteristics of Some Popular Agency Issues

Type of Issue	Minimum Denomination	Initial Maturity	Tax Status*		
			Federal	State	Local
Federal Farm Credit System	$ 1,000	13 months to 15 years	T	E	E
Federal Home Loan Bank	10,000	1 to 20 years	T	E	E
Federal Land Banks	1,000	1 to 10 years	T	E	E
Farmers Home Administration	25,000	1 to 25 years	T	T	T
Federal Housing Administration	50,000	1 to 40 years	T	T	T
Federal Home Loan Mortgage Corp.** ("Freddie Mac")	25,000	18 to 30 years	T	T	T
Federal National Mortgage Association** ("Fannie Mae")	25,000	1 to 30 years	T	T	T
Government National Mortgage Association** (GNMA—"Ginnie Mae")	25,000	12 to 40 years	T	T	T
Student Loan Marketing Association	10,000	3 to 10 years	T	E	E
Tennessee Valley Authority (TVA)	1,000	5 to 50 years	T	E	E
U.S. Postal Service	10,000	25 years	T	E	E
Federal Financing Corp.	1,000	1 to 20 years	T	E	E

*T = taxable; E = tax-exempt.
**Mortgage-backed securities.

HOT

For more information on municipal bonds, go to investinginbonds.com. Scroll down the left and click on [MuniBonds] under "Investors Guide".

www.investinginbonds.com/muni_bond_prices.htm

bond market where the individual investor plays a major role: About 40% of all municipal bonds are directly held by individuals (which excludes the 36% that are held by mutual funds). These bonds are often issued as *serial obligations*, which means that the issue is broken into a series of smaller bonds, each with its own maturity date and coupon.

general obligation bonds municipal bonds backed by the full faith, credit, and taxing power of the issuer.

revenue bonds municipal bonds that require payment of principal and interest only if sufficient revenue is generated by the issuer.

Municipal bonds ("munis") are brought to the market as either general obligation or revenue bonds. **General obligation bonds** are backed by the full faith, credit, and taxing power of the issuer. **Revenue bonds**, in contrast, are serviced by the income generated from specific income-producing projects (e.g., toll roads). Although general obligations used to dominate the municipal market, the vast majority of munis today come out as revenue bonds (accounting for about 70% to 75% of the new-issue volume).

The distinction between a general obligation bond and a revenue bond is important for a bondholder, because the issuer of a revenue bond is obligated to pay principal and interest *only if a sufficient level of revenue is generated.* If the funds aren't there, the issuer does not have to make payment on the bond. General obligation bonds, however, are required to be serviced in a prompt and timely fashion irrespective of the level of tax income generated by the municipality. Obviously, revenue bonds involve a lot more risk than general obligations, and because of that, they provide higher yields. Regardless of the type, municipal bonds are customarily issued in $5,000 denominations.

municipal bond guarantees guarantees from a party other than the issuer that principal and interest payments will be made in a prompt and timely manner.

A somewhat unusual aspect of municipal bonds is the widespread use of **municipal bond guarantees.** With these guarantees, a party other than the issuer assures the bondholder that principal and interest payments will be made in a prompt and timely manner. The third party, in essence, provides an additional source of collateral in the form of insurance, placed on the bond at the date of issue, that is nonrevocable over the life of the obligation. As a result of the guarantee, bond quality is improved. The three principal insurers are the Municipal Bond Investors Assurance Corporation (MBIA), the American Municipal Bond Assurance Corporation (AMBAC), and the Financial Guaranty Insurance Company (FGIC). These guarantors will normally insure any general obligation or revenue bond as long as it carries an S&P rating of triple-B or better. (We'll explore bond ratings later in this chapter.) Municipal bond insurance results in higher ratings (usually triple-A) and improved liquidity for these bonds, which are generally more actively traded in the secondary markets. Insured bonds are especially common in the revenue market, and insurance markedly boosts their attractiveness. Whereas an uninsured revenue bond lacks certainty of payment, a guaranteed issue is very much like a general obligation bond because the investor knows that principal and interest payments will be made on time.

Tax Advantages Without a doubt, the thing that makes municipal securities unique is the fact that, in most cases, their interest income is exempt from federal income taxes. That's why these issues are known as *tax-free*, or *tax-exempt*, bonds. Normally, the obligations are also exempt from state and local taxes *in the state in which they were issued*. For example, a California issue is free of California tax if the bondholder lives in California, but its interest income is subject to state tax if the investor resides in Arizona. Note that *capital gains on municipal bonds are not exempt from taxes.*

Individual investors are the biggest buyers of municipal bonds, and tax-free yield is certainly a major draw. Table 10.4 shows what a taxable bond would have to yield to equal the net yield of a tax-free bond. *It demonstrates how the yield attractiveness of municipals varies with an investor's income level.* Clearly, the higher the individual's tax bracket, the more attractive municipal bonds become. Generally speaking, an investor has to be in one of the higher federal tax brackets (28% to 35%) before municipal bonds offer yields that are competitive with fully taxable issues. This is so because municipal yields are (almost always) lower than those available from fully taxable issues (such as corporates). So, unless the tax effect is sufficient to raise the yield on a municipal to a figure that equals or surpasses taxable rates, it doesn't make much sense to buy municipal bonds.

Taxable Equivalent Yields We can determine the level of return a fully taxable bond would have to provide in order to match the after-tax return of a lower-yielding, tax-free issue by computing what is known as a municipal's **taxable equivalent yield.** Indeed, use of the taxable equivalent yield is standard convention in the market, as it facilitates comparing the return on a given municipal bond to any number of fully taxable issues. This measure can be calculated according to the following simple formula:

taxable equivalent yield the return a fully taxable bond would have to provide to match the after-tax return of a lower-yielding, tax-free municipal bond.

Equation 10.1

$$\text{Taxable equivalent yield} = \frac{\text{Yield on municipal bond}}{1 - \text{Federal tax rate}}$$

For example, if a municipal offered a yield of 6.5%, then an individual in the 35% tax bracket would have to find a fully taxable bond with a yield of 10.0% (i.e., 6.5%/0.65 = 10.0%) to reap the same after-tax returns as the municipal.

Note, however, that Equation 10.1 considers *federal taxes only*. As a result, the computed taxable equivalent yield applies only to certain situations:

TABLE 10.4 Taxable Equivalent Yields for Various Tax-Exempt Returns

Taxable Income*			Tax-Free Yield					
Joint Returns ($000)	Individual Returns ($000)	Federal Tax Bracket	5%	6%	7%	8%	9%	10%
$0–$14.0	$0–$7.0	10%	5.55%	6.66%	7.77%	8.88%	10.00%	11.11%
$14.0–$56.8	$7.0–$28.4	15	5.88	7.06	8.24	9.41	10.59	11.76
$56.8–$114.6	$28.4–$68.8	25	6.67	8.00	9.33	10.67	12.00	13.33
$114.6–$174.7	$68.8–$143.5	28	6.94	8.33	9.72	11.11	12.50	13.89
$174.7–$311.9	$143.5–$311.9	33	7.46	8.96	10.45	11.94	13.43	14.92
$311.9 and above	$311.9 and above	35	7.69	9.23	10.77	12.31	13.85	15.38

*Taxable income and federal tax rates effective January 1, 2003.

(1) to states that have no state income tax, (2) to situations where the investor is looking at an out-of-state bond (which would be taxable by the investor's state of residence), or (3) where the investor is comparing a municipal bond to a Treasury (or agency) bond—in which case *both* the Treasury and the municipal bonds are free from state income tax. Under any of these conditions, the only tax that's relevant is federal income tax, so using Equation 10.1 is appropriate. But what if the investor is comparing an in-state bond to, say, a corporate bond? In this case, the in-state bond would be free from both federal and state taxes, but the corporate bond would not. As a result, Equation 10.1 could not be used. Instead, the investor should use a form of the equivalent yield formula that considers *both* federal and state income taxes:

Equation 10.2

$$\text{Taxable equivalent yield for both federal and state taxes} = \frac{\text{Municipal bond yield}}{1 - \left[\text{Federal tax rate} + \text{State tax rate}\left(1 - \text{Federal tax rate}\right)\right]}$$

When both federal and state taxes are included in the calculations, the net effect is to *increase* the taxable equivalent yield. Of course, the size of the increase depends on the level of state income taxes. In a high-tax state like California, for example, the impact can be substantial. Return to the 6.5% municipal bond introduced above. If a California resident in the maximum federal and state tax brackets (35% and 11%, respectively) were considering a corporate issue, she would have to get a yield of 11.25% on the corporate to match the 6.5% yield on the California bond:

$$\text{Taxable equivalent yield for both federal and state taxes} = \frac{6.5}{1 - [0.35 + 0.11(1 - 0.35)]}$$

$$= \frac{6.5}{1 - [0.35 + 0.072]}$$

$$= \underline{\underline{11.25\%}}$$

This yield compares to a taxable equivalent yield of 10.0% when only federal taxes were included in the calculation. That's a difference of more than one full percentage point—certainly *not* an insignificant amount.

Corporate Bonds Corporations are the major nongovernmental issuers of bonds. The market for corporate bonds is customarily subdivided into four segments: *industrials* (the most diverse of the groups), *public utilities* (the dominant group in terms of volume of new issues), *rail and transportation bonds*, and *financial issues* (e.g., banks, finance companies). Not only is there a full range of bond qualities available in the corporate market, but there is also a wide assortment of different types of bonds. These range from first-mortgage obligations to convertible bonds (which we'll examine in Chapter 12), debentures, subordinated debentures, senior subordinated issues, capital notes (a type of unsecured debt issued by banks and other financial institutions), and income bonds. Interest on corporate bonds is paid semiannually, and sinking funds are fairly common. The bonds usually come in $1,000 denominations and are issued on a term basis with a single maturity date. Maturities usually range from 25 to 40 years or more. Many corporates, especially the longer ones, carry call deferment provisions that prohibit prepayment for the first 5 to 10 years. Corporate issues are popular with individuals because of their relatively attractive yields.

Most corporates fit the general description above. One that does not is the *equipment trust certificate*, a security issued by railroads, airlines, and other transportation concerns. The proceeds from equipment trust certificates are used to purchase equipment (e.g., jumbo jets and railroad engines) that serves as the collateral for the issue. These bonds are usually issued in serial form and carry uniform annual installments throughout. They normally carry maturities that range from 1 year to a maximum of 15 to 17 years. An attractive feature of equipment trust certificates is that despite a near-perfect payment record that dates back to pre-Depression days, these issues generally offer above-average yields to investors.

Specialty Issues

In addition to the basic bond vehicles described above, investors can choose from a number of *specialty issues*—bonds that possess unusual issue characteristics. For the most part, these bonds have coupon or repayment provisions that are out of the ordinary. Most are issued by corporations, although they are being used increasingly by other issuers as well. Four of the most actively traded specialty issues today are zero-coupon bonds, mortgage-backed securities, asset-backed securities, and high-yield junk bonds. All four of these rank as some of the more popular bonds on Wall Street. Let's now take a closer look at each of these specialty issues.

zero-coupon bonds
bonds with no coupons that are sold at a deep discount from par value.

Zero-Coupon Bonds As the name implies, **zero-coupon bonds** have no coupons. Rather, these securities are sold at a deep discount from their par values and then increase in value over time at a compound rate of return so that at maturity, they are worth much more than their initial investment. Other things being equal, the cheaper the zero-coupon bond, the greater the return an investor can earn: For example, a bond with a 6% yield might cost $420, but one with a 10% yield might cost only $240.

Because they don't have coupons, these bonds do not pay interest semiannually. In fact, they pay *nothing* to the investor until the issue matures. As strange as it might seem, this feature is the main attraction of zero-coupon bonds. Because there are no interest payments, investors do not have to worry about reinvesting coupon income twice a year. Instead, the fully compounded rate of return on a zero-coupon bond is virtually guaranteed at the rate that existed when the issue was purchased. For example, in mid-2003, U.S. Treasury zero-coupon bonds with 10-year maturities were available at yields of around 4.8%. Thus, for around $600, you could buy a bond that would be worth $1,000 at maturity in 10 years. And that 4.8% yield is a fully compounded rate of return that's *locked in* for the life of the issue—or what's left of it (10 years in this case).

HOT LINKS

To read about Treasury strips, go to:

www.bondsonline.com/asp/treas/zeros.asp

The foregoing advantages notwithstanding, zeros do have some serious disadvantages. One is that if rates do move up over time, you won't be able to participate in the higher return (you'll have no coupon income to reinvest). In addition, zero-coupon bonds are subject to tremendous price volatility: If market rates climb, you'll experience a sizable capital loss as the prices of zero-coupons plunge. (Of course, if interest rates *drop*, you'll reap enormous capital gains if you hold long-term zeros. Indeed, such issues are unsurpassed in capital gains potential.) A final disadvantage is that the IRS has ruled that zero-coupon bondholders must report *interest as it is accrued*, even though no interest is actually received. For this reason, most fully taxable zero-coupon bonds should either be used in tax-sheltered investments, such as IRAs, or be held by minor children who are likely to be taxed at the lowest rate, if at all.

Treasury strips (strip-Ts)
zero-coupon bonds created from U.S. Treasury securities.

Zeros are issued by corporations, municipalities, and federal agencies. You can even buy U.S. Treasury notes and bonds in the form of zero-coupon securities. They're known as **Treasury strips,** or **strip-Ts,** for short. Actually, the Treasury does *not* issue zero-coupon bonds. Instead, it *allows government securities dealers to sell regular coupon-bearing notes and bonds in the form of zero-coupon securities*. Essentially, the coupons are stripped from the bond, repackaged, and then sold separately as zero-coupon bonds. For example, a 10-year Treasury note has 20 semiannual coupon payments, plus one principal payment. These 21 cash flows can be repackaged and sold as 21 different zero-coupon securities, with maturities that range from 6 months to 10 years. Because they sell at such large discounts, Treasury strips are often sold in minimum denominations (par values) of $10,000. But with their big discounts, you'll probably pay only about half that amount (or less) for $10,000 worth of 10-year strip-Ts. Because there's an active secondary market for Treasury strips, investors can get in and out of these securities with ease just about any time they want. Strip-Ts offer the maximum in issue quality, a wide array of different maturities, and an active secondary market—all of which explains why they are so popular.

mortgage-backed bond
a debt issue secured by a pool of home mortgages; issued primarily by federal agencies.

Mortgage-Backed Securities Simply put, a **mortgage-backed bond** is a debt issue that is secured by a pool of residential mortgages. An issuer, such as the Government National Mortgage Association (GNMA), puts together a pool of home mortgages and then issues securities in the amount of the total mortgage pool. These securities, also known as *pass-through securities* or *participation certificates*, are usually sold in minimum denominations of $25,000. Though their maturities can go out as far as 30 years, the average life is generally much shorter (perhaps as short as 8 to 10 years) because many of the mortgages are paid off early.

As an investor in one of these securities, you hold an undivided interest in the pool of mortgages. When a homeowner makes a monthly mortgage payment, that payment is essentially passed through to you, the bondholder, to pay off the mortgage-backed bond you hold. Although these securities come with normal coupons, *the interest is paid monthly rather than semiannually*. Actually, the monthly payments received by bondholders are, like mortgage payments, made up of both principal and interest. Because the principal portion of the payment represents return of capital, it is considered tax-free. The interest portion, however, is subject to ordinary state and federal income taxes.

HOT LINKS

For additional information on agency issues and mortgage-backed securities, visit Fidelity Investment. Also visit Fitch Ratings and click on [structured finance] to look at some collateral mortgage obligations and other asset-backed securities. Fitch also lists specific issues of a variety of fixed income securities. Click the links on top and then look at the selections on the left.

personal.fidelity.com/products/fixedincome/bond_offerings.shtml
www.fitchratings.com

Mortgage-backed securities are issued primarily by three federal agencies. Although there are some state and private issuers (mainly big banks and S&Ls), agency issues dominate the market and account for 90% to 95% of the activity. The major agency issuers of mortgage-backed securities (MBSs) are:

- ***Government National Mortgage Association (GNMA).*** Known as Ginnie Mae, it is the oldest and largest issuer of MBSs.
- ***Federal Home Loan Mortgage Corporation (FHLMC).*** Known as Freddie Mac, it was the first to issue pools containing conventional mortgages. Stock in FHLMC is publicly owned and traded on the NYSE.
- ***Federal National Mortgage Association (FNMA).*** Known as Fannie Mae, it's the newest agency player and the leader in marketing seasoned/older mortgages. Its stock is also publicly owned and traded on the NYSE.

One problem with mortgage-backed securities is that they *are self-liquidating investments;* that is, a portion of the monthly cash flow to the investor is repayment of principal. Thus, the investor is always receiving back part of the original investment capital, so at maturity there is *no* big principal payment. To counter this problem, a number of *mutual funds* were formed that invest in mortgage-backed securities *but* automatically reinvest the capital/principal portion of the cash flows. Mutual fund investors therefore receive only the interest from their investments and are thus able to preserve their capital.

collateralized mortgage obligation (CMO)
mortgage-backed bond whose holders are divided into classes based on the length of investment desired; principal is channeled to investors in order of maturity, with short-term classes first.

Collateralized Mortgage Obligations Loan prepayments are another problem with mortgage-backed securities. In fact, it was in part an effort to defuse some of the prepayment uncertainty in standard mortgage-backed securities that led to the creation of **collateralized mortgage obligations** (CMOs). Normally, as pooled mortgages are prepaid, all bondholders receive a prorated share of the prepayments. The net effect is to sharply reduce the life of the bond. A CMO, in contrast, divides investors into classes (called "tranches," which is French for "slice"), depending on whether they want a short-, intermediate-, or long-term investment. Although interest is paid to all bondholders, all principal payments go first to the shortest tranche until it is fully retired. Then the next class in the sequence becomes the sole recipient of principal, and so on, until the last tranche is retired.

Basically, CMOs are *derivative securities* created from traditional mortgage-backed bonds, which are placed in a trust. Participation in this trust is then sold to the investing public in the form of CMOs. The net effect of this transformation is that CMOs look and behave very much like any other bond:

They offer predictable interest payments and have (relatively) predictable maturities. However, although they carry the same triple-A ratings and implicit U.S. government backing as the mortgage-backed bonds that underlie them, CMOs represent a quantum leap in complexity. Some types of CMOs can be as simple and safe as Treasury bonds. But others can be far more volatile—and risky—than the standard MBSs they're made from. That's because when putting CMOs together, Wall Street performs the financial equivalent of gene splicing: Investment bankers isolate the interest and principal payments from the underlying MBSs and rechannel them to the different tranches. It's not issue quality or risk of default that's the problem here, but rather prepayment, or call, risk. All the bonds will be paid off; it's just a matter of when. Different types of CMO tranches have different levels of prepayment risk. The overall risk in a CMO cannot, of course, exceed that of the underlying mortgage-backed bonds, so in order for there to be some tranches with very little (or no) prepayment risk, others have to endure a lot more. The net effect is that while some CMO tranches are low in risk, others are loaded with it.

securitization
the process of transforming lending vehicles such as mortgages into marketable securities.

asset-backed securities (ABS)
securities similar to mortgage-backed securities that are backed by a pool of bank loans, leases, and other assets.

Asset-Backed Securities The creation of mortgage-backed securities and CMOs quickly led to the development of a new market technology—the process of **securitization**, whereby various lending vehicles are transformed into marketable securities, much like a mortgage-backed security. Investment bankers are now selling billions of dollars worth of pass-through securities, known as **asset-backed securities (ABS)**, which are backed by pools of auto loans, credit card bills, and home equity lines (three of the principal types of collateral), as well as computer leases, hospital receivables, small business loans, truck rentals, and even royalty fees. These securities, first introduced in the mid-1980s, are created when an investment banker bundles together some type of debt-linked asset (such as loans or receivables), and then sells investors—via asset-backed securities—the right to receive all or part of the future payments made on that debt. For example, GMAC, the financing arm of General Motors, is a regular issuer of collateralized *auto loan* securities. When it wants to get some of its car loans off its books, GMAC takes the monthly cash flow from a pool of auto loans and pledges them to a new issue of bonds, which are then sold to investors. In similar fashion, *credit card receivables* are regularly used as collateral for these bonds (indeed, they represent the biggest segment of the ABS market), as are *home equity loans*, the second-biggest type of ABS.

Investors are drawn to ABSs for a number of reasons. One is the relatively *high yields* they offer. Another is their *short maturities*, which often extend out no more than 3 to 5 years. A third is the *monthly, rather than semiannual, principal/interest payments* that accompany many of these securities. Also important to investors is their *high credit quality*. That's due to the fact that most of these deals are backed by generous credit protection. For example, the securities are often overcollateralized, which means that the pool of assets backing the bonds may be 25% to 50% larger than the bond issue itself. For whatever reason, the vast majority of ABSs receive the highest credit rating possible (triple-A) from the leading agencies.

junk bonds
high-risk securities that have low ratings but high yields.

Junk Bonds **Junk bonds** (or *high-yield bonds*, as they're also called) are highly speculative securities that have received low, sub-investment-grade ratings (typically Ba or B). These bonds are issued primarily by corporations and, also, by municipalities. Junk bonds often take the form of *subordinated debentures*,

INVESTING IN ACTION

At Last—Bonds for the Little Guy

Did the stock market's topsy-turvey performance over the past few years make you jittery about buying stocks? Perhaps you wanted to purchase bonds but didn't want to tie up your money for 20 years, or you would rather hold individual bonds instead of paying fees to a mutual fund. Now you have another option: *medium-term* or *direct access notes (DANs)*, original-issue corporate bonds designed for individual investors. Major companies such as Banc of America, Boeing, Diageo PLC, Dow Chemical, GE Capital, Household Finance, IBM, and UPS have all sold this new type of debt security through a network of more than 300 brokerage firms. Current offerings range in maturity from 18 months to 25 years.

These notes are sold at face value ($1,000), so you know the coupon and cost before you make a purchase. The broker buys the bonds from the issuer at a discount, so you don't pay a commission on your purchase. As with any fixed-income security, yields vary based on the issuers' credit ratings and maturity. New issues are offered every Monday. Because the $1,000 offering price is available for the entire first week, investors can take the time to consider which DANs are best suited for their portfolios. Many DANs pay interest monthly, rather than the more typical semiannual payments of traditional corporate bonds. This steady income stream makes them attractive to retired people. Another special feature is the "death put," or survivor's option. If you inherit a DAN, you can ask the issuing company to redeem the bond at its par value—regardless of its current price.

While DANs offer higher yields than Treasury notes, they have the same interest rate and credit risks as other bond investments:

- Rising interest rates will cause the price of the bond in the secondary market to drop.
- You must assess the company, or credit, risk—that is, the issuer's ability to repay both interest and principal.

DANs have a limited secondary market, which may make it difficult to sell the note before maturity. Most investors who buy DANs plan to hold them to maturity. Some of these notes also carry call provisions. Advantages of these securities include greater investor control and flexibility. You can choose the maturities, yields, and payment dates that are best for your needs. To get greater diversification, as you would with a bond fund, investors can buy several issues instead of just one DAN.

For more information about DANS, go to www.directnotes.com or www.internotes.com.

Critical Thinking Question Summarize the advantages and disadvantages of DANs. Would they be a good choice for your portfolio? Explain.

Sources: David McNaughton, "Some Bonds Entice Individuals," *Atlanta Journal and Constitution*, December 8, 2002, p. H6; Direct Access Notes, La Salle Broker Dealer Services, www.directnotes.com, accessed September 24, 2003; and Jeff D. Opdyke and Carrick Mollenkamp, "Corporate Bonds for the Little Guy," *The Wall Street Journal*, July 30, 2002, pp. D1, D2.

which means the debt is unsecured and has a low claim on assets. These bonds are called "junk" because of their high risk of loss. The companies that issue them generally have excessive amounts of debt in their capital structures, and their ability to service that debt is subject to considerable doubt. Probably the most unusual type of junk bond is something called a **PIK-bond.** PIK stands for *payment in kind* and means that rather than paying the bond's coupon in cash, the issuer can make annual interest payments in the form of additional debt. This "financial printing press" usually goes on for 5 or 6 years, after which time the issuer is supposed to start making interest payments in real money.

PIK-bond
a payment-in-kind junk bond that gives the issuer the right to make annual interest payments in new bonds rather than in cash.

Traditionally, the term *junk bond* was applied to issues of troubled companies, which might have been highly rated when first issued but slid to low ratings through corporate mismanagement, heavy competition, or other factors. That all changed during the 1980s, when the vast majority of junk bonds originated not with troubled companies but with a growing number of mature (fairly well-known) firms that used enormous amounts of debt to finance takeovers and buyouts. These companies would change overnight from investment-grade firms to junk as they piled on debt to finance a takeover—or the threat of one. (Wall Street refers to these firms as "fallen angels.")

Why would any rational investor be drawn to junk bonds? The answer is simple: They offer very high yields. Indeed, in a typical market, relative to investment-grade bonds, you can expect to pick up anywhere from 2.5 to 5 percentage points in added yield. For example, not long ago, investors were getting 11% or 12% yields on junk bonds, compared to 7% or 8% on investment-grade corporates. Obviously, *such yields are available only because of the correspondingly higher exposure to risk*. However, as we saw earlier in this chapter, there's more to bond returns than yield alone: The *returns* you actually end up with don't always correspond to the *yields* you went in with. Junk bonds are subject to a good deal of risk, and their prices are unstable. Indeed, unlike investment-grade bonds, whose prices are closely linked to the behavior of market interest rates, junk bonds tend to behave more like stocks. As a result, the returns you actually end up with are highly unpredictable. Accordingly, only investors who are thoroughly familiar with the risks involved, and who are comfortable with such risk exposure, should use these securities.

A Global View of the Bond Market

Globalization has hit the bond market, just as it has the stock market. Foreign bonds have caught on with U.S. investors because of their high yields and attractive returns. There are risks with foreign bonds, of course, but high risk of default is *not* one of them. Instead, the big risk with foreign bonds has to do with the impact that currency fluctuations can have on returns in U.S. dollars.

By mid-year 2003, the total value of the world bond market had reached some $33 trillion. The United States has the biggest debt market, accounting for about 52% of the total. Following the United States is *Euroland*, which accounts for about 20% of the market (principally in Germany, Italy, and France). Close behind is Japan at 16%, followed by the United Kingdom (at 3%) and Canada (at less than 2%). Together, these issuers account for slightly more than 90% of the world bond market. Worldwide, various forms of government bonds (e.g., Treasuries, agencies, and munis) dominate the market, accounting for about 55% of the total.

U.S.-Pay Versus Foreign-Pay Bonds There are several ways to invest in foreign bonds (*excluding* foreign bond mutual funds, which we'll examine in Chapter 13). From the perspective of a U.S. investor, foreign bonds can be divided into two broad categories on the basis of the currency in which the bond is denominated: *U.S.-pay* (or dollar-denominated) bonds and *foreign-pay* (or non-dollar-denominated) bonds. All the cash flows—including purchase price, maturity value, and coupon income—from dollar-denominated foreign bonds are in U.S. dollars, whereas the cash flows from nondollar bonds are designated in a foreign currency, such as the euro, British pound, or Swiss franc.

Yankee bonds
bonds issued by foreign governments or corporations but denominated in dollars and registered with the SEC.

Eurodollar bonds
foreign bonds denominated in dollars but not registered with the SEC, thus restricting sales of new issues.

THE DREAM FACTORY—Want to own a piece of a rock star or a best-selling author? Thanks to Wall Street financier David Pullman and his "Bowie bonds," you can! These asset-backed securities were based on royalties of David Bowie songs, rather than mundane financial assets like portfolios of home mortgages, credit card receivables, or corporate loans. Since their introduction, Pullman's firm and others have offered more than $250 million of bonds secured by the works of stars like James Brown, Marvin Gaye, and the Isley Brothers. Others have jumped into the arena with Pullman: In August 2002, DreamWorks announced a $1 billion film securitization deal, and FIFA, the governing organization for world soccer, pledged receipts from the 2002 World Cup.

Sources: Matthew Benz, "Bowie Bonds: One-off or a Sound Vision for the Future," *Billboard*, June 20, 2001, downloaded from www.pullmanco.com/article136.htm; DigiCirc Web site, www.digicirc.com/XcAuctionPro.asp; and "Who's Who in Bowie Bonds," downloaded from www.ex.ac.uk/~RDavies/arian/bowiebonds.html, September 24, 2003.

Dollar-Denominated Bonds Dollar-denominated foreign bonds are of two types: Yankee bonds and Eurodollar bonds. **Yankee bonds** are issued by foreign governments or corporations or by so-called supernational agencies, like the World Bank and the InterAmerican Bank. These bonds are issued and traded in the United States; they're registered with the SEC, and all transactions are in U.S. dollars. Buying a Yankee bond is really no different from buying any other U.S. bond: These bonds are traded on U.S. exchanges and the OTC market, and *because everything is in dollars, there's no currency exchange risk to deal with*. The bonds are generally very high in quality (which is not surprising, given the quality of the issuers) and offer highly competitive yields to investors.

Eurodollar bonds, in contrast, are issued and traded outside the United States. They are denominated in U.S. dollars, but they are not registered with the SEC, which means underwriters are legally prohibited from selling new issues to the U.S. public. (Only "seasoned" Eurodollar issues can be sold in this country.) The Eurodollar market today is dominated by foreign-based investors (though that is changing) and is primarily aimed at institutional investors.

Foreign-Pay Bonds From the standpoint of U.S. investors, foreign-pay international bonds encompass all those issues denominated in a currency other than dollars. These bonds are issued and traded overseas and are not registered with the SEC. Examples are German government bonds, which are payable in euros; Japanese bonds, issued in yen; and so forth. When investors speak of *foreign bonds*, it's this segment of the market that most of them are thinking of.

Foreign-pay bonds are subject to changes in currency exchange rates, which can dramatically affect total returns to U.S. investors. The returns on foreign-pay bonds are a function of three things: (1) the level of coupon (interest) income earned on the bonds; (2) the change in market interest rates, which determine the level of capital gains (or losses); and (3) the behavior of currency exchange rates. The first two variables are the same as those that drive bond returns in this country and are, of course, just as important to foreign bonds as they are to domestic bonds. Thus, if you're investing overseas, you still want to know what the yields are today and where they're headed. *It's really the third variable that separates the return behavior of dollar-denominated from foreign-pay bonds.*

We can assess returns from foreign-pay bonds by employing the same (modified) holding period return formula first introduced in our discussion of foreign stock returns. (See Equation 6.6 in Chapter 6.) For example, assume a U.S. investor purchased a Swedish government bond, in large part because of the attractive 7½% coupon it carried. If the bond was bought at par and market rates fell over the course of the year, the security itself would have provided a return in excess of 7½% (because the decline in rates would provide some capital gains). However, if the Swedish krona (SEK) fell relative to the dollar, the total return (in U.S. dollars) could have actually ended up at a lot less than 7½%, depending on what happened to the U.S. $/SEK exchange rate. To find out exactly how this investment turned out, you could use Equation 6.6, and make a few (very minor) modifications to it (e.g., use interest income in place of dividends received). Like foreign stocks, *foreign-pay bonds can pay off from both the behavior of the security and the behavior of the currency*. That combination, in many cases, means superior returns to U.S.

investors. Knowledgeable investors find these bonds attractive not only because of their competitive returns but also because of *the positive diversification effects they have on bond portfolios.*

CONCEPTS IN REVIEW

10.7 Briefly describe each of the following types of bonds: (a) *Treasury bonds,* (b) *agency issues,* (c) *municipal securities,* and (d) *corporate bonds.* Note some of the major advantages and disadvantages of each.

10.8 Briefly define each of the following and note how they might be used by fixed-income investors: (a) *zero-coupon bonds,* (b) *CMOs,* (c) *junk bonds,* and (d) *Yankee bonds.*

10.9 What are the special tax features of (a) *Treasury securities,* (b) *agency issues,* and (c) *municipal bonds?*

10.10 Describe an *asset-backed security* (ABS) and identify some of the different forms of collateral used with these issues. Briefly note how an ABS differs from a MBS. What is the central idea behind securitization?

10.11 Identify the six or seven biggest bond markets in the world. How important is the U.S. bond market relative to the rest of the world?

10.12 What's the difference between dollar-denominated and non-dollar-denominated (foreign-pay) bonds? Briefly describe the two major types of U.S.-pay bonds. Can currency exchange rates affect the total return of U.S.-pay bonds? Of foreign-pay bonds? Explain.

Trading Bonds

LG 6

In large part as a result of the perceived safety and stability of bonds, many individual investors view bond investing as a relatively simple process. Such thinking, however, can often lead to unsatisfactory results, even losses. The fact is that not all bonds are alike, and picking the right security for the time is just as important for bond investors as it is for stock investors. Indeed, success in the bond market demands a thorough understanding not only of the different types of bonds but also of the many technical factors that drive bond yields, prices, and returns—things like call features, refunding provisions, and the impact that coupon and maturity can have on bond price volatility. Also, because bond ratings are so important to a smooth-running bond market, investors should become thoroughly familiar with them. Let's now take a look at these ratings and at the quotation system used for bonds.

Bond Ratings

bond ratings
letter grades that designate investment quality and are assigned to a bond issue by rating agencies.

Bond ratings are like grades: A letter grade that designates investment quality is assigned to an issue on the basis of extensive, professionally conducted financial analysis. They denote the amount of *credit risk* embedded in a bond and are widely used by fixed-income investors. Indeed, these ratings are an important part of the municipal and corporate bond markets, where issues are regularly evaluated and rated by one or more of the rating agencies. Even some agency issues, like the Tennessee Valley Authority (TVA), are rated, though they always receive ratings that confirm the obvious—that the issues are prime grade. The two largest and best-known rating agencies are Moody's and Standard & Poor's; another lesser known but still important bond-rating agency is Fitch Investors Service.

INVESTOR FACTS

BETTING ON AN UPGRADE—"You say *potayto* and I say *potahto*," as the old song goes. It turns out that some corporate bonds appear to be of investment-grade quality to one credit rating agency but look like junk to another. Such bonds—which are given a low *investment-grade* rating by one agency and a lower *junk bond* rating by another—are known as *crossover bonds*, and they are proving to be popular with investors. For one thing, they usually pay higher interest rates than a purely investment-grade bond, because one rating agency thinks the credit risk is greater. But they also offer investors the opportunity for capital appreciation. The reason: Often, the rating agency that called the bond junk eventually upgrades its credit rating, making the bond more valuable.

How Ratings Work Every time a large new issue comes to the market, it is analyzed by a staff of professional bond analysts to determine default risk exposure and investment quality. (A fee, usually ranging from $1,000 to $15,000 and paid by the issuer or the underwriter of the securities, is charged for rating each bond.) The rating agency thoroughly studies the financial records of the issuing organization and assesses its future prospects. Although the specifics of the actual credit analysis conducted by the rating agencies change with each issue, several major factors enter into most bond ratings. With a corporate issue, for example, these factors include an analysis of the issue's indenture provisions, an in-depth study of the firm's earning power (including the stability of its earnings), a look at the company's liquidity and how it is managed, a study of the company's relative debt burden, and an in-depth exploration of its coverage ratios to determine how well it can service both existing debt and any new bonds that are being contemplated or proposed. As you might expect, the firm's financial strength and stability are very important in determining the appropriate bond rating. Although, there is far more to setting a rating than cranking out a few financial ratios, the fact is a strong relationship exists between the operating results and financial condition of the firm and the rating its bonds receive. Generally, higher ratings are associated with more profitable companies that rely *less* on debt as a form of financing, are more liquid, have stronger cash flows, and have no trouble servicing their debt in a prompt and timely fashion.

Table 10.5 lists the various ratings assigned to bonds by the two major services. In addition to the standard rating categories noted in the table, Moody's uses numerical modifiers (1, 2, or 3) on bonds rated double-A to B, while S&P uses plus (+) or minus (−) signs on the same rating classes to show relative standing within a major rating category. For example, A+ (or A1) means a strong, high A rating, whereas A− (or A3) indicates that the issue is on the low end of the A rating scale. Except for slight variations in designations (Aaa versus AAA), the meanings and interpretations are basically the same.

Note that the top four ratings (Aaa through Baa, or AAA through BBB) designate *investment-grade* bonds. Such ratings are highly coveted by issuers, as they indicate financially strong, well-run companies. The next two ratings (Ba/B or BB/B) are reserved for junk bonds. These ratings mean that although *the principal and interest payments on the bonds are still being met in a timely fashion*, the risk of default is relatively high. The issuers of these bonds generally lack the financial strength that backs investment-grade issues. (Sometimes the Caa1/CCC1 category is counted as part of the junk category, although technically the C rating class is meant to designate bonds that are already in default or getting very close to it.) Most of the time, Moody's and S&P assign identical ratings. Sometimes, however, an issue carries two different ratings. These **split ratings** are viewed simply as "shading" the quality of an issue one way or another. For example, an issue might be rated Aa by Moody's but A or A+ by S&P.

split ratings
different ratings given to a bond issue by the two major rating agencies.

Also, just because a bond is given a certain rating at the time of issue doesn't mean it will keep that rating for the rest of its life. Ratings change as

TABLE 10.5 Bond Ratings

Moody's	S&P	Definition
Aaa	AAA	*High-grade investment bonds.* The highest rating assigned, denoting extremely strong capacity to pay principal and interest. Often called "gilt-edge" securities.
Aa	AA	*High-grade investment bonds.* High quality by all standards but rated lower primarily because the margins of protection are not quite as strong.
A	A	*Medium-grade investment bonds.* Many favorable investment attributes, but elements may be present that suggest susceptibility to adverse economic changes.
Baa	BBB	*Medium-grade investment bonds.* Adequate capacity to pay principal and interest but possibly lacking certain protective elements against adverse economic conditions.
Ba	BB	*Speculative issues.* Only moderate protection of principal and interest in varied economic times. (This is one of the ratings carried by junk bonds.)
B	B	*Speculative issues.* Generally lacking desirable characteristics of investment bonds. Assurance of principal and interest may be small; this is another junk-bond rating.
Caa	CCC	*Default.* Poor-quality issues that may be in default or in danger of default.
Ca	CC	*Default.* Highly speculative issues, often in default or possessing other market shortcomings.
C		*Default.* These issues may be regarded as extremely poor in investment quality.
	C	*Default.* Rating given to income bonds on which no interest is paid.
	D	*Default.* Issues actually in default, with principal or interest in arrears.

Source: Moody's *Bond Record* and Standard & Poor's *Bond Guide.*

the financial condition of the issuer changes. In fact, all rated issues are reviewed on a regular basis to ensure that the assigned rating is still valid. Many issues do carry a single rating to maturity, but it is not uncommon for ratings to be revised up or down. As you might expect, the market responds to rating revisions by adjusting bond yields accordingly. For example, an upward revision (e.g., from A to AA) causes the market yield on the bond to drop, as a reflection of the bond's improved quality. One final point: Although it may appear that the firm is receiving the rating, it is actually the *issue* that receives it. As a result, a firm's different issues can have different ratings. The senior securities, for example, might carry one rating and the junior issues another, lower rating.

HOT LINKS

For further explanation of Moody's bond ratings, go to:

www.bondpickers.com/?cmd=ratings

What Ratings Mean Investors pay close attention to agency ratings, because ratings can affect not only potential market behavior but comparative market yields as well. Specifically, *the higher the rating, the lower the yield*, other things being equal. For example, whereas an A-rated bond might offer a 7.5% yield, a comparable triple-A issue would probably yield something like 7%. Furthermore, investment-grade securities are far more interest-sensitive and tend to exhibit more uniform price behavior than junk bonds and other lower-rated issues. Perhaps most important, *bond ratings serve to relieve individual investors of the drudgery of evaluating the investment quality of an issue on their own.* Large institutional investors often have their own staff of credit analysts who independently assess the creditworthiness of various corporate and municipal issuers; individual investors, in contrast, have little if anything to gain from conducting their own credit analysis. After all, credit analysis is time-consuming and costly, and it demands a good deal more expertise than the average individual investor possesses. Most important, the ratings are closely adhered to by a large segment of the bond investment community, in large part because it has been shown that *the rating agencies do a remarkably good job of assessing bond quality*. Thus individual investors can depend on assigned agency ratings as a viable measure of the creditworthiness of the issuer and an issue's risk of default. A word of caution is in order, however: Bear in mind that bond ratings are intended to measure only an issue's *default risk*, which has no bearing whatsoever on an issue's exposure to *market risk*. Thus, if interest rates increase, even the highest-quality issues go down in price, subjecting investors to capital loss and market risk.

Reading the Quotes

One thing you quickly learn in the bond market is that transactions are not always as easy to conduct as they may seem. In the first place, many bonds have relatively "thin" markets. Indeed, some issues may trade only five or ten bonds a week, and many have no secondary market at all. There are, of course, numerous high-volume issues, but even so, you should pay particularly close attention to an issue's trading volume—especially if you're looking for lots of price action and need prompt order executions. In addition, it's not always easy to obtain current information on bond prices. That's because most bonds trade in over-the-counter markets rather than on centralized exchanges; and except for Treasury securities, the financial pages provide little information on general market activity and even less on particular securities. Indeed, daily price quotes are widely available on only a few of the thousands of publicly traded corporate and municipal bonds. Finally, investors often have to look to both brokers and bankers to complete transactions. Most brokerage houses tend to confine their activities to new issues and to secondary market transactions of listed Treasury obligations, agency issues, and corporate bonds. Commercial banks, in contrast, are still the major dealers in municipal bonds and are active in Treasury and agency securities as well.

HOT LINKS

Two great sites for getting bond quotes, as well as a lot of other information about bonds, are:

www.bondsonline.com
www.investinginbonds.com

Except for municipal issues (which are usually quoted in terms of the yield they offer), bonds are quoted on the basis of their dollar prices. Such quotes are always interpreted as a *percent of par*. Thus, a quote of 97 does not mean \$97.00 but, instead, means that the issue is trading at 97% of the par value of the obligation. In the bond market, it's assumed that we're dealing with bonds that have par values of \$1,000—or some multiple thereof. Accordingly, a quote of 97 translates into a dollar price of \$970. (With bond quotes, 1 point = \$10.) As you can see in Figures 10.5 and 10.6 (on pages 445 and 447), one quotation system is used for corporate bonds and another for governments. (Treasuries and agencies are quoted the same.)

Corporate Bond Quotes To understand the system used with corporate bonds, take a look at Figure 10.5. These quotes appeared in the *Wall Street Journal* on August 1, 2003, and represent trades that occurred the day before, on Thursday, July 31. Looking at the highlighted Sara Lee quote, we can see that the name of the issuer is followed parenthetically by the company's ticker symbol (in this case, SLE). The next two items are self-explanatory: This particular issue carries a coupon of 3.875% and will mature on June 15, 2013

FIGURE 10.5 **Price Quotations for Corporate Notes and Bonds**

Like most fixed-income securities, corporate notes and bonds are quoted as a percentage of their par values. Listed here are *Wall Street Journal* quotes for the 40 most actively traded (fixed-rate) corporate bonds; the *Journal* doesn't devote any space to thinly traded issues for the simple reason that there are just too many of them (literally hundreds of NYSE-listed bonds, for example, trade just 5 or 10 bonds a day). These quotes are for transactions that took place either on listed markets (like the NYSE) or, more likely, in the OTC market. (*Source: Wall Street Journal*, August 1, 2003.)

Corporate Bonds

Thursday, July 31, 2003

Forty most active fixed-coupon corporate bonds

COMPANY (TICKER)	COUPON	MATURITY	LAST PRICE	LAST YIELD	EST SPREAD	UST	EST $ VOL (000's)
General Motors (GM)	8.375	Jul 15, 2033	93.455	9.008	365	30	340,425
Bank of America (BAC)	3.250	Aug 15, 2008	96.625	3.997	78	5	194,555
Bank of America (BAC)	4.750	Aug 15, 2013	95.398	5.348	94	10	146,190
General Motors (GM)	7.125	Jul 15, 2013	97.628	7.465	305	10	146,096
General Electric (GE)	5.000	Feb 01, 2013	98.037	5.265	85	10	144,634
Comcast Cable Communications Holdings (CMCSA)	8.375	Mar 15, 2013	118.129	5.878	147	10	135,940
General Motors (GM)	8.250	Jul 15, 2023	95.410	8.738	335	30	117,653
Ford Motor Credit (F)	7.250	Oct 25, 2011	98.903	7.428	301	10	117,617
Goldman Sachs Group (GS)	4.750	Jul 15, 2013	93.669	5.588	119	10	111,659
Citigroup (C)	3.500	Feb 01, 2008	98.772	3.800	58	5	104,746
DaimlerChrysler North America Holding (DCX)	4.050	Jun 04, 2008	96.129	4.960	168	5	99,620
Morgan Stanley (MWD)	5.300	Mar 01, 2013	97.882	5.588	118	10	93,529
Wal-Mart Stores (WMT)	4.550	May 01, 2013	96.497	5.008	54	10	88,205
Sara Lee (SLE)	3.875	Jun 15, 2013	90.546	5.106	63	10	85,019 ← Sara Lee Issue (note)
American Express (AXP)	4.875	Jul 15, 2013	97.153	5.246	83	10	83,560
General Electric Capital (GE)	3.500	May 01, 2008	98.251	3.907	62	5	82,391
General Motors Acceptance (GMAC)	8.000	Nov 01, 2031	92.482	8.718	336	30	81,937
Comcast Holdings (CMCSA)	5.300	Jan 15, 2014	95.530	5.875	147	10	80,008
Household Finance (HSBC)	4.750	Jul 15, 2013	93.210	5.652	123	10	77,682
Ford Motor Credit (F)	7.375	Oct 28, 2009	102.108	6.949	373	5	74,962
General Dynamics (GD)	4.250	May 15, 2013	93.395	5.116	71	10	71,113
Household Finance (HSBC)	6.500	Jan 24, 2006	108.740	2.811	53	3	70,691
Sprint Capital (FON)	8.750	Mar 15, 2032	109.755	7.885	254	30	67,855
General Electric Capital (GE)	5.450	Jan 15, 2013	100.252	5.415	90	10	65,319
Citigroup (C)	5.625	Aug 27, 2012	102.275	5.305	80	10	64,782
DaimlerChrysler North America Holding (DCX)	8.500	Jan 18, 2031	110.332	7.598	225	30	62,075
Bank of America (BAC)	4.875	Jan 15, 2013	96.507	5.351	93	10	60,155
Lehman Brothers Holdings (LEH)	6.625	Jan 18, 2012	109.515	5.218	68	10	59,943
AT&T Wireless Services (AWE)	8.125	May 01, 2012	114.634	5.951	155	10	57,225
Wells Fargo (WFC)	6.625	Jul 15, 2004	104.919	1.364	n.a.	n.a.	54,683
Citigroup (C)	6.000	Feb 21, 2012	106.012	5.122	69	10	54,483
Tenet Healthcare (THC)	7.375	Feb 01, 2013	94.500	8.221	372	10	51,310
Ford Motor Credit (F)	6.875	Feb 01, 2006	105.095	4.682	245	3	51,085
General Motors Acceptance (GMAC)	4.500	Jul 15, 2006	100.270	4.399	219	3	50,093
Bank of America (BAC)	7.400	Jan 15, 2011	114.869	4.984	50	10	50,048
Washington Mutual Bank (WM)	6.875	Jun 15, 2011	111.644	5.060	64	10	49,328

(thus, it has 10 years to maturity). Next is the "last price" at which the issue traded on July 31; in other words, the last trade for the day was made at 90.546% of par. Unless you're a big-time investor, this is probably *not* the price you'd pay to buy the bond, as these prices are for minimum *trades of $1 million or more*. Buy in smaller lots and a "dealer spread" will be tacked on, meaning you'll buy at a higher price or sell at a lower price than the one quoted here.

Following the last price is the "last yield" (of 5.106%), which represents the bond's closing *yield-to-maturity* (a fully compounded measure of return that captures both current income and capital gains or losses, and which will be examined in detail in the next chapter). Note that this issue is trading at a *discount* (its price of 90.546 is less than par), because the market yield on the bond (5.106%) is more than its coupon (3.875%). The next two columns ("Est. Spread" and "UST") show the spread (or differential) between the yield on the Sara Lee bond and a comparable U.S. Treasury security. The spread is measured in "basis points," where 1 basis point = 1/100 of 1%; in other words, there are 100 basis points in a percentage point. Note in Figure 10.5 that SLE's last yield was 63 basis points higher than a comparable 10-year Treasury; the 10 in the "UST" column indicates that a 10-year Treasury is used as the benchmark issue in the yield spread measure. Finally, as can be seen in the last column, some $85 million worth of these SLE bonds changed hands on July 31, 2003.

Government Bond Quotes In contrast to corporates (and munis), U.S. government bonds (Treasuries as well as agency issues) are listed in thirty-secondths of a point. With government bonds, the figures to the right of the colon (:) indicate the number of thirty-seconds in the fractional bid or ask price. For example, look at the ask price of the highlighted 9.25% Treasury issue in Figure 10.6: It is being quoted at 141:08 (ask). Translated, that means the bond is being quoted at 141$\frac{8}{32}$, or 141.25% of par. Thus, if you wanted to buy, say, $15,000 worth of this issue, you would have to pay $21,187.50 (i.e., $15,000 × 1.4125). Here again, these quotes are for minimum trades of $1 million or more, so the amount you'd actually pay would likely be more than that after dealer spreads and other transaction costs are tacked on. Also note that this bond is trading at a very big premium (of some 41% *above* its par value). This, of course, would be due to the fact that market interest rates have fallen well below the bond's coupon—in this case, the bond's yield is about half the coupon.

As can be seen in Figure 10.6, the quotes on Treasury (and agency) securities include not only the coupon (see the "Rate" column), but also the month and year of maturity. In addition, note that the securities are quoted in bid/ask terms. The bid price signifies what the bond dealers are willing to pay for the securities (which is how much you can sell them for), whereas the ask price is what the dealers will sell the issues for (or what you'd have to pay to buy them). Again, keep in mind that these bid/ask prices ignore dealer spreads/transaction costs. When these costs are factored in, you'll end up getting *less* than the quoted price when you sell and paying *more* than the quoted price when you buy. Finally, the last two columns in the quotes include the change ("CHG") in the ask price and the yield-to-maturity on the issue, based on the latest ask price ("ASK YLD").

Quotes on Zero-Coupon Bonds Also included in Figure 10.6 are quotes for some zero-coupon bonds. You'll find these listed under the heading "U.S. Treasury Strips." As we discussed earlier in this chapter, these securities are created by "stripping" the coupons from their bond issues and selling them separately from the principal. Thus the principal and interest *cash flows* can be sold on their own. (Look at the quotes: A *ci* behind the maturity date means the issue is made up of coupon/interest cash flow, whereas an *np* or *bp* means it is made up of principal from a note or bond.) The prices of most zeros are quite low compared to regular coupon bonds. For example, note the highlighted strip-T of February 2010. This issue is trading at an ask price of 76$\frac{31}{32}$, or at less than $770 for each $1,000 in par value. The same issue in coupon form is the highlighted 6½% U.S. Treasury note of February 2010, which is trading at an ask price of just under 115½. Thus, the strip-T version is selling

FIGURE 10.6 **Price Quotes for U.S. Treasury Securities**

Listed here are *Wall Street Journal* quotes for some coupon-bearing and zero-coupon Treasury securities. Note that Treasuries are quoted in fractions of thirty-secondths of a point, rather than in decimals (like corporate bonds). You can also see here that both coupon and maturity play vital roles in the quotation system. For example, look at the Treasury quotes (the one on the left) and you'll find no less than five issues that mature in 2007, yet these bonds have five different (ask) prices. The reason: five different coupons. If you look back at Figure 10.5, you'll find the same thing with corporates. (*Source: Wall Street Journal*, August 1, 2003.)

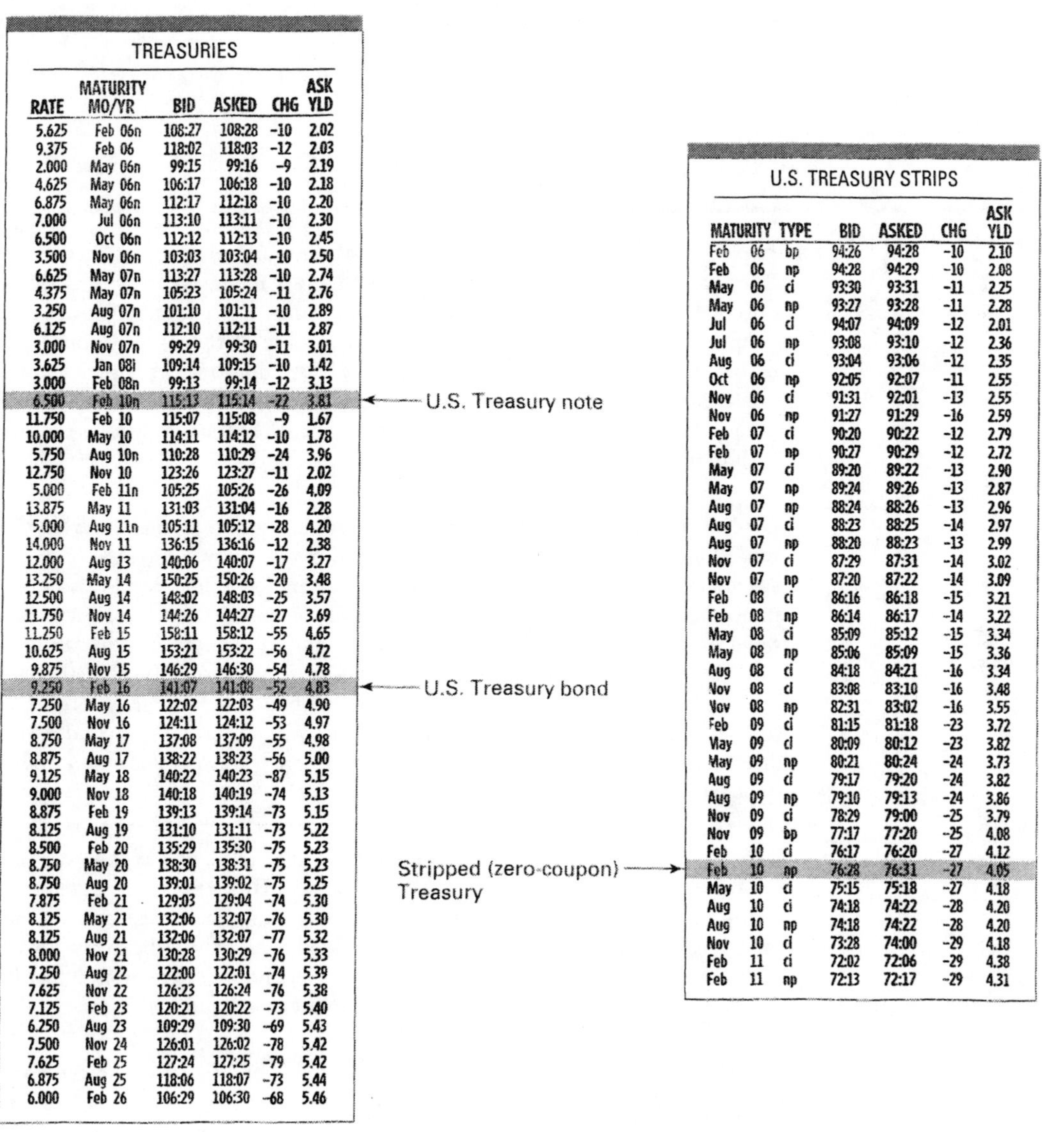

TREASURIES

RATE	MATURITY MO/YR	BID	ASKED	CHG	ASK YLD
5.625	Feb 06n	108:27	108:28	-10	2.02
9.375	Feb 06	118:02	118:03	-12	2.03
2.000	May 06n	99:15	99:16	-9	2.19
4.625	May 06n	106:17	106:18	-10	2.18
6.875	May 06n	112:17	112:18	-10	2.20
7.000	Jul 06n	113:10	113:11	-10	2.30
6.500	Oct 06n	112:12	112:13	-10	2.45
3.500	Nov 06n	103:03	103:04	-10	2.50
6.625	May 07n	113:27	113:28	-10	2.74
4.375	May 07n	105:23	105:24	-11	2.76
3.250	Aug 07n	101:10	101:11	-10	2.89
6.125	Aug 07n	112:10	112:11	-11	2.87
3.000	Nov 07n	99:29	99:30	-11	3.01
3.625	Jan 08i	109:14	109:15	-10	1.42
3.000	Feb 08n	99:13	99:14	-12	3.13
6.500	Feb 10n	115:13	115:14	-22	3.81
11.750	Feb 10	115:07	115:08	-9	1.67
10.000	May 10	114:11	114:12	-10	1.78
5.750	Aug 10n	110:28	110:29	-24	3.96
12.750	Nov 10	123:26	123:27	-11	2.02
5.000	Feb 11n	105:25	105:26	-26	4.09
13.875	May 11	131:03	131:04	-16	2.28
5.000	Aug 11n	105:11	105:12	-28	4.20
14.000	Nov 11	136:15	136:16	-12	2.38
12.000	Aug 13	140:06	140:07	-17	3.27
13.250	May 14	150:25	150:26	-20	3.48
12.500	Aug 14	148:02	148:03	-25	3.57
11.750	Nov 14	144:26	144:27	-27	3.69
11.250	Feb 15	158:11	158:12	-55	4.65
10.625	Aug 15	153:21	153:22	-56	4.72
9.875	Nov 15	146:29	146:30	-54	4.78
9.250	Feb 16	141:07	141:08	-52	4.83
7.250	May 16	122:02	122:03	-49	4.90
7.500	Nov 16	124:11	124:12	-53	4.97
8.750	May 17	137:08	137:09	-55	4.98
8.875	Aug 17	138:22	138:23	-56	5.00
9.125	May 18	140:22	140:23	-87	5.15
9.000	Nov 18	140:18	140:19	-74	5.13
8.875	Feb 19	139:13	139:14	-73	5.15
8.125	Aug 19	131:10	131:11	-73	5.22
8.500	Feb 20	135:29	135:30	-75	5.23
8.750	May 20	138:30	138:31	-75	5.23
8.750	Aug 20	139:01	139:02	-75	5.25
7.875	Feb 21	129:03	129:04	-74	5.30
8.125	May 21	132:06	132:07	-76	5.30
8.125	Aug 21	132:06	132:07	-77	5.32
8.000	Nov 21	130:28	130:29	-76	5.33
7.250	Aug 22	122:00	122:01	-74	5.39
7.625	Nov 22	126:23	126:24	-76	5.38
7.125	Feb 23	120:21	120:22	-73	5.40
6.250	Aug 23	109:29	109:30	-69	5.43
7.500	Nov 24	126:01	126:02	-78	5.42
7.625	Feb 25	127:24	127:25	-79	5.42
6.875	Aug 25	118:06	118:07	-73	5.44
6.000	Feb 26	106:29	106:30	-68	5.46

U.S. TREASURY STRIPS

MATURITY		TYPE	BID	ASKED	CHG	ASK YLD
Feb	06	bp	94:26	94:28	-10	2.10
Feb	06	np	94:28	94:29	-10	2.08
May	06	ci	93:30	93:31	-11	2.25
May	06	np	93:27	93:28	-11	2.28
Jul	06	ci	94:07	94:09	-12	2.01
Jul	06	np	93:08	93:10	-12	2.36
Aug	06	ci	93:04	93:06	-12	2.35
Oct	06	np	92:05	92:07	-11	2.55
Nov	06	ci	91:31	92:01	-13	2.55
Nov	06	np	91:27	91:29	-16	2.59
Feb	07	ci	90:20	90:22	-12	2.79
Feb	07	np	90:27	90:29	-12	2.72
May	07	ci	89:20	89:22	-13	2.90
May	07	np	89:24	89:26	-13	2.87
Aug	07	np	88:24	88:26	-13	2.96
Aug	07	ci	88:23	88:25	-14	2.97
Aug	07	np	88:20	88:23	-13	2.99
Nov	07	ci	87:29	87:31	-14	3.02
Nov	07	np	87:20	87:22	-14	3.09
Feb	08	ci	86:16	86:18	-15	3.21
Feb	08	np	86:14	86:17	-14	3.22
May	08	ci	85:09	85:12	-15	3.34
May	08	np	85:06	85:09	-15	3.36
Aug	08	ci	84:18	84:21	-16	3.34
Nov	08	ci	83:08	83:10	-16	3.48
Nov	08	np	82:31	83:02	-16	3.55
Feb	09	ci	81:15	81:18	-23	3.72
May	09	ci	80:09	80:12	-23	3.82
May	09	np	80:21	80:24	-24	3.73
Aug	09	ci	79:17	79:20	-24	3.82
Aug	09	np	79:10	79:13	-24	3.86
Nov	09	ci	78:29	79:00	-25	3.79
Nov	09	bp	77:17	77:20	-25	4.08
Feb	10	ci	76:17	76:20	-27	4.12
Feb	10	np	76:28	76:31	-27	4.05
May	10	ci	75:15	75:18	-27	4.18
Aug	10	ci	74:18	74:22	-28	4.20
Aug	10	np	74:18	74:22	-28	4.20
Nov	10	ci	73:28	74:00	-29	4.18
Feb	11	ci	72:02	72:06	-29	4.38
Feb	11	np	72:13	72:17	-29	4.31

at about two-thirds the price of the comparable coupon-bearing security. Keep in mind that these quotes occurred at a time when market yields were at near-40-year lows. As a result, the market prices are abnormally high. Several years ago, in early 2000, when market yields were more like 6% or 7%, this same February 2010 strip-T was trading at something closer to $525.

CONCEPTS IN REVIEW

10.13 What are *bond ratings*, and how can they affect investor returns? What are *split ratings?*

10.14 From the perspective of an individual investor, what good are bond ratings? Do bond ratings indicate the amount of market risk embedded in a bond? Explain.

10.15 Bonds are said to be quoted "as a percent of par." What does that mean? What is 1 point worth in the bond market?

10.16 Why should an aggressive bond trader be concerned with the trading volume of a particular issue?

Summary

LG 1 **Explain the basic investment attributes of bonds and their use as investment vehicles.** Bonds are publicly traded debt securities that provide investors with two basic sources of return: (1) current income and (2) capital gains. Current income is derived from the coupon (interest) payments received over the life of the issue. Capital gains can be earned whenever market interest rates fall. In addition to their yields and returns, bonds can be used to shelter income from taxes and for the preservation and long-term accumulation of capital. Just as important, the diversification properties of bonds are such that they can greatly enhance portfolio stability.

LG 2 **Describe the essential features of a bond and distinguish among different types of call, refunding, and sinking-fund provisions.** All bonds carry some type of coupon, which specifies the annual rate of interest to be paid by the issuer. Bonds also have predetermined maturity dates: Term bonds carry a single maturity date, and serial bonds have a series of maturity dates. Every bond is issued with some type of call feature, be it freely callable, noncallable, or deferred callable. Call features spell out whether an issue can be prematurely retired and, if so, when. Some bonds (temporarily) prohibit the issuer from paying off one bond with the proceeds from another by including a refunding provision. Others are issued with sinking-fund provisions, which specify how a bond is to be paid off over time.

LG 3 **Describe the relationship between bond prices and yields, and explain why some bonds are more volatile than others.** The price behavior of a bond depends on the issue's coupon and maturity and on the movement in market interest rates. When interest rates go down, bond prices go up, and vice versa. However, the extent to which bond prices move up or down depends on the coupon and maturity of an issue. Bonds with lower coupons and/or longer maturities generate larger price swings.

LG 4 **Identify the different types of bonds and the kinds of investment objectives these securities can fulfill.** The bond market is divided into four major segments: Treasuries, agencies, municipals, and corporates. Treasury bonds are issued by the U.S. Treasury and are virtually default-free. Agency bonds are issued by various political subdivisions of the U.S. government and make up an increasingly important segment of the bond market. Municipal bonds are issued by state and local governments in the form of either general obligation or revenue bonds. Corporate bonds make up the major non-government sector of the market and are backed by the assets and profitability of the issuing companies. Generally speaking, Treasuries are attractive because of their high quality, agencies and corporates because of the added returns they provide, and munis because of the tax shelter they offer.

LG 5 **Discuss the global nature of the bond market and the difference between dollar-denominated and non-dollar-denominated foreign bonds.** There's growing investor interest in foreign bonds, particularly foreign-pay securities, because of their highly competitive yields and returns. Foreign-pay bonds cover all those issues that are denominated in some currency other than U.S. dollars. These bonds have an added source of return: currency exchange rates. In addition, there are dollar-denominated foreign bonds—Yankee bonds and Eurodollar bonds. These have no currency exchange risk because they are issued in U.S. dollars.

LG 6 **Describe the role that bond ratings play in the market and the quotation system used with various types of bonds.** Municipal and corporate issues are regularly rated for bond quality by independent rating agencies. A rating of Aaa indicates an impeccable record. Lower ratings, such as A or Baa, indicate more risk. As with all investments, the returns required of lower-quality instruments generally are higher than those required of high-quality bonds. The bond market also has its own quotation system, wherein bonds are quoted as a percent of par.

Putting Your Investment Know-How to the Test

1. Which of the following statements regarding interest rates is *false?*
   a. The longer the maturity of the bond, the higher the interest rate risk.
   b. There is an inverse relationship between bond prices and interest rates.
   c. The higher the coupon rate on the bond, the higher the interest rate risk.
   d. Bond prices fall less when interest rates rise than they rise when interest rates fall.
2. Which of the following Standard and Poor's bond ratings would be considered junk grade?
   a. A rating
   b. BBB rating
   c. BB rating
   d. All of the above
3. All else being equal, which one of the following bonds will sell for the lowest price (or highest yield)?
   a. Callable subordinated debentures
   b. Noncallable senior bonds
   c. Callable mortgage bonds
   d. Noncallable debentures

4. The refunding provision of an indenture allows bonds to be retired *unless*
   a. They are replaced with a new issue having a lower interest cost.
   b. The remaining time to maturity is less than 5 years.
   c. The stated time period in the indenture has not passed.
   d. The stated time period in the indenture has passed.

5. To a taxpayer in the 34% tax bracket, a municipal bond available at a price of 100 and a coupon rate of 10% has a taxable equivalent yield of
   a. 6.6%.
   b. 10.0%.
   c. 13.4%.
   d. 15.2%.
6. A collateral trust bond is
   a. Unsecured.
   b. Secured by other securities held outside the firm.
   c. Secured by real estate owned by the firm.
   d. Secured by the equipment owned by the firm.

7. A revenue bond is distinguished from a general obligation bond in that revenue bonds
   a. Are issued by counties, special districts, cities, towns and state-controlled authorities, whereas general obligation bonds are only issued by the states themselves.
   b. Are typically secured by limited taxing power, whereas general obligation bonds are secured by unlimited taxing power.
   c. Are issued to finance projects and are secured by the revenues of the project being financed.
   d. Have first claim to any revenue increase of the tax authority issuing the bonds.

8. Bonds that are issued in the currency of one country but sold in other national markets are called
   a. Eurodollar bonds.
   b. Samurai bonds.
   c. Yankee bonds.
   d. Foreign-pay bonds.

9. The dollar value of a U.S. Treasury bond quoted at 92.24 is
   a. $92.24.
   b. $922.40.
   c. $927.50.
   d. None of the above.

10. What is true about the U.S. agency bonds?
   a. They are backed by the "full faith and credit" of the U.S. government.
   b. Their interest is exempt from federal and state taxes.
   c. All else constant, they provide higher yields than U.S. Treasury bonds.
   d. All of the above.

Answers: 1. c; 2. b; 3. a; 4. a; 5. d; 6. b; 7. c; 8. d; 9. c; 10. c

Discussion Questions

LG 1

Q10.1 Using the bond returns in Tables 10.1 and 10.2 as a basis of discussion:
   a. Compare the returns during the 1970s to those produced in the 1980s. How do you explain the differences?
   b. How did the bond market do in the 1990s? How does the performance in this decade compare to that in the 1980s? Explain.
   c. What do you think would be a fair rate of return to expect from bonds in the future? Explain.

LG 1

Q10.2 Use the data in Tables 6.1 and 6.2 (for stocks) and Tables 10.1 and 10.2 (for bonds) to compare returns for stocks and bonds during the '70s, '80s, and '90s.
   a. Using both annual and holding-period returns, how would you describe the comparative performance of these two markets over each of the three decades? Which market was more volatile? How did the return performance of bonds compare to stocks over the 3½-year period from 2000 through mid-2003?
   b. In view of these comparative returns, develop an argument for why investors *should* hold bonds. Can you think of any reason(s) why investors should *not* hold bonds? What are they?
   c. Assume that you're out of school and hold a promising, well-paying job. How much of your portfolio (in percentage terms) would you, personally, want to hold in bonds? Explain. What role do you see bonds playing in your own portfolio, particularly as you go farther and farther into the future?

LG 4

Q10.3 Identify and briefly describe each of the following types of bonds.
   a. Agency bonds
   b. Municipal bonds
   c. Zero-coupon bonds
   d. Junk bonds
   e. Foreign bonds
   f. Collateralized mortgage obligations (CMOs)

What type of investor do you think would be most attracted to each?

LG 1 LG 4

Q10.4 "Treasury securities are guaranteed by the U.S. government. Therefore, there is no risk in the ownership of such bonds." Briefly discuss the wisdom (or folly) of this statement.

LG 4 LG 5

Q10.5 Select the security in the left-hand column that best fits the investor desire described in the right-hand column.

a. 5-year Treasury note.	1. Lock in a high coupon yield.
b. A bond with a low coupon and a long maturity.	2. Accumulate capital over a long period of time.
c. Yankee bond.	3. Generate a monthly income.
d. Insured revenue bond.	4. Avoid a lot of price volatility.
e. Long-term Treasury strips.	5. Generate tax-free income.
f. Noncallable bond.	6. Invest in a foreign bond.
g. CMO.	7. Go for the highest yield available.
h. Junk bond.	8. Invest in a pool of credit-card receivables.
i. ABS.	9. Go for maximum price appreciation.

LG 6

Q10.6 Using the quotes in Figures 10.5 and 10.6, answer the following questions.

a. What's the dollar (bid) price of the November 10 Treasury strip bond, and when does it mature?
b. What's the yield on the November 10 Treasury strip issue?
c. Which is higher priced: Sprint Capital 8.75% bond of 2032 or the 8.75% U.S. Treasury of August 20? (Use the ask price with the Treasury issue.) Both bonds carry the same coupons; so why don't they sell for about the same price?
d. What's the dollar (ask) price of the 14% U.S. Treasury of November 11? Why is that issue priced so high?
e. Which bond was more actively traded, GE 5% of 2013 or the GMAC 8% of 2031?
f. Which of the following bonds has the highest yield-to-maturity: the Citigroup 3½% of 2008, the 13¼% U.S. Treasury of May 14, or the February 9 strip-T? Which one would produce the most dollar amount of annual interest income (per $1,000 par bond)?

Problems

LG 6

P10.1 A 6%, 15-year bond has 3 years remaining on a deferred call feature (the call premium is equal to 1 year's interest). The bond is currently priced in the market at $850. What is the issue's current yield?

LG 3

P10.2 A 12%, 20-year bond is currently trading at $1,250. What is the current yield?

LG 3

P10.3 Charlie buys a 10% corporate bond with a current yield of 6%. How much did he pay for the bond?

LG 4

P10.4 An investor is in the 28% tax bracket and lives in a state with no income tax. He is trying to decide which of two bonds to purchase. One is a 7½% corporate bond that is selling at par. The other is a municipal bond with a 5¼% coupon that is also selling at par. If all other features of these two bonds are comparable, which should the investor select? Why? Would your answer change if this were an *in-state* municipal bond and the investor lived in a place with high state income taxes? Explain.

LG 4

P10.5 An investor lives in a state where her tax rate on interest income is 8%. She is in the 33% federal tax bracket. She owns a 7% corporate bond trading at par. What is her after-tax current yield on this bond?

LG 4

P10.6 Sara Jordan is a wealthy investor who's looking for a tax shelter. Sara is in the maximum (35%) federal tax bracket and lives in a state with a very high state income tax. (She pays the maximum of 11½% in state income tax.) Sara is currently looking at two municipal bonds, both of which are selling at par. One is a double-A-rated *in-state* bond that carries a coupon of 6⅜%. The other is a double-A-rated *out-of-state* bond that carries a 7⅛% coupon. Her broker has informed her that comparable fully taxable corporate bonds are currently available with yields of 9¾%. Alternatively, long Treasuries are now available at yields of 9%. She has $100,000 to invest, and because all the bonds are high-quality issues, she wants to select the one that will give her maximum after-tax returns.

a. Which one of the four bonds should she buy?
b. Rank the four bonds (from best to worst) in terms of their taxable equivalent yields.

LG 4

P10.7 Rob is looking for a fixed-income investment. He is considering two bond issues:

a. A Treasury with a yield of 5%.
b. An in-state municipal bond with a yield of 4%.

Rob is in the 33% federal tax bracket and the 8% state tax bracket. Which bond would provide Rob with a higher tax-adjusted yield?

LG 6

P10.8 Which of the following three bonds offers the highest current yield?

a. A 9½%, 20-year bond quoted at 97¾.
b. A 16%, 15-year bond quoted at 164⅜.
c. A 5¼%, 18-year bond quoted at 54.

LG 6

P10.9 Assume that an investor pays $850 for a long-term bond that carries a 7½% coupon. Over the course of the next 12 months, interest rates drop sharply. As a result, the investor sells the bond at a price of $962.50.

a. Find the current yield that existed on this bond at the beginning of the year. What was it by the end of the 1-year holding period?
b. Determine the holding period return on this investment. (See Chapter 5 for the HPR formula.)

LG 3

P10.10 Charlie buys a 10% corporate bond with a current yield of 6%. When he sells the bond 1 year later, the current yield on the bond is 7%. How much did Charlie make on this investment?

LG 1

P10.11 In early January 1998, an investor purchased $30,000 worth of some Baa-rated corporate bonds. The bonds carried a coupon of 8⅞% and mature in 2015. The investor paid 94⅛ when she bought the bonds. Over the 5-year period from 1998 through 2002, the bonds were priced in the market as follows:

	Quoted Prices		
Year	Beginning of the Year	End of the Year	Year-End Bond Yields
1998	94⅛	100⅝	8.82%
1999	100⅝	102	8.70
2000	102	104⅝	8.48
2001	104⅝	110¼	8.05
2002	110¼	121⅛	7.33

Coupon payments were made on schedule throughout the 5-year period.

a. Find the annual holding period returns for 1998 through 2002. (See Chapter 5 for the HPR formula.)

b. Use the return information in Table 10.1 to evaluate the investment performance of this bond. How do you think it stacks up against the market? Explain.

LG 4

P10.12 Richie purchased a 13% zero-coupon bond with a 15-year maturity and a $20,000 par value 15 years ago. The bond matures tomorrow. How much will Richie receive in total from this investment, assuming all payments are made on these bonds as expected?

LG 4

P10.13 Archie purchased an interest-bearing security last year, planning to hold it until maturity. He received interest payments, and, to his surprise, a sizable amount of the principal was paid back in the first year. This happened again in year 2. What type of security did Archie purchase?

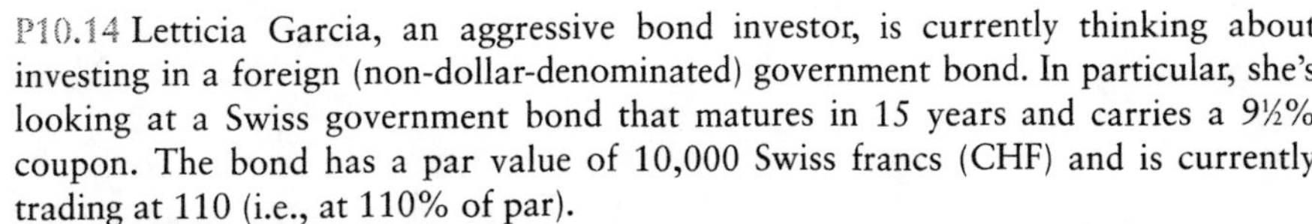

P10.14 Letticia Garcia, an aggressive bond investor, is currently thinking about investing in a foreign (non-dollar-denominated) government bond. In particular, she's looking at a Swiss government bond that matures in 15 years and carries a 9½% coupon. The bond has a par value of 10,000 Swiss francs (CHF) and is currently trading at 110 (i.e., at 110% of par).

Letticia plans to hold the bond for a period of 1 year, at which time she thinks it will be trading at 117½—she's anticipating a sharp decline in Swiss interest rates, which explains why she expects bond prices to move up. The current exchange rate is 1.58 CHF/U.S. $, but she expects that to fall to 1.25 CHF/U.S. $. Use the foreign investment return formula introduced in Chapter 6 (Equation 6.6) to answer the questions below.

a. Ignoring the currency effect, find the bond's total return (in its local currency).

b. Now find the total return on this bond in *U.S. dollars*. Did currency exchange rates affect the return in any way? Do you think this bond would make a good investment? Explain.

LG 6

P10.15 Red Electrica Espana SA (E.REE) is refinancing its bank loans by issuing Eurobonds to investors. You are considering buying $10,000 of these bonds, which will yield 6%. You are also looking at a U.S. bond with similar risk that will yield 5%. You expect that interest rates will not change over the next year, after which you will sell the bonds you purchase.

a. How much will you make on each bond if you buy it, hold it for 1 year, and then sell it for $10,000 (or the Eurodollar equivalent)?

b. Assume the dollar/euro exchange rate goes from 1.11 to 0.98. How much will this currency change affect the proceeds from the Eurobond? (Assume you receive annual interest at the same time you sell the Eurobond.)

See the text Web site (www.aw-bc.com/gitman_joehnk) for Web exercises that deal with *fixed-income securities*.

Case Problem 10.1 Max and Heather Develop a Bond Investment Program

LG 4 LG 6

Max and Heather Peters, along with their two teenage sons, Terry and Thomas, live in Portland, Oregon. Max is a sales rep for a major medical firm, and Heather is a personnel officer at a local bank. Together, they earn an annual income of around $100,000. Max has just learned that his recently departed rich uncle has named him in his will to the tune of some $250,000 after taxes. Needless to say, the family is elated. Max intends to spend $50,000 of his inheritance on a number of long-overdue family items (like some badly needed remodeling of their kitchen and family room, the down payment on a new Porsche Boxster, and braces to correct Tom's overbite). Max wants to invest the remaining $200,000 in various types of fixed-income securities.

Max and Heather have no unusual income requirements or health problems. Their only investment objectives are that they want to achieve some capital appreciation and they want to keep their funds fully invested for a period of at least 20 years. They would rather not have to rely on their investments as a source of current income but want to maintain some liquidity in their portfolio just in case.

Questions

a. Describe the type of *bond investment program* you think the Peters family should follow. In answering this question, give appropriate consideration to both return and risk factors.

b. List several different types of bonds that you would recommend for their portfolio, and briefly indicate why you would recommend each.

c. Using a recent issue of the *Wall Street Journal* or *Barron's*, construct a $200,000 bond portfolio for the Peters family. *Use real securities* and select any bonds (or notes) you like, given the following ground rules:

1. The portfolio must include at least one Treasury, one agency, and one corporate bond; also, in total, the portfolio must hold at least 5, but no more than 8 bonds or notes.
2. No more than 5% of the portfolio can be in short-term U.S. Treasury bills (but note that if you hold a T-bill, that limits your selections to just 7 other notes/bonds).

Security Issuer-Coupon-Maturity	Latest Quoted Price	Number of Bonds Purchased	Amount Invested	Annual Coupon Income	Current Yield
Example: U.S. Treas - 8½%-'15	96⅝32	25	$ 24,062	$ 2,125	8.83%
1.					
2.					
3.					
4.					
5.					
6.					
7.					
8.					
Totals	—	____	$200.000	$ ____	____%

3. Ignore all transaction costs (i.e., invest the full $200,000) and assume all securities have par values of $1,000 (though they can be trading in the market at something other than par).
4. Use the latest available quotes to determine how many bonds/notes/bills you can buy.

d. Prepare a schedule listing all the securities in your recommended portfolio. *Use a form like the one shown on the previous page*, and include the information it calls for on each security in the portfolio.

e. *In one brief paragraph*, note the key investment attributes of your recommended portfolio and the investment objectives you hope to achieve with it.

Case Problem 10.2 *The Case of the Missing Bond Ratings*

LG 6

While a lot goes into a bond rating, it's probably safe to say that there's nothing more important in determining a bond's rating than the underlying financial condition and operating results of the company issuing the bond. Just as financial ratios can be used in the analysis of common stocks, they can also be used in the analysis of bonds—a process we refer to as *credit analysis*. In credit analysis, attention is directed toward the basic liquidity and profitability of the firm, the extent to which the firm employs debt, and the ability of the firm to service its debt.

The following financial ratios are often helpful in carrying out such analysis: (1) current ratio, (2) quick ratio, (3) net profit margin, (4) return on total capital, (5) long-term debt to total capital, (6) owners' equity ratio, (7) pretax interest coverage, and (8) cash flow to total debt. The first two ratios measure the liquidity of the firm, the next two its profitability, the following two the debt load, and the final two the ability of the firm to service its debt load. (For ratio 5, the *lower* the ratio, the better. For all the others, the *higher* the ratio, the better.) The following table lists each of these ratios for six different companies.

A Table of Financial Ratios
(All ratios are real and pertain to real companies)

Financial Ratio	Company 1	Company 2	Company 3	Company 4	Company 5	Company 6
1. Current ratio	1.13 ×	1.39 ×	1.78 ×	1.32 ×	1.03 ×	1.41 ×
2. Quick ratio	0.48 ×	0.84 ×	0.93 ×	0.33 ×	0.50 ×	0.75 ×
3. Net profit margin	4.6%	12.9%	14.5%	2.8%	5.9%	10.0%
4. Return on total capital	15.0%	25.9%	29.4%	11.5%	16.8%	28.4%
5. Long-term debt to total capital	63.3%	52.7%	23.9%	97.0%	88.6%	42.1%
6. Owners' equity ratio	18.6%	18.9%	44.1%	1.5%	5.1%	21.2%
7. Pretax interest coverage	2.3 ×	4.5 ×	8.9 ×	1.7 ×	2.4 ×	6.4%
8. Cash flow to total debt	34.7%	48.8%	71.2%	20.4%	30.2%	42.7%

Notes: Ratio (2)—Whereas the current ratio relates current assets to current liabilities, the quick ratio considers only the most liquid current assets (cash, short-term securities, and accounts receivable) and relates them to current liabilities.
Ratio (4)—Relates pretax profit to the total capital structure (long-term debt + equity) of the firm.
Ratio (6)—Shows the amount of stockholders' equity used to finance the firm (stockholders' equity ÷ total assets).
Ratio (8)—Looks at the amount of corporate cash flow (from net profits + depreciation) relative to the total (current + long-term) debt of the firm
The other four ratios are as described in Chapter 6.

Questions

a. Three of these companies have bonds that carry investment-grade ratings. The other three companies carry junk-bond ratings. Judging by the information in the table, which three companies have the investment-grade bonds and which three have the junk bonds? Briefly explain your selections.

b. One of these six companies is a AAA-rated firm and one is B-rated. Identify those two companies. Briefly explain your selection.

c. Of the remaining four companies, one carries a AA rating, one carries an A rating, and two are BB-rated. Which companies are they?

Excel with Spreadsheets

The cash flow components of bond investments is made up of the annual interest payments and the future redemption value or its par value. Just like other time-value-of-money considerations, the bond cash flows are discounted back in order to determine their present value.

In comparing bonds to stocks, many investors look at the respective returns. The total returns in the bond market are made up of both current income and capital gains. Bond investment analysis should include the determination of the current yield as well as a specific holding period return.

On January 13, 2004, you gather the following information on three corporate bonds issued by the General Motors Acceptance Corp (GMA). Remember that corporate bonds are quoted as a percent of their par value. Assume the par value of each bond to be $1,000. These debentures are quoted in eighths of a point. Create a spreadsheet that will model and answer the following three bond investment problems.

Bonds	Current Yield	Volume	Close
GMA 5.3 07	?	25	105 7/8
GMA 6.65s 14	?	45	103
GMA 7.4 16	?	37	104 6/8

Questions

a. Calculate the current yields for these three GMA corporate debentures.
b. Calculate the holding period returns under the following three scenarios:
   1. Purchased the 5.3 bonds for 990 on January 13, 2003.
   2. Purchased the 6.65s for 988 on January 13, 2003.
   3. Purchased the 7.4 bonds for 985 on January 13, 2001.

c. As of January 13, 2004, GMA common stock had a close price of $26.20. The price of GMA stock in January 2001 was $25.25. The stock paid a 2002 dividend of $.46, a 2003 dividend of $.46, and a 2004 dividend of $.46.
   1. Calculate the current (January 13, 2004) dividend yield for this security.
   2. Assuming you purchased the stock in January 2001, what is the holding period return as of January 2004?

Fundamentals of Investing

CHAPTER 13

MUTUAL FUNDS: PROFESSIONALLY MANAGED PORTFOLIOS

CHAPTER 13

MUTUAL FUNDS: PROFESSIONALLY MANAGED PORTFOLIOS

LEARNING GOALS

After studying this chapter, you should be able to:

LG 1 Describe the basic features of mutual funds, and note what they have to offer as investment vehicles.

LG 2 Distinguish between open- and closed-end funds, as well as other types of professionally managed investment companies, and discuss the various types of fund loads, fees, and charges.

LG 3 Discuss the types of funds available and the variety of investment objectives these funds seek to fulfill.

LG 4 Discuss the investor services offered by mutual funds and how these services can fit into an investment program.

LG 5 Gain an appreciation of the investor uses of mutual funds, along with the variables to consider when assessing and selecting funds for investment purposes.

LG 6 Identify the sources of return and compute the rate of return earned on a mutual fund investment.

Back in 1976, John Bogle, founder of the Vanguard Group, had a radical idea: create a mutual fund that would hold only stock in the Standard & Poor's 500 stock index of large companies. Unlike many other mutual funds, the Vanguard 500 Index fund wouldn't try to outperform the equities market, but rather would strive to keep pace with the returns offered by the S&P 500 index. Instead of constantly buying and selling a diversified portfolio of equities, Vanguard would limit itself to the small number of trades necessary to mirror changes in the S&P index. Investors would be rewarded with an unimaginative portfolio that Bogle promised would offer consistent returns and low operating costs.

Flash forward to today. The Vanguard 500 Index fund is the largest mutual fund in the world, with net assets exceeding $84 billion. Just as Bogle predicted, the fund's emphasis on limited stock turnover has kept its operating expenses low. For every $1,000 an investor places in the fund, Vanguard extracts just $1.80 per year for operating costs, compared with a mutual fund industry average of $15 annually per $1,000 invested. Even more impressive to investors seeking steady, long-term growth, the Vanguard 500 Index fund has offered predictable returns, averaging 9.10% per year since 1992, just below the 9.18% average annual return of the S&P 500 index itself.

If the Vanguard 500 Index fund's investment strategy doesn't appeal to you, you can choose from more than 8,300 mutual funds sold by Vanguard and other mutual fund firms in the United States. Your choices range from funds that track other market indexes to funds focusing on companies in a particular industry sector—for instance, pharmaceutical companies—to emerging markets funds that invest in stocks in developing economies. Other options include funds that buy and sell a broad range of stocks, bonds, and even shares in other mutual funds in an attempt to maximize investor profits. Before choosing a mutual fund, however, it's important to understand how such funds are managed and the factors affecting their performance. As you'll learn in this chapter, with this information under your belt, mutual funds can help you reach your investment goals.

Sources: Geoffrey Colvin, "The Pressure Is On at Vanguard," *Fortune*, December 8, 2003, p. 5[illegible]; Robert Frick, "The New Spin on Indexing," *Kiplinger's Personal Finance Magazine*, March 1, 2003, pp. 34–38; Michael Maiello and James M. Clash, "Beating the Broad Market," *Forbes*, February 3, 2003, p. 80; and Jody Yen, "Risky Business," *Forbes*, February 3, 2003, p. 94.

The Mutual Fund Phenomenon

LG 1 LG 2

Questions of which stock or bond to select, when to buy, and when to sell have plagued investors for as long as there have been organized securities markets. Such concerns lie at the very heart of the mutual fund concept and in large part explain the growth that mutual funds have experienced. Many investors lack the time, know-how, or commitment to manage their own portfolios, so they turn to professional money managers and simply let them decide which securities to buy and when to sell. More often than not, when investors look for professional help, they look to mutual funds.

mutual fund
an investment company that invests its shareholders' money in a diversified portfolio of securities.

Basically, a **mutual fund** is a type of financial services organization that receives money from its shareholders and then invests those funds on their behalf in a diversified portfolio of securities. Thus, when investors buy shares in a mutual fund, they actually become *part owners of a widely diversified portfolio of securities*. In an abstract sense, a mutual fund can be thought of as the *financial product* sold to the public by an investment company. That is, the investment company builds and manages a portfolio of securities and sells ownership interests—shares of stock—in that portfolio through a vehicle known as a mutual fund.

Recall from Chapter 5 that portfolio management deals with both asset allocation and security selection decisions. By investing in mutual funds, investors delegate some, if not all, of the *security selection decisions* to professional money managers. As a result, they can concentrate on key asset allocation decisions—which, of course, play a vital role in determining long-term portfolio returns. Indeed, it's for this reason that *many investors consider mutual funds to be the ultimate asset allocation vehicle*. For with mutual funds, all investors have to do is decide where they want to invest—in large-cap stocks, for example, or in technology stocks, high-yield bonds, the S&P 500 index, or international securities—and then let the professional money managers at the mutual funds do the rest (i.e., decide which securities to buy and sell, and when).

Mutual funds have been a part of the investment landscape for over 75 years. The first one (MFS) was started in Boston in 1924 and is still in business today. By 1940 the number of mutual funds had grown to 68, and by 1980 there were 564 of them. But that was only the beginning: The next 20 years saw unprecedented growth in the mutual fund industry, as assets under management grew from less than $100 billion in 1980 to some $6.4 *trillion* in 2002. Indeed, by 2002, *there were nearly 8,300 publicly traded mutual funds*. (Actually, counting duplicate and multiple fund offerings from the same portfolio, there were more like *15,000 funds available*.) To put that number in perspective, *there are more mutual funds in existence today than there are stocks listed on the New York and American exchanges combined*. The mutual fund industry has grown so much, in fact, that it is now *the largest financial intermediary* in this country—even ahead of banks.

An Overview of Mutual Funds

Mutual funds are big business in the United States and, indeed, all over the world. As the year 2003 began, an estimated 95 million individuals in 54 million U.S. households owned mutual funds. That's nearly half of all U.S. households! Table 13.1 (on page 542) provides some additional statistics about mutual funds in this country and abroad. Clearly, mutual funds appeal to a lot

TABLE 13.1 Some Mutual Fund Statistics

I. Total Number of U.S. Shareholder Accounts (in millions)

	1990*	2002*
Stock funds	22.2	164.4
Bond funds	13.6	25.6
Money market funds	23.0	45.5
Other funds	3.2	15.5
Total	62.0	251.0

II. Total Number of Funds

	1990*	2002*
Stock funds	1,099	4,756
Bond funds	1,046	2,036
Money market funds	741	989
Other funds	193	475
Total—U.S. funds	3,079	8,256
Number of funds in other countries**	N/A	44,870
Total—worldwide	N/A	53,126

III. Total Net Assets Under Management (in billions of dollars)

	1990*	2002*
Stock funds	$239.5	$2,667.1
Bond funds	291.3	1,125.1
Money market funds	498.3	2,272.0
Other funds	31.1	327.4
Total—U.S. funds	$1,065.2	$ 6,391.6
Net assets under mgmt. in other countries**	N/A	$ 4,828.6
Total—worldwide	N/A	$11,220.2

IV. Composition of Mutual Fund Ownership in the United States (relative to total mutual fund assets)

	1990*	2002*
Owned by U.S. households		
in dollars	$790 billion	$4.7 trillion
% of total	74.0%	74.0%
Owned by institutions		
in dollars	$275 billion	$1.7 trillion
% of total	26.0%	26.0%

Notes: *All data are for year-end 1990 and 2002.

**Totals for 38 countries, the major ones being Canada, France, Germany, United Kingdom, Japan, Italy, Korea, Spain, Ireland, and Luxembourg..

Source: 2003 Mutual Fund Fact Book, Investment Company Institute, 2003; obtained from www.ici.org.

of investors—investors from all walks of life and all income levels. They range from inexperienced to highly experienced investors who all share a common view: Each has decided, for one reason or another, to turn over at least a part of his or her investment management activities to professionals.

Pooled Diversification As noted above, an investment in a mutual fund really represents *an ownership position in a professionally managed portfolio of securities.* To appreciate the extent of such diversification, take a look at

FIGURE 13.1 A Partial List of Portfolio Holdings

This exhibit represents just *two pages* of security holdings for this particular fund. The total list of holdings goes on for 21 pages and includes stocks in hundreds of different companies. Certainly, this is far more diversification than most individual investors could ever hope to achieve. (*Source: Fidelity Contrafund,* June 30, 2003.)

Investments (Unaudited) – continued

Common Stocks – continued

	Shares	Value (Note 1) (000s)
INDUSTRIALS – continued		
Electrical Equipment – 0.1%		
American Power Conversion Corp.	1,128,200	$ 17,589
Cooper Industries Ltd. Class A	139,400	5,757
Rockwell Automation, Inc.	235,500	5,614
		28,960
Industrial Conglomerates – 3.4%		
3M Co.	7,623,490	983,278
Tomkins PLC	2,966,800	11,147
Tyco International Ltd.	1,783,100	33,843
		1,028,268
Machinery – 1.3%		
CUNO, Inc. (a)	4,000	144
Danaher Corp.	3,489,420	237,455
Dionex Corp. (a)	53,400	2,123
Donaldson Co., Inc.	513,000	22,803
ESCO Technologies, Inc. (a)	204,900	9,016
PACCAR, Inc.	1,643,430	111,030
Pall Corp.	327,900	7,378
Wabash National Corp. (a)	604,400	8,480
		398,429
Marine – 0.0%		
CP Ships Ltd.	140,900	2,347
Road & Rail – 0.3%		
Canadian National Railway Co.	306,120	14,781
Canadian Pacific Railway Ltd.	218,350	4,910
Heartland Express, Inc. (a)	1,494,231	33,247
Knight Transportation, Inc. (a)	682,550	16,995
Landstar System, Inc. (a)	294,074	18,483
Norfolk Southern Corp.	7,900	152
P.A.M. Transportation Services, Inc. (a)	78,600	1,974
		90,542
Trading Companies & Distributors – 0.0%		
Fastenal Co.	59,488	2,019
MSC Industrial Direct Co., Inc. Class A (a)	131,900	2,361
		4,380
TOTAL INDUSTRIALS		3,906,170

See accompanying notes which are an integral part of the financial statements.

Semiannual Report 16

Common Stocks – continued

	Shares	Value (Note 1) (000s)
INFORMATION TECHNOLOGY – 10.1%		
Communications Equipment – 1.0%		
Adtran, Inc. (a)	230,072	$ 11,800
Avocent Corp. (a)	742,633	22,227
Cisco Systems, Inc. (a)	78,700	1,314
Comverse Technology, Inc. (a)	1,631,400	24,520
NetScreen Technologies, Inc. (a)	2,659,200	59,965
Nokia Corp. sponsored ADR	7,900	130
QUALCOMM, Inc.	411,300	14,704
SafeNet, Inc. (a)	38,400	1,074
Scientific-Atlanta, Inc.	2,746,100	65,467
Sycamore Networks, Inc. (a)	3,739,300	14,322
Telefonaktiebolaget LM Ericsson ADR (a)	4,117,391	43,768
UTStarcom, Inc. (a)	835,300	29,712
		289,003
Computers & Peripherals – 1.0%		
Apple Computer, Inc. (a)	2,012,500	38,479
ATI Technologies, Inc. (a)	939,500	9,341
Avid Technology, Inc. (a)	234,900	8,238
Cray, Inc. (a)	486,500	3,843
Dell Computer Corp. (a)	1,129,300	36,092
Electronics for Imaging, Inc. (a)	744,721	15,110
Hutchinson Technology, Inc. (a)	133,700	4,397
Lexmark International, Inc. Class A (a)	260,100	18,407
Logitech International SA (Reg.) (a)	200,592	7,541
SanDisk Corp. (a)	79,100	3,192
Seagate Technology	4,351,300	76,800
Storage Technology Corp. (a)	383,700	9,876
Western Digital Corp. (a)	7,267,500	74,855
		306,171
Electronic Equipment & Instruments – 0.6%		
CDW Corp. (a)	39,200	1,795
Flextronics International Ltd. (a)	2,079,500	21,606
Flir Systems, Inc. (a)(c)	2,911,200	87,773
Lexar Media, Inc. (a)	474,300	4,525
National Instruments Corp. (a)	82,995	3,136
Roper Industries, Inc.	46,300	1,722
Symbol Technologies, Inc.	4,194,100	54,565
Thermo Electron Corp. (a)	336,800	7,080
Waters Corp. (a)	318,000	9,263
		191,465

See accompanying notes which are an integral part of the financial statements.

17 Semiannual Report

Figure 13.1. It provides a partial list of the securities held in the portfolio of a major mutual fund. (The exhibit shows just two pages out of a 21-page list of security holdings.) Note that in June 2003, this fund owned anywhere from 4,000 shares of CUNO, Inc., to more than 7.6 *million* shares of 3M Company. Furthermore, note that within each industry segment, the fund diversified its holdings across a number of different stocks. Clearly, this is far more diversification than most investors could ever attain. Yet each investor who owns shares in this fund is, in effect, a part owner of this diversified portfolio.

Of course, not all funds are as big or as widely diversified as the one depicted in Figure 13.1. But whatever the size of the fund, as the securities held by it move up and down in price, the market value of the mutual fund shares moves accordingly. And when dividend and interest payments are received by the fund, they too are passed on to the mutual fund shareholders and distributed

pooled diversification
a process whereby investors buy into a diversified portfolio of securities for the collective benefit of the individual investors.

on the basis of prorated ownership. Thus, if you own 1,000 shares in a mutual fund and that represents 1% of all shares outstanding, you will receive 1% of the dividends paid by the fund. And when a security held by the fund is sold for a profit, the capital gain is also passed on to fund shareholders on a prorated basis. The whole mutual fund idea, in fact, rests on the concept of **pooled diversification.** This process works very much like health insurance, whereby individuals pool their resources for the collective benefit of all the contributors.

INVESTOR FACTS

WHO OWNS THE FUNDS, AND WHY?—Mutual funds are one of the most popular investments in the United States, with about 95 million individuals in nearly half of all households owning one or more funds. The average mutual fund shareholder is 45 years old, married, college educated, and employed, with $69,000 of household income, $74,400 in mutual fund assets, and $199,000 in total financial assets. Almost 90% own equity mutual funds, and about half own money market funds.

Almost all mutual fund investors consider their holdings to be long-term savings, with retirement and education being their primary investment objectives. The top four reasons they select mutual funds are professional management, investment diversification, potential for high returns, and ease of making investment.

Source: 2003 Mutual Fund Fact Book (Washington, DC: Investment Company Institute, May 2000), downloaded from www.ici.org.

Attractions and Drawbacks of Mutual Fund Ownership The attractions of mutual fund ownership are numerous. One of the most important is *diversification.* It benefits fund shareholders by spreading out holdings over a wide variety of industries and companies, thus reducing risk. Another appeal of mutual funds is *full-time professional management,* which relieves investors of many of the day-to-day management and record-keeping chores. What's more, the fund is probably able to offer better investment expertise than individual investors can provide. Still another advantage is that most mutual fund investments can be started with a *modest capital outlay.* Sometimes no minimum investment is required, and after the initial investment additional shares can usually be purchased in small amounts. The *services that mutual funds offer* also make them appealing to many investors: These include automatic reinvestment of dividends, withdrawal plans, and exchange privileges. Finally, mutual funds offer *convenience.* They are relatively easy to acquire; the funds handle the paperwork and record keeping; their prices are widely quoted; and it is possible to deal in fractional shares.

There are, of course, some major drawbacks to mutual fund ownership. One of the biggest disadvantages is that mutual funds in general can be costly and involve *substantial transaction costs.* Many funds carry sizable commission fees ("load charges"). In addition, a **management fee** is levied annually for the professional services provided. It is deducted right off the top, regardless of whether the fund has had a good or a bad year. And, in spite of all the professional management and advice, it seems that *mutual fund performance* over the long haul is at best about equal to what you would expect from the market as a whole. There are some notable exceptions, of course, but most funds do little more than keep up with the market. And in many cases, they don't even do that.

management fee
a fee levied annually for professional mutual fund services provided; paid regardless of the performance of the portfolio.

Figure 13.2 shows the investment performance for 12 different types of equity (or equity-oriented) funds over the 10½-year period from January 1993 through mid-2003. The reported returns are average, fully compounded annual rates of return. They assume that all dividends and capital gains distributions are reinvested into additional shares of stock. Note that when compared to the S&P 500, only four fund categories outperformed the market, whereas several fell far short. The message is clear: *Consistently beating the market is no easy task,* even for professional money managers. Although a handful of funds have given investors above-average and even spectacular rates of return, most mutual funds simply do not meet those levels of performance. This is not to say that the long-term returns from mutual funds are substandard or that they fail to equal what you could achieve by putting your money in, say, a savings account or some other risk-free investment outlet. Quite the contrary: The long-term returns from mutual funds have been substantial (and perhaps even better than what a lot of

HOT

To see the corrosive effect that fees paid have on return (or profit), use the fee analyzer at:

www.smartmoney.com/fundfeeanalyzer/

FIGURE 13.2 The Comparative Performance of Mutual Funds Versus the Market

Even with the services of professional money managers, it's tough to outperform the market. In this case, the average performance of 8 out of the 12 fund categories failed to meet the market's standard of return (for the period from January 1993 to mid-2003). (*Source: Morningstar,* June 2003.)

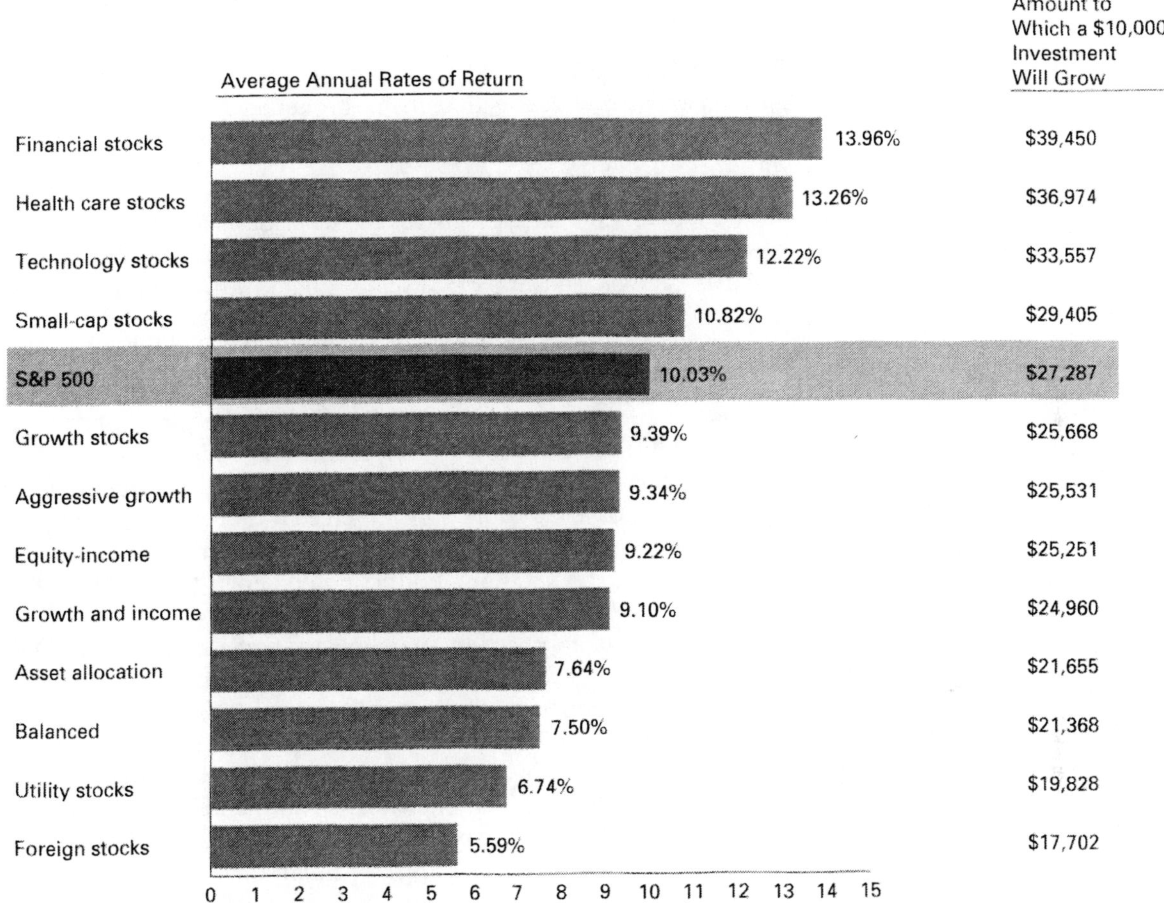

individual investors could have achieved on their own), but most of these returns can be traced to strong market conditions and/or to the reinvestment of dividends and capital gains.

How Mutual Funds Are Organized and Run Although it's tempting to think of a mutual fund as a single large entity, that view is not really accurate. Various functions—investing, record keeping, safekeeping, and others—are split among two or more companies. To begin with, there's the fund itself, which is organized as a separate corporation or trust and is *owned by the shareholders*, not by the firm that runs it. In addition, there are several other major players:

- The *management company* runs the fund's daily operations. Management companies are the firms we know as Fidelity, Vanguard, T. Rowe Price, American Century, and Dreyfus. They are the ones that create the funds in the first place. Usually, the management firm also serves as investment adviser.

- The *investment adviser* buys and sells stocks or bonds and otherwise oversees the portfolio. Usually, three parties participate in this phase of the operation: (1) *the money manager,* who actually runs the portfolio and makes the buy and sell decisions; (2) *securities analysts*, who analyze securities and look for viable investment candidates; and (3) *traders*, who buy and sell big blocks of securities at the best possible price.
- The *distributor* sells the fund shares, either directly to the public or through authorized dealers (like major brokerage houses and commercial banks). When you request a prospectus and sales literature, you deal with the distributor.
- The *custodian* physically safeguards the securities and other assets of the fund, without taking a role in the investment decisions. To discourage foul play, an independent party (usually a bank) serves in this capacity.
- The *transfer agent* keeps track of purchase and redemption requests from shareholders and maintains other shareholder records.

All this separation of duties is designed to protect the mutual fund investor/shareholder. Obviously, as a mutual fund investor, you will lose money if your fund's stock or bond holdings go down in value. But that's really the only risk of loss you face with a mutual fund. The chance of your ever losing *money from a mutual fund collapse* is almost nonexistent. Here's why: In addition to the separation of duties noted above, the only formal link between the mutual fund and the company that manages it is a contract that must be renewed—and approved by shareholders—on a regular basis. One of the provisions of this contract is that the fund's assets—stocks, bonds, cash, or other securities in the portfolio—can *never be in the hands of the management company.* As still another safeguard, each fund must have a board of directors, or trustees, who are elected by shareholders and are charged with keeping tabs on the management company and renewing its contract. Unfortunately, as the *Ethics* box on pages 548–549 explains, the mutual fund industry did come close to a crisis in 2003, when it was revealed that a handful of fund families were allowing some big investors to execute questionable—if not illegal—transactions in their funds. But note that even here, *the integrity of the fund portfolios was never at risk;* rather, the scandal revolved around some highly questionable trades that took place in the funds.

Mutual Fund Regulations We discussed securities regulations in Chapter 2, but it might be helpful to review some of the major regulatory provisions that apply to mutual funds. To begin with, the *Securities Act of 1933* requires the filing of full information about a mutual fund with the SEC. This act also requires the fund to provide potential investors with a fund profile or current prospectus. This document discloses the fund's management, its investment policies and objectives, and other essential data. In addition, the purchase and sale of mutual fund shares are subject to the antifraud provisions of the *Securities Exchange Act of 1934,* while the *Investment Advisers Act of 1940* regulates the activities of the investment advisers that work for mutual funds. Most importantly, to qualify for investment company status, a fund must comply with the provisions of the *Investment Company Act of 1940.* That comprehensive piece of legislation provides the foundation for the regulation of the mutual fund industry and, among other things, establishes standards of income distribution, fee structures, and diversification of assets.

From a tax perspective, a mutual fund can be treated as an essentially tax-exempt organization (and thereby avoid the double taxation of dividends and income) so long as it qualifies under *Subchapter M* of the Internal Revenue Code of 1954. Briefly, to operate as a regulated investment company and enjoy the attendant tax benefits, a fund must annually distribute to its shareholders all of its realized capital gains and at least 90% of its interest and dividend income. That way, the fund will pay *no* taxes on any of its earnings, whether they're derived from current income or capital gains.

Open- or Closed-End Funds

Although investing in mutual funds has been made as simple as possible, investors nevertheless should have a clear understanding of what they're getting into. For starters, it's essential that you be aware of the different organizational structures, particularly with regard to open- and closed-end funds, as well as a type of fund that combines the characteristics of both open- and closed-end funds, the so-called exchange-traded fund.

open-end investment company
a type of investment company in which investors buy shares from, and sell them back to, the mutual fund itself, with no limit on the number of shares the fund can issue.

Open-End Investment Companies The term *mutual fund* is commonly used to describe an open-end investment company. In an **open-end investment company,** investors buy their shares from, and sell them back to, the mutual fund itself. When an investor buys shares in an open-end fund, the fund issues new shares of stock and fills the purchase order with those new shares. There is no limit, other than investor demand, to the number of shares the fund can issue. (Occasionally, funds *temporarily* close themselves to new investors—they won't open any new accounts—in an attempt to keep fund growth in check.) All open-end mutual funds stand behind their shares and buy them back when investors decide to sell. There is never any trading between individuals.

HOT

American Association of Individual Investors glossary of mutual fund terms is at:

www.aaii.com/mfunds/glossary/

Open-end mutual funds are the dominant type of investment company and account for well over 95% of the assets under management. All the statistics cited above, including those in Table 13.1, pertain to these types of funds. Many of these funds are very large and hold *billions* of dollars' worth of securities. Indeed, in 2003, the typical stock or bond fund held an average portfolio of some $550 million, and there were nearly 600 billion-dollar funds.

Both buy and sell transactions in (open-end) mutual funds are carried out at prices based on the current market value of all the securities held in the fund's portfolio. (Technically, this would also include the book value of any other assets, such as cash and receivables from securities transactions, that the fund might hold at the time, though for all practical purposes, these other assets generally account for only a tiny fraction of the fund's total portfolio.) Known as the fund's **net asset value (NAV),** this current market value is calculated at least once a day and represents the underlying value of a share of stock in a particular mutual fund. NAV is found by taking the total market value of all assets held by the fund, less any liabilities, and dividing this amount by the number of fund shares outstanding. For example, if the market value of all the assets held by the XYZ mutual fund on a given day equaled $10 million, and if XYZ on

net asset value (NAV)
the underlying value of a share of stock in a particular mutual fund.

When Mutual Funds Behave Badly

For the nearly 95 million Americans who own them, mutual funds were once considered a relatively safe place to invest money. That remained true until September 2003, when New York Attorney General Eliot Spitzer shook the mutual fund industry with allegations of illegal after-hours trading, special deals for large institutional investors, market timing in flagrant violation of funds' written policies, and an array of other abuses. These violations could be costing long-term fund investors billions of dollars.

Executives and portfolio managers from several industry giants, including Putnam Investments, Alliance Capital, Strong Capital, PBHG, Nations Funds, Wachovia/Prudential, and Fred Alger Management, have either resigned or now face civil and criminal charges. Several other big names in the securities industry, such as Charles Schwab, American Express, Morgan Stanley, Bank One, and Janus Capital, are either under investigation by the SEC and the New York State Attorney General's office or have decided to settle the charges of improper behavior.

Many mutual fund abuses stem from *market timing,* a practice in which short-term traders seek to exploit differences between hours of operations of various global markets. For example, when the U.S. market rallies on strong economic news, short-term traders buy shares of U.S.-based international funds with large Asian holdings just before the close of the market at 4 PM EST. Prices of these funds, often calculated between 4 and 6 PM, reflect current prices of the U.S. securities but previous-day prices of Asian-based stocks, which typically close around 2 AM. When the next-day Tokyo and other Asian markets rally following Wall Street's lead, the market timer sells shares of Asian holdings at the higher price, pocketing the profits. Most funds strictly prohibit this kind of activity, yet exceptions have been made for large institutional investors who may trade millions of dollars' worth of fund shares.

Under federal law, investors can purchase or sell shares of a mutual fund at today's price as long as the fund receives the order before 4 PM EST. Mutual fund shares bought or sold after 4 PM are priced at the next day's closing net asset value. Yet many institutional investors in the past were able to profit by placing a late order after the market close when news came out that was likely to move stocks higher or lower the next day. The investor could use this information to purchase or sell shares at the 4 PM closing price. According to regulators, this practice resembles betting on a winning horse after the horse race is over. Although *late trading* is illegal, many mutual funds did not enforce that rule for some of their privileged clients.

continued on next page

that particular day had 500,000 shares outstanding, the fund's net asset value per share would be \$20 (\$10,000,000 ÷ 500,000). This figure, as we will see, is then used to derive the price at which the fund shares are bought and sold.

closed-end investment companies
a type of investment company that operates with a fixed number of shares outstanding.

Closed-End Investment Companies Although the term *mutual fund* is supposed to be used only with open-end funds, it is also commonly used to refer to closed-end investment companies. **Closed-end investment companies** operate with a fixed number of shares outstanding, and do not regularly issue new shares of stock. In effect, they have a capital structure like that of any other corporation, except that the corporation's business happens to be investing in marketable securities. Shares in closed-end investment companies, like those of any other common stock, are actively traded in the secondary market. But

ETHICS IN INVESTING

continued from previous page

Another form of abuse involved the use of index funds for *ultra-fast computer trading* when powerful computer programs detected minuscule differences (measured in fractions of a percentage point) between the prices of index futures and underlying indexes. If the price of an index future exceeded the value of the underlying stock index, the investor could sell short an index future and simultaneously purchase the corresponding index fund. When both the index and the index future converged in price, the investor would close out the short position and sell the index fund, locking in the difference in price as profit. For an institutional investor able to commit more than $100 million on each transaction, this arbitrage activity repeated several times in a week might result in substantial profits earned almost on a risk-free basis as index and index futures prices converged each day at the market close.

The abuses did not stop there. The National Association of Securities Dealers and the SEC cracked down on widespread abuses in mutual fund sales practices that overcharged investors on sales charges, or loads. NASD estimates that at least $86 million is owed to investors for 2001 and 2002. Also, several funds closed to new investors charged their existing shareholders millions of dollars in marketing and sales fees. Some fund managers—like Gary Pilgrim of PBHG Funds, for example—not only tolerated market timing and other trading abuses but also handsomely profited from them by investing millions of dollars of their own money in the market timing schemes.

Although people's savings invested in the funds were never at stake, investors suffered losses because *these abuses resulted in higher fund expenses and trading costs as well as sub-par returns resulting from the funds' higher than necessary cash positions needed to accommodate frequent purchases and redemptions by professional traders.* These costs were borne not by the fund or its management that permitted these practices, but rather by the fund's long-term investors. However, many funds that settled with the regulators promised to reimburse the existing stockholders for losses resulting from overcharging fees or trading abuses.

CRITICAL THINKING QUESTION The SEC has proposed several regulations intended to curb mutual trading abuses. They include strict enforcement of trading hours and the imposition of 2% redemption fees if a fund is sold in less than 90 days after the purchase. Do you think this will eliminate trading abuses?

unlike open-end funds, *all trading in closed-end funds is done between investors in the open market.* The fund itself plays no role in either buy or sell transactions. Once the shares are issued, the fund is out of the picture. By far, most closed-end investment companies are traded on the New York Stock Exchange, a few are traded on the American Exchange, and occasionally some are traded in the OTC market or on some other exchange. Even so, while these shares are traded (on the NYSE, AMEX, or Nasdaq) like any other stock, their quotes are listed separately—in the *Wall Street Journal* at least. Figure 13.3 (on page 550) shows the quotes for a small sample of closed-end funds listed on the NYSE, including Gabelli Equity Trust (one of the bigger closed-end investment companies). These quotes are grouped by the exchange on which the funds are traded, and include little more than share prices and dividends.

FIGURE 13.3

Stock Quotations for Closed-End Investment Companies

The quotes for closed-end investment companies are listed separately from other common stocks. As can be seen, they provide only a minimal amount of information, including the fund's abbreviated name and symbol, the latest annual dividend, the latest closing price, and the net change in price. (*Source: Wall Street Journal*, November 18, 2003.)

CLOSED-END FUNDS

STOCK (SYM)	DIV	LAST	NET CHG
FstFnlFd **FF**	2.96e	18.20	-0.35
FstIsrael **ISL**	.35e	11.15	-0.03
FlrtyClayPfdSec **FFC** n	2.07	26.33	0.03
FlrtyPfd Income **PFD**	1.10a	17.34	0.69
FlrtyPfdIncomOp **PFO**	.88a	13.31	0.11
FlrtyClayTotRet **FLC** n	.16p	25.71	0.11
FltngRteIncoFd **FRA** n		20.19	0.19
FtDearborn **FTD**	.80	14.79	-0.04
40/86StrInco **CFD**	.94e	10.90	-0.01
FraGrthFd **FRF**		7.18	-0.19
FrnklnMulti **FMI**	.42	7.15	-0.06
FrnklnUnvlTr **FT**	.36	5.53	...
GabelliConv **GCV**	.80	10.22	0.03
GabelliConv pfB n	.78e	25.02	-0.23
GabelliTr **GAB**	.56a	7.68	-0.04
GabelliTr pfB	1.80	26.95	...
GabelliTr pfD n		24.97	0.04
GabelliMlti **GGT**		8.39	-0.09
GabelMlti pfB n	.73e	25.30	0.06
GabelliUtilTr **GUT**	.72a	9.01	-0.07
GenAmInv **GAM**	.86e	28.22	-0.37
GermanyFd **GER**	e	6.91	-0.07
NewGrmnyFd **GF**	.00e	6.67	-0.13
GlblHiInco **GHI**	1.83e	17.44	0.14

Gabelli Equity Trust (GAB) →

A closed-end fund is, in many respects, both a common stock and an investment company. As the original form of investment company, closed-end funds have enjoyed a long history that dates back to nineteenth-century England and Scotland. In the United States, closed-end funds were actively traded during the 1920s bull market, when they far outnumbered their open-end relatives. During that freewheeling era, however, they were highly leveraged and consequently were hit hard during the Crash of 1929, earning a bad reputation with investors. They remained something of an oddity for decades afterward. It wasn't until the bull market that began in the early 1980s that closed-end funds came back into fashion.

Many of the investment advisers that today run closed-end funds (like Nuveen, MFS, Eaton Vance, Dreyfus, PIMCO, and Franklin-Templeton) also manage open-end funds, often with similar investment objectives. They offer both closed- and open-end funds because they are really *two different investment products*. For although it may not appear so at first glance, there are some major differences between these two types of funds. To begin with, closed-end funds have a fixed amount of capital to work with. Therefore, they don't have to be concerned about keeping cash on hand (or readily available) to meet redemptions. Equally important, because there is no pressure on portfolio managers to cash in these securities at inopportune times, they can be more aggressive in their investment styles by investing in obscure yet attractive securities that may not be actively traded. And, of course, because they don't have new money flowing in all the time, portfolio managers don't have to worry about finding new investments. Instead, they can concentrate on a set portfolio of securities.

Of course, this also puts added pressures on the money managers, since their investment styles and fund portfolios are closely monitored and judged by the market. That is, the share prices of closed-end companies are determined not only by their net asset values but also by general supply and demand conditions in the market. As a result, depending on the market outlook and investor expectations, closed-end companies generally trade at a discount or premium to NAV. (They almost never trade at net asset value.) Share price discounts and premiums can at times become quite large. In fact, it's not unusual for such spreads to amount to as much as 25% to 30% of net asset value (occasionally more) depending on market judgments and expectations. (We'll discuss closed-end funds in more detail later in this chapter.)

Exchange-Traded Funds

Combine some of the operating characteristics of an open-end fund with some of the trading characteristics of a closed-end fund, and what you'll end up with is something called an *exchange-traded fund*. These securities are being promoted as the newest product to hit the fund world, but they're really a recreation of a product that's been around since the early 1990s. Technically, an **exchange-traded fund (ETF)** is a type of open-end mutual fund that trades as a listed security on one of the stock exchanges (mostly the AMEX). Actually, all ETFs thus far (mid-year 2003) have been structured as *index funds* set up to match the performance of a certain segment of the market. They do this by owning all, or a representative sample, of the stocks in a targeted market segment or index. (We'll examine traditional index funds in more detail later in this chapter.) Thus, ETFs offer the professional money management of traditional mutual funds *and* the liquidity of an exchange-traded stock.

exchange-traded fund (ETF) an open-end mutual fund that trades as a listed security on a stock exchange.

Even though these securities are like closed-end funds in that ETFs are traded on listed exchanges, *they are in reality open-end mutual funds,* where the number of shares outstanding can be increased or decreased in response to market demand. That is, although ETFs can be bought or sold like any stock on a listed exchange, *the ETF distributor can also create new shares or redeem old shares.* This is done through a special type of security known as a *payment-in-kind creation unit.* (Without getting into all the messy details, these units are created by exchange specialists, or so-called "authorized participants", who deposit with a trustee a portfolio, or market basket, of stocks that track an index. The authorized participant then receives from the trustee new ETF shares, on the index, to be sold in the open market. To redeem shares, the authorized participant simply turns in ETF shares in exchange for the underlying stocks.) This is all done to ensure an efficient and orderly market, and to prevent the fund shares from trading at (much of) a discount or premium, thereby avoiding one of the pitfalls of closed-end funds. Individual investors, of course, are *not* involved in the creation of these fund shares (that's handled by big institutional investors). Instead, they buy and sell ETFs in the secondary market by placing orders with their brokers, as they would normally do with any stock.

HOT

Which are the most active index shares—Nasdaq 100 index shares, SPDRs, Midcap SPDRs, or Diamonds? To find out, visit:

amex.com

By mid-2002, there were more than 100 ETFs listed on the American Stock Exchange, and all but a handful of them were based on some domestic or international stock market index. The biggest and oldest (started in 1993) are based on the S&P 500 and are known as *spiders*. In addition to spiders, there are *diamonds* (which are based on the DJIA) and *qubes* (based on the Nasdaq 100 and so-named because of their QQQ ticker symbol). There also are ETFs based on 39 international markets (from Australia and Canada to Germany, Japan, and the United Kingdom), and 8 that are based on bond measures. Just about every major U.S. index, in fact, has its own ETF. So do a lot of minor indexes (some of which were created by the distributors) that cover very specialized (and sometimes fairly small) segments of the market.

The net asset values of ETFs are set at a fraction of the underlying index value at any given time. For example, if the S&P 500 index stands at, say, 1064.46, the EFT on that index will trade at around 106.50 (that is, at about 1/10 of the index). Likewise, the ETF on the Dow is set at 1/100 of the DJIA. (Thus, when the DJIA is at say, 10449.30, the EFT will trade at around 104.50). At year-end 2002, the market value of all outstanding ETFs amounted to more than $100 billion, though just two of them, the S&P 500 spiders and Nasdaq qubes, accounted for nearly 60% of that total.

ETFs combine many of the advantages of closed-end funds with those of traditional (open-end) index funds. As with closed-end funds, you can buy and sell ETFs at *any time of the day* by placing an order through your broker (and paying a standard commission, just as you would with any other stock). In contrast, you *cannot* trade a traditional open-end fund on an intraday basis; all buy and sell orders for those funds are filled at the end of the trading day, at closing prices. What's more, because ETFs are passively managed, they offer all the advantages of any index fund: low cost, low portfolio turnover, and low taxes. In fact, the fund's tax liability is kept very low, because ETFs rarely distribute any capital gains to shareholders. Thus, you could hold one of these things for decades and never pay a dime in capital gains taxes (at least not until you sell the shares). The *Investing in Action* box on pages 554–555 provides some additional information about ETFs—information that might help you decide whether they are right for you.

Some Important Considerations

load fund
a mutual fund that charges a commission when shares are bought; also known as a *front-end load fund*.

no-load fund
a mutual fund that does not charge a commission when shares are bought.

low-load fund
a mutual fund that charges a small commission (2% to 3%) when shares are bought.

When you buy or sell shares in a *closed-end* investment company (or in *ETFs*, for that matter), you pay a commission, just as you would with any other listed or OTC stock. This is not the case with open-end mutual funds, however, as the cost of investing in an open-end fund depends on the types of fees and load charges that the fund levies on its investors.

Load and No-Load Funds The *load charge* on an open-end fund is the commission the investor pays when buying shares in a fund. Generally speaking, the term **load fund** is used to describe a mutual fund that charges a commission when shares are bought. (Such charges are also known as *front-end loads*.) In a **no-load fund** no sales charges are levied. Load charges can be fairly substantial and can amount to as much as 8½% of the *purchase price* of the shares. However, very few funds charge the maximum. Instead, many funds charge commissions of only 2% or 3%. Such funds are known as **low-load funds.**

Although there may be little or no difference in the performance of load and no-load funds, *the cost savings with no-load funds tend to give investors a head start in achieving superior rates of return.* Unfortunately, the true no-load fund is becoming harder to find, as more and more no-loads are becoming *12(b)-1 funds.* While these funds do not directly charge commissions at the time of purchase, they *annually* assess what are known as 12(b)-1 charges to make up for any lost commissions. (These charges are more fully described below.) Overall, less than 30% of the funds sold today are pure no-loads; the rest charge some type of load or fee.

back-end load
a commission charged on the *sale* of shares in a mutual fund.

12(b)-1 fee
a fee levied annually by many mutual funds to cover management and other operating costs; amounts to as much as 1% of the average net assets.

Occasionally, a fund will have a **back-end load,** which means commissions are levied when shares are sold. These loads may amount to as much as 7¼% of the value of the shares sold, although back-end loads tend to decline over time and usually disappear altogether after 5 or 6 years from date of purchase. The stated purpose of back-end loads is to enhance fund stability by discouraging investors from trading in and out of the funds over short investment horizons. In addition, a substantial (and growing) number of funds charge something called a **12(b)-1 fee** that's assessed annually for as long as you own the fund. Known appropriately as *hidden loads,* these fees are designed to help funds (particularly the no-loads) cover their distribution and marketing costs. They can amount to as much as 1% per year of assets under management. In good markets and bad, these fees are paid right off the top, and that can take its toll. Consider, for instance, $10,000 invested in a fund that charges a 1% 12(b)-1 fee. That translates into a charge of $100 per year—certainly not an insignificant amount of money.

The latest trend in mutual fund fees is the so-called *multiple-class sales charge.* You'll find such arrangements at firms like Dreyfus, Merrill Lynch, MFS, Evergreen, Franklin/Templeton, Scudder, and Putnam. The mutual fund simply issues different classes of stocks on the same portfolio of securities, with each class having a different fee structure. For example, class A shares might have normal front-end loads; class B shares might have no front-end loads but substantial back-end loads along with maximum annual 12(b)-1 fees; and class C shares might carry only 12(b)-1 fees of up to 1% per year. In other words, you "choose your own poison."

To try to bring some semblance of order to fund charges and fees, in 1992 the SEC instituted a series of caps on mutual fund fees. Under the 1992 rules, a mutual fund cannot charge more than 8½% in *total sales charges and fees,* including front- and back-end loads as well as 12(b)-1 fees. Thus, if a fund charges a 5% front-end load and a 1% 12(b)-1 fee, it can charge a maximum of only 2½% in back-end load charges without violating the 8½% cap. In addition, the SEC set a 1% cap on annual 12(b)-1 fees and, perhaps more significantly, stated that true no-load funds cannot charge more than 0.25% in annual 12(b)-1 fees. If they do, they have to drop the no-load label in their sales and promotional material.

INVESTOR FACTS

THE ABC's OF FUND FEES—
A shares, B shares, C shares—what's an investor to do? Here's a guide to use in deciding which type of mutual fund share is best for you.

1. **A shares**: Usually involve modest front-end load charges and perhaps a small 12(b)-1 fee (typically 0.25%). *These shares usually make the most sense for long-term investors.*
2. **B shares**: Normally have substantial back-end loads for a period of up to 6 years, plus maximum 12(b)-1 fees of 1% per year. The lack of a front-end load make them look attractive to investors, but the fact is *most investors should steer clear of them—they are a bad deal!*
3. **C shares**: Usually a small back-end load if you sell within a year, plus a 12(b)-1 fee of up to 1%. *These shares are normally a better deal than B shares.*

Bottom line: If you're a long-term investor, go for the A shares; if not, go for the C shares.

Other Fees and Costs Another cost of owning mutual funds is the *management fee.* This is the compensation paid to the professional managers who administer the fund's portfolio. It must be paid regardless of whether a fund is load or no-load, and whether it is an open- or closed-end fund, or an exchange-traded fund. Unlike load charges, which are one-time costs, management fees and 12(b)-1 charges, if imposed, are levied annually. They are paid

INVESTING IN ACTION

ADDING ETFs TO YOUR INVESTMENT PORTFOLIO

Want to buy some diamonds? Or maybe spiders or qubes are more your style. These exchange-traded funds (ETFs) are similar to index mutual funds but trade like stocks. Each share represents a basket of securities that closely tracks one specific index. Investors can choose from about 120 different types of ETFs that trade on the American Stock Exchange. They include diamonds, a basket of the Dow Jones Industrial Average stocks; spiders (SPDRS), S&P 500 Depository Receipts; qubes (QQQs), a basket of Nasdaq 100 Index stocks; and even bond ETFs, that track the Lehman Brothers and other bond indexes. New ETFs are introduced regularly; two recent offerings targeted Treasury Inflation-Protected Securities and the 50 highest dividend-yielding stocks in the Dow averages.

Because ETFs trade on the stock market, it's easy to buy and sell them through a brokerage account during the entire day—not just after the markets close, as with mutual funds. ETFs also have extremely low costs because they have no research or management fees and minimal back-office costs. "Basically, a computer manages the ETF fund rather than some $5 million-a-year portfolio manager," says Jeff Seely, chief executive officer of the Seattle online brokerage ShareBuilder Securities Corporation. For example, annual expenses for SPDRS are just 0.11%, well below the 1.4% fee charged by the average actively managed mutual fund. Another benefit comes from their tax status. Because they are not actively managed, ETFs have minimal turnover and generate little or no taxable income and capital gains distributions. Investors do not incur a tax liability until they sell the ETF at a profit.

Performance has been attractive as well, helped by ETFs' low expense ratios. ETFs that track broad stock indexes, such as the S&P 500, the DJIA, or the Wilshire 5000, have generally achieved higher returns than about 75% of actively managed funds.

ETFs do have some drawbacks, however. While fees are low, investors incur brokerage commissions when they trade ETFs, as well as a small bid/ask spread. Frequent trades can quickly wipe out any profits. ETFs do not offer dividend reinvestment or monthly investment programs. And, whereas traditional mutual funds can reinvest dividends and capital gains immediately to continuously compound their gains, ETFs can reinvest the cash only monthly or quarterly.

Despite the downside, ETFs provide investors with a quick way to get exposure to a market

continued on next page

regardless of the fund's performance. In addition, there are the administrative costs of operating the fund. These are fairly modest and represent the normal cost of doing business (e.g., the commissions paid when the fund buys and sells securities). The various fees that funds charge generally range from less than 0.5% to as much as 3% or 4% of average assets under management. Total expense ratios bear watching, because high expenses take their toll on performance. As a point of reference, in 2003, domestic stock funds had average expense ratios of around 1.50%, foreign stock funds of around 1.90%, stock index funds of around 0.70%, and domestic bond funds of around 1.10%. In addition to these management fees, some funds may charge an *exchange fee*, assessed whenever an investor transfers money from one fund to another within the same fund family, and/or an *annual maintenance fee*, to help defer the costs of providing service to low-balance accounts.

A final cost of mutual funds is the taxes paid on securities transactions. To avoid double taxation, nearly all mutual funds operate as *regulated investment*

INVESTING IN ACTION

continued from previous page

segment. They offer diversification and precise market tracking, and they appeal to both active traders and long-term investors. It's easy to add a specific equity component based on one of the following factors:

- **Style**: Choose an ETF that tracks a growth or value index such as the S&P 400 Mid Cap Barra Growth or the S&P 600 Small Cap Value.
- **Size**: Market capitalization is another ETF segmentation strategy. You will find ETFs that track small-, mid-, and large-cap companies, using the S&P, Dow, Nasdaq, and Russell indexes.
- **Sector**: Many ETFs, including Barclays' iShares and Merrill Lynch's HOLDRS, target specific industries or sectors such as biotechnology, real estate investment trusts, pharmaceuticals, telecommunications, health care, energy, noncyclical companies, and subsectors of the Internet industry. They offer exposure to a small part of an industry that mutual funds may not cover, yet broader coverage than an investor would gain by buying several individual stocks.
- **Region**: ETFs make it easy to achieve geographical diversification, whether for just one country or an entire region, without the high loads and fees imposed by most foreign stock funds. Examples include Barclays' iShares, such as the Webs (World Equity Benchmark shares) that track the Morgan Stanley Capital International (MSCI) indexes for 20 countries, and regional ETFs that track the S&P Europe 350 and Global 100 and MSCI European Monetary Union. However, international index funds are a less costly way to get broad exposure.

Investors can track ETF total returns and compare them to the returns for traditional mutual funds in similar sectors at Morningstar.com (www.morningstar.com) and with the *Wall Street Journal*'s monthly Mutual Fund Report.

CRITICAL THINKING QUESTIONS What are four ways of structuring exchange-traded funds? What investment advantages do ETFs offer?

Sources: Jeff Brown, "Exchange-Traded Funds Can Be Gentle Alternative to Mutual Funds," *Philadelphia Enquirer*, December 9, 2003, downloaded from www.infotrac.com; Bill Deener, "Exchange-Traded Funds Remain Worth a Look for Investors," *Dallas Morning News*, December 1, 2003, downloaded from www.infotrac.com; Christopher J. Traulsen, "Four New ETFs on Tap," *Morningstar.com*, August 28, 2003, downloaded from www.morningstar.com; and "What Are iShares," *iShares*, www.ishares.com, downloaded December 10, 2003.

companies. This means that all (or nearly all) of the dividend and interest income is passed on to the investor, as are any capital gains realized when securities are sold. The mutual fund therefore passes the tax liability on to its shareholders. This holds true whether such distributions are reinvested in the company (in the form of additional mutual fund shares) or paid out in cash. Mutual funds annually provide each stockholder with a summary report on the amount of dividends and capital gains received and the amount of taxable income earned by the fund shareholder.

Keeping Track of Fund Fees and Loads Critics of the mutual fund industry have come down hard on the proliferation of fund fees and charges. Some argue that the different charges and fees are meant to do one thing: Confuse the investor. A lot of funds were going to great lengths (lowering a cost here, tacking on a fee there, hiding a charge somewhere else) to make themselves look like something they weren't. The funds were following the letter of the law, and were fully disclosing all their expenses and fees. The trouble was that the funds were able to hide all but the most conspicuous charges in "legalese." Fortunately, steps have been taken to bring fund fees and loads out into the open.

HOT LINKS

Study the impact of load, expense ratio, 12(b)-1 fee, and taxes on fund performance at:

www.smartmoney.com/fundfeeanalyzer/

For one thing, fund charges are more widely reported now than they were in past. Most notably, today you can find detailed information about the types and amounts of fees and charges on just about any mutual fund by accessing a variety of Web sites, such as www.quicken.com/investments/mutualfunds, www.kiplinger.com/investing/funds/, or www.morningstar.com/Funds/. Figure 13.4 provides excerpts from one of these sites and shows the kind of information that's readily available, at no charge, on the Web.

Alternatively, you can use the mutual fund quotes that appear daily in most major, large-city newspapers or in the *Wall Street Journal.* For example, look at the *Wall Street Journal* quotations in Figure 13.5 (on page 558). Note the use of the letters *r, p,* and *t* behind the name of the fund. An *r* behind a fund's name means that the fund charges some type of redemption fee, or back-end load, when you sell your shares. This is the case, for example, with the Fidelity Aggressive Growth Fund. A *p* in the quotes means that the fund levies a 12(b)-1 fee, which you'll have to pay, for example, if you invest in the Diversified Equity Growth Fund. Finally, a *t* indicates funds that charge both redemption fees and 12(b)-1 fees. Note, for example, that the Cohen & Steers Equity Income Fund is one such fund.

The quotations, of course, tell you only the *kinds* of fees charged by the funds. They do not tell you *how much* is charged. To get the specifics on the amount charged, you'll have to turn to other sources. Furthermore, these published quotes (which are fairly representative of what you'd find in other major newspapers) *tell you nothing about the front-end loads,* if any, charged by the funds. Refer once again to the quotes in Figure 13.5, and compare the Dodge & Cox Balanced and FPA Paramount Funds. They look alike, don't they? But they're not. For even though neither of them charges redemption or 12(b)-1 fees, only one of them is a no-load fund. Dodge & Cox does not charge a front-end load, and is in fact a no-load fund. The FPA fund, in contrast, comes with a hefty 5¼% front-end load. As a point of interest, the other three funds highlighted in Figure 13.5—Cohen & Steers Equity Income, Diversified Equity Growth, and Fidelity Aggressive Growth—don't charge front-end loads either, but you'd never know that from the quotes. (It should be noted that the *Wall Street Journal* also publishes a *Monthly Mutual Fund Review* on the first or second Monday of each month. Among other things, it provides some specifics on front-end loads and annual expense charges, including 12(b)-1 fees.)

In addition to the public sources noted above, the mutual funds themselves are required by the SEC to fully disclose all of their fees and expenses in a standardized, easy-to-understand format. Every fund profile or prospectus must contain, up front, a fairly detailed *fee table,* much like the one illustrated in Table 13.2 (on page 559). This table has three parts. The first specifies *all shareholder transaction costs.* In effect, this tells you what it's going to cost to buy and sell shares in the mutual fund. The next section lists the *annual operating expenses* of the fund. Showing these expenses as a percentage of average net assets, the fund must break out management fees, 12(b)-1 fees, and any

FIGURE 13.4 Fund Fees and Charges on the Web

The Internet has become the motherlode of information on just about any topic imaginable, including mutual fund fees and charges. Here's an example of information taken from the Morningstar Web site. These excerpts show, among other things, all the fees and expenses levied by each fund. The two funds in the exhibit provide a stark contrast in fees and expenses. The A shares for the PF Putnam Equity Income fund carry both a high (5½%) front-end load and a ½% 12(b)-1 fee, along with a substantial total management fee/expense ratio (of 1.90%). The Vanguard Small Cap Index fund, on the other hand, provides a vivid example of a truly low-cost fund: no loads or fees and a *very low* total management fee/expense ratio (of 0.27%). (*Source:* www.morningstar.com/fund/fees, November 18, 2003. © 2003 Morningstar, Inc. Used with permission.)

MORNINGSTAR.com

PF Putnam Equity Income A(PFAEX)

Fees and Expenses

Maximum Sales Fees %		**Total Cost Projections**	Cost per $10,000
Initial	5.50	3-Year	$1114
Deferred	None	5-Year	$
Redemption	None	10-Year	$

Maximum Fees %		**Actual Fees %**	
Administrative	0.00	12b-1	0.50
Management	0.95	Management	0.95
12b-1	0.50	Total Expense Ratio (03-31-03)	1.90
		(Category Average)	1.40

Vanguard Small Cap Index (NAESX)

Fees and Expenses

Maximum Sales Fees %		**Total Cost Projections**	Cost per $10,000
Initial	None	3-Year	$87
Deferred	None	5-Year	$152
Redemption	None	10-Year	$343

Maximum Fees %		**Actual Fees %**	
Administrative	0.00	12b-1	0.00
Management	0.24	Management	0.24
12b-1	0.00	Total Expense Ratio (12-31-02)	0.27
		(Category Average)	1.57

other expenses. The third section provides a rundown of *the total cost over time* of buying, selling, and owning the fund. This part of the table contains both transaction and operating expenses and shows what the total costs would be over hypothetical 1-, 3-, 5-, and 10-year holding periods. To ensure consistency and comparability, the funds must follow a rigid set of guidelines when constructing the illustrative costs.

FIGURE 13.5

Mutual Fund Quotes

Open-end mutual funds are listed separately from other securities. They have their own quotation system, an example of which, from the *Wall Street Journal*, is shown here. Note that these securities are quoted in dollars and cents and that the quotes include not only the fund's NAV but year-to-date (YTD) and 3-year returns as well. Also included is an indication of whether the fund charges redemption and/or 12(b)-1 fees. (*Source: Wall Street Journal*, November 18, 2003.)

Mutual Fund Quotations

FUND	NAV	NET CHG	YTD %RET	3-YR %RET
Citizens Funds				
CitCGSt p	17.80	-0.15	18.7	-13.5
CitEmGrSt	12.39	-0.13	27.3	-18.5
CitGblSt	14.47	-0.17	13.4	-15.8
Clipper	84.50	-0.45	11.6	8.4
Cohen & Steers				
EqIncA p	14.14	-0.02	29.5	19.6
EqIncB t	13.73	-0.02	28.8	18.8
EqIncC t	13.73	-0.02	28.8	18.8
InstlRlty	37.44	-0.09	32.5	16.0
RltyShrs	55.47	-0.14	32.6	15.8
Colo Bonds	9.32	...	5.7	6.7
Diversified Funds				
AggrEq p	11.16	-0.13	24.4	-16.3
Balance p	13.12	-0.06	12.3	-2.1
CoreBond p	12.82	0.02	3.7	7.3
EqGrow p	17.14	-0.11	20.7	-12.0
Gro&Inc p	16.51	-0.10	16.1	-13.4
HiQual p	11.80	0.01	1.5	5.5
HiYldBd p	9.38	0.01	23.1	9.5
InLHorSA	10.74	-0.05	15.5	-1.8
IntGvt p	11.35	0.01	0.8	5.6
IntHorSA	10.77	-0.04	12.2	0.7
IntlEq p	12.30	-0.23	22.3	-6.7
LgHorSA	9.00	-0.07	18.1	-5.9
SpecEq p	22.65	-0.30	37.6	1.2
StHorSA	11.01	0.01	5.5	5.5
StkIdx p	8.15	-0.05	19.8	-7.8
Val&Inc p	20.87	-0.13	17.0	0.6
Dodge & Cox				
Balanced	69.99	-0.43	17.6	10.2
Income	12.95	0.03	5.1	9.6
Intl Stk	21.50	-0.46	36.0	NS
Stock	106.41	-0.99	22.5	9.2
FFTW Funds				
LtdDur	10.05	0.01	2.2	5.8
US Sht	9.44x	...	1.3	2.7
WWFxdIn	9.90	0.01	8.8	10.0
FMI CommonStock	21.20	-0.09	17.8	13.1
FMI FocusFd	31.60	-0.32	37.6	2.5
FPA Funds				
Capit	35.25	-0.61	31.2	20.3
FPACres	20.96	-0.14	20.9	21.5
NwInc	11.26	-0.01	6.9	8.6
Parmt	11.82	-0.13	39.1	16.7
Peren	27.80	-0.25	36.2	16.7
Fidelity Invest				
A Mgr	15.24	-0.04	12.5	-0.4
AggrGr r	14.24	-0.17	27.3	-29.1
AggrInt	13.93	-0.30	29.8	0.3
AMgrAggr	9.64	-0.13	39.1	-8.9
AMgrGr	13.82	-0.07	15.5	-3.4
AMgrIn	12.01	-0.03	12.6	4.6
Balanc	15.99	-0.10	21.8	4.9
BluCh	37.62	-0.24	18.2	-11.6
Canad r	25.28	-0.12	39.5	8.6
CapAp	22.79	-0.32	40.9	0.3
ChinaReg	14.96	-0.21	37.8	1.3

NAV: The price you get when you *sell* shares, or what you pay when you *buy* no-load funds.

Cohen & Steers Equity Income: A fund with both a redemption fee and a 12(b)-1 fee (t).

Diversified Equity Growth: A fund with a 12(b)-1 fee (p).

Dodge & Cox Blanced: A true no-load fund (no front-end, back-end, or 12(b)-1 fees).

FPA Paramount: A fund with a $5^1/_4$% front-end load, but no redemption or 12(b)-1 fees.

Fidelity Aggressive Growth: A fund with a redemption fee (r).

TABLE 13.2 Mutual Fund Fee Table (Required by Federal Law)

The following table describes the fees and expenses that are incurred when you buy, hold, or sell shares of the fund.

Shareholder Fees (paid by the investor directly)	
Maximum sales charge (load) on purchases (as a % of offering price)	3%
Sales charge (load) on reinvested distributions	None
Deferred sales charge (load) on redemptions	None
Exchange fees	None
Annual account maintenance fee (for accounts under $2,500)	$12.00
Annual fund operating expenses (paid from fund assets)	
Management fee	0.45%
Distribution and service (12b-1) fee	None
Other expenses	0.20%
Total annual fund operating expenses	0.65%

Example

This example is intended to help an investor compare the cost of investing in different funds. The example assumes a $10,000 investment in the fund for one, three, five, and ten years and then a redemption of all fund shares at the end of those periods. The example also assumes that an investment returns 5 percent each year and that the fund's operating expenses remain the same. Although actual costs may be higher or lower, based on these assumptions an investor's costs would be:

1 year	$364
3 years	$502
5 years	$651
10 years	$1,086

Other Types of Investment Companies

In addition to open-end, closed-end, and exchange-traded funds, there are four other types of investment companies: (1) unit investment trusts, (2) real estate investment trusts, (3) annuities, and (4) hedge funds. Unit investment trusts, annuities, and hedge funds are similar to mutual funds to the extent that they, too, invest primarily in marketable securities, such as stocks and bonds. Real estate investment trusts, in contrast, invest primarily in various types of real estate–related investments, like mortgages. We'll look at unit investment trusts and hedge funds in this section. The other two types of investment companies are discussed in detail at the book's Web site.

HOT

For a detailed discussion of two other types of investment companies—real estate investment trusts and annuities—see our Web site, at:

www.aw-bc.com/gitman_joehnk

unit investment trust (UIT)
a type of investment vehicle whereby the trust sponsors put together a fixed/unmanaged portfolio of securities and then sell ownership units in the portfolio to individual investors.

Unit Investment Trusts A **unit investment trust** (UIT) represents little more than an interest in an *unmanaged* pool of investments. UITs are like mutual funds to the extent that they involve a portfolio of securities. But that's where the similarity ends. Once a portfolio of securities is put together, it is simply held in safekeeping for investors under conditions set down in a trust agreement. Traditionally, these portfolios were made up of various types of *fixed-income securities*, with long-term municipal bonds being the most popular type of investment vehicle. There is no trading in the portfolios, so the returns, or yields, are fixed and fairly predictable—at least for the short term. Not surprisingly, these unit investment trusts appeal mainly to income-oriented investors looking for a safe, steady stream of income.

At year-end 1990, taxable and tax-free bond trusts accounted for about 95% of total UIT assets outstanding. About this time, however, brokerage firms began aggressively marketing a new type of investment product—the *stock-oriented UIT*. These new equity trusts caught on quickly and by year-end 1999, accounted for about 65% of the $90 billion UIT market. But then the 2000–2002 bear market hit. Not surprisingly, these products quickly fell out of favor. Indeed, by 2002, equity trusts outstanding fell to $14.6 billion and represented just 40% of the total market—which by then had also fallen, to only $36 billion. Except for the shorter terms (1 to 5 years for equity trusts versus 15 to 30 years for fixed-income products), these trusts are no different from the traditional bond-oriented UITs: Once the portfolios are put together, they usually remain untouched for the life of the trust.

Various sponsoring brokerage houses put together these pools of securities and then sell units of the pool to investors. (Each unit is like a share in a mutual fund.) For example, a brokerage house might put together a pool of corporate securities that amounts to, say, $100 million. The sponsoring firm would then sell units in this pool to the investing public at anywhere from $250 (for many equity trusts) to $1,000 per unit (common for fixed-income products). The sponsoring organization does little more than routine record-keeping. It services the investments by collecting coupons or dividends and distributing the income (often on a monthly basis) to the holders of the trust units.

hedge fund
a type of unregulated investment vehicle that invests money for a very select group of institutional and high-net-worth individual investors; the investment objectives usually are to not only preserve capital, but also deliver positive returns in all market conditions.

Hedge Funds First of all, in spite of the name similarities, it is important to understand that hedge funds are *not* mutual funds. They are totally different types of investment products! **Hedge funds** are set up as private entities, usually in the form of *limited partnerships* and, as such, are *largely unregulated*. The *general partner* runs the fund and directly participates in the fund's profits—often taking an "incentive fee" of 10–20% of the profits, in addition to a base fee of 1–2% of assets under management. The *limited partners are the investors* and consist mainly of institutions, such as pension funds, endowments, and private banks, as well as high-income individual investors. Because hedge funds are unregulated, they can be sold only to "accredited investors," meaning the individual investor must have a net worth in excess of $1 million and/or an annual income (from qualified sources) of at least $200,000 to $300,000. Many hedge funds are, by choice, even more restrictive and limit their investors to only *very*-high-net-worth individuals; in addition, some hedge funds limit the number of investors they'll let in (often to no more than 100 investors).

These practices, of course, stand in stark contrast to the way mutual funds perform. That is, while hedge funds are largely unregulated, mutual funds are very highly regulated and monitored. In addition, individuals don't need to qualify or be accredited to invest in mutual funds. Although some mutual funds do have minimum investments of $50,000 to $100,000 or more, they are the exception rather than the rule. Not so with hedge funds—many of them have minimum investments that can run into the millions of dollars! Also, mutual fund performance is open for all to see, whereas hedge funds simply don't divulge such information, at least not to the general public. Indeed, mutual funds are required by law to provide certain periodic and standardized pricing and valuation information to investors, as well as the general public, while hedge funds are totally free from such requirements. Try to get a price quote or a public report on a hedge fund and you're likely to run into a brick wall—that world (of hedge funds) is very secretive and about as *non-transparent* as you can get.

Hedge funds and mutual funds are similar in one respect, however: Both are pooled investment vehicles that accept investors' money and invest those funds on a collective basis. Put another way, *both sell shares (or participation) in a professionally managed portfolio of securities.* Most hedge funds structure their portfolios so as to reduce volatility and risk, while trying to preserve capital (i.e., "hedge" against market downturns) and still deliver positive returns under different market conditions. They do so by taking often very complex market positions that involve both long and short positions, the use of various arbitrage strategies (to lock in profits), as well as the use of options, futures, and other derivative securities. Indeed, hedge funds will invest in almost any opportunity in almost any market so long as impressive gains are believed to be available at reasonable levels of risk. Thus, these funds are anything but low-risk, fairly stable investment vehicles. In 2002, it was *estimated* (because hedge funds are largely unregulated, no accurate records are available) that there were approximately 4,200 hedge funds in existence, which in total had about $550 billion under management.

IN REVIEW

CONCEPTS

13.1 What is a *mutual fund?* Discuss the mutual fund concept, including the importance of diversification and professional management.

13.2 What are the attractions and drawbacks of mutual fund ownership?

13.3 Briefly describe how a mutual fund is organized. Who are the key players in a typical mutual fund organization?

13.4 Define each of the following:

a. Open-end investment companies
b. Closed-end investment companies
c. Exchange-traded funds
d. Unit investment trusts
e. Hedge funds

13.5 What is the difference between a *load fund* and a *no-load fund?* What are the advantages of each type? What is a 12(b)-1 fund? Can such a fund operate as a no-load fund?

13.6 Describe a *back-end load,* a *low load,* and a *hidden load.* How can you tell what kind of fees and charges a fund has?

Types of Funds and Services

LG 3 LG 4

Some mutual funds specialize in stocks, others in bonds. Some have maximum capital gains as an investment objective, some high current income. Some funds appeal to speculators, others are of interest primarily to income-oriented investors. Every fund has a particular investment objective, and each fund is expected to do its best to conform to its stated investment policy and objective. Categorizing funds according to their investment policies and objectives is a common practice in the mutual fund industry. The categories indicate similarities in how the funds manage their money, and also their risk and return characteristics. Some of the more popular types of mutual funds are growth, aggressive growth, value, equity-income, balanced, growth-and-income, bond, money market, index, sector, socially responsible, asset allocation, and international funds.

Of course, it's possible to define fund categories based on something other than stated investment objectives. For example, Morningstar, the industry's leading research and reporting service, has developed *a classification system based on a fund's portfolio position*. Essentially, the firm carefully evaluates the make-up of a fund's portfolio to determine where its security holdings are concentrated. It then uses that information to classify funds on the basis of investment style (growth, value, or blend), market segment (small-, mid-, or large-cap), or other factors. Such information has been found to be especially useful in helping *mutual fund investors make informed asset allocation decisions* when structuring or rebalancing their own portfolios. That benefit notwithstanding, let's stick with the investment-objective classification system noted above, and examine the various types of mutual funds to see what they are and how they operate.

Types of Mutual Funds

growth fund
a mutual fund whose primary goals are capital gains and long-term growth.

Growth Funds The objective of a **growth fund** is simple: capital appreciation. Long-term growth and capital gains are the primary goals. Growth funds invest principally in well-established, large- or mid-cap companies that have above-average growth potential. They may offer little (if anything) in the way of dividends and current income. Because of the uncertain nature of their investment income, growth funds may involve a fair amount of risk exposure. They are usually viewed as long-term investment vehicles most suitable for the more aggressive investor who wants to build up capital and has little interest in current income.

aggressive growth fund
a highly speculative mutual fund that seeks large profits from capital gains.

Aggressive Growth Funds Aggressive growth funds are the so-called performance funds that tend to increase in popularity when markets heat up. **Aggressive growth funds** are highly speculative investment vehicles that seek large profits from capital gains. Most are fairly small (60% of these funds have assets under management of less than $50 million), and their portfolios consist mainly of "high-flying" common stocks. These funds often buy stocks of small, unseasoned companies, stocks with relatively high price/earnings multiples, and common stocks whose prices are highly volatile. They seem to be especially fond of turnaround situations and may even use leverage in their portfolios (i.e., buy stocks on margin); they also use options fairly aggressively, various hedging techniques, and perhaps even short selling. These techniques are designed, of course, to yield big returns. But aggressive funds are also highly speculative and are among the most volatile of all mutual funds. When the markets are good, aggressive growth funds do well; conversely, when the markets are bad, these funds often experience substantial losses.

value fund
a mutual fund that seeks stocks that are undervalued in the market by investing in shares that have low P/E multiples, high dividend yields, and promising futures.

Value Funds **Value funds** confine their investing to stocks considered to be *undervalued* by the market. That is, the funds look for stocks that are fundamentally sound but have yet to be discovered. These funds hold stocks as much for their underlying intrinsic value as for their *growth potential*. In stark contrast to growth funds, value funds look for stocks with relatively low price/earnings ratios, high dividend yields, and moderate amounts of financial leverage. They prefer undiscovered companies that offer the potential for growth, rather than those that are already experiencing rapid growth.

HOT LINKS

For more information on fund objectives, go to the sites below and read the sections on investment strategy.

www.fool.com/school/mutualfunds/basic/read.htm
www.wachovia.com/misc/0,,133,00.html
www.axaonline.com/rs/3p/sp/5058.html

Value investing is not easy. It involves extensive evaluation of corporate financial statements and any other documents that will help fund managers uncover value (investment opportunities) *before the rest of the market does* (that's the key to the low P/Es). And the approach seems to work. For even though value investing is generally regarded as *less risky* than growth investing (lower P/Es, higher dividend yields, and fundamentally stronger companies all translate into reduced risk exposure), the long-term return to investors in value funds is competitive with that from growth funds and even aggressive growth funds. Thus, value funds are often viewed as a viable investment alternative for relatively conservative investors who are looking for the attractive returns that common stocks have to offer, yet want to keep share price volatility and investment risk in check.

equity-income fund
a mutual fund that emphasizes current income and capital preservation and invests primarily in high-yielding common stocks.

Equity-Income Funds **Equity-income funds** emphasize current income by investing primarily in high-yielding common stocks. Capital preservation is also important, and so are capital gains, although capital appreciation is not a primary objective of equity-income funds. These funds invest heavily in high-grade common stocks, some convertible securities and preferred stocks, and occasionally even junk bonds or certain types of high-grade foreign bonds. As far as their stock holdings are concerned, they lean heavily toward blue chips (including perhaps even "baby blues"), public utilities, and financial shares. They like securities that generate hefty dividend yields but also consider potential price appreciation over the longer haul. In general, because of their emphasis on dividends and current income, these funds tend to hold higher-quality securities that are subject to less price volatility than the market as a whole. They're generally viewed as a fairly low-risk way of investing in stocks.

balanced fund
a mutual fund whose objective is to generate a balanced return of both current income and long-term capital gains.

Balanced Funds **Balanced funds** tend to hold a balanced portfolio of both stocks and bonds for the purpose of generating a well-balanced return of both current income and long-term capital gains. In many respects, they're much like equity-income funds, but balanced funds usually put more into fixed-income securities; generally, they keep at least 25% to 50% of their portfolios in bonds. The bonds are used principally to provide current income, and stocks are selected mainly for their long-term growth potential.

The funds can, of course, shift the emphasis in their security holdings one way or the other. Clearly, the more the fund leans toward fixed-income securities, the more income-oriented it will be. For the most part, balanced funds tend to confine their investing to high-grade securities, including growth-oriented blue-chip stocks, high-quality income shares, and high-yielding investment-grade bonds. Balanced funds are usually considered a relatively safe form of investing, in which you can earn a competitive rate of return without having to endure a lot of price volatility. (*Note:* Equity-income funds and the more income-oriented balanced funds, as well as certain types of bond funds, are sometimes all lumped together and referred to as *income funds*, because of their emphasis on generating high levels of current income.)

growth-and-income fund
a mutual fund that seeks both long-term growth and current income, with primary emphasis on capital gains.

Growth-and-Income Funds Growth-and-income funds also seek a balanced return made up of both current income and long-term capital gains, but they place a greater emphasis on growth of capital. Unlike balanced funds, growth-and-income funds put most of their money into equities. In fact, it's not unusual for these funds to have 80% to 90% of their capital in common stocks. They tend to confine most of their investing to quality issues, so growth-oriented blue-chip stocks appear in their portfolios, along with a fair amount of high-quality income stocks. Part of the appeal of these funds is the fairly substantial returns many have generated over the long haul. Of course, these funds involve a fair amount of risk, if for no other reason than the emphasis they place on stocks and capital gains. Thus growth-and-income funds are most suitable for those investors who can tolerate the risk and price volatility.

bond fund
a mutual fund that invests in various kinds and grades of bonds, with income as the primary objective.

Bond Funds As the name implies, **bond funds** invest exclusively in various types and grades of bonds—from Treasury and agency bonds to corporates and municipals. Income is the primary investment objective, although capital gains are not ignored. There are three important advantages to buying shares in bond funds rather than investing directly in bonds. First, the bond funds are generally more liquid than direct investments in bonds. Second, they offer a cost-effective way of achieving a high degree of diversification in an otherwise expensive investment vehicle. (Most bonds carry minimum denominations of $1,000 to $5,000.) Third, bond funds will automatically reinvest interest and other income, thereby allowing the investor to earn fully compounded rates of return.

Bond funds are generally considered to be a fairly conservative form of investment. But they are not without risk; that's because *the prices of the bonds held in the fund's portfolio fluctuate with changing interest rates.* Many bond funds are managed pretty conservatively, but a growing number are becoming increasingly aggressive. In fact, a lot of the growth that bond funds have experienced recently can be attributed to this more active investment posture. Some of that growth, however, can also be traced to the 2000–2002 bear market in stocks. During that time investors drew a lot of their money out of stocks and put it into safer and higher-yielding bonds. Indeed, from year-end 1999 to year-end 2002, the amount of assets under management in bond funds grew from some $800 billion (or 12% of total mutual fund assets) to more than $1.1 trillion (nearly 18% of total assets).

In today's market, investors can find everything from high-grade government bond funds to highly speculative funds that invest in nothing but junk bonds or even in highly volatile derivative securities. Here's a list of the different types of domestic bond funds available to investors:

- *Government bond funds,* which invest in U.S. Treasury and agency securities.
- *Mortgage-backed bond funds,* which put their money into various types of mortgage-backed securities of the U.S. government (e.g., GNMA issues). These funds appeal to investors for several reasons: (1) They provide diversification. (2) They are an affordable way to get into mortgage-backed securities. (3) They allow investors (if they so choose) to reinvest the principal portion of the monthly cash flow, thereby enabling them to preserve rather than consume their capital.
- *High-grade corporate bond funds,* which invest chiefly in investment-grade securities rated triple-B or better.

- *High-yield corporate bond funds,* which are risky investments that buy junk bonds for the yields they offer.
- *Convertible bond funds,* which invest primarily in securities (domestic and possibly foreign) that can be converted or exchanged into common stocks. These funds offer investors some of the price stability of bonds, along with the capital appreciation potential of stocks.
- *Municipal bond funds,* which invest in tax-exempt securities and are suitable for investors who seek tax-free income. Like their corporate counterparts, municipal funds can be packaged as either high-grade or high-yield funds. A special type of municipal bond fund is the so-called *single-state fund,* which invests in the municipal issues of only one state, thus producing (for residents of that state) interest income that is *fully exempt* from both federal and state taxes (and possibly even local/city taxes as well).
- *Intermediate-term bond funds,* which invest in bonds with maturities of 7 to 10 years or less and offer not only attractive yields but relatively low price volatility as well. Shorter (2- to 5-year) funds are also available; these shorter-term funds are often used as substitutes for money market investments by investors looking for higher returns on their money, especially when short-term rates are way down.

Clearly, no matter what you're looking for in a fixed-income security, you're likely to find a bond fund that fits the bill. The number and variety of such funds have skyrocketed in the past 15 years or so, and by mid-2003, there were over 2,000 publicly traded bond funds that together had more than $1.1 *trillion* worth of bonds under management.

money market mutual fund (money fund)
a mutual fund that pools the capital of investors and uses it to invest in short-term money market instruments.

Money Market Funds The first **money market mutual fund,** or **money fund** for short, was set up in November 1972 with just $100,000 in total assets. It was a new idea that applied the mutual fund concept to the buying and selling of short-term money market instruments—bank certificates of deposit, U.S. Treasury bills, and the like. For the first time, investors with modest amounts of capital were given access to the high-yielding money market, where many instruments require minimum investments of $100,000 or more. The idea caught on quickly, and the growth in money funds was nothing short of phenomenal. That growth temporarily peaked in 1982, when the introduction of money market deposit accounts by banks and S&Ls caused money fund assets to level off and eventually decline. It didn't take long for the industry to recover, however, and by mid-2003, there were some 1,000 money funds that together held nearly $2.3 trillion in assets.

There are several different kinds of money market mutual funds:

- *General-purpose money funds,* which invest in any and all types of money market investment vehicles, from Treasury bills and bank CDs to corporate commercial paper. The vast majority of money funds are of this type. They invest their money wherever they can find attractive short-term yields.
- *Government securities money funds,* which were established as a way to meet investor concerns for safety. They effectively eliminate any risk of default by confining their investments to Treasury bills and other short-term securities of the U.S. government, or its agencies.

- *Tax-exempt money funds,* which limit their investing to very short (30- to 90-day) tax-exempt municipal securities. Because their income is free from federal income taxes, they appeal predominantly to investors in high tax brackets. The yields on these funds are about 20% to 30% below the returns on other types of money funds, so you need to be in a high enough tax bracket to produce a competitive after-tax return. Some tax-exempt funds confine their investing to the securities of a single state so that residents of high-tax states can enjoy income that's free from both federal and state taxes.

Just about every major brokerage firm has at least four or five money funds of its own, and hundreds more are sold by independent fund distributors. Most require minimum investments of $1,000 (although $2,500 to $5,000 minimums are not uncommon). Because the maximum average maturity of their holdings cannot exceed 90 days, money funds are highly liquid investment vehicles. They're also very low in risk and virtually immune to capital loss, because at least 95% of the fund's assets must be invested in top-rated/prime-grade securities. On the other hand, since the fund's interest income tends to follow general interest rate conditions, the returns to shareholders are subject to the ups and downs of market interest rates. Even so, the yields on money funds are highly competitive with those of other short-term securities. And with the check-writing privileges they offer, money funds are just as liquid as checking or savings accounts. They are viewed by many investors as a convenient, safe, and (reasonably) profitable way to accumulate capital and temporarily store idle funds.

index fund
a mutual fund that buys and holds a portfolio of stocks (or bonds) equivalent to those in a specific market index.

Index Funds "If you can't beat 'em, join 'em." That saying pretty much describes the idea behind index funds. Essentially, an **index fund** is a type of mutual fund that buys and holds a portfolio of stocks (or bonds) equivalent to those in a market index like the S&P 500. An index fund that's trying to match the S&P 500, for example, would hold the same 500 stocks that are held in that index, in exactly (or very nearly) the same proportions. Rather than trying to beat the market, as most actively managed funds do, *index funds simply try to match the market.* That is, they seek to match the performance of the index on which the fund is based. They do this through low-cost investment management. In fact, in most cases, the whole portfolio is run almost entirely by a computer that matches the fund's holdings with those of the targeted index.

The approach of index funds is strictly buy-and-hold. Indeed, about the only time an index-fund portfolio changes is when the targeted market index alters its "market basket" of securities. (Occasionally an index will drop a few securities and replace them with new ones.) A pleasant by-product of this buy-and-hold approach is that the funds have extremely low portfolio turnover rates and, therefore, very little in *realized* capital gains. As a result, aside from a modest amount of dividend income, these funds produce very little taxable income from year to year, which leads many high-income investors to view them as a type of tax-sheltered investment.

In addition to their tax shelter, these funds provide something else: By simply trying to match the market, index funds actually produce *highly competitive returns.* It's very tough to outperform the market, whether you are a professional money manager or a seasoned individual investor. Index funds readily acknowledge this fact and don't even try to outperform the market;

instead, all they try to do is match market returns. Surprisingly, the net result of this strategy, combined with *a very low cost structure*, is that most index funds outperform the vast majority of all other types of stock funds. Historical data show that only about 20% to 25% of stock funds outperform the market. Because an index fund pretty much matches the market, these funds tend to produce better returns than 75% to 80% of competing stock funds. Granted, every now and then the fully managed stock funds will have a year (or two) when they outperform index funds. But these are the exception rather than the rule, especially when you look at multi-year returns, covering periods of 3 to 5 years or more—indeed, over most multi-year periods, the vast majority of fully managed stock funds just can't keep up with index funds.

Besides the S&P 500, which is the most popular index, a number of other market indexes are used, including the S&P Midcap 400, the Russell 2000 Small Stock, and the Wilshire 5000 indexes, as well as value-stock indexes, growth-stock indexes, international-stock indexes, and even bond indexes. When picking index funds, be sure to avoid high-cost funds, as such fees significantly *reduce* the chance that the fund will be able to match the market. Also, avoid index funds that use gimmicks as a way to "enhance" yields: That is, rather than follow the index, these funds will "tilt" their portfolios in an attempt to outperform the market. Your best bet is to buy a *true* index fund (one that has no added "bells and whistles"), and a low-cost one at that.

sector fund
a mutual fund that restricts its investments to a particular segment of the market.

Sector Funds One of the hottest products on Wall Street is the so-called **sector fund,** a mutual fund that restricts its investments to a particular sector (or segment) of the market. These funds concentrate their investment holdings in one or more industries that make up the sector being aimed at. For example, a health care sector fund would focus on such industries as drug companies, hospital management firms, medical suppliers, and biotech concerns. The portfolio of a sector fund would consist of promising growth stocks from these particular industries. Among the more popular sector funds are those that concentrate their investments in technology, financial services, leisure and entertainment, real estate (REITs), natural resources, electronics, chemicals, computers, telecommunications, utilities, and, of course, health care—all the "glamour" industries.

The overriding investment objective of a sector fund is *capital gains*. A sector fund is similar to a growth fund in many respects and should be considered speculative. The sector fund concept is based on the belief that the really attractive returns come from small segments of the market. So rather than diversifying your portfolio across the market, put your money where the action is! It's an interesting notion that may warrant consideration by investors willing to take on the added risks that often accompany these funds.

Socially Responsible Funds For some, investing is far more than just cranking out financial ratios and calculating investment results. To these investors, the security selection process doesn't end with bottom lines, P/E ratios, growth rates, and betas. Rather, it also includes the *active, explicit consideration of moral, ethical, and environmental issues*. The idea is that social concerns should play just as big a role in investment decisions as do profits and other financial matters. Not surprisingly, a number of funds cater to such investors: Known as **socially responsible funds,** they actively and directly incorporate ethics and morality into the investment decision. Their investment decisions, in effect, revolve around *both* morality and profitability.

socially responsible fund
a mutual fund that actively and directly incorporates ethics and morality into the investment decision.

Socially responsible funds consider only certain companies for inclusion in their portfolios. If a company doesn't meet the fund's moral, ethical, or environmental tests, fund managers simply won't consider buying the stock, no matter how good the bottom line looks. Generally speaking, these funds refrain from investing in companies that derive revenues from tobacco, alcohol, gambling, or weapons, or that operate nuclear power plants. In addition, the funds tend to favor firms that produce "responsible" products or services, that have strong employee relations and positive environmental records, and that are socially responsive to the communities in which they operate. Although these screens might seem to eliminate a lot of stocks from consideration, these funds (most of which are fairly small) still find plenty of securities to choose from. As far as performance is concerned, the general perception is that there's a price to pay, in the form of lower average returns, for socially responsible investing. For example, in late 2003, year-to-date returns on 149 socially responsible funds averaged slightly less than 14.0%, whereas domestic stock funds in general turned in year-to-date returns of 20.6%. Such comparative performance should come as no surprise, however, for whenever you add more investment hurdles, you're likely to reduce return potential. But to those who truly believe in socially responsible investing, the sacrifice apparently is worth it.

Asset Allocation Funds Studies have shown that the most important decision an investor can make is where to allocate his or her investment assets. As we saw in Chapter 5, *asset allocation* involves deciding how you're going to divide up your investments among different types of securities. For example, what portion of your money do you want to devote to money market securities, what portion to stocks, and what portion to bonds? Asset allocation deals in broad terms (types of securities) and does not address individual security selection. Strange as it may seem, asset allocation has been found to be a far more important determinant of total portfolio returns than individual security selection.

asset allocation fund
a mutual fund that spreads investors' money across stocks, bonds, money market securities, and possibly other asset classes.

Because many individual investors have a tough time making asset allocation decisions, the mutual fund industry has created a product to do the job for them. Known as **asset allocation funds**, these funds spread investors' money across different types of markets. That is, whereas most mutual funds concentrate on one type of investment—whether stocks, bonds, or money market securities—asset allocation funds put money into all these markets. Many of them also include foreign securities in the asset allocation scheme. Some even include inflation-resistant investments, such as gold or real estate. By mid-year 2003, there were nearly 200 asset allocation funds in existence. All were designed for people who want to hire fund managers not only to select individual securities but also to allocate money among the various markets.

Here's how a typical asset allocation fund works. The money manager establishes a desired allocation mix, which might look something like this: 50% of the portfolio goes to U.S. stocks, 30% to bonds, 10% to foreign securities, and 10% to money market securities. Securities are then purchased for the fund in these proportions, and the overall portfolio maintains the desired mix. Actually, each segment of the fund is managed almost as a separate portfolio. Thus securities within, say, the stock portion are bought, sold, and held as the market dictates.

What really separates asset allocation funds from the rest of the pack is that *as market conditions change over time, the asset allocation mix changes as well.* For example, if the U.S. stock market starts to soften, funds will be moved out of stocks to some other area. As a result, the stock portion of the portfolio might drop to, say, 35%, and the foreign securities portion might increase to 25%. Of course, there's no assurance that the money manager will make the right moves at the right time, but the expectation is that he or she will. (It's interesting to note that *balanced funds* are really a form of asset allocation fund, except that they tend to follow a *fixed-mix* approach to asset allocation. That is, the fund may put, say, 60% of the portfolio into stocks and 40% into bonds, and then pretty much stick to that mix, no matter what the markets are doing.)

Asset allocation funds are supposed to provide investors with one-stop shopping. That is, rather than buying a couple of stock funds, a couple of bond funds, and so on, you find an asset allocation fund that fits your needs and invest in it. The success of these funds rests not only on how well the money manager picks securities but also on how well he or she times the market and moves capital among different segments of the market.

international fund
a mutual fund that does all or most of its investing in foreign securities.

International Funds In their search for higher yields and better returns, U.S. investors have shown a growing interest in foreign securities. Sensing an opportunity, the mutual fund industry has been quick to respond with a proliferation of so-called **international funds**—a type of mutual fund that does all or most of its investing in foreign securities. Just compare the number of international funds that are around today with those in existence a few years ago: In 1985 there were only about 40 of these funds; by 2003, the number had grown to more than 750. The fact is that a lot of people would like to invest in foreign securities but simply don't have the experience or know-how to do so. International funds may be just the vehicle for such investors, *provided they have at least a basic appreciation of international economics.* Because these funds deal with the international economy, balance-of-trade positions, and currency valuations, investors should have a fundamental understanding of what these issues are and how they can affect fund returns.

Technically, the term *international fund* describes a type of fund that invests *exclusively in foreign securities*. Such funds often confine their activities to specific geographic regions (e.g., Mexico, Australia, Europe, or the Pacific Rim). In contrast, *global funds* invest not only in foreign securities but also in U.S. companies—usually multinational firms. As a rule, global funds provide more diversity and, with access to both foreign and domestic markets, can go wherever the action is.

Regardless of whether they're global or international (we'll use the term *international* to apply to both), you'll find just about any type of fund you could possibly want in the international sector. There are international stock funds, international bond funds, even international money market funds. There are aggressive growth funds, balanced funds, long-term growth funds, high-grade bond funds, and so forth. There are funds that confine their investing to large, established markets (like Japan, Germany, and Australia) and others that stick to the more exotic (and risky) emerging markets (such as Thailand, Mexico, Chile, and even former Communist countries like Poland). No matter what your investment philosophy or objective, you're likely to find what you're looking for in the international area.

Basically, these funds attempt to take advantage of international economic developments in two ways: (1) by capitalizing on changing market conditions and (2) by positioning themselves to benefit from devaluation of the dollar. They can make money either from rising share prices in a foreign market or, perhaps just as important, from a falling dollar (which in itself produces capital gains for U.S. investors in international funds). Many of these funds, however, attempt to protect their investors from currency exchange risks by using various types of *hedging strategies*. That is, by using foreign currency options and futures, or some other type of derivative product (some of which are discussed in Chapters 15 and 16), the fund tries to eliminate (or reduce) the effects of fluctuating currency exchange rates. Some funds, in fact, do this on a permanent basis: In essence, these funds try to hedge away exchange risk so that they can concentrate on the higher returns offered by the foreign securities themselves. Others use currency hedges only occasionally, when they feel there's a real chance of a substantial swing in currency values. But even with currency hedging, international funds are still considered fairly high-risk investments and should be used only by investors who understand and are able to tolerate such risks.

Investor Services

Ask most investors why they buy a particular mutual fund and they'll probably tell you that the fund provides the kind of income and return they're looking for. Now, no one would question the importance of return in the investment decision, but there are some other important reasons for investing in mutual funds, not the least of which are the valuable services they provide. Some of the most sought-after *mutual fund services* are automatic investment and reinvestment plans, regular income programs, conversion and phone-switching privileges, and retirement programs.

automatic investment plan
a mutual fund service that allows shareholders to automatically send fixed amounts of money from their paychecks or bank accounts into the fund.

Automatic Investment Plans It takes money to make money. For an investor, that means being able to accumulate the capital to put into the market. Unfortunately, that's not always easy. But mutual funds have come up with a program that makes savings and capital accumulation as painless as possible. The program is the **automatic investment plan.** This service allows fund shareholders to automatically funnel fixed amounts of money *from their paychecks or bank accounts* into a mutual fund. It's much like a payroll deduction plan.

This fund service has become very popular, because it enables shareholders to invest on a regular basis without having to think about it. Just about every fund group offers some kind of automatic investment plan for virtually all of its stock and bond funds. To enroll, you simply fill out a form authorizing the fund to siphon a set amount (usually a minimum of $25 to $100 per period) from your bank account or paycheck at regular intervals, such as monthly or quarterly. Once enrolled, you'll be buying more shares every month or quarter (most funds deal in fractional shares). Of course, if it's a load fund, you'll still have to pay normal sales charges on your periodic investments. To remain diversified, you can divide your money among as many funds (within a given fund family) as you like. Finally, you can get out of the program at any time, without penalty, by simply calling the fund. Although convenience is perhaps the chief advantage of automatic investment plans, they also make solid investment sense: One of the best ways of building up a sizable amount of capital is to *add funds to your investment program system-*

atically over time. The importance of making regular contributions to your investment portfolio cannot be overstated; it ranks right up there with compound interest.

Automatic Reinvestment Plans An automatic reinvestment plan is another of the real draws of mutual funds and is offered by just about every open-end fund. Whereas automatic investment plans deal with money the shareholder is putting into a fund, automatic *re*investment plans deal with the dividends the funds pay to their shareholders. Much like the dividend reinvestment plans we looked at with stocks (in Chapter 6), the **automatic reinvestment plans** of mutual funds enable you to keep your capital fully employed. Through this service, dividend and/or capital gains income is automatically used to buy additional shares in the fund (most funds deal in fractional shares). Such purchases are often commission-free. Keep in mind, however, that even though you may reinvest all dividends and capital gains distributions, the IRS still treats them as cash receipts and taxes them as investment income in the year in which they were received.

automatic reinvestment plan
a mutual fund service that enables shareholders to automatically buy additional shares in the fund through the reinvestment of dividends and capital gains income.

Automatic reinvestment plans are especially attractive because they enable you to earn fully compounded rates of return. That is, by plowing back profits, you can essentially put them to work in generating even more earnings. Indeed, the effects of these plans on total accumulated capital over the long run can be substantial. Figure 13.6 (on page 572) shows the long-term impact of one such plan. (These are the actual performance numbers for a *real* mutual fund, Vanguard Health Care.) In the illustration, we assume the investor starts out with $10,000 and, except for the reinvestment of dividends and capital gains, *adds no new capital over time.* Even so, note that the initial investment of $10,000 grew to $145,000 over a 15-year period (which amounts to a compounded rate of return of almost 20%). Of course, not all periods will match this performance, nor will all mutual funds be able to perform as well, even in strong markets. The point is that as long as care is taken in selecting an appropriate fund, *attractive benefits can be derived from the systematic accumulation of capital offered by automatic reinvestment plans.*

Regular Income Although automatic investment and reinvestment plans are great for the long-term investor, what about the investor who's looking for a steady stream of income? Once again, mutual funds have a service to meet this need. Called a **systematic withdrawal plan,** it's offered by most open-end funds. Once enrolled in one of these plans, an investor automatically receives a predetermined amount of money every month or quarter. Most funds require a minimum investment of $5,000 or more to participate. The size of the minimum payment must normally be $50 or more per period (with no limit on the maximum). The funds will pay out the monthly or quarterly income first from dividends and realized capital gains. If this source proves to be inadequate and the shareholder so authorizes, the fund can then tap the principal or original paid-in capital to meet the required periodic payments.

systematic withdrawal plan
a mutual fund service that enables shareholders to automatically receive a predetermined amount of money every month or quarter.

Conversion Privileges and Phone Switching Sometimes investors find it necessary to switch out of one fund and into another. For example, an investor's objectives or the investment climate itself may have changed. **Conversion** (or **exchange**) **privileges** were devised to meet such needs conveniently and economically. Investment management companies that offer a

conversion (exchange) privilege
feature of a mutual fund that allows shareholders to move money from one fund to another, within the same family of funds.

FIGURE 13.6 The Effects of Reinvesting Income

Reinvesting dividends or capital gains can have a tremendous impact on one's investment position. This graph shows the results of a hypothetical investor who initially invested $10,000 in Vanguard Health Care and, for a period of 15 years, reinvested all dividends and capital gains distributions in additional fund shares. (No adjustment has been made for any income taxes payable by the shareholder, which is appropriate so long as the fund was held in an IRA or Keogh account.) (*Source: Morningstar Principia for Mutual Funds*, June 30, 2003.)

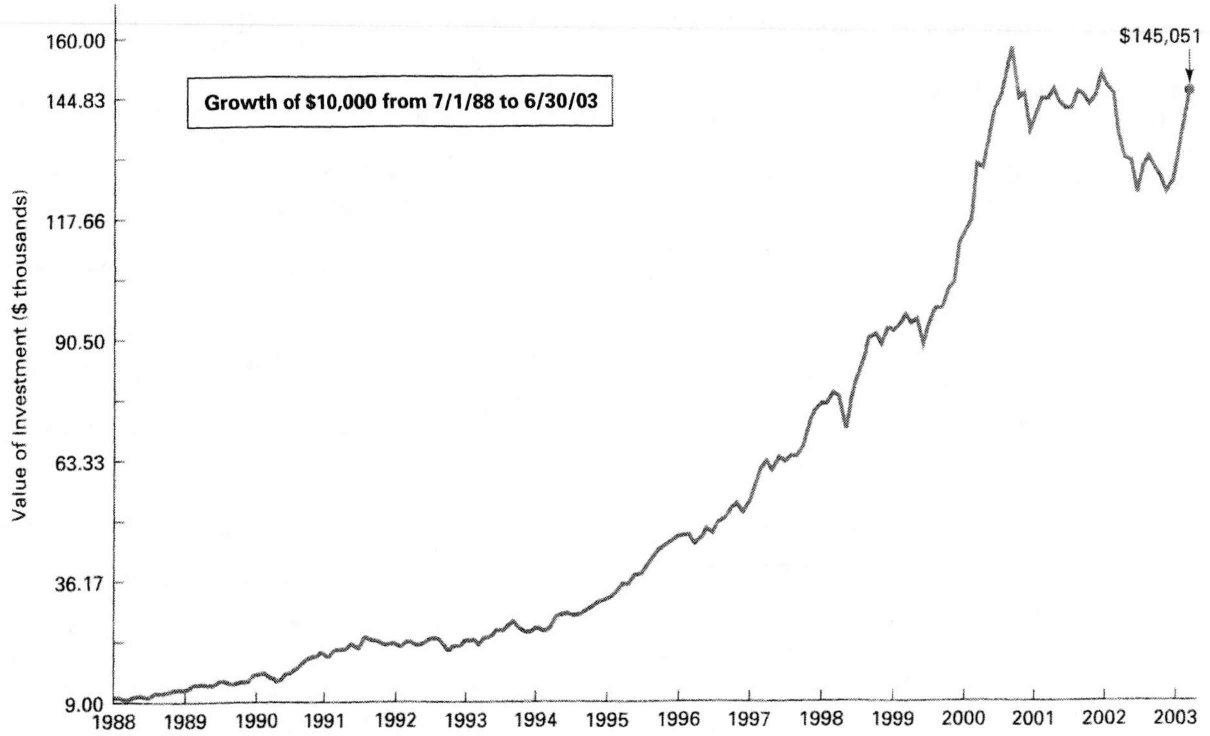

fund families
different kinds of mutual funds offered by a single investment management company.

number of different funds—known as **fund families**—often provide conversion privileges. These enable shareholders to move easily from one fund to another. With *phone switching* you simply pick up the phone to move money among funds. The only constraint is that the switches must be confined to the same *family* of funds. For example, you can switch from a Dreyfus growth fund to a Dreyfus money fund, or any other fund managed by Dreyfus.

With some fund families, the alternatives open to investors seem almost without limit. Indeed, some of the larger families offer literally hundreds of funds. Fidelity has over 300 different funds in its family: from high-performance stock funds to bond funds, tax-exempt funds, a couple of dozen sector funds, and a couple of dozen money funds. More than 400 fund families are in operation today. The two biggest—Fidelity and Vanguard—each has more than *half-a-trillion dollars* in assets under management, and that *excludes* their money market funds. Other big fund families include American Funds ($400 billion under management), Franklin/Templeton ($175 billion), Putnam ($150 billion), and PIMCO ($140 billion). Each of these, and all the other fund families, provide low-cost conversion/phone-switching privileges. Some even provide these privileges for free, although most have limits on the number of times such switches can occur each year.

Conversion privileges are usually considered beneficial for shareholders, as they allow investors to meet their ever-changing long-term goals. They also permit investors to manage their mutual fund holdings more aggressively by allowing them to move in and out of funds as the investment environment changes. Unfortunately, there is one major drawback: For tax purposes, the exchange of shares from one fund to another is regarded as a sale transaction followed by a subsequent purchase of a new security. As a result, if any capital gains exist at the time of the exchange, the investor is liable for the taxes on that profit, even though the holdings were not truly "liquidated."

HOT

You can obtain details on the various IRA programs, as well as other tax-sheltered retirement plans at the book's Web site. Click on the Web chapter titled "Tax-Advantaged Investments" and then on "Tax Deferred Retirement Programs." To access our Web site, go to:

www.aw-bc.com/gitman_joehnk

Retirement Programs As a result of government legislation, self-employed individuals are permitted to divert a portion of their pretax income into self-directed retirement plans. And all working Americans, whether or not they are self-employed, are allowed to establish individual retirement arrangements (IRAs). Indeed, with legislation passed in 1997, *qualified investors* can now choose between deductible and nondeductible (Roth) IRAs. Even those who make too much to qualify for one of these programs can set up special non- deductible IRAs. Today all mutual funds provide a special service that allows individuals to set up tax-deferred retirement programs as either IRA or Keogh accounts—or, through their place of employment, to participate in a tax-sheltered retirement plan, such as a 401(k). The funds set up the plans and handle all the administrative details so that the shareholder can easily take full advantage of available tax savings.

IN REVIEW

CONCEPTS

13.7 Briefly describe each of the following types of mutual funds:
a. Aggressive growth funds
b. Equity-income funds
c. Growth-and-income funds
d. Bond funds
e. Sector funds
f. Socially responsible funds

13.8 What is an *asset allocation fund,* and how does it differ from other types of mutual funds?

13.9 If growth, income, and capital preservation are the primary objectives of mutual funds, why do we bother to categorize funds by type? Do you think such classifications are helpful in the fund selection process? Explain.

13.10 What are *fund families?* What advantages do fund families offer investors? Are there any disadvantages?

13.11 Briefly describe some of the investor services provided by mutual funds. What are *automatic reinvestment plans,* and how do they differ from *automatic investment plans?* What is phone switching, and why would an investor want to use this service?

Investing in Mutual Funds

LG 5 LG 6

Suppose you are confronted with the following situation: You have money to invest and are trying to select the right place to put it. You obviously want to pick a security that meets your idea of acceptable risk and will generate an attractive rate of return. The problem is that you have to make the selection from a list of nearly 8,300 securities. Sound like a "mission impossible"? Well that's basically what you're up against when trying to select a suitable mutual fund. However, if you approach the problem systematically, it may not be so formidable a task. First, it might be helpful to examine more closely the various investor uses of mutual funds. With this background, we can then look at the selection process and at several measures of return that can be used to assess performance. As we will see, it is possible to whittle down the list of alternatives by matching your investment needs with the investment objectives of the funds.

Investor Uses of Mutual Funds

Mutual funds can be used in a variety of ways. For instance, performance funds can serve as a vehicle for capital appreciation, whereas bond funds can provide current income. Regardless of the kind of income a mutual fund provides, investors tend to use these securities for one of three reasons: (1) as a way to accumulate wealth, (2) as a storehouse of value, or (3) as a speculative vehicle for achieving high rates of return.

INVESTOR FACTS

SOME MUTUAL FUND FACTS EVERY INVESTOR SHOULD KNOW . . .

- Even bad funds sometimes rank as top performers.
- Stock funds that get hit hard in market crashes aren't necessarily bad investments.
- Even great funds have bad years now and then.
- Most stock (and bond) funds fail to beat the market.
- You don't need a broker to buy mutual funds.
- A fund that doesn't charge a sales commission isn't necessarily a no-load fund.
- If you own more than a dozen different funds, you probably own too many.
- Mutual fund names can be misleading.
- Funds with high yields don't necessarily produce high returns.
- Money funds are not risk-free (you never know what kind of return you're going to earn with these things).

Accumulation of Wealth Accumulation of wealth is probably the most common reason for using mutual funds. Basically, the investor uses mutual funds over the long haul to build up investment capital. Depending on investor goals, a modest amount of risk may be acceptable, but usually preservation of capital and capital stability are considered important. The whole idea is to form a "partnership" with the mutual fund in building up as big a pool of capital as possible: *You provide the capital by systematically investing and reinvesting in the fund, and the fund provides the return by doing its best to invest your resources wisely.*

Storehouse of Value Investors also use mutual funds as a storehouse of value. The idea is to find a place where investment capital can be fairly secure and relatively free from deterioration yet still generate a relatively attractive rate of return. Short- and intermediate-term bond funds are logical choices for such purposes, and so are money funds. Capital preservation and income over the long term are very important to some investors. Others might seek storage of value only for the short term, using, for example, money funds as a place to "sit it out" until a more attractive opportunity comes along.

Speculation and Short-Term Trading Although speculation is becoming more common, it is still not widely used by mutual fund investors. The reason, of course, is that most mutual funds are long-term in nature and thus not meant to be used as aggressive trading vehicles. However, a growing number of funds (e.g., sector funds) now cater to speculators. Some investors have found that mutual funds are, in fact, attractive outlets for speculation and short-term trading.

One way to do this is to trade in and out of funds aggressively as the investment climate changes. Load charges can be avoided (or reduced) by dealing in families of funds offering low-cost conversion privileges and/or by dealing only in no-load funds. Other investors might choose to invest in funds for the long run but still seek high rates of return by investing in aggressive mutual funds. A number of funds follow very aggressive trading strategies, which may appeal to investors willing to accept substantial risk exposure. These are usually the fairly specialized, smaller funds. Examples are sophisticated enhanced-yield funds, leverage funds, option funds, emerging-market funds, small-cap aggressive growth funds, and sector funds. In essence, investors in such funds are simply applying the basic mutual fund concept to their investment needs by letting professional money managers handle their accounts in a way they would like to see them handled: *aggressively.*

The Selection Process

When it comes to mutual funds, there is one question every investor has to answer right up front: Why invest in a mutual fund to begin with—why not just go it alone by buying individual stocks and bonds directly? For beginning investors and investors with little capital, the answer is simple: With mutual funds, investors are able to achieve far more diversification than they could ever get on their own, and they get the help of professional money managers at a very reasonable cost. For more seasoned investors, the answers are probably a bit more involved. Certainly, diversification and professional money management come into play, but there are other reasons as well. The competitive returns offered by mutual funds are a factor with many investors, as are the services they provide. Many seasoned investors simply have decided they can get better returns over the long haul by carefully selecting mutual funds than by investing on their own. As a result, they put all or a big chunk of their money into funds. Some of these investors use part of their capital to buy and sell individual securities on their own and use the rest *to buy mutual funds that invest in areas they don't fully understand or don't feel well informed about.* For example, they'll use mutual funds to get into foreign markets, to buy mortgage-backed securities, to buy junk bonds (where diversification is so very important), or to buy value funds (because that's such a tricky and time-consuming way to invest).

Once you have decided to use mutual funds, you have to decide which fund(s) to buy. In many respects, the selection process is critical in determining how much success you will have with mutual funds. It means putting into action all you know about funds, in order to gain as much return as possible from an acceptable level of risk. The selection process begins with an assessment of your own investment needs, which sets the tone of the investment program. Obviously, what you want to do is select from those 8,300 or so funds the one or two (or six or eight) that will best meet your total investment needs.

Objectives and Motives for Using Funds Selecting the right investment means finding those funds that are most suitable to your investment needs. The place to start is with your own investment objectives. In other words, why do you want to invest in a mutual fund, and what are you looking for in a fund? Obviously, an attractive rate of return would be desirable, but there is also the matter of a tolerable amount of risk exposure. Probably, when you look at your own risk temperament in relation to the various types of mutual funds available, you will discover that certain types of funds are more appealing to

INVESTOR FACTS

KNOWING WHERE TO LOOK IS HALF THE BATTLE—If mutual fund prospectuses seemed daunting in the past, you might want to give them another try. The fund industry, in response to new SEC rules, now prepares more readable, streamlined prospectuses and offers fund profiles, briefer documents that provide key information in a tidy 2 to 6 pages. Here are some guidelines to help sort through the material:

Expenses: This critical section lists all fees and their amounts.

Investment Objectives: Here you will find a description of the fund's investment style and perhaps some information on the types of securities it will buy.

Long-Term Total Returns: Are they consistent or volatile? If they are missing from the prospectus, be wary: They might be low.

Management: Look at the fund manager's biography. How long has he or she managed the fund?

you than others. For instance, aggressive growth or sector funds are usually *not* attractive to individuals who wish to avoid high exposure to risk.

Another important factor in the selection process is the intended use of the mutual fund. That is, do you want to invest in mutual funds as a means of accumulating wealth, as a storehouse of value, or to speculate for high rates of return? This information puts into clearer focus the question of exactly what you are trying to do with your investment dollars. Finally, there is the matter of the types of services provided by the fund. If you are particularly interested in certain services, you should be sure to look for them in the funds you select. Having assessed what you are looking for in a fund, you are ready to look at what the funds have to offer.

What the Funds Offer Just as each individual has a set of investment needs, each fund has its own *investment objective,* its own *manner of operation,* and its own *range of services.* These three parameters are useful in helping you to assess investment alternatives. But where do you find such information? One obvious place is the fund's *profile,* or its prospectus, which supplies information on investment objectives, portfolio composition, management, and past performance. Publications such as the *Wall Street Journal, Barron's, Money, Fortune,* and *Forbes* also offer useful information about mutual funds. These sources provide a wealth of operating and performance statistics in a convenient and easy-to-read format. For instance, each year *Forbes* rates a couple thousand mutual funds, and every quarter *Barron's* publishes an extensive mutual fund performance report.

A number of reporting services also provide background information and assessments on funds. Among the best in this category are *Morningstar Mutual Funds* (a sample of which is shown in Figure 13.7), Wiesenberger's *Investment Companies* (an annual publication with quarterly updates), and *Value Line Mutual Fund Survey* (which produces a mutual fund report similar to its stock report). In addition, all sorts of performance statistics are available on disks and on the Internet for easy use on home computers. For example, quarterly or annually updated software is available, at very low cost, from Morningstar or from the American Association of Individual Investors (AAII). Using sources like these, investors can obtain information on such things as investment objectives, load charges and annual expense rates, summary portfolio analyses, services offered, historical statistics, and reviews of past performance.

Whittling Down the Alternatives At this point, fund selection becomes a process of elimination. A large number of funds can be eliminated from consideration simply because they fail to meet stated needs. Some funds may be too risky; others may be unsuitable as a storehouse of value. Thus, rather than trying to evaluate 8,300 different funds, you can narrow down the list to two or three *types* of funds that best match your investment needs. From here, you can whittle down the list a bit more by introducing other constraints. For example, because of cost considerations, you may want to deal only in no-load or low-load funds (more on this topic below). Or you may be seeking certain services that are important to your investment goals.

Now we introduce the final (but certainly not the least important) element in the selection process: the *fund's investment performance.* Useful information includes (1) how the fund has performed over the past 5 to 7 years, (2) the type of return it has generated in good markets as well as bad, (3) the level and

FIGURE 13.7 Some Relevant Information About Specific Mutual Funds

Investors who want in-depth information about the operating characteristics, investment holdings, and market behavior of specific mutual funds, such as the Clipper Fund profiled here, can usually find what they're looking for in publications like *Morningstar Mutual Funds* or, as shown here, from computer-based information sources like *Morningstar's Principia.* (*Source:* Morningstar, Inc., *Principia,* release date: June 30, 2003.)

Data through May 31, 2003 For internal and/or client reporting purposes only.

Clipper

Ticker	Load	NAV	Yield	Total Assets	Mstar Category
CFIMX	None	$79.63	1.3%	$4,659 mil	Large Value

Manager Strategy

This fund's management searches for established companies with dominant franchises but only buys ones trading at discounts of at least 30% to its estimates of intrinsic value. Management uses discounted cash-flow analysis to estimate a company's worth but uses the sale price of comparable companies if the latter value is more conservative. The managers also look for factors such as insiders who are buying company stock and share-repurchase programs. The fund is concentrated, holding just 20 to 30 names. It eschews pricey sectors such as technology, and it will sit on big bond or cash stakes if the managers can't find stocks cheap enough and financially strong enough to meet their criteria.

Portfolio Manager(s)

James H. Gipson. Since 02-84.
Michael C. Sandler. Since 02-84.
Bruce Veaco. Since 01-86.
Peter Quinn. Since 08-87.
Kelly Sucoka. Since 04-02.

Historical Profile
Return: High
Risk: Below Avg
Rating: ★★★★★ Highest

Investment Style: Equity

▼ Manager Change
∇ Partial Manager Change

Fund Performance vs. Category Average
Quarterly Fund Return
+/- Category Average
— Category Baseline

Performance Quartile (within Category)

1992	1993	1994	1995	1996	1997	1998	1999	2000	2001	2002	05-03	History
				76%	59%	72%	74%	66%	70%	92%	89%	Stock %
51.74	50.05	46.09	60.74	67.57	76.86	75.37	65.28	79.25	83.53	75.73	79.63	NAV
15.90	11.26	-2.51	45.22	19.43	30.44	19.20	-2.02	37.40	10.26	-5.51	5.15	Total Return %
8.28	1.20	-3.82	7.68	-3.51	-2.91	-9.38	-23.06	46.50	22.14	16.58	-5.19	+/-S&P 500
2.09	-6.86	-0.52	6.87	-2.14	-4.74	3.56	-9.38	30.39	15.85	10.01	-5.04	+/-Russ 1000 VI
1.99	1.46	1.41	1.64	1.37	2.01	2.26	2.98	2.86	1.36	1.29	0.00	Income Return %
13.91	9.80	-3.92	43.58	18.06	28.43	16.94	-5.00	34.54	8.90	-6.80	5.15	Capital Return %
12	68	75	1	56	24	9	83	1	3	1	97	Total Rtn % Rank Cat
0.95	0.75	0.71	0.76	0.83	1.36	1.63	2.25	1.87	1.08	1.08	0.00	Income $
3.02	6.73	2.00	5.42	4.27	9.83	12.86	6.16	8.38	2.75	2.11	0.00	Capital Gains $
1.12	1.11	1.11	1.11	1.08	1.08	1.06	1.10	1.09	1.08	1.07	—	Expense Ratio %
2.02	1.41	1.41	1.39	1.32	1.84	2.13	2.54	2.88	1.72	1.65	—	Income Ratio %
46	64	45	31	24	31	65	63	46	23	48	—	Turnover Rate %
210	240	247	404	543	824	1,234	961	1,366	2,685	5,002	4,659	Net Assets $mil

Performance 05-31-03

	1st Qtr	2nd Qtr	3rd Qtr	4th Qtr	Total
1999	-3.34	7.37	-4.31	-1.34	-2.02
2000	-3.03	5.55	16.20	15.54	37.40
2001	1.03	3.02	-2.52	8.67	10.26
2002	5.71	-6.22	-12.34	8.73	-5.51
2003	-10.17	—	—	—	—

Trailing	Total Return%	+/- S&P 500	+/- Russ 1000 VI	%Rank All	%Rank Cat	Growth of $10,000
3 Mo	15.24	0.21	-0.79	30	46	11,524
6 Mo	2.03	-1.84	-3.39	86	89	10,203
1 Yr	-6.93	1.13	0.92	54	13	9,307
3 Yr Avg	13.15	24.00	15.29	3	1	14,488
5 Yr Avg	10.67	11.74	9.60	2	1	16,599
10 Yr Avg	15.46	5.53	4.68	1	1	42,088
15 Yr Avg	15.26	3.61	3.31	2	2	84,139

Tax Analysis	Tax-Adj Rtn%	%Rank Cat	Tax-Cost Rat	%Rank Cat
3 Yr Avg	10.97	1	1.93	81
5 Yr Avg	7.61	1	2.76	90
10 Yr Avg	12.29	2	2.75	80

Potential Capital Gain Exposure: 0% of assets

Rating and Risk

Time Period	Load-Adj Return %	Morningstar Rtn vs Cat	Morningstar Risk vs Cat	Morningstar Risk-Adj Rating
1 Yr	-6.93			
3 Yr	13.15	High	Avg	★★★★★
5 Yr	10.67	High	Avg	★★★★★
10 Yr	15.46	High	Avg	★★★★★
Incept	15.75			

Other Measures	Standard Index S&P 500	Best Fit Index Russ 1000 VI
Alpha	18.6	14.6
Beta	0.52	0.80
R Squared	38	70

Standard Deviation	17.81
Mean	13.15
Sharpe Ratio	0.58

Portfolio Analysis 03-31-03

Share change since 12-02 Total Stocks:32	Sector	PE	YTD Ret%	% Assets
⊕ Freddie Mac	Financial	7.8	-14.82	8.73
⊕ Tyco Intl	Ind Mtrls	—	10.94	8.16
⊕ Electronic Data Sys	Business	9.6	23.46	6.71
⊕ Fannie Mae	Financial	16.3	6.85	5.44
⊕ Altria Group	Goods	7.9	11.74	5.03
⊕ Tenet Healthcare	Health	9.0	-26.77	4.15
⊕ American Express	Financial	20.7	19.45	4.03
⊕ El Paso	Energy	—	17.95	3.37
⊕ Equity Residential Prope	Financial	35.8	7.45	3.35
⊕ USI, Inc.	Goods	—	10.00	2.94
⊕ Wyeth	Health	13.2	28.07	2.71
⊕ Pfizer	Health	21.1	16.83	2.54
AOL Time Warner	Media	—	18.63	2.43
⊕ McDonald's	Consumer	24.3	39.12	2.40
⊕ Sara Lee	Goods	11.8	-14.64	2.36
⊕ Kraft Foods	Goods	16.5	-15.81	2.33
⊕ Safeway	Consumer	15.7	-15.28	2.17
⊕ CVS	Consumer	14.9	6.32	2.14
⊕ Merrill Lynch	Financial	16.5	21.49	2.09
⊕ Kroger	Consumer	10.3	2.91	1.93

Current Investment Style

Value Blnd Growth; Large Mid Small

Market Cap %	
Giant	26.7
Large	52.9
Mid	20.4
Small	0.0
Micro	0.0

Median $mil: 26,579

Value Measures		Rel S&P 500
Price/Earnings	9.8	0.6
Price/Book	1.4	0.6
Price/Sales	0.7	0.5
Price/Cash Flow	0.8	0.1
Dividend Yield %	3.1	1.8

Growth Measures	%	Rel S&P 500
Long-Term Erngs	15.9	1.2
Book Value	7.1	1.1
Sales	8.3	3.3
Cash Flow	27.8	4.2
Historical Erngs	13.2	1.2

Profitability	%	Rel S&P 500
Return on Equity	16.8	1.1
Return on Assets	8.2	1.2
Net Margin	8.5	0.9

Sector Weightings	% of Stocks	Rel S&P 500	3 Year High	3 Year Low
Info	2.7	0.1	—	—
Software	0.0	0.0	0	0
Hardware	0.0	0.0	0	0
Media	2.7	0.8	3	0
Telecom	0.0	0.0	0	0
Service	68.4	1.5	—	—
Health	12.4	1.0	12	0
Consumer	11.4	1.4	17	11
Business	11.5	2.8	17	11
Financial	33.1	1.6	39	33
Mfg	28.9	0.9	—	—
Goods	14.6	1.3	24	11
Ind Mtrls	10.5	0.9	12	6
Energy	3.8	0.6	4	0
Utilities	0.0	0.0	0	0

Composition

Cash	7.7
Stocks	88.8
Bonds	2.3
Other	1.1
Foreign (% of Stock)	9.2

Morningstar's Take by Christopher Traulsen 06-15-03

Clipper Fund's current malaise comes with the territory.

This fund is up just 6.6% for the year to date through June 13, 2003, and it trails 99% of all large-value funds for the period. A lack of technology exposure has hurt. But by far the bigger issue has been stock-specific problems. One of the biggest is Freddie Mac, the fund's top holding as of March 31. Freddie is mired in scandal. Earnings are to be restated, a criminal probe is under way, and top executives have been shown the door. The stock is down 14%.

The managers' response to the Freddie debacle is telling. They didn't panic and sell. Instead, they held and tried to analyze the real risks of the situation. When all is said and done, they decided there's more smoke than fire here and think any earnings restatements should be in an upward direction. Such a measured response is typical; the team's value approach often leads it to buy controversial names. Tenet Healthcare, El Paso, and Tyco were all purchases in 2002. Such companies limit the fund's price risk but expose it to substantial business risk. The latter is magnified by the fund's concentrated portfolio.

Fortunately, the managers here have proved themselves strong stock-pickers over time. They've built one of the finest long-term records in the mutual fund world, largely by using sell-offs to build positions in cheap companies. The fund is also a good diversifier, with a low R-squared relative to the S&P 500. Investors should note, however, that although the fund has been less volatile than its typical peer, its concentration and patience with struggling companies make it ill-suited for those with short time horizons.

This fund's minimum for taxable accounts has increased to $25,000 from $5,000. Those who don't want to put that much here could go with PBHG Clipper Focus instead, which has much lower minimums. Its portfolio is nearly the same as this fund's, but it is kept fully invested.

Address:	9601 Wilshire Boulevard Suite 828, Beverly Hills, CA 90210, 800-776-5033	Minimum Purchase:	$25000	Add: $1000	IRA: $3000
		Min Auto Inv Plan:	$25000	Add: $150	
		Sales Fees:	No-load		
Web Address:	www.clipperfund.com	Management Fee:	1.00%		
Inception:	02-29-84	Actual Fees:	Mgt:1.00%	Dist: —	
Advisor:	Pacific Financial Research, Inc.	Expense Projections:	3Yr:$350	5Yr:$606	10Yr:$1340
Subadvisor:	None	Income Distrib:	Annually		
NTF Plans:	Fidelity Retail-NTF, CommonWealth NTF	Total Cost (relative to category):	Below Avg		

MORNINGSTAR® Mutual Funds

stability of dividend and capital gains distributions, and (4) the amount of volatility/risk in the fund's return. Note that the dividend and capital gains distribution is an important indication not only of how much current income the fund distributes annually but also of the fund's *tax efficiency.* As a rule, funds that have low dividends and low asset turnover expose their shareholders to less taxes and therefore have higher tax-efficiency ratings. And while you're looking at performance, it probably wouldn't hurt to check out the fund's *fee structure.* Be on guard for funds that charge abnormally high management fees; they can really hurt returns over time. Another important consideration is *how well a particular fund fits into your portfolio.* If you're trying to follow a certain asset allocation strategy, then be sure to take that into account when you're thinking about adding a fund (or two) to your portfolio. You can easily do so by using the fund categories developed by Morningstar (for example, look in the upper-right corner of Figure 13.7 and you'll find the "Mstar Category" for Clipper—it's a large-cap value fund).

Note that in this decision process, considerable weight is given to *past performance.* As a rule, the past is given little or no attention in the investment decision. After all, it's the future that matters. Although the *future performance* of a mutual fund is still the variable that holds the key to success, investors should look carefully at past investment results to see how successful the fund's investment managers have been. In essence, the success of a mutual fund rests in large part on the *investment skills of the fund managers.* Therefore, look for consistently good performance, in up as well as down markets, over *extended* periods of time (5 years or more). Most important, check whether the same key people are still running the fund. Although past success is certainly no guarantee of future performance, a strong team of money managers can have a significant bearing on the level of fund returns.

Stick with No-Loads or Low-Loads There's a long-standing "debate" in the mutual fund industry regarding load funds and no-load funds. Do load funds add value? If not, then why pay the load charges? As it turns out, empirical results generally do not support the idea that load funds provide added value. Load fund returns, in general, don't seem to be any better than the returns from no-load funds. In fact, in many cases, the funds with abnormally high loads and 12(b)-1 charges often produce returns that are far less than what you can get from no-load funds. In addition, because of compounding, the differential returns tend to widen with longer holding periods. But that should come as no surprise, because big load charges and/or 12(b)-1 fees reduce your investable capital—and therefore the amount of money you have working for you. In fact, the only way a load fund can overcome this handicap is to produce *superior returns,* which is no easy thing to do, year in and year out. Granted, a handful of load funds have produced very attractive returns over extended periods of time, but they are the exception rather than the rule.

Obviously, it's in your best interest to pay close attention to load charges (and other fees). As a rule, to maximize returns, you should *seriously consider sticking to no-load funds or to low-loads* (funds that have total load charges, including 12(b)-1 fees, of 3% or less). At the very minimum, you should consider a more expensive load fund *only* if it has a much better performance record (and offers more return potential) than a less expensive fund. There may well be times when the higher costs are justified. But far more often than not, you're better off trying to minimize load charges. That shouldn't be difficult to do, however, because there are literally thousands of no-load and low-load funds to choose from. And they come in all types and sizes. What's more, most of the top-performing funds are found in the universe of no-loads or low-loads. So why would you even want to look anywhere else?

Investing in Closed-End Funds

The assets of closed-end funds (CEFs) represent only a fraction of the $6.4 trillion invested in open-end funds. Indeed, by year-end 2002, there were only about 560 CEFs, which together held total assets of some $155 billion (less than 2% of the amount held by open-end funds). Like open-end funds, CEFs come in a variety of types and styles, including funds that specialize in municipal bonds, taxable bonds, various types of equity securities, and international securities, as well as regional and single-country funds. Both taxable and tax-free bonds dominate the CEF universe, and account for nearly 80% of assets under management. In fact, municipal bonds alone account for about 56% of CEF assets. In addition to bonds and the domestic equity market, many closed-end funds target foreign stock markets. For example, regional funds focus on a group of countries within a broad geographic area, such as Europe or Latin America. In contrast, *single-country funds* target either *emerging markets* (such as Brazil, China, the Czech Republic, India, Indonesia, Mexico, the Philippines, and Turkey) or *developed markets* (such as France, Germany, Japan, and the United Kingdom).

Some Key Differences Between Closed-End and Open-End Funds Because closed-end funds trade like stocks, you must deal with a broker to buy or sell shares, and the usual brokerage commissions apply. Open-end funds, in contrast, are bought from and sold to the fund operators themselves. Another important difference between open- and closed-end funds is their liquidity. You can buy and sell relatively large dollar amounts of an open-end mutual fund at its net asset value (NAV) without worrying about affecting the price. However, a relatively large buy or sell order for a CEF could easily bump its price up or down. Thus, the greater liquidity of open-end funds gives them a distinct advantage. Like open-end funds, most CEFs offer dividend reinvestment plans, but in many cases, that's about it. CEFs simply don't provide the full range of services that mutual fund investors are accustomed to.

All things considered, probably the most important difference is the way these funds are priced in the marketplace. This is important because it *directly affects* investor costs and returns. That is, whereas open-end funds can be bought and sold at NAV (plus any front-end load or minus any redemption charge), CEFs *have two values*—a market value (or stock price) and a NAV. The two are rarely the same, because CEFs typically trade at either a premium or a discount. A *premium* occurs when a fund trades for more than its NAV; a *discount* occurs when it trades for less. As a rule, CEFs trade at discounts. Indeed, at mid-year 2003, the typical CEF traded at an average *discount of around 5% to 10%*. In addition to normal competitive pressures in the marketplace, other factors that can lead to discounts (or premiums) include the fund's *relative performance*, its annual payout or yield, the *name recognition* of the fund's manager, a significant amount of *illiquid* holdings in the fund's portfolio, and/or a substantial amount of *unrealized* appreciation sitting in the fund's portfolio. Premiums (+) and discounts (−), along with NAVs and

FIGURE 13.8

Selected Performance on CEFs

As can be seen here, the market prices of closed-end funds often exceed or fall short of the fund's NAV. *Premiums* occur when the fund's (closing) price is greater than its NAV; *discounts* occur when the fund's NAV is greater than its closing price. To find the "PREM/DISC" as reported in the quotes, simply divide the fund's quoted "CLOSE" by its quoted "NAV," and then subtract 1. (*Source: The Wall Street Journal*, November 18, 2003.)

CLOSED-END FUNDS

STOCK (SYM)	EXCH	NAV	CLOSE	NET CHG	VOL 100s	PREM /DISC	DIV	52 WK TTL RET
General Equity Funds								
AdamsExp **ADX**	N	14.24	12.66	0.00	732	-11.1	1.30	17.8
AllncAll **AMO**	N	14.31	15.15	-0.09	36	5.9	1.32	18.9
BlueChipVal **BLU**	N	5.36	6.03	-0.14	432	12.5	.49	37.4
BoulderGro **BIF** h	N	6.53	5.44	0.00	84	-16.7	.07	8.0
BouldrTotR **BTF**	N	17.34	14.39	0.08	30	-17.0	.03	17.8
CntlSec **CET**	A	23.10	20.21	-0.13	40	-12.5	2.55	22.1
CornstnStrat **CLM**	A	6.59	8.46	-0.03	248	28.4	1.04	66.0
CornrstnTtlRtn Fd **CRF**	A	13.33	16.73	0.27	304	25.5	2.11	64.4
Equus II **EQS**	N	12.49	8.60	0.06	505	-31.1	.72	30.7
GabelliTr **GAB**	N	7.46	7.72	0.02	1649	3.5	.56	17.9
GenAmInv **GAM**	N	31.83	28.59	-0.05	345	-10.2	.86	16.0
LibtyASE **USA**	N	8.55	9.42	-0.01	2073	10.2	.97	41.6
LibtyASG **ASG**	N	6.32	6.60	-0.08	402	4.4	.72	36.7
RoyceFocus **FUND**	O	9.12	8.39	-0.08	z28085	-8.0	.09	62.1
RycMcroCap **OTCM**	O	13.01	12.90	0.00	z36055	-0.8	.94	64.3
RoyceValTr **RVT**	N	16.66	16.87	-0.22	1020	1.3	1.31	30.0
S&P 500 Fd **PEFX**	N	9.64	8.69	0.08	z24426	-9.9	.01	3.9
SlBrosFd **SBF**	N	13.22	11.35	-0.07	755	-14.1	.11	21.0
SourceCap **SOR**	N	56.85	59.53	-0.16	21	4.7	3.50	16.0
TriContl **TY**	N	18.48	15.75	-0.13	818	-14.8	.19	13.7
ZweigFd **ZF**	N	5.50	4.72	0.00	5546	-14.2	.50	-0.6

Gabelli Equity Trust **(GAB)** →

Note: "EXCH" = Exchange fund is traded on: N = NYSE; A = AMEX; O = OTC.

52-week total returns are reported weekly (on Mondays) in the *Wall Street Journal*, an example of which appears in Figure 13.8.

The premium or discount on CEFs is calculated as follows:

Equation 13.1

$$\text{Premium (or discount)} = (\text{Share price} - \text{NAV})/\text{NAV}$$

Suppose Fund A has a NAV of \$10. If its share price is \$8, it will sell at a 20% discount. That is,

$$\text{Premium (or discount)} = (\$8 - \$10)/\$10$$

$$= \$2/\$10 = .20 = \underline{\underline{-20\%}}$$

Because this value is negative, the fund is trading at a *discount* (or below its NAV). On the other hand, if this same fund were priced at \$12 per share, it would be trading at a *premium* of 20%—that is, (\$12 − \$10)/\$10 = \$2/\$10 = 0.20. Because the value is positive, the fund is trading at a premium (above its NAV).

What to Look for in a Closed-End Fund If you know what to look for and your timing and selection are good, you may find that some *deeply discounted CEFs* provide a great way to earn attractive returns. For example, if a fund trades at a 20% discount, you pay only 80 cents for each dollar's worth of assets. If you can buy a fund at an abnormally wide discount (say, more than 10% to 15%) and then sell it when the discount narrows or turns to a premium, you can enhance your overall return. In fact, even if the discount does not narrow, your return will be improved, because the yield on your investment is higher than it would be with an otherwise equivalent open-end fund. The reason: You're investing less money. Here's a simple example. Suppose a CEF trades at $8, a 20% discount from its NAV of $10. If the fund distributed $1 in dividends for the year, it would yield 12.5% ($1 divided by its $8 price). However, if it was a no-load, open-end fund, it would be trading at its higher NAV and therefore would yield only 10% ($1 divided by its $10 NAV). Thus, when investing in CEFs, pay special attention to the size of the premium and discount. In particular, keep your eyes open for funds trading at deep discounts, because that feature alone can enhance potential returns.

For the most part, except for the premium or discount, a CEF should be analyzed just like any other mutual fund. That is, check out the fund's expense ratio, portfolio turnover rate, past performance, cash position, and so on. In addition, study the history of the discount. Information on closed-end funds can be found in such publications as *Morningstar Closed-End Funds* and *Value Line Investment Survey.* Also, keep in mind that with CEFs, you probably won't get a prospectus (as you might with an open-end fund), because they do not continuously offer new shares to investors.

One final point to keep in mind when developing a closed-end fund investment program: Stay clear of new issues (IPOs) of closed-end funds and funds that sell at steep *premiums.* Never buy new CEFs when they are brought to the market as IPOs. Why? Because IPOs are always brought to the market at *hefty premiums.* You therefore face the almost inevitable risk of losing money as the shares fall to a discount within a month or two. This drop in price occurs because the IPO funds have to be offered at a premium just to cover the amount of the underwriting spread. You also want to avoid funds that are trading at premiums—especially at steep premiums—such as volatile single-country portfolios. That too can lead to built-in losses when, if sentiment sours, these premiums quickly turn into discounts.

Measuring Performance

As in any investment decision, return performance is a major dimension in the mutual fund selection process. The level of dividends paid by the fund, its capital gains, and its growth in capital are all important aspects of return. Such return information enables you to judge the investment behavior of a fund and to appraise its performance in relation to other funds and investment vehicles. Here, we will look at different measures that mutual fund investors use to assess return. Also, because risk is so important in defining the investment behavior of a fund, we will examine mutual fund risk as well.

Sources of Return An open-end mutual fund has three potential sources of return: (1) dividend income, (2) capital gains distribution, and (3) change in the price (or net asset value) of the fund. Depending on the type of fund, some mutual funds derive more income from one source than another. For example, we would normally expect income-oriented funds to have much higher dividend income than capital gains distributions.

TABLE 13.3 A Report of Mutual Fund Income and Capital Changes (For a share outstanding throughout the year)

	2004	2003	2002
1. **Net asset value, beginning of period**	$24.47	$27.03	$24.26
2. **Income from investment operations:**			
3. Net investment income	$0.60	$0.66	$0.50
4. Net gains on securities (realized and unrealized)	6.37	(1.74)	3.79
5. Total from investment operations	6.97	(1.08)	4.29
6. **Less distributions:**			
7. Dividends from net investment income	($0.55)	($0.64)	($0.50)
8. Distributions from realized gains	(1.75)	(.84)	(1.02)
9. Total distributions	(2.30)	(1.48)	(1.52)
10. **Net asset value, end of period**	$29.14	$24.47	$27.03
11. **Total return**	28.48%	(4.00%)	17.68%
12. **Ratios/supplemental data**			
13. Net assets, end of period ($000)	$307,951	$153,378	$108,904
14. Ratio of expenses to average net assets	1.04%	0.85%	0.94%
15. Ratio of net investment income to average net assets	1.47%	2.56%	2.39%
16. Portfolio turnover rate*	85%	144%	74%

**Portfolio turnover rate* relates the number of shares bought and sold by the fund to the total number of shares held in the fund's portfolio. A high turnover rate (in excess of 100%) means the fund has been doing a lot of trading.

Open-end mutual funds regularly publish reports that recap investment performance. One such report is the *Summary of Income and Capital Changes*, an example of which is provided in Table 13.3. This statement is found in the fund's profile or prospectus, and gives a brief overview of the fund's investment activity, including expense ratios and portfolio turnover rates. Of interest to us here is the top part of the report (which runs from "net asset value, beginning of period" to "net asset value, end of period"—lines 1 to 10). This part reveals the amount of dividend income and capital gains distributed to the shareholders, along with any change in the fund's net asset value.

dividend income
income derived from the dividend and interest income earned on the security holdings of a mutual fund.

Dividend income (see line 7 of Table 13.3) is derived from the dividend and interest income earned on the security holdings of the mutual fund. It is paid out of the *net investment income* that's left after all operating expenses have been met. When the fund receives dividend or interest payments, it passes these on to shareholders in the form of dividend payments. The fund accumulates all of the current income it has received for the period and then pays it out on a prorated basis. Thus, if a fund earned, say, $2 million in dividends and interest in a given year and if that fund had 1 million shares outstanding, each share would receive an annual dividend payment of $2. Keep in mind that because the mutual fund itself is tax exempt, any taxes due on dividend earnings are payable by the individual investor. For funds that are not held in tax-deferred accounts, like IRAs or 401(k)s, the amount of taxes due on dividends will depend on the source of such dividends. That is, *if these distributions are derived from dividends earned on the fund's common stock holdings, then they are subject to a preferential tax rate of 15%, or less*. However, if these distributions are derived from interest earnings on bonds, dividends from REITs, or dividends from most types of preferred stocks, then such dividends *do not qualify for the preferential tax treatment*, but instead are taxed as ordinary income.

capital gains distributions
payments made to mutual fund shareholders that come from the profits that a fund makes from the sale of its securities.

Capital gains distributions (see line 8) work on the same principle, except that these payments are derived from the *capital gains actually earned* by the fund. It works like this: Suppose the fund bought some stock a year ago for \$50 and sold that stock in the current period for \$75 per share. Clearly, the fund has achieved capital gains of \$25 per share. If it held 50,000 shares of this stock, it would have realized a total capital gain of \$1,250,000 (\$25 × 50,000 = \$1,250,000). Given that the fund has 1 million shares outstanding, each share is entitled to \$1.25 in the form of a capital gains distribution. (From a tax perspective, if the capital gains are long-term in nature, then they qualify for the preferential tax rate of 15%, or less; if not, then they're treated as ordinary income.) Note that these (capital gains) distributions apply only to *realized* capital gains (that is, the security holdings were actually sold and the capital gains actually earned).

unrealized capital gains (paper profits)
a capital gain made only "on paper"—that is, not realized until the fund's holdings are sold.

Unrealized capital gains (or **paper profits**) are what make up the third and final element of a mutual fund's return. When the fund's holdings go up or down in price, the net asset value of the fund moves accordingly. Suppose an investor buys into a fund at \$10 per share and sometime later the fund is quoted at \$12.50. The difference of \$2.50 per share is the unrealized capital gains. It represents the profit that shareholders would receive (and are entitled to) if the fund were to sell its holdings. (Actually, as Table 13.3 shows, some of the change in net asset value can also be made up of undistributed income.)

The return on *closed-end* investment companies is derived from the same three sources as that of open-end funds and from a *fourth source* as well: changes in price discounts or premiums. But because the discount or premium is already embedded in the share price of a fund, it follows that, for a closed-end fund, the third element of return—change in share price—is made up not only of change in net asset value but also of change in price discount or premium.

What About Future Performance? There's no doubt that a statement like the one in Table 13.3 provides a convenient recap of a fund's past behavior. Looking at past performance is useful, but it doesn't tell you what the future will be. Ideally, you want an indication of what the same three elements of return—dividend income, capital gains distribution, and change in NAV—*will be*. But it's extremely difficult—if not impossible—to get a firm grip on what the future holds in dividends, capital gains, and NAV. This is because a mutual fund's future performance is directly linked to the *future make-up of the securities in its portfolio*, something that is next to impossible to get a clear reading on. It's not like evaluating the expected performance of a share of stock, in which case you're keying in on one company. With mutual funds, investment performance depends on the behavior of many different stocks and bonds.

HOT

You can research risk, price history, and managers of mutual funds at the MSN site:

moneycentral.msn.com/investor/research/wizards/FRW.asp?Funds=1

Where, then, do you look for insight into future performance? Most market observers suggest that the first place to look is the market itself. In particular, try to get a fix on the future direction of *the market as a whole*. This is important because the behavior of a well-diversified mutual fund tends to reflect the general tone of the market. Thus, if the feeling is that the market is going to be drifting up, so should the investment performance of mutual funds. Also spend some time evaluating the *track records* of mutual funds in which you are interested. Past performance has a lot to say about the investment skills of the fund's money managers. In essence, look for funds that you think will be able to capture the best of what the future market environment holds.

Measures of Return A simple but effective measure of performance is to describe mutual fund return in terms of the three major sources noted above: dividends earned, capital gains distributions received, and change in price. When dealing with investment horizons of 1 year or less, we can easily convert these fund payoffs into a return figure by using the standard holding period return (HPR) formula. The computations necessary are illustrated below using the 2004 figures from Table 13.3. Referring to the exhibit, we can see that in 2004, this hypothetical no-load, open-end fund paid 55 cents per share in dividends and another $1.75 in capital gains distributions. It had a price at the beginning of the year of $24.47 that rose to $29.14 by the end of the year. Thus, summarizing this investment performance, we have

Price (NAV) at the *beginning* of the year (line 1)	$24.47
Price (NAV) at the *end* of the year (line 10)	29.14
Net increase	$ 4.67
Return for the year:	
Dividends received (line 7)	$ 0.55
Capital gains distributions (line 8)	1.75
Net increase in price (NAV)	4.67
Total return	$ 6.97
Holding period return (HPR) (Total return/beginning price)	**28.48%**

This HPR measure (which is shown in Table 13.3 as "Total Return" on line 11) not only captures all the important elements of mutual fund return but also provides a handy indication of yield. Note that the fund had a total dollar return of $6.97. On the basis of a beginning investment of $24.47 (the initial share price of the fund), the fund produced an annual return of nearly 28.5%.

HPR with Reinvested Dividends and Capital Gains Many mutual fund investors have their dividends and/or capital gains distributions reinvested in the fund. How, then, do you obtain a measure of return when you receive your (dividend/capital gains) payout in additional shares of stock rather than cash? With slight modifications, you can continue to use holding period return. The only difference is that you have to keep track of the number of shares acquired through reinvestment. To illustrate, let's continue with the example above and assume that you initially bought 200 shares in the mutual fund. Assume also that you were able to acquire shares through the fund's reinvestment program at an average price of $26.50 a share. Thus, the $460 in dividends and capital gains distributions [($.55 + $1.75) × 200] provided you with another 17.36 shares in the fund ($460/$26.50). Holding period return under these circumstances would relate the market value of the stock holdings at the beginning of the period with the holdings at the end:

Equation 13.2

$$\text{Holding period return} = \frac{\left(\begin{array}{c}\text{Number of}\\ \text{shares at } \textit{end}\\ \text{of period}\end{array} \times \begin{array}{c}\text{Ending}\\ \text{price}\end{array}\right) - \left(\begin{array}{c}\text{Number of}\\ \text{shares at } \textit{beginning}\\ \text{of period}\end{array} \times \begin{array}{c}\text{Initial}\\ \text{price}\end{array}\right)}{\left(\begin{array}{c}\text{Number of shares}\\ \text{at } \textit{beginning} \text{ of period}\end{array} \times \begin{array}{c}\text{Initial}\\ \text{price}\end{array}\right)}$$

Thus, the holding period return on this investment would be

$$\text{Holding period return} = \frac{(217.36 \times \$29.14) - (200 \times \$24.47)}{(200 \times \$24.47)}$$

$$= \frac{(\$6,333.87) - (\$4,894.00)}{(\$4,894.00)} = \underline{\underline{29.4\%}}$$

This holding period return, like the preceding one, provides a rate-of-return measure that can now be used to compare the performance of this fund to those of other funds and investment vehicles.

Measuring Long-Term Returns Rather than using 1-year holding periods, it is sometimes necessary to assess the performance of mutual funds over extended periods of time. In these cases, it would be inappropriate to employ holding period return as a measure of performance, because it ignores the time value of money. Instead, when faced with multiple-year investment horizons, we can use the present-value-based *internal rate of return* (IRR) procedure to determine the fund's average annual compound rate of return. To illustrate, refer once again to Table 13.3. Assume that this time we want to find the annual rate of return over the full 3-year period (2002 through 2004). In this case, we see that the mutual fund had the following annual dividends and capital gains distributions:

	2004	2003	2002
Annual dividends paid	$ .55	$ .64	$ .50
Annual capital gains distributed	$1.75	$ .84	$1.02
Total distributions	$2.30	$1.48	$1.52

Now, given that the fund had a price of $24.26 at the beginning of the period (1/1/02) and was trading at $29.14 at the end of 2004 (3 years later), we have the following time line of cash flows:

Initial Cash Flow	Subsequent Cash Flows: Year 1	Year 2	Year 3
$24.26 (Beginning Price)	$1.52 (Distributions)	$1.48 (Distributions)	$2.30 + $29.14 (Distributions + Ending Price)

The idea is to find the discount rate that will equate the annual dividends/capital gains distributions *and* the ending price in year 3 to the beginning (2002) price of the fund ($24.26).

Using standard present-value calculations, we find that the mutual fund in Table 13.3 provided its investors with an annual rate of return of 13.1% over the 3-year period from 2002 through 2004. That is, at 13.1%, the present value of the cash flows in years 1, 2, and 3 equals the beginning price of the fund ($24.26). Such information helps us assess fund performance and compare the return performance of one fund to other funds and investment vehicles. According to SEC regulations, if mutual funds report historical return behavior, they must do so in a standardized format that employs fully compounded, total-return figures similar to those obtained from the above present value-based measure of return. The funds are not required to report such information, but if they do cite performance in their promotional material, they must follow a full-disclosure manner of presentation that takes into account not only dividends and capital gains distributions but also any increases or decreases in the fund's NAV that have occurred over the preceding 1-, 3-, 5-, and 10-year periods.

Returns on Closed-End Funds The returns of CEFs have traditionally been reported on the basis of their NAVs. That is, *price premiums and discounts were ignored when computing return measures.* It is, however, becoming increasingly common to see return performance expressed in terms of *actual market prices*, a practice that captures the impact of changing market premiums or discounts on holding period returns. As you might expect, the greater the premiums or discounts and the greater the changes in these values over time, the greater their impact on reported returns. It's not at all uncommon for CEFs to have different market-based and NAV-based holding period returns. When NAVs are used, you find the returns on CEFs in exactly the same way as you do the returns on open-end funds. In contrast, when market values (i.e., actual market prices) are used to measure return, all you need do *is substitute the market price of the fund* (with its embedded premium or discount) *for the corresponding NAV in the holding period or internal rate of return* measures. Some CEF investors like to run *both* NAV-based and market-based measures of return to see how changing premiums (or discounts) have added to or hurt the returns on their mutual fund holdings. Even so, as a rule, NAV-based return numbers are generally viewed as the preferred measures of performance. Because fund managers often have little or no control over changes in premiums or discounts, NAV-based measures are felt to give a truer picture of the performance of the fund itself.

The Matter of Risk Because most mutual funds are so diversified, their investors are largely immune to the business and financial risks normally present with individual securities. Even with extensive diversification, however, the investment behavior of most funds is still exposed to a considerable amount of *market risk*. In fact, because mutual fund portfolios are so well diversified, they often tend to perform very much like the market—or some segment of the market that's being targeted by the fund. Although a few funds, like gold funds, tend to be defensive (countercyclical), market risk is still an important behavioral ingredient for most types of mutual funds, both open- and closed-end. Investors should be aware of the effect the general market has on the investment performance of a mutual fund. For example, if the market is trending downward and you anticipate that trend to continue, it might be best to place any new investment capital into something like a money fund until the market reverses itself. At that time, you can make a more long-term commitment.

Another important risk consideration revolves around *the management practices of the fund itself*. If the portfolio is managed conservatively, the risk of a loss in capital is likely to be much less than that for aggressively managed funds. Obviously, the more speculative the investment goals of the fund, the greater the risk of instability in the net asset value. But, a conservatively managed portfolio does not necessarily eliminate all price volatility. The securities in the portfolio are still subject to inflation, interest rate, and general market risks. However, these risks are generally reduced or minimized as the investment objectives and portfolio management practices of the funds become more conservative.

CONCEPTS IN REVIEW

13.12 How important is the general behavior of the market in affecting the price performance of mutual funds? Explain. Why is a fund's past performance important to the mutual fund selection process? Does the future behavior of the market matter in the selection process? Explain.

13.13 What is the major/dominant type of closed-end fund? What is the difference between regional funds and single-country funds? How do CEFs differ from open-end funds?

13.14 Identify three potential sources of return to mutual fund investors and briefly discuss how each could affect total return to shareholders. Explain how the discount or premium of a closed-end fund can also be treated as a return to investors.

13.15 Discuss the various types of risk to which mutual fund shareholders are exposed. What is the major risk exposure of mutual funds? Are all funds subject to the same level of risk? Explain.

Summary

LG 1

Describe the basic features of mutual funds, and note what they have to offer as investment vehicles. Mutual fund shares represent ownership in a diversified, professionally managed portfolio of securities. Many investors who lack the time, know-how, or commitment to manage their own money turn to mutual funds. Mutual funds shareholders benefit from a level of diversification and investment performance they might otherwise find difficult to achieve. In addition, they can establish an investment program with a limited amount of capital and obtain a variety of investor services not available elsewhere.

LG 2

Distinguish between open- and closed-end mutual funds, as well as other types of professionally managed investment companies, and discuss the various types of fund loads, fees, and charges. Open-end funds have no limit on the number of shares they may issue. Closed-end funds have a fixed number of shares outstanding and trade in the secondary markets like any other share of common stock. Exchange-traded funds possess characteristics of both open-end and closed-end funds. Other types of investment companies are unit investment trusts, hedge funds (a type of private, unregulated investment vehicle available to institutional and high-net-worth individual investors), REITs (which invest primarily in various types of real estate products), and variable annuities. Mutual fund investors face an array of loads, fees, and charges, including front-end loads, back-end loads, annual 12(b)-1 charges, and annual management fees. Some of these costs are one-time charges (e.g., front-end loads). Others are paid annually [e.g., 12(b)-1 and management fees]. Investors should understand fund costs, which can be a real drag on fund performance and return.

LG 3 **Discuss the types of funds available and the variety of investment objectives these funds seek to fulfill.** Each fund has an established investment objective that determines its investment policy and identifies it as a certain type of fund. Some of the more popular types of funds are growth funds, aggressive growth funds, value funds, equity-income funds, balanced funds, growth-and-income funds, asset allocation funds, index funds, bond funds, money funds, sector funds, socially responsible funds, and international funds. The different categories of funds have different risk-return characteristics.

LG 4 **Discuss the investor services offered by mutual funds and how these services can fit into an investment program.** Mutual funds also offer special services, such as automatic investment and reinvestment plans, systematic withdrawal programs, low-cost conversion and phone-switching privileges, and retirement programs.

LG 5 **Gain an appreciation of the investor uses of mutual funds, along with the variables to consider when assessing and selecting funds for investment purposes.** Mutual funds can be used to accumulate wealth, as a storehouse of value, or as a vehicle for speculation and short-term trading. The fund selection process generally starts by assessing the investor's needs and wants. The next step is to consider what the funds have to offer, particularly with regard to investment objectives, risk exposure, and investor services. The investor then narrows down the alternatives by aligning his or her needs with the types of funds available and, from this short list of funds, applies the final selection tests: fund performance and cost.

LG 6 **Identify the sources of return and compute the rate of return earned on a mutual fund investment.** The payoff from investing in a mutual fund includes dividend income, distribution of realized capital gains, growth in capital (unrealized capital gains), and—for closed-end funds—the change in premium or discount. Various measures of return recognize these elements and provide simple yet effective ways of gauging the annual rate of return from a mutual fund. Risk is also important to mutual fund investors. A fund's extensive diversification may protect investors from business and financial risks. But considerable market risk still remains because most funds tend to perform much like the market, or like that segment of the market in which they specialize.

Putting Your Investment Know-How to the Test

1. A charge on the sale of shares in mutual fund is called a
   a. Front-end load.
   b. Back-end load.
   c. 12(b)-1 charge.
   d. Management fee.
2. Which of the following investment companies invests in a portfolio that is fixed for the life of the fund?
   a. A mutual fund
   b. A money market fund
   c. A unit investment trust
   d. An asset allocation fund

CHARTERED CFA FINANCIAL ANALYST

3. The structure of an investment company is *least likely* to be characterized by
   a. A corporate form of organization.
   b. Investment of a pool of funds from many investors in a portfolio of investments.

c. An annual management fee ranging from 3% to 5% of the total value of the fund.
d. A board of directors who hires a separate investment management company to manage the portfolio of securities and to handle other administrative duties.

4. The net asset value (NAV) of a mutual fund is defined as the
   a. Book value of assets divided by the number of shares outstanding.
   b. Book value of assets minus liabilities divided by the number of shares outstanding.
   c. Market value of assets divided by the number of shares outstanding.
   d. Market value of assets minus liabilities divided by the number of shares outstanding.

5. Consider a no-load mutual fund with $200 million in assets, $20 million in debt, and 20 million shares at the beginning of the year; and $300 million in assets, $25 million in debt, and 25 million shares at the end of the year. During the year investors receive combined dividends and capital gains distributions of $0.70 per share. What is the annual rate of return on this fund?
   a. 22.2% b. 25.0%
   c. 28.7% d. 30.0%

6. The ZYX fund is a closed-end fund with assets currently worth $300 million. It has liabilities of $15 million and 10 million shares outstanding. If the shares sell for $31, what is its percentage premium (or discount) to its net asset value (NAV)?
   a. 8.8% premium
   b. 3.3% premium
   c. 8.8% discount
   d. 3.3% discount

7. Sector funds concentrate their investment portfolios in
   a. Government securities.
   b. Bonds of a particular maturity.
   c. Securities issued by firms in a particular industry.
   d. Municipal bonds from certain geographic areas.

8. Mutual funds whose goal is to generate both current income and long-term capital appreciation by holding a portfolio of stocks and bonds in relatively stable proportions are called
   a. Growth-and-income funds.
   b. Balanced funds.
   c. Index funds.
   d. Equity-income funds.

9. The ABC Fund sells class A shares with a front-end load of 6% and class B shares with a 1% 12(b)-1 annual fee and a 1% redemption charge voided after 10 years. If you plan to sell the fund after 8 years, which shares offer a better choice?
   a. Class A.
   b. Class B.
   c. There is no difference between the two.
   d. Not enough information is given to calculate the returns.

10. Which of the following is *not* an exchange-traded fund?
    a. Diamond b. Qube
    c. Cobra d. Spider

Answers: 1. a; 2. c; 3. c; 4. b; 5. d; 6. a; 7. c; 8. b; 9. a; 10. c

Discussion Questions

LG 1 LG 2

Q13.1 Contrast *mutual fund ownership* with *direct investment in stocks and bonds.* Assume your class is going to debate the merits of investing through mutual funds versus investing directly in stocks and bonds. Develop some arguments on each side of this debate and be prepared to discuss them in class. If you had to choose one side to be on, which would it be? Why?

LG 2

Q13.2 Based on the mutual fund quotes in Figure 13.5, answer the questions listed below for each of the following five funds:

(1) Clipper Fund (Clipper).
(2) Diversified High Yield Bonds (HiYldBd).
(3) Fidelity Canada (Canad).
(4) Cohen & Steers Equity Income/C shares (EqIncC).
(5) FMI Focus Fund (FMI Focusfd).

Based on the information reported in Figure 13.5:

a. How much would you receive for each fund if you were selling them?
b. Which of the five listed funds have 12(b)-1 fees?
c. Which funds have redemption fees?
d. Do any of the funds have both 12(b)-1 and redemption fees?
e. Can you tell whether any of the funds are no-loads?
f. Which fund has the highest front-end load?
g. Which fund has the highest year-to-date return? Which has the lowest?

LG 3

Q13.3 For each pair of funds listed below, select the one that is likely to be the *less* risky. Briefly explain your answer.

a. Growth versus growth-and-income funds.
b. Equity-income versus high-grade corporate bond funds.
c. Balanced versus sector funds.
d. Global versus value funds.
e. Intermediate-term bonds versus high-yield municipal bond funds.

LG 2 LG 3

Q13.4 Describe an ETF and explain how these funds combine the characteristics of both open-end and close-end funds. Consider the Vanguard family of funds. Which of its funds most closely resembles a "spider" (SPDR)? In what respects are the Vanguard fund (that you selected) and spiders the same? How are they different? If you could invest in only one of them, which would it be? Explain.

LG 2 LG 6

Q13.5 In the absence of any load charges, open-end mutual funds are priced at (or very close to) their net asset values, whereas closed-end funds rarely trade at their NAVs. Explain why one type of fund would normally trade at its NAV while the other type (CEFs) usually does not. What are price premiums and discounts, and in what segment of the mutual fund market will you usually find them? Look in a recent edition of the *Wall Street Journal* (*Hint:* pick one that comes out on Mondays), and find five funds that trade at a discount and five funds that trade at a premium. List all 10 of them, including the sizes of their respective discounts and premiums. What's the biggest price discount you could find? How about the biggest price premium? What would cause a fund to trade at a discount? At a premium?

LG 3 LG 5

Q13.6 Imagine that you've just inherited $20,000. Now you're faced with the "problem" of how to spend it. You could make a down payment on a condo, or you could buy that sports car you've always wanted. Or you could build a mutual fund portfolio. After some soul-searching, you decide to build a $20,000 mutual fund portfolio. Using actual mutual funds and actual quoted prices, come up with a plan to invest as much of the $20,000 as you can in a portfolio of mutual funds. (In addition to one or more open-end funds, include at least one CEF *or* one ETF.) Be specific! Briefly describe your planned portfolio, including the investment objectives you are trying to achieve.

Problems

LG 6

P13.1 A year ago, an investor bought 200 shares of a mutual fund at $8.50 per share. Over the past year, the fund has paid dividends of 90 cents per share and had a capital gains distribution of 75 cents per share.

a. Find the investor's holding period return, given that this no-load fund now has a net asset value of $9.10.
b. Find the holding period return, assuming all the dividends and capital gains distributions are reinvested into additional shares of the fund at an average price of $8.75 per share.

LG 6

P13.2 A year ago, the Really Big Growth Fund was being quoted at a NAV of $21.50 and an offer price of $23.35. Today it's being quoted at $23.04 (NAV) and $25.04 (offer). What is the holding period return on this load fund, given that it was purchased a year ago and that its dividends and capital gains distributions over the year have totaled $1.05 per share? (*Hint:* You, as an investor, buy fund shares at the offer price and sell at the NAV.)

LG 6

P13.3 The All-State Mutual Fund has the following 5-year record of performance.

	2003	2002	2001	2000	1999
Net investment income	$ 0.98	$ 0.85	$ 0.84	$ 0.75	$ 0.64
Dividends from net investment income	(0.95)	(0.85)	(0.85)	(0.75)	(0.60)
Net realized and unrealized gains (or losses) on security transactions	4.22	5.08	(2.18)	2.65	(1.05)
Distributions from realized gains	(1.05)	(1.00)	—	(1.00)	—
Net increase (decrease) in NAV	$ 3.20	$ 4.08	($ 2.19)	$ 1.65	($ 1.01)
NAV at beginning of year	12.53	8.45	10.64	.99	10.00
NAV at end of year	$15.73	$12.53	$ 8.45	$10.64	$ 8.99

Find this no-load fund's 5-year (1999–2003) average annual compound rate of return. Also find its 3-year (2001–2003) average annual compound rate of return. If an investor bought the fund in 1999 at $10.00 a share and sold it 5 years later (in 2003) at $15.73, how much total profit per share would she have made over the 5-year holding period?

LG 6

P13.4 You've uncovered the following per-share information about a certain mutual fund.

	2002	2003	2004
Ending share prices:			
Offer	$46.20	$64.68	$61.78
NAV	43.20	60.47	57.75
Dividend income	2.10	2.84	2.61
Capital gains distribution	1.83	6.26	4.32
Beginning share prices:			
Offer	55.00	46.20	64.68
NAV	51.42	43.20	60.47

On the basis of this information, find the fund's holding period return for 2002, 2003, and 2004. (In all three cases, assume you buy the fund at the beginning of the year and sell it at the end of each year.) In addition, find the fund's average annual compound rate of return over the 3-year period, 2002–2004. What would the 2003 holding period return have been if the investor had initially bought 500 shares of stock and reinvested both dividends and capital gains distributions into additional shares of the fund at an average price of $52.50 per share?

LG 2 LG 6

P13.5 Listed is the 10-year, per-share performance record of Larry, Moe, & Curly's Growth Fund, as obtained from the fund's May 30, 2004, prospectus.

	Years Ended March 31									
	2004	2003	2002	2001	2000	1999	1998	1997	1996	1995
1. Net asset value, beginning of period	$58.60	$52.92	$44.10	$59.85	$55.34	$37.69	$35.21	$34.25	$19.68	$29.82
2. Income from investment operations:										
3. Net investment income	$1.39	$1.35	$1.09	$0.63	$0.42	$ 0.49	$ 0.79	$0.37	$ 0.33	$0.38
4. Net gains on securities (realized and unrealized)	8.10	9.39	8.63	(6.64)	11.39	19.59	5.75	2.73	15.80	(0.02)
5. Total from investment operations	9.49	10.74	9.72	(6.01)	11.81	20.08	6.54	3.10	16.13	0.36
6. Less distributions:										
7. Dividends from net investment income	($0.83)	($1.24)	($0.90)	($0.72)	($0.46)	($0.65)	($0.37)	($0.26)	($0.33)	($0.58)
8. Distributions from realized gains	(2.42)	(3.82)	—	(9.02)	(6.84)	(1.78)	(3.69)	(1.88)	(1.23)	(9.92)
9. Total distributions	(3.25)	(5.06)	(0.90)	(9.74)	(7.30)	(2.43)	(4.06)	(2.14)	(1.56)	(10.50)
10. Net asset value, end of period	$64.84	$58.60	$52.92	$44.10	$59.85	$55.34	$37.69	$35.21	$34.25	$19.68

Use this information to find LM&C's holding period return in 2004 and 2001. Also find the fund's rate of return over the 5-year period 2000–2004, and the 10-year period 1995–2004. Finally, rework the four return figures assuming the LM&C fund has a front-end load charge of 3% (of NAV). Comment on the impact of load charges on the return behavior of mutual funds.

LG 3 LG 6

P13.6 Using the resources available at your campus or public library (or those available on the Internet), select five mutual funds—a growth fund, an equity-income fund, an international (stock) fund, an index fund, and a high-yield corporate bond fund—that you feel would make good investments. Briefly explain why you selected these funds. List the funds' holding period returns for the past year and their annual compound rates of return for the past 3 years. (Use a schedule like the one in Table 13.3 to show relevant performance figures.)

LG 6

P13.7 One year ago, Super Star Closed-End Fund had a NAV of $10.40 and was selling at an 18% discount. Today its NAV is $11.69 and it is priced at a 4% premium. During the year, Super Star paid dividends of 40 cents and had a capital gains distribution of 95 cents. On the basis of the above information, calculate each of the following.

a. Super Star's NAV-based holding period return for the year.
b. Super Star's market-based holding period return for the year. Did the market premium/discount hurt or add value to the investor's return? Explain.
c. Repeat the market-based holding period return calculation, except this time assume the fund started the year at an 18% *premium* and ended it at a 4% *discount*. (Assume the beginning and ending NAVs remain at $10.40 and $11.69, respectively.) Is there any change in this measure of return? Why?

LG 6

P13.8 The Well Managed Closed-End Fund turned in the following performance for the year 2004.

	Beginning of the Year	End of the Year
NAV	$7.50	$9.25
Market price of the fund shares	$7.75	$9.00
Dividends paid over the year	—	$1.20
Capital gains distributed over the year	—	$0.90

a. Based on this information, what was the NAV-based HPR for the WMCEF in 2004?
b. Find the percentage (%) premium or discount at which the fund was trading at the beginning of the year and at the end of the year.
c. What was the market-based HPR for the fund in 2004? Did the market premium or discount add to or hurt the holding period return on this CEF? Explain.

LG 6

P13.9 Three years ago, you invested in the Future Investco Mutual Fund by purchasing 1,000 shares of the fund at a net asset value of $20.00 per share. Because you did not need the income, you elected to reinvest all dividends and gains distributions. Today, you sell your 1,100 shares in this fund for $22.91 per share. What is the compounded rate of return on this investment over the three-year period?

LG 6

P13.10 Refer to Problem 13.9 above. If there were a 3% load on this fund, assuming you purchased the same number of shares, what would your rate of return be?

LG 6

P.13.11 You invested in the no-load OhYes Mutual Fund one year ago by purchasing 1,000 shares of the fund at the net asset value of $25.00 per share. The fund distributed dividends of $1.50 and capital gains of $2.00. Today, the NAV is $26. What was your holding period return?

LG 6

P13.12 Refer to Problem 13.11 above. If OhYes was a load fund with a 2% front end load, what would be the HPR?

LG 6

P13.13 Refer to Figure 13.8. You purchased shares of AdamsExp (**ADX**) at the end of the day quoted. The fund pays the same dividend this year as that quoted, and at the end of the year the fund is quoted as having a NAV of $15.00 and a close of $14.50. What is your holding period return?

LG 6

P13.14 Refer to Problem 13.13 above. Now assume that you hold your shares of AdamsExp for three years. Each year you receive the same dividend, and at the end of year three, the fund has a NAV of $15.00 and a close of $15.68. What is the compound annual rate of return for the three-year period?

LG 6

P13.15 You are considering the purchase of shares of a closed end mutual fund. The NAV is equal to $22.50 and the latest close is $20.00. Is this fund trading at a premium or a discount? How big is the premium or discount?

LG 6

P13.16 You purchased 1,000 shares of MutualMagic one year ago for $20.00 per share. During the year, you received $2.00 in dividends, half of which were from dividends on stock the fund held and half of which was from interest earned on bonds in the fund portfolio. Assuming your federal marginal tax rate is 25%, how much will you owe in federal taxes on the distributions you received this year (your answer should be in dollars).

See the text Web site (www.aw-bc.com/gitman_joehnk) for Web exercises that deal with *mutual funds*.

Case Problem 13.1 *Reverend Robin Ponders Mutual Funds*

LG 3 LG 5

Reverend Robin is the minister of a church in the San Antonio area. He is married, has one young child, and earns a "modest income." Because religious organizations are not notorious for their generous retirement programs, the reverend has decided he should do some investing on his own. He would like to set up a program that enables him to supplement the church's retirement program and at the same time provide some funds for his child's college education (which is still some 12 years away). He is not out to break any investment records but wants some backup to provide for the long-run needs of his family.

Although he has a modest income, Reverend Robin believes that with careful planning, he can probably invest about $250 a quarter (and, with luck, increase this amount over time). He currently has about $15,000 in a savings account that he would be willing to use to begin this program. In view of his investment objectives, he is not interested in taking a lot of risk. Because his knowledge of investments extends to savings accounts, Series EE savings bonds, and a little bit about mutual funds, he approaches you for some investment advice.

Questions

a. In light of Reverend Robin's long-term investment goals, do you think mutual funds are an appropriate investment vehicle for him?

b. Do you think he should use his $15,000 savings to start a mutual fund investment program?

c. What type of mutual fund investment program would you set up for the reverend? Include in your answer some discussion of the types of funds you would consider, the investment objectives you would set, and any investment services (e.g., withdrawal plans) you would seek. Would taxes be an important consideration in your investment advice? Explain.

Case Problem 13.2 *Tom Yee Seeks the Good Life*

LG 3 LG 4 LG 5 LG 6

Tom Yee is a widower who recently retired after a long career with a major Midwestern manufacturer. Beginning as a skilled craftsman, he worked his way up to the level of shop supervisor over a period of more than 30 years with the firm. Tom receives Social Security benefits and a generous company pension. Together, these two sources amount to over $4,500 per month (part of which is tax-free). The Yees had no children, so he lives alone. Tom owns a two-bedroom rental house that is next to his home, and the rental income from it covers the mortgage payments for both the rental house and his house.

Over the years, Tom and his late wife, Camille, always tried to put a little money aside each month. The results have been nothing short of phenomenal. The value of Tom's liquid investments (all held in bank CDs and passbook savings accounts) runs well into the six figures. Up to now, Tom has just let his money grow and has not used any of his savings to supplement his Social Security, pension, and rental income. But things are about to change. Tom has decided, "What the heck, it's time I start living the good life!" Tom wants to travel and, in effect, start reaping the benefits of his labors. He has therefore decided to move $100,000 from one of his savings accounts to one or two high-yielding mutual funds. He would like to receive $1,000–$1,500 a month from the fund(s) for as long as possible, because he plans to be around for a long time.

Questions

a. Given Tom's financial resources and investment objectives, what kinds of mutual funds do you think he should consider?

b. What factors in Tom's situation should be taken into consideration in the fund selection process? How might these affect Tom's course of action?

c. What types of services do you think he should look for in a mutual fund?

d. Assume Tom invests in a mutual fund that earns about 10% annually from dividend income and capital gains. Given that Tom wants to receive $1,000 to $1,500 a month from his mutual fund, what would be the size of his investment account 5 years from now? How large would the account be if the fund earned 15% on average and everything else remained the same? How important is the fund's rate of return to Tom's investment situation? Explain.

Excel with Spreadsheets

In the Wall Street Journal, open-ended mutual funds are listed separately from other securities. They have their own quotation system where two primary data variables are the net asset value (NAV) and the year-to-date returns. The NAV represents the price you get when you sell shares, or what you pay when you buy no-load funds.

Create a spreadsheet model similar to the spreadsheet for Table 13.3, which you can view at www.aw-bc.com/gitman_joehnk, to analyze the following three years of data relating to the MoMoney Mutual Fund. It should report the amount of dividend income and capital gains distributed to the shareholders, along with any other changes in the fund's net asset value.

	A	B	C	D	E
1		2003	2002	2001	
2	NAV, beginning of period	$ 35.24	$ 37.50	$ 36.25	
3	Net investment income	$ 0.65	$ 0.75	$ 0.60	
4	Net gains on securities	$ 5.25	$ 4.75	$ (3.75)	
5	Dividends from net investment income	$ 0.61	$ 0.57	$ 0.52	
6	Distributions from realized gains	$ 1.75	$ 2.01	$ 1.55	

Questions

a. What is the total income from the investment operations?
b. What are the total distributions from the investment operations?
c. Calculate the net asset value for MoMoney Fund as of the end of the years 2002, 2001, and 2000.
d. Calculate the holding period returns for each of the years 2003, 2002, and 2001.

Part Two: Money, the Financial System, and the Economy

Taken from:
Money, the Financial System, and the Economy, Fifth Edition
by R. Glenn Hubbard

Contents: Money, the Financial System, and the Economy

CHAPTER 3 Overview of the Financial System 351

CHAPTER 5 The Theory of Portfolio Allocation 379

CHAPTER 11 Reducing Transactions Costs and Information Costs 397

CHAPTER 12 What Financial Institutions Do 415

CHAPTER

3 Overview of the Financial System

Throughout 2001 and during the course of the congressional campaign in 2002, many investors and businesspeople complained that the financial system was simply not working during the recession. Corporate accounting scandals made investors concerned about the values of financial assets. Businesspeople worried about the availability of credit. Politicians and economists began to take a hard look at how well the U.S. financial system brought together borrowers with good ideas and savers with money to lend.

Although you might not march to Washington to express your views about the financial system, the way the financial system works affects your well-being. At times in your life, you will be a saver, as when you put aside money for your children's education or your retirement. At other times, you will be a borrower. You may borrow to buy a home or car or to build a factory to produce your great invention. The financial system channels funds from savers to borrowers and makes it possible for both to achieve their objectives. When the financial system works efficiently, it increases the health of the economy: Borrowers obtain funds for consumption and investment, and savers are rewarded by earning extra funds that they might not have otherwise.

What does the financial system do? How does it accomplish its objectives? We begin to answer these questions in this chapter by introducing the playing field—*financial markets*—and some key players—*financial institutions*. To answer these questions in full, we need more than a single chapter. We continue our investigation of financial markets and financial institutions in Parts 2, 3, and 4. This chapter will give you the ground rules and background for your study of the financial system.

What Is the Purpose of the Financial System?

You probably don't think you have much in common with a farmer, an inventor, or the federal government. But you do. All of you at one time or another may need more funds than you have on hand. You may want to go to graduate school and delay your entry into the job market. A farmer may need money for spring planting. An inventor may want to finance the start of a new high-technology company. The federal government may run a budget deficit, spending more than it collects in taxes. Those finding themselves with a mismatch between income and desired spending may be willing to pay for the funds they need.

At the same time, others spend less than their incomes. Your parents may save for their retirement or for your education. A business receiving a big payment on a government contract may decide not to spend all the funds at once. Even the federal government currently collects more in taxes than it needs immediately. Those who have surplus funds may be willing to let someone else use their savings if they are compensated for doing so.

The mismatch between income and spending for individuals and organizations creates an opportunity to trade. The inventor can use the funds saved by your parents to start a business now. The inventor would be better off by earning a profit from investing funds in a new venture. Your parents would be better off by receiving the return that the inventor pays them for "renting" their funds. They would not have earned this extra income if they had kept their savings in a shoebox in a closet.

Not all financial transactions involve investing in a new project or business venture. Suppose that you have a good job and decide to buy a house. There's only one problem: You earn $30,000 per year, and the house you want to buy costs $100,000. You could rent an apartment and save your money slowly until you accumulate enough to buy the house. That would probably take many years, though, and you and your family may want to enjoy owning a home sooner. As an alternative, someone could lend you the money to buy the house now. Just as you would be better off by being able to enjoy the benefits of homeownership sooner, the person who loaned you the money would be better off, too. The interest that you pay the lender would be extra income—income that the lender would not have received without making the loan.

Now you can begin to see what functions the financial system provides in the economy. It moves funds from those who want to spend less than they have available to those who have a desire to purchase durable goods or those who have productive investment opportunities. This matching process increases the economy's ability to produce goods and services. In addition, it makes households and businesses better off by allowing them to time purchases according to their needs and desires. A smoothly functioning financial system thus improves the economy's efficiency and people's economic welfare.

The **financial system** provides channels to transfer funds from individuals and groups who have saved money to individuals and groups who want to borrow money. **Savers** (or lenders) are suppliers of funds, providing funds to borrowers in return for promises of repayment of even more funds in the future. **Borrowers** are demanders of funds for consumer durables, houses, or business plant and equipment, promising to repay borrowed funds based on their expectation of having higher incomes in the future. These promises are financial **liabilities** for the borrower—that is, both a source of funds and a claim against the borrower's future income. Conversely, the promises, or IOUs, are financial **assets** for savers—that is, both a use of funds and a claim on the borrower's future income. For example, your car loan is an asset (use of funds) for the bank and a liability (source of funds) for you. If you buy a house, the mortgage is your liability and your lender's asset. If your uncle buys Treasury bonds for his retirement account, the bonds are assets for him and liabilities for the U.S. government.

Web Site Suggestions:
http://www.nyse.com
http://www.reuters.com/markets.jhtml
http://finance.yahoo.com/?
Offer information and quotes from financial markets in the U.S. and overseas.

Figure 3.1 shows that the financial system channels funds from savers to borrowers and channels returns back to savers, both directly and indirectly. Savers and borrowers can be households, businesses, or governments, both domestic and foreign. **Financial markets**, such as the stock market or the bond market, issue claims on individual borrowers directly to savers. **Financial institutions or intermediaries**, such as banks, mutual funds, and insurance companies, act as go-betweens by holding a portfolio of assets and issuing claims based on that portfolio to savers. We discuss the participants in these activities and their roles later in this chapter. First, however, let's consider the financial services that motivate savers and borrowers to use the financial system.

FIGURE 3.1 **Moving Funds Through the Financial System**

The financial system transfers funds from savers to borrowers. Borrowers transfer returns back to savers through the financial system. Savers and borrowers include domestic and foreign households, businesses, and governments.

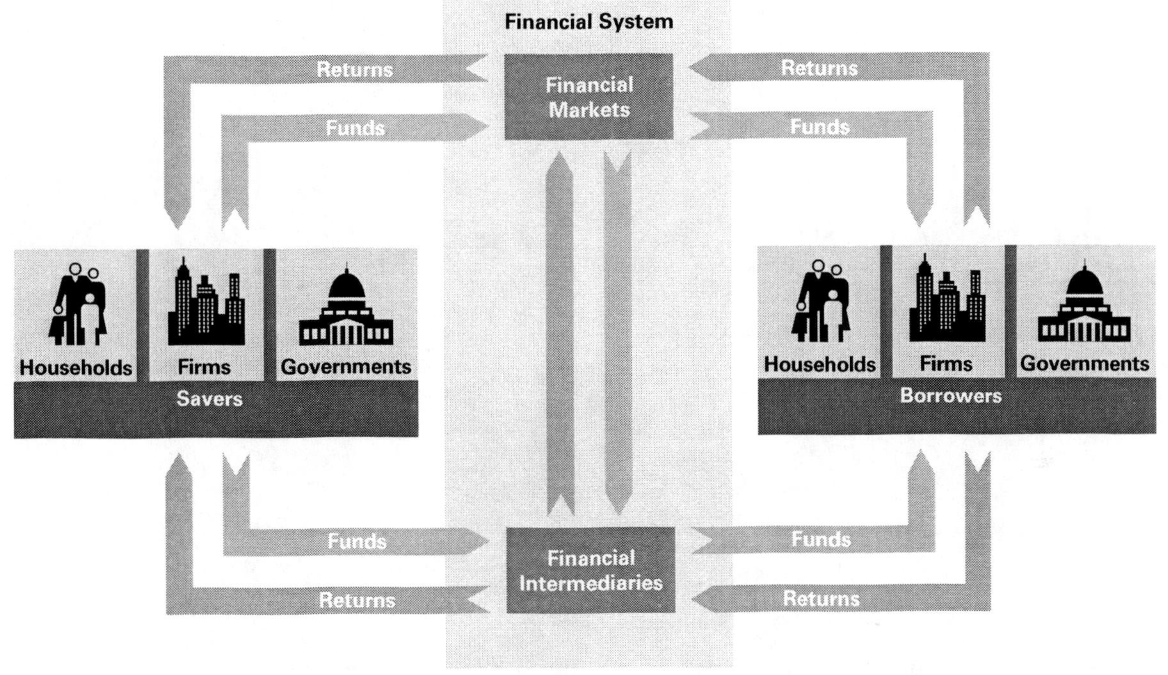

CHECKPOINT

As a saver, what sort of claims might you hold? You can hold claims on many borrowers. Your checking account is a claim on your bank. If you have savings bonds, you own a claim on the U.S. government. Money market accounts with Fidelity, Merrill Lynch, or any of their competitors are claims on a portfolio of assets held by the brokerage firm. If your aunt left you a Disney bond, you own a claim against that firm. ◆

Key Services Provided by the Financial System

In addition to matching individuals who have excess funds with those who need them, the financial system provides three key services for savers and borrowers. These services are *risk sharing*, *liquidity*, and *information*. Figure 3.2, a modified version of Fig. 3.1, emphasizes these services. Financial markets and financial intermediaries provide these services in different ways, making various financial assets and financial liabilities more attractive to individual savers and borrowers. Many financial decisions made by savers and borrowers are shaped by the availability of these services.

FIGURE 3.2 Key Services Provided by the Financial System
The financial system provides risk-sharing, liquidity, and information services. These services are valued by savers and borrowers.

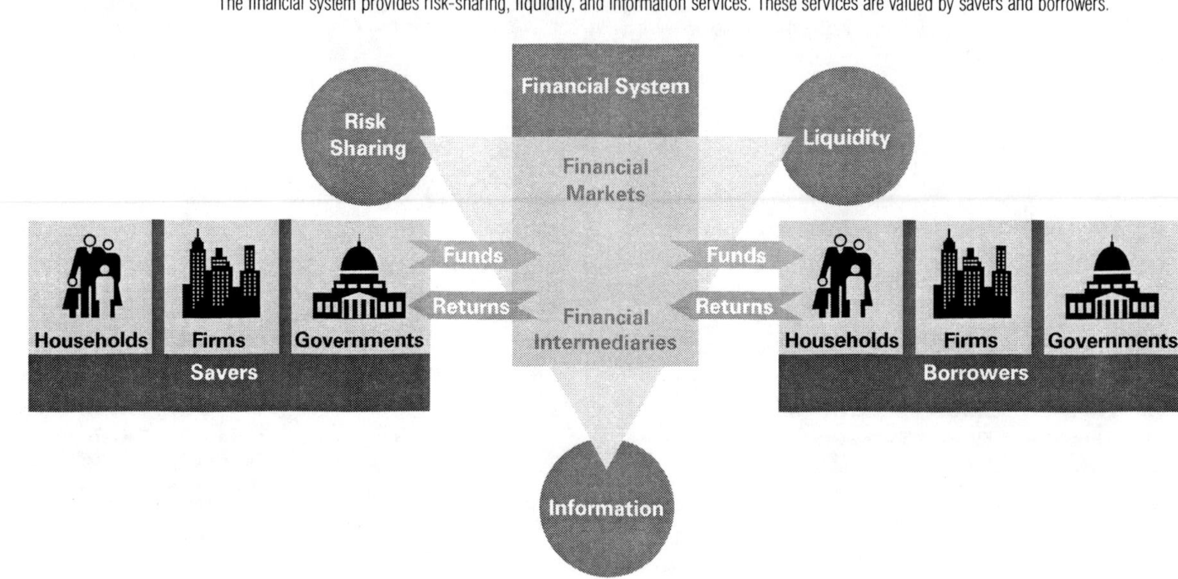

Risk Sharing

Your brother-in-law asks you to invest all your savings in shares of stock in his new company. You know that it's a risky proposition. If the economy booms, sales of the product—glow-in-the-dark earrings—might make you rich. But if the economy sours, those earrings might not be such a great product. You would like to invest in the business, but you're not convinced that you should tie up all your savings in such an investment. Are you being too cautious?

Probably not. One advantage of using the financial system to match individual savers and borrowers is that it allows the sharing of risks. *Risk* is the chance that the value of financial assets will change relative to what you expect. For example, if you buy a bond of Okayco for $1000, that bond might be worth $900 or $1100 in one year's time, depending on fluctuations in interest rates and Okayco's prospects. Most individual savers are not gamblers and seek a steady return on their assets rather than erratic swings between high and low earnings. Indeed, individuals prefer stable returns on the collection of assets they hold. A collection of assets is called a **portfolio.** For example, you might hold some U.S. savings bonds, some shares of stock, and some shares in a mutual fund. Although one asset or set of assets may perform well and another not so well, overall the returns tend to average out. This splitting of wealth into many assets is known as **diversification.** As long as the individual returns do not vary in the same way, the risk of severe fluctuations in a portfolio's value will be reduced. The financial system provides **risk sharing** by allowing savers to hold many assets.

We demonstrate the advantages of diversification in Chapter 5 and describe ways in which the financial system enables individuals to *transfer risk*. Financial markets can create instruments to transfer risk from savers or borrowers who do not like uncertainty in returns or payments to savers or investors who are willing to bear risk. For example, you might be willing to accept a lower return on your investment in your brother-in-law's business if he or one of his other investors guaranteed you that return. You have transferred some of your risk as a saver to the borrower—but the transfer comes at a cost: the lower return.

The ability of the financial system to provide risk sharing makes savers more willing to buy borrowers' IOUs. This willingness, in turn, increases borrowers' ability to raise funds in the financial system.

Liquidity

The second service that the financial system offers savers and borrowers is **liquidity,** which is the ease with which an asset can be exchanged for money to purchase other assets or exchanged for goods and services. Savers view the liquidity of financial assets as a benefit. When they need their assets for their own consumption or investment, they want to exchange them easily. In general, the more liquid an asset, the easier it is to exchange the asset for something else. You can easily exchange the dollar bill in your pocket for a hamburger because a dollar bill is highly liquid. You could also cash a check within a short period of time to buy clothes. Selling your car, however, takes more time because personal property is not very liquid. By holding financial claims (such as stock or bonds) on a factory, individual investors have more liquid savings than they would if they owned the machines in the factory. The reason is that the investor can more easily sell the claim than a specialized machine in order to buy other assets or goods. Liquid assets allow an individual or firm to respond quickly to new opportunities or unexpected events. Financial assets created by the financial system, such as stocks, bonds, or checking accounts, are more liquid than cars, machinery, or real estate.

Financial markets and intermediaries provide trading systems for making financial assets more liquid. In addition to creating financial assets, the financial system provides systems for increasing the liquidity of financial assets. In the United States, for instance, investors can readily sell their holdings in government securities and stocks and bonds of large corporations, making those assets very liquid. During the past two decades, the financial system has made many other assets liquid besides stocks and bonds. Thirty years ago, for example, financial intermediaries had to hold mortgage loans and loans made to businesses until the loans were paid off. Now, those institutions can sell the loans to other investors and buy loans made by other institutions. As a result, mortgages and other loans have become more desirable assets for savers to hold. Savers are willing to accept a lower return on assets with greater liquidity, reducing the costs of borrowing obligations for less well-known firms. One measure of the efficiency of the financial system is the extent to which it can transform illiquid assets into the liquid claims that savers want.

Information

A third service of the financial system is the collection and communication of **information,** or facts about borrowers and expectations about returns on financial assets. The first informational role the financial system plays is to gather information. That includes finding out about prospective borrowers and what they will do with borrowed funds. Joe's neighbor wants to borrow the money that Joe has set aside for his daughter's education and promises to pay it back when she starts college. Should Joe lend his neighbor his nest egg? To make a wise decision, Joe needs to know more about the loan. What will the neighbor do with the funds? How likely is it that Joe will be paid back in time for the first tuition payment? Obtaining such information would be costly and time-consuming for savers, who of course want all the facts before lending their money. Working through the financial system, Joe is likely to learn more about the borrower than he would if he tried to make the investment on his own.

Another problem that exists in most transactions is **asymmetric information.** This means that borrowers possess information about their opportunities or activities that they don't disclose to lenders or creditors and can take advantage of this information. Sometimes, financial arrangements have to be structured so that borrowers do not take advantage of asymmetric information at the expense of lenders. Fast Eddie might seek a $10,000 loan that he claims he will use to launch a new line of billiard cues, but he really plans to use the funds for a first-class cruise to Europe. Clearly, Fast Eddie knows more about the actual use of the funds than the potential lender. Parts of the financial system specialize in information gathering and monitoring, and specialized arrangements exist for solving problems of asymmetric information.

The second informational role that the financial system plays is *communication* of information. If you read a newspaper headline announcing that a pharmaceutical company had found a cure for cancer, how would you determine the effect of this discovery on the company's financial position? Financial markets do that job by incorporating information into the prices of stocks, bonds, and other financial assets. In this example, the expectation of higher future profits would boost the prices of the pharmaceutical company's outstanding stocks and bonds.

Savers and borrowers receive the benefits of information from the financial system by looking at asset returns. As long as financial market participants are informed, the information works its way into asset returns and prices. Information is communicated to borrowers as well as to savers. For example, if the price of the pharmaceutical company's stock goes up, the company may decide to sell more shares and invest the proceeds in new research projects. The incorporation of available information into asset returns is the distinguishing feature of well-functioning financial markets.

Financial Markets in the Financial System

Financial markets bring savers and borrowers together directly. When you buy a new share of Boomco stock for $100, you are investing the $100 directly in Boomco to finance its growth. In this form of finance, known as **direct finance,** an individual saver holds financial claims issued directly by an individual borrower. These direct finance arrangements take place through financial markets, markets in which investors lend their savings directly to borrowers. To analyze the role played by financial markets, we focus on the two principal tasks of the financial system: (1) matching savers and borrowers and (2) providing risk-sharing, liquidity, and information services.

Matching Savers and Borrowers: Debt and Equity

Primary markets are those in which newly issued claims are sold to initial buyers by the borrower. Businesses use primary markets to raise funds for new ventures, and governments use them to finance budget deficits. Borrowers can raise funds in a primary financial market in two ways—by borrowing or by selling shares—which result in different types of claims on the borrower's future income. The first and most commonly used claim is **debt,** which requires the borrower to repay the amount borrowed, the

principal, plus a rental fee, or **interest.**[†] The other type of claim is **equity,** which is an ownership claim to a share in the profits and assets of a firm.

Debt instruments are promises to repay the principal and interest, all at once or in periodic payments over a fixed period of time. The length of the period of time before the debt instrument expires is its **maturity,** or term. The maturity can be a short period of time (30 days or even overnight) or a long period of time (10 years or more). **Short-term debt** instruments have a maturity of less than one year. **Intermediate-term debt** instruments have a maturity between 1 year and 10 years. **Long-term debt** instruments have a maturity of 10 years or more. Debt instruments include student loans, government bonds, corporate bonds, and loans by financial institutions.

Debt instruments offer borrowers certain advantages. Suppose that you take out a student loan to study business, and when you graduate, you land a Wall Street position paying $50,000 per year. The fact that you got such a good job does not mean that you have to pay back more than the agreed-upon loan amount. In general, in a debt contract, a lender does not get more than the amount promised even if the borrower does exceptionally well. However, the lender may get less than the amount promised. If, for example, you cannot find a job and consequently can't pay back your loan, the lender gets less than the full amount of the loan. Lenders face the risk that borrowers will **default,** or not be able to repay all or part of their obligations.

The second means of raising funds—equity—allows for variable payments from the borrower to the lender. A good example is common stock, which entitles stockholders in a business to get their share of the firm's profits after all expenses, including payments of principal and interest to debtholders, have been settled. For example, if you own 100 shares of Bigco, which has 1 million shares outstanding, you own the right to 1/10,000 (100/1 million) of the firm's profits and assets. Equity owners generally receive periodic payments (usually once each quarter) from the firm, known as **dividends.** If the business does exceptionally well, equity owners receive more, while the debtholders still get only their promised payment. However, if the business's profits are weak, there may be nothing left after payments to debtholders are made. If you buy shares in Oopsco and it loses money, do you have to pay the firm's losses? No. Shareholders in corporations can lose only the amount of funds they invest in the venture. Firms also have strong reasons for issuing a particular mix of equity and debt. In Chapter 11, we examine the relative merits of using equity or debt to finance businesses, and we use economic intuition to explain major developments in the use of debt or equity.

Although you hear about the stock market's fluctuations each night on the evening news, debt instruments actually account for more of the funds raised in the financial system. In early 2003, the value of debt instruments was about $32.3 trillion compared to $11.9 trillion for equities.

Providing Risk-Sharing, Liquidity, and Information Services

Risk-sharing, liquidity, and information services are provided in **secondary markets,** markets in which claims that have already been issued are sold by one investor to

[†]The formula for computing how much interest is paid can be either an agreed-upon percentage, as is used for your bank account or student loan, or an indexed percentage, tied to some economic indicator such as the inflation rate or some published interest rate. Many business loans made by banks—especially in international lending—fall into the second category.

another. Suppose, for example, that you start a software company, Hitechco, which after a few years is growing rapidly but is in need of new capital for expansion. If you sell shares in Hitechco, you are turning to a primary market for new funds. Once Hitechco shares are issued, investors trade the shares in the secondary market. Note that as an owner of Hitechco, you do not receive any new funds when your company's shares are traded in secondary markets.

Most of the news about events in financial markets concerns secondary markets rather than primary ones. Most primary market transactions are sales of new debt or equity instruments to initial buyers and are conducted behind closed doors. The most widely reported secondary markets—such as the New York, American, and Tokyo Stock Exchanges—are those in which already-issued equities are traded. Even larger volumes of secondary market transactions take place in the bond market, in which U.S. government and corporate debt instruments are traded. Secondary markets are also important for global foreign-exchange transactions. Regardless of the type of instrument being traded, the buyer of the instrument in a secondary market pays money to the seller. The *initial* seller of the instrument—a corporation or government agency, for example—does *not* receive the proceeds. The initial issuer receives only the proceeds from the sale of the instrument in the primary market.

If the initial seller of a financial instrument raises funds from a lender only in the primary market, why are secondary markets so important? The answer incorporates risk-sharing, liquidity, and information services. Smoothly functioning secondary markets make it easier for investors to reduce their exposure to risk by holding a diversified portfolio of stocks, bonds, and other assets. Secondary markets also promote liquidity for stocks, bonds, foreign exchange, and other financial instruments so that it is easier for investors to sell the instruments for cash. This liquidity makes investors more willing to hold financial instruments, thereby making it easier for the issuing firm or government agency to sell the securities in the first place. Finally, secondary markets convey information to both savers and borrowers by determining the price of financial instruments. When the price of your shares of Hitechco rises, you are richer, which tells you that you can spend more if you want to. Likewise, the managers of Hitechco can get information on how well the market thinks they are doing from secondary market prices. For example, a major increase in Hitechco's stock price conveys the market's good feelings about the firm's investment possibilities and management skills, and the firm may decide to issue new debt or equity and expand. Hence secondary market prices are valuable sources of information for corporations that are considering issuing new debt or equity. As a result, we will focus mainly on secondary markets in our discussion.

There is no single "secondary market." Indeed, we can categorize secondary markets by (1) what maturity level characterizes the claims being traded, (2) how trading takes place, and (3) when settlement takes place.

Web Site Suggestions:
http://www.federal reserve.gov
Presents interest rate data in money and capital markets.

Maturity: money and capital markets. Debt instruments that have a maturity of greater than one year are traded in **capital markets.** Equities, which have no fixed maturity, are also traded in capital markets. Short-term instruments, with a maturity of less than one year, are traded in **money markets.** Where do these instruments come from? Borrowers seeking funds for long-term investments in housing or business investment issue long-term financial instruments in capital markets. When the government or well-known corporations need funds to finance inventories or to meet short-term needs, they issue money market instruments. (The principal money and capital market instruments are described in the appendix to this chapter.)

How do investors decide which instruments to buy? There are three differences between money market and capital market instruments that result from differences in risk, liquidity, and information. First, short-term instruments have relatively small increases or decreases in price, so they are less risky as investments than long-term instruments are. As a result, financial institutions and corporations typically invest short-term surplus funds in money markets. Some financial institutions, such as pension funds and insurance companies, are willing to hold assets for a long time and risk price fluctuations in capital markets. Second, money market instruments are generally more liquid than capital market instruments because their trading volume is greater and the cost of buying and selling is low. Thus households and businesses can invest their funds for a short period of time relatively cheaply. Finally, information costs are lower for money market instruments because the borrowers are well known and the length of time for which funds are loaned is relatively short.

Web Site Suggestions:
http://www.nyse.com
http://www.nasdaq.com
Give information on the U.S. stock exchange.

Trading places: auction and over-the-counter markets. Secondary financial markets can also be categorized according to how assets are traded between buyers and sellers. The first category is **auction markets,** in which prices are set by competitive bidding by a large number of traders acting on behalf of individual buyers or sellers. The most common auction markets are **exchanges,** or central locations at which buyers and sellers trade. They include the New York and American Stock Exchanges, the Tokyo Stock Exchange, the London Stock Exchange, and others.

Secondary markets also can be organized as **over-the-counter (OTC) markets,** in which there is no centralized place for exchanges. Over-the-counter dealers buy and sell stocks and bonds through computerized trading to anyone who is willing to accept their posted prices. Close electronic contact keeps the over-the-counter market competitive. You are unlikely to pay a much higher price for a share of stock of Apple Computer at one dealer than at another.

The equities of the largest corporations are traded on exchanges, as are the bonds of the best-known corporations. The shares of smaller, less well-known firms are generally traded in over-the-counter markets, as are U.S. government bonds. The market for these bonds has the largest trading volume of any debt or equity market. Other major OTC markets include those for foreign exchange, federal funds, and negotiable certificates of deposit.

Web Site Suggestions:
http://www.cbot.com
Describes futures information in U.S. markets.

Settlement: cash and derivative markets. Finally, financial markets can be categorized by whether the claims traded are direct or derivative. **Cash markets** are those markets in which actual claims are bought and sold with immediate settlement: The buyer pays money to the seller in exchange for the asset. Examples include the stock and bond markets. Alternatively, in **derivative markets,** trades are made now, but settlement is made at a later date. For example, an investor could agree to buy a Treasury bond from a bond dealer one year from now at a prespecified price. Why would anyone want to do this? The reason is that households and businesses use derivative markets to reduce their exposure to the risk of price fluctuations in cash markets (and sometimes even to bet on future price fluctuations).

Derivative claims, the value of which is determined by (derived from) underlying assets (such as stocks, bonds, or foreign exchange), include financial futures and options. **Financial futures** require settlement of a purchase of a financial instrument at a specified future date, with the price determined at the outset. **Options** on financial contracts, as the name suggests, confer on the trader the right (or option) to buy or sell a particular asset (shares of stock, bonds, or units of foreign currency, for example) within a specified time at a specified price.

CHECKPOINT

Using the categories describing financial markets, how would you characterize a transaction in which you buy 100 shares of Growthco from someone through a dealer? *Debt or equity:* Shares of stock are equities. *Primary or secondary market:* The stock is already outstanding, so the transaction takes place in a secondary market. *Money or capital market:* The equities have no fixed maturity and so are traded in the capital market. *Auction or over-the-counter market:* The transaction takes place through a dealer rather than through an exchange, so it is conducted in an over-the-counter market. *Cash or derivative market:* You pay money to the dealer and receive the stock now, so the transaction takes place in a cash market. ♦

Financial Intermediaries in the Financial System

The financial system also channels funds from savers to borrowers indirectly through intermediaries. These institutions facilitate financial trade by raising funds from savers and investing in the debt or equity claims of borrowers. This indirect form of finance is known as **financial intermediation.** Like financial markets, financial intermediaries have two tasks: (1) matching savers and borrowers and (2) providing risk-sharing, liquidity, and information services.

Matching Savers and Borrowers

When you deposit funds in your checking account, the bank may lend the funds (together with the funds of other savers) to Jane's Sub Shop to open a new store. In this intermediated transaction, your checking account is an asset for you and a liability for the bank. The loan becomes Jane's liability and the bank's asset. Rather than your holding a loan to Jane's Sub Shop as an asset directly, the bank acts as a go-between for you and Jane. Financial intermediaries, such as banks, insurance companies, pension funds, and mutual funds, also make investments in stocks and bonds on behalf of savers.

Intermediaries pool the funds of many small savers to lend to many individual borrowers. The intermediaries pay interest to savers in exchange for the use of savers' funds and earn a profit by lending money to borrowers and charging borrowers a higher rate of interest on the loans. For example, a bank might pay you as a depositor a rate of interest of 5% while lending the money to a local business at an interest rate of 8%.

Providing Risk-Sharing, Liquidity, and Information Services

Intermediation adds an extra layer of complexity and cost to financial trade. Why don't savers just deal directly with borrowers, bypassing the costs of financial intermediation? Again, the three main reasons are risk sharing, liquidity, and information. First, as a saver, you want to share risk. If you had $5000 in cash, you could loan it to your neighbor. But how do you know that your neighbor will pay you back? If you deposit your $5000 in the bank, the bank puts your money to work by making various

CASE STUDY

Where Do Households Put Their Savings?

The Federal Reserve System publishes quarterly and annual data on assets and liabilities of sectors of the U.S. economy. Clues about trends in direct finance and indirect intermediary finance are provided by examining the Fed's data on household holdings of financial assets.

The table reports holdings of assets in financial markets and of assets supplied by financial intermediaries. These data show the importance of financial intermediation for savers. About one-half of household financial assets are held through financial intermediaries. Note particularly the increasing share of mutual funds and pension funds, which helped to increase the percentage of financial assets in indirect finance from 46.3% in 1978 to 54.0% in 2003.

These data come from the Fed's publication entitled *Flow of Funds Accounts, Financial Assets and Liabilities*, which you can find in the library.

Household Holdings of Selected Financial Assets
(Billions of Dollars, Various Years)

	1978	1985	2003
Financial Assets in Financial Markets			
U.S. government securities	148.6	447.5	735.1
State and local government securities	94.0	305.0	640.7
Corporate bonds	57.0	18.9	862.8
Mortgages	76.0	127.4	114.3
Commercial paper	31.4	128.7	34.9
Corporate equities	663.9	1700.0	4165.9
Equity in unincorporated businesses	1398.9	2040.6	5068.7
Miscellaneous assets	68.0	132.5	551.8
Subtotal	**2537.8**	**4900.6**	**12,174.2**
% in direct finance	*53.7%*	*50.8%*	*40.4%*
Financial Assets in Financial Intermediaries			
Bank deposits	1280.1	2306.7	5234.0
Money market mutual fund shares	9.4	211.1	1062.7
Mutual fund shares	41.1	206.9	2610.0
Life insurance reserves	196.0	256.7	968.7
Pension fund reserves	661.5	1794.5	7936.1
Subtotal	**2188.1**	**4775.9**	**17,811.5**
% in indirect finance	*46.3%*	*49.2%*	*59.4%*
Total Financial Assets	**$4725.9**	**$9676.5**	**$29,985.7**

loans and investments. Because banks have a large quantity of deposits and access to numerous borrowers and investments, they can diversify and provide risk-sharing services to you at a lower cost than you could obtain on your own. Second, bank deposits and other intermediary claims are liquid. Therefore, if your car breaks down, you can easily withdraw funds from your bank account to pay for repairs. (Your neighbor would probably not be able to pay you back early or appreciate having to do so.) Finally, financial intermediaries provide information services that are important to savers who may not have the time or resources to research investments on their own. You can easily get information about the likely return on a U.S. Treasury bond or a bond issued by a major corporation such as Exxon. More difficult, however, is obtaining information about the likely financial prospects of individuals or small and medium-sized businesses.

Your local bank is an information warehouse. It collects information on borrowers by monitoring their income and spending as reflected in their checking account transactions. Borrowers fill out detailed loan applications, and the bank's loan officers determine how well each borrower is doing financially. Because the bank collects and processes information on behalf of you and other depositors, its costs for information gathering are lower than yours would be if you tried to gather information on a pool of borrowers. The intermediary's profits from lending compensate it for investing in information.

Financial intermediaries are the largest group in the financial system. They move more funds between savers and borrowers than do financial markets in the United States and in most other countries. Many economists believe that intermediaries' advantage in reducing information costs accounts for this pattern globally as well as nationally. Even in the United States, where financial markets are the most highly developed, businesses raise much more of their external funds from intermediaries than they do directly from financial markets.

CHECKPOINT

Why might you be willing to buy a bond issued by IBM but prefer to lend to the local computer store through a bank? Your preference results from differences in information costs. Information about IBM is readily available, but you would have to incur significant costs to investigate the creditworthiness of the computer store. A bank can collect information on behalf of many small savers, reducing the cost of lending to the computer store and reducing the chance that you will invest your savings in a losing proposition. ♦

Competition and Change in the Financial System

Let's say that you've sold your car and have decided not to buy a new one. What will you do with the proceeds from the sale? Your choices are many: Depending on how much you have to invest, you might buy debt or equity claims in a financial market or place your funds in a financial institution. As in other industries, financial markets and financial intermediaries compete for your funds and more generally for market share in the financial system. Their tools for competition are the risk-sharing, liquidity, and information services they offer to savers and borrowers.

Mutual funds and banks, for example, offer savers the chance to hold a diversified portfolio of assets at a lower cost than savers could arrange individually (a risk-sharing service). Mutual funds offer assets that are money market or capital market instruments, whereas a bank's assets are the loans originated and monitored by the bank. Banks and mutual funds compete for savers' funds, and these are but two of many choices savers have.

Borrowers can also choose from an array of financial arrangements. A firm could seek short-term finance through money markets or from an intermediary such as a bank. A firm could raise long-term funds through capital markets or from an intermediary such as a life insurance company.

Financial Innovation

With all the competition among financial markets and institutions, how do savers and borrowers choose among them? They base their decisions on the risk-sharing, liquidity, and information characteristics that are best suited for their needs. A saver who values a low degree of risk, for example, might turn to financial markets that match savers with low-risk borrowers, such as the U.S. government or well-known corporations. Savers who want a diversified portfolio without doing their own research might turn to intermediaries such as banks, which specialize in reducing information costs and have an accumulated stock of information about borrowers. However, the types of services offered by markets and intermediaries change over time.

Changes in costs of providing risk-sharing, liquidity, or information services or changes in demand for these services encourage financial markets and intermediaries to alter their operations and to offer new types of financial assets and liabilities. These improvements in the financial system are called **financial innovation.** Financial innovation can benefit everyone. Indeed, financial markets and institutions that have survived and thrived are those that combine low operation costs with high demand (meeting households' and firms' demand for risk-sharing, liquidity, and information services). Shifts in the cost of and demand for financial services can also alter the competitive balance among markets and institutions in the financial system.

Changes in Financial Integration and Globalization

Financial systems in the United States and around the world become linked more closely every day. The funds in your checking account can help finance a car loan in your hometown, a new drill press in Chicago, a new steel mill in Seoul, or a loan to the government of Brazil. Bringing together savers and borrowers from around the country and around the world helps the global economy.

Integration. One measure of the system's efficiency is its degree of **financial integration,** or the way in which financial markets are tied together geographically. Early nineteenth-century U.S. financial markets were fragmented geographically. Because of the high costs of gathering and communicating information, eastern capital to a large extent was used in the East; similarly, western or southern capital was used in the West or South. Hence interest rates charged to borrowers tended to be different in different parts of the country, making the financing of a high-quality investment project more costly in the West than in the East. As a result, savers sank too much capital in mansions and silver tea sets in Boston while potentially profitable mining and industrial ventures in California lacked funds.

The increasing ease of communicating information has enabled U.S. financial markets to become much more integrated. Now borrowers who raise funds through securities have access to national markets.

Globalization. A major development during recent decades has been the global integration of financial markets. Just as capital became more mobile among regions in the United States, moving capital between countries has become increasingly important

CONSIDER THIS . . .

Financial Innovation: Home Mortgages or Rock Star Bonds?

For most of us, the largest transaction we will make is financing the purchase of a home. A generation ago, home mortgage loans were generally made and held by local savings and loan institutions and mortgage bankers. As a result, housing finance tended to be a regional business, making diversification of mortgage loans into different geographical areas difficult for lenders.

In the early 1980s, however, the situation changed. The federal government's credit agencies developed secondary markets to improve the liquidity of home mortgages by increasing their desirability for investors. Mortgage pools could package mortgages from different original lenders and sell claims on the package to savers, a process known as *securitization*. These claims are traded in secondary markets. You may be able to obtain funds from a lender to purchase a house at a lower cost than your parents could obtain 20 years ago.

Securitization has marched on and now includes cash flows beyond mortgages, such as business loans and consumer credit card loans. By the early 2000s, more exotic securitizations included rights to a slice of royalties by rock stars such as David Bowie and Rod Stewart. Pop or flop? Some analysts worry about rock star securitization, which subtracts pooling and adds moral hazard (how hard will the star work when paid up front?) to the old idea.

In early 2003, some analysts floated the idea of securitizing Iraqi oil revenues to raise funds for reconstructing that war-ravaged economy.

since the 1970s. New York's Citigroup can raise funds in London as easily as it can in Brooklyn, and it can lend money to finance an industrial development project in Queensland, Australia, or in Queens, New York. The globalization of financial markets improves the ability of the financial system to channel savers' funds to the highest-value borrowers, wherever they may be.

Over most of the period following World War II, U.S. financial markets dominated financial markets elsewhere. This dominance eroded substantially during the 1980s and 1990s for two reasons. First, rapid postwar economic growth in Japan and in Europe increased the pool of savings brought to foreign financial markets. Second, during the past decade, many countries lifted regulations that kept their citizens from exporting their savings or foreigners from importing it, thereby enabling savers to transfer their funds to borrowers around the world. In the early 1990s, capital market funds crossed national borders at a rate of several trillion dollars per year. Indeed, the foreign-exchange market now has a volume of trading of more than $1 trillion per day.

The globalization of financial markets has two effects. First, the easy flow of capital across national boundaries helps countries with productive opportunities to grow, even if their current resources are insufficient. For instance, the U.S. economy grew rapidly in the 1980s and 1990s, but domestic saving was insufficient to fund the demand for investment. Foreign funds filled the gap between U.S. investment and U.S. saving. Second, increasing financial integration around the world reduces the cost of allocating savers' funds to the highest-valued uses, wherever they may be. That is what the financial system is supposed to do.

CHECKPOINT

Why do you think many experts have encouraged emerging market economies in Eastern Europe to develop financial intermediaries before relying on financial markets? Financial intermediaries can reduce the information costs of lending in these countries while offering risk-sharing and liquidity services to savers. After information about companies becomes better known to savers, financial markets will become more important. ◆

Financial Regulation

Countries' governments around the world regulate financial markets and institutions. This regulation occurs for three reasons. First, governments want to ensure that all participants in the financial system have access to information and that markets and intermediaries give savers and borrowers accurate and timely information. Without such information, it is difficult to make prudent financial decisions. Second, governments regulate the financial system to maintain financial stability. Stock market crashes, bank failures, and other financial disasters can undermine the efficiency with which the economy's resources are allocated. Finally, the government can advance economic policy by interacting with the financial system. Actions of the Federal Reserve, for example, affect the banking system and promote monetary policy. Over time, regulations imposed by governments change, causing the services and instruments offered by markets or institutions to change.

Provision of Information

The quality of many products—from fish in the supermarket to clothing in a department store—is relatively easy to assess. The quality of other goods and services—from cars to legal services—is more problematic to judge. Even more difficult to evaluate are debt and equity instruments traded in financial markets. A small investor cannot easily judge whether shares or bonds issued by a business are safe investments. The investor could pay a financial analyst or an accounting firm to evaluate corporations that issue stocks and bonds, but the cost of gathering this information is likely to be prohibitive. Because of the demand for this type of service, private firms have organized to collect information on the quality of financial instruments. (Moody's Investor Service and Standard & Poor's Corporation are leading examples.) These firms earn profits by selling the information to individual investors.

OTHER TIMES, OTHER PLACES ...

The Growth of International Bond and Stock Markets

Before the 1960s, the term "international bond market" referred to *foreign bonds*, or bonds sold in another country and denominated in that country's currency. Since the 1960s, a new form of finance known as a *Eurobond* has grown rapidly. Unlike foreign bonds, Eurobonds are denominated in a currency other than that of the country where they are sold, usually in U.S. dollars. Currently, about 85% of new issues in the international bond market are Eurobonds, and the value of new issues in the Eurobond market exceeds the value of new issues of the U.S. corporate bond market. Historically the center of foreign borrowing, London has retained its dominance as a center for Eurolending, but competition from other European nations and Japan is expected in the new century.

In the mid-1980s, another new market developed, this time in *Euroequities*, or new equity issues sold to investors abroad. This market has grown rapidly relative to domestic equity issues. Cross-border equity trading is now substantial. The tremendous increase in cross-border equity trading has improved the ability of the financial system to match savers' funds with the highest-value users. But it exposes savers to risks that were unfamiliar a generation ago. For example, a stock market crash in Japan could affect a Japanese bank's ability to pay its creditors around the world.

Global stock and bond transactions are likely to become even more important over the next 10 years. Although bonds continue to account for most financial market capital flows, the multitrillion-dollar equity flows are growing for two reasons. First, equities proved to be lucrative investments in the 1990s (though less so since 2001). Second, as many countries shift toward private pension schemes, the funds that are available for equity investments are increasing. The internationally integrated financial markets in New York, London, Tokyo, and other cities are making the financial system truly global.

However, private firms are not always able to collect truthful information. As a result, the federal government has intervened in financial markets to require issuers of financial instruments to disclose information about their financial condition and to impose penalties on issuers that do not comply. The leading federal regulatory body for financial markets in the United States is the Securities and Exchange Commission (SEC). It was established by the Securities Act of 1933 in response to investors' concerns over the stock market crash of 1929 and fraud by securities dealers during the 1920s. The SEC mandates that corporations issuing bonds or stocks disclose information about earnings, sales, assets, and liabilities. It also limits trading by managers owning large amounts of a firm's stock or others having privileged information (this type of trading is called *insider trading*). These regulations ensure that securities dealers communicate information and that investors are protected from fraud. The Sarbanes-Oxley Act of 2002 strengthens the SEC's hand in prosecutors presenting misleading accounting data to the investing public. In derivative markets, the Commodities Futures Trading Commission (CFTC) guards against fraud in futures trading.

Maintenance of Financial Stability

Most regulation of the financial system is concerned with its stability, meaning the ability of financial markets and intermediaries to provide the three key services (risk sharing, liquidity, and information) in the face of economic disturbances. For example, if the stock market were to cease functioning efficiently, stock liquidity would be reduced, and individuals' willingness to hold stocks would diminish. Companies would have difficulty raising capital for investment and job creation. Reductions in the ability of the financial system to provide the three key services raise the cost of moving funds from savers to borrowers. In fact, many economists link the severity of the Great Depression of the 1930s to the breakdown in the banking system's ability to provide financial services. A sudden collapse of a segment of the financial system can lead to sharp reductions in economic activity. Such dramatic instances can prompt new government regulation. Indeed, the length and depth of the Great Depression were responsible for the development of current U.S. financial regulations.

Because most financial assets are held by intermediaries such as banks, pension funds, or insurance companies, policymakers are concerned about the financial soundness of those intermediaries. The federal government has implemented four types of regulations that address such concerns: disclosure of information, prevention of fraud, limitations on competition, and safety of investors' funds. We analyze these regulations in Part 4.

Advancement of Other Policy Objectives

Financial regulation also may be used to further public policy objectives that are unrelated to the efficiency of the financial system. These objectives include controlling the money supply and encouraging particular activities, such as home ownership.

Controlling the money supply. Because banks affect movements in the money supply, which in turn influence the economic variables that affect people's daily lives, policymakers have implemented rules to facilitate control of the quantity of money. For example, the Federal Reserve System requires banks to hold a specified fraction of their deposits in cash or in accounts with the Fed, giving the Fed some control over the money supply.

Encouraging particular activities. Several regulations are designed to promote home ownership, a politically popular objective. One way in which the federal government fosters home ownership is by allowing the deduction of interest paid on a home mortgage from income subject to federal income taxes, something the taxpayer can no longer do for interest on a car loan or credit card debt. In addition, Congress created large government-sponsored financial intermediaries to make home mortgages accessible to many borrowers and, before 1980, restricted savings and loan associations and mutual savings banks to mortgage loans. This restriction was intended to make more funds available for mortgage lending; in fact, it made these institutions vulnerable to certain types of risks. Regulators weakened these limitations in the 1980s. Many economists and policymakers question whether regulations designed to direct savings to finance home mortgages have improved the efficiency of the financial system.

The federal government has also intervened in credit markets to subsidize lending for agriculture, college tuition, and other activities that it regards as beneficial to the economy. In each case, the interventions created specialized intermediaries and provided guarantees for certain types of loans.

Effects of Regulation

Regulation affects the ability of financial markets and institutions to provide risk-sharing, liquidity, and information services. Restrictions on the types of instruments that can be traded in markets affect liquidity. Regulations limiting the ability of financial institutions to hold certain types of assets or to operate in various geographic locations affect risk sharing and the potential for diversification. Policymakers should consider the effects of regulation on the financial system's ability to provide risk-sharing opportunities, liquidity, and information. Stringent limits placed on these activities in domestic markets create opportunities for international competition. Table 3.1 summarizes current regulation of U.S. financial institutions and markets and its effects on their key services.

Financial regulation in other industrial economies, such as Japan, Canada, the United Kingdom, and Western European countries, is broadly similar to that in the United States. The ability of financial markets to provide risk-sharing, liquidity, and information services is enhanced by regulators promoting financial disclosure. The vitality of financial intermediaries is bolstered by licensing and examination of banks and other financial institutions.

These broad similarities notwithstanding, significant differences exist in investor protection in financial markets and in bank regulation. Some industrial countries, among them France, offer weaker protection of creditor claims and outside equity investors, making securities markets for bonds and stocks less important for financing enterprises there than in the United Kingdom or United States. In the area of banking regulation, the United States stands out historically because of its restrictions on branching and on the types of assets banks can hold. Although U.S. branching restrictions were eliminated in 1994, U.S. banks still lack the ability to hold direct equity stakes in firms of the size permitted in Germany, for example.

TABLE 3.1 **Regulation of Financial Institutions and Markets in the United States**

	Effect of Regulation on Key Services of the Financial System		
Regulatory body	**Risk sharing**	**Liquidity**	**Information**
Securities and Exchange Commission (SEC)	—	Supervises trading in organized exchanges	Mandates information disclosure and financial markets
Commodities Futures Trading Commission (CFTC)	—	Sets rules for trading in futures markets	—
Office of the Comptroller of the Currency (OCC)	Restricts assets held by federally chartered commercial institutions (e.g., banks)	—	Charters and examines federally chartered banks
Federal Deposit Insurance Corporation (FDIC)	Provides insurance to bank depositors	Promotes liquidity of bank deposits	Examines insured banks
Federal Reserve System	Restricts assets of participating financial institutions	Promotes liquidity of bank deposits	Examines commercial banks in Federal Reserve System
State banking and insurance commissions	Impose restrictions on assets held by banks; impose restrictions on bank branching	—	Charter and examine state-chartered banks and insurance companies
Office of Thrift Supervision (OTS)	Restricts assets held by savings and loan associations	—	Examines savings and loan associations
National Credit Union Administration	Restricts assets held by credit unions	—	Charters and examines federally chartered credit unions

KEY TERMS AND CONCEPTS

- Assets
- Asymmetric information
- Auction markets
- Borrowers
- Capital markets
- Cash markets
- Debt
  - Default
  - Interest
  - Intermediate-term debt
  - Long-term debt
  - Maturity
  - Principal
  - Short-term debt
- Derivative markets
- Direct finance
- Diversification
- Dividends
- Equity
- Exchanges
- Financial futures
- Financial innovation
- Financial institutions
- Financial integration
- Financial intermediation
- Financial markets
- Financial system
- Information
- Intermediaries
- Liabilities
- Liquidity
- Money markets
- Options
- Over-the-counter (OTC) markets
- Portfolio
- Primary markets
- Risk sharing
- Savers
- Secondary markets

SUMMARY

1. The basic motivation for financial trade, and hence for the development of a financial system, is that individuals, businesses, and governments sometimes need to save and at other times need to borrow. The financial system channels funds from savers to borrowers, giving savers claims on borrowers' future income.
2. The financial system provides three key services: risk sharing, liquidity, and information. These services make financial claims attractive to savers and can lower the cost of finance for borrowers. Differences in the demand for and the cost of providing these services partially explain changes in the U.S. financial system over time, as well as differences among financial systems internationally.
3. The financial system brings together savers and borrowers in two ways. In direct finance through financial markets, individual savers hold the claims issued by individual borrowers. In indirect finance through financial intermediaries, claims held by savers are claims against intermediaries that are backed by their portfolios of assets, which are claims on the borrowers.
4. Financial markets for debt and equity include primary markets, in which claims are newly issued, and secondary markets, in which outstanding claims are traded. In secondary markets, some claims mature in less than one year (money market), whereas others mature in more than one year (capital market); some claims are traded by auction, whereas others are traded over the counter; and some claims are traded in cash markets, whereas others are traded in derivative markets.
5. Financial intermediaries act as go-betweens for savers and borrowers. These institutions acquire funds from savers and then make loans to or purchase financial instruments issued by borrowers. In the process, financial intermediaries provide risk-sharing, liquidity, and information services that especially benefit small savers and borrowers.
6. Changes in the financial system are called financial innovations. Shifts in the demand for and cost of providing risk-sharing, liquidity, and information services lead to changes in the operation of financial markets and institutions.
7. An important measure of the financial system's efficiency is its degree of integration, or the way in which markets are tied together geographically. Financial markets have become much more integrated over many years in the United States and are now becoming integrated globally.
8. Another cause of differences and changes in financial systems is government regulation. Governments regulate financial markets for three reasons: (a) to guarantee provision of information, (b) to maintain the stability of the financial system, and (c) to advance other policy objectives.

REVIEW QUESTIONS

1. Why do households save? Why do businesses borrow? Why are the financial services of risk sharing, liquidity, and information valued by savers and borrowers?
2. Explain why financial assets are considered to be uses of funds from the point of view of savers and sources of funds from the point of view of borrowers.
3. Why are money market assets typically more liquid than capital market assets? Does the relative illiquidity of capital market assets have any consequences for the banking system?
4. Under what circumstances does financial regulation improve the efficiency of the financial system?
5. What is meant by *integration* of financial markets? What effect would increased integration of financial markets, domestically and internationally, have on returns for savers? On costs to borrowers?
6. What are the benefits to savers and borrowers if financial markets communicate all available information about financial instruments via their prices?

In Questions 7–12, categorize the transactions described according to whether they (a) rely on financial markets or intermediaries, (b) occur in the primary or secondary market or, (c) are carried out in the money or capital market.

7. A bank makes a 30-year mortgage loan to a household.
8. The bank sells a mortgage loan to a government-sponsored financial intermediary.
9. ABC Corporation opens for business by selling shares of stock to 10 private investors.
10. Joan Robinson sells her shares of ABC stock to someone else.

MOVING FROM THEORY TO PRACTICE . . .

THE NEW YORK TIMES MARCH 19, 2003

Small Loans, Big Idea

Guadalupe Castillo Ureña was widowed at 31, left alone with five children when her husband died trying to get to the United States from their hut here in the foothills of Mexico's southern Sierras.

She was among the poorest of the poor—scrapping by, like half the people in Mexico, and half the world's six billion people, on $2 a day or less, barely surviving.

Then an organization called Finca came to the village. It asked the women there—and only the women—whether they would be interested in borrowing a little money, at the stiff interest rate of 6 percent a month, to start their own businesses.

Change came. With a loan of about $250, Ms. Ureña, now 35, started making hundreds of clay pots this winter. With Finca's help, they were sold in bulk to a wholesaler, who sells them in the city. She pocketed $15 to $20 a week in profit. That sum, the first real money she had ever earned, was enough to help feed her children and pay their school expenses . . . .

These small loans, known as microcredit or microfinance, are not a charity. They are a growing business that is producing wealth in some of the world's poorest countries . . . .

In Mexico, the best-run little village lenders have grown into something closely resembling banks. That is something new in Mexico. Commercial banks in this country are for rich people. They almost never serve the middle class or the poor, rarely if ever providing them with savings accounts, much less loans or credit . . . .

The established small loan groups like Finca, whose name means farm, and Compartamos have learned some fundamental lessons about what works and what does not work when it comes to fighting poverty.

What works, first of all, is loaning money to women.

"When you walk into a village, you do not consult the mayor and you do not consult the priest," said **a** John Hatch, Finca's executive director. "You ask, 'Who is the woman in this community that everyone most respects?' Then you ask that woman, 'Would you be willing to convene a meeting at your house?' And at the meeting we start the bank." . . .

The women in San Marcos Acteopan said they reacted with a rainbow of emotions after Finca came to town last year, from fear to fascination. The idea that someone was going to lend them money to start businesses was riveting.

What is also working—and this is very new—goes beyond lending money **b** to providing poor people with the ability to save and invest. This has become possible under a new federal law in Mexico providing a legal architecture and regulations for village banks and small loans . . . .

This fact qualifies as something of a revelation to economists: that given the chance, poor people would put their money into **c** a certificate of deposit, rather than spending it, stashing it under a mattress, or fattening a pig for market . . . .

ANALYZING THE NEWS . . .

This link arises not just from moving funds between savers and borrowers, but from providing risk-sharing, liquidity, and information services that enhance savers' returns and reduce the cost of funds to borrowers.

In industrial countries, entrepreneurship—starting and operating one's own business—is a prominent route to improving one's income and wealth. Many financing arrangements from financial institutions are available in countries like the United States for business formation and expansion. The article discusses a type of financial institution in Mexico and other emerging economies that is arising to meet borrowers' needs and ultimately to provide a broader array of financial services.

a While Mexican conventional financial institutions cater to high-income families, institutions like Finca pool funds of poorer individuals (with some external assistance) to make loans to potential entrepreneurs. An important part of financial intermediation is gathering information about borrowers and their projects so that lenders and savers know how much to charge for risk. Without this investment in *reducing information costs*, uninformed savers might not lend to potential entrepreneurs with no track record.

b By holding a portfolio of loans, Finca offers *risk-sharing* services to its depositors and investors, as the risk of default for the collection of loans is almost certainly less than the risk of default on one particular loan. This risk sharing enables Finca to offer funds to borrowers at a lower cost than a single saver might charge.

c Financial institutions like Finca can offer services to savers, too. Returns on the loan portfolio are more attractive than holding cash. Eventually, the institution may grow sufficiently to provide savers easier access to their funds—that is, provide liquidity services, too.

For further thought...

Given what you know about regulation of financial markets and institutions in the United States, is there a role for public policy in Mexico to encourage financial intermediation for low-income savers and borrowers? How?

Source: Excerpted from "With Little Loans, Mexican Women Overcome," *The New York Times*, March 19, 2003, page A8.

11. The DEF money market mutual fund buys $100,000 of three-month Treasury bills in the government's weekly auction.

12. DEF buys $100,000 of three-month Treasury bills from First Bank.

ANALYTICAL PROBLEMS

13. An attribute of financial assets that investors sometimes overlook is the asset's tax treatment. Suppose that you are an investor with a choice among three assets that are identical in every way except in their rate of return and rate of taxation. Which asset yields the highest after-tax return?

    A: interest rate 10%, interest taxed at a 40% rate.

    B: interest rate 8%, interest taxed at a 25% rate.

    C: interest rate 6.5%, no tax on interest.

14. Suppose that asset A in Problem 13 paid 11%. Would your answer change?

15. What is "insider trading"? Analyze the consequences for securities markets of legalizing insider trading.

16. The text states that because of financial integration and globalization: "The funds in your checking account can help finance a car loan in your hometown, a new drill press in Chicago, a new steel mill in Seoul, or a loan to the government of Brazil." Is the possibility that U.S. savings might be loaned to foreign businesses or governments a good or bad development from the point of view of the U.S. economy?

17. Why do people want to share risk? After all, the only way to get rich is to take risks.

18. Do banks and other financial intermediaries like high interest rates? Why or why not?

19. Traditionally, financial markets in Germany and Japan have played a smaller role in financing businesses than markets in the United States and Great Britain, while financial institutions play a larger role as a source of long-term funds. What factors determine whether businesses rely more heavily on financial markets or financial institutions to raise funds needed for investment in plant and equipment?

20. You have not yet studied the effects of financial regulation on incentives for borrowers and savers. Do you think that insuring savers against fluctuations in the value of claims on financial institutions necessarily makes the financial system more efficient? Why or why not?

DATA QUESTIONS

21. In a current issue of *The Wall Street Journal,* try to find financial instruments traded in money and capital markets, auction and over-the-counter markets, and cash and derivative markets. Compare the yields on these different assets. Can you explain the different yields?

22. On of the more popular venues through which savers and investors meet are stock exchanges, and the New York Stock Exchange (http://www.nyse.com) is the most well-known financial intermediaries. Go to this site and look up the program trading statistics for 2003 and compare it with 2000. Which statistics appear higher, on average? Given your knowledge of the state of the business cycle during these two years, explain the difference.

23. The Chicago Board of Trade, now in its third century, deals primarily in futures and options markets. Go to its web site at http://www.cbot.com, and find its most recent data for corn futures (under the agricultural futures heading). Based on the information displayed, in what direction do the futures markets expect corn prices to be over the next two years? Do these expectations fluctuate with the crop cycle? Explain.

APPENDIX

Financial Instruments

Financial instruments are the vehicles by which financial markets channel funds from savers to borrowers and provide returns to savers. In this appendix, we compare major instruments, or securities, traded in the financial system. For convenience, we analyze money market and capital market instruments separately. (Recall that money market claims mature in less than a year and capital market claims mature in more than a year.) Both money market and capital market assets are actively traded in U.S. financial markets. We describe the issuers and the characteristics of the most widely used instruments here and discuss them in more detail in Parts 2 and 3.

Money Market Instruments

The short maturity of money market assets doesn't allow much time for their returns to vary. Therefore these instruments are safe investments for short-term surplus funds of households and firms. However, in making investment decisions, savers must still consider the possibility of default—the chance that the borrower will be unable to repay all the amount borrowed plus interest at maturity.

U.S. Treasury bills. U.S. Treasury securities are short-term debt obligations of the U.S. government. They are also the most liquid money market instrument because they have the largest trading volume. The federal government can raise taxes and issue currency to repay the amount borrowed, so there is virtually no risk of default.[†] Treasury securities with maturities of less than one year are called Treasury bills (T-bills). Although individuals can hold them, the largest holders of T-bills are commercial banks, followed by other financial intermediaries, businesses, and foreign investors.

Commercial paper. Commercial paper provides a liquid, short-term investment for savers and a source of funds for corporations. High-quality, well-known firms and financial institutions use commercial paper to raise funds. Because these borrowers are generally the most creditworthy, the default risk is small, but the interest rate is higher than that on Treasury bills. The growth in the commercial paper market during the past two decades is part of a shift by many corporations toward direct finance (and away from bank loans).

Bankers' acceptances. Designed to facilitate international trade, bankers' acceptances are instruments that establish credit between parties who do not know each other. A banker's acceptance is a checklike promise that the bank will pay the amount of funds indicated to the recipient. It is issued by a firm (usually an importer) and is payable on a date indicated. The bank that marks the draft "accepted" guarantees the payment to the recipient (usually an exporter or its representing bank). The issuing firm is required to deposit funds in the bank sufficient to cover the draft; if it does not do so, the bank is still obligated to make good on the draft. The bank's good name is likely to enable an importer to buy goods from an overseas exporter that lacks knowledge about whether the importer will be able to pay. In recent years, acceptances

[†] Technically, in the United States, the Federal Reserve issues currency.

have generally been resold in secondary markets and held by other banks, households, and businesses.

Repurchase agreements. Repurchase agreements, also known as repos or RPs, are used for cash management by large corporations. They are very short-term loans, typically with maturities of less than two weeks. In many cases, a firm loans a bank money overnight. For example, if a large firm such as IBM has idle cash, it purchases T-bills from a bank that agrees to buy them back the next morning at a higher price, reflecting the accumulated interest. The T-bills serve as collateral; that is, if the borrower defaults, the lender receives the T-bills. Since their inception in 1969, repurchase agreements have become a significant source of funds for banks.

Federal (Fed) funds. Federal funds instruments represent overnight loans between banks of their deposits with the Federal Reserve System (the U.S. central bank). Banking regulations require that banks deposit a percentage of their deposits as reserves with the Fed. If a bank is temporarily low on reserves, it can borrow funds from another bank that has reserves greater than the required level. The federal funds market reflects the credit needs of commercial banks, so money market analysts watch the *federal funds rate* (the interest rate charged on these overnight loans) closely. When it is high, banks need additional funds; when it is low, banks have low credit needs.

Eurodollars. Eurodollars are U.S. dollars deposited in foreign branches of U.S. banks or in foreign banks outside the United States (not necessarily in Europe). Rather than being converted into the currency of the foreign country, the deposits remain denominated in dollars. U.S. banks can then borrow these funds. Eurodollar funds raised abroad have become an important source of funds for U.S. banks.

Negotiable bank certificates of deposit. A certificate of deposit (CD) is a fixed-maturity instrument sold by a bank to depositors; it pays principal and interest at maturity. You might, for example, take the $1000 you earned over vacation and put it in a CD for six months at 5% interest (an annual rate). After six months, your investment would be worth $1025. Before 1961, CDs were illiquid because they were nonnegotiable; that is, the depositors could not sell them to someone else before redemption. In 1961, Citibank created the *negotiable certificate of deposit*—a CD in a large denomination (over $100,000, and today typically over $1,000,000) that could be sold again in a secondary market. Negotiable CDs are an important source of funds for banks today and are held principally by mutual funds and nonfinancial corporations.

Concluding remarks. Figure 3A.1 shows the amounts of the principal money market instruments outstanding in 1970, 1980, and 2003. Information on interest rates for these instruments appears each business day in the Money Rates column of *The Wall Street Journal.* Note the especially rapid growth in commercial paper and negotiable certificates of deposit. In Part 4, we show that this growth reflects important changes in the business of banking during the past two decades.

Capital Market Instruments

Because capital market instruments have longer maturities than money market instruments, they are subject to greater fluctuations in their returns. For this reason, borrowers who seek to use funds for a long period of time and savers with long investment horizons

FIGURE 3A.1

Money Market Instruments in the United States

U.S. Treasury bills, commercial paper, and negotiable CDs are the leading money market instruments. Since 1980, commercial paper issues have grown relative to negotiable CD issues.

Sources: Federal Reserve Flow of Funds Accounts; Council of Economic Advisers, *Economic Report of the President; Federal Reserve Bulletin.*

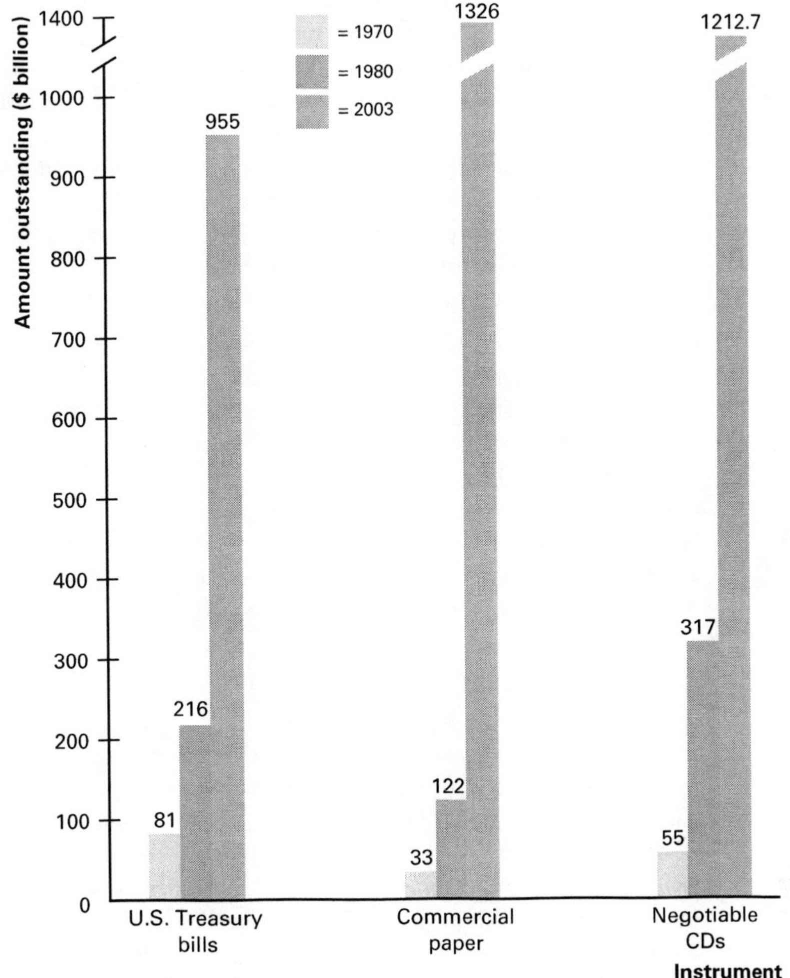

invest in them. With the exception of U.S. government obligations, all capital market debt instruments contain some risk of default.

U.S. Treasury securities. Intermediate-term and long-term U.S. Treasury securities are bonds issued by the federal government to finance budget deficits. They are widely traded and hence are liquid. Since 1997, these instruments have included inflation-indexed notes and bonds. These government securities are held by domestic banks and households, foreigners, and the Federal Reserve System.

U.S. government agency securities. U.S. government agency securities are intermediate-term or long-term bonds issued by the federal government or government-sponsored agencies. For example, the Farm Credit System issues bonds to raise money to finance agricultural activities, and the Government National Mortgage Association (GNMA) issues bonds to finance home mortgages. Many such securities are officially guaranteed by the government (with a pledge of the government's "full faith and credit"); others are implicitly guaranteed, so the default risk is still low.

State and local government bonds. State and local government bonds (often called municipal bonds) are intermediate-term or long-term bonds issued by municipalities and state governments. These governmental units use the funds borrowed to build schools, roads, and other large capital projects. The bonds are exempt from federal income taxation (and typically also income taxation by the issuing state). These bonds are often held by high-tax-bracket households, commercial banks, and life insurance companies. Although generally considered safe, these instruments do have some default risk. In the early 1930s, for example, many state and local governments defaulted on their bonds. In 1994, Orange County, California's default sent shock waves through the municipal bond market.

Stocks. Stocks are issued as equity claims by corporations and represent the largest single category of capital market assets. However, new stock issues are not a major source of funding for nonfinancial businesses in the United States and many other countries. From the end of World War II through 1980, new share issues accounted for about 5% of total funds raised. During the late 1980s, new share issues were substantially *negative* (–30% of funds raised in 1988, for example), as U.S. corporations used funds raised with debt to buy back shares. That trend reversed in the early 1990s, but share repurchases increased again in the late 1990s and early 2000s.

Corporate bonds. Corporate bonds are intermediate-term and long-term obligations issued by large, high-quality corporations to finance plant and equipment spending. Typically, corporate bonds pay interest twice each year and repay the principal amount borrowed at maturity. There are many variations, however. *Convertible bonds*, for example, allow the holder to convert the debt into equity (for a specified number of shares). By using such variations, firms can sometimes lower their borrowing costs by giving bond buyers an extra return if the firm does exceptionally well. Corporate bonds are not as liquid as government securities because they are less widely traded. Corporate bonds have greater default risk than government bonds, but they generally fluctuate less in price than corporate equities.

Although the corporate bond market is smaller than the stock market in the United States, it is more important for raising funds because corporations issue new shares infrequently. Most funds raised through financial markets take the form of corporate bonds. Investors in corporate bonds are a diverse group, including households, life insurance companies, and pension funds.

Mortgages. Mortgages are loans (usually long-term) to households or businesses to purchase buildings or land, with the underlying asset (house, plant, or piece of land) serving as collateral. In the United States, the mortgage market is the largest debt market. Residential mortgages, the largest component, are issued by savings institutions and commercial banks. Mortgage loans for industrial and agricultural borrowers are made by life insurance companies and commercial banks. Since World War II, the growth of the mortgage market has been spurred by federal government interventions to encourage homeownership by creating a liquid secondary national mortgage market. Three government-sponsored enterprises—Federal National Mortgage Association (FNMA), Government National Mortgage Association (GNMA), and the Federal Home Loan Mortgage Corporation (FHLMC)—borrow in bond markets to provide funds for mortgage financing by securitizing mortgages.

Commercial bank loans. Commercial bank loans include loans to businesses and consumers made by banks and finance companies. Secondary markets for commercial bank loans are not as well developed as those for other capital market instruments, so these loans are less liquid than mortgages. In Chapter 13, we show how recent developments in banking and financial markets are improving the liquidity of these loans.

Concluding remarks. Figure 3A.2 summarizes the amounts of principal capital market instruments outstanding in 1970, 1980, and 2003. Note the enormous growth in U.S. government and government agency securities. This growth reflects the borrowing necessitated by large federal budget deficits in the 1980s and early 1990s and the increasing prominence of federal credit agencies in the capital market.

FIGURE 3A.2 Capital Market Instruments in the United States

The leading capital market instruments are corporate stocks, residential mortgages, and U.S. government securities. Since 1970, the share of outstanding capital market instruments represented by U.S. government securities has doubled.

Sources: Federal Reserve Flow of Funds Accounts; Federal Reserve Bulletin.

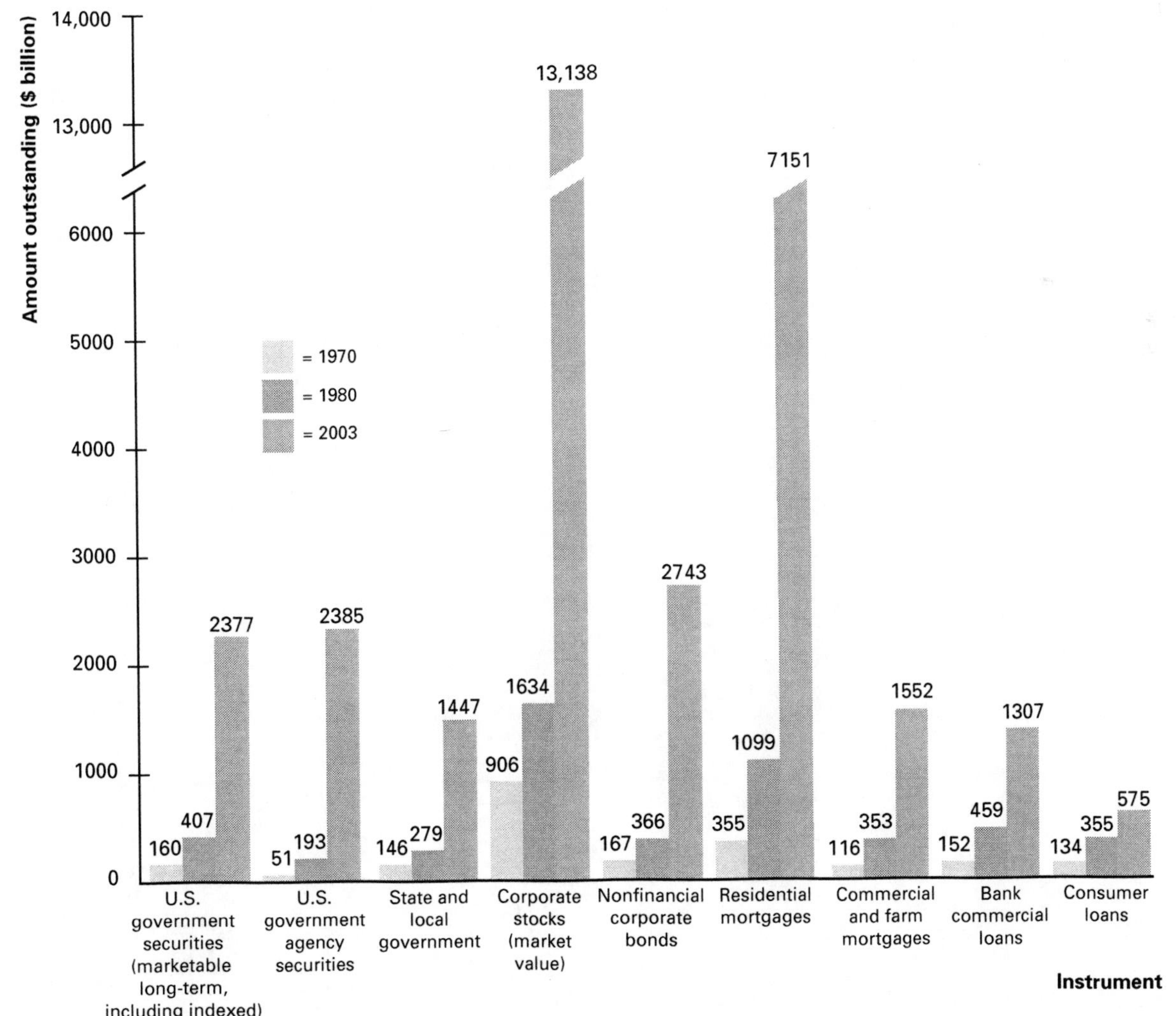

CHAPTER 5

The Theory of Portfolio Allocation

If you turn to Section C of *The Wall Street Journal*, you will see ads for financial services companies, offerings for bonds or stocks, and listings of financial assets ranging from the common stock of *Fortune* 500 firms to junk bonds used to finance leveraged buyouts to a staggering array of mutual funds. Each of these assets offers savers the potential for future returns and a reward in the form of interest or capital gains for postponing consumption. How can savers choose among these financial assets in deciding where to invest their funds?

Individuals may be motivated to save for several reasons: to smooth spending over time, to purchase durable goods, to accumulate precautionary (or emergency) funds for retirement, and to leave bequests. In meeting these needs, savers are concerned about the expected return on their savings. They also care about how easily their savings can be converted into a secure and steady source of income to finance future spending.

In this chapter, we explore portfolio allocation to understand how savers decide to allocate their wealth among alternative assets. The theory of portfolio allocation describes why savers behave as they do when selecting one asset rather than another. But this is not the only choice savers must make. Suppose you find the perfect financial asset—bonds issued by Golden Horizons, Inc. Should you put all your savings into Golden Horizons? The answer is no. The second theme of this chapter is to demonstrate why investing in a group of assets, or a *portfolio*, allows investors to reduce their risk. The decisions they make about asset allocation affect the performance of the entire portfolio. A third theme of this chapter is to describe why investing in a portfolio of assets allows investors to reduce their risk. Our subsequent analysis in later chapters of interest rate determination, the behavior of financial institutions, and innovation in financial markets and institutions builds on the concepts presented in this chapter.

Determinants of Portfolio Choice

Web Site Suggestions: http://www.federalreserve.gov/releases/Z1 *Z1, Flow of Funds* describes households' portfolio allocation.

The financial system offers savers an array of assets from which to choose. Such assets are stores of value; that is, they can be sold when the saver needs the funds to spend on goods and services. The types of financial assets that savers have held, on average, are shown in Fig. 5.1. Americans in 2003 held 1.7% of their financial assets in checkable deposits, another 16.3% in bank savings and time deposits, 11.2% in equity mutual funds, 17.9% in stocks directly held, 4.2% through life insurance reserves, and 34.1% through pension fund reserves. A generation ago, things were different. In 1970, households kept a larger share of their savings in bank checking and saving accounts and life insurance reserves and a smaller share in mutual funds and pension reserves. Two generations ago, in 1950, households held most of their financial assets in bank accounts, government securities, and stocks; mutual funds and pension reserves were not major stores of household wealth.

Figure 5.1 shows two patterns. The first pattern is that savers divide their assets among different financial assets, and the second pattern is that these allocations change over time. Our focus in this section is on the decisions that an individual saver makes in deciding which assets to include in a portfolio, or collection of assets, and how much a saver will devote to each asset in a portfolio. Later in the chapter, we describe the reason for the changes in asset allocation over time.

To begin, how would you invest $1000? You might choose to invest in stocks, a bond, a money market fund, or physical assets (such as commodities, real estate, gold, machines, or paintings) or hold it as cash. What influences your choice?

The **theory of portfolio allocation** seeks to answer questions about portfolio choice and predicts how a saver distributes his or her savings across alternative investments. According to this theory, savers evaluate five criteria when deciding what investments to make and how much to invest in each alternative. These **determinants of portfolio choice** are

- the saver's *wealth* or total stock of savings to be allocated,
- the *expected return* from the investment as compared with the expected return from other investments,
- the degree of *risk* of the asset as compared to the risk of other assets,
- the *liquidity* of the asset as compared to other assets, and
- the *cost of acquiring information* about the asset as compared to gathering information about other assets.

FIGURE 5.1 Portfolios of U.S. Households: 2003, 1970, 1950

Source: Board of Governors of the Federal Reserve System, *Flow of Funds Accounts*, various issues.

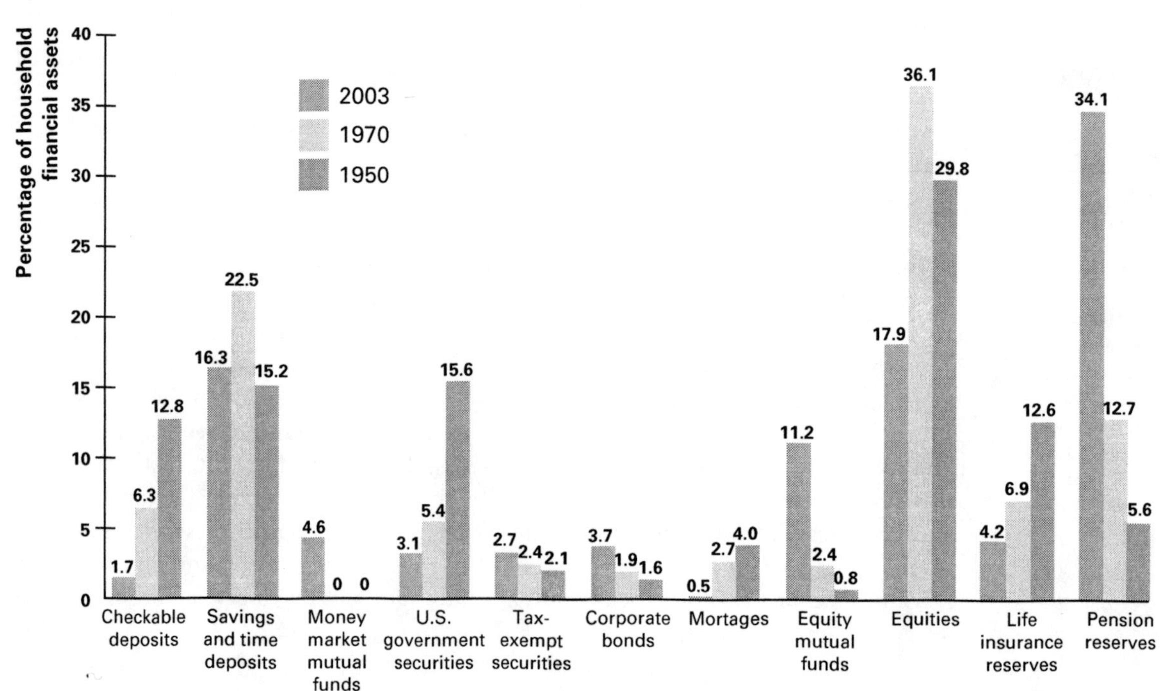

Wealth

As people become wealthier, the size of their portfolio of assets increases because they have more savings to allocate to the acquisition of assets. As people grow richer, they do not increase the quantities of all they have in their portfolios; rather, they choose to increase their purchases of some assets rather than others. Which assets do they choose? To begin answering this question, consider the asset mix you would purchase if your total wealth were \$1000; you might hold 10%, or \$100, in cash. If your total wealth were \$1 million, however, you probably would not hold \$100,000 in cash. Cash holdings would make up a smaller percentage of your wealth, and you would increase your relative holdings in other assets, such as stocks. Although holding many shares of different high-quality stocks with wealth of only \$1000 is difficult, you might well own a variety of stocks with \$1 million.

The **wealth elasticity of demand** describes how responsive the percentage change in the quantity of an asset chosen is to a percentage change in wealth. The wealth elasticity of demand does not depend on the actual dollar value of your wealth. Rather, it equals the percentage increase in the quantity of an asset you demand divided by the percentage increase in your total wealth; that is,

$$\begin{array}{c}\text{Wealth elasticity of demand}\\ \text{for an asset}\end{array} = \frac{\text{\% change in quantity demanded of the asset}}{\text{\% change in wealth}}.$$

Let's use this definition to find the wealth elasticity of your demand for cash when your wealth increases from \$1000 to \$1 million. With \$1000, you might hold 10%, or \$100, of your wealth as cash if your total wealth were \$1000. When your wealth reaches \$1 million (be optimistic!), you might hold 0.1%, or \$1000, in cash. Thus your wealth elasticity of demand for cash is 0.01, which is less than 1. Hence an increase in wealth generates a decrease in percentage terms of cash held. However, your wealth elasticity of demand for stocks and other assets is greater than 1. Hence an increase in wealth generates an increase in percentage terms of stocks and other assets held.

A *necessity asset* is one for which the wealth elasticity of demand is less than 1. Savers demand necessity assets, such as cash or checking accounts, in order to conduct regular transactions. A *luxury asset*, however, is one for which the wealth elasticity of demand exceeds 1. What makes some assets luxuries? They are assets, such as stocks, that are held for investment rather than for facilitating transactions. Savers also must consider the high fixed cost of owning a luxury asset, such as real estate taxes and insurance costs for a \$1 million house, or the high transactions costs of acquiring the asset, such as stockbroker or dealer fees for stocks. For savers with less wealth, these costs make up a larger percentage of their investment than for savers with more wealth. Thus acquiring some assets, such as buying a famous painting, is feasible only for wealthy individuals.

To summarize, as wealth increases, savers hold more of their wealth in luxury assets and less in necessity assets.

Expected Returns on Assets

What factors determine how savers, whether wealthy or poor, choose to allocate their wealth among assets? Given the choice between two otherwise similar assets, a saver will pick the one with the higher expected return. The correct measure of expected return is the expected *real* rate of return.

Savers must assess the impact of inflation on returns because changes in the value of money will affect the real value of returns. We encountered the problem of converting nominal returns to real returns in Chapter 4 when we studied rates of returns on bonds. The expected real return savers consider equals the nominal return less expected inflation. Savers use real returns as the measure of their gain in an investment because those returns adjust for changes in purchasing power.

Because savers care about expected returns for financing current and future spending, they also focus on the amount that they can keep after taxes; that is, they compare expected real after-tax returns. Taxation of returns on savings varies significantly in the United States. Interest on private corporate bonds, bank deposits, and dividends from holdings of corporate stock are taxed at the federal, state, and local levels (though dividends are taxed at a lower rate than interest). Interest received from U.S. Treasury securities is subject to federal income taxation but not to state and local income taxation. The obligations of state and local governments (called municipal bonds) generally are exempt from all taxation and often are called *tax-exempt bonds.* All such differences affect savers' portfolio decisions.

When assets are similar—that is, all other factors being held constant—an increase in the expected return on one asset relative to other assets makes the asset more desirable to savers. The remaining three determinants of portfolio choice—risk, liquidity, and information costs—are attributes that we use to compare two assets.

CHECKPOINT

Interest received from municipal bonds is tax-exempt in the United States. Should you switch your savings from taxable assets to municipal bonds to take advantage of their favorable tax treatment? Not necessarily. Investors compare expected *after-tax* returns when making their investment decisions. Suppose that a taxable bond pays an interest rate of 10%. If investors face a tax rate of 30%, this after-tax return is equivalent to the return on the tax-exempt bond of 10% − 0.3(10%) = 7%. If the tax-exempt rate were higher (say, 8%), the expected return on the tax-exempt bond would exceed that on the taxable bond. Investors would increase their demand for tax-exempt bonds, bidding up their price and reducing their yield. (Recall that bond prices and yields are inversely related.) At a tax rate of 15%, investors would prefer to invest in the taxable bond because they could receive an expected after-tax return of 10% − 0.15(10%) = 8.5%. This is greater than the 7% expected rate of return on the tax-exempt bond. Investors who are subject to high tax rates are more likely to invest in tax-exempt bonds than are investors who are subject to low tax rates. ◆

Risk Associated with Asset Returns

In making investment decisions, savers evaluate the variability of (fluctuations up and down in) the expected return as well as the size of the return. Because households use their assets largely to smooth their spending over time, they want to avoid having assets fall in value just when they need funds.

To demonstrate the impact of variability on expected returns, suppose that you have $1000 to invest in stocks and are comparing the shares of Solid Enterprises and Rollercoaster Industries. Solid Enterprises' shares yield a return of 10% all the time (with certainty), whereas Rollercoaster Industries' shares yield a return of 20% half the time and 0% half the time. We calculate the expected return on Rollercoaster's shares using a weighted average of its possible returns:

$$\left(\frac{1}{2}\right)(0.20) + \left(\frac{1}{2}\right)(0) = 0.10, \quad \text{or} \quad 10\%.$$

Solid's expected return, 10%, is the same. How do you choose between the two investments?

The answer lies in the degree of risk or variability associated with the two investments. Although Solid and Rollercoaster have equal expected returns, the likelihood that an investor in Rollercoaster will earn 10% is less certain than the return from an equivalent investment in Solid. The greater potential variation in Rollercoaster's return means that it is a riskier investment. The investor's view of risk determines which asset the investor will buy. Most people are **risk-averse savers.** They seek to minimize variability in the return on their savings and prefer security in their investments. A risk-averse saver would even accept a lower return from Solid Enterprises because of this desire for stability. **Risk-neutral savers** judge assets only on their expected returns; variability of returns is not a concern. A few individuals are **risk-loving savers,** who actually prefer to gamble by holding a risky asset with the possibility of maximizing returns.

Empirical evidence on expected returns from financial markets confirms the risk-averse behavior of most investors. For example, annual real rates of return (adjusted for inflation) on U.S. common stocks averaged 8.2% from 1926 to 1999, while annual real rates of return on long-term government bonds averaged only 2.0%.[†] Why do investors accept such low returns on government bonds when they could earn more by investing in stocks? The principal reason is that government bonds have less risk. Stocks offer higher potential returns to compensate savers for taking the higher risk associated with equity investment. Nevertheless, many economists have argued that the *equity premium* implied by the gap between the return on stocks and bonds is too large to be explained by risk considerations alone.

Because savers are generally risk-averse, an increase in the risk of one asset relative to other assets leads to a decline in the quantity of that asset chosen.

Liquidity of Assets

Assets with greater liquidity help savers to smooth spending over time or to draw down funds for emergencies. For example, if you maintain some savings in financial assets to meet unanticipated medical expenses, you want to be able to sell those assets quickly if you need the money for an operation.

Obviously, cash is the most liquid asset. Many marketable securities, such as U.S. government bonds or shares of IBM, are very liquid assets because finding a buyer for them with minimal transactions costs is easy. Real estate, coins, and fine paintings are relatively illiquid assets because their sale incurs substantial transactions costs. For example, a saver who wants to sell a house might need to wait months or even years before finding a buyer who is willing to pay the full asking price.

CHECKPOINT

Certificates of deposit (CDs) offered by banks have a penalty for early withdrawal. For example, if you invest $1000 in a one-year CD paying 5% interest, you receive less interest if you withdraw your savings before the end of a year. Why are investors willing to accept a lower interest rate (say, 3.25%) on savings accounts without a penalty for early withdrawal? Savers are generally willing to sacrifice some portion of expected return to be able to convert an asset to cash quickly to finance unplanned or emergency spending. ♦

[†]The calculations are based on data from Roger C. Ibbotson and Rex A. Sinquefield, *Stocks, Bonds, and Inflation: 2000 Yearbook*, Chicago: Ibbotson Associates, 2000.

CASE STUDY

How Much Risk Should You Tolerate in Your Portfolio?

Although all investments are risky, you can take steps to understand and manage risk when building your own portfolio. Financial planners encourage their clients to evaluate their financial situation and their willingness to bear risk in determining whether an investment is appropriate.

In assessing the volatility of returns, financial planners recommend that you determine how far ahead your savings goal extends.

The longer your time horizon, the more you can focus on the growth potential of investments in stocks. Over the period from 1926 to 1999, one-year returns on stocks ranged between −43% and 54%, while 20-year returns ranged between 3% and 18%. For most people, an important savings goal is retirement, and retirement savings make up a significant component of their wealth. If your retirement is many years away, you can take advantage of the long-term gains from riskier investments such as common stock without much concern for short-term variability in returns. Then as you approach retirement, you should adopt a more conservative strategy to reduce the risk of losing a substantial portion of your savings. Here are two typical financial plans that differ in the time horizon and savings goal of younger and older savers:

Younger Saver

Description:

Below age 50 and wishes to build his or her net worth over a relatively long time.

Goal:

Accumulate funds by earning high long-term return.

Portfolio plan:

Select portfolio based on maximizing expected real return with only limited concern for variability.

Older Saver

Description:

Close to retirement age with a portfolio at or near the amount needed to retire.

Goal:

Conserve existing funds to earn a return slightly above the inflation rate.

Portfolio plan:

Reduce risk by selecting safe assets to earn an expected real return of about zero.

Finally, in assessing the volatility of your returns, you must consider the effects of inflation and taxes. Your investment returns are (generally) subject to taxation, and your real returns lop off inflation. With these considerations in mind, over the period mentioned above, "safe" nominal government bonds would have brought you a much lower and less-than-volatile average annual yield relative to common stocks.[†]

Understanding the types of risk that influence your investment will help you to reduce emotional reactions to market volatility and to make informed investment decisions.

[†]The calculations are based on data from Roger C. Ibbotson and Rex A. Sinquefield, *Stocks, Bonds, and Inflation: 2000 Yearbook*, Chicago: Ibbotson Associates, 2000.

The average investor favors assets that are liquid over those that are not. The investor must weigh the benefits of liquidity against the lower returns that are generally available on liquid assets when selecting assets for a portfolio.

Costs of Acquiring Information

Savers seek to lower the risk associated with an asset but want to do so without devoting time or resources to assessing the issuer's creditworthiness or monitoring the borrower's actions. For some assets, such as cash or government securities, information is

TABLE 5.1 **Determinants of Asset Allocation**

An increase in ...	Causes the quantity of the asset in the portfolio chosen to ...	Because ...
wealth	rise	savers have greater stock of savings to allocate
expected return on asset relative to expected returns on other assets	rise	savers gain more from holding asset
risk (variability of returns)	fall	savers are generally risk-averse
liquidity (ease with which an asset can be converted to cash)	rise	the asset can be cheaply converted to cash to finance consumption
information costs	fall	savers must spend more resources acquiring and analyzing data on the asset and its returns

readily available to the public at low cost. For example, if you want to buy a government bond, you can easily find prices and returns in *The Wall Street Journal*. Similarly, savers can gather information about the stocks and bonds of large corporations inexpensively because financial analysts publicize information about these assets.

If a new company issues financial claims, however, investors must spend time and resources to collect and analyze information about the company before deciding to invest. Therefore savers prefer to hold assets with low information costs. An increase in the information cost for an asset raises the required rate of return on the asset; a decrease in information costs reduces the required rate of return. Specialists in the financial system acquire and analyze information about issuers of financial assets and make this information available for a fee. Other factors being held constant, a higher cost of information for an asset relative to other assets leads to a decrease in the quantity of that asset demanded.

Table 5.1 summarizes the principal determinants of portfolio choice. The underlying assumption for the effects listed in the second column of the table is that all other factors remain constant. Given the discussion of each factor, you can think about how these determinants shape your own financial decisions. As we discuss in Part 4, the same factors affect the portfolio allocation decisions of businesses and financial intermediaries.

Advantages of Diversification

Savers purchase assets with the expectation that these assets will increase in value over time, but not all assets appreciate in this way. From our description of a saver's behavior in selecting an asset, you might expect that a saver could sort through the maze of available assets and find one that does increase in value and is a "best" choice for the saver's investment dollars. But implicit in our discussion of the theory of portfolio allocation is the importance given to each asset the saver decides to include in a portfolio. Why did we assume that the saver would hold more than one asset if he or she could locate the perfect investment? The answer is that the real world is full of uncertainty, and despite all the analysis and careful decision making, a saver cannot be certain that an asset will perform as expected. To compensate for the inability to find a perfect asset, individuals typically hold various types of assets, including financial instruments, property, and durable goods. Even within categories of financial assets (stocks, for example), investors usually hold many individual issues. Allocating savings among many different assets is known as **diversification.**

In the real world, returns on assets do not move together perfectly because their risks are imperfectly correlated. That is, assets do not all fare well or poorly at the same time. Thus the return on a diversified portfolio is more stable than the returns on the individual assets making up the portfolio. Diversification effectively allows the investor to divide risk into smaller and thus less potentially harmful pieces. Research on the benefits of diversification led to three Nobel Prizes in economics: to James Tobin of Yale University, Harry Markowitz of Baruch College, and William Sharpe of Stanford University.

How does diversification reduce portfolio risk? Let's use an example to answer this question. Suppose that you want to invest \$1000 in stocks and are choosing between two investments—shares in Boomco, Inc., and shares in Bustco, Inc.—whose returns vary with the economy's performance in different ways. Suppose that Boomco does well half the time and not so well the other half. When the economy does well, Boomco prospers. Its shares have a rate of return of 20%, and you earn \$200. But in a weak economy, sales of Boomco's products are poor. Then the stock's rate of return is 0%, and you have nothing. The expected amount you will earn on your \$1000 investment in Boomco is

$$\left(\frac{1}{2}\right)(\$200) + \left(\frac{1}{2}\right)(\$0) = \$100.$$

If you invest only in Boomco, you can expect a rate of return of 10% (100/1000).

Suppose that Bustco's returns follow an opposite pattern. The rate of return on Bustco shares is high (20%) when the economy is weak, and you earn \$200. When the economy does well, you earn nothing (0%). Like Boomco shares, Bustco shares have an expected return of

$$\left(\frac{1}{2}\right)(\$0) + \left(\frac{1}{2}\right)(\$200) = \$100.$$

If you invest only in Bustco, you can expect a rate of return of 10%. Of course, if you invest only in Boomco shares or only in Bustco shares, you incur risk because the returns vary with the economy's performance.

Now consider what happens if you invest equal amounts in Boomco and Bustco shares. In good times, Boomco's rate of return is 20% and Bustco's rate of return is 0%. Therefore your total rate of return in good times is

$$\left(\frac{1}{2}\right)(\text{Boomco return}) + \left(\frac{1}{2}\right)(\text{Bustco return}) = 10\%,$$

or

$$(\$500)(0.20) + (\$500)(0) = \$100.$$

Similarly, in bad times, you earn

$$\left(\frac{1}{2}\right)(\text{Boomco return}) + \left(\frac{1}{2}\right)(\text{Bustco return}) = 10\%,$$

or

$$(\$500)(0) + (\$500)(0.20) = \$100.$$

By this strategy you earn the same expected return (10%) as you would earn from buying the shares of only one of the companies. However, you lessen the risk affecting your portfolio's returns by limiting the influence of one source of variability: the economy. The strategy of dividing risk by holding multiple assets ensures steadier income.

Savers cannot eliminate risk entirely because assets share some common risk called **market** (or **systematic**) **risk.** For example, general fluctuations in economic conditions can increase or decrease returns on stocks collectively. Assets also carry their own unique risk called **idiosyncratic** (or **unsystematic**) **risk.** For example, the price of an individual stock may be influenced by factors such as discoveries, strikes, or lawsuits that influence the profitability of the firm and its share value. Diversification can eliminate idiosyncratic risk but not systematic risk.†

Diversification reduces the riskiness of the return on a portfolio unless assets' returns move together perfectly. The less the returns on assets move together, the greater the benefit savers reap from diversification in reducing portfolio risk. Because savers generally are risk-averse, they amass portfolios containing an array of different assets.

Figure 5.2 illustrates the results of a study to determine how much risk can be eliminated through diversification in a portfolio of stocks traded on the New York Stock Exchange. It illustrates the relationship between the average annual variability on equally weighted portfolios and the different numbers of stocks (selected randomly) in the portfolios. Although a single security had an average annual variability (measured by the standard deviation) of about 49%, holding two stocks reduced the variability by about one-quarter, to just over 37%.†† Holding eight stocks cuts the average annual variability in half, to just less than 25%. Increasing the number of assets to 20 cuts the average

FIGURE 5.2

Reducing Risk through Stock Portfolio Diversification

Increasing the number of New York Stock Exchange–listed stocks held in a portfolio decreases the variability of the portfolio's return. While diversification can reduce individual risk, there is a certain amount of risk that cannot be reduced.

Source: Based on calculations presented in Meir Statman, "How Many Stocks Make a Diversified Portfolio?" *Journal of Financial and Quantitative Analysis,* 22:353–364, 1980.

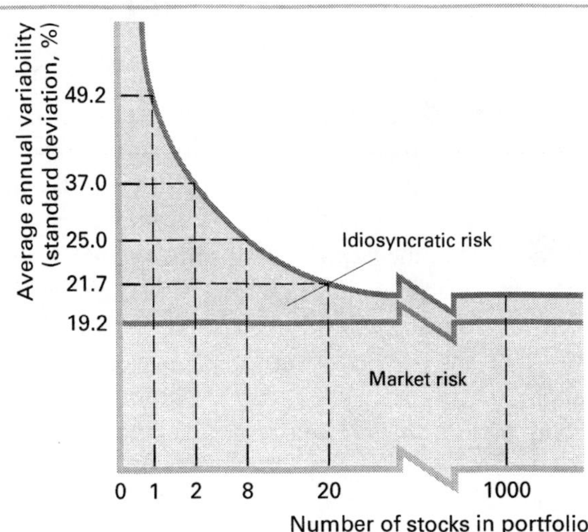

†Indeed, even if asset returns are independent (completely uncorrelated), increasing the number of assets held in a portfolio reduces overall risk.

†† The variance of a portfolio return is the squared deviation from the expected return. The standard deviation is the square root of the variance.

annual variability further to about 21.7%. Holding the entire portfolio of stocks listed on the New York Stock Exchange reduces the average annual variability to 19.2%. This remaining variability is traceable to market risk and cannot be eliminated by holding additional stocks; that is, the risk is nondiversifiable. In the (unlikely) event that returns are perfectly and positively correlated, adding additional assets does not reduce the variability of the portfolio.

To measure systematic risk, financial economists calculate a variable called **beta,** the responsiveness of a stock's expected return to changes in the value of the complete market portfolio of that stock—that is, the collection of all stocks. For example, if a 1% increase in the value of the market portfolio leads to a 0.5% increase in the value of the asset, the asset's beta is calculated to be 0.5. If the value of the asset rises by 1.5% when the market portfolio rises by 1%, then the asset's beta equals 1.5.

The market portfolio faces no idiosyncratic risk, only systematic risk. Hence, when an asset has a high value of beta, its return has a lot of systematic risk. This systematic risk is scaled by beta; a beta of 1.5 implies three times the systematic risk as a beta of 0.5. Because systematic risk cannot be diversified away, investors are less willing to hold an asset with a high beta, all other factors being equal. Hence assets with higher values of beta must have a higher expected return to compensate investors for their higher risk.

Savers' ability to diversify is limited by the cost of acquiring information about alternative assets and the transactions costs of buying and selling individual assets. Another potential limit to diversification comes from legal restrictions on the assets that can be held by individual savers or by certain financial intermediaries on their behalf. For example, individuals face limits on their investments in derivative securities depending on their net worth and financial sophistication. Commercial banks are not allowed to invest depositors' funds in corporate equities.

Putting It All Together: Explaining Portfolio Allocation

At the beginning of the chapter we looked at current and past patterns of asset allocation by households. We can use the determinants of portfolio choice and the principle of diversification to explain how portfolio composition changes over time.

One pattern in Fig. 5.1 is that, in looking at the allocation of savings to different assets over time, the popularity of some assets has increased among savers, whereas that of others has declined. For example, there has been a sharp decrease in the proportion of savers' portfolios devoted to checkable deposits. One reason for this is the increase in wealth that has occurred over the post–World War II period. Checking accounts are an example of a necessity asset. As U.S. households have become much wealthier over the postwar period, their balances of checking accounts have fallen relative to other asset holdings.

Another reason for the changes is the tax treatment of different assets. Savers compare expected returns on alternative assets when making decisions about portfolio allocation. One component of differences in expected returns is different tax treatment. When a household buys stocks or bonds directly, it pays income taxes on returns. Savings through life insurance reserves receive favorable tax treatment because no tax is paid as earnings on reserves accrue. Pension fund reserves receive similarly favorable tax treatment and an additional benefit: households' contributions to pension plans are

CASE STUDY

Modeling Risk Premiums in Financial Markets

An increase in the risk of an asset's return makes investors less willing to hold the asset, other things being equal. This useful qualitative prescription has stimulated major efforts to model risk premiums. In what follows, we consider two of these developments: the *capital asset pricing model (CAPM)* and the *arbitrage pricing theory (APT)*.

The CAPM was developed by William Sharpe of Stanford University and the late John Lintner of Harvard University in the 1960s. It begins with the idea that the risk contributed by an individual asset (say, Exxon stock) to a well-diversified portfolio of stocks reflects the magnitude of its systematic risk. This magnitude is measured by beta. The larger is beta, the greater is the systematic risk and therefore the higher is the expected return required by investors for being willing to hold the asset. In the CAPM the expected return on asset j, R^e_j, depends on the default-risk-free interest rate, R_f, and the expected return on the market portfolio, R^e_m. Specifically,

$$\underbrace{R^e_j}_{\substack{\text{Expected}\\\text{return on}\\\text{asset } j}} = \underbrace{R_f}_{\substack{\text{Risk-free}\\\text{rate}}} + \underbrace{\underbrace{\beta_j}_{\substack{\text{Beta of}\\\text{asset } j}} \underbrace{\left(R^e_m \quad R_f\right)}_{\substack{\text{Risk premium on}\\\text{the market portfolio}}}}_{\text{Risk premium on asset } j}$$

In other words, the expected return on asset has two components: the default-risk-free rate and the risk premium for that asset. The risk premium compensates the investor for the risk that the security will not generate the expected return. In the CAPM the risk premium equals the risk premium on the market portfolio scaled by beta. Suppose, for example, that an asset has a beta of 1.0. Then its risk premium equals $1.0 \times (R^e_m - R_f)$, or the risk premium on the market portfolio. If the asset has a beta of 1.5, then its risk premium is one and one-half times that of the market portfolio. In this case, for example, if the expected return on the market portfolio is 8% and the risk-free rate is 2%, then the risk premium on the market portfolio is 8%, and the risk premium on the individual asset is 1.5 × 6%, or 9%.

A key element in the simplicity of the CAPM is its assumption of a single source of market risk—that is, the systematic risk of the market portfolio. There may, however, be multiple sources of systematic risk in the economy. Examples include aggregate inflation or aggregate output. In the arbitrage pricing theory, developed by Stephen Ross of Yale University, each of these factors has an associated beta. The beta values are found by estimating how sensitive the expected return is to a change in the factor. To see how the APT refines the CAPM, we can substitute for the market return R^e_m the expected return from each factor R^e_{FAC}. Hence in the arbitrage pricing theory,

$$\underbrace{R^e_j}_{\substack{\text{Expected return}\\\text{on asset } j}} = \underbrace{R_f}_{\substack{\text{Risk-free}\\\text{rate}}} + \underbrace{\underbrace{\beta_{j1}\left(R^e_{FAC1} \quad R_f\right)}_{\substack{\text{Contribution to risk}\\\text{premium from factor 1}}} + \underbrace{\beta_{j2}\left(R^e_{FAC2} \quad R_f\right)}_{\substack{\text{Contribution to risk}\\\text{premium from factor 2}}} + \cdots \underbrace{\beta_{jN}\left(R^e_{FACN} \quad R_f\right)}_{\substack{\text{Contribution to risk}\\\text{premium from factor } N}}}_{\text{Risk premium on asset } j}$$

In this theory, an increase in the sensitivity of the assets to each factor increases the risk premium.

While they have been extended in many ways, both the CAPM and the APT are used by practitioners in financial markets. Although each theory offers technical interpretations for calculating risk premiums, the central insight is common: An increase in systematic risk raises an asset's risk premium and the return investors require for holding the asset.

from pre-tax dollars; no individual-level tax is paid on the earnings contributed. Since 1950, as pension plan eligibility has expanded, households have held more assets through pension plans to take advantage of higher after-tax returns. Direct holdings of U.S. government bonds, corporate bonds, and equities have declined in relative importance over the same period.

In 1950, U.S. households held less than 1% of their financial assets in stock mutual funds; that figure more than doubled by 1970 to 2.4%, then more than quadrupled again by 2003 to 11.2%. One reason for their increase is that mutual funds reduce risk and information costs for small investors and increase the liquidity of owning stock.

One way in which mutual funds help savers to reduce overall exposure to risk is by facilitating diversification. One barrier to diversification is the cost of buying and selling financial assets. On the one hand, transactions costs of direct purchases and sales can be high for small savers. For example, brokerage commissions to buy a few shares of GM stock are very high. On the other hand, investors in a mutual fund buy shares in diversified portfolios of assets from financial markets. Because a mutual fund has a great quantity of funds to invest (the collective funds of the individual savers), it offers lower transactions costs. Thus mutual funds can offer diversified portfolios of stocks. Mutual funds offer diversification possibilities beyond stocks—to government or corporate bonds and money market instruments such as Treasury bills or commercial paper.

In addition to offering a way for savers to pool risk, mutual funds allow maintenance of liquidity through low transactions costs and, in some cases, check-writing features. They

OTHER TIMES, OTHER PLACES . . .

Are Investors (Globally) Well Diversified?

In domestic equity markets, investors can reduce their exposure to risk by diversifying—that is, by holding many individual stocks whose returns do not rise or fall at the same time. Investors can apply this principle even further by diversifying in *international* markets: Because equities in different national markets do not always move precisely together, investors can improve their portfolio diversification by holding stocks from many countries. Kenneth French of Dartmouth College and James Poterba of M.I.T. have shown that equity returns on stocks from the United States, Japan, United Kingdom, France, Germany, and Canada do not move together, indicating that investors could significantly reduce risk by holding a portfolio made up of stocks from more than one of these countries.[†] Although the benefits of global diversification have long been known, most savers nonetheless hold the vast majority of their wealth in domestic assets. The study by French and Poterba of the world's five largest stock markets—United States, Japan, United Kingdom, Germany, and France—indicates that domestic investors account for about 90% of ownership, with the exception of Germany, which has about 80% domestic ownership.

Why are investors missing the potential for significant gains from more global diversification of their portfolios? One possible explanation is *institutional barriers*, such as government regulations that limit investment abroad. Although this explanation may have been plausible in the 1970s when such controls were widespread, capital controls are not widely used by industrial countries today. Another theory suggests that there are different *transactions costs* between domestic and foreign markets and that investors seek the lowest transactions costs. However, since such costs are lower in very liquid markets such as New York, this explanation does not fit the fact that most investors keep their investments in their home market. The most likely explanation relates to *information costs*: Investors may assign extra "risk" to foreign stocks simply because they know less about foreign firms and markets. Therefore they choose the less risky option of domestic investment. Country-specific mutual funds, which give investors access to broad groups of foreign stocks and have been growing in popularity, might help to overcome this barrier to diversification.

[†]See Kenneth R. French and James M. Poterba, "Investor Diversification and International Equity Markets," *American Economic Review*, 81:222–226, 1991.

also reduce savers' information costs by economizing on costs of research and information collection about the assets in the portfolio.

Why do mutual funds provide these services that have accounted for their rapid growth? The funds earn a profit for the fund managers, as investors are willing to sacrifice some of the expected return on investments to obtain these benefits. While diversification is a worthwhile investment goal, be careful not to invest in too many similar funds. When you buy a mutual fund, you are already diversifying by investing in a group of securities. If you invest in too many similar funds, you may be racking up extra costs in fees and recordkeeping.

To summarize, we can explain trends in the way in which savers allocate their funds among different assets by applying the theory of portfolio choice and diversification. As the wealth of the population grows, investors are more likely to substitute luxury assets for necessity assets. Investments that reduce risk and information costs and increase liquidity become popular vehicles for savers who seek high expected returns. Shifts in taxation or differences in taxation among assets cause investors to favor some securities over others.

KEY TERMS AND CONCEPTS

Beta
Determinants of portfolio choice
Diversification
Idiosyncratic (unsystematic) risk
Market (systematic) risk
Risk-averse savers
Risk-loving savers
Risk-neutral savers
Theory of portfolio allocation
Wealth elasticity of demand

SUMMARY

1. The theory of portfolio allocation helps to predict how savers select assets to hold as investment. A saver's allocation of savings in a particular asset is determined by (1) wealth (with greater responsiveness for luxury assets than for necessity assets); (2) expected return on the asset relative to expected returns on other assets; (3) risk of the return on the asset relative to the returns on other assets; (4) liquidity of the asset relative to other assets; and (5) cost of gathering information about the asset relative to information costs associated with other assets.
2. Diversification (holding more than one asset) reduces the risk of the return on a portfolio unless the returns on the individual assets move together perfectly. The less the returns on assets move together, the greater is the reduction in risk provided by diversification. This reduction in risk is valued by risk-averse savers, who are concerned not only about the expected return on their savings (portfolio of assets), but also about the variability of that return.

REVIEW QUESTIONS

1. What are the five key determinants of demand for a particular asset?
2. What is the difference between a necessity asset and a luxury asset? Give some examples of each.
3. What are the differences in being *risk-averse*, *risk-neutral*, and *risk-loving*? Which type of saver is likely to own only stocks and stock options? Which type of saver is likely to hold more bonds and cash than stocks?
4. U.S. citizens invest mostly in the U.S. stock market; Japanese citizens invest mostly in the Japanese stock market. Why do they do so if there are gains to diversification?
5. The saying "You shouldn't put all your eggs in one basket" is an example of what principle in investing? What does it mean?

MOVING FROM THEORY TO PRACTICE . . .

THE WALL STREET JOURNAL SEPTEMBER 18, 2002

Europe's Tender Equity Culture

While the bear market has prompted greater regulatory scrutiny in the U.S., it could have a deeper effect on Europe.

Evidence is growing that big and small business, government and individuals are retreating from a push toward stock-market capitalism that began about five years ago. . . .

Certainly, a bear market is a normal part of a mature equity culture, and Europe may quickly resume its nascent move toward stock-market capitalism once markets turn around. "What alternative is there?" asks Jean Lemierre, the president of the European Bank for Reconstruction and Development.

But for many Europeans, the past few years have been the worst bear market of their lifetimes. Since its peak in March 2000, the stock-market fall has wiped away more than $5 trillion from the value of European companies. As a percentage of gross domestic product, that's a bigger decrease than either the 1987 crash or the bear market of the early 1970s, according to Credit Suisse First Boston.

a Fear of market forces has returned. "We didn't have a real risk culture here," says Bodo Heiss, the founder and chief executive of Tonxx. . . .

The last time Europe suffered such stock-market woes, some 70 years ago, a seemingly well-developed stock-market culture unraveled. In 1913, initial public offerings, equity issues and bank deposits in several European countries all exceeded those in the U.S., relative to GDP. But then the 1929 stock-market crash and ensuing Depression, the rise of the trade-union movement, and World War II turned sentiment and governments in Europe against market forces. b Over the next two decades, the role of government in European economies grew, as leaders sought to protect citizens from the whims of stock prices and foreign capital. . . .

The market slump is undermining another huge undertaking: revamping Europe's pension systems. In recent years, governments have acknowledged that the widely used pay-as-you-go system—in which workers and employers pay a percentage of wages each month to support current retirees—isn't sustainable. c When the equity culture was spreading a few short years ago, governments began introducing market-financed elements, similar to the U.S. 401(k) plan. As the stock market boomed in the late 1990s, even skeptical unions ceded ground.

Europe's new start-up culture may need a while to get going again as well. Venture-capital firms invested nearly $50 billion in European start-ups in 2000, seven times the total of just four years earlier. This year, money has dried up.

All of this is crimping Europe's banks, which went on a hiring binge as IPO volume rose from 1995 to 2000. Then everything stopped. Banks are in the midst of laying off tens of thousands. . . .

ANALYZING THE NEWS ...

Investors compare alternative assets by considering expected returns, risk, liquidity, and information costs. Many financial planners in the United States recommend that individuals place a significant portion of their retirement savings (the bulk of most households' financial assets) in stocks. A majority of U.S. households own stocks either directly or through mutual funds. Likewise, stockholding is popular in the United Kingdom as well. Continental European portfolio allocation remains much less weighted toward equities. A budding equity culture in the 1990s was dealt a harsh blow by the decline in stock indices around the world over the 2000–2002 period. European households may be passing up higher expected returns and diversification over the long run (and a weak equity market makes it difficult for companies to raise equity capital). The determinants of portfolio choice offer some explanations.

a One possibility is that European investors (say, in France or Germany) have a different attitude toward risk than U.S. investors—in particular, Germans are more risk-averse. If European investors dislike risk, stocks—with sometimes quite variable returns—will be less preferred than bonds.

b When a stock market is illiquid, investors incur high costs of buying and selling shares, lowering their returns. Because the market for many European government bonds has much lower costs of buying and selling for individual investors, European households may be more likely to choose bonds.

c Tax breaks for retirement saving—like IRAs and 401(k) plans in the United States—can give a stimulus to the mutual fund business. While transactions costs for equities may eliminate the expected return differential for households, intermediaries such as mutual funds face lower transactions costs, which, when passed on to individual investors, increase the demand for stocks. Investors in the United States went through this transformation during the 1960s–1990s.

For further thought...

Why might households' unwillingness to hold stocks depress venture capital funding of emerging companies?

Source: Excerpted from Christopher Rhoads, "Europe's Tender Equity Culture," *The Wall Street Journal*, September 18, 2002.

6. If the equity premium implied by the gap between the return on stocks and the return on bonds is too large to be explained by risk considerations alone, how might it be explained?
7. What advantages do small investors see in owning stock mutual funds as opposed to holding individual stocks?
8. Despite the stock market boom of the 1990s, the fraction of household financial assets directly invested in equities declined by 10 percentage points between 1970 and 1998. Can you think of reasons why this happened?
9. What is the difference between market risk and idiosyncratic risk? Which type of risk can be reduced by diversification?
10. Why don't all risk-averse investors hold a fully diversified portfolio?
11. Would you expect the variability of returns on individual stocks traded on the New York Stock Exchange to be greater or less than the variability of the return on a portfolio consisting of all stocks traded on the exchange? Why or why not?

ANALYTICAL PROBLEMS

12. Suppose that your wealth elasticity of demand for IBM stock is 2, you own 1000 shares of IBM stock, and your total wealth is $1 million. You earn a $100,000 bonus at work. How much more IBM stock will you buy?
13. Suppose that you are an investor with a choice of three assets that are identical in every way except in their rate of return and taxability. Which asset yields the highest after-tax return?

    Asset 1: interest rate 10%, interest taxed at a 40% rate
    Asset 2: interest rate 8%, interest taxed at a 25% rate
    Asset 3: interest rate 6.5%, no tax on interest
14. Suppose that Asset 1 in Problem 13 had a return of 11%. Would your answer change? If so, in what way?
15. U.S. government bonds with 30-year maturities used to be sold with a call provision: After 25 years, the government could call the bonds and make a final interest payment plus principal repayment. When the government eliminated the call provision in 1985, it found that it could offer a different interest rate on the bonds than it could before. Was the interest rate higher or lower? Why? When was the government likely to call the outstanding callable bonds?
16. Suppose that you have invested $1000 in Acme Widget. Half of the time you earn a 20% return on your Acme shares and half of the time you earn a 0% return. Suppose that you have studied the returns on the shares of Amalgamated Gidget and it turns out that in years when the return on Acme's shares was 20%, half the time the return on Amalgamated's shares was also 20% and half the time the return was 0%. Similarly, in years when the return on Acme's shares was 0%, half the time the return on Amalgamated's shares was 20% and half the time the return was 0%. Would you be better off selling $500 worth of your Acme shares and investing the funds in Amalgamated or would you be better off keeping all of your funds invested in Acme?
17. In the mid-1980s, a new technique was developed that divides payments on government coupon bonds into two parts: One part consists of the coupon interest payments on the bonds, and the other part consists of the principal repayment on the bonds. Sold separately, the two parts are worth more to investors than the entire bond. Why?
18. Suppose that you are investing money in a portfolio of stocks and are choosing from among Badrisk Company, which returns 30% in good years and loses 50% in bad years; Worserisk Company, which returns 30% in good years and loses 75% in bad years; Norisk Company, which returns 10% all the time; and Lowrisk Company, which returns 20% in good years and loses 5% in bad years.
    a. If you were completely risk-averse and your only goal was to minimize your risk, which stock(s) would you buy?
    b. If you were risk-neutral, and good years and bad years each occurred half the time, which stock(s) would you buy?
    c. If you were somewhat risk-averse, would you ever have both Badrisk and Worserisk in your portfolio? Why or why not?
    d. If you decided on a portfolio consisting of one- third Badrisk, one-third Norisk, and one-third Lowrisk, what would be your rate of return in good years? In bad years? What would be your average rate of return over all years if good years and bad years each

occurred half the time? If good years occurred 80% of the time and bad years 20% of the time?

19. Suppose that you want to hold a stock portfolio for just one year. You have $1000 to invest in stocks, and you can choose to invest in Topgunner, Inc., which has returns of 20% in good years and –10% in bad years, or in Lowrunner, Inc., which has returns of 35% in good years and –15% in bad years.

    a. What is your return in a good year if you buy just Topgunner? In a bad year? What is your return in a good year if you buy just Lowrunner? In a bad year? What is your return in a good year if you put half your money in Topgunner and half in Lowrunner? In a bad year?

    b. Now suppose that, for every stock you buy, you must pay transactions costs equal to $50. Repeat (a) with your return reduced by these transactions costs. What happens to your portfolio choice?

20. You are a member of an investment club that owns shares in a firm that manufactures men's clothing. Explain the arguments for and against buying

    a. shares in a company that manufactures women's clothing.

    b. shares in a chemical manufacturing concern.

    Which investment is more likely to decrease the overall risk of your club's portfolio? Why?

21. Using the theory of portfolio allocation, state why you would be more willing or less willing to buy a share of IBM stock if you

    a. win $1 million in the state lottery.

    b. expect that stock prices will become more volatile.

    c. expect the price of IBM shares to increase over the next year.

    d. read about new developments increasing the liquidity of the bond market.

22. Using the theory of portfolio allocation, state why you would be more willing or less willing to buy corporate bonds if you

    a. expect interest rates on bonds to rise.

    b. expect a large capital loss next month on the sale of your house.

    c. learn that the transactions costs of selling bonds will increase.

    d. expect inflation to increase significantly in the future.

DATA QUESTIONS

23. You can find information about mutual funds through advertisements in *The Wall Street Journal.* Such ads invite you to write to the fund manager to obtain a copy of the *prospectus,* which contains information about the fund's portfolio, management strategy, and fees. Find a prospectus on the World Wide Web, or locate one in your library for a fund specializing in equities, and examine the list of stocks held. Is the fund well diversified? How can you tell?

24. The Federal Reserve periodically publishes a summary of assets and liabilities of U.S. households and businesses. Locate a recent copy of *Balance Sheets for the U.S. Economy* in your library. Calculate for the most recent year available the ratio of foreign corporate equities held to total corporate equities held. Using the theory of portfolio allocation, explain why such a small fraction of equity holdings of U.S. residents are in non–U.S. stocks.

25. The Federal Reserve's Flow of Funds Accounts report provides quarterly information on household's portfolio allocation decisions. Table 100 of each issue breaks down this information on an annualized basis over the most previous eight-year period. Look at this table in the most recent release of this report at http://www.federalreserve.gov/releases/z1/current/data.htm. How has households' allocation of various investment vehicles changed during this time period? How do these changes relate to changes in the business cycle during this period of time?

26. Information on mutual funds is ubiquitous. A popular internet site is Morningstar's. Look at Morningstar's "Family Fund Data Pages" via http://www.morningstar.com/Cover/Funds.html?topnav=funds and click on a cross section of funds listed. Look at each fund's sector breakdown, and then evaluate the degree of portfolio allocation in terms of risk and return. Which funds would be preferred by investors most concerned about wealth maximization? Expected return? Degree of risk? Explain.

CHAPTER 11

Reducing Transactions Costs and Information Costs

The collapse of communist governments in the former Soviet Union and Eastern Europe in the early 1990s led to much rejoicing and hope for the emergence of individual freedom, political democracy, and market economies. As attention turned to getting private businesses started, financial analysts foresaw a daunting task. Savers seemed unwilling to lend their funds to local borrowers, preferring to invest in government bonds or foreign exchange. Borrowers found financial markets too poorly developed to be of much use. Hungary and Poland made strides in developing financial markets. Russia still struggled in the late 1990s and in the new century to do so. One prominent economist noted wearily that "hundreds of billions of dollars were being left on the table" because eager entrepreneurs were unable to fund new businesses while savers were unable to earn returns on their savings. Most financial experts suggested that efforts should focus on organizing financial intermediaries.

Financial markets in the United States and many other industrial economies perform the task of matching savers and borrowers more effectively than do those in newly emerging economies, but there are still obstacles to the efficient channeling of funds from savers to borrowers. In 2001 and 2002, major corporate accounting scandals in the United States drove this point home. In our discussions of financial markets, we assumed that borrowers were successful in raising funds in financial markets and that savers could use the information contained in market prices to make informed portfolio allocation decisions. Financial markets don't function quite as smoothly as we implied. In this chapter, we describe the obstacles that exist in financial markets—transactions costs and information costs—to see how they are mitigated in our financial system. Often, financial intermediaries such as banks reduce information costs more effectively than financial markets do, as we will explain here.

Obstacles to Matching Savers and Borrowers

Suppose that you saved $3000 from working part-time and you want to invest it. Should you invest the money in stocks? A stockbroker will tell you that the commissions you must pay will be large relative to the size of your purchases because you are investing a small amount of money. This cost is particularly high if you are attempting to diversify by buying a few shares each of different stocks. Should you turn instead to the bond market to buy, say, a Treasury bill? Your broker will tell you: sorry, but the minimum face value is $10,000.

Undaunted, you decide to bypass financial markets. Conveniently, your roommate's brother-in-law needs $3000 to develop a potentially successful new Internet browser. But how do you know that he is the best person to write and market this computer application? Perhaps you should seek out other borrowers and evaluate their plans. If you decide to lend your money to the fledgling entrepreneur, your lawyer tells you that to draw up the contract describing the terms of your investment will cost

$1500, or half the amount you have to invest. Hence you give up on the investment. The cost that you face and your decision not to invest also hurt the browser designer, who will have the same difficulty raising funds from other individual investors.

This example demonstrates **transactions costs,** the costs of buying or selling a financial instrument, such as a stock or a bond. **Information costs** are the costs that savers incur to determine the creditworthiness of borrowers and to monitor how borrowers use the acquired funds. These costs increase the cost of funds that borrowers must pay and lower the expected returns to savers, reducing the efficiency of financial markets. This inefficiency creates profit opportunities for individuals and institutions that can reduce transactions and information costs.

Transactions Costs

Brokerage commissions, minimum investment requirements, and lawyers' fees are all examples of transactions costs. There is obviously a need for a channel to match small savers and borrowers, and financial intermediaries have satisfied a need that financial markets are not filling. For example, mutual funds sell shares to many individual savers and, in turn, invest in a diversified portfolio of bonds or stocks. Banks accept deposits from individual savers and lend the funds to household and business borrowers. The economy also benefits from the growth generated by financial intermediaries, while the intermediaries earn a profit by charging savers and borrowers fees for reducing transactions costs.

Financial intermediaries reduce transactions costs by exploiting **economies of scale,** the reduction of costs per unit that accompanies an increase in volume. In the case of transactions costs, intermediaries' costs fall as the size of the funds raised increases. Transactions costs per dollar of investment decline as the size of transactions increases. For example, the transactions cost of buying $1,000,000 of Treasury bonds is not much greater than that of buying $10,000 of bonds. Individual investors can reduce transactions costs by combining their purchases through an intermediary. Thus 100 investors with $10,000 each to invest face lower costs per dollar if together they buy $1,000,000 of bonds than if they purchased the bonds individually.

There are other ways in which intermediaries benefit from economies of scale—for example, in drawing up legal contracts. Financial intermediaries spread legal costs among many individual savers so that each saver who wants to invest in an invention, the corner drugstore, or an IBM bond doesn't have to seek costly, customized legal advice. Financial intermediaries also take advantage of economies of scale to purchase sophisticated computer systems that provide financial services, such as automatic teller machine networks.

In Chapters 12 and 13, we examine in more detail how mutual funds, banks, and other financial intermediaries reduce transactions costs for savers and borrowers.

Asymmetric Information and Information Costs

In describing transactions in financial markets, we have assumed that savers and borrowers have the same information, or *symmetric information.* That is, individuals buying shares in or bonds of a company have the same information as the company's managers. This assumption does not mean that the parties will have perfect information; conditions may unfold differently from their initial expectations. For example, a change in consumers' tastes might mean that the borrower faces a more challenging market than expected and must default on bond payments. When the lender and borrower exchanged funds for a security, neither could perfectly anticipate market conditions or economic events, but both had the same information and could make informed decisions.

In the real world, borrowers may have private information. A company issuing bonds may be aware of a potential lawsuit or other unfavorable conditions, but the buyer of those bonds may be uninformed. **Asymmetric information** describes the situation in which one party in a transaction has better information than the other. Most typically, the borrower has better information than the lender. The existence of asymmetric information makes it costly for savers and borrowers to make exchanges in financial markets. In the next two sections, we describe two costs arising from asymmetric information:

Adverse selection: a lender's problem of distinguishing the good-risk applicants from the bad-risk applicants before making an investment.

Moral hazard: a lender's verification that borrowers are using their funds as intended.

In some cases, the cost of adverse selection and moral hazard can be so great that a lender will lend only to the government or other well-known borrowers. However, more generally there are practical solutions to these problems, in which the markets or financial intermediaries lower the cost of information needed to make investment decisions.

Adverse Selection

The used car market demonstrates the problems that adverse selection can pose for buyers and sellers in a market.† Suppose that your parents are trying to sell their 2003 Ford Taurus. Among all the 2003 Ford Tauruses in the newspaper ads, some are good cars and others are "lemons" (cars that are constantly in the repair shop). Sellers, such as your parents, know the quality of their cars, but uninformed readers of newspaper ads do not. Because these potential buyers can't distinguish good cars from lemons, they will offer the price of an *average-quality* 2003 Taurus to sellers of all 2003 Tauruses. Your parents view this price as too low and consider their good Taurus to be *undervalued.* The price delights the Sunkists down the street, who own a lemon. Their Taurus is *overvalued* at the average price, and the Sunkists can hardly wait to unload it. As a result of this pricing process, owners of good Tauruses may decide not to sell their cars. Therefore the available pool of used Tauruses consists of cars of below-average quality, resulting in an adverse selection of potential used cars. In the used car market, buyers and sellers find trading among themselves costly.

To reduce the costs of adverse selection, car dealers act as intermediaries between buyers and sellers. To maintain their reputations with buyers, dealers are less willing to take advantage of their private information about the quality of the used cars that they are selling than are individual sellers. As a result, dealers sell both lemons and good cars for their true values. In addition, government regulations require that car dealers disclose information about the cars to consumers.

†This example of adverse selection was first described by George Akerlof of the University of California, Berkeley. George A. Akerlof, "The Market for 'Lemons': Quality Uncertainty and the Market Mechanism," *Quarterly Journal of Economics,* 84:488–500, 1970.

"Lemons Problems" in Financial Markets

Just as in the used car market, lemons problems make lending in financial markets more costly, and financial information disclosure regulations again come to the rescue. How does adverse selection affect the stock and bond markets' ability to channel funds from savers to borrowers? First, let's look at the stock market. Suppose that Hitechco is a new maker of computer chips. If the firm obtains capital, it will be able to finance an exciting new technological development in chip making. If Hitechco issues new shares of stock, it can pursue the chip-making project. If it doesn't, it loses the opportunity.

At the same time, Lemonco is seeking funds to develop a product similar to Hitechco's, but, unknown to the market, Lemonco's product is inferior. In fact, on the basis of available information, investors can't determine the quality of the firms' scientific expertise and their productive capabilities. When Hitechco tries to sell stock, then, the market will assign the same value to it as to Lemonco's stock, and Hitechco's shares will be undervalued. Hitechco's cost of funds is higher than it would be if potential shareholders had all the information the firm possessed.

Adverse selection is present in the bond market as well. Suppose that Hitechco and Lemonco know more about the risk of their projects than do investors in the bond market. If an increase in interest rates on default-risk-free Treasury bonds makes them a more attractive investment than Hitechco or Lemonco bonds, lenders raise the interest rate they require to hold Hitechco and Lemonco bonds. In this situation, as lenders generally raise their required returns on bonds, adverse selection occurs. The reason is that, at high interest rates, only very risky borrowers, such as Lemonco, will be likely to borrow funds: If their projects are successful, both lenders and borrowers win big; if (as is more likely) they aren't, the lenders suffer. Lenders are aware of this problem and may restrict the availability of credit rather than raise rates to the level at which the quantities of funds demanded and supplied are equal. This restricting of credit is known as **credit rationing.** When lenders ration credit, borrowed funds become more costly for unknown firms—both good and bad.

Adverse selection is costly for the economy. When good firms have difficulty communicating information to financial markets, their external financing costs rise. This situation forces firms to grow primarily through investment of internal funds, or investment by firm insiders and accumulated profits.[†] Because the firms that are most affected are usually in dynamic, emerging sectors of the economy, opportunities for growth of physical capital, employment, and production are likely to be restricted.

Reducing Information Costs

The costs to savers and borrowers of adverse selection make it difficult for good borrowers to raise money in financial markets and lower the returns obtained by savers. Similarly, good borrowers are willing to pay to communicate information about their prospects. Some financial market participants charge fees for their services—to savers who seek information about borrowers and to borrowers who wish to communicate information about their prospects to savers—but these fees are lower than the information costs of adverse selection. Other costs can be mitigated by regulation of financial

[†] If entrepreneurs have to avoid high information costs associated with external financing by investing most of their savings in their businesses, they lose risk-sharing benefits of diversification.

markets. As we will see later, these costs can also be reduced by financial intermediaries who can provide savers with information about the quality of potential borrowers.

Direct disclosure of information. In most industrialized countries, government agencies set requirements for information disclosure for firms that desire to sell securities in financial markets. In the United States, government regulations promulgated by the Securities and Exchange Commission† require publicly owned companies to report their performance in financial statements prepared by using standard accounting methods. Such disclosure reduces the information costs of adverse selection, but it doesn't eliminate them, for two reasons. First, some good firms may be too young to have much information for potential investors to evaluate. Second, lemon firms will try to present the required information in the best possible light so that investors will overvalue their securities.

Private firms have tried to reduce the costs of adverse selection by collecting information on individual borrowers and selling the information to savers. As long as the information-gathering firm does a good job, savers purchasing the information will be better able to judge the quality of borrowers, improving the efficiency of lending. Although savers must pay for the information, they can benefit from the information by earning higher returns. Companies specializing in information—including Moody's Investor Service, Standard & Poor's Corporation, Value Line, and Dun and Bradstreet—collect information from businesses' income statements, balance sheets, and investment decisions and sell it to subscribers. Buyers include individual investors, libraries, and financial intermediaries. You can find some of these publications in your college library or through on-line information services. Private information-gathering firms cannot eliminate adverse selection, but they can help to minimize its cost.

Although only subscribers pay for the information collected, others can benefit without paying for it. Individuals who gain access to the information without paying for it are **free riders.** That is, they obtain the same benefits but do not incur the costs. The *free-rider problem* hurts the information-gathering firm and lessens its effectiveness. Suppose that you subscribe to Infoperfect, a service that gives you the best possible information on the stocks and bonds of many companies. You are willing to pay a fee to subscribe to Infoperfect because it enables you to profit by buying undervalued stocks and bonds (using information that is better than other investors have). While you are reminding yourself of your cleverness and foresight, Freeda Frieryde and her colleagues decide to buy and sell particular stocks and bonds whenever you do. Because Freeda broadcasts your every move, others are sharing in your profits. As a result, you are willing to pay less to Infoperfect, as are other investors. Deprived of the additional revenue, Infoperfect is less willing to collect as much information to sell to savers.

When direct disclosure of information fails to provide enough information to reduce the likelihood of adverse selection, lenders can redesign financial contracts to reduce information costs by focusing on borrowers' collateral and net worth.

Roles of collateral and net worth. When borrowers invest little of their own money in their business, their loss is small if they default on their bonds. To make it

†The SEC also mandates firms' ongoing disclosure of material information to the investor community. In August 2000, the SEC went further by approving Regulation Fair Disclosure (FD), which required U.S. companies to release material information to the general public at the same time it is issued to Wall Street professionals. Many economists argue that the regulatory change makes information dissemination to the institutional investors and analysts more difficult, while proponents see the new rule as empowering individual investors.

more costly for borrowers to take advantage of their asymmetric information, lenders often require borrowers to pledge some of their own assets as **collateral,** which the lender claims if the borrower defaults. Suppose that Eleanor Riche wants to borrow $10,000 to start a home improvement business called Newvo Riche. If she owns a house worth $250,000, a lender might not hesitate to lend her the money. In the event that Eleanor defaults, a lender could claim the house or other assets that she might have pledged as collateral. Collateral reduces the likelihood of adverse selection—lemon borrowers are unlikely to pledge their own funds—and is widely used in debt contracts for individuals and businesses.

Net worth, the difference between assets and liabilities, satisfies the same assurance that collateral does. If lenders can make a claim against net worth if the borrower defaults on its loans, the firm will be more cautious about making risky investments. When a firm's net worth is high, the chance that it will default is low: Bondholders must be paid off—from the firm's net worth, if necessary—before funds can be distributed to shareholders. As a result, costs of adverse selection are less likely in lending to borrowers with high net worth.

Concluding remarks. Adverse selection increases the information costs of channeling funds from savers to borrowers in financial markets. Increased information costs in turn increase the demand for financing arrangements in which information about borrowers can be collected at a lower cost. These arrangements include direct information disclosure and collateral and net worth.

CHECKPOINT

As you read about the possibilities offered by the World Wide Web, you decide you want to invest some of your savings in an Internet service provider. You note that many small firms appear to be making a lot of money, but rating agencies haven't followed them closely. What information costs do you face if you go ahead with your investment plans? Because it is likely to be difficult to distinguish good and lemon Internet service providers, adverse selection may occur. Some of the firms rushing to sell shares may be lemons. You will incur costs of acquiring information about the firms as a result. ◆

Moral Hazard

Even though a lender might gather information about the borrower—when deciding to make an investment or a loan or structure a bond agreement that minimizes the effects of adverse selection—the lender's information problems haven't ended. There is always the chance that, after the borrower receives the funds, the funds will not be used as intended. This situation, known as moral hazard, is more likely to occur when the borrower has an incentive to conceal information or act in a way that does not reflect the lender's interests. Moral hazard arises because of asymmetric information: The borrower knows more than the lender does about how the borrowed funds will actually be used, and the resulting problems increase the lender's costs.

Moral Hazard in Equity Financing

Monitoring problems increases the information costs of raising funds through stock issues. For example, say that you buy stock in Bigdream, Inc. How do you know whether the firm is investing the funds in its research and development laboratory or in wood paneling for

CASE STUDY

Recent Regulatory Changes to Improve Information Disclosure

The accounting scandals at Enron, WorldCom, and other large U.S. corporations in 2001 and 2002 raised concerns that *corporate governance*—the system of checks and balances that guides the decisions of corporate managers—was not working well. For market prices to provide the right signals for saving and investment, they should reflect the best available information. Questionable accounting practices and a lack of transparency can reduce market liquidity and market prices—harming investors and employees through losses of wealth and harming firms through a higher cost of capital.

The private sector's response to the scandals was almost immediate. In addition to reexamination of corporate governance practices at many corporations, the New York Stock Exchange and the NASDAQ put forth initiatives to ensure the accuracy and accessibility of information. In March 2002, President Bush announced a ten-point plan to improve incentives for honest and transparent information disclosure. Much of the president's proposal became law that summer in the *Sarbanes-Oxley Act of 2002*. The Sarbanes-Oxley Act may promote the timeliness and accuracy of financial information. New disclosure requirements mandate that directors and officers disclose their transactions in company stock more quickly to enable investors to react. Financial analysts and auditors must disclose whether any conflicts of interest might exist to limit their independence from considerations other than the desire to serve shareholders' interests. Companies must make more information available about the quality of internal control structures. The Act promotes management accountability by specifying responsibilities of corporate officers and increasing penalties for managers who do not meet their responsibilities.

Perhaps the most noticeable corporate governance reform under the Sarbanes-Oxley Act is the creation of the Public Company Accounting Oversight Board, a special national board to oversee the auditing of public companies' financial reports. The board's mission is to promote the independence of auditors to ensure accurate information disclosure. Whether the Sarbanes-Oxley Act will be successful in achieving its objectives is the subject of vigorous debate.† Proponents note that more accurate and transparent information can promote more liquid markets, higher equity prices, and a lower cost of capital. Some skeptics note that companies might have responded with similar changes on their own in the wake of the scandals and laws already on the books would be used to punish fraudulent reporting at Enron or WorldCom. Also, ambiguity in many of the law's provisions may invite litigation and decrease executives' desire to take risk. Finally, some economists argue that the law does not address the need to provide better incentives for institutional investors, who control a majority of U.S. corporate equities, to be more engaged in corporate governance. On balance, most observers acknowledge that the Sarbanes-Oxley Act brought back confidence in 2002 and 2003 in the U.S. corporate governance system, though questions remain for the future.

Outside the United States, the European Commission released plans in 2003 to tighten corporate governance rules, while Japan debated such reforms as well. The OECD recommended better governance practices for several Asian economies.

†The disagreement extends even to the two namesakes. A year after the law's passage, Senator Paul Sarbanes celebrated that companies were cleaning up their act, while Congressman Michael Oxley worried that the law might make managers too cautious and limit investment (see Deborah Solomon, "Sarbanes and Oxley Agree to Disagree," *The New York Times*, July 24, 2003). For a general discussion of pros and cons, see Chapter 4 of the 2003 *Economic Report of the President* and Bengt Holmstrom and Steven N. Kaplan, "The State of U.S. Corporate Governance: What's Right and What's Wrong?," *Journal of Applied Corporate Finance*, Spring 2003, pp. 8–20.

the new executive dining room? The investment in research and development is likely to increase Bigdream's profits and your returns; the wood paneling is not. To find out whether the firm is using funds in a way that will benefit you, you need to spend time and money monitoring its activities. When Bigdream's managers tell you that your $1000 investment earned no returns, how do you know whether the claims are true? Once you have bought the stock, the firm has an incentive to understate profits and reduce your

CONSIDER THIS . . .

Are Stock Market Signals Affected by Adverse Selection?

In an efficient capital market, the value of a company's stock provides the best signal to managers about the profitability of new investments. Stock prices increase in response to good news, suggesting that more capital should be allocated to the firm's lines of business. Similarly, a decline in stock prices reflects news about market pessimism regarding the firm's prospects.

How does asymmetric information affect these relationships? In the case of adverse selection, or the lemons problem, for the stock market, share prices of a good firm can be too low, sending inaccurate signals about its prospects. In such a situation, management knows that the firm's prospects are better than the market price signals and will not turn to the market. Instead, the firm might choose to avoid the market altogether and use internal funds to finance future growth.

A study of some 300 manufacturing firms during the 1970s and 1980s found that firms that rely heavily on internal funds tend to be young, rapidly growing firms. Moreover, these firms' capital spending is closely tied to their internal funds. In contrast, capital spending by more mature firms that are capable of raising funds in financial markets is not. Hence adverse selection affects financing and investment decisions for many U.S. firms.

Source: Steven M. Fazzari, R. Glenn Hubbard, and Bruce C. Petersen, "Financing Constraints and Corporate Investment," *Brookings Papers on Economic Activity,* 1:143–195, 1988; and the review in R. Glenn Hubbard, "Capital-Market Imperfections and Investment," *Journal of Economic Literature,* 36:196–229, 1998.

dividend payments. To police such underreporting, outside suppliers of funds must audit the firm's finances every time an earnings report is issued—and such audits are costly.

The federal government and the business community itself regulate reporting by firms to reduce the chance of fraud. In addition to regulating annual reports for the benefit of owners and potential investors, the Securities and Exchange Commission and the Public Company Accounting Oversight Board—government agencies—and the Financial Accounting Standards Board—a private agency—have set standard accounting principles for firms to use in reporting their earnings and overall financial condition. These accounting principles are designed to help investors understand the financial condition of the firms in which they have invested. In addition, federal laws have made misreporting or stealing profits belonging to shareholders a federal offense, punishable by large fines or prison terms, or both.

Another information problem results from the behavior of a firm's agents, who have different goals than the principals. The shareholders, who *own* the firm's net worth, are the **principals**, and the managers, who *control* the firm's assets, are the **agents.** Called the **principal-agent problem,** this type of moral hazard may arise when managers do not own much of the firm's equity and thus do not have the same incentive to maximize the firm's value as the owners do. Because a firm's shareholders have a residual claim on its earnings, improvements in profitability (and hence in the firm's stock price) accrue to them and not to the managers who are charged with controlling the firm's assets. In the United States, for example, the majority of private economic activity occurs in large public corporations, whose managers do not own a significant part of the firm. Indeed, the stake of top management in a firm's ownership usually is less than 5%. Because management stakes in large U.S. corporations are typically less than 5%, an increase in management stakes might benefit their shareholders, though evidence is mixed.[†]

[†]For evidence in favor of the claim, see Randall Mørck, Andrei Shleifer, and Robert Vishny, "Management Ownership and Market Valuation," *Journal of Financial Economics,* 20:293–315, 1988. For a dissenting view, see Charles P. Himmelberg, R. Glenn Hubbard, and Darius Palia, "Understanding the Determinants of Managerial Ownership and the Link Between Ownership and Performance," *Journal of Financial Economics,* 53:353–384, 1999.

An example will demonstrate the principal-agent problem in stock ownership. Suppose that your neighbor, Reed Moore, asks you to join him in his new business venture, a bookstore. He needs \$50,000 to open the bookstore, but he has only \$2500. He read in the newspaper that you won the lottery and knows that you could invest \$47,500. After you make the investment, you own 95% of the bookstore, and Reed owns the other 5%. You're pleased with the investment. If Reed provides savvy tips on the best books and chats with the customers over coffee, the bookstore could make \$50,000 each year after paying his salary. Your share would be \$47,500, a 100% return; Reed's share would be \$2500 (in addition to his salary). But maybe not. Reed might decide to buy mahogany bookcases and oriental rugs and chat with customers over champagne, leaving no profit. Although Reed would forgo the \$2500 in profits, he would still receive a salary—and enjoy working in plush surroundings. Nothing would be left over for you.

The principal-agent problem exists in most equity contracts. Many uses of corporate funds by managers are highly visible (such as spending on large-scale investment projects), but many are hidden from view (such as expenses for research, maintenance, management, and organizational efficiency). Although not fraudulent, expenses such as corporate art collections, mahogany desks, limousines, and jets do not directly benefit shareholders. Managers often run firms to satisfy their personal goals, which might include accruing prestige and power. If managers aren't motivated to maximize a firm's value, nonmanagement shareholders may get shortchanged.

The shareholders own the firm, so why can't they just fire bad managers? To determine whether management is using corporate funds efficiently requires detailed and costly audits. No individual small shareholder has an incentive to pay these monitoring costs. Even if some individual shareholder offered to do so, others might take a free ride on his or her efforts, preferring to wait and see what the individual learns. As a result, most small investors lack the ability and motivation to evaluate managers.

Moral Hazard in Debt Financing

One way to decrease the information costs arising from moral hazard is to use debt rather than equity financing. For example, rather than investing \$47,500 in equity in Reed Moore's bookstore and receiving 95% of the bookstore's profits, you could lend Reed \$47,500 and require him to pay you a fixed interest rate of 10%. In this case, you would get \$4750 each year. Because the debt promises a fixed payment, you (or your accountant) don't need to audit Reed's operation of the bookstore unless he fails to meet the interest and principal payments and defaults on the loan. As long as Reed keeps making debt payments to you, it doesn't matter to you whether the bookstore reports earnings of \$10,000 or \$100,000 each year. The lower costs of monitoring make debt more attractive than equity in many cases.[†]

Even though debt financing can reduce moral hazard problems relative to equity financing in many cases, it does not eliminate moral hazard. Because a debt contract allows the borrower to keep any profits that exceed the fixed amount of the debt payment, borrowers have an incentive to assume greater risk to earn these profits than is in the interest of the lender. To demonstrate, suppose that you think you are lending money to Reed to finance the purchase of bookcases and a computer system.

[†]Many analysts believe that the dramatic increase in corporate borrowing and the decrease in the use of equity finance by corporations in the 1980s reflected an attempt to reduce the costs of principal-agent problems for shareholder value.

CONSIDER THIS . . .

Can Falling Prices Raise Information Costs?

High levels of borrower net worth reduce information costs associated with adverse selection and moral hazard. However, sudden reductions in borrower net worth can increase information costs of lending, sometimes to levels that sharply reduce borrowers' ability to raise funds for new plant and equipment and job creation. The classic example of this link among net worth, financing, and the economy is *debt deflation*. In debt deflation, falling prices raise the real value of firms' outstanding debt, reducing their net worth. As a result, savers know that the likelihood of adverse selection and moral hazard increases, and they reduce their willingness to lend to all but the safest borrowers (for example, the government). Faced with severe credit declines, firms significantly cut their spending, reducing economic activity.

The best-known example of debt deflation came during the Great Depression of the early 1930s. Declining prices increased the real debt burdens of borrowers by nearly 40% between 1929 and 1933. The combined effect of declining output and deflation sharply reduced borrowers' net worth, constraining borrowers' ability to obtain credit and leading to a collapse in lending, investment, and employment. More recent episodes of debt deflation in particular sectors include the collapse in Midwest farmland values in the early 1980s, the fall in oil prices in the mid-1980s, and the sharp decline in commercial real estate prices in Boston and New York in the late 1980s and early 1990s. In each case, the collapse in borrower net worth initiated by debt deflation raised the cost of funds to borrowers because of the increased severity of adverse selection and moral hazard.

However, once the money is in Reed's hands, he decides to invest the money in a machine that sends subliminal messages to shoppers, telling them to buy expensive books. If the machine works, the bookstore—and Reed—will make a fortune. In the more likely case that it doesn't work, he won't be able to repay you. Even with a debt contract, the risk of moral hazard is present. Financial markets use restrictive covenants in debt contracts to combat moral hazard in debt financing.

The basic problem caused by moral hazard that you encountered in making a loan to Reed was that he might use the proceeds for risky purposes. Even if he does not have $25,000 of net worth to commit to the venture, you may be able to reduce the likelihood of moral hazard by placing in the debt contract restrictions, known as **restrictive covenants,** on Reed's management activities. The most typical restrictive covenant in business lending is a limit on the borrower's risk taking. For example, the lender can restrict the borrower to buying only particular goods or prohibit the borrower from buying other businesses.

A second type of restrictive covenant requires that the borrower maintain a certain minimum level of net worth. For example, if you apply for a mortgage loan to buy a house, the bank may ask you to take out sufficient life insurance to pay off the loan in the event that you die before the mortgage is repaid. Businesses may be required to maintain a certain level of net worth, particularly in liquid assets, to reduce incentives to take on too much risk.

Financial markets often address moral hazard in debt contracts by insisting that entrepreneurs or managers of firms place their own funds at risk. In that case, taking on risky projects increases the chance that insiders like Reed Moore will lose their own money if they make bad decisions, thereby reducing the incentive to use outside investors' funds in risky ways. Suppose that Reed invested $25,000, rather than $2500 of his own net worth (his assets less his liabilities) in the bookstore. He is likely to be much more cautious in making management decisions. Thus, in general, the greater the net worth (equity capital) contributed by a firm's managers, the less likely is a problem caused by moral hazard to occur, and thus the greater is the firm's ability to borrow.

At quite low levels of invested net worth, problems arising from moral hazard may prevent borrowing altogether.

A third type of restrictive covenant, common in consumer lending, requires the borrower to maintain the value of any collateral offered to the lender. For example, if you take out a loan to buy a new car, you will have to carry a minimum amount of insurance against theft and collision, and you can't sell the car to a friend if you haven't paid off the loan. If you take out a mortgage loan to buy a house, you will have to carry insurance on the house, and you can't sell your house without first repaying your mortgage loan.

However, restrictive covenants complicate debt contracts and reduce their marketability in secondary markets for savers. The cost of monitoring whether firms actually are complying with restrictive covenants further hampers marketability and liquidity. Finally, restrictive covenants cannot protect a lender against every possible risky activity in which the borrower might engage.

CHECKPOINT

Firms in cyclical industries—those whose profits rise and fall with economy-wide booms and busts—tend to borrow less than firms in noncyclical industries do. If monitoring costs are lower for debt financing than for equity financing, why don't all firms rely on debt? The strategy of using debt financing to reduce moral hazard problems is based on the assumption that fluctuations in the borrowing firm's profits reflect the efforts of its managers. If most of the profit swings reflect movements in economy-wide profitability, too much debt could cause a firm to go bankrupt when its profits slump and it cannot repay debtholders. As a result, the use of debt is concentrated in firms whose profitability depends less on economic movements. ♦

Information Costs and Financial Intermediaries

The presence of transactions costs and information costs increases the cost of funds that borrowers must pay and lowers the expected returns to lenders, reducing the efficiency of financial markets. We have examined the costs of adverse selection and moral hazard in equity and debt financing. In addition to responses by financial market participants to reduce those costs, financial intermediaries play key roles in the United States and most other industrial economies.

Recall that businesses raise most of their funds from current and accumulated profits, not from financial markets. Since World War II, nonfinancial corporations in the United States have raised more than two-thirds of the funds they needed internally. A similar pattern holds for other key industrialized countries. In Germany, Japan, and the United States, firms do not raise a substantial fraction of their financing from financial markets for stocks and bonds. Most external funds needed are raised through financial intermediaries such as banks, as shown in Table 11.1.

Financial Intermediaries and Adverse Selection

Financial intermediaries, particularly banks, specialize in gathering information about the default risk of many borrowers. Banks raise funds from depositors and, using their superior information, lend them to borrowers that represent good risks. Because banks are better able than individual savers to distinguish qualified borrowers from lemons, banks earn a profit by charging a higher rate on their loans than the interest rate they pay to depositors.

TABLE 11.1 **Sources of Finance for Business Firms**

Business firms rely more heavily on financial markets to raise external funds.

	Financial Markets	Financial Intermediaries
United States	45%	55%
Germany	12%	88%
Japan	14%	86%

Source: Data cover the period 1970–1996. U.S. data are from Board of Governors of the Federal Reserve System, *Flow of Funds Accounts*, various issues. Data for Germany and Japan are taken from Reinhard H. Schmidt, "Differences Between Financial Systems in European Countries: Consequences for EMU," in Deutsche Bundesbank, *The Monetary Transmission Process: Recent Developments and Lessons for Europe*, Hampshire: Palgrave Publishers, 2001, p. 222.

Banks generally avoid the free-rider problem by holding the loans they make. Thus investors can't observe banks' activities and profit by mimicking them. By mainly holding loans that are not traded in financial markets, banks earn a profit on information collection.

Banks' information advantage in reducing costs of adverse selection accounts in large part for their role in providing external financing. Their specialization in evaluating borrowers to reduce the likelihood of adverse selection also explains why largely unknown small and medium-sized businesses depend on banks when they need a loan, whereas large, mature corporations have access to stock and bond markets.

CHECKPOINT

Why might the founder of a young firm in the growing biotechnology industry not raise funds by selling new shares in the firm, even to finance a very profitable investment opportunity? Adverse selection causes firms in emerging, growing industries to have the highest information costs. Faced with the high information costs of distinguishing between good firms and lemons, savers investing in financial markets require a higher return on investments in all firms in these industries to compensate them for the risk of investing in lemons. As a result, shares of good firms will be undervalued, and entrepreneurial firms will prefer to grow by using internal funds or loans from banks, which specialize in reducing problems of adverse selection. ◆

Financial Intermediaries and Moral Hazard

Large investors often have more success than small investors in reducing the free-rider problem that arises in gathering information on the behavior of corporate managers. If a large investor, such as a financial intermediary, holds a large block of shares, the investor has an incentive to monitor closely how agents use their funds.

Some **venture capital firms,** which raise equity capital from investors and invest in emerging or growing entrepreneurial business ventures, use this method successfully. Venture capital firms insist on holding large equity stakes and sitting on the firm's board of directors to observe management's actions closely. In addition, when a venture capital firm acquires equity in a new firm, it holds the shares; that is, the shares are not marketable to other investors. As a result, the venture capital firm avoids the free-rider problem: Other investors are unable to take advantage of its monitoring efforts. The venture capital firm is then able to earn a profit from its monitoring activities, reducing the information costs of moral hazard and improving the allocation of funds from savers to borrowers.

Web Site Suggestions: http://www.ventureeconomics.com Offers information on trends in venture capital.

Not all efforts by intermediaries to reduce the costs of principal-agent problems are directed at young firms. **Corporate restructuring firms** raise equity capital to acquire large blocks of the equity in mature firms to reduce free-rider problems (see the case study at www.awlonline.com/hubbard). The leaders of many such firms (including Ivan Boesky, Carl Icahn, T. Boone Pickens, and Henry Kravis) became rich and famous (or notorious) in the 1980s.

Whenever monitoring is costly—as it is, for example, in debt financing when lenders must ensure that borrowers adhere to restrictive convenants—free-rider problems may occur. As an individual saver, you would find monitoring the activities of Reed Moore or General Motors (if you bought a GM bond) to be very expensive. Therefore you and others like you are likely to try to seek a free ride on the monitoring efforts of others. Borrowers who are aware of the difficulties that you and others like you have in monitoring their efforts, and who believe that lenders will not incur monitoring costs, may be tempted to violate restrictive covenants.

Financial intermediaries, particularly banks, reduce this problem and earn a profit by acting as *delegated monitors* for many individual savers, who deposit their funds with the intermediary. (We examine this role for banks in Chapter 13.) When an intermediary such as a bank holds the loans it makes, other investors are unable to gain a free ride on the intermediary's monitoring efforts. As delegated monitors, financial intermediaries reduce the information costs of moral hazard and improve the channeling of funds from savers to borrowers. This result is a major reason that most lending takes place through financial intermediaries rather than through the direct issuance of marketable securities.

Figure 11.1 summarizes the remedies used to fight problems of moral hazard and adverse selection.

OTHER TIMES, OTHER PLACES ...

Investor Protection and Economic Growth

Recent research by economists using cross-country data has documented a link between financial development and economic growth. Robert King of the University of Virginia and Ross Levine of the World Bank, for example, presented the intriguing possibility that the institutional factors responsible for financial development were also important for the efficient accumulation and allocation of capital.[†] Their work raises an important question: Might cross-country differences in investor protection against adverse selection and moral hazard partly explain differences in economic performance?

In a series of papers, Rafael La Porta, Florencio Lopez-di-Silanes, and Andrei Shleifer of Harvard University and Robert Vishny of the University of Chicago document a wide variation across countries in protection of minority shareholders and creditors and in the efficiency of the judicial system in adjudicating disputes.[††] Those researchers show that in countries with weaker investor protection, such as France and Spain, firm insiders hold a much larger share of the firm's equity than do firm insiders in countries with stronger investor protection, such as the United Kingdom and the United States.

Do these cross-country differences matter for economic performance? Yes. Poor investor protection against adverse selection and moral hazard is associated with less well-developed financial markets, and entrepreneurs tend to hold poorly diversified portfolios in such economies, as they must hold more of their firm's shares. One recent study also concludes that the firms' cost of capital for investment and growth can be substantially higher in countries with weaker investor protection than in countries with stronger protection.[§] This link suggests important influences of policies to reduce information costs on economic growth.

[†] Robert G. King and Ross Levine, "Finance and Growth: Schumpeter Might Be Right," *Quarterly Journal of Economics*, 108:717–737, 1993.

[††] Rafael La Porta, Florencio Lopez-di-Silanes, Andrei Shleifer, and Robert W. Vishny, "Law and Finance," *Journal of Political Economy*, 106:1133–1155, 1998.

[§] Charles P. Himmelberg, R. Glenn Hubbard, and Inessa Love, "Investor Protection, Ownership, and Investment: Some Cross-Country Evidence," Working Paper, Columbia University, 2000.

FIGURE 11.1 Remedies for Problems of Adverse Selection and Moral Hazard

When borrowers and savers have private information about their prospects or use of funds, information costs to savers arise. With adverse selection, savers can't tell good risks from bad risks; with moral hazard, savers can't monitor how funds are used. These problems impede the flow of funds to borrowers and returns to savers.

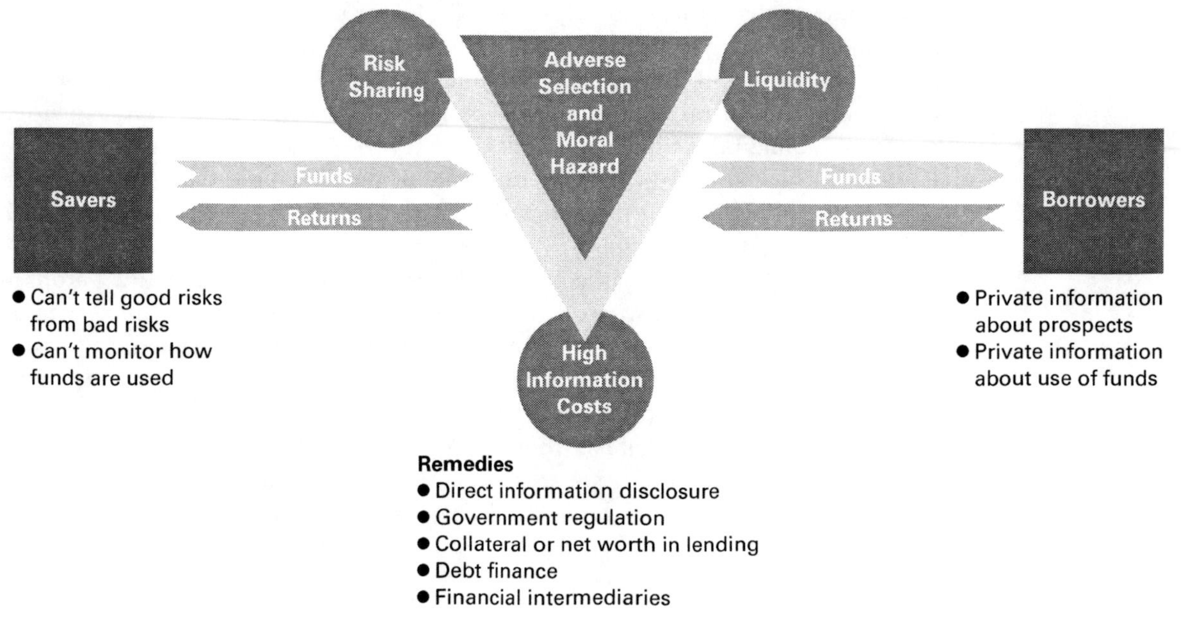

KEY TERMS AND CONCEPTS

- Asymmetric information
  - Adverse selection
  - Moral hazard
- Collateral
- Corporate restructuring firms
- Credit rationing
- Economies of scale
- Free riders
- Information costs
- Net worth
- Principal-agent problem
  - Agents
  - Principals
- Restrictive covenants
- Transactions costs
- Venture capital firms

SUMMARY

1. Financial markets do not efficiently match savers and borrowers when the transactions and information costs of lending are high.

2. Transactions costs make investing in debt and equity instruments in financial markets costly for small savers. Financial intermediaries take advantage of economies of scale by pooling savers' funds to lower transactions costs. As a result, individual savers are able to earn a higher return on their savings, and borrowers realize a lower cost of funds.

3. Information costs result from two problems of asymmetric information: adverse selection—difficulty in knowing the true prospects of the borrower before the transaction—and moral hazard—the need to monitor the borrower's use of funds after the transaction. Information costs arising from adverse selection and moral hazard reduce returns for savers and increase the cost of funds for borrowers.

4. Strategies to reduce costs of adverse selection in financial markets include direct disclosure of information and the use of collateral and net worth provisions in financial contracts.

5. The principal-agent problem, in which managers (agents) do not have the same incentive to maximize

profits that shareholders (principals) have, illustrates moral hazard in equity financing. Solutions to the principal-agent problem include regulation of information disclosure and use of debt instead of equity financing.

6. Costs of moral hazard problems in debt financing are reduced by net worth requirements and use of restrictive covenants.

7. The important role played by financial intermediaries in channeling funds from savers to borrowers is explained by their relative success in lowering costs of adverse selection and moral hazard in financial markets.

REVIEW QUESTIONS

1. What advantages do financial intermediaries have over small savers in dealing with the transactions costs involved in making loans?

2. Distinguish symmetric information from asymmetric information, and state why the distinction is important for the financial system.

3. What is the difference between moral hazard and adverse selection? How does each contribute to making information asymmetric?

4. Explain why information collection in financial markets is subject to the free-rider problem. How do banks overcome the free-rider problem?

5. Explain what the "lemons problem" is. How does the lemons problem lead many firms to borrow from banks rather than from individual investors?

6. Why might the number of loans that aren't repaid to banks rise as interest rates rise? What might be a better strategy for banks than raising interest rates?

7. Suppose that a bank makes a loan to a business and that the loan contract specifies that the business is not to engage in certain lines of business. What is this type of provision called? Why would the bank make such a provision?

8. What is the name of the main problem associated with the separation of ownership from management? What do managers do that owners don't like? What types of solutions are available?

9. Is a large firm with thousands of shareholders more or less likely to suffer a principal-agent problem than a small firm with just a few shareholders? Explain.

10. Describe opportunities for specialized investors or financial institutions in mitigating financing problems associated with adverse selection and moral hazard.

ANALYTICAL PROBLEMS

11. At a used car lot, a nearly new car with only 2000 miles on the odometer is selling for half the car's original price. The salesperson tells you that the car was "driven by a little old lady from Pasadena" who had it for two months and then decided that she "didn't like the color." The salesperson assures you that the car is in great shape and has had no major problems. What type of asymmetric information problem is present here? How can you get around this problem?

12. Why don't insurance companies sell income insurance? That is, if a person loses his or her job or doesn't get as big a raise as anticipated, that person would be compensated under his or her insurance coverage.

13. In which of the following situations is moral hazard likely to be less of a problem? Explain.
    (a) A manager is paid a flat salary of $150,000.
    (b) A manager is paid a salary of $75,000 plus 10% of the firm's profits.

14. A banker is thinking of making a loan to a small business. The owner of the business also owns a house and has a $40,000 investment in stocks and bonds. What kind of loan contract should the banker write to minimize costs of moral hazard?

15. Describe some of the information problems in financial markets that lead firms to rely more heavily on internal funds than external funds for investment. Do these problems necessarily imply that, as a result, too little good investment is being made? Why or why not?

MOVING FROM THEORY TO PRACTICE . . .

THE BANKER MAY 2003

Glasnost in the Boardroom

Lack of good corporate governance is a problem worldwide for investors, but the risks in Russia are very different from those experienced in the U.S. and Europe post-Enron. . . .

[T]he emphasis in Russia is very much on governance standards and this month *The Banker* publishes a chart (overleaf), drawn from Troika Dialog research, listing leading Russian corporates according to governance standards.

Loose accounting standards are not necessarily a problem if companies are audited professionally and with rigor. However this is often not the case in Russia. While the Ministry of Finance is now sole supervisor of the audit industry, it is estimated that only 40% of audit firms follow a clear set of audit procedures and nothing has been done as yet to prevent "single client" firms who are so dependent on one large client that their independence must be questioned. Nearly 10% of the RAS audit market is run by "single client" firms—the firm with the largest market share within this has Surgutneftegaz (ranked 27 in our table) to thank for this.

Using auditors for consultancy services and the use of off-balance sheet liabilities is common practice in Russia as in the U.S. While stock options are not, they can be simulated by "phantom shares" to circumnavigate legislation. Loans to directors are unheard of, partly because a director's remuneration is large and confidential. Recently LUKoil (ranked nine), in a run up to an aborted American Depositary Receipt (ADR) placement, revealed its CEO's annual salary to be $1.5m, while the newly elected non-executive directors would be paid nothing.

a In fact the strongest driver for reform of Russian governance has not been the state regulatory system, but the market itself. In a desire to raise capital abroad, firms are switching to International Accounting Standards (IAS). A total of 39 of the top 57 companies now use IAS, 33 of which have ADRs outstanding. Ten new firms switched to these or GAAP standards in the 2001 reporting year (Bashinformsvyaz ranked 23, Lenenergo ranked two, Magnitogorsk Metal ranked 35, to mention a few). . . .

Securing foreign ownership may encourage transparency and greater financial discipline, but is still open to abuse. Many ADR holders do not realize they have voting rights and so do not ask their custodian to exercise them. Russian directors often have an agreement with the custodians that they may use unexercised votes themselves—known as "discretionary voting." They can therefore push through proposals that may not be in the best interests of shareholders. b

Despite all this it seems that corporate governance has improved in Russia and is likely to improve in the future. There has been more shareholder representation on boards of directors such as Central Telecom (ranked 10) and Lenenergo (ranked 2). Charters have been revised to give independent non-executives approval over major decisions, as in the case of Norilsk Nickel (ranked 44), or limit the CEO's powers to approve deals in the company's assets, as in the case of Aeroflot (ranked 25). c

ANALYZING THE NEWS ...

Capital markets perform well in matching borrowers and savers when information costs are low. When investors have poor information from business owners and managers about the prospects and risks of the firm, costs of adverse selection depress equity values and raise the cost of finance. In cases in which managers lack strong incentives to act in shareholders' interest, costs of moral hazard also make raising funds expensive. Both private and governmental actions can reduce information costs and strengthen capital markets, offering risk-sharing, liquidity, and information services to savers and borrowers. In the year after the collapse of the Soviet Union, Russia's capital markets struggled to become more efficient. While the United States was not immune to corporate governance concerns—as the corporate accounting scandals in 2001 and 2002 made clear—Russia in 2003 faced tough hurdles in decreasing information costs in its capital markets.

a The need to raise capital—particularly from foreign investors—means that Russian firms must reduce information costs to levels acceptable in international capital markets. The lack of rigorous audits makes investors wary of the quality of information and adds costs of adverse selection to costs of external financing.

b The use of International Accounting Standards reduces monitoring costs and costs of raising funds. Even in this case, to provide incentives for managers to act in shareholders' interests, large shareholders need to be actively involved in corporate governance and executive pay should reflect performance. The legal system can decrease the scope for moral hazard by limiting opportunities for insiders to transfer wealth from outside shareholders to themselves.

c These changes in governance, welcome in any economy suffering from costs of corruption and weak capital markets, can spell good news for Russia's economy. Lower information costs enable Russian companies to raise funds more cheaply and grow more rapidly. Entrepreneurs can diversify their wealth more easily as markets in which they can sell their equity flourish. Savers in Russia—and abroad—can benefit from higher returns as Russia grows.

For further thought...

Suppose that to raise additional revenue, the Russian government raised taxes significantly on dividends paid by corporations to their shareholders. How might such a policy change affect information costs and corporate governance?

Source: Excerpted from Alex Foreman-Peck, *The Banker*, May 2003.

16. Do you think that lemons problems are likely to be important in emerging stock and bond markets in Eastern Europe? Why or why not?
17. Suppose that you own some corporate bonds issued by the Buyusout Company. Would you be happy if the company underwent a leveraged buyout? Why or why not? Would you be happy if the company were taken over by a much larger firm, reducing its default risk? Why or why not?
18. In the early twentieth century J. P. Morgan placed representatives from his firm on the boards of directors of most of the companies in which his firm invested. He was often denounced for what some commentators saw as the excessive control he exercised in the business and financial world. Is it possible that, given the existence of asymmetric information problems, Morgan's policy of placing his men on many boards of directors may have improved the workings of the financial system?
19. On average, Japanese nonfinancial corporations have greater leverage than U.S. corporations do. Does that imply that Japanese firms are more financially fragile than U.S. firms? Why or why not?

DATA QUESTIONS

20. Suppose you believe that adverse selection problems are important in the stock market. If a firm announces that it will issue new shares, what pattern would you look for in data on the price of the firm's outstanding shares following the announcement? Explain.
21. Thomson Financial's Venture Economics division provides information about the venture capital industry. Review Venture Economics Web site at www.ventureeconomics.com. What does this site provide that helps savers and investors deal with potential moral hazard and adverse selection problems in this industry? Look at the site's "Statistics" link and look up the most recent venture capital activity reported for your state. What trends do you see? How would the degree of taxes, regulation, and property right protection affect your state's ability to attract venture capital?

CHAPTER

12 What Financial Institutions Do

What Financial Institutions Do

The late 1990s and early 2000s were challenging times for financial institutions. Competition, bad management, and poor decisions caused the failure of many savings institutions and banks in the early 1990s. Many surviving banks merged to increase their markets and to cut costs by exploiting economies of scale. The 1995 merger of banking giants Chase and Chemical formed the biggest bank in the United States—until 1998 mergers of Citicorp and Travelers, Bank America and NationsBank, and Deutsche Bank and Bankers Trust created still larger firms. New laws passed by Congress in 1994 and 1995 ushered in new competition between banks and other financial institutions. In 1994, Mellon Bank acquired Dreyfus, a leading mutual fund company; the 1998 Citicorp–Travelers merger created a financial supermarket. All of these changes blurred the distinctions among the types of financial institutions, creating new opportunities for financial institutions and offering new or improved services to savers and borrowers. Indeed, the three largest financial institutions in the world (by assets) in 2003—Citigroup, Mizuho, and UBS—are active in most financial services.

In Part 4 of the text—and in this chapter—we examine the role of financial institutions in the financial system. To understand the changes that have taken place and that will continue to occur, we describe the traditional roles of the following organizations in the financial system:

1. *Securities market institutions:* investment banks, brokerage firms, and organized exchanges
2. *Investment institutions:* mutual funds and finance companies
3. *Contractual saving institutions:* insurance companies and pension funds
4. *Depository institutions:* commercial banks, savings institutions, and credit unions
5. *Government financial institutions*

Although securities market institutions are not financial intermediaries, we include them in our discussion of financial institutions because they help to match savers and borrowers in the financial system. Our focus in this chapter is on the risk-sharing, liquidity, and information functions of financial institutions and their role in matching savers and borrowers. We also describe the challenges each institution has faced and how institutions have adapted.

Financial intermediaries manage a sizable share of the assets in the financial system. Table 12.1 lists the share of each and the changes in assets each has held over approximately the past 40 years. These changes reflect competition, regulation, and financial innovation, as we will see. We can understand the changes and their impact only if we first know what the traditional roles for each organization are. This chapter will present that information and analyze major regulatory and competitive changes in the environment that have caused each institution to adapt—either by offering new products to savers and borrowers or by changing the way each does business.

Web Site Suggestions: http://www.federalreserve.gov/releases Supplies the latest data on financial institutional holdings (Z.1).

TABLE 12.1 **Financial Intermediaries in the United States†**

Class of institution	Assets ($ billions) 2003	% of total assets of intermediaries 1960	1970	1980	1990	2003
Mutual funds						
Money market mutual funds	2156	0.0	0.0	1.8	4.4	7.2
Other mutual funds	3587	2.9	3.5	1.6	5.7	11.9
Finance companies	2478	4.7	4.7	4.9	5.4	8.2
Insurance companies						
Life insurance companies	3358	19.4	14.8	11.0	12.1	11.1
Property and casualty companies	925	4.4	3.7	4.3	4.7	3.1
Pension funds						
Private pension funds	3603	6.3	8.1	12.0	14.4	12.0
State and local government retirement funds	1940	3.3	4.4	4.7	6.5	6.4
Depository institutions						
Commercial banks	7502	38.2	37.2	35.7	29.3	24.9
Savings institutions	1408	18.8	18.8	18.8	12.1	4.7
Credit unions	585	1.1	1.4	1.5	1.9	2.0
Government financial institutions	2598	1.0	3.4	4.2	3.7	8.6
	Total: $30.1 trillion					

† Data are as of March 31, 2003.

Source: Board of Governors of the Federal Reserve System, *Flow of Funds Accounts: Flows and Outstandings*, June 5, 2003.

Securities Market Institutions

Securities market institutions—in particular, investment banks, brokers and dealers, and organized exchanges—contribute to the efficiency of financial markets. These institutions reduce the costs of matching savers and borrowers and provide risk-sharing, liquidity, and information services that enable financial markets to function smoothly—and well-functioning markets, you'll recall, generate price information for market participants and help investors make intelligent portfolio allocation decisions. Securities market institutions are not financial intermediaries, because they do not acquire funds from savers to invest in borrowers; they simply make it easier for investors to locate suitable borrowers and to reduce borrowers' costs in raising funds.

We discuss securities market institutions in two steps. First, we explain how investment banks gather information and help borrowers to raise funds in primary markets for debt and equity. Then we discuss the contributions of brokers, dealers, and organized exchanges in providing liquidity in secondary markets. Liquid secondary markets provide information to savers and borrowers as well as risk-sharing services for savers.

Information: Investment Banking

Underwriting. **Investment banks** assist businesses in raising new capital in primary markets, and advise them on the best way to do so: either by recommending a stock issue or by structuring debt contracts to attract investors. One way in which investment bankers earn income is by **underwriting** a firm's new stock or bond issue.

Underwriters guarantee a price to the issuing firm, sell the issue at a higher price, and keep the profit, known as the *spread.* In exchange for this spread, the underwriting investment bank assumes the risk of not being able to resell the securities to investors.

In addition to underwriting, the investment bank might sell the issue under other conditions. For example, the investment bank might not guarantee prices of very risky new issues. The risk of price fluctuations may cause investment banks to be wary of making a fixed commitment to the issuing firm. Rather than guaranteeing the price, the investment bank will sell the issue on an *all-or-none* basis. In this case, the company issuing the securities receives nothing unless the investment bank sells the complete issue at the offering price. Another alternative, called *best efforts*, allows the investment bank to make no guarantee, requiring it to sell to investors only as much of the issue as it can.

Relatively small issues may be underwritten by a single investment banker, whereas large issues are sold by groups of underwriting investment banks called **syndicates.** In a syndicated sale, the lead investment bank acts as manager and keeps part of the spread. The remainder of the spread is split among the syndicate members buying the issue and to brokerage firms selling the issue to the public. Investment bankers market new issues to institutional investors (such as pension funds or insurance companies) or to individual savers through advertisements in *The Wall Street Journal.* Leading underwriting firms include major securities firms, such as Merrill Lynch, Goldman Sachs, and CS First Boston.

Underwriting lowers information costs between lenders and borrowers because investment banks put their reputations behind the firms they underwrite. Underwriters give investors confidence about a new issue. In addition, regulations require issuers of securities to disclose information about the stocks or bonds to inform investors of risks and to prevent fraud. Public issues in the United States must be registered with the Securities and Exchange Commission (SEC), a federal government regulatory body authorized by the Securities and Exchange Acts of 1933 and 1934 in response to disreputable underwriting practices in the 1920s. Firms issuing securities are required to file a prospectus with the SEC disclosing information on long-term issues of publicly traded securities.

During the 1980s, risks associated with underwriting bond issues rose because of the higher volatility of interest rates. At the same time, underwriting fees dropped. This occurred in large part because of SEC Rule 415, which allows a firm to register a new issue with the SEC and then wait as long as two years before selling it. During the waiting period, issuers can sell securities when underwriting fees are expected to be low, thus fostering competition. Another way in which Rule 415 increased competition among underwriters was by allowing issuers to choose an underwriter after registration, permitting the firm greater flexibility in bargaining with investment bankers. In the mid-1980s and later, bargaining led to reductions in fee income for underwriters, encouraging them to supplement their income by taking positions in bonds on their own account.

Investment banks during the 1980s also engineered corporate restructurings, mergers, and acquisitions in which substantial amounts of the firms' equity were bought with risky bonds. Financiers used investment banks to raise large amounts of risky debt through junk bonds, bonds with ratings of less than Baa (Moody's Investor Service) or BBB (Standard & Poor's). Also in the 1980s, investment banks engaged in *merchant banking*—that is, they placed their own funds at risk by investing in firms that were undergoing restructuring.

Recent trends. In the 1990s, investment banks became masters of *deleveraging*, helping firms to raise equity in public markets to reduce their debt burdens. Also, trading profits and fees from managing clients' funds and from advising are more important sources of investment banks' earnings. As investment banks' core business of underwriting became less profitable, their success in offering services to savers and borrowers allowed them to remain a force in matching savers with firms seeking external financing. The sharp drop in U.S. equity prices in 2000, 2001, and 2002 significantly reduced investment banking activity. In addition, some investment banking firms were sanctioned for their roles in corporate accounting scandals in 2001 and 2002. The industry sought ways to separate more effectively research activities of analysts from underwriting to avoid conflicts of interest. By 2003, growth areas for investment banking lie in part in Europe, where possibilities for initial public offerings and restructurings are on the rise.

CHECKPOINT

Why do many issuers of bonds and stocks use underwriters? Successful underwriters are skilled in collecting financial market information and communicating it to their clients. Investment bankers collect information on issuing firms and put their reputations on the line in issues they underwrite. An investment bank's endorsement is particularly valuable for issuers that are less well known to small investors than to the major investment banking firms. ♦

Liquidity and Risk Sharing: Secondary Markets

The ability to buy and sell issues at low cost after their original issue increases the liquidity of stocks, bonds, and other financial instruments. For example, a saver might not want to buy stock in SolidState Corporation if she could not be certain of being able to sell the stock when she needed money. She might turn to other investments, such as bank deposits, that she would be able to convert to cash more easily. The existence of an arena in which securities can be converted easily to cash improves their liquidity. Secondary markets are this arena.

Brokers and dealers. Brokers and dealers facilitate the exchange of securities in financial markets by locating buyers when sellers want to convert securities to cash. The decrease in time and cost required to match buyers and sellers in secondary markets improves liquidity in those markets. **Brokers** earn commissions by matching ultimate buyers and sellers in a particular market. **Dealers** trade between ultimate buyers and sellers; they hold inventories of securities and sell them for a price higher than they paid for them, earning the spread between the bid and asked price. The largest firms in securities markets, such as Merrill Lynch, act as both brokers and dealers (and often as investment bankers as well). The fortunes of such "broker-dealers" rise and fall with stock and bond prices and trading opportunities. Their profits were very high in the mid-1980s, fell to zero by 1990, rebounded to high levels in most of the 1990s, and fell again in the 2000–2002 period, recovering somewhat in 2003.

To enhance the liquidity of services offered by brokers and dealers, the SEC strictly regulates brokers and dealers to ensure disclosure of information, prevent fraud, and restrict trading based on **insider information.** Insider information is available to individuals within an organization or to parties in a transaction (say,

USING THE NEWS ...

A Tombstone for Something New?

To learn about major financial offerings arranged by investment banks, you need only consult *The Wall Street Journal*. Advertisements for offerings—known as *tombstones*—state the size and price of the issue and the investment banks involved. In the tombstone shown here, Needham & Company and A.G. Edwards, respected investment banking firms, are managing the sale of 2,070,000 shares of stock in Ceradyne.

Some of the offering may be sold to foreign investors abroad through overseas affiliates of the investment banking firms. This underscores the importance of international borrowing and lending in today's financial system.

Ceradyne ad that appeared in *The Wall Street Journal*, August 14, 2003. Reprinted with permission.

This announcement is neither an offer to sell nor a solicitation of an offer to buy these securities.
The offer is made only by the Prospectus.

July 1, 2003

2,070,000 Shares

Common Stock

Price $17.50 Per Share

Copies of the Prospectus may be obtained in any State in which this announcement is circulated from only such of the undersigned as may legally offer these securities in such State.

Needham & Company, Inc. **A.G. Edwards & Sons, Inc.**

D.A. Davidson & Co. **Fahnestock & Co. Inc.** **Friedman Billings Ramsey**

The Seidler Companies Incorporated **C.E. Unterberg, Towbin**

members of two firms engaged in a merger discussion) but unavailable to the general public. Historically—from the 1930s until 1975—the SEC also regulated brokerage commissions. As a result of increased competition since 1975, investors now pay significantly lower commissions—especially large institutional investors and individual investors using discount brokers; thus liquidity is improved in secondary markets. Discount brokers such as Charles Schwab offer lower commissions but fewer services (for example, no investment information libraries and minimal advice) than those offered by full-service firms such as Merrill Lynch. Trading volume expanded dramatically after commissions were lowered in 1975. Similarly, deregulation of commissions in England in 1986 (known as the "big bang"), as well as in Canada (1983), Australia (1984), France (1988), the Netherlands (1990), and Japan (beginning in 1998), generally expanded trading volume.

Exchanges. Securities may be traded in one of two ways: through exchanges or in over-the-counter markets. An **exchange** is a physical location at which securities are traded. Essentially, an exchange is an institution providing an auction market for securities: assets are bought from the offerer of the lowest price and sold to the bidder of the highest price. Exchanges don't set prices but provide a way for buyers and sellers of financial assets to trade anonymously, lowering information costs for savers.

The best-known U.S. exchanges are the New York Stock Exchange (NYSE) and the American Stock Exchange (AMEX) in New York. There are also various regional exchanges. The exchanges themselves, together with the SEC, regulate trading practices and enforce prohibition of insider trading. Around the world, there are 142 exchanges. Among the oldest and best known are (with their dates of formal establishment) London (1773), Paris (1802), Tokyo (1818), and Sydney (1872). Following the euro's arrival in 1999, analysts expected exchanges in Europe to consolidate. In 2000, the Paris Bourse, the Amsterdam Exchange, and the Brussels Exchange formed Euronext, an integrated European stock exchange. Among electronic startups, Virt-X—a joint venture of a London-based electronic market and the Swiss Stock Exchange—offers trading in more U.K. and continental European equities.

The size of the issuing firm determines the exchange on which a stock is listed. The securities of the oldest and largest U.S. firms are listed on the NYSE; those of less well-known firms are listed on the AMEX; and those of the smallest and youngest business firms are generally traded in over-the-counter markets, which we discuss shortly.

In the New York Stock Exchange, buyers and sellers are matched on the floor of an exchange by a broker-dealer known as a **specialist,** who represents one or more stocks. For example, suppose that you place an order for 100 shares of General Motors stock. Your broker sends the order to a specialist in GM stock. Acting as a broker, the specialist puts together buy and sell orders at the same price. Then, acting as a dealer, the specialist uses inventory to match your buy order with someone else's sell order. The specialist system generally works well, but it can lead to a fragile market during a panic, as occurred during the stock market crash of October 19, 1987.

Web Site Suggestions: http://www.gpoaccess.gov/eop/index.html Offers in Chapter 2 a review of regulatory issues for exchanges.

Over-the-counter trading. Broker-dealers also match buyers and sellers in **over-the-counter (OTC) markets,** in which trading takes place over the telephone and by computer. OTC trading has grown dramatically owing to advances in computer technology. Traders keep track of the market by examining the activity in individual issues on their computer screens. Under the Securities Amendment Act of 1975, the SEC fostered development of a consolidated arrangement for trading securities: the National Market System. Member broker-dealers regulate themselves through the National Association of Securities Dealers (NASD). The National Market System provides computerized quotes through the National Association of Securities Dealers' Automated Quotation (NASDAQ) system, developed in 1971. In November 1998, NASD and AMEX merged, yielding a firm with both auction market and over-the-counter capabilities. Outside the United States, Frankfurt's Neuer Markt exchange was briefly successful after its launch in 1997 in bringing younger German firms to market. NASDAQ, in turn, took a small stake in EASDAQ, a Brussels-based exchange founded in 1996 as a "NASDAQ for Europe."

Trading bonds. The market for U.S. Treasury bonds and U.S. government agency securities is the most liquid market in the world, with small bid-asked spreads. However, the market for most individual bonds is relatively illiquid, though some issues for prominent companies (such as GM and IBM) have liquid markets. These firms' bonds are usually traded on organized exchanges, such as the NYSE. The vast majority of secondary market trading of corporate bonds is done in over-the-counter markets. Owing to their relative illiquidity, the bid-asked spreads for corporate bonds are higher than those for U.S. government securities. (The same is true in growing corporate bond markets in Europe and Japan.) For corporate bonds, the more highly rated bonds typically have lower bid-asked spreads than lower-rated bonds do.

Recent trends. The activities of brokers, dealers, and exchanges improve liquidity in secondary markets. Around the world, these organizations are being reshaped in response to the revolution in computing technology. Many brokers and dealers offer more opportunities for electronic communication among investors. Exchanges have also been affected by changes in technology. In 1971, the NYSE accounted for almost three-fourths of shares traded in U.S. exchanges; by 1991, it accounted for only about half of such trades.

Electronic auctions for large buyers and sellers in networks outside the NYSE improve liquidity by executing trades at lower cost. This competition from electronic trading reduced the value of seats on major exchanges in the late 1990s. Outside the United States, electronic trading has been introduced in exchanges in Toronto, Paris, London, Brussels, Madrid, Sydney, and Copenhagen. The latest source of competition for exchanges around the world has come from on-line *e-trading*, providing efficient service, low costs, and the comfort of trading from home.

Most analysts believe that electronic trading will eventually dominate traditional floor trading, diminishing the power of individual exchanges. Whereas traditional exchanges rely on a specialized class of liquidity suppliers effectively tied to the exchange, anyone with cash and a computer can supply liquidity in an electronic market. This phenomenon can be seen in the publicized actions of *day traders*, individuals trading electronically and eroding profit margins of traditional brokerage firms.

At the frontier of large-scale e-trading, *electronic communications networks* (ECNs) are redefining U.S. equity markets. ECNs are innovative stock-trading systems that rely on computer software to match buy and sell orders—typically with lower transactions costs than with traditional exchanges—generally for institutional investors. In 2003, ECNs were largely NASDAQ players. Many analysts believe, however, that ECNs will become important executors of transactions of exchange-traded stocks in the near future.

Investment Institutions

Investment institutions, which raise funds to invest in loans and securities, include mutual funds and finance companies.

Mutual Funds

Mutual funds are financial intermediaries that convert small individual claims into diversified portfolios of stocks, bonds, mortgages, and money market instruments by pooling the resources of many small savers.

Mutual funds obtain savers' money by selling shares in portfolios of financial assets and then using the funds of many savers to maintain and expand those portfolios. Mutual funds offer savers the advantage of reducing transactions costs. Rather than buying numerous stocks, bonds, or other financial instruments individually—each with its own transactions costs—a saver can buy into all the shares in the fund with one transaction. Mutual funds provide risk-sharing benefits by offering a diversified portfolio of assets and liquidity benefits by guaranteeing to quickly buy back a saver's shares. Moreover, the company managing the fund—the fund manager (say, Fidelity)—specializes in gathering information about different investments.

The mutual fund industry in the United States dates back to the organization of the Massachusetts Investors Trust (managed by Massachusetts Financial Services, Inc.) in March 1924. The fund's marketing stressed the usefulness of mutual funds for achieving a diversified portfolio for retirement savings. Later in 1924, the State Street Investment Corporation was organized; in 1925, Putnam Management Company introduced its Incorporated Investment Fund. These three investment managers are still major players in the mutual fund industry.

Web Site Suggestions: http://www.ici.org Presents information on mutual funds.

Types of funds. Mutual funds operate as either closed-end or open-end funds. In **closed-end mutual funds,** the mutual fund company issues a fixed number of nonredeemable shares, which investors may then trade in over-the-counter markets like common stock. The price of these shares fluctuates with the value of the underlying assets. Owing to differences in the quality of fund management or the liquidity of the shares, fund shares may sell at a discount or a premium relative to the market value of the underlying assets. More common are **open-end mutual funds,** which issue redeemable shares at a price tied to the underlying value of the assets.

Most mutual funds are called **no-load funds** because they earn income only from management fees (typically about 0.5% of assets), not from sales commissions. The alternative, **load funds,** charge commissions for purchases and sales.

The largest category of mutual funds, with assets of $3587 billion in 2003, consists of funds offering claims against portfolios of capital market instruments, such as stocks and bonds. Large mutual fund management companies, such as Fidelity, Vanguard, and Dreyfus, offer many alternative stock and bond funds. Some funds hold a wide range of stocks or bonds; others specialize in securities issued by a particular industry or sector; still others invest as an *index fund* in a fixed market basket of securities (say, shares of S&P 500 firms). Large mutual fund firms also often offer funds specializing in foreign securities, making it a convenient way for small investors to participate in foreign financial markets.

The greatest growth in mutual funds has been in **money market mutual funds,** which hold high-quality, short-term assets, such as Treasury bills, negotiable certificates of deposit, and commercial paper. Representing only about 8% of the total mutual fund market in 1975, these funds (generally offered by the same fund management companies that offer stock and bond funds) made up more than 38% of the market in 2003, with assets of $2156 billion. The underlying instruments in these funds have short maturities, so their asset values do not fluctuate much. Hence the funds provide savers with a liquid account that pays market interest rates. Most money market mutual funds allow savers to write checks above a specified minimum ($500, for example) against their accounts.

Regulation of the mutual fund industry. Heavy losses during the stock market crash of 1929 led investors to call for regulation of the mutual fund industry. With passage of the Securities Act of 1933, funds' shares had to be registered with the SEC prior to sale. The act also required disclosure to potential investors of information about portfolio holdings and investment policies and objectives. Mutual funds were prohibited from advertising anticipated returns, though they could state past returns. Congress and the SEC have amended the regulations governing mutual funds several times since 1933; more recent regulations also are generally intended to ensure disclosure of information and to prevent fraud. The Investment Company Act of 1940 assigned regulatory jurisdiction over mutual funds to the SEC. Subsequent regulation increased competition among mutual funds; amendments to the Investment Company Act in the 1970s reduced sales loads, and the Garn–St. Germain Act of 1982 allowed banks to offer money market deposit accounts.

In the early and mid-1990s, the SEC unveiled several regulatory proposals representing the most significant changes in mutual fund regulation in the United States since the 1940 Investment Company Act. One significant proposal is a requirement that the majority of the directors of any individual mutual fund be independent of the fund's sponsor, compared to 40% of the directors under existing law. (A company such as Fidelity or Vanguard offers several different funds and hence is the sponsor.) The idea is to limit the cost of administering the funds, particularly the increases in salaries that managers can vote for themselves when they sit on the board. The same proposal would amend the 1940 Act to set standards for maintaining liquidity of mutual funds and to require shareholder approval for any change in the fund's investment objectives. Some high-profile scandals at mutual funds, in which "after hours" trading by some investors diluted the value of most investors' shares, led the SEC in 2003 to propose additional regulatory reform.

Recent trends. Over the 1980s, 1990s, and early 2000s, the role of mutual funds in capital markets has increased dramatically. Competition among hundreds of mutual funds firms gave investors thousands of funds from which to choose by 2003. Analysts predict major changes in the mutual fund industry in years to come. Expensive needed investments in technology to manage marketing and investor record keeping will give a significant advantage to large firms. The turn of the century will likely see fewer but very large mutual fund "families," along with smaller niche funds. The growth in self-directed retirement accounts (such as IRAs and 401(k) plans) will continue to propel the growth of mutual funds. Outside the United States, U.S. mutual fund firms began making significant inroads in Japan and Europe in the late 1990s and early 2000s.

Finance Companies

Finance companies are intermediaries that raise large amounts of money through the sale of commercial paper and securities. They then use these funds to make (generally) small loans to households and businesses. Finance companies had assets of about $2478 billion in 2003. Before making loans, finance companies must gather and monitor information about borrowers' default risks. Because finance companies do not issue deposits as banks do, however, federal and state governments generally have found little need for regulation beyond information disclosure to prospective borrowers and fraud prevention. However, some states regulate the terms of finance company loan contracts. The lower degree of regulation allows finance companies to provide loans tailored to match the particular needs of borrowers more closely than do the standard loans that other, more regulated institutions can provide.

Types of finance companies. The three main types of finance companies are consumer finance, business finance, and sales finance firms. Consumer finance companies make loans to enable consumers to buy cars, furniture, and appliances; to finance home improvements; and to refinance household debts. Finance company customers have higher default risk than good-quality bank customers do and so are charged higher interest rates.

Business finance companies engage in factoring—that is, the purchase of accounts receivable of small firms at a discount. The finance company holds the receivables until maturity to earn a profit. For example, Moneybags Finance Company might buy $100,000 of short-term accounts receivable of Axle Tire Company for $90,000—effectively lending Axle $90,000 and earning a $10,000 return when the accounts receivable are collected. Axle Tire is willing to sell its receivables to Moneybags because it needs the cash to pay for inventory and for labor costs, and it might have a cash-flow problem if it waited for all its customers to pay their bills. Another activity of business finance companies is to purchase expensive equipment (airplanes, for example) and then lease it to businesses over a fixed length of time. In this activity, finance companies specialize in gathering information about the value of collateral. Factoring loans are generally short-term, but leasing contracts can be for five years or more.

Sales finance companies are affiliated with companies that manufacture or sell big-ticket goods. Their purpose is to promote the business of the underlying manufacturer or retailer. For example, General Motors Acceptance Corporation (GMAC) offers financing to customers when they buy new GM cars. Department stores issue credit cards with which customers finance purchases at those stores (Sears or J.C. Penney, for example). This convenient credit is part of the selling effort of the manufacturer or retailer.

Recent trends. Over the 1980s, 1990s, and early in the 2000s, finance companies have increased their role in consumer and business lending. Many analysts think that finance companies have an advantage in monitoring the value of collateral, making them logical players in lending for consumer durables, inventories, and business equipment.

Contractual Saving: Insurance Companies

Some events impose significant financial hardship when they occur, such as a medical emergency, a car accident, or the death of a spouse. **Contractual saving institutions** allow individuals (1) to pay money to transfer the risk of financial hardship to someone else or (2) to save in a disciplined manner for retirement. We discuss the first type of contractual saving institution—insurance companies—in this section. The second type—pension funds—is described in the next section.

Insurance companies are financial intermediaries that specialize in writing contracts to protect their policyholders from the risk of financial loss associated with particular events. Insurers obtain funds by issuing promises to pay under certain conditions and then lending the money to borrowers. The prospect of financial hardship leads many people to pay insurance companies fees, called *premiums*, so that the insurance company assumes risk. Consider an example: An individual may pay $1000 for a premium on life insurance, which the life insurance company will lend to a hotel chain.

Web Site Suggestions: http://www.iii.org/media/industry Presents financial data for the U.S. insurance industry.

In terms of premium income, U.S. insurance companies such as Allstate, Aetna, and Prudential are the largest insurers in the world, and U.S. premium income generally accounts for more than one-third of the global total. However, rapid growth in insurance coverage in the late 1990s came from Europe, Asia, and the emerging market economies of Eastern Europe.

The insurance industry has two segments. **Life insurance companies** sell policies to protect households against a loss of earnings from disability, retirement, or death of the insured person. *Property and casualty companies* sell policies to protect households and firms from the risks of illness, theft, fire, accidents, or natural disasters. Insurance companies' profitability depends in large part on their ability to reduce information costs of adverse selection and moral hazard. Hence, before we analyze these two types of insurance companies in greater detail, we need to discuss how insurance companies reduce information costs in providing insurance.

Principles of Insurance Management

In 2003, the U.S. insurance industry controlled assets of almost $4.3 trillion. Insurance companies make profits from the excess of premiums over claims payments and from investments in businesses. These institutions have long been important participants in the financial system, investing policyholders' premiums in capital markets, usually in stocks, bonds, mortgages, and direct loans to firms known as *private placements*. Insurance companies have fueled U.S. industrial expansion for more than 150 years by holding capital market instruments as assets and issuing insurance policies as liabilities.

Risk pooling. Insurance companies can comfortably predict when and how much compensation savers will claim by taking advantage of the *law of large numbers*. This statistical concept states that although the death, illness, or injury risks of an individual cannot be predicted, the average occurrences of any such event for large numbers of people can generally be predicted. Thus, by issuing a sufficient number of policies, insurance companies take advantage of risk pooling and diversification to estimate the size of reserves needed for potential claims. Statisticians known as *actuaries* compile probability tables to help predict event risk in the population.

Insurance company problems. There is more to insurance management than simple risk pooling, however. An insurance company faces costs associated with asymmetric information because individuals or firms seeking insurance are likely to have information that the insurance company does not have. Insurers also face both adverse selection and moral hazard. For an insurance company, adverse selection occurs when the buyers who are most eager to purchase insurance are individuals whose probability of requiring an insurance payout over some period of time is highest. For example, if you learned that you had cancer, you probably would want to take out a generous health insurance policy. Moral hazard arises in insurance when individuals assume greater risk when covered by insurance than they would without it. With complete fire insurance on your business, for example, you might be tempted to save money by not buying fire extinguishers or flame-retardant office furniture. Insurance company procedures are aimed at reducing costs due to adverse selection and moral hazard.

Adverse selection and screening. Because adverse selection results from the policyholder's private information, insurance company managers gather information to screen out poor insurance risks. If you apply for health insurance on your own (that is, not through a group plan offered by your employer), you have to disclose information about your health history to the insurance company. Similarly, if you try to buy automobile insurance, you have to supply information about your driving record, including speeding tickets and accidents. When you buy life insurance—especially if you want to purchase a large policy—you have to answer detailed questions about your health history and personal habits (such as smoking and alcohol or drug use) and undergo urine and blood tests. These procedures may seem intrusive, but they allow insurance companies to reduce problems of adverse selection.

Risk-based premiums. A longstanding practice of insurance management to avoid adverse selection is to charge individuals **risk-based premiums,** premiums based on the probability of their collecting claims. Suppose that the Egalite Insurance Company charges drivers the same premium, based on the average risk in the population, while Varyem Insurance Company charges risk-based premiums. If Stanley Stolid applies for auto insurance with a record of no speeding tickets (he won't drive faster than 40 mph) and Gary Gunem applies to the same company with a record of 32 speeding tickets in the last 12 months, Gunem should pay a higher premium. Choosing between policies offered by Egalite and Varyem, Stanley would say "no thanks" to Egalite and buy insurance from Varyem. Gary would say "sure," leaving Egalite with a potential loss. This version of the lemons problem (Chapter 11) explains why private insurance companies vary premiums according to differences in risk.

Moral hazard complicates insurance company managers' decisions to offer policies to consumers. Recall that the financial system develops new financial arrangements to reduce information costs related to moral hazard. For insurance companies, these arrangements include such policy provisions as deductibles, coinsurance, and restrictive covenants.

Deductibles. One way to ensure that the policyholder exercises some care to prevent the insured event is to place some of the policyholder's own money at risk. Insurance companies do so by requiring a **deductible,** a specified amount to be deducted from the policyholder's loss when a claim is paid. A $500 deductible in your health insurance or automobile insurance policy, for example, holds you responsible for the first $500 of claimable expenses; the insurance company will pay the rest. The use of deductibles enables an insurance company to align policyholders' interests with its own. Because deductibles reduce costs of moral hazard, insurance companies are able to lower the premiums that policyholders must pay.

Coinsurance. Although the policyholder is at risk for the amount of a deductible, the insurance company is still responsible for 100% of all allowable claims above that

CONSIDER THIS . . .

Can Investors Keep "Captives" at Bay?

Property and casualty insurance companies use economic principles of risk management to price risks. They also make a profit and offer a narrow set of insurance products—creating a combustible mix of possibilities for financial innovation.

Many large firms are taking a complete inventory of the risks they face and analyzing the risks as parts of a portfolio. Some companies hope to manage their risks with little or no outside insurance. Far-fetched? No. Companies in such diverse businesses as energy, telecommunications, and luxury goods are working with risk-management consulting firms to develop internal risk-management models for collections of risks. These models are then used by large firms that pool their risks internally in *captive insurance subsidiaries* instead of buying insurance from property and casualty insurers.

Will the captives carry the day? Likely, yes and no. Firms using a portfolio approach to defining risk may still be interested in transferring that risk. Even if companies do not want policies for individual risks (such as fire), they may want to cap the net risk of a portfolio of exposures—"portfolio insurance" of a sort.

Will commercial insurers seize the day? Perhaps. Insurers laughed in the 1960s at the notion of captive insurance subsidiaries (which now number more than 4000). In the early 1990s, they laughed at the packaging of risks into bonds traded in financial markets. Portfolio approaches to risk management . . . ?

amount. To give the policyholder further incentive to hold down costs, insurance companies may offer **coinsurance** as an option. This option requires the policyholder to pay a certain percentage of the costs of a claim in addition to the deductible amount. For example, when you choose among the health insurance options that are available through your employer, some may offer you a lower premium in exchange for your agreeing to pay, say, 20% of insured expenses after you pay the deductible. Hence coinsurance aligns policyholders' interests with the interest of the company.

Restrictive covenants. To cope with moral hazard, insurers also sometimes use **restrictive covenants,** which limit risky activities by the insured if a subsequent claim is to be paid. For example, a fire insurance company may refuse to pay a business's claim if the business failed to install and maintain smoke alarms, fire extinguishers, or a sprinkler system in accordance with its contract. By forcing the policyholder to restrict risky activities so as to claim insured losses, restrictive covenants act as a valuable management tool in helping insurance companies to reduce moral hazard.

Other insurance policy provisions. Insurance companies use other practices to reduce moral hazard. First, most insurance policies include limits on individual claims paid, such as the lifetime claim limit imposed by health insurance companies. Second, insurance companies reserve the right to cancel policies if the policyholder engages in excessively risky behavior. Finally, insurance companies safeguard against fraud—as, for example, when policyholders seek reimbursement for theft or medical expenses that never took place—by hiring seasoned claims adjustors to investigate claims.

Having explored ways in which insurance companies reduce information costs in providing risk-sharing services, we are ready to look more closely at the services offered by life insurance companies and property and casualty insurance companies.

Life Insurance Companies

Life insurance companies provide insurance (and savings plans) to protect against financial hardship for the policyholder's survivors. In the United States in 2003, life insurance firms had assets totaling about $3.3 trillion. Two types of firms characterize this industry: (1) *mutual companies*, which are owned by the policyholders, and (2) *stock companies*, which are owned by the shareholders. The largest U.S. life insurance firms are generally mutual companies, which account for over half the industry's assets. However, these large companies represent only 10% of all life insurance companies; more than 90% are organized as stock companies. By the mid-1990s, some large mutual companies were contemplating a conversion to stock companies to strengthen their capital base by issuing stock in financial markets. Metropolitan Life announced in 1998 that it intended to go public, and other conversions followed.

Most policies issued are *whole life* or *term life*. For whole life insurance, the policyholder pays a constant premium over the life of the policy; cash value (the excess of the premium over the expected cost of payout) accrues in early periods and declines subsequently as the risk of death rises. Individuals can use whole life policies to save for the future. Policyholders can borrow against the cash value, and individuals can either withdraw the total *cash value* at retirement or turn that value into annual payments, known as *annuities*. Saving through whole life insurance receives favorable tax treatment in the United States: Accumulated returns from investing the premiums are not taxed. This favorable treatment has particularly encouraged the growth of saving through annuities provided by most insurance companies. In addition, they allow the saver to withdraw accumulated savings in a lump sum at retirement, thereby deferring taxes on the accumulated investment income.

Term life insurance, by contrast, pays off only at the death of the policyholder; the policies have no cash value. Hence premiums reflect only the probability of the policyholder's dying during the insured interval, or term. Financial innovations over the past decade have given households investment opportunities with higher returns than those on whole life investments. For this reason and because investors have questions about the financial condition of insurers, term life insurance has grown in popularity over whole life insurance.

Since the 1980s, life insurance companies have met the challenge of reduced demand for whole life policies by restructuring their business to manage assets for pension funds. Indeed, more than one-half of the assets under life insurance company management are for pension funds, not for insurance reserves. Table 12.1 shows the success of this strategy. While life insurance companies' market share of intermediated assets fell sharply from 1960 to 1980, their market share stabilized somewhat between 1980 and 2003. Figure 12.1 shows that life insurance companies invest most of their funds in stocks, bonds, and loans to policyholders.

Property and Casualty Insurance Companies

Property and casualty insurance companies in the United States, controlling assets of $925 billion in 2003, insure policyholders against events other than death. They also are organized as both stock and mutual companies. They sell insurance to cover losses

FIGURE 12.1

Financial Assets of U.S. Insurance Companies

The differing mix of assets held by life insurance companies and property and casualty insurance companies reflects the difference in risk-sharing services they provide. (The data are as of March 31, 2003. Assets are listed by type and by percentage of total funds invested.)

Source: Federal Reserve, *Flow of Funds Accounts.*

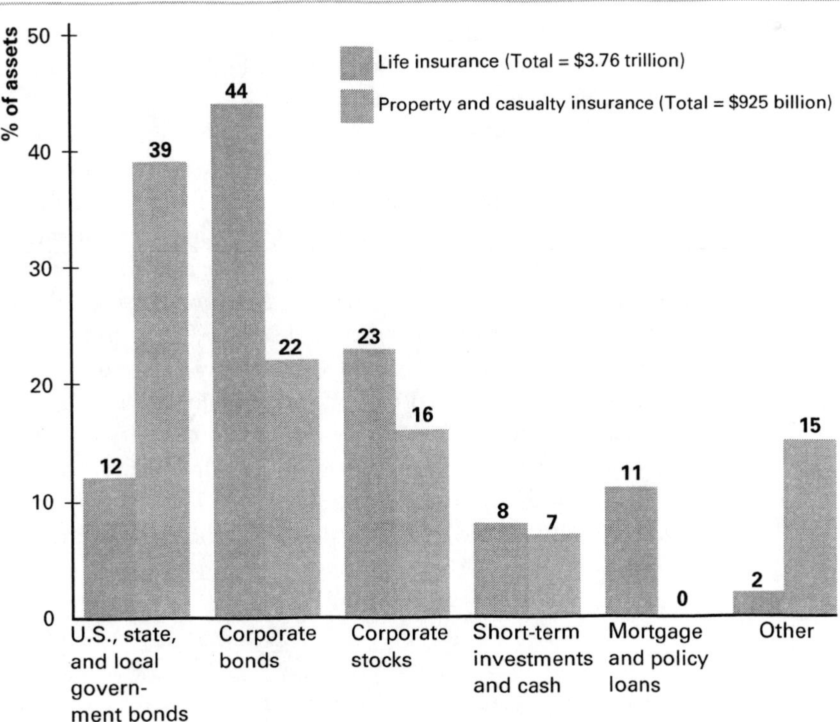

from such risks as theft, illness, fire, earthquakes, and car accidents. The premiums that are charged correspond to the chance of the event occurring. For example, high-risk drivers who are more likely to have accidents pay more than low-risk drivers do for automobile insurance.

The asset portfolios of property and casualty insurance companies differ from those of life insurance companies. Because events such as fires and earthquakes are more difficult to predict statistically than are death rates in the population, the portfolios of property and casualty insurers largely contain liquid assets, such as short-term and long-term credit market instruments (see Fig. 12.1). In addition, property and casualty insurance companies differ from life insurance companies in the way they are taxed. Life insurance companies pay no tax on their income, whereas property and casualty insurers pay U.S. income tax on their net income but with allowances for tax-free reserves.[†]

A possible insurance crisis loomed in this segment of the insurance industry as claims and premiums rose dramatically during the 1980s and 1990s. Proposals for reform would limit the size of the awards in settling certain lawsuits—particularly for negligence or malpractice. The large claims against insurance companies may encourage them to acquire riskier assets or engage in activities to increase their current returns, practices that increase their financial fragility. Terrorism risk after 2001 became a significant concern.

Regulation of Insurance Companies and Recent Trends

Most states establish insurance commissions to regulate insurance companies. Regulations typically require insurance companies to disclose the components of their portfolios (to reduce policyholders' information costs about the solvency of insurers), to submit to examinations to minimize fraud, to restrict holdings of risky assets, and to limit premiums.

The early and mid-1990s were turbulent times for both life insurance companies and property and casualty insurers. Some life insurance companies promised policyholders high returns on the saving component of whole life insurance in the mid-1980s when interest rates were relatively high. When interest rates fell in the 1990s, many of those promises led to losses for many insurers. For property and casualty companies, large losses from 1992's Hurricane Andrew caused policyholders to doubt insurers' ability to weather the next major disaster. These problems are prompting state insurance regulators and the Congress to review ways to ensure that insurance companies can honor their financial obligation to policyholders. In the meantime, financial markets are innovating ways for property and casualty companies to spread catastrophic risks. In 2000, some property and casualty insurers faced lawsuits stemming from "Y2K" information technology problems. The temporary federal *terrorism risk insurance* program passed in 2002 posed a major challenge for the industry.

[†] Historically, these companies were allowed a deduction for funds set aside for future obligations, and much of their income was tax-exempt income in the form of interest on state and local government securities, for example. The U.S. Tax Reform Act of 1986 restricted these deductions, though property and casualty companies are still more lightly taxed than manufacturing companies are.

CHECKPOINT

Why are property and casualty companies more exposed to the risk of large unexpected insurance losses than life insurance companies are? Life insurance companies face relatively low risk in the aggregate, owing to the law of large numbers. In property and casualty insurance, a single event—Hurricane Andrew, for example—may lead to claims by a large number of policyholders at the same time. ◆

Contractual Saving: Pension Funds

For many people, saving for retirement is the most important form of saving. People can accumulate retirement savings in two ways: through pension funds sponsored by employers or through personal savings accounts. **Pension funds** invest contributions of workers and firms in stocks, bonds, and mortgages to provide for pension benefit payments during workers' retirement. Representing about $5.5 trillion in assets in the United States in 2003, private and state and local government pension funds are the largest institutional participants in capital markets. Because retirements are predictable, pension funds can invest in long-term capital market instruments. Indeed, as Fig. 12.2 shows, private pension plans invest most of their assets in stocks, long-term bonds, and mortgages. With about 18% of all U.S. financial assets under their control, pension funds hold about 20% of the nation's publicly traded equities and about 11% of the value of corporate bonds.

Like insurance companies, pension funds are not deposit-taking intermediaries. An employee receives pension benefits from pension funds only if the employee is vested. *Vesting* is the length of service required before an employee is entitled to future benefits, and the required amount of time varies among plans.

Employees may prefer to save through pension plans provided by employers rather than through savings accounts for three reasons. First, pension funds may be able to manage a financial portfolio more efficiently, with lower transactions costs, than employees can. Second, pension funds may be able to provide benefits such as

FIGURE 12.2 **Assets of Pension Funds**

Pension funds concentrate their investments in long-term capital market instruments. Data are as of March 31, 2003.

Source: Federal Reserve, *Flow of Funds Accounts.*

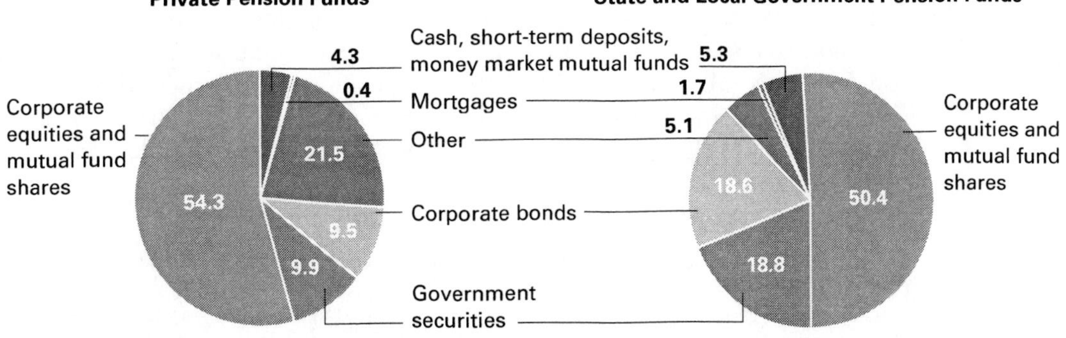

life annuities, which are costly for individual savers to obtain. Third, the special tax treatment of pensions can make pension benefits more valuable than cash wages to employees.†

Ownership of Pension Funds Assets

A key distinction among pension plans is whether they have *defined contributions* or *defined benefits*. In a **defined contribution plan,** contributions are invested for the employees, who own the value of the funds in the plan. If the pension plan's investments are profitable, pension income during retirement will be high; if the pension plan's investments are not profitable, retirement income will be low. The pension fund for most college professors is an example of a defined contribution plan. It invests pension contributions in stocks, bonds, mortgages, and money market instruments.

Pension assets in *employee stock ownership plans* (ESOPs) are invested primarily in employer securities. The value of pension assets depends on the performance of the firm, as measured by the value of employer securities. Such plans are designed to do more than help employees accumulate savings for retirement; they also may increase productivity by providing employees with a stake in company profitability.

Other types of defined contribution plans in which employers or employees contribute an amount based on earnings are more diversified. In some plans, contributions are invested in a pool that is similar to a mutual fund. In others, participants may choose to allocate their assets among a limited number of investment funds. For example, a plan might offer three investment choices: one that purchases U.S. Treasury securities, a second that purchases private bonds, and a third that purchases a portfolio of common stocks. Proposals to "privatize" Social Security, such as that announced by President George W. Bush in his 2000 campaign, generally would incorporate such a retirement pension option for households.

Web Site Suggestions:
http://www.pbgc.gov
Offers information on the regulation of defined benefit plans.

In a **defined benefit plan**—the more common type for most employees, particularly those in unions—the employee is promised an assigned benefit based on earnings and years of service. The benefit payments may or may not be indexed for inflation. If the funds in the pension plan exceed the amount promised, the excess accrues to the issuing firm or institution. If the funds in the pension plan are insufficient to pay the promised benefit, the issuing firm is liable for the difference.

Funding of Pension Plans

The principal difference between defined contribution and defined benefit plans is the method of **plan funding** that guarantees retirement benefits. For a defined contribution plan, funding is not an issue. By definition, these plans are *fully funded* by the employees who make the contributions and receive the returns on them. However, a defined benefit plan is fully funded only when the contributions, together with the projected future earnings, are sufficient to pay the projected assigned benefits. If the plan lacks these resources, it is underfunded. For a private firm, an underfunded defined benefit

† Your contribution to a pension fund can be excluded from your current income for tax purposes; your employer's matching contribution is tax-deductible for your employer. In addition, you can't be taxed on the investment earnings of a pension fund. Your taxation is deferred until you receive your pension benefits. You also have the option of transferring certain pension benefit payments into an individual retirement account (IRA) or other favorable distribution plan, which can reduce the tax you would otherwise owe on a lump-sum payment.

plan is a shareholder liability; an underfunded public plan is a taxpayer liability. As the efficient markets hypothesis would predict, the stock market lowers the value of the shares of firms with underfunded pension liabilities because those liabilities reduce the firms' value.

Regulation of Private Pension Plans

To reduce information costs for both defined contribution and defined benefit plans, pension funds disclose the composition of their portfolios. Regulations for defined contribution plans require information disclosure on the fund's portfolio of assets against fraud and mismanagement. Regulation of defined benefit plans is more complex because these pension funds may be underfunded, leaving workers without the retirement income they were promised. In response to difficulties in administering pension plans, Congress passed the Employee Retirement Income Security Act (ERISA) in 1974. This landmark legislation set national criteria for pension plan vesting and funding, restricted plans' ownership of certain types of risky investments, and enacted standards for information reporting and disclosure.

The act authorized creation of the Pension Benefit Guaranty Corporation (PBGC, or "Penny Benny") to insure pension benefits up to a limit if a company cannot meet its unfunded obligations (because of bankruptcy, for example). The PBGC charges companies a premium on pension liabilities and has an implicit line of credit from the U.S. Treasury. Many analysts are worried that, because the PBGC's premiums do not completely reflect differences in plan risk, government pension insurance may increase risk taking by firms' defined benefit pension plans. Because U.S. private pension plans collectively are underfunded by tens of billions of dollars, the PBGC must monitor carefully the health of the nation's pension plans. Some economists fear that a pension insurance disaster—like that which occurred for bank deposit insurance in the late 1980s—is on the horizon.

Public Pension Plans

Like private companies, governments provide pension plans for their employees. At the federal level, these include civil service and military plans. (Social Security is a general retirement benefit plan.) State and local governments also provide plans, which closely resemble private plans, for their employees. In the late 1980s, underfunding became an important problem in many states, resulting in downgrading of bond ratings for some states. The improving stock market and state finances in the 1990s mitigated the extent of underfunding, though declining equity valuations in the early 2000s again raised the problem.

Recent Trends

Fewer and fewer workers have the option of joining a traditional company pension plan, in which a retired worker collects a benefit based on earnings and years of service. While defined contribution plans have become more important, one segment of defined contribution plans is emerging as a major force in retirement saving: 401(k) plans. Named after the section of the Internal Revenue Code in which they are described, 401(k) plans are giving many employees a chance to be their own pension plan managers.

In a 401(k) plan, an employee can make tax-deductible contributions through regular payroll deductions (subject to an annual limit) and pay no tax on accumulated earnings until retirement. Employers can (and generally do) supplement employee contributions. Indeed, many employers match fully the employee contributions. Contributions to 401(k) plans have grown rapidly. Total contributions grew threefold in real terms over the decade after 1984; by the late 1990s, contributions equaled more than one-third of personal saving.

The employee can choose from a menu of options how funds are to be invested. These pension accounts are "portable"; you can take the funds with you as you change jobs. There is a risk: How much you have at retirement depends on how much you are willing to contribute when you are working and how well your investments have performed.

If you participate in a 401(k) plan, you may have to become your own pension manager. In this case, you can apply principles of investing and asset allocation discussed in Chapter 5. First, if your time horizon until retirement is a long one, you should invest your funds largely in stocks, which have generally higher returns than bonds or money market funds over long periods of time. Second, remember the advantages of diversification. Many 401(k) participants invest through mutual funds, which enable them to hold a large collection of assets at a modest cost.

CHECKPOINT

In the United States, direct ownership of equities supposedly is concentrated in the hands of the wealthiest individuals. One argument against this claim is that workers collectively own large amounts of stock through their companies' pension plans. Is this reasoning correct? Yes, for defined contribution plans, in which plan participants own the assets of the plan. However, more workers are covered by defined benefit plans. Because benefits are contractually specified, participants in these plans neither benefit from an increase in the market valuation of the pension plan's portfolio nor lose from a decrease in the market valuation. The shareholders of the firm benefit or lose, respectively. Hence participation in pension plans that own shares does not imply concentration of equity ownership in the hands of workers. ◆

Depository Institutions

Depository institutions are commercial banks, savings and loan associations, mutual savings banks, and credit unions. These institutions accept deposits and make loans, acting as intermediaries in matching lenders and borrowers. They are introduced briefly here. Their lines of business, regulation, and recent trends are explored in much greater detail in Chapters 13–16.

Commercial Banks

Web Site Suggestions: http://www.federalreserve.gov/releases Presents data on bank assets and liabilities (H8).

Commercial banks—the largest category of depository institutions—are financial intermediaries that accept deposits and make loans, offering risk-sharing, liquidity, and information services that benefit savers and borrowers. Savers obtain risk-sharing benefits from banks' diversified portfolios of loans; borrowers can obtain needed funds to finance the purchase of cars, inventories, or plants and equipment. Banks also provide liquidity services through checking accounts, in which savers' deposits are available on demand.

Banks have stiff competition from other financial institutions in the provision of risk-sharing and liquidity services. Today, savers can deposit their cash in a money market fund that invests, say, in Treasury bills, a transaction that was limited to large savers in the past. Savers can also purchase a diversified portfolio by buying shares in a mutual fund. However, many borrowers can't raise funds easily through bond or stock markets or other nonbank financial institutions. Commercial banks thus serve a special function in providing credit to particular types of borrowers by reducing the transactions and information costs of lending.

Transactions costs. One reason that borrowers with small or medium-sized credit needs do not rely on stock or bond markets is the high transactions cost of issuing such securities. Many transactions costs are fixed (for example, payments for SEC registration and investment bankers' services), so the average cost per dollar of funds raised may be too high to justify the effort. Averaging about 4% of funds raised for large issues of stock or bonds (say, more than $50 million), these costs can range from 13% to 20% for small issues (say, $500,000 or less).

Information costs. High information costs also restrict access to financial markets for households and small and medium-sized businesses. In fact, the most significant reason for the existence of commercial banks is their ability to reduce information costs. Recall that investors face high information costs in coping with adverse selection and moral hazard in financial markets. Banks, on the other hand, specialize in gathering information about borrowers' default risk, thereby reducing costs imposed by adverse selection. In the United States, bank loans are the dominant method of external financing for small and medium-sized firms but are much less important for large firms. This pattern holds for most industrialized countries. Banks reduce information costs associated with moral hazard by monitoring borrowers' activities. For the small saver to monitor borrowers' activities would be cumbersome and expensive. Banks act as delegated monitors for many individual savers and lenders who deposit their funds with the bank.

Savings Institutions

In the United States, **savings institutions** (savings and loan associations and mutual savings banks) originated as building and loan societies, in which individuals pooled money to be loaned to members to build homes. The modern savings and loan industry emerged in the 1930s as part of a general federal government policy of subsidizing home ownership. Savings institutions reduce problems of asymmetric information and default risk by requiring a down payment to make sure that the borrower maintains an economic interest in the value of the house. These savings institutions took on relatively short-term deposits to finance long-term home mortgages, thereby exposing themselves to risk in the event of market interest rate fluctuations. The mismatch of maturity assets and liabilities was a major factor in the deposit insurance crisis for U.S. savings institutions during the 1980s and early 1990s, which we address in Chapter 15. Over the 1980s, 1990s, and early 2000s, savings institutions have declined significantly in importance relative to commercial banks.

Credit Unions

Consumer loans are subject to potentially severe private information problems and associated monitoring costs. One way for a lender to reduce information costs is to concentrate on making loans to groups about which the lender has good information. **Credit**

unions are another specialized intermediary in consumer lending, taking deposits from and making loans to individuals who are well known to one another and who typically work at the same firm or in the same industry. Except for relatively small consumer loans, credit union assets are invested primarily in mortgage loans to members. The profits earned by credit unions are exempt from income taxes; this increases their attractiveness to savers in comparison with banks.

Table 12.2 summarizes the risk-sharing, liquidity, and information services offered by private financial intermediaries.

CHECKPOINT

Why are mutual funds more likely to invest in stocks, bonds, or Treasury securities than in loans to households and small businesses, which is the business of banks? Most mutual funds issue very liquid claims to savers, so they invest in assets that can be bought and sold with low transactions costs. Because converting loans to households and small businesses into marketable securities is costly, investors in mutual funds would face the risk of having assets sold at a discount to meet withdrawal demands. ♦

Government Financial Institutions

The U.S. government participates in financial intermediation both *directly*, through government-sponsored financial institutions, and *indirectly*, through guarantees of loans made by private financial intermediaries.

Direct Role: Federal Credit Agencies

Federal credit agencies are **government financial institutions** that make loans in the interest of public policy—most notably agricultural finance, housing finance, and student loans. In 2003, they held assets that were worth $2598 billion.

Government lending to farmers is the oldest form of U.S. government participation in financial intermediation. The Farm Credit System issues bonds and commercial paper in financial markets and uses the proceeds to make crop, equipment, and mortgage loans to farmers. Made up of a network of regional Banks for Cooperatives, Federal Land Banks, and Federal Intermediate Credit Banks, the Farm Credit System required a multibillion-dollar taxpayer bailout in 1987 as farm loan defaults soared.

Government intermediation for housing is the largest of the government lending activities. The Federal National Mortgage Association (FNMA, or "Fannie Mae"), the Federal Home Loan Mortgage Company (FHLMC, or "Freddie Mac"), and the Government National Mortgage Association (GNMA, or "Ginnie Mae") are government agencies that issue bonds in financial markets and use the proceeds to supply funds to the mortgage market. Only GNMA is a federal agency. Although their debt is not explicitly guaranteed by the federal government, most market participants believe that the Treasury would not permit FNMA or FHLMC to default on their obligations. These two agencies experienced very robust portfolio growth in the late 1990s and the early 2000s, drawing substantial criticism from other private-sector competitors.

To encourage lending to students for educational expenses, the government created a special charter for the Student Loan Market Association (SLMA, or "Sallie Mae") to purchase student loans made by private financial intermediaries under the auspices of the

TABLE 12.2 **Services Provided By Private Financial Intermediaries**

Financial institution	Risk sharing	Liquidity	Information
Commercial banks	Offer claims on diversified portfolios of assets, reducing transactions costs for individual savers	Offer liquid claims on portfolios of assets as well as some less liquid saving methods	Offer lower transactions and information costs than financial markets for many savers and borrowers; specialize in resolution of information problems (adverse selection and moral hazard)
Savings institutions	Similar to banks	Similar to banks	—
Credit unions	Similar to banks	Similar to banks	Similar to banks
Investment banks	—	Participate in securities trading	Evaluate securities in the underwriting process and advise firms on external financing
Securities firms	Similar to banks, but with money market accounts	Participate in securities trading; offer liquid claims on portfolios of money and capital instruments	—
Mutual funds	Similar to banks, but with money market accounts	Offer liquid claims on portfolios of money and capital instruments	—
Finance companies	—	—	Collect information for credit analysis for borrowers (often similar to bank borrowers)
Insurance companies	Offer advantages of risk pooling against financial hardship from death or specified unforeseen events	—	Gather and monitor information on policyholders and on some of the less well-known firms to which they lend
Pension funds	Offer claims on (typically) diversified portfolio of assets for retirement saving	—	—

guaranteed Student Loan Program. In the late 1980s and early 1990s, SLMA experienced significant losses from loan defaults. In 1994, President Clinton signed a law directing the Department of Education to conduct a five-year test to determine whether the government could manage the student loan program more cheaply than the private sector. In 1995, the Congress rejected the expanded role for the government, and in 2001, the incoming Bush administration made review of the federal credit agencies a priority.

Indirect Role: Loan Guarantees

A second role for the federal government in intermediation is to guarantee loans made by private financial institutions. Such guarantees are analogous to insurance, because the lender (a private financial institution) is not harmed if the borrower defaults. As with direct intermediation, loan guarantees are administered by many agencies. The Farmers Home Administration (FmHA) guarantees certain loans to farmers; the Federal Housing

CASE STUDY

What Kind of Financial Institution Is a Hedge Fund?

Just a year after winning Nobel Prizes in economics, Robert Merton and Myron Scholes found themselves less pleasantly in the news—as high-profile partners in Long-Term Capital Management (LTCM), the "hedge fund" whose spectacular crash and rescue in the fall of 1998 captured headlines around the world. As a hedge fund, LTCM joined the ranks of a recently popular (if misunderstood) class of financial institutions. Mahaathir Mohamad, Malaysia's stormy prime minister, has called hedge fund managers "highwaymen of the global economy." Many journalists and policymakers share similar, if less colorfully stated, views. The LTCM case has the trappings of drama—Nobel Prize winners, multibillion-dollar losses, very rich investors, and a Federal Reserve-orchestrated rescue.

A *hedge fund* is a hybrid institution, a largely unregulated investment entity (generally organized as private partnerships) specializing in putting together short sales (borrowing a security and selling it in the hope of being able to repurchase it more cheaply before repaying the lender) and leverage (purchasing securities with borrowed funds) in a manner that mitigates risk. Such investment vehicles have been around in various forms since the 1950s. Hedge funds make profits from speculation, but they usually operate on both the "long" and "short" sides of the market at the same time (hence the name—from "hedging" their positions to prosper whichever way the market moves). This sort of activity can lead to significant leverage that can be magnified using derivatives.

LTCM used these funds to place some rather large bets. The firm specialized in detecting discrepancies among bond prices and predicting which way prices would move. As the Asian financial crisis emerged, LTCM decided to short U.S. Treasury securities (wagering that their prices would fall) and go long on risky U.S. corporate bonds and European government bonds (wagering that their prices would rise). The bet went badly, however. A classic "flight to quality" during the Asian crisis pushed up prices of U.S. Treasuries, ravaging risky corporate bond and European government bond markets and reducing those markets' liquidity. LTCM's large borrowings from banks and its central role in key bond markets led the Federal Reserve Bank of New York to bring LTCM's creditors together to rescue the firm in 1998.

Mutual funds also pool funds from individual investors to invest in securities, but hedge funds differ in important ways—from the small numbers of players to the $10 million minimum investment requirements to the lax disclosure requirements.[†] In addition, hedge fund managers tie up most of their own capital in the fund and earn 15% to 20% of the funds' profits over and above a management fee (which a mutual fund manager would also receive). Hedge funds are smaller than mutual funds, with an estimated collective capital holding of $120 billion at the time of the LTCM debacle. These differences do not imply that hedge funds are a bad deal for wealthy households and institutional investors, which enjoyed very significant net returns from hedge fund investing in the 1990s. One lesson of mutual fund management—the importance of market liquidity for investment strategies—applies to hedge funds, though. As LTCM learned, trading is costly when markets become illiquid.

In 2003, the SEC initiated a discussion of whether hedge funds should be regulated. Many economists expressed concern over regulation of the industry.

[†] For a comparison of mutual fund and hedge fund regulation, see Franklin R. Edwards and R. Glenn Hubbard, "The Growth of Institutional Ownership: A Promise Unfulfilled," *Journal of Applied Corporate Finance*, 13:92–104, 2000.

CASE STUDY

What Kind of Financial Institution Is a Venture Capital Fund?

Venture capital funds have played a starring role in America's new economy, financing large-scale new ventures and consolidating more mature firms. While wealthy individuals known as "angels" invest funds directly in new ventures, venture capital funds (VCs) act as intermediaries. They raise funds from institutional investors and very wealthy individuals (who commit funds as an illiquid investment for periods as long as 10 years), then invest those funds in portfolio companies. From a base of $3 billion in investments in VCs in 1990, investors pumped a record $56 billion into U.S. VCs in 1999 (though venture funding declined sharply in the early 2000s). In addition, some large corporations invest funds in their own venture firms.

What accounts for VCs' popularity? Nothing succeeds like success. Annual returns on funds under management were very high in the middle and late 1990s, in part because of the boom in initial public offerings of VCs' portfolio companies (especially in the technology and telecommunications sectors). Will the good times continue to roll? Perhaps a bit less robustly in the near term. As the market for individual public offerings slowed in 2000 and in 2001, VCs found harvesting built-up gains more difficult.

The success of some venture capital funds reflects the special skill of their managers (called "general partners" in the typical VC organized as a partnership, with the outside investors being "limited partners"),† who specialize in reducing costs of adverse selection and moral hazard in entrepreneurial finance. Because screening and monitoring are time-consuming, VCs cannot profitably invest funds on as large a scale as do mutual funds, insurance companies, or pension funds.

What does the future hold? Although 2000 was a bad year for initial public offerings and many VCs, economists widely support the notion that the future of the venture capital industry is bright because of their role in the finance and governance of emerging companies.

† Venture firms are generally organized as partnerships because the Investment Company Act of 1940 imposes very stringent regulations on public firms that are essentially an investment portfolio.

Administration (FHA) and the Department of Veterans Affairs (VA) guarantee certain mortgage loans; and the Department of Education guarantees student loans.

Recent Trends

By the 1990s, many analysts questioned the advisability of maintaining or increasing the government's direct participation in financial intermediation. Private financial institutions have complained about the inroads of federally sponsored credit agencies into mortgage and other lending activities. Nonetheless, in the 1990s, proposals were being made in the Congress for new agencies to administer such activities as municipal road-building loans, mortgage insurance for veterans, and insurance for pollution control bonds.

The tenfold growth in loan guarantees during the past two decades and recent increases in defaults trouble many analysts and policymakers. The reason is that overly generous loan guarantees encourage moral hazard; private institutions will not be as careful in screening and monitoring borrowers in the presence of loan guarantees. These problems, in turn, cost taxpayers money. In the midst of the expensive bailout of federal deposit insurance in banking, the General Accounting Office (GAO) informed the Congress in 1990 that taxpayer losses from government loan guarantees may eventually exceed $100 billion. Since that time, losses have materialized from student loan guarantees and from defaults on the loan guarantees of the Department of Housing and Urban Development. Many analysts worry that, without reforms, taxpayer losses on guaranteed loans will be significant.

Financial Institutions: Blurring the Lines

We have explained why various types of financial institutions—securities market institutions, investment institutions, contractual savings institutions, depository institutions, and government financial institutions—came into being and how they serve the needs of savers and borrowers. During the 1930s, laws and regulations built barriers that protected the services offered by each type of institution from competition. As deregulation of the financial services industry proceeded during the 1980s and 1990s, more providers of various services emerged.

The landmark *Gramm-Leach-Bliley Financial Services Modernization Act of 1999* removed many of the regulatory lines among financial institutions. Responding to competitive developments in markets for insurance, commercial banking, and securities, the act permits the acquisition of commercial banks by insurance companies and firms in the securities business and gives banks the right to conduct real estate activities and to underwrite insurance and securities. As a consequence, the services provided by different types of financial institutions now overlap greatly.

In the current environment, the provision of financial services is being organized more by function—delivery of risk-sharing, liquidity, and information services—than by the identity of the provider. The equivalent of checkable deposits can be maintained not only at commercial banks, but also at savings institutions, brokerage firms, and mutual funds, and nonbank alternatives often offer greater returns for depositors. Banks are using their relationships with depositors to compete head to head with insurance companies in selling life insurance and vice versa. Finance companies are exploiting their ability at evaluating collateral and making inroads into banks' business lending activities. As regulations separating commercial and investment banking activities break down following the passage of the Gramm-Leach-Bliley Act, commercial banks are relying on their information collection strengths to compete aggressively with investment banks for underwriting business. Citigroup—formed from Citicorp and Travelers—worked in 1998 to create a financial supermarket. In 2000, securities giant Merrill Lynch and insurance powerhouse State Farm prepared to enter the banking business.

While most funds flowing between lenders and borrowers use the services of intermediaries, the market shares of individual intermediaries have changed significantly over the past few decades, as Table 12.1 shows. These changes in part reflect competition by function, as regulatory separation of institutions has been reduced. For example, the market shares (of intermediated assets) of commercial banks, savings institutions, and credit unions were stable over the period from 1960 to 1980 but fell sharply over the period from 1980 to 2003.

What accounts for this change? Depository institutions faced competition for checking account customers from more remunerative money market mutual funds, whose market share more than doubled. Households also switched funds out of bank savings accounts to stock and bond mutual funds. Banks also face strong competition for loans from finance companies, pension funds, and government financial institutions.

Common needs for the regulation of financial institutions and intermediaries emerge as competition induces distinctions among them to blur. As early as 1995, the White House, the Congress, and the Federal Reserve began urging the regulation of financial services by function. Under the Gramm-Leach-Bliley Act, regulatory oversight of multifunction financial institutions will be spread among the Treasury Department's Office of the Comptroller of the Currency (which has regulatory authority for bank subsidiaries engaged in securities underwriting), the SEC (which continues its regulatory oversight of securities activities), the Federal Reserve (which continues monitoring bank holding companies with insurance, real estate, and securities operations), and states (which maintain their regulatory authority over insurance businesses).

More generally, transmitting information is an important activity for all financial intermediaries. When information costs are relatively unimportant, regulations guaranteeing disclosure of asset portfolios, investment management practices, and supervision and examination are likely to be sufficient. However, for financial institutions and intermediaries that are involved in reducing information costs in financial markets, such regulations alone may be insufficient. Additional regulatory interventions focusing on the lending activities of banks and insurance firms, as well as the market-making activities of securities firms and exchanges, may be necessary.

KEY TERMS AND CONCEPTS

Contractual saving institutions
- Coinsurance
- Deductible
- Defined benefit plan
- Defined contribution plan
- Insurance companies
- Life insurance companies
- Pension funds
- Plan funding
- Property and casualty insurance companies
- Restrictive covenants
- Risk-based premiums

Depository institutions
- Commercial banks
- Credit unions
- Savings institutions

Government financial institutions

Insider information

Investment institutions
- Closed-end mutual funds
- Finance companies
- Load funds
- Money market mutual funds
- Mutual funds
- No-load funds
- Open-end mutual funds

Securities market institutions
- Brokers
- Dealers
- Exchange
- Investment banks
- Over-the-counter (OTC) markets
- Specialist
- Syndicates
- Underwriting

SUMMARY

1. Investment banks assist firms in raising funds in primary financial markets by underwriting new issues of debt and equity. Brokers and dealers match buyers and sellers in secondary financial markets. Financial instruments such as stocks and bonds are traded in organized exchanges and over-the-counter markets.
2. Mutual funds convert small individual claims into diversified portfolios of money and capital market instruments. In addition to providing diversification, funds economize on costs associated with securities transactions.
3. Finance companies make loans to consumers and firms with funds they raise in money and capital markets. Some such firms—sales finance companies—are tied to companies that manufacture or sell goods.
4. Life insurance companies and property and casualty insurance companies provide risk-sharing services to savers and are large investors in financial markets. Insurance companies reduce information costs of adverse selection and moral hazard by gathering and monitoring information about policyholders.
5. Private and public pension funds invest contributions of employees and firms to provide retirement benefits. The two broad categories of pension plans are defined benefit and defined contribution plans. In a defined benefit plan, employees receive a specified schedule of benefits, irrespective of the market performance of pension fund assets. In a defined contribution plan, participants receive the returns on their contributions, accepting the residual claim on fund earnings and the associated risk.
6. Depository institutions (commercial banks, savings institutions, and credit unions) accept deposits and make loans and investments. Like mutual funds, they issue liquid deposit claims against a portfolio of loans and investments. However, as borrowers may have

MOVING FROM THEORY TO PRACTICE . . .

THE WALL STREET JOURNAL MARCH 12, 2003

"Unforecastable Shock"

Housing, particularly owner-occupied housing, has long been a public policy issue in the United States. . . .

The original Federal National Mortgage Association—Fannie Mae, as it came to be unofficially and affectionately called—was organized in February 1938 to increase the volume of residential construction and develop a secondary market in government-insured or guaranteed mortgages. To achieve the first objective, from its inception Fannie Mae purchased mortgages and issued its own debt. Initially, Fannie Mae was funded through the sale of preferred stock to the Treasury.

As the presence of savings institutions in the residential mortgage market receded, the financing void was filled by U.S. government agencies. . . . Recent data indicate that their market share is 42.5% as of the end of the third quarter of 2002. Clearly, the efficiency and stability of the government agencies has become a critical factor in the financing of residential construction. . . . **a**

Given the current magnitude of mortgage debt outstanding relative to total credit market debt, any serious instability in the financing of the residential capital stock has the potential for significant effects not only on the housing industry and house prices but also on the entire economy.

A little-discussed but critically important dimension of systemic risk is the uncertainty about how the government and regulators will respond to a major unforeseen event. No one should underestimate the potential importance of **b** the ambiguity over the financial status of the government-sponsored enterprises. Would "too big to fail" be extended to GSEs in a crisis, and if so how would it be effected in the absence of a federal insurance agency with an unlimited line of credit? How quickly could such a rescue be implemented? . . .

In the case of the GSEs, the enormous scale of their liabilities could create a massive problem in the credit markets. If the market value of GSE debt were to fall sharply, because of ambiguity about the financial soundness of GSEs and about the willingness of the federal government to backstop the debt, what would happen? I do not know, and neither does anyone else.

Capital on the books of Fannie Mae and Freddie Mac is well below the levels **c** required of regulated depository institutions. The capital adequacy standards applying to these two GSEs were established by the Federal Housing Enterprises Financial Safety and Soundness Act of 1992. The core capital requirement is 2.5% of on-balance sheet securities and other off-balance sheet publications. The off-balance sheet obligations have a capital requirement because they are guaranteed by Fannie and Freddie. . . .

Today, the housing finance system is heavily concentrated. Just three firms—Fannie Mae, Freddie Mac and Ginnie Mae—account for over 40% of the residential mortgage market. Ginnie Mae is backed by the full faith and credit of the U.S. government. Fannie Mae and Freddie Mac are not so backed, and hold capital far below that required of regulated banking institutions. Should either firm be rocked by a mistake or by an unforecastable shock, in the absence of robust contingency arrangements the result could be a crisis in U.S. financial markets that would inflict considerable damage.

ANALYZING THE NEWS . . .

Federal credit agencies, sometimes known as government-sponsored enterprises, are increasingly important financial intermediaries. This statement is particularly true in the case of housing finance. Fannie Mae and Freddie Mac purchase mortgages and sell packages of mortgages as securities, after guaranteeing payment of interest and principal.

a Private financial institutions develop to fill particular niches in matching savers and borrowers and to provide particular risk-sharing, liquidity, and information services to savers. Government financial institutions emerge to fill important niches not satisfied by private intermediaries or to advance public policy objectives, such as promoting home ownership. The activities of Fannie Mae and Freddie Mac have lowered mortgage costs for home buyers and generated significant profits for their shareholders.

b To the extent that there is an implicit government guarantee, taxpayers are exposed to the risk of losses when the value of federal credit agencies' mortgages fall (when market interest rates rise, for example). The value of this implicit guarantee is the subject of vigorous debate. Taxpayer risk is compounded to the degree that private lenders find it more difficult to compete with federal credit agencies.

c Is this expanding intervention a win-win situation, raising profits and implementing the public purpose? As we showed in this chapter and Chapter 11, one purpose of financial arrangements is to make sure that borrowers or insured individuals have appropriate incentives to perform. If investors in mortgage securities packaged by Fannie Mae and Freddie Mac believe that they are "insured," they have no incentive to monitor managers of the federal credit agencies. How can taxpayers' interests be safeguarded? One option is to require shareholders in government-sponsored enterprises to place more of their own capital at risk, giving them an incentive to monitor the managers more closely. Alternatively, the GSEs could disclose more information on their hedging transactions in derivatives markets. Many economists and analysts believe that proper hedging could significantly lower risks for the GSEs, and perhaps taxpayers, though at the cost of lower profits for the GSEs.

For further thought . . .

If the federal government insured all mortgages, would the risk of fluctuating mortgage values be eliminated? Explain.

Source: Excerpted from William Poole, "Unforecastable Shock." Reprinted by permission of *The Wall Street Journal*, March 12, 2003.

private information about their prospects or their plans for using the borrowed funds, lenders at arm's length face high information costs. Bank lending requires an investment in gathering and monitoring information about the borrower.

7. The U.S. government participates in financial intermediation directly, through government-sponsored financial institutions known as federal credit agencies. It is also involved indirectly, through guarantees of loans made by private financial intermediaries.

REVIEW QUESTIONS

1. What are the five main groups of financial institutions? Which institutions belong in each group?
2. What role do underwriters play in bringing savers' funds to borrowers?
3. If you buy 100 shares of IBM stock on the New York Stock Exchange, does IBM get the money? Why or why not?
4. If you want to buy a $10,000 U.S. Treasury bond and a securities firm sells you one from its own holdings, is it acting as a broker or a dealer? If it arranges for you to buy one from someone else, is it acting as a broker or a dealer?
5. What is e-trading? What effect has it had on the value of seats on the major stock exchanges?
6. What are the different types of finance companies, and who uses them?
7. What is the moral hazard problem in insurance? How do insurance companies attempt to reduce the moral hazard problem?
8. How do insurance companies know how high their premiums should be for life and accident insurance? What kinds of problems do they face in assessing risks?
9. Why do property and casualty insurance companies invest more heavily in short-term assets than life insurance companies do?
10. What is the advantage of saving for retirement through a pension plan at work as opposed to saving on your own?
11. How do banks address adverse selection problems?
12. What types of depository institutions specialize in loans to consumers and homeowners? How are they different from commercial banks?
13. Describe how mutual funds provide services related to risk sharing and liquidity. Distinguish a mutual fund from a bank. What do the differences you highlighted imply about the need for regulation of mutual funds as opposed to banks?
14. Why do sales finance companies exist? Why might the General Motors Acceptance Corporation at certain times offer a lower interest rate on loans to buy GM cars than commercial banks would?

ANALYTICAL PROBLEMS

15. Explain how life insurance companies and private pension funds provide risk-sharing services for savers. Why do individuals not choose to self-insure—that is, insure their lives or retirement incomes on their own?
16. Suppose that a state has a number of low-income neighborhoods in its cities that have difficulty attracting businesses to locate there because the businesses find it problematic to secure fire insurance. Insurance companies say they are reluctant to write fire insurance policies in these neighborhoods because of the prevalence of arson fires. If the state legislature passes a law forbidding insurance companies from taking into account the arson experience of a neighborhood when deciding whether to offer fire insurance policies to businesses, predict the likely effect on the insurance market.
17. A country with restrictions on bank loan and deposit rates is more likely than other countries to develop significant markets in mutual funds for short-term claims. Would such mutual funds completely undo the interest rate regulations—that is, serve the same savers and borrowers equally well? Explain.
18. Is a compulsory government-sponsored Social Security retirement annuity system as subject to adverse selection as a private insurance company that offers individual annuity contracts? Explain.
19. If you believe the stock market is an efficient market, would you prefer to invest in an index mutual fund or in a mutual fund that is actively managed?
20. What type of financial institution would each of the following people be most likely to do business with?

a. A person with $10,000 in savings who would like to earn a decent return at low risk and who does not know much about the stock and bond markets.

b. A person with $350 who needs a checking account.

c. A person who needs a $10,000 loan to open a pizza shop.

d. A person who is recently married, is starting a family, and wants to make sure that his children are well taken care of in the future.

e. The president of a small company who wants to list it on the stock exchange to obtain additional capital.

f. Someone who has just received a large inheritance and wants to invest it in the stock market.

g. A person with no credit history who is buying her first car.

h. A family needing a mortgage loan to buy a house.

i. A person who has declared bankruptcy in the past and is looking for a loan to pay off some past-due bills.

21. Suppose that you have a choice of one of three stock mutual funds. Fund One boasts an average return over the last five years of 8.33%, Fund Two has returned 8.10%, and Fund Three has earned 7.95%. You might think that Fund One is the best, but are there some reasons why Fund Two or even Fund Three might be better?

22. As an employee in a large firm, you are given the choice between a defined benefit pension plan and a defined contribution pension plan. What are the advantages and disadvantages of each?

23. The earnings on savings through whole life insurance policies are not taxed. The policy provides both insurance (it pays a benefit when the policyholder dies) and savings (policyholders can cash in the policy before death). If the investment earnings on policy contributions were taxed, what would happen to the relative demand for term life and whole life policies?

DATA QUESTIONS

24. In *The Wall Street Journal,* look at the listings of mutual funds. What types of funds are they, closed-end funds or open-end funds? How can you tell? Suppose that the price of a share in a mutual fund is less than the value of a share of the fund's portfolio. Should you buy into the fund?

25. Compare the federal government-related debt instruments with those of the private sector by locating the most recent historical data found in the *Flow of Funds Accounts* of the United States compiled by the Federal Reserve (found at http://www.federalreserve.gov/releases/). In the table entitled "Credit Market Borrowing by Financial Sector," compute the ratio of private financial sector borrowing to federal government-related borrowing for the last several years. How does this ratio differ during years of economic booms with those of recessions?

26. The Investment Company Institute is a nonprofit, privately funded organization that analyzes the mutual fund industry in the United States. Locate its most recent annual issue of its *Mutual Fund Fact Book* (from http://www.ici.org/stats/latest/index.html). Of all U.S. corporate equity, what percentage is held by mutual funds? Compare the difference between retail and institutional cash flow to money market funds. How do they differ? Why do you think they differ?

27. One important role played by contractual savings is risk reduction—a role specifically filled by the insurance industry, which has been especially impacted by both the events of September 11, 2001, and the war on terrorism that followed. Calculate the industry's earned premium to expense ratios on an annual basis via the Insurance Information Institute's "Industry Financials and Outlook" section of its Web site (http://www.iii.org). (Look specifically at that the "Year End Results" reports.) What conclusions do you draw?

28. Locate the Pension Benefit Guaranty Corp.'s defined benefit plan fact sheet at its Web site, http://www.pbgc.gov. How many American workers currently hold such plans? How many such plans does the PBGC insure? Now consult a recent issue of the *Pension Insurance Data Book* (http://www.pbgc.gov/publications/databook/default.htm). What types of industries provide defined benefit plans? What role might unions play in the maintenance of such plans? Explain.

CHAPTER 14

The Banking Industry

The Banking Industry

If we compare the size of U.S. banks, number of U.S. banking firms, and concentration of assets held by U.S. banks with banks in other large economies, we develop a profile of the U.S. banking industry. Although the United States has the world's largest economy, U.S. banks are not as large by international standards. Indeed, as recently as 1995, only one of the top 30 banks in the world (ranked by assets) was a U.S. bank (then Citicorp). Between 1995 and 2000, mergers propelled two U.S. banks into the ranks of the top ten—Citigroup and BankAmerica. In 2003, U.S.-based Citigroup was the world's largest bank by assets; J. P. Morgan Chase was the only other U.S. bank in the top ten.

Another difference between the U.S. banking industry and those in most other countries is that the U.S. banking industry has an enormous number of banking firms. In 2003, there were about 7900 commercial banking firms in the United States (down from 14,404 in 1980). Currently, the United States has about 27 banks per million people, significantly more than in other industrial economies such as Japan and Canada. Many U.S. banks are also small by international standards: 54% have less than $100 million in assets.

Third, the U.S. banking industry traditionally has been much less concentrated as that in other countries: The share of U.S. deposits held by the five largest banks has been far less than that held by its counterparts in Japan, Canada, and Germany, which hold much higher percentages of their countries' deposits. However, these figures do not mean that U.S. households and businesses receive more *banking services* than their counterparts in other countries do. The United States does not have more bank offices, including branches, per capita—only more separately owned *banking firms* per capita.

The 1990s and early 2000s saw a major structural change in the U.S. banking industry. The industry consolidated significantly, with the number of domestically chartered commercial banks falling by about one-third, even as industry assets rose by about one-third. Over the 1990s, the 10 largest banking firms almost doubled their share of domestic deposits and total assets. By 2000, banks with more than $10 billion of assets (0.9% of banks) held approximately 68% of total bank assets and 65% of bank equity capital, whereas small banks with less than $100 million of assets (60% of banks) held just 4% of assets and 5% of equity capital.

Web Site Suggestions:
http://www2.fdic.gov/sdi/sob/
Offers a wealth of information on the U.S. banking industry from the Federal Deposit Insurance Corporation (FDIC).

Government regulation and regulatory changes are the primary reason for the differences in the U.S. banking industry and the changes in the U.S. banking structure and activities over the past decade. In this chapter, we describe the reasoning behind those regulations, the government agencies that monitor banks, and the tools the government uses to regulate bank activities. Recent trends in the banking industry have encouraged mergers and changed the services that banks provide for their customers. Regulations have been changing as well—in response to competition among different bank and nonbank financial intermediaries in providing financial services—stimulating consolidation in the industry. The business of banking is no longer the staid enterprise it once was, and we describe the changes that occurred in the past decade that will continue to shape the banking industry in the United States and in other industrial economies in the future.

Origins of Today's U.S. Banking Industry

We can trace the role of banks in the financial system to the cultural and political views held by many leaders and citizens in the early decades of the United States. Many people, particularly those in rural areas, feared big-city banking interests, particularly those in New York City. In 1791, Treasury Secretary Alexander Hamilton tried to establish a nationwide banking system, with the Bank of the United States in Philadelphia as the leading bank, to provide the nation with an efficient system of intermediation. Although the bank's 20-year charter was renewed (after a five-year hiatus) as the Second Bank of the United States in 1816, its survival was threatened by legislators from agricultural states. After his election, President Andrew Jackson, a populist hero, allowed the charter of the Second Bank to expire in 1836.

Although the establishment of a national banking system was doomed, states were given the right to control banks within their borders after 1836. This was the start of the Free Banking Period, during which banking was conducted with little government intervention. Some contemporary observers believe that the free banks were relatively successful intermediaries in matching savers and borrowers. The Free Banking Period lasted until passage of the National Banking Act during the Civil War.

The National Banking Act of 1863 established the current **dual banking system** in the United States, in which banks are chartered by either the federal government or a state government. Federally chartered banks, known as **national banks,** are supervised by the Office of the Comptroller of the Currency (OCC) in the U.S. Treasury Department and originally were allowed to issue bank notes as currency. To eliminate the ability of state-chartered banks, known as **state banks,** to issue bank notes as currency, Congress imposed a prohibitive tax on state bank notes in the National Banking Act of 1863. Congress intended to eliminate competition for national banks by drying up state-chartered banks' source of funds. However, state banks came up with a close substitute for currency—a **demand deposit,** or an account against which checks convertible to currency can be written. National banks adopted this innovation, and as a result, the two types of banks coexist today.

Legislation affecting banking did not end with the National Banking Act of 1863. Economic crises resulting from waves of bank failures, in which savers lost their deposits and borrowers found it difficult to raise funds, led to the creation of the Federal Reserve System in 1913. The severe banking crisis of the 1930s prompted the introduction of federal deposit insurance, through which most depositors' funds are guaranteed. Other regulations beginning in the 1930s shaped the competitive landscape of banking. As we will see, regulation of the banking industry is being hotly debated. We describe these regulations, explain why they exist, and describe the agencies that charter and examine banks in the next section.

Who Regulates Banks

The banking industry is highly regulated in the United States, as it is in most countries. Regulators are responsible for chartering banks and examining their operations. We first describe what this regulation entails and then describe the agencies that are responsible

OTHER TIMES, OTHER PLACES . . .

Lessons from the Free Banking Period

Banking was not really "free" during the Free Banking Period. To obtain a state banking charter, banks typically had to agree to (1) pay gold to depositors on demand, (2) accept double liability for bank shareholders (that is, they would be responsible for twice the value of their contributed capital), and (3) deposit designated bonds (usually state bonds) with the state banking authority.

Historians often use the term "wildcat banking" to describe the Free Banking Period. They allege that banks frequently failed despite regulatory attempts to protect them, causing substantial losses to users of bank currency. Much of the subsequent debate in the United States about the instability of free market banking came from the experience of this period.

Arthur Rolnick and Warren Weber, economists at the Federal Reserve Bank of Minneapolis, have vigorously challenged this view in their study of banking during that period in Indiana, Minnesota, New York, and Wisconsin.† They found that about half the free banks closed but that fewer than one-third of those ultimately failed to redeem bank notes at face value. In general, losses on notes were small—on average, about one cent per dollar. The wave of bank failures during that period can be attributed to default on the bonds backing the bank notes rather than to loss of consumer confidence in banks.

Two lessons emerge from that period. First, regulations are necessary to provide information to the public about the quality of the bank assets that back bank notes. Second, given the public's knowledge of problems in assets backing the notes of a bank, bank failures are rational and reflect large swings in the value of banks' assets. Government intervention in the banking industry may be needed to help it adjust to such large variations in asset values.

† See Arthur J. Rolnick and Warren E. Weber, "The Free Banking Era: New Evidence on Laissez-Faire Banking," *American Economic Review*, 73:1080–1091, 1983.

for regulating commercial banks, savings institutions, and credit unions. As a result of the dual banking system, bank regulation is enforced by many regulators with overlapping authority for these institutions.

Chartering and Examination

How does someone establish a bank? Individuals who want to start a bank must file an application for a federal charter with the Office of the Comptroller of the Currency. For a state charter, the would-be bankers must file an application with the appropriate state banking authority. When the federal or state regulatory agency evaluates the application, it considers the amount of equity capital supplied by the owners, the qualifications of the bank's proposed managers, and the bank's prospects for making profits. Before the late 1970s, the federal or state chartering authority also investigated whether the proposed bank's community "needed" a new bank. Often, an authority refused to grant the charter because it thought that the profits of existing banks would be harmed significantly, potentially causing them to fail. Since the 1980s, chartering authorities generally have not turned down applications on anticompetitive grounds.

A chartered bank must file quarterly reports of its earnings, assets and liabilities, and operations (called *Call Reports*); it also is subject to periodic examination of its financial condition by regulators. The FDIC examines banks at least every three years and generally more often. The Fed conducts examinations about every 18 months. Large national banks may be examined several times each year by the Office of the Comptroller of the Currency. These regulatory bodies often cooperate and accept each other's examination reports.

Examiners also make unexpected visits to banks to ensure that the banks are complying with all applicable laws and regulations. Examiners have fairly wide latitude to force a bank to sell risky investments or to write off the value of a worthless loan. An examiner who finds problems with excessive risk taking or low net worth may classify the bank as a "problem bank" and subject it to more frequent examinations. Although examiners help to control risky or dishonest bank management practices, some analysts believe that allowing examiners too much discretion forces banks to be too conservative in their lending practices. Regulators generally try to strike a balance.

In current practice, regulators use examinations to monitor compliance with capital standards and restrictions on permissible activities. After examination, a bank receives a grade in the form of a C (capital adequacy), A (asset quality), M (management), E (earnings), L (liquidity), and S (sensitivity to market risk) score. A sufficiently low *CAMELS rating* can lead to "cease and desist" orders to change behavior, a means of restraining moral hazard. Such a system mimics the way private markets approach moral hazard by inserting restrictive covenants in financial contracts.

Regulating Commercial Banks

As of 2003, the Office of the Comptroller of the Currency supervised the national banks that are members of the Federal Reserve System. These banks hold most of the assets in the U.S. commercial banking system. The state banks that are members of the Federal Reserve System are jointly supervised by the Fed and state banking regulators. The Fed also has supervisory responsibility for **bank holding companies,** which are companies that own more than one bank. Most of the remaining (smaller) banks are state banks that are not members of the Federal Reserve System but are covered by FDIC insurance; these are supervised by the FDIC. Some very small state banks with no FDIC insurance are supervised solely by state banking regulators.

This network of commercial bank regulatory authorities occasionally results in duplication of effort. Some analysts believe that regulation by more than one agency decreases the chance of lapses in supervision. They also believe that individual regulatory agencies may serve the banking industry better than they serve the interests of savers and borrowers. Since 1999, regulation of banking firms' activities in banking, securities, and insurance has been divided among federal and state banking, securities, and insurance regulators, as described later.

Regulating Savings Institutions

Savings institutions, comprising savings and loan associations and mutual savings banks, also are supervised by multiple regulatory agencies. Savings and loan associations (S&Ls) can be chartered by federal or state authorities. The majority of S&Ls are members of the Federal Home Loan Bank System (FHLBS), which was founded in 1932 as a "Federal Reserve" for S&Ls. The Office of Thrift Supervision, which is similar to the OCC, supervises the 12 district Federal Home Loan Banks of the FHLBS. It also charters and supervises federally chartered S&Ls. The FDIC provides federal deposit insurance to S&Ls through its Savings Association Insurance Fund (SAIF). [Before 1989, savings institutions were insured by the Federal Savings and Loan Insurance Corporation (FSLIC).]

About half the mutual savings banks are chartered by the states, and about half are chartered by the federal government. The primary regulators of mutual savings banks are state banking authorities. However, those with FDIC insurance must follow the FDIC's rules for state-chartered banks. The remainder of mutual savings banks generally have deposits insured by state deposit insurance funds.

Regulating Credit Unions

Web Site Suggestions: http://www.ncua.gov Presents information and data on U.S. credit unions.

Unlike commercial banks and savings institutions, both of which take deposits from any saver and make loans to any borrower, U.S. credit unions are cooperative lending associations for a particular group, usually employees of a particular firm or governmental unit. As a result, most credit unions are small, although shareholders of a credit union may live in many states (or even in many countries, as in the case of the Navy Federal Credit Union). Both federal and state charters are available, but most credit unions are chartered and regulated by the federal government's National Credit Union Administration (NCUA). Federal deposit insurance is provided by the National Credit Union Share Insurance Fund (NCUSIF), a subsidiary of the NCUA.

The federal and state laws that created multiple regulatory authorities have shaped the U.S. banking industry in terms of the risks to which banks are exposed and their activities as financial intermediaries. Table 14.1 summarizes the chartering and supervisory responsibilities for banking activities of U.S. depository institutions. In 2002 and 2003, Congress and the Bush administration debated plans for regulatory consolidation.

CHECKPOINT

Mutual funds with short-term money market assets don't require much ongoing supervision as long as the funds truthfully disclose to savers the contents of their portfolio of assets. By this reasoning, can we say that if banks disclose the identity of loans in their asset portfolios, ongoing supervision won't be needed? The answer is no. Ongoing supervision is necessary because bankers use private information in making loans that cannot be evaluated well by outsiders. In contrast, mutual funds own more well-known assets. ♦

Why the Banking Industry Is Regulated

Why is the banking industry in the United States and other countries subject to so much regulation relative to other financial intermediaries and markets? One possibility is that banks assume special risks in their activities as intermediaries. We know that a difference in the maturities of banks' assets and liabilities can expose banks to interest rate risk, the chance that banks' net worth will decline if market interest rates rise. By itself, however, interest rate risk isn't currently much of a problem for banks. They can use instruments traded in financial markets to reduce their exposure to it. Even if deposit insurance didn't exist, banks could compensate depositors for the risk that the bank might fail because of interest rate risk by paying depositors a risk premium on their deposits.

Instead, the government's concern for the health of banking institutions has focused on *information problems* and *liquidity risk* associated with unanticipated withdrawals of deposits. Banks hold reserves as a cushion against anticipated and unanticipated withdrawals by savers. Savers, however, cannot know the true health of the bank because the bank has private information about its loan portfolio. Because banks have private information, depositors may lose confidence in even financially healthy banks. When enough savers lose confidence in a bank's portfolio of assets, a bank run can occur.

Bank Runs

Depositors begin to lose confidence in a bank when they question the value of the bank's underlying assets. Often, the reason for a loss of confidence is bad news,

TABLE 14.1 **Regulation and Supervision of U.S. Depository Institutions**†

Type of institution	Chartered by . . .	Supervised by . . .	Examined by . . .	Insured by . . .
Commercial Banks				
National banks	Comptroller of the Currency	Comptroller of the Currency	Comptroller of the Currency	FDIC
State-chartered banks (members of the Federal Reserve System)	State authorities	The Fed	The Fed	FDIC
State-chartered banks (not members of the Federal Reserve System)	State authorities	FDIC	FDIC	FDIC
State-chartered banks (not insured by FDIC)	State authorities	State authorities	State authorities	
Savings Institutions				
Federal associations (insured)	Office of Thrift Supervision (OTS)	Office of Thrift Supervision (OTS)	Office of Thrift Supervision (OTS)	FDIC
State savings associations (insured)	State authorities	OTS and state authorities	OTS and state authorities	FDIC
State savings associations (not federally insured)	State authorities	State authorities	State authorities	
Credit Unions				
Federal credit unions (insured)	National Credit Union Administration (NCUA)	National Credit Union Administration (NCUA)	National Credit Union Administration (NCUA)	National Credit Union Share Insurance Fund (NCUSIF)
State credit unions (not federally insured)	State authorities	State authorities	State authorities	NCUSIF or state authorities

† Regulatory authority as of January 2001. Securities activities of commercial banks are regulated by federal and state securities regulators, and insurance activities are regulated by state insurance regulators.

whether true or false. Suppose that the major loans of Anytown Bank are likely to default. The assistant bank manager discovers the problem and tells two friends, who tell everyone they know. Fearing that the bank probably will not be able to repay them in full, many (if not all) of the depositors rush to the bank to get their money back. Because it must pay on demand, Anytown Bank will pay depositors in full on a first-come, first-serve basis until its liquid funds are exhausted. This sequence of events is known as a **bank run.** In this case, the bad news is true, and a run forces the bank to close its doors.

Moreover, bad news about one bank can snowball and affect other banks. Suppose that State Bank of Anytown has no insolvency problem. Its loans are likely to be repaid in full and on time. However, as rumors spread that Anytown Bank will run out of funds and be unable to repay depositors, many of State Bank's depositors do not want to take any chances. They begin demanding *their* money back. If State Bank's assets are largely illiquid, it will be forced to liquidate its loans at deep discounts to raise money quickly as its reserves run out. As a result, it cannot repay its depositors in full and is forced to close its doors also. In this case, the bad news about State Bank is false, but the rumors made the news seem true and led to a second bank failure.

The Cost of a Bank Run

This spreading of bad news about one bank to include other banks is known as **contagion.** Even if the rumors are unfounded, solvent banks such as State Bank of Anytown can fail during a bank run because of the costs associated with a forced liquidation of their assets. A bank run feeds on a self-fulfilling perception: If depositors *believe* that the bank is in trouble, it *is* in trouble.

The underlying problem in bank runs and contagion lies in the private information about banks' loan portfolios. The private information makes it difficult for depositors to determine which banks are strong and which are weak. This situation is similar to adverse selection in financial markets, in which lenders cannot distinguish good from bad loan prospects. Because of the private information that banks obtain when acquiring assets, savers have little basis for assessing the quality of their banks' portfolios and distinguishing solvent from insolvent banks. Hence bad news about one bank can raise fears about the financial health of others. Figure 14.1 shows the anatomy of a bank run.

Policymakers wish to maintain the health of the banking industry because of banks' importance in reducing information costs in the financial system. The failure of financially healthy banks hurts the ability of less well-known borrowers (households and small and medium-sized businesses) to obtain loans, thereby reducing the efficiency with which savers and borrowers are matched. In financial markets, government intervention focuses on reducing information costs through disclosure of information and prevention of fraud. For financial institutions—banks in particular—government intervention is intended to maintain the financial health of the lender.

CHECKPOINT

How does asymmetric information contribute to bank runs? Would runs be as likely to occur if banks held only marketable securities? Banks acquire private information while evaluating and monitoring borrowers. As a result, uninformed depositors may be unable to determine the quality of a strong bank's assets and a weak bank's assets, and their withdrawals could force the liquidation of the bank's loan portfolio at a loss. If banks held only marketable securities, the value of their assets would be known. Depositors would not make a run on an institution they knew to be solvent. ◆

Government Intervention in the Banking Industry

The government has intervened in the banking system to ensure that banks serve savers and borrowers and to promote the efficiency of the financial system. Three regulatory interventions after the National Banking Act shaped the modern U.S. banking industry. In 1913, Congress created the **Federal Reserve System** (the Fed) to promote stability in the banking industry—by serving as a lender of last resort during banking crises. The Fed was given a monopoly in issuing currency, now known as Federal Reserve Notes. All national banks were required to join the system and obey its regulations. State banks were allowed to choose whether they wanted to belong to the Federal Reserve System; most chose not to, owing to the costs of complying with the Fed's regulations.

The second major intervention came during the Great Depression in the form of **federal deposit insurance,** a federal government guarantee of certain types of bank

FIGURE 14.1 Bank Runs and Bank Failures

Bank runs can cause good banks to fail as well as bad banks. Bank failures are costly because they reduce credit availability for households and small firms.

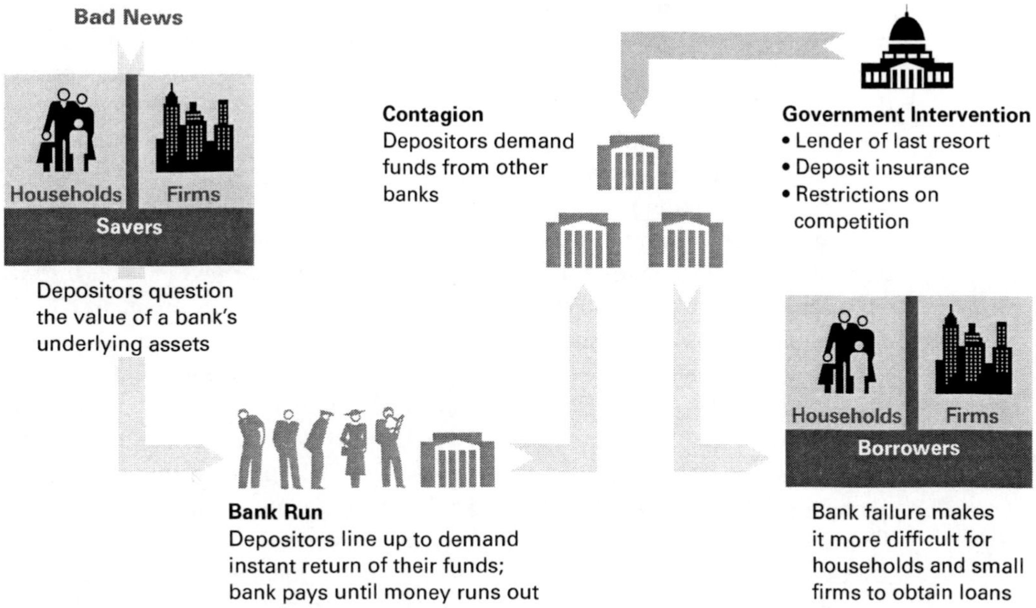

deposits. Thousands of bank failures had destroyed the savings of many depositors and eroded their confidence in the banking system. In 1934, Congress responded by creating the Federal Deposit Insurance Corporation (FDIC) to guarantee deposits at commercial banks. [At the same time, Congress created the Federal Savings and Loan Insurance Corporation (FSLIC) to insure deposits at savings institutions.] The act required banks that were members of the Federal Reserve System to purchase deposit insurance. Nonmember banks were given a choice. Virtually all banks were eventually covered by deposit insurance. The purchase of deposit insurance subjected banks to additional regulation by the FDIC.

Another significant government intervention in the banking industry is restrictions on bank competition, to stabilize the banks' profitability. The first such measures imposed **branching restrictions,** geographic limitations on banks' ability to open more than one office or branch. (Such restrictions are no longer a feature of U.S. banking regulation.) The National Banking Act of 1863 gave states the authority to restrict branch banking within their borders. Indeed, some states prohibited branch banking. By giving banks a monopoly over certain activities and limiting bank competition in local markets, the law sought to ensure a low cost of funds to banks and to stabilize the banking system. A second branching restriction, the McFadden Act of 1927, prohibited national banks from operating branches outside their home states. The act further required national banks to abide by state branching restrictions, thus placing them on an equal footing with state-chartered banks. These regulations led to a larger number of banking firms in the United States than would have existed otherwise. Anticompetitive restrictions also prevented banks from competing with investment banks, brokers, and dealers in the securities industry.

Lender of Last Resort

Bank runs and collapses of commercial credit were unavoidable, often devastating events in the U.S. financial system during the nineteenth and early twentieth centuries. During the National Banking Period (from 1863 to 1913), at least five major **banking panics,** or waves of severe bank runs, reduced the availability of credit to borrowers. The panics culminated in several deep business recessions. Simultaneously, stock and bond market prices fell, further spurring depositors to question the net worth of business borrowers and their ability to repay bank loans. Banking panics raised information costs for uninformed savers, leading them to withdraw funds from banks to invest in gold or high-quality bonds.

What the banking industry was missing during this period was a "banker's bank," or **lender of last resort,** to serve as an ultimate source of credit to which banks could turn during a panic. Many small banks that were particularly vulnerable during a panic exacerbated the problem. The lender of last resort advances credit to solvent banks using a bank's good, but illiquid, loans as collateral. Insolvent banks are allowed to fail.

Prominent private bankers such as J. P. Morgan and George F. Baker understood the severity of the problems of bank runs and contagion and the need for a lender of last resort. In the late nineteenth century, they and several other New York City bankers used the New York Clearing House to attack the problem of contagion. Member banks agreed to lend funds to banks that were threatened with a run during a panic. To provide cash to satisfy the public's demand for currency instead of bank deposits, the clearing house issued *loan certificates*, which could be used to settle transactions among member banks without using currency. To reduce the chance of a run on individual banks, the clearing house reported information about its balance sheet as a group, rather than for member banks separately. In theory, if the bad news hit all members of the clearing house at the same time, the members would have to break their promise of full convertibility of bank deposits into cash and issue certificates that would be usable at other member banks to supplement their cash reserves.

Despite their significant advantages over individual banks in dealing with panics, private arrangements such as the New York Clearing House cannot easily cope in practice with *common shocks*—that is, shocks to the members as a whole. Hence the clearing house could not make a credible promise to lend during a common downturn. The severe panic of 1907 and associated business recession led President Woodrow Wilson and the Congress to create the Federal Reserve System. The Fed was designed to be a lender of last resort to prevent general banking panics. Member banks were compelled to keep reserve deposits at the Fed and could borrow from the Fed through discount loans. The Fed's resources, including gold, member bank reserves, and the statement of "full faith and credit of the U.S. government," enable it to deal with disturbances to the banking system better than private arrangements can. With the exception of its weak performance during the banking panics of the early 1930s, the Federal Reserve System's credible record as lender of last resort financially stabilized the banking industry. The Fed's role as lender of last resort has expanded over the years to include ensuring general financial stability. For example, the Fed's lending to banks during the stock market crash of October 1987 helped to forestall the failure of securities firms. In 1998, the Fed brought together creditors of Long-Term Capital Management, a large and financially troubled hedge fund, to avoid contagion.

Federal Deposit Insurance

The basic idea behind deposit insurance is to guarantee the value of savers' deposits—to promise that if a bank fails, the insuring authority will reimburse the saver for funds

Web Site Suggestions: http://www.fdic.gov/deposit/insurance/index.html
Gives information on deposit insurance funds and ideas for reform of deposit insurance.

lost. As with the lender of last resort, federal deposit insurance reduces the information costs incurred by savers in evaluating a bank's assets. To be credible, the guarantee must be backed by sufficient funds to calm the fears of bank depositors during a panic.

Numerous bank failures during the 1920s and early 1930s led to the creation of the Federal Deposit Insurance Corporation (FDIC) in 1934. During the financial crisis from 1930 to 1933, more than one-third of all U.S. banks failed (about 2000 each year). These failures meant delays in receiving funds and, in many cases, outright losses for depositors. Following the establishment of the FDIC, calmer days resulted for the banking industry, with failure rates averaging fewer than 10 per year between 1934 and 1981.

The FDIC initially insured deposits up to $2500; it now insures deposits up to $100,000. Thus the FDIC protects any depositor with less than $100,000 in a bank account from loss in the event of bank failure. As a result, most depositors have little incentive to withdraw their money and cause the bank to fail if there are questions about the bank's strength. Although about 99% of all depositors are fully insured, the remaining 1% account for more than one-fourth of all deposits. Hence savers with more than $100,000 in deposits still have reason to question a bank's financial condition and demand their funds when they are in doubt about it. For example, if Cindy Croesus holds a $1 million negotiable CD at Doubtful Bank, $900,000 of her investment is at risk, and she will understandably withdraw her funds at a moment's notice if she is worried about her bank's financial health.

The FDIC participated in the resolution of a number of bank failures during the 1980s. Bank failures accelerated in the 1980s, climbing from 10 in 1981 to 79 in 1984, when the giant Continental Illinois National Bank, one of the 10 largest U.S. banks at the time, failed. The rate of failures increased later in the 1980s, peaking in 1989 at 206. Whereas 168 banks failed in 1990, only 31 banks have failed since 1997.

How the FDIC deals with bank failure. The FDIC generally handles bank failures in one of two ways: It pays off depositors, or it purchases and assumes control of the bank.

In some cases of bank failure, the FDIC closes the bank and pays off the insured depositors immediately. To recover its funds, the FDIC draws payments from the bank's remaining funds and net worth, including the sale of the bank's assets. If those funds are insufficient, the FDIC makes up the difference from its insurance reserves. After compensating insured depositors, any remaining funds are paid to uninsured depositors. Although the FDIC doesn't use this method often, it did so occasionally during the 1980s. For example, when the FDIC closed the Penn Square Bank of Oklahoma, uninsured depositors lost, on average, only about 20% of their deposits.

The FDIC prefers to keep a failed bank running by purchasing the bank and assuming control over it. The FDIC then tries to find a financial institution that is willing to take over the bank to gain entry into new geographic markets and access to the failed bank's goodwill (its network of customer relationships). Banks became especially interested in acquiring other banks after the Banking Act of 1982 permitted acquisition of failed banking institutions across state lines. When the FDIC purchases and assumes control of a failed bank, the transition typically costs the FDIC money. Generally, it tries to find an acquiring bank to take on *all* of the failed bank's deposits. In that case, the FDIC subsidizes the assumption by providing loans at low rates of interest or buying problem loans in the failed bank's portfolio.

The FDIC must assess the relative costs of the two methods of dealing with a failed bank. Paying off depositors has the advantage of low cost to the deposit insurance fund because only insured depositors are compensated. As long as the perceived value of the insolvent bank's goodwill is less than the value of uninsured depositors' claims, the FDIC saves money by compensating depositors. However, because banks have a special role in the intermediation process, forcing all failed banks to close their doors may not be in the best interests of borrowers or the economy. Although keeping banks open by purchasing them and assuming their assets may be costly, some economists argue that this policy may actually be cheaper for the FDIC in the short run. Its reserves do not have to shrink, and regulators do not have to report operating losses. (We return to this point in Chapter 15 when we analyze the 1980s crisis in federal deposit insurance, in which insolvent institutions continued to operate, losing even more money, with regulators' approval—a process that foreshadowed events in Japan in the 1990s and early 2000s.)

Stability of the bank insurance fund. The FDIC earns income through the insurance premiums paid by insured banks and investment earnings (since 1996, assessments have been minimal for banks, with funds coming principally from investment earnings, though savings institutions still pay premiums). It receives no regular appropriation from Congress. At the end of the 1980s, however, the FDIC was unable to make good on its guarantee of commercial bank deposits without significant regulatory reforms or a cash infusion from the Treasury. In 1988, the FDIC's outflows exceeded inflows from bank insurance premiums for the first time in its history. The FDIC's Bank Insurance Fund held $13.2 billion at the end of 1990, or about 0.7% of total insured bank deposits. The FDIC paid out more than $9 billion in 1990, bringing reserves down to about 0.2% of insured deposits. It then paid out $11 billion in 1991, making its net worth a *negative* $7 billion at the end of 1991, or about 0.4% of total insured bank deposits. In November 1991, Congress approved the Treasury Department's emergency request for an infusion of $70 billion into the fund, including a $30 billion line of credit. As a result of a fall in the number of bank failures and an increase in deposit insurance premiums in the early 1990s, the Bank Insurance Fund restored its funding level required by the Congress. Indeed, in November 1995, the FDIC voted to eliminate remaining premiums for most banks (92%, accounting for 95% of U.S. insured deposits), replacing them with a $2000 annual fee. Premiums for the weakest banks fell to $0.27 per $100 of insured deposits from $0.31. Fees currently vary from zero to $0.27 per $100 of insured deposits, according to how well-capitalized the bank is and whether bank examinations reveal any weakness. Since 2000, proposals by the FDIC to increase coverage to $200,000 have been greeted skeptically by most economists, who feared that the large resulting increase in insured deposits would increase the likelihood of another deposit insurance crisis.

Should these ups and downs of the Bank Insurance Fund cause you to withdraw all your money from the bank? The answer is no, because the size of the FDIC's insurance fund is not what maintains public confidence in it. The true deposit insurance is the implicit guarantee of the U.S. Treasury and the Federal Reserve System. In addition to the Treasury's recent rescue of the FDIC, the Fed on numerous occasions has lent large sums of money to troubled banks (including $5 billion in one transaction in the rescue of Continental Illinois).

Monitoring banks, capital requirements, and evaluating risk. In Chapter 13, we noted that, because bankers have private information about the quality of their loan portfolios, savers should monitor bankers. However, the introduction of federal deposit insurance reduces the need for savers with large deposits to monitor banks and eliminates it for savers with small deposits. As a result, legislation and regulations have had to provide ways to monitor banks, primarily reducing costs of moral hazard.

Insured banks have an incentive to make risky loans and investments. Therefore banking laws and regulations limit this behavior by restricting the types of assets that banks can hold. For example, banks are not allowed to invest deposits in common stocks. To ensure that bank examiners are doing their job, the *Federal Deposit Insurance Corporation Improvement Act of 1991* (FDICIA) requires the FDIC, as insurer, to monitor the supervisory evaluation of the bank's federal or state examiner. In addition, the FDIC considers other information that is appropriate for evaluating risk, including results of statistical monitoring systems. Bank examiners for the FDIC may instruct bankers to sell risky assets to remove them from their portfolios.

Banking laws and regulations also require banks to maintain a minimum level of net worth, or equity capital. The bank's equity capital is its cushion against losses on loans and investments. Banks want to hold as little capital as necessary, to increase the return on their equity. For example, if a bank with $250 million in assets and $20 million in capital earns $2 million, it achieves a 10% return on equity. But if it could earn $2 million with only $10 million in capital, the return would jump to 20%. In the absence of federal deposit insurance, to reduce the costs of moral hazard, savers would insist that bankers place their own net worth at risk. With deposit insurance, individual savers are less concerned about the value and quality of a bank's assets, giving banks an incentive to hold less equity capital. FDICIA strengthened capital requirements for U.S. banks. However, even with a minimum level of capital requirement, capital–asset ratios for commercial banks are only about half their 1930 level (before the introduction of federal deposit insurance).

During most of the FDIC's existence, minimum capital requirements were stated as a fixed percentage of a bank's assets. However, as bank failures increased in the mid-1980s, regulators discovered that the requirements did not reflect differences in banks' risk taking, especially the risk of their off-balance-sheet activities, such as trading in financial futures and options and interest rate swaps. In 1988, regulators from many countries worked under the auspices of the Bank for International Settlements (BIS) in Basel, Switzerland, and agreed to design more stringent, default-risk-based capital requirements.† Since that time, the BIS has proposed that banks develop their own systems to assess their exposure to interest rate risk.

While the 1988 Basel I accord provided a framework for capital regulation, it is (arguably) too simple to address the risks in large, complex financial institutions today. Since 1998, a Basel II framework has evolved to reflect improved techniques for measuring and managing risks. Basel II brings together a minimum capital requirement against credit risk and a capital requirement against operational risk. In 2003, many analysts doubted whether banks have the time and resources to have the new requirements in place by the framework's goal year of 2007. In the United States, regulators have supported imposing the new requirements only for the very largest banks. European regulators are likely to follow the approaches to credit risk and operational risk dictated by U.S. regulators for U.S. banks.

---

†International coordination is important. Otherwise, banks in a country that has a high capital requirement may be put at a short-term competitive disadvantage against banks in a country that has a low capital requirement.

FDICIA legislated a new supervisory framework connecting enforcement actions to the bank's level of capital. This approach, known as "prompt corrective action," attempts to link the extent of supervisory intervention to the extent of capital inadequacy. Under FDICIA, federal banking agencies assign a bank to one of five categories: well capitalized, adequately capitalized, undercapitalized, significantly undercapitalized, and critically undercapitalized. Banks that fall into one of the last three categories face mandatory enforcement actions.

To assign banks to capital categories, regulators consider ratios of capital to risk-weighted assets (*risk-based capital requirement*) and capital to total average assets (*leverage* ratio). Banking agencies use two definitions of capital. Tier 1 capital includes the most permanent types of capital (common stockholders' equity) to absorb losses. Tier 2 capital components offer some protection against loss but have a limited life and may carry an interest obligation (including subordinated debt and intermediate-term preferred stock). For an institution to be considered well capitalized, it must have total capital of at least 10% of risk-weighted assets and Tier 1 capital of at least 6% of risk-weighted assets.[†] To avoid prompt corrective action, total capital must exceed 6% of total risk-weighted assets, and Tier 1 capital must exceed 3% of total risk-weighted assets. The leverage ratio must exceed 5% for the bank to be considered well capitalized and must be at least 4% to avoid prompt corrective action. Although capital standards are an important discipline against moral hazard, economists argue that such standards have limitations in dealing with the complex activities of banks in the new century.

While bank examinations and capital standards have figured prominently in bank regulation in recent years, regulators in the United States and other industrial countries have increasingly focused their attention on assessments of banks' internal risk management. Judging a bank's risk position by examining its current balance sheet ignores the fact that, in today's financial system, given the many new financial instruments, taking very large bets quickly is relatively easy. In this setting, an institution judged to be healthy from a capital adequacy standpoint can assume large risks and fail quickly if outcomes are adverse, as was the case in Barings' spectacular failure in 1995 (discussed in Chapter 9).

Accordingly, regulators now emphasize the quality of the bank's internal models for evaluating and controlling exposure to risk. In the United States, the Fed and the Comptroller of the Currency feed risk management process ratings into the CAMELS system. In addition, banks are required to consider interest-rate risk exposure in deciding capital requirements. They must establish limits on internal risks and designate personnel to monitor and manage the risks.

Finally, as we saw for analyses of financial markets in Chapter 11, disclosure requirements can play a valuable role in producing information on bank risk, which

---

[†] Two other types of capital requirements have been used in recent practice. First, minimum capital standards must be connected to the bank's exposure to risks in off-balance-sheet activities, including trading positions in derivatives and interest rate swaps. Under the auspices of the Bank for International Settlements, industrial countries coordinate their capital requirements for "risk-weighted" assets. Second, because large U.S. banks are also engaged in substantial trading activities, the Federal Reserve requires that banks develop internal risk analysis models to forecast the largest trading loss they could sustain over a 10-day period. Banks must hold incremental equity capital amounting to at least three times this potential loss, and the capital may be held in standard equity capital or Tier 3 capital—that is, short-term securities that cannot be converted to cash upon maturity should the bank be judged to be undercapitalized relative to the new requirement.

can in turn improve the ability of bank depositors, shareholders, and regulators to evaluate bank performance. In 1994, the Eurocurrency Standing Committee of the G-10 central banks recommended that financial risk assessments produced by banks' risk management models be included in public disclosures.

Restrictions on Banking Industry Competition

The final category of government intervention in the banking industry is restrictions on competition. In the United States, these restrictions have taken two forms: (1) geographic branching restrictions and (2) restrictions on permissible activities of banks. Both restrictions have been loosened significantly in recent years.

Branching restrictions. Branching restrictions figured prominently in federal and state banking regulation until recently. To promote competition among banks, the McFadden Act prohibited national banks from establishing branches across state lines. In addition, it compelled national banks to comply with the branching restrictions in the states in which they are located. State branching regulations traditionally assumed one of three forms: restricting banks to a single bank (unit banking), to branches within a narrow geographic area (limited branching), or to branches within a single state (statewide branching). As early as 1995, no state still enforced unit banking, and 45 states plus the District of Columbia allowed statewide branching.

The combination of state branching restrictions and the McFadden Act protected small banks by limiting the ability of large banks to expand outside their regions or states. Branching restrictions for savings institutions and credit unions are more lenient. Almost all states allow branching for savings and loan associations and mutual savings banks. Since 1980, federally chartered S&Ls have been permitted to establish branches statewide in all 50 states. Since 1981, mergers of financially troubled S&Ls have been allowed across state lines.

Geographic restrictions may push banks toward local lending, lowering the costs of providing risk-sharing, liquidity, and information services to individuals and businesses in a region. However, geographic restrictions also reduce banks' ability to diversify assets, raising their exposure to credit risk. For example, a bank in an agricultural state may make most of its loans to farmers. If farm prices are low, then the bank faces the prospect of default on many of its loans. The effects of recessions are also often regional. If all firms in a region face adverse conditions, then loans to those firms lack diversification and raise credit risk.

In addition, because the fixed costs of funding a bank (for example, computer systems, regulatory reporting, and so on) are high, branching restrictions may reduce banks' profitability. Indeed, in the debate over branching restrictions in the early 1990s, California-based Bank of America estimated that elimination of branching restrictions alone would save it $50 million per year in duplicated overhead costs. (In 1998, Bank of America merged with NationsBank.) Thus limited competition may lead to bank inefficiency and lower rates of return for investors, with significant costs to the economy.

Advocates of limited branching argued that the large number of U.S. banks benefits the banking system because it promotes competition. In fact, the opposite is true. When a bank's territory is protected by regulation, it may operate inefficiently yet still compete successfully against more efficient banks. Why has this anticompetitive inefficiency persisted so long? The answer lies in the politics of U.S. finance mentioned at the

CONSIDER THIS ...

Is Bank Consolidation Good for Business?

Consolidation of the U.S. banking industry is occurring rapidly, fueled in part by regulatory changes permitting nationwide banking. Advocates of consolidation point to improved diversification of bank assets and lower overhead costs as benefits of this trend. For example, California, which has allowed statewide branching in a geographically large and economically diverse state since 1909, avoided the banking crises related to agriculture that other states experienced in the mid-1980s. There are many fewer banks per capita in California as well. Some critics of consolidation argue, however, that the emergence of fewer and much larger banks will dampen competition and reduce lending to small business borrowers.

Most economists side with the advocates of consolidation. Competition is generally enhanced by nationwide banking, because banks formerly protected from out-of-state competition now must provide better service and lower costs to stay in business.

While larger banks will emerge, banking economists suggest that there will be at least 10 banks with assets exceeding a threshold of $100 billion. Small community banks are unlikely to be driven out of business where knowledge of local markets is important. California and New York, for example, have a number of community banks even though small and large banks have competed within the states for a long time. These smaller banks plus focused lending departments of larger banks lead most economists to be skeptical of the notion that small-business lending will suffer greatly as a result of consolidation, although some decline may well occur.

Analysts await news of how stronger diversification in nationwide banks will fare in a downturn. In a more expansionary setting, some commentators worry that rapid expansion of banks across geographic boundaries may increase risk taking and make bank failures more likely.

beginning of the chapter. Americans have long and continually distrusted large, big-city banks. Indeed, the states with the strongest populist, anti-big-bank sentiment in the nineteenth century—usually agricultural states in the Midwest and South—were more likely to have restrictive branching regulations after that time. The large number of relatively small commercial banks reflects in large part the legacy of those political struggles.

Competitive forces in the banking industry are difficult to restrain. Innovations by financial institutions, including bank holding companies, nonbank banks, and automated teller machines, steadily eroded restrictions on geographic competition.

As early as the 1950s, banks began to get around branching restrictions by forming *bank holding companies (BHCs)*. A bank holding company is a large firm with many different banks as subsidiaries. Congress relaxed branching restrictions in the Bank Holding Company Act of 1956, permitting bank holding companies to provide nonbank financial services on an interstate basis. The act directed the Fed to regulate the new activities of *multibank* holding companies, so a loophole existed for expansion into nonbanking activities by *one-bank* holding companies. Congress closed this loophole in the 1970 Amendment to the Bank Holding Company Act, but the period since 1970 has been one of significant expansion by bank holding companies. Virtually all large banks are owned by bank holding companies, and banks in holding companies hold more than 90% of commercial bank deposits.

For many years, financial institutions circumvented branching restrictions through BHCs. The Bank Holding Company Act of 1956 defined a bank as a financial institution that accepts demand deposits and makes commercial loans. Financial institutions got around the regulation by splitting these two functions: They created **nonbank offices,** which did not take demand deposits but made loans, and **nonbank banks,** which took demand deposits but did not make loans. The regulatory response to this activity was the Competitive Equality Banking Act of 1987, which forbade opening additional nonbank banks, although it allowed additional nonbank offices to be opened.

During the 1980s, banks further broke branching restrictions by expanding the use of **automated teller machines (ATMs)**, which spread rapidly in the 1980s and 1990s. The development of ATMs was made possible by the combination of falling computer costs and regulatory opportunity. Because ATMs technically are not bank branches, they are not subject to branching restrictions. These facilities can be located some distance from the main bank and actually function as bank branches, accepting deposits, processing withdrawals, making loans through credit cards, and conducting various other transactions. Many ATMs are linked through electronic banking networks such as NYCE or CIRRUS.

After the mid-1970s, limits imposed by branching restrictions faded significantly before their eventual repeal—both within states (as noted above) and across states. In 1975, Maine became the first state to allow complete interstate banking. In 1982, Massachusetts and other New England states entered into a regional compact to permit growth of larger banking organizations in New England. Such regional arrangements in New England and elsewhere spawned *superregional banks*. Indeed, some superregional banks approach *money center banks* (large, established national banks in major cities) in size and profitability. By 1995, 49 states and the District of Columbia allowed some degree of interstate banking; 37 had legislated nationwide entry.

The **Riegle-Neal Interstate Banking and Branching Efficiency Act of 1994** provided a consistent nationwide standard for interstate expansion after September 1995. As of that time, states could permit interstate mergers within their own borders, and bank holding companies could begin acquiring banks in other states. As of July 1997, banks could begin merging with institutions in any state that has not declined to participate in interstate branching. The 1998 merger of NationsBank and Bank of America produced the first bank with branches on both coasts.

Bankers and bank analysts cheer the favorable climate for nationwide branching. First, interstate branching will permit many banks to create single institutions, instead of series of state-by-state affiliates, saving money through new efficiencies and reducing their regulatory burdens. Second, the shares of some regional banking groups will likely rise in response to newly permitted acquisitions. The 1990s witnessed a significant decline in the number of banks.[†] This decline was driven largely by consolidation, with bank failures playing a secondary role. From 1985 to 1992—a tough time for the U.S. banking industry—the number of banks fell by about 3000 (more than twice the number of failures that occurred during the same period). In the healthier period for the industry from 1992 to 2003, the number of U.S. commercial banks declined by about 3600, with fewer than 3% being accounted for by failures. Consolidation within and across regions has driven the decline in the number of banking firms. Many analysts predict that the changed regulatory climate will continue to reduce the number of banks.

Restrictions on the scope of bank activities. Before 1933, commercial banks were securities market financial institutions as well as depository institutions. In particular, some banks underwrote corporate securities, selling good-quality issues to the

[†] Allen Berger of the Federal Reserve Board, Anil Kashyap of the University of Chicago, and Joseph Scalise of the Federal Reserve Board estimated in 1995 that the number of independent U.S. banking firms would fall to between 3500 and 5000 by 2005. Allen N. Berger, Anil K. Kashyap, and Joseph M. Scalise, "The Transformation of the U.S. Banking Industry: What a Long, Strange Trip It's Been," *Brookings Papers on Economic Activity*, 2:55–218, 1995.

public and placing poor-quality issues in trust accounts for individuals or pensions in its care. As a result, banks earned investment banking fees for risky activities, the risk being borne in part by their depositors.†

The wave of bank failures during the 1930s and the public outcry over abusive banking practices led Congress to reduce conflicts of interest by limiting the scope of permissible activities for commercial banks. The Banking Act of 1933 (known as the Glass-Steagall Act) prohibited commercial banks from participating in underwriting corporate securities and broker-dealer activities, although banks were allowed to continue selling new issues of government securities (see Fig. 14.2). In addition, banks could hold only those debt securities that were approved by regulatory agencies. Thus the Glass-Steagall Act erected a wall between commercial banking and investment banking, forcing a wave of divestitures by financial institutions. Figure 14.3 illustrates how the wall has broken down over time. For example, J. P. Morgan, then a commercial bank, spun off Morgan Stanley, an investment bank, and First National Bank of Boston spun off First Boston Corporation.

The Glass-Steagall Act separated ownership of financial institutions and nonfinancial firms to limit the concentration of power—that is, to prevent financiers from being able to monopolize major industries and reward affiliates while starving their competitors' credit needs. Some policymakers justified their fear of such activity by pointing to J. P. Morgan and other financiers, who used their financial power to create

FIGURE 14.2

The Glass-Steagall Wall

The Glass-Steagall Act of 1933 sought to reduce conflicts of interest by creating a wall separating the permissible activities of commercial banking and investment banking.

†Economists have generally been skeptical about the conflict-of-interest argument for separating commercial and investment banking, as under Glass-Steagall. See, for example, the review in Randall Kroszner, "Rethinking Bank Regulation: A Review of the Historical Evidence," *Journal of Applied Corporate Finance*, 11:48–58, 1998.

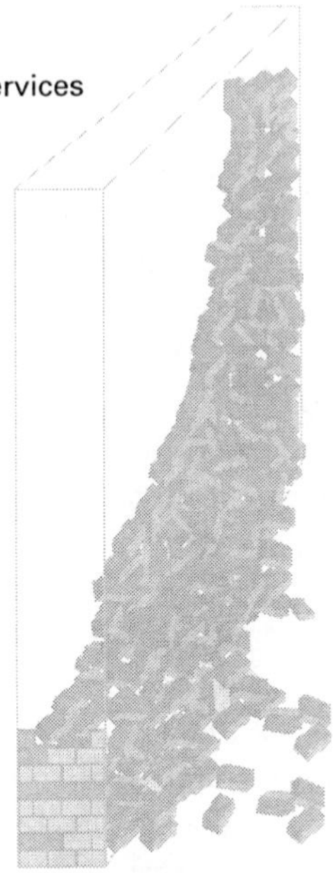

FIGURE 14.3

Breaking Down the Glass-Steagall Wall

Beginning in the 1970s, commercial banks and investment banks introduced innovations that allowed them to offer competing services. These innovations continue to steadily erode the wall created by the Glass-Steagall Act. Over time, this financial innovation has been ratified by changes in regulation, culminating in the Gramm-Leach-Bliley Financial Services Modernization Act of 1999.

monopolies in the late nineteenth and early twentieth centuries. However, such activities are much less likely today because of greater competition in finance and industry.

The debate over retaining these restrictions. In today's regulatory environment, many analysts believe that the fears of the early 1930s about abusive banking practices are unwarranted. They argue that the SEC and federal banking regulatory agencies—and banks' concern for their reputations—limit the potential for problems. In principle, the Glass-Steagall Act was designed to protect depositors of commercial banks from risky investment activities by the banks. In practice, however, it has protected the investment banking industry from competition, enabling it to earn higher profits than the commercial banking industry. As a result, borrowers pay more for issuing new securities than they would if competition from banks were allowed.

Opponents of breaking down the wall between commercial and investment banking point out that commercial banks have a cost advantage in obtaining funds because bank deposits are generally insured by the FDIC. Securities firms have no such insurance and pay a higher cost for funds, usually in the form of loans from banks themselves. Allowing commercial banks to participate in risky broker-dealer and investment banking activities exposes the FDIC—and, through it, taxpayers' funds—to additional risk. Some compromises are possible. They include charging risk-based premiums for bank deposit insurance or increasing net worth requirements for banks that engage in securities market activities.

Regulation still prohibits banking firms from entering the markets of nonfinancial firms. Allowing banks to participate in nonfinancial activities is called **universal banking.**

Although not permitted in the United States, full universal banking exists in other countries (notably Germany). Where banks own shares of companies to which they grant loans and may influence the management of those firms, advocates of universal banking argue that creating a role for commercial banks in corporate finance improves information gathering and monitoring, thereby reducing problems of adverse selection and moral hazard. If a bank holds shares in a nonfinancial firm and is represented on its board of directors, the information gap shrinks, and monitoring the firm's activities becomes easier and more efficient. One problem with integrating financial and commercial activities in the United States is the safety net afforded banks by deposit insurance; risky activities by banks could generate large taxpayer losses through deposit insurance. Further debate over whether expanding risk taking by banks is a good idea and whether U.S. banks are big enough to compete in the world banking is taking place after the passage of comprehensive banking industry reform legislation.

During the past two decades, commercial banks to a large degree have overcome the restrictions that kept them from offering investment services, as shown in Fig. 14.3. Because the role of banking in finance is to generate information, investment banking and raising long-term capital for corporations are logical extensions of banking. Hence banks have been major players in underwriting commercial paper. Because the Glass-Steagall Act was passed before international banking networks became firmly established, it does not regulate the overseas activities of banks. Therefore Eurobonds could always be written by U.S. banks. In June 1988, the Supreme Court allowed the Federal Reserve System to authorize bank affiliates to underwrite commercial paper, municipal revenue bonds, and mortgage-backed and consumer-debt-backed securities. Revenue from underwriting is restricted to 5% of the affiliate's gross revenue. In June 1989, the Fed gave some commercial banks limited power to underwrite corporate bonds, allowing them to compete with investment bankers. These activities were required to be conducted in separate subsidiaries within a bank holding company, with no access to insured bank deposits.

Banks also offered investment advice and brokerage services. In 1983, the Fed permitted bank holding companies to provide discount brokerage services. In 1987, the Office of the Comptroller of the Currency approved full-service brokerage powers for national banks. In 1987 and 1988, the Fed extended these powers to bank holding companies. Finally, in 1992, the Fed relaxed existing barriers between banks and their securities affiliates by lifting restrictions on the cross-marketing of banking and securities services. This action enables customers to deal with one institution whether discussing a bank loan or raising funds by selling commercial paper or issuing stock. Hence, from the banking side, the line between the banking and the securities industries is thin indeed.

By the early 1990s, banks had begun to compete with securities firms in setting up proprietary mutual funds, in which they act as investment advisors and in selling funds managed by other financial services companies. In addition to their significant role in managing money market mutual funds, banks participate increasingly in managing stock and bond mutual funds.

The clamor to eliminate Glass-Steagall restrictions was heard from the other direction as well. Securities firms, such as Fidelity and Merrill Lynch, have long been active sellers of money market mutual funds, which provide a close substitute for bank deposits. Merrill Lynch and others have purchased banks and turned them into nonbanks. Regulators halted this activity in 1987, but securities firms have continued to establish nonbanks by acquiring failing savings institutions.

The separation of finance from commerce also is breaking down. Nonfinancial firms already engage in significant financial sector activities. For example, General Motors, Ford, and Chrysler have long offered financial services by providing credit to customers to purchase automobiles, and each owns insurance companies. Through its GE Capital arm, GE has become a leader in financial services.

While financial innovation and regulatory response served to erode the effects of Glass-Steagall restrictions on banks, full-scale repeal came in 1999. Virtually every session of Congress during the 1990s witnessed a legislative attempt to tear down the Glass-Steagall wall between banking and other financial services. The megamerger of Citicorp and Travelers in 1998 brought the pressure to the boiling point, and Glass-Steagall abolition came soon thereafter. The landmark **Gramm-Leach-Bliley Financial Services Modernization Act of 1999** repealed Glass-Steagall by allowing ownership of banks by securities and insurance firms and allowed banks to participate in securities, insurance, and real estate activities.† The Gramm-Leach-Bliley Act pursues a "functional" approach to regulation: Federal and state banking regulators regulate banking activities; federal and state securities regulators regulate securities activities; and state insurance regulators regulate insurance activities.

Did the Gramm-Leach-Bliley Act go far enough in liberating banks from restrictions on the scope of activities? Perhaps not. On the one hand, the act made U.S. banking laws conform more closely to the banking laws of other industrial countries. On the other hand, it still allows fewer activities for banks and their subsidiaries than for financial holding companies, and generally separates banking and commerce. Most other countries also permit banks greater discretion in choosing the organizational form in which they conduct securities activities. Recent research suggests that countries with greater restrictions on banks' participation in securities activities and commerce have less efficient banks and a greater likelihood of a banking crisis, all else being equal.

In the aftermath of spectacular corporate financial scandals at Enron and other large U.S. firms in 2001 and 2002, some policymakers questioned whether the Gramm-Leach-Bliley Act's repeal of Glass-Steagall had gone too far. The fear is that some large financial institutions might have let their commercial bank lending standards slip in order to win lucrative investment banking business from Enron. Economists were generally skeptical of these concerns, favoring information disclosure instead and pointing to rapid market responses as financial institutions seek to avoid conflicts that hurt their reputation and brand value.

CHECKPOINT

Suppose that commercial banks are allowed to enter all investment banking and securities activities. What do you predict would happen to profit margins in underwriting services and to the salaries and bonuses of investment bankers? Full-scale entry by banks into investment banking and securities businesses likely would reduce the profitability of underwriting and related investment banking businesses, reducing investment bankers' compensation. ◆

†For excellent overviews of the act and its likely consequences, see James R. Barth, R. Dan Brumbaugh, Jr., and James A. Wilcox, "The Repeal of Glass-Steagall and the Advent of Broad Banking," *Journal of Economic Perspectives*, 14:191–204, 2000; and Edward G. Boehne, "Financial Modernization: Vastly Different or Fundamentally the Same?," Federal Reserve Bank of Philadelphia *Business Review*, 3–14, July–August 2000.

The Banking Industry in Other Countries

Outside the United States, banks perform different services in the economy, in large part because of differences in regulations. However, the worldwide trends of competition among financial intermediaries and financial deregulation are shaping the banking industry in other industrial economies in ways that are similar to those in the United States.

The role of banks in lowering costs of matching savers and borrowers suggests that several beneficial links can be developed between banking and industry: (1) financing growth opportunities in sectors with information problems, (2) making sure that managers of large-scale enterprises are working to maximize the long-run value of those firms, and (3) reducing costs of financial distress for firms that are having difficulty meeting their current obligations to banks and other creditors. These activities lower transactions and information costs.

The rapid growth of the Japanese and German economies since World War II can be traced in part to the close cooperation of banks and commercial and industrial firms. After World War II, many new firms and industries in Japan and Germany entered new markets, creating problems of asymmetric information and a demand for bank financing. The banks in those countries took advantage of the opportunities presented for intermediation. We now evaluate how Japanese and German banks filled industry's needs following World War II and then briefly examine the prospects for the integration of banking in Europe.

Japanese Banking

Government regulation in Japan of capital markets and financial institutions historically made it easier for firms to obtain financing from banks. In addition, the cooperative organizational structure of Japanese industry influences the role of Japanese banks.

Regulation. For much of the post–World War II period, government regulation kept Japanese firms from issuing securities internationally or issuing risky debt instruments in domestic financial markets. Hence firms turned to banks for financing, making Japanese nonfinancial corporations largely dependent on bank loans. Government authorities—in particular, the (then) Ministry for Trade and Industry (MITI) and the Ministry of Finance (MOF)—greatly influenced the channeling of funds to industries by banks. Short-term banking was the province of city and regional banks. Long-term credit banks were the only institutions allowed to make long-term loans (usually three- to five-year unsecured loans), but they could not make short-term loans. Finally, small mutual banks, known as *sogos*, were created to ensure that local small firms had access to credit.

Structure. The structure of Japanese industry differs significantly from that of U.S. industry. Many large Japanese firms have been affiliated with industrial groups, or *keiretsu*. The six major keiretsu—Mitsubishi, Mitsui, Sumitomo, Fuyo, Daiichi Kangyo, and Sanwa—were established during the 1950s, but some trace their origins to the prewar period. These large groups are diversified and vertically integrated. In the early 1980s, such group firms accounted for about half of Japanese sales in the natural resources, primary metals, industrial machinery, chemicals, and cement industries. Moreover, group firms traded much more with other group members than with nongroup firms.

CASE STUDY

Is Banking a Declining Industry?

As we noted in Chapter 12, banks lost ground to other intermediaries in the share of assets under their control since the 1980s. Indeed, the rapid growth of nonbank sources of credit and the increase in bank failures during the 1980s led many analysts to conclude that banking is a declining industry. Regulatory burdens and increasing competition have *changed* the business of banking over the past two decades. But is the banking industry in decline?

On the one hand, banks' assets made up less than 25% of all assets held by private financial institutions in 2003, down from 50% as recently as 1974. On the other hand, the ratio of bank assets to gross domestic product remained at about the same level in 1974 and 1994; these data do not suggest a decline in banking relative to the overall level of economic activity.

Another way to assess whether banking is a declining industry is to examine the trend in lending to nonfinancial businesses, the traditional activity of banks. Allen Berger of the Federal Reserve Board, Anil Kashyap of the University of Chicago, and Joseph Scalise of the Federal Reserve Board note that over the period from 1979 to 1995, U.S. banks' share of real lending to nonfarm, nonfinancial corporate business fell by one quarter from 20% to 15%, with most of the decline occurring in the 1989–1992 period.[†] However, more than offsetting this fall in U.S. bank lending over the period was an increase in lending to U.S. corporations by foreign banks. Hence, taken together, U.S. and foreign banks' share of corporate lending shows no significant decline.

Banks experienced strong competition in both their lending and deposit-taking activities in the 1980s and 1990s, owing to four key innovations. On the lending side, the growth of the commercial paper market has made it possible for large, high-quality corporate borrowers to raise more funds outside of bank loans. In addition, finance companies can tap the commercial paper market for funds, then lend the proceeds to businesses and households. The expansion of the junk bond market during the 1980s also enabled many lower-quality corporate borrowers to raise funds outside of bank loans. On the deposit side, banks face aggressive competition from money market mutual funds, which allow savers to write checks and pay higher rates of return than those typically offered on bank checking accounts.

Finally, *securitization*—the transformation of traditional illiquid financial assets (such as loans and residential mortgages) into marketable securities for trade on capital markets—has emerged because of declines in transactions costs and information costs. Banks can bundle portfolios of loans into standardized amounts to diversify risk and earn a return from servicing the loans (that is, collecting interest and principal payments from borrowers and paying them to lenders). Beginning with mortgages, securitized transactions cover certain leases, credit card receivables, and car loans. Securitization makes traditional banking with on-balance-sheet loans and capital to support them less attractive.

In addition, when markets dry up, even very large firms turn to banks seeking liquidity. In the second half of 1998, for example, when risk spreads increased and volume fell sharply in the commercial paper market as a result of adverse events in international securities markets, large firms drew down funds from backup bank lines of credit. When market liquidity became too expensive, banks came through as a reliable source of liquidity for nonfinancial companies.

Focusing just on traditional lending and deposit-taking activities probably understates banks' importance relative to nonbank competitors. The growth of off-balance-sheet activities—the biggest change in banks' business in the past two decades—has helped banks to unbundle information and monitoring services from lending activities. Likewise, banks' provision of derivative instruments, notably interest rate swaps, increases bank involvement in information and risk management.

How important are these new activities? Between 1980 and 2000, banks' noninterest income (that from off-balance-sheet activities) doubled. Hence, while banks' direct lending role (measured by interest income) declined relative to other financial institutions, their indirect role expanded.

[†] See Allen N. Berger, Anil K. Kashyap, and Joseph M. Scalise, "The Transformation of the U.S. Banking Industry: What a Long, Strange Trip It's Been," *Brookings Papers on Economic Activity*, 2:55–218, 1995.

John Boyd of the Federal Reserve Bank of Minneapolis and Mark Gertler of New York University constructed a revised measure of total bank assets that adjusted for off-balance-sheet activities.[†] Their adjustments remove about half of the unadjusted decline noted earlier in banks' share of total assets since 1974. Indeed, they note that, viewed from the period since the 1950s, banks' share of intermediated assets has been fairly stable. They concluded that banking—broadly defined—is not in decline.

Nevertheless, traditional banking—that is, making loans funded with demand and time deposits—is no longer so prominent in the financial system. The reason is that the relatively healthy profitability of banks since 1992 reflects the increased importance of profitable off-balance-sheet activities. Because the overall profitability of banks has not increased in recent years, the increase in earnings from off-balance-sheet activities must be matched by a decline in the profitability of traditional deposit-taking and lending activities of banks.

The factors behind the financial innovations described above are the culprits in the decline of traditional banking. Shifts in regulation, improvements in information technology, and the rise of alternative assets to be required and traded in capital markets have all reduced the competitive advantages of banking.

How will banks respond? To maintain the profit levels required to give shareholders a reasonable return on equity, banks must either change those lines of business or increase their willingness to take risk. In fact, banks have done a bit of both. As we saw in Chapter 13, banks have developed new off-balance-sheet lines of business. In addition, the overall risk of bank loan portfolios has increased, with a greater fraction of lending taking place in commercial real estate loans, telecommunications loans, and loans for corporate restructurings. Such loans are typically riskier than traditional business loans.

Is this quest for new lines of business healthy? From one standpoint, yes. Competition has transformed banks, enabling them to exploit their competitive advantage in reducing transactions costs and information costs without depending on less profitable lines of business. These changes are not without concerns, however. Increased risk taking in banking requires regulators—who must worry about the integrity of the financial system and costs of deposit insurance—to monitor banks' new activities.

The patterns we have noted for the United States are also occurring around the world, as deregulation, financial innovation, and the rise of securities markets have exposed banks to greater competitive pressure. Indeed, banks in Europe and Japan experienced low levels of returns on assets and returns on equity in the late 1990s and in the early 2000s, leading to consolidation and, in some cases, government bailouts.

The U.S. case also makes clear the importance of political and regulatory support for financial consolidation. To the extent that the American experience is instructive, Europe may receive similar benefits and costs from consolidation, although many analysts argued even in 2003 that European consolidation may be limited by structural differences among regulations, capital markets, and tax policies of European nations. Likewise, in Japan, with some exceptions, political forces have attempted to resist market pressures for consolidation.

[†]See John H. Boyd and Mark Gertler, "Are Banks Dead? Or, Are the Reports Greatly Exaggerated?" Federal Reserve Bank of Minneapolis *Quarterly Review*, Summer 1994.

Two organizing principles of group finance are of interest. First, the extensive trading relationships are reinforced by cross-shareholding within the group; that is, firms with close ties often hold large equity stakes in each other. Second, each group has a **main bank** that (1) owns some equity in the member firms, (2) is a primary source of credit for group firms, (3) monitors the activities of member firms, in some instances even placing key bank personnel in managerial positions in the firms, and (4) helps member firms recover from financial distress, taking the lead in organizing financial restructurings (other banks defer to the main bank's leadership in this respect). In sum, the main banks' relationships with borrowers are structured to reduce costs of adverse selection and moral hazard.

Benefits and costs. Economists have studied the value to savers and borrowers of this relationship between industry and banking. They found convincing evidence that group firms with access to main bank credit invest more and grow faster than their often credit-rationed, nongroup counterparts do. In addition, group firms that are in financial distress recover faster in terms of investment and sales growth than do similarly situated nongroup firms. This success is attributed to the role of main banks, which provide supplementary credit and write down the value of their loans without a bankruptcy proceeding. Because the main banks actively monitor the firms, the main banks have good information about the firms' prospects for long-term recovery and growth.

However, these relationships also have costs: Interest rates on loans are often higher than market interest rates on bonds, and banks may restrict some of the firms' activities. Owing to these costs, Japanese firms pressed for and received relief from the government in the form of the Foreign Exchange Law Reform of 1980. It allowed firms to issue bonds abroad without government permission. Then, in January 1983, deregulation permitted firms to issue bonds without collateral. Many firms subsequently went outside their main bank relationships to obtain funds from securities markets in Japan and abroad. The share of external funds raised by bank borrowing fell from 80% in 1980 to about 50% in 1985 and has continued to decline.

Web Site Suggestions:
http://www.fsa.go.jp/indexe.html
Presents information on Japanese banks and regulations.

Current status. Recent trends in Japanese banking resemble trends in the U.S. banking industry. As a consequence of financial deregulation, Japanese banks have lost many of their large-firm customers to financial markets. The large Japanese city banks—among the world's largest in terms of assets—earned low returns on assets relative to many large U.S. banks in the 1990s. In the mid- and late 1990s, many large Japanese banks were financially weak, owing to rising default rates and the collapsing stock market. Indeed, since 1998, the Japanese government has taken on a major commitment to shore up the troubled industry. Japanese banks' strategy in the 1990s was to move into the securities business while remaining close enough to Japanese industry to lend money and provide advice. Recently, more successful Japanese banks such as Shinsei are becoming more like their U.S. counterparts. In a law patterned after the Glass-Steagall Act, Japan officially separated commercial and investment banking. Nonetheless, Japanese banks have expanded into foreign securities operations. Japanese banks also consolidated assets, as with the merger of the Bank of Tokyo and Mitsubishi. In 2002 and 2003, the Financial Services Agency put forth new rules to reform lending standards and resolve Japan's large nonperforming loan problem.

German Banking

Germany is one of only a few countries that allow full universal banking; others are France, Luxembourg, and the Netherlands. (British-style universal banking, found in the United Kingdom, Canada, and now the United States, allows bank participation in securities, but significant bank holdings of common stocks are less common.) Recall that universal banking allows banks to carry out banking and many nonbanking activities within a single firm. In Germany, for example, Deutsche Bank owns a significant stake in Daimler-Benz, a large automobile manufacturer (now Daimler-Chrysler). German universal banking requires that bank participation in nonfinancial firms include direct voting rights for bank-owned shares. The significant reinforcement of proxy votes for shares held by the bank as custodian for its clients is also required.

Banking and industry developed together in Germany, with establishment of the first joint-stock bank in 1848. Initially, banks relied on their own capital to make long-term loans. Later, Deutsche Bank became the first major bank to seek deposits, although at that time, it invested deposits only in safe and liquid short-term loans to merchants. Large national banks emerged in the late nineteenth century. Because of the strong role of banks for most of this century, securities markets are less well developed in Germany than in the United Kingdom or the United States.

Benefits and costs. Many observers have concluded that the close alliance between banking and industry helped to accelerate industrialization and growth in post–World War II Germany. They contend that universal banking benefits German industry by extending to it the information-related strengths of commercial banking arrangements. However, other experts suggested potential problems of conflict of interest and unfair loan pricing. Recall that the fear of conflict of interest prompted the separation of commercial and investment banking by the Glass-Steagall Act in the United States. However, strict supervision, coupled with vigorous competition in financial and product markets, can counterbalance this problem. A second and more important problem regards the pricing of bank loans in Germany. Without aggressive competition from securities markets, banks may charge higher interest rates to firms than they could in the face of competition. A final significant reservation is that the relationship between industry and banks under universal banking might require a wider role for the new European Central Bank in a financial crisis: If deposits in financial institutions are insured to protect depositors from losses when banks fail, commercial or industrial firms that own financial institutions also may need to be covered by insurance.

Current status. Complementing the few very large banks in Germany—such as Deutsche Bank—are numerous smaller banks. Current developments in German banking resemble those in the United States, Japan, and elsewhere. Increasing volatility of interest rates and exchange rates has generated a trend toward securitization. In addition, investment banking is emerging as an important activity within commercial banks, and German banks are facing strong competition from other European banks and from U.S. banks. In 1998, Deutsche Bank acquired U.S.-based Bankers Trust.

Integration of European Banking

In the past, only very restricted bank branching across national borders has been allowed in Europe. The European Community (EC) began removing national barriers to trade in goods and financial markets in 1992. It is also gradually shifting to a banking industry that resembles interstate banking in the United States. The goal is a uniform charter for banking operations. Hence, as with relaxed U.S. branching restrictions, substantial bank consolidation is occurring. Indeed, the Second Banking Directive would have a long-run effect similar to that of financial modernization in the United States à la the Riegle-Neal and Gramm-Leach-Bliley Acts.

What predictions can we make as to the effect of European integration on the banking industry? Integration should promote risk sharing and lead to greater diversification. In addition, activities of banks, securities firms, and insurance firms are likely to become more interconnected. In Europe, as in the United States, banks have successfully ventured into broader securities and investment activities. As capital markets develop further in Europe, the information-gathering and monitoring skills of banks, as well as their branch networks, make them formidable competitors in Europe's increasingly important securities and insurance markets. As in the United States, European financial regulators must monitor banks closely as banking markets become more competitive.

KEY TERMS AND CONCEPTS

- Automated teller machines (ATMs)
- Bank holding companies
- Bank run
- Banking panics
- Branching restrictions
- Contagion
- Demand deposit
- Dual banking system
  - National banks
  - State banks
- Federal deposit insurance
- Federal Reserve System
- Gramm-Leach-Bliley Financial Services Modernization Act of 1999
- Lender of last resort
- Main bank
- Nonbank banks
- Nonbank offices
- Riegle-Neal Interstate Banking and Branching Efficiency Act of 1994
- Universal banking

SUMMARY

1. The United States has a dual banking system: Commercial banks are chartered and examined both by the federal government and by states. Regulatory agencies that are responsible for commercial bank regulation include the Federal Deposit Insurance Corporation (FDIC), the Office of the Comptroller of the Currency, the Federal Reserve System, and state banking authorities. Savings and loan associations generally are insured by the FDIC and regulated by the Office of Thrift Supervision. Mutual savings banks are also insured by the FDIC but regulated by state authorities. Credit unions generally are insured by the National Credit Union Share Insurance Fund and regulated by the National Credit Union Administration.
2. Loss of confidence by depositors in a bank can lead to a bank run, in which the bank is forced to liquidate its assets to pay depositors and close its doors. Because of private information in banking, bank runs can cause solvent banks as well as insolvent banks to fail. If sound banks fail after a run, the economy suffers because banks lose their effectiveness as financial intermediaries.
3. To promote stability, government has intervened in the banking industry by (a) creating a lender of last resort, (b) introducing federal deposit insurance, and (c) restricting permissible bank activities.
4. Federal deposit insurance was introduced in the United States in the 1930s to guarantee bank deposits and guard against bank runs. Until the early 1980s, it was very successful in reducing bank failures. In response to the greater number of bank failures in the 1980s and early 1990s, the FDIC and other regulatory agencies now require banks to hold greater minimum amounts of net worth, or equity capital, than before and to refrain from participation in risky activities.
5. Because of the McFadden Act, which prohibits branching across state lines, and state branching restrictions, the United States has traditionally had a large number of relatively small commercial banks. In recent years, banks have circumvented branching restrictions by forming bank holding companies, creating nonbank offices and nonbank banks, and introducing automated teller machines. In addition, states have relaxed their branching restrictions, and federal legislation has been passed to permit nationwide banking.
6. The Glass-Steagall Act separated commercial banking from investment banking and brokerage businesses. The act's restrictions on banks' activities were circumvented by bank holding companies that can now underwrite many types of securities and engage in brokerage activities. Conversely, securities firms competed with banks for deposits. The Glass-Steagall Act was finally repealed by the Gramm-Leach-Bliley Financial Services Modernization Act of 1999. Although some nonfinancial firms have entered the financial services industry, the separation of banking and commerce in the United States remains relatively strong.

MOVING FROM THEORY TO PRACTICE . . .

THE ECONOMIST JULY 26, 2003

Guiding the Pack

In the past 20 years or so, banking crises and financial instability have come around with depressing frequency and at considerable cost. According to estimates by the International Monetary Fund, more than a dozen banking crises in the past 15 years have cost the countries afflicted 10% or more of their GDP. Latin America seems to suffer about once a decade. The miracle economies of East Asia were caught in the late 1990s. Not even rich countries are immune, as the Japanese have come to know only too well.

The blame is often—and rightly—laid on macroeconomic policy: an unsustainable exchange rate, poor budgetary control and so forth. Yet bank regulators, too, should do more to ward off crises in the banking system. If they did their job differently, might financial systems and economies be more stable? In a recent paper[†] Claudio Borio, an economist at the Bank for International Settlements (BIS), argues that they might. Bank regulation, he says, has two basic components. First, there is what he calls a "microprudential" element. This concentrates on avoiding problems at individual banks, and at protecting depositors when things go wrong. The second, "macroprudential" component is concerned with stopping the banking system as a whole getting into trouble, and thus with limiting the damage to the economy. . . .

One reason for shifting to a more macro footing is the huge economic costs of systemic crises. Although deposit insurance can protect people's savings, it cannot insulate them from the possibly far greater costs of widespread financial distress, such as unemployment. A second reason is that deposit insurance (a) might make bank failures and financial distress more likely, by fostering moral hazard. Knowing that their savings are safe in almost any event, depositors are less likely to monitor how wisely bankers use their money. If bankers believe that regulators will not let their institutions collapse, they may not worry enough about the riskiness of their assets.

A third reason stems from the way in which financial crises happen. One common view is that a crisis starts when a single bank collapses. Trouble then spreads to other banks: maybe those that have lent to it are hit, or maybe a general panic takes hold. . . . But another way that systemic crises start is when a country's banks are exposed to the same common risks.  For example, suppose that they have borrowed a lot of dollars, but most of their loans are to local companies, in local currency. If the dollar appreciates, all the banks will be in a similar pickle. If this scenario is closer to reality, regulators ought to worry more about system-wide risks and less about the balance sheets of individual banks. . . .

New rules on bank capital, known as Basel II, are due to come into force in 2007. But there is a risk that, in one respect at least, Basel II will make the system less, not more stable. As now, the emphasis will remain on individual banks, not whole systems; and regulators will put more weight on credit ratings in assessing the sturdiness of banks. The trouble is that ratings, along with other measures of the riskiness of banks, such as credit spreads, are cyclical:  they look best at the top of a boom, when things are about to turn bad, and worst at the bottom of a slump, when business is about to pick up. . . .

[†] "Towards a Macroprudential Framework for Financial Supervision and Regulation," BIS Working Papers, no. 128, February 2003: http://www.bis.org/publ/work128.htm

ANALYZING THE NEWS ...

The costs of systemic risk in banking crises has led to significant regulation of banks and other financial institutions in most economies. U.S. experience in the 1930s and more recent banking crises in emerging economies and in Japan have been costly. Disruptions of bank intermediation can disrupt credit flows, leading to declines in consumption, investment, and overall economic activity.

Bank regulation in the United States and other major economies has focused on ways to maintain the liquidity and solvency of individual banking firms—capital requirements to guard against moral hazard in banks, for example. More recently, capital requirements in the Basel I and Basel II frameworks have capital requirements on the riskiness of banks' assets and activities. Deposit insurance protects depositors (within limits), should a bank fail anyway.

Given the importance of macroeconomic shocks in recent high-profile episodes of banking crises in emerging economies, some economists have speculated that we need to think more carefully about bank regulation.

a Deposit insurance raises a moral hazard problem of its own, as insured depositors have no incentive to monitor banks in which their funds are depositors. Such monitoring is done mainly by regulators, who must keep up with the banks to measure how risky their assets and off-balance-sheet activities are.

b To the extent that banking crises are caused by macroeconomic shocks—a falling price level or currency valuation changing the credit risk of portfolios—the problem is less the bank run problem envisioned by current regulation and more one of how to guard against systemwide failures. In the example given, a depreciation in the dollar value of local currency increases the credit risk of all banks' borrowers.

c Tightening capital requirements during a boom would put a check on credit expansion against assets whose higher values might nonetheless be risky. Loosening capital requirements during a bust might promote credit availability when collateral values and internal funds are low. Realistically, regulators could start by measuring risks over periods of time longer than a year (current practice) and by raising capital requirements on very large institutions making disproportionately large contributions to systemwide risk.

For further thought...

Suppose that in an emerging market economy, most nonbank borrowing is in dollars. How might regulators protect the banking industry from the effects of sudden changes in the exchange rate between the local currency and the dollar?

Source: Excerpted from "Guiding the Pack," *The Economist*, July 26, 2003.

7. The banking industry differs by country in response to differences in bank regulation. Banks in Japan and Germany are permitted to have closer relationships with borrowers than are U.S. banks; some analysts argue that these relationships contributed to the rapid growth of investment and output in these countries since World War II. Nonetheless, as domestic financial systems become more integrated internationally, banking industries in various countries appear to be becoming more similar.

REVIEW QUESTIONS

1. What is the dual banking system? Why does it persist?
2. What is the main function of federal deposit insurance?
3. Why does the United States have so many banks?
4. What is meant by contagion? What problems does it pose for the stability of the banking system?
5. If bank runs closed only insolvent banks, should anyone care? Why might bank runs create a need for regulation?
6. How did the establishment of the Federal Reserve System reduce the chance of banking panics?
7. What are the advantages and disadvantages of the payoff method compared to the purchase-and-assumption method of dealing with failed banks?
8. How do risk-based capital requirements work?
9. Which government regulations restrict bank competition? How did they come about? Are they likely to continue into the future?
10. What are the costs to banks of geographic restrictions on bank competition? To savers? To borrowers? In a banking system with banks of different sizes, which banks stand to gain from geographic restrictions? To lose?
11. How have banks tried to get around restrictions on branching? What was the regulatory response to these attempts?
12. What is the difference between a nonbank office and a nonbank bank?
13. Which law forced the separation of commercial banking from investment banking in the United States? Why was it enacted? Is it still in force? Explain.
14. How does the U.S. experience of separating commerce from banking compare to that of countries having universal banking?
15. What can banks do to link banking and industry more beneficially?
16. How does universal banking work in Germany? What concerns might taxpayers have if universal banking were tried in the United States and banks were still covered by FDIC insurance?

ANALYTICAL PROBLEMS

17. How did private bankers attempt to deal with the problems of bank runs and contagion during the National Banking Period? Under which circumstances were these private attempts to deal with these problems likely to be successful and under which circumstances were they likely to be unsuccessful?
18. Evaluate this statement: "The recent wave of bank mergers has eliminated many smaller banks. This is bad news for small businesses, because they receive most of their loans from small banks."
19. Why was the Fed concerned about the possible failure of Long-Term Capital Management? What negative consequences may result from the Fed's actions in this situation?
20. Evaluate the following statement: The United States has about 8900 banks, whereas Canada has only a few, so the U.S. banking industry must be more competitive.
21. The ceiling on the size of an account covered by federal deposit insurance is $100,000. If you heard that your bank might be in trouble, what would you do if you had $10,000 in the bank? If you had $200,000 in the bank? Does deposit insurance fulfill its role in reducing failures if a bank has many large depositors? Why or why not?
22. Suppose that banks, preparing for increased international competition, are trying to improve their capital by making fewer loans, buying more securities, and holding more cash. Suddenly, bank funding for several large (and solvent) corporations is in jeopardy. What would you do if you were the Chairman of the Federal Reserve Board?

ANALYTICAL PROBLEMS

23. By the 1980s, the level of bank net worth (equity capital) relative to bank assets had declined significantly from pre-1934 levels. All other things being equal, could the introduction of federal deposit insurance in 1934 account for this change? Explain.

24. Evaluate the following statement: A banking system with deposit insurance needs more supervision from third-party examiners than does a banking system without guarantees for depositors.

DATA QUESTIONS

25. Find the most recent issue of the *World Almanac* in your library and locate historical data on the number of U.S. bank failures each year. In the four decades following the introduction of federal deposit insurance (by the Banking Act of 1933), what happened to the number of bank failures relative to the number in the decade before the introduction of deposit insurance? On the basis of this information, can you conclude that deposit insurance made financial intermediaries healthier? Explain.

26. The Federal Deposit Insurance Corp. is charged with guaranteeing the value of savers' deposits. What is the total amount of assets that the FDIC insures? To locate this information, look at the historical trends data on the FDIC's Web site, at http://www.fdic.gov/bank/statistical/stats/index.html. Is there a relationship between the number of institutions insured, the amount of assets, and insurance fund balance? Do you think the number of failures is compatible with a competitive industry? Explain.

27. Like banks and savings and loans, credit unions have experienced increased competitive pressures in recent years. Consider the information found at the National Credit Union Association's Web site at http://www.ncua.gov. From the "Credit Union Data" link, click on "Statistics for FICUs" (Federally Insured Credit Unions) and then look at the most recent year-end statistics report. Calculate the number of credit unions to asset ratios for the past five years. How has this industry changed during this time period?

28. The Financial Services Agency is the official deposit insurance provider for Japanese banks. Compare the status of the Japanese banking industry with that of the U.S. banking industry (based on your findings from question 25 above). Go to the FSA's Web site at http://www.fsa.go.jp/indexe.html and click on the "References" link. Click on "Recent Developments in the Japanese Financial Sector," and then look at the "Existing NPLs and Ratio of NPLs to Total Loans." Do the U.S. and Japanese banking industries appear to perform similarly during the time period reported? Explain.

CHAPTER 19

Organization of Central Banks

Will he or won't he? In early 2003, analysts speculated about whether President George W. Bush would nominate Alan Greenspan for a fifth term as Chairman of the Board of Governors of the Federal Reserve System, the "CEO" of the U.S. central bank. Financial markets were worried that the failure to reappoint Greenspan would deprive the central bank of the services of a well-respected leader. President Bush then signaled his early support for Greenspan's reappointment, though buzz over who would be the next chairman continued. In 2003, a similar tug-of-war took place around the world, as Chairman Greenspan, Bank of Japan Governor Fukuí, and European Central Bank President Duisenberg (and soon-to-be President Trichet) struggled to balance monetary policy objectives and political pressures.

Why should the choice of a central bank chairman be the subject of political controversy and an event that can trouble financial markets? You know from earlier chapters that the Fed plays an active role in the money supply process. But in learning about the money supply process, we viewed the Fed as a "black box." That is, we observed the results of the Fed's actions in managing the monetary base, setting reserve requirements, and making discount loans, but we didn't look inside the Fed to see *why* those decisions were made and implemented. That is our mission in this chapter and the next two chapters. In this chapter, we begin our study of the way the Fed conducts monetary policy by looking at the structure of the Fed. The Federal Reserve chairman has often been called the second most important person in the nation. The reason is that the Fed is in control of monetary policy a set of decisions that affect the well-being of individuals and firms during economic downturns and upturns. It is little wonder, then, that speculation on Greenspan's appointment caused some jitters on Wall Street.

Our specific objectives in this chapter are to learn about the Fed's organization and structure and its role as an economic policymaking body. We also describe the political arena in which the Fed operates and the debate over the independence of the central bank. We then examine the organization and independence of central banks outside the United States, including the European Central Bank.

Power Sharing in the Federal Reserve System

Few countries have as complex a structure for their central bank as the United States has in its Federal Reserve System. The Fed's organization was shaped by the same political struggle that gave the United States a fragmented banking system: advocates of strong economic institutions versus those who feared large, powerful economic interests. To understand why the Fed is organized as it is, we need to look back in history at the nation's earlier attempts to create a central bank.

Creation of the System

Not long after the United States won its independence, Treasury Secretary Alexander Hamilton organized the Bank of the United States, which was meant to function as a central bank but had both government and private shareholders. Distrust of the Bank of the United States by Southern and Western agrarian and small-business interests resulted in the bank's demise in 1811. In 1816, the Second Bank of the United States was formed, but populist President Andrew Jackson did not renew its national charter when it expired in 1836. (The bank survived for a time as a state-chartered bank in Pennsylvania.)

Abolition of the Second Bank of the United States left the nation without an official lender of last resort for banks. The void was filled by private institutions such as the New York Clearing House, but severe nationwide financial panics in 1873, 1884, 1893, and 1907—and accompanying economic downturns—raised fears in Congress that the U.S. financial system was unstable. After the 1907 panic and economic recession, Congress considered options for government intervention. Many officials worried that bankers such as New York financier J. P. Morgan, who had served as a de facto lender of last resort, would be unable to manage future crises. Congress appointed a National Monetary Commission to begin formal studies leading to the design of a central bank. With the support of President Woodrow Wilson, the Federal Reserve Act became law in 1913.

The Federal Reserve Act of 1913 created a central bank for the United States, the **Federal Reserve System.** The act provided for checks and balances that were designed to diffuse economic power in three ways: among bankers and business interests, among states and regions, and between government and the private sector. The act and subsequent legislation created four groups within the system, each empowered in theory to perform separate duties: the Federal Reserve banks, member banks, the Board of Governors, and the Federal Open Market Committee (FOMC). The responsibilities that were assigned to each reflected the original intent of the 1913 act to give the central bank control over the amount of currency outstanding and the volume of discount loans to member banks (the lender-of-last-resort function). In theory, the President and Congress didn't envision that the Fed would control monetary policy, broadly defined. In practice, however, over time, the Fed has assumed the lead role in making monetary policy. In the rest of this section, we describe the roles of the principal groups within the Federal Reserve System in conducting open market operations, setting reserve requirements, and making discount loans.

Federal Reserve Banks

The Federal Reserve Act divided the United States into 12 Federal Reserve districts, each of which has a **Federal Reserve bank** in one city (and, in most cases, additional branches in other cities in the district) to conduct discount lending. Figure 19.1 shows the Federal Reserve districts and locations of the Federal Reserve banks. The map may appear strange at first glance: No state (not even California or New York) is a single Federal Reserve district. Some states are split by district boundaries, and economically dissimilar states are grouped in the same district. Most Federal Reserve districts contain a mixture of urban and rural areas, as well as manufacturing, agriculture, and service business interests. This arrangement is intentional, to prevent any one interest group or one state from obtaining preferential treatment from the district Federal Reserve bank. Nor can a district easily have its way at the expense of other districts, owing to supervision by the Board of Governors and the Federal Open Market Committee. If one district is suffering from a recession, it cannot singlehandedly alter Fed money and credit policies to meet its needs. Some cities (New York, Chicago, and San Francisco) clearly were population centers in 1914 and so were chosen as locations for Federal Reserve banks. Other cities were chosen because of political pressure during

Web Site Suggestions:
http://www.federalreserve.gov/otherfrb.htm
Offers contact numbers and e-links to the reserve banks.

FIGURE 19.1

Federal Reserve Districts and Banks

The division of the 50 states into 12 Federal Reserve districts was designed so that each district contained a mixture of urban and rural areas and manufacturing, agriculture, and service business interests.

Source: Federal Reserve Bulletin, December 2000, p. A74.

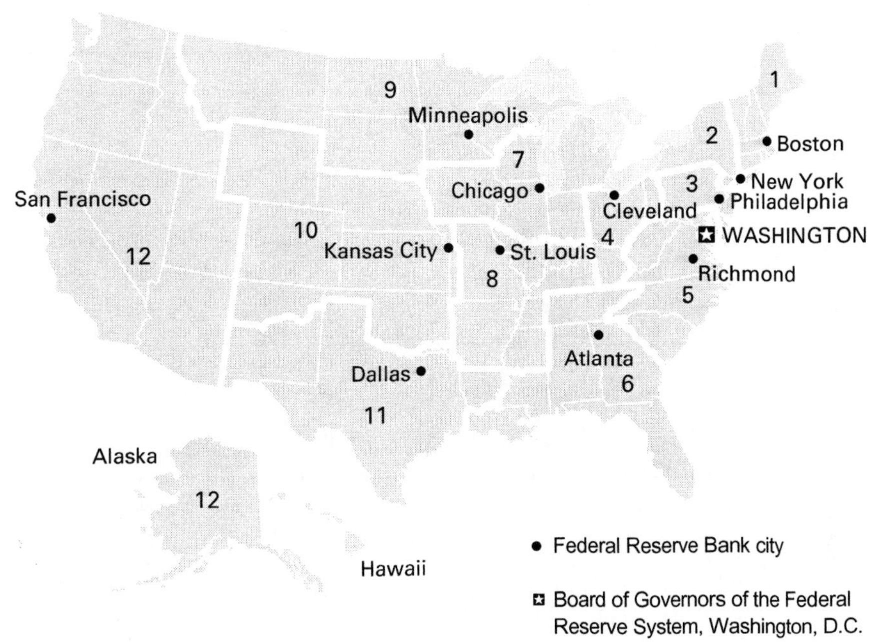

the debate over the Federal Reserve Act. (For example, Richmond, Virginia, was the home of Carter Glass, one of the legislative architects of the Federal Reserve System.)

Who owns the Federal Reserve banks? In principle, the private commercial banks in each district that are members of the Federal Reserve System own the district bank. In fact, each Federal Reserve bank is a private–government joint venture. Member banks receive dividends (limited to 6%) on the shares of stock they own in the district bank.

A guiding principle of the 1913 Federal Reserve Act was that one constituency (for example, finance, industry, commerce, or agriculture) would not be able to exploit the central bank's economic power at the expense of another constituency. Therefore Congress restricted the composition of the boards of directors of the Federal Reserve banks. The directors represent the interests of three groups: banks, businesses, and the general public. Member banks elect three bankers (*Class A directors*) and three leaders in industry, commerce, and agriculture (*Class B directors*). The Fed's Board of Governors appoints three public interest directors (*Class C directors*). Subject to the Board's approval, the nine directors of a Federal Reserve bank elect the president of that bank.

The 12 Federal Reserve banks carry out duties related to the Fed's roles in the payments system, monetary control, and financial regulation. Specifically, the district banks

- manage check clearing in the payments system;
- manage currency in circulation by issuing new Federal Reserve Notes and withdrawing damaged notes from circulation;
- conduct discount lending by making and administering discount loans to banks within the district;
- perform supervisory and regulatory functions such as examining state member banks and evaluating merger applications; and

- provide services to businesses by collecting and making available data on district business activities and by publishing articles on monetary and banking topics written by professional economists employed by the banks.

The Federal Reserve district banks engage in monetary policy both directly (through discount lending) and indirectly (through membership in Federal Reserve committees). In theory, Federal Reserve banks establish the discount rate and determine the amounts that individual (member and nonmember) banks are allowed to borrow.† The district banks indirectly influence policy through their representatives on the Federal Open Market Committee, which sets guidelines for open market operations (purchases and sales of securities by the Fed to affect the monetary base), and the Federal Advisory Council, a consultative body composed of district bankers.

Member Banks

The Federal Reserve Act required all national banks to become **member banks** of the Federal Reserve System. State banks may elect to become members; currently, only about one in seven state banks is a member. About one-third of all banks in the United States now belong to the Federal Reserve System. These member banks hold a substantial majority of all bank deposits.

Historically, one reason for the low voluntary membership rate was the cost. The Fed's reserve requirements compel banks to keep part of their deposits as idle funds, effectively imposing a tax on bank intermediation. In contrast, when banks are chartered by states rather than the federal government, their reserves can earn interest. As nominal interest rates rose during the 1960s and 1970s, the opportunity cost of Fed membership increased, and fewer state banks elected to become or remain members.

During the 1970s, the Fed argued that the so-called reserve tax on member banks placed them at a competitive disadvantage relative to nonmember banks. It claimed that declining bank membership eroded its ability to influence the money supply and urged Congress to compel all commercial banks to join the Federal Reserve System. Although Congress has not yet legislated such a requirement, the Depository Institutions Deregulation and Monetary Control Act (DIDMCA) of 1980 required that all banks (by 1987) maintain reserve deposits with the Fed on the same terms. This legislation gave member and nonmember banks equivalent access to discount loans and to payments system (check-clearing) services. It effectively blurred the distinction between member and nonmember banks and halted the decline in Fed membership. Today, about 3000 banks are Federal Reserve System members.

CHECKPOINT

Suppose that City National Bank pays a 7% annual interest rate on checkable deposits, subject to a reserve requirement of 10%. What is City National's effective cost of funds? Against \$100 of deposits, City National must hold \$10 in reserves (in vault cash or deposits with the Fed), leaving \$90 to invest. The bank must pay depositors (0.07)(\$100) = \$7 to obtain \$90 in funds to invest in loans or securities, so its effective cost of funds is not 7%, but 7/90 = 7.8%. Thus reserve requirements impose a tax on bank intermediation, raising City National's cost of funds from 7% to 7.8%. ♦

†In practice, the discount rate is reviewed and approved for each Federal Reserve district by the Board of Governors in Washington, D.C.

Board of Governors

The **Board of Governors** is headquartered in Washington, D.C. Its seven members are appointed by the President of the United States and confirmed by the U.S. Senate. To provide for central bank independence, the terms of board members were set so that one U.S. President generally cannot appoint a full Board of Governors. Governors serve a nonrenewable term of 14 years; their terms are staggered so that one term expires every other January.† Geographical restrictions ensure that no one Federal Reserve district is overrepresented.

Currently, many board members are professional economists from business, government, or academia. Chairmen of the Board of Governors since World War II have come from various backgrounds, including Wall Street (William McChesney Martin), academia (Arthur Burns), business (G. William Miller), public service (Paul Volcker), and economic forecasting (Alan Greenspan). The chairman serves a four-year term and may be reappointed or serve out the balance of a 14-year member's term.

The Board of Governors administers monetary policy to influence the nation's money supply through open market operations, reserve requirements, and discount lending. Since 1935, it has had the authority to determine reserve requirements within limits set by Congress. The Board of Governors also effectively sets the discount rate (which is in principle established by the Federal Reserve banks) through its review and determination procedure. It holds seven of the 12 seats on the Federal Open Market Committee and therefore influences the setting of guidelines for open market operations. In addition to its formal responsibilities relating to monetary control, it informally influences national and international economic policy decisions. The chairman of the Board of Governors advises the President and testifies before Congress on economic matters.

The Board of Governors has certain responsibilities relating to financial regulation. Before the elimination of Regulation Q in 1986, the board administered interest rate regulations. It also sets *margin requirements*, or the proportion of the purchase price of securities that an investor must pay in cash rather than buying on credit. In addition, it determines permissible activities for bank holding companies and approves bank mergers. Finally, it exercises certain administrative controls over individual Federal Reserve banks, reviewing their budgets and setting the salaries of their presidents and officers.

Federal Open Market Committee

Web Site Suggestions: http://www.federalreserve.gov/fomc Describes the FOMC, and its members and statements.

The 12-member **Federal Open Market Committee (FOMC)** gives direction to the Fed's open market operations. Members of the FOMC are the chairman of the Board of Governors, the other Fed governors, the president of the Federal Reserve Bank of New York, and the presidents of four of the other 11 Federal Reserve Banks (who serve on a rotating basis). Only five Federal Reserve bank presidents are voting members of the FOMC, but all 12 attend meetings and participate in discussions. The committee meets eight times each year.

The Fed influences the monetary base primarily through open market operations. Therefore, in practice, the FOMC is the centerpiece of Fed policymaking. Prior to the meeting, the FOMC members receive a national economic forecast for the next two years prepared by the Board staff in the "green book." The public "beige book"

†Technically, a governor could resign before the term expired and then be reappointed, thereby lengthening the term. Since 1970, this practice has been rare.

prepared by reserve banks is also available, as is the "blue book" with projections for monetary aggregates from the Board staff. The FOMC doesn't literally buy or sell securities for the Fed's account. Instead, it summarizes its views in a public statement of the *balance of risks* (between higher inflation or a weaker economy) and a directive issued to the Fed's trading desk at the Federal Reserve Bank of New York. There, the manager for domestic open market operations communicates each day with members of the FOMC (and their staffs) about execution of the directive.

Power and Authority Within the Fed

Because Congress configured the Federal Reserve System with many formal checks and balances to ensure that no one group could effectively control it, central (or national) control of the system was virtually nonexistent during the Fed's first 20 years. After the severe banking crisis of the early 1930s, many analysts concluded that the decentralized district bank system could not adequately respond to national economic and financial disturbances. The Banking Acts of 1933 and 1935 gave the Board of Governors authority to set reserve requirements and the FOMC the authority to direct open market operations. The Banking Act of 1935 also centralized the Fed's participation in the money supply process, giving the Board of Governors a majority (seven of 12) of seats on the FOMC and thereby great influence in implementing monetary policy.

The Board of Governors and the FOMC exert most of the Fed's formal influence on monetary policy. However, many Fed watchers believe that the informal authority of the chairman, the staff of the Board, and the FOMC predominates. In other words, the informal power structure within the Fed may be more concentrated and influential than the formal power structure. Because the Federal Reserve Bank of New York always occupies a seat on the FOMC, the president of that bank also can be quite influential. Figure 19.2 shows the organizational and power-sharing arrangements within the Fed, both in theory and in practice.

Member banks, the nominal owners of Federal Reserve banks, have little actual influence within the system. The distinction between *ownership* and *control* within the Federal Reserve System is clear. Member banks own shares of stock in the Federal Reserve banks, but shareholding confers none of the rights that are typically granted to shareholders of private corporations. Member banks receive at most a 6% annual dividend, regardless of the Fed's earnings, and so do not have the residual claim that is normally granted to equity. Moreover, member banks have virtually no control over how their stakes in the system are used because the Board of Governors in Washington formulates policy directives. Although member banks elect the six Class A and Class B directors, there is generally only one candidate per position, whom the Federal Reserve bank or Board of Governors suggests.

Although there is no direct evidence as to who actually holds power in the Fed, the impressions of experienced insiders are revealing. On the basis of his personal experience as a Fed official, economist Sherman Maisel estimated the relative influence of groups within the Fed in setting monetary policy: the chairman of the Board of Governors, 45%; the staff of the Board and the FOMC, 25%; and other governors and the Federal Reserve banks, not particularly powerful.[†] Those impressions were recorded in the 1970s, but current actions support them. Some board members and district bank presidents on the FOMC may challenge the chairman's agenda, but the chairman's influence still dominates.

[†]Sherman J. Maisel, *Managing the Dollar.* New York: W. W. Norton, 1973.

FIGURE 19.2 Organization and Authority of the Federal Reserve System

The Federal Reserve Act of 1913 established the Federal Reserve System but incorporated a series of checks and balances into the system. Part (a) shows that in theory, its economic power is diffuse. Part (b) shows that informal power within the Fed is more concentrated in the hands of the chairman of the Board of Governors than the formal structure suggests.

7-Member Board of Governors

Appointed by the President and confirmed by the Senate. The key role of the board is to administer monetary policy.

- Holds seven of twelve seats on the FOMC.
- Sets reserve and margin requirements.
- Reviews discount rate set by FRBs.

Federal Open Market Committee (FOMC)

The twelve members consist of five FRB presidents, including the president of the FRB New York, and the seven governors; their key role is to direct the Fed's open market operations.

- Issues policy directives to the Fed's trading desk at the FRB New York.

12 Federal Reserve Banks (FRB)

The nine directors are evenly split between business, banking, and public interest backgrounds. The banks' key role is performing supervisory and regulatory functions.

- Hold five of twelve voting seats on the FOMC.
- "Establish" the discount rate and decide which banks can obtain discount loans.
- Manage currency in circulation by issuing new FR notes and collecting damaged notes.

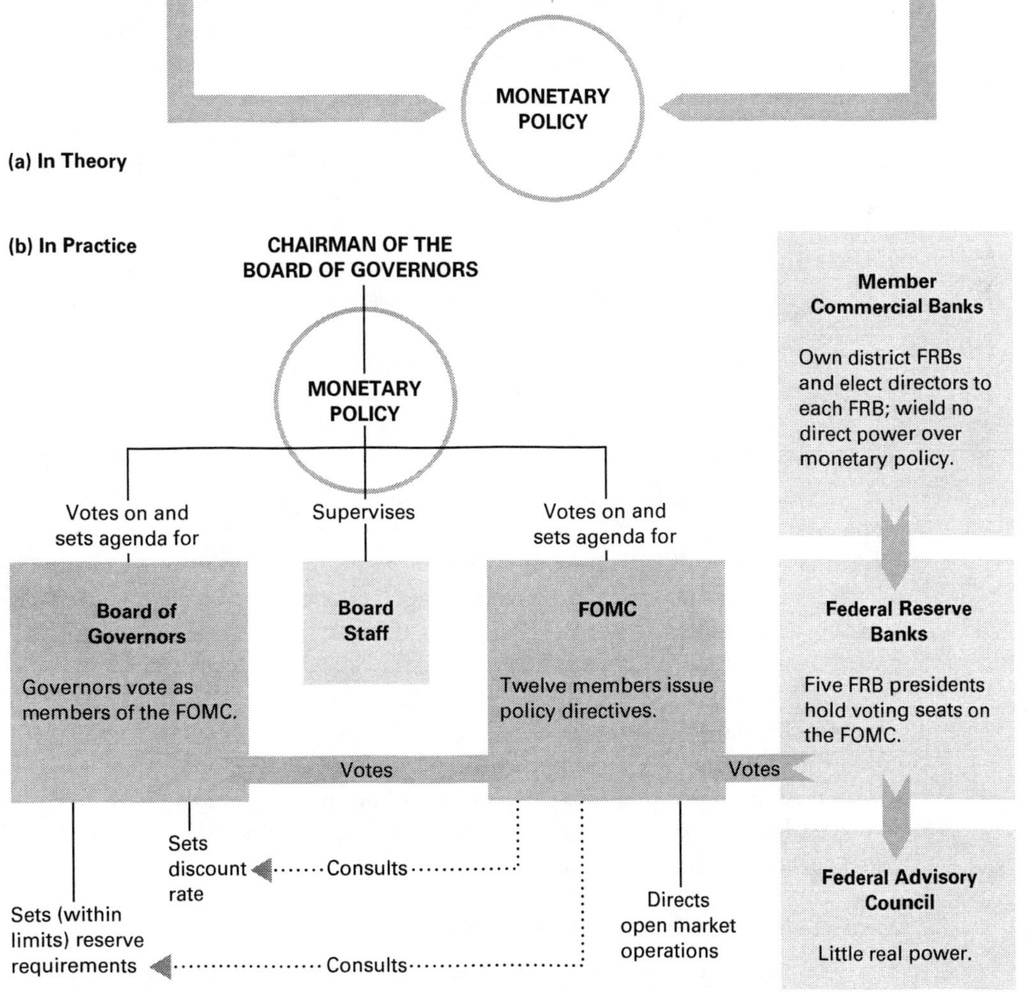

How the Fed Operates

The government created the Fed to manage the banking system and the money supply. Lacking a constitutional mandate, the Fed operates in a political arena, and it is subject to pressure by legislators and officials. The central bank also exerts power in economic policymaking because of its role in the money supply process. In this section we describe how the Fed operates in the political environment, and we discuss the debate over the independence of the central bank.

Handling External Pressure

Congress intended the Federal Reserve System generally to operate independently of external pressures (for example, from the President, Congress, the banking industry, or business groups). Board members are appointed for long, nonrenewable terms of office, reducing any one President's influence on the Board's composition and the temptation for governors to take actions merely to please the President and Congress.

The Fed's financial independence allows it to combat external pressure. Generally, federal agencies are subject to the annual appropriations process, during which Congress scrutinizes budgetary requests, authorizes funds, and then appropriates the funds. Not only is the Fed exempt from this process, but it is also a profitable organization, contributing funds to the Treasury rather than receiving funds from it. Most of the Fed's earnings come from interest on the securities it holds; smaller amounts come from interest on discount loans and fees that are received from financial institutions for check-clearing and other services. In recent years, the Fed's net income has exceeded $25 billion annually—substantial profits when compared even to the largest U.S. corporations.

Despite the attempt to give the Fed independence, it isn't completely insulated from external pressure. First, the President can exercise control over the membership of the Board of Governors. Often, governors do not serve their full 14-year terms, because they can earn higher incomes in private business. Therefore a President who serves two terms in office may be able to appoint several governors. Additionally, the President may appoint a new chairman every four years an appointment that can sometimes make or break his presidency. A chairman who is not reappointed may serve the remainder of his or her term as a governor but traditionally resigns, thereby giving the President another vacancy to fill.

Second, although the Fed's significant net income exempts it from the appropriations process (Congress's "power of the purse"), the Fed remains a creation of Congress. The U.S. Constitution does not specifically mandate a central bank, so Congress can amend the Fed's charter and powers or even abolish it entirely. Members of Congress usually are not shy about reminding the Fed of this fact. Nor is Congressional oversight merely rhetoric. In the middle and late 1970s, Congress forced the Fed to explain its goals and procedures. Passed in 1975, House Concurrent Resolution 133 requires the Fed to announce targets for the growth of monetary aggregates. In addition, the Humphrey-Hawkins Act (officially the Full Employment and Balanced Growth Act of 1978) requires the Fed to explain how these targets are consistent with the President's economic objectives. Nevertheless, in practice, the Congress has not often successfully challenged the Fed's policies.

Examples of Treasury–Fed Conflict

Elected officials lack formal control of monetary policy, and this lack of control at times has resulted in conflicts between the Fed and the President, who is often represented by the Secretary of the Treasury. During World War II, the administration increased its control over the Fed. To help finance wartime budget deficits, the Fed agreed to hold interest rates on Treasury securities at low levels. It could do so by buying bonds that were not purchased by private investors, thereby predetermining (pegging) the rates. After the war, the Treasury wanted to continue this policy, but the Fed didn't agree. The Fed's concern was inflation: Larger purchases of Treasury securities by the Fed increased the monetary base, potentially increasing the money supply growth rate and inflation. Price controls that had restrained inflation during the war were lifted after the war ended.

Chairman of the Board of Governors Marriner Eccles particularly objected to the rate-fixing policy. His opposition to the desires of the Truman administration cost him the Fed chairmanship in 1948, although he continued to fight for Fed independence during the remainder of his term as a governor. On March 4, 1951, the wartime policy of fixing the interest rates on Treasury securities was formally abandoned with the Treasury–Federal Reserve Accord.

Conflicts between the Treasury and the Fed didn't end with that accord, however. For example, President Ronald Reagan and Federal Reserve Chairman Paul Volcker argued over who was at fault for the severe business recession of the early 1980s. Reagan blamed the Fed's contractionary monetary policy. Volcker held that the Fed could not expand money supply growth until the budget deficit—which results from policy actions of the President and Congress—was reduced.

Early in the George H. W. Bush administration, the conflict was less severe, even though the Treasury typically argued for a more expansionary monetary policy than the Fed wanted. During the debate in 1991 over reforms of U.S. banking regulations, the Treasury and the Fed argued over which would have greater responsibility in overseeing the banking system. Finally, in late 1991 and early 1992, the Treasury pressured the Fed to reduce short-term interest rates. Although the Fed did reduce the discount rate, there is no way of knowing whether Treasury pressure influenced its decision. In early 1993, the Clinton Treasury argued that the Fed should not raise short-term interest rates in the face of the administration's budget package; and in 1994, the administration challenged the Fed's repeated increases in the federal funds rate. In 1996, some members of Congress questioned whether the Fed was sufficiently stringent in its operating budget in light of cutbacks in government budgets. In the George W. Bush administration in 2003, some commentators worried about a conflict between the Treasury and the Fed over the administration's tax policy.

Factors That Motivate the Fed

We have shown that the Fed has considerable power over monetary policy. Let's now examine alternative explanations of how the Fed decides to use its power. We consider two views of Fed motivation: the public interest view and the principal-agent view.

The public interest view. The usual starting point for explaining the motivation of business managers is that they act in the interest of the constituency they serve: the shareholders. The **public interest view** of Fed motivation holds that the Fed, too, acts in the interest of its primary constituency (the general public) and that it seeks to achieve economic goals that are in the public interest. Examples of such goals are price and employment stability and economic growth.

Does the evidence support the public interest view? It doesn't appear to with regard to price stability. The record of persistent inflation since World War II undercuts the claim that the Fed has emphasized price stability. Similarly, some economists dispute the Fed's contributions to the stability of other economic indicators.

CONSIDER THIS ...

Importance of Selecting a Fed Chairman

In the summer of 1979, President Jimmy Carter perceived the failure of his economic policies to roll back inflation as a huge stumbling block in his quest for reelection. Inflation was accelerating, and the value of the dollar was declining sharply on foreign-exchange markets. To try to turn the economy around before the election, Carter sought to replace Federal Reserve Chairman G. William Miller (who was leaving to become Secretary of the Treasury) with a champion of price stability. On July 24, 1979, Carter offered the Fed chairmanship to Paul Volcker, the president of the Federal Reserve Bank of New York and former undersecretary of the Treasury for monetary affairs. Volcker's views on Fed policies were well known. Earlier in 1979, he had argued for a contractionary monetary policy, with a significant increase in the federal funds rate, to fight inflation. The inflation challenge led Volcker to accept the new post (despite having to take a pay cut from $116,000 to $57,500).

In October 1979, the Volcker Fed began a restrictive policy of significantly lower money supply growth that resulted in a dramatic increase in the federal funds rate. High interest rates and a sagging economy were major factors in President Carter's campaign woes. By 1982, the rate of inflation had declined significantly, but the decline came too late for Jimmy Carter. Carter had appointed Federal Reserve Chairman Volcker, but the short-term effects of his policies had helped to hand the 1980 presidential election to Republican Ronald Reagan.

The principal-agent view. Many economists view organizations as having conflicting goals. Although they are created to serve the public and perform a public service, government organizations also have internal goals that might not match their stated mission. In effect, public organizations face the agency problem just as private corporations do. In this section, we describe goals other than those outlined in the Federal Reserve Act that might influence the Fed's decisions and the way in which it exerts its economic power.

Recall that when managers (agents) have little stake in their businesses, their incentives to maximize the value of shareholders' (principals') claims may be weak; in that situation, the agents don't always act in the interest of the principals. James Buchanan and Gordon Tullock of George Mason University formulated a **principal-agent view** of motivation in bureaucratic organizations such as the Fed. They contend that bureaucrats' objective is to maximize their personal well-being—power, influence, and prestige—rather than the well-being of the general public. Hence the principal-agent view of Fed motivation predicts that the Fed acts to increase its power, influence, and prestige as an organization, subject to constraints placed on it by principals such as the President and Congress.

How can we determine whether the principal-agent view accurately explains the Fed's motivation? If it does, we might conclude that the Fed would fight to maintain its autonomy. Unquestionably, it does so; the Fed has resisted congressional attempts to control its budget many times. In fact, the Fed is one of the most successful bureaucratic organizations in mobilizing constituents (such as bankers and business executives) in its own defense.

Proponents of the principal-agent view also think that the Fed would avoid conflicts with groups that could limit its power, influence, and prestige. For example, the Fed could manage monetary policy to assist the reelection efforts of presidential incumbents who are unlikely to limit its power. The result would be a **political business cycle,** in which the Fed would try to lower interest rates to stimulate credit demand and economic activity before an election to make the Fed look good. After the election, the economy would pay the piper when the Fed contracted economic activity to reduce the inflationary pressure caused by its earlier expansion—but, by then, the President who was sympathetic to the Fed would have been reelected. The facts for the United States don't generally support the political business cycle theory, however. For example, expansion of money supply growth preceded President Nixon's reelection in 1972, but contraction of money supply growth preceded President Carter's and President Bush's unsuccessful bids for reelection in 1980 and 1992, respectively.

Nevertheless, the President's desires may subtly influence Fed policy. One study of the influence of politics on changes in monetary policy from 1979 through 1984 measured the number of signals of desired policy from the administration in articles appearing in *The Wall Street Journal.* The author found a close correlation between changes in monetary policy and the number of administration signals.[†]

One criticism of the principal-agent view addresses the need to separate the Fed's intentions from external pressure: The Fed itself might want to act in one way, whereas Congress and the President might try to get the Fed to pursue other goals. The principal-agent view also fails to explain why Congress allows the Fed to be relatively independent through self-financing. Some economists suggest that the Fed may provide Congress with long-run benefits through self-financing. If self-financing gives the Fed an incentive to conduct more open market purchases, thereby expanding the money supply, more residual revenue will accrue to the Treasury for appropriation by Congress.

Fed Independence

Usually, the political issue of Fed independence arises not because of academic disagreement over monetary policy or even the role of the Fed in managing monetary policy, but because of the public's negative reaction to Fed policy. For example, legislation introduced in Congress in 1982 to decrease the Fed's autonomy stemmed from public reaction to high interest rates. We now analyze the arguments for and against Fed independence.

Arguments for independence. The main argument for Fed independence is that monetary policy—which affects inflation, interest rates, exchange rates, and economic growth—is too important and technical to be determined by politicians. Because of the frequency of elections, politicians may be myopic, concerned with short-term benefits without regard to potential long-term costs. Short-term and long-term interests often clash after inflation. Supporters argue that monetary policy tends to be too expansionary if it is left to policymakers with short horizons, leading to inflation. Therefore the Fed cannot assume that politicians' objectives reflect public sentiment. The public may well prefer that the experts at the Fed, rather than politicians, make monetary policy decisions.

Another argument for Fed independence is that complete control of the Fed by elected officials increases the likelihood of political business cycle fluctuations in the money supply. For example, those officials might pressure the Fed to assist the Treasury's borrowing efforts by buying government bonds, increasing the money supply and fueling inflation.

Arguments against independence. The importance of monetary policy for the economy is also the main argument against central bank independence. Supporters claim that in a democracy, elected officials should make public policy. Because the public holds elected officials responsible for perceived monetary policy problems, some analysts advocate giving the President and Congress more control over monetary

---

[†]Thomas Havrilesky, "Monetary Policy Signaling from the Administration to the Federal Reserve," *Journal of Money, Credit, and Banking*, 20:83–101, February 1988.

OTHER TIMES, OTHER PLACES . . .

Conflicts Between the Treasury and the Central Bank in Japan over Independence

The United States isn't the only country in which tensions between the Treasury and the central bank influence monetary policy. Japanese monetary policy during the late 1980s and early 1990s provides another good example. During the mid-1980s, Bank of Japan Governor Satoshi Sumita conducted an expansionary monetary policy. Mr. Sumita, a former vice minister of finance (the Ministry of Finance is akin to the U.S. Treasury), favored low interest rates. Yasushi Mieno, appointed to head the Bank of Japan in 1989, pursued a more contractionary policy. *The Wall Street Journal* reported that "Mr. Mieno took away the *sake* bowl just as the party started getting rambunctious."† That is, Japanese money growth would be reduced, leading to concerns that the runup in Japanese stock prices would end.

During 1990, increases in the Bank of Japan's discount rate sent Japanese stock market prices plunging and threatened some highly leveraged firms with financial distress. The surprise decision by the Bank of Japan to reduce its discount rate from 6% to 5.5% on July 1, 1991, caused Japanese central bank watchers to worry that Mieno was currying favor with Finance Minister Ryutaro Hashimoto. The finance minister was a strong candidate to be the Japanese prime minister, and Mieno's actions seemed to create a political business cycle.

Like Federal Reserve actions in the United States, the Bank of Japan's actions can be viewed as reflecting responsible, independent behavior: The bank may have tried to ease the likelihood of a financial crisis in Japan induced by high interest rates, even though it could attempt relatively contractionary policies over the medium term. In more recent years, the Bank of Japan became formally independent of the government.

† Marcus W. Brauchli and Clay Chandler, "Financial Shift: In a Major Reversal, the Bank of Japan Cuts Its Key Interest Rate," *The Wall Street Journal*, July 2, 1991.

policy. The counterargument to the view that monetary policy is too technical for elected officials is that national security and foreign policy also require sophisticated analysis and a long-term horizon, and these functions are entrusted to elected officials. In addition, critics of Fed independence argue that placing the central bank under the control of elected officials could confer benefits by coordinating and integrating monetary policy with government taxing and spending policies.

Those who argue for greater congressional control make the case that the Fed has not always used its independence well. For example, some critics note that the Fed, because of its deflationary bias, failed to assist the banking system during the economic contraction of the early 1930s. Another example that many economists cite is that Fed policies were too inflationary in the 1960s and 1970s. Finally, some analysts believe that the Fed acted too slowly in addressing credit problems during the recession of the early 1990s.

Concluding remarks. Economists and politicians don't universally agree on the merits of Fed independence. Under the present system, however, the Fed's independence is not absolute, and so it sometimes satisfies one or the other group of critics. In practice, debates center on proposals to limit Fed independence in some respects, not to eliminate its formal independence. Some recent proposals include shortening the term of office of governors, making the chairman's term coincide more closely with that of the President, and placing the Secretary of the Treasury on the FOMC. Enacting any of these proposals would tend to make the Fed's economic policies more consistent with the President's.

Central Bank Independence Outside the United States

The degree of central bank independence varies greatly from country to country. When we compare the structure of the Fed with that of central banks in Canada, Europe, and

Japan, four patterns emerge. First, in countries where central bank board members serve fixed terms of office, none is as long as the 14-year term for Federal Reserve governors, implying nominally greater independence for the Fed. Second, in those countries, the head of the central bank has a longer term of office than the four-year term of office of the chairman of the Board of Governors in the United States. Third, of these countries, only Germany has had a federal structure for the central bank (we discuss the European Central Bank below).

Finally, the overall degree of independence of the central bank varies. An independent central bank is free to pursue its goals without direct interference from other government officials and legislators. Most economists believe that an independent central bank can more freely focus on keeping inflation low (we discuss this goal in more detail in Chapter 21). The European Central Bank is, in principle, extremely independent, whereas the central banks of Japan and the United Kingdom traditionally have been less independent, though by 1998, both had become more independent and more focused on price stability.

Web Site Suggestions: http://www.bankofengland.co.uk Presents the Bank of England's Web site.

The Bank of England, the world's oldest central bank (founded in 1694), obtained the power to set interest rates independent of the government in 1997. While the government can overrule the Bank in "extreme circumstances," such deviation is unlikely. The Bank of England's inflation target is set by the Chancellor of the Exchequer. Interest rate determination falls to the Monetary Policy Committee, whose members are the Governor, two Deputy Governors, two members appointed by the Governor (after consulting with the Chancellor of the Exchequer), and four external economic experts named by the Chancellor.

Web Site Suggestions: http://www.boj.or.jp/en/ Presents the Bank of Japan's Web site.

The Bank of Japan Law, in force since April 1998, gives the Policy Board more autonomy to pursue price stability. Policy board members include the Governor, two Deputy Governors, and six outside members named by the cabinet and confirmed by the Diet. While the government may send representatives to meetings of the policy board, it lacks a vote. The Ministry of Finance does, however, retain control over parts of the Bank of Japan's budget unrelated to monetary policy.

Web Site Suggestions: http://www.bank-banque-canada.ca Presents the Bank of Canada's Web site.

The Bank of Canada has an inflation target as a goal for monetary policy, but that target is set jointly by the Bank of Canada and the government. While the government has had since 1967 the final responsibility for monetary policy, the Bank has generally controlled monetary policy. While the finance minister can direct the bank's action, such direction must be written and public, and none has been issued up to this time.

The push for central bank independence to pursue a goal of low inflation has increased in recent years. Indeed, in most of the industrialized world, central bank independence from the political process is gaining ground as the way to organize monetary authorities. In practice, the degree of actual independence in the conduct of monetary policy varies across countries. What conclusions should we draw from differences in central bank structure? Many analysts believe that an independent central bank improves the economy's performance by lowering inflation without raising output or employment fluctuations. Calculations by Alberto Alesina and Lawrence Summers of Harvard University indicate that the countries that have the most independent central banks (Germany and Switzerland) had the lowest average rates of inflation during the 1970s and 1980s. New Zealand, Italy, and Spain, with much less independent central banks, had significantly higher rates of inflation.

What constitutes meaningful central bank independence? Economists emphasize that declarations of independence are insufficient. The central bank must be able to conduct policy without direct interference from the government. The central bank also must be able to set nonconflicting goals for which it can be held accountable. The leading example of such a goal is a target for inflation. Central banks in Canada, Finland, New Zealand, Sweden, and the United Kingdom have official inflation targets. A number of European countries, including France and Germany, had informal inflation targets (prior to the emergence of the European Central Bank), and the European Central Bank does now. Many economists urge that the U.S. Fed adopt an inflation target.

Web Site Suggestions: http://www.ecb.int Provides information on and data from the European Central Bank.

As part of the move toward economic integration in Europe, the *European Central Bank (ECB)* is charged with conducting monetary policy for Europe (that is, for the 11 countries participating in European Monetary Union). Representatives of many European nations signed an important agreement in Maastricht, the Netherlands, in December 1991. This agreement detailed a gradual approach to monetary union to be completed between 1994 and 1999. Although the monetary union became effective only on January 1, 1999, groundwork for the ECB had been laid in advance. Indeed, European nations coordinated an expansionary monetary policy in late 1998.

The ECB's organization is in some respects similar to that of the U.S. Fed. The ECB's executive board, chaired initially by Wim Duisenberg (a former Dutch finance minister), has six members who work exclusively for the bank. Board members (a Vice President and four others) are appointed by the heads of state and government, based on the recommendation of the Council of Ministers of Economics and Finance, after consulting the European Parliament and the Governing Council of the ECB. Executive board members serve nonrenewable eight-year terms (although Executive Board President Duisenberg tentatively agreed to step aside after four years). Also participating in the governance of the ECB are the Governors of each of the 11 member national central banks, each of whom will have a term of at least five years. The long terms of office are designed to increase the political independence of the ECB.

In principle, the ECB has a high degree of overall independence, with a clear mandate to emphasize price stability, following the lead of the Bundesbank (Germany's central bank), and it is free from European Union and national governments in the conduct of policy. Moreover, the ECB's charter can only be accomplished by changing the Maastricht Treaty, which would require the assent of all countries signing the original treaty. Whether legal independence will translate into actual independence is difficult to say, however. Such a translation requires observing the new institution for a period of time.

Based on the historical experience of the Federal Reserve, there may be cause for concern. The decentralized central banking system envisioned in the original Federal Reserve Act of 1913 led to power struggles within the system and offered no mechanism to achieve consensus during the financial crisis of the early 1930s. National central banks have considerable power in the ECB. The Governors of the European System of Central Banks (ESCB) hold a majority of votes in the ECB's governing council, 11 votes against the six held by the Executive Board. Although the ECB began with only about 500 staff members, national central banks had more than 60,000 employees in 1999.

Where might conflict arise? While the ECB statute emphasizes price stability, countries have argued—and likely will continue to argue—over the merits of expansionary or contractionary monetary policy. Also, no consensus has been reached on the way the ECB will function as the lender of last resort in dealing with domestic financial crises. Optimists believe that the united ECB and monetary union forces Europe to confront key structural economic weaknesses, such as an oversized public sector and inflexible labor markets. Pessimists argue that monetary unions generally require a broader political union (the case for the Fed, but not for the ECB) to be successful. One thing is clear—all eyes are on the ECB.

KEY TERMS AND CONCEPTS

Federal Reserve System
- Board of Governors
- Federal Open Market Committee (FOMC)

Federal Reserve bank

Member banks

Political business cycle

Principal-agent view

Public interest view

SUMMARY

1. The Federal Reserve Act of 1913 created the U.S. Federal Reserve System (the Fed). Its three principal components are the Federal Reserve banks, the Board of Governors, and the Federal Open Market Committee (FOMC).
2. The Fed's formal activities are conducting open market operations, setting reserve requirements, and making discount loans. The FOMC issues guidelines for open market operations. The Board of Governors sets reserve requirements. Depository institutions obtain discount loans through district Federal Reserve banks, although the Board of Governors essentially determines the discount rate (the interest rate charged on discount loans).
3. In practice, power within the Federal Reserve System is more centralized than is apparent from the official structure. The Board of Governors, especially its chairman, typically dominates monetary policy decisions.
4. The Fed is relatively independent of the political process, owing to the long-term appointments of members of the Board of Governors and to the Fed's financial independence. However, because the Federal Reserve System was created by legislation, not by the Constitution, Congress could enact legislation to reduce its power (or even to eliminate it).
5. The public interest view of Fed motivation argues that the Fed pursues monetary policies and financial regulation in the broad national interest. Alternatively, the principal-agent view stresses that the Fed is more interested in enhancing its own well-being as an organization than in the national interest.
6. Should the Fed be independent? Some argue that it should because its longer time horizon (relative to those of elected officials) enables it to pursue monetary policies in the long-term interest of the nation. Critics of central bank independence note that monetary policy is an important part of the national policy agenda and hence should be controlled by elected officials.
7. The degree of independence from the political process and the general procedures for appointing governors vary for central banks of other industrialized countries. Countries having relatively independent central banks generally have lower inflation rates than do countries having less independent central banks.

REVIEW QUESTIONS

1. Why did Congress pass the Federal Reserve Act in 1913 when the United States had gotten along without a central bank since 1836?
2. What are the Board of Governors' duties and responsibilities with regard to monetary policy?
3. Who are the voting members of the Federal Open Market Committee?
4. Where does most of the Fed's income come from?
5. What features of the Fed help to make it independent of political pressure? How does the U.S. Constitution protect the Fed?
6. How many district Federal Reserve banks are there? Where are they located?
7. Who guides the open market operations of the Fed?
8. Why do Federal Reserve districts cut across some state lines, and why do the directors of the district banks represent business, banking, and the general public?

MOVING FROM THEORY TO PRACTICE . . .

FINANCIAL TIMES MARCH 19, 2003

A New BoJ Chief and Deflation

Toshihiko Fukui, who takes over as governor of the Bank of Japan tomorrow, signalled that he is prepared to adopt a more aggressive monetary policy, although he said the central bank could not tackle deflation alone. . . .

In confident testimony before parliament yesterday, Mr. Fukui said the BoJ would consider broadening the range of assets it buys—comments taken by analysts to refer to the possible purchase of property-backed securities or exchange-traded funds, a proxy for the stock market.

Mr. Fukui also said he would look favourably on requests from politicians for the BoJ to raise the Y2,000bn ($16.9bn) limit on the amount of shares it can buy from commercial banks. The BoJ broke a taboo last September when it said it would purchase shares from banks but Masaru Hayami, who steps down as governor today, has been openly nervous about the effect this could have on the institution's credibility.

Paul Sheard, senior economist at Lehman Brothers, said: "[Mr.] Fukui did a pretty good day's work. No one would have blamed him for being quite tight-lipped but he sent a strong message that he is not complacent about the current deflationary environment."

On the controversial topic of whether the BoJ should set an inflation target, Mr. Fukui was less dismissive of the idea than Mr. Hayami [the former governor], although he said it would be foolhardy to set such a target without making clear how it was to be achieved.

"I think inflation targeting can be an important policy tool for a central bank," he said. "I still need to debate with the BoJ policy board members whether the conditions are in place for such a policy."

Kazumasa Iwata, one of two incoming deputy governors, supported an inflation target, saying: "Targeting price stability would allow the BoJ to explain the responsibility for its actions."

Mr. Iwata said that because the consumer price index underestimated deflation, an inflation target should be set between zero and 2 percent. The BoJ has not set a deadline for beating deflation, which has been chipping away at prices since 1995. . . .

Mr. Fukui said the government had an important role in tackling deflation, both through fiscal measures and through tackling bad debts in the financial system, the ossification of which the BoJ regards as the principal obstacle to effective monetary policy.

He implied that recent moves by banks to raise capital in the markets would be inadequate and that state capital injections might eventually prove necessary.

Toshiro Muto, vice-finance minister until January, said he would try to  help improve co-ordination between government and BoJ policy.

ANALYZING THE NEWS ...

Central bank leadership appointments are widely watched around the world and are the subject of intense political (and sometimes financial) speculation in individual countries. Japan's experience with deflation and sluggish economic growth since the early 1990s led to calls within Japan and from many economists and policymakers around the world for a change in monetary policy. In 2003, the outgoing Governor of the Bank of Japan, Masaru Hayami, was criticized in many quarters for not focusing the Bank of Japan's attention on "price stability." Traditionally, an emphasis on price stability was designed to restrain inflation. In Japan's case, deflation was the problem. In March 2003, Toshihiko Fukui was tapped by Prime Minister Koizumi to be the new Governor of the Bank of Japan.

a The Bank of Japan has official independence in selecting its goal—price stability. To be credible, however, the Bank must take steps to stave off deflation, just as a central bank would take steps to reduce inflation. While the Policy Board of the Bank sets monetary policy, the Governor's informal power to signal changes in policy direction can be substantial. The new Governor spoke about his concern about deflation, but analysts awaited tangible steps from the central bank.

b Many economists have urged that Japan adopt an inflation target to provide a beacon in arresting deflation and a future anchor for inflationary expectations. The support for such an idea by Deputy Governor Kazumasa Iwata, with little formal support from Governor Fukui, likely heralds a struggle within the Bank over how to guide monetary policy.

c Incoming Deputy Governor Toshiro Muto's comments could imply a welcome coordination of fiscal and monetary policy to attack deflation in Japan. Some commentators worried, though, that a new battle might emerge over how independent the Bank of Japan should be from the Ministry of Finance. Some Bank officials worried that expansionary policies to combat deflation might require financial assistance from the Ministry of Finance, something for which they have been hesitant to ask since independence was granted.

For further thought...

Under what circumstances is central bank independence likely to foster better economic outcomes? Explain.

Source: Excerpted from David Pilling, "New BoJ Chief Prepared to Use More Aggressive Monetary Policy," *Financial Times*, March 19, 2003.

9. Is speculation in shares of stock of the Federal Reserve banks possible? Why or why not?
10. What are the duties of Federal Reserve banks?
11. "It is impossible to know where the true power and authority in an organization lie just from examining the formal structure of the organization." Does this observation apply to the Federal Reserve System? Explain.
12. *Evaluate:* The Federal Reserve System is independent of the political process in the United States.
13. *Evaluate:* To conduct monetary policy in the national interest, the Federal Reserve System should be independent of the political process in the United States.
14. *Evaluate:* The Fed's independence from the government's appropriations process necessarily rules out the principal-agent view of Fed motivation.

ANALYTICAL PROBLEMS

15. Is it easier for a central bank to be independent in a modern, industrial country or in a less developed country? What implications does your answer have for what the average inflation rate is likely to be in modern, industrial countries as opposed to less developed countries?
16. Suppose that you are the president of the country Moolah and that you are writing a new constitution for it. Would you give monetary policymakers complete independence from your government? Why or why not?
17. Research shows that 9 to 18 months after the Fed eases monetary policy, the economy shows increased real growth. Suppose that 18 months before a presidential election, the Fed announces a reduction of the discount rate by 1 percentage point. What would you conclude about the Fed's motivation? Would your conclusion change if, six months earlier, real output growth had been forecast to be 3% but the economy weakened and real output grew by only 1%?
18. Why might the President not want to appoint a tough-minded, independent chairman of the Federal Reserve Board of Governors but prefer someone with whom he or she had previous political ties?
19. Are the high rates of inflation that the United States experienced during the 1970s consistent with the public interest view of the Fed's motivation?
20. Is the principal-agent view of the Fed's motivation believable if Fed policymakers routinely turn down jobs on Wall Street that would double or triple their salaries?
21. A recent proposal would remove the presidents of the Federal Reserve banks from the FOMC and add the Secretary of the Treasury and the chairperson of the President's Council of Economic Advisers to the FOMC. What would such a proposal do to the Fed's independence? Would it make the Fed more accountable for its actions? How would regional concerns and information be communicated to the Fed?
22. Suppose that economic conditions worsen and the Fed considers easing monetary policy. But before the Fed can act, the President's chief economic advisor holds a press conference and states that the Fed should ease its policy to stimulate the economy. Does this statement make easing the policy less or more difficult for the Fed? Why?
23. According to an article in *The Wall Street Journal*, early in 1999: "Germany's determined finance minister, Oskar Lafontaine, urged the new European Central Bank to cut interest rates to boost corporate profits and, most important of all, create jobs." What impact do you believe the fact that the European Central Bank had been newly created would have on the likelihood of its accepting the advice of the German finance minister?
24. In Japan, the central bank is not formally independent. Yet Japan's inflation rate is much lower than that of the United States. Does this condition suggest that low inflation doesn't really depend on central bank independence? Why or why not?
25. *Evaluate:* The Fed's occasional mobilization of banking interests to defend itself against legislative attacks is inconsistent with the public interest view of Fed motivation.
26. During the debate in 1991 over reform of U.S. banking regulations, the Treasury advocated the removal of barriers between banking and commerce (for example, allowing nonfinancial firms to own depository institutions), but the Fed opposed such a move. Offer an explanation of the Fed's response in terms of (a) the public interest view of Fed motivation and (b) the principal-agent view of Fed motivation.

DATA QUESTIONS

27. In the *Federal Reserve Bulletin,* the Federal Reserve Open Market Transactions table lists the changes in the Fed's holdings of U.S. government and other securities in the System Open Market Account. Determine how much its holdings have changed during the past three years. In which year was monetary policy the "easiest"? In which year was it the "tightest"?

28. In the latest *Annual Report of the Board of Governors of the Federal Reserve System,* look up the table that reports historical data on "Income and Expenses" of Federal Reserve banks. Find the column that lists payments to the U.S. Treasury—the Fed's profits that are returned to the government. What is the total amount of the Fed's profits for the past three years? Now determine the total amount of U.S. federal government revenue for the past three years from the *Economic Report of the President.* What proportion of the government's total revenue was the Fed's income?

29. Look for articles in *The Wall Street Journal* in which the President or the Treasury Department (or another arm of the administration) delivers strong policy suggestions to the Fed, and then watch for the Fed's response.

30. One of the claims for central bank independence is that it reduces the likelihood of inflationary policies. One well-known study of this issue, by Harvard University economists Alberto Alesina and Lawrence Summers, strongly supports this contention. (Summers is the current president of Harvard University.) Consider a graph depicting the results of their research from a paper published by the Federal Reserve Bank of St. Louis, "Central Bank Independence and Economic Performance" (by Patricia S. Pollard) found at http://research.stlouisfed.org/publications/review/93/07/Bank_Jul_Aug1993.pdf. (The graph is on page 23 of the document.) Based solely on the graph, does there appear to be an inverse relationship between inflation and independence? Which countries appear to have high inflation and low independence? Which appear to have low inflation and high independence?

31. The Federal Reserve presents an annual report of its activities on an annual basis to Congress. Find the most recent issue (from http://www.federalreserve.gov/boarddocs/rptcongress/) and find the total amount of the Fed's profits over the last three years (under the heading for payments to the Treasury). Compare your answers with the amount of U.S. federal government revenue over the last three years (from the most recent issue of the *Economic Report of the President*—http://www.gpoaccess.gov/eop/index.html). What proportion of the U.S. government's revenue is made up of the Fed's income?

CHAPTER

20 Monetary Policy Tools

Monetary Policy Tools

In the fall of 2001, the Federal Reserve made headlines again and again. In the immediate aftermath of the terrorist attacks in New York and Washington on September 11, 2001, the Fed's expanded discount lending ensured the smooth operation of commercial banks in affected areas. The $45 *billion* in discount loans outstanding on September 12 dwarfed the $59 *million* average for the prior ten weeks. On September 17, the Fed cut the federal funds rate by one-half percentage point just before the New York Stock Exchange reopened, boosting confidence. The Fed reacts to the economic environment in setting monetary policy, and changes in monetary policy (implemented with open market operations, discount lending, or setting reserve requirements) affect interest rates, output, and inflation.

In this chapter, we describe the implementation of the Fed's monetary policy tools and see how they can be used to affect short-term interest rates. This chapter extends our study of monetary policy tools from Chapters 17 and 18, in which we described how those tools could change the monetary base and the money supply. As you might expect, the Fed's actions and uses of its policy tools are not without their critics. We also include some of the controversy about the Fed's use of monetary policy tools and alternatives that economists have proposed to improve monetary decisions.

Another theme of this chapter is *Fed watching*: Many individuals and organizations scrutinize the actions of the Fed to forecast changes in interest rates and to predict economic changes. Leading banks and Wall Street firms rely on in-house analysis of the Fed's intentions and actions in guiding lending and investment decisions. Individuals watch the Fed's moves to guide decisions about buying a home or making investments. As you will see, understanding how the Fed uses its policy tools is an important component of Fed watching.

Open Market Operations

Open market operations, the purchases and sales of securities in financial markets by the Fed, are the dominant means by which the Fed changes the monetary base. Recall from Chapter 17 that an open market purchase increases the monetary base (generally by increasing bank reserves) and that an open market sale decreases the monetary base. If the money multiplier is relatively stable, the Fed can use open market operations to regulate the money supply by changing the monetary base.

The original Federal Reserve Act didn't specifically mention open market operations, because they weren't well understood in financial markets at that time. The Fed began to use open market purchases as a policy tool during the 1920s when it acquired World War I Liberty Bonds from banks, enabling banks to finance more business loans. Before 1935, district Federal Reserve banks conducted limited open market operations in securities markets, but these transactions lacked central coordination to achieve a monetary policy goal. The lack of concerted intervention by the Fed during the banking crisis of the early 1930s led Congress to establish the Federal Open Market Committee (FOMC) to guide open market operations.

Web Site Suggestions: http://www.federalreserve.gov/fomc/ Describes the work of the FOMC and lists its current members.

The Fed generally conducts open market operations in liquid Treasury securities markets, affecting interest rates in those markets. An open market purchase of Treasury securities increases their price, all else being equal, thereby decreasing their yield and expanding the money supply. An open market sale decreases the price of Treasury securities, thereby increasing their yield and contracting the money supply. Open market purchases tend to reduce interest rates and so are viewed as *expansionary*; open market sales tend to increase interest rates and so are viewed as *contractionary*.

The Fed's actions influence interest rates on other securities. Although the differences in yields on different assets depend on their risk, liquidity, and information costs, the change in the interest rate on Treasury securities has an immediate impact on their yield and return. When the news media say that the Fed sets interest rates, they are implicitly summarizing this process.

We now turn to actions that the FOMC takes to carry out open market transactions.

Implementing Open Market Operations

How does the FOMC guide open market operations? It meets eight times per year (roughly every six weeks) and issues a **general directive** stating its overall objectives for interest rates. The directive also describes instructions for open market operations. These directives are less precise than reserve requirement and discount rate policies. Lacking perfect foresight, the FOMC can't determine in advance the exact actions that are needed to achieve its objectives for changes in interest rates and monetary aggregates.

The Federal Reserve System's account manager (a vice president of the Federal Reserve Bank of New York) is responsible for carrying out open market operations that fulfill the FOMC's objectives. The **Open Market Trading Desk,** a group of traders at the Federal Reserve Bank of New York, trades government securities over the counter electronically with primary dealers. *Primary dealers* are private securities firms selected by the Fed that trade government securities and are permitted to trade directly with the Fed. Before making transactions, the trading desk notifies all the dealers at the same time, asks them to submit offers, and gives them a deadline. The Fed's account manager goes over the list, accepts the best offers, and then has the trading desk buy or sell the securities until the volume of reserves reaches the Fed's desired goal. These securities are either added to or subtracted from the portfolios of the various Federal Reserve banks according to their shares of total assets in the system.

How does the account manager know what to do? The manager interprets the FOMC's most recent directive, holds daily conferences with two members of the FOMC, and personally analyzes financial market conditions. Then the manager compares the level of reserves in the banking system with the desired level recommended by the directive. If the level that the directive suggests is greater than actual bank reserves, the account manager purchases securities to raise the level of bank reserves toward the desired level. If the level that the directive suggests is less than actual reserves, the account manager sells securities to lower reserves toward the desired level. The desk is connected to its trading partners through an electronic system called the Trading Room Automated Processing System, or TRAPS.

One way the account manager conducts open market operations is through **outright purchases and sales** of Treasury securities of various maturities by the trading desk—that is, by buying from or selling to dealers. More commonly, the manager uses

Federal Reserve repurchase agreements (analogous to commercial bank repos, discussed in Chapter 13). Through these agreements, the Fed buys securities from a dealer in the government securities market, and the dealer agrees to buy them back at a given price at a specified future date, usually within one week. In effect, the government securities serve as collateral for a short-term loan. For open market sales, the trading desk often engages in **matched sale-purchase transactions** (sometimes called *reverse repos*), in which the Fed sells securities to dealers in the government securities market and the dealers agree to sell them back to the Fed in the near future.

In conducting the Fed's open market operations, the trading desk makes both dynamic and defensive transactions. Open market operations that are intended to change monetary policy as desired by the FOMC are known as **dynamic transactions.** A much greater volume of open market transactions are **defensive transactions,** which the Fed's traders use to offset fluctuations in the monetary base arising from portfolio allocation preferences of banks and the nonbank public, financial markets, and the economy. In other words, the Fed uses defensive transactions to offset the effects of disturbances to the monetary base, not to change monetary policy.

Defensive open market operations may be used to compensate for either predictable or unexpected events that change the monetary base. For example, the nonbank public predictably increases its demand for currency before Christmas and other holidays and in response to seasonal preferences for travel. The Fed can also predict certain types of borrowing: Borrowing within the banking system occurs periodically to satisfy reserve requirements; and the U.S. Treasury, foreign governments, and large corporations often sell or buy blocks of securities at announced intervals. Other, less predictable, disturbances come from the Treasury or the Fed. Although the Treasury attempts to synchronize withdrawals from its bank accounts with its bill paying (to avoid large shifts in the currency or reserves), it doesn't always succeed. Disruptions in the Fed's own balance sheet caused by Federal Reserve float or changes in discount loans, the amount of Treasury coins outstanding, or the Treasury's holdings of Federal Reserve Notes also produce short-term fluctuations in the monetary base. Fluctuations in Treasury deposits with the Fed and in Federal Reserve float are the most important of the unexpected disturbances to the monetary base.

There are other reasons for defensive transactions besides those needed to correct fluctuations in the monetary base. Even if the monetary base remains constant, movements of currency between the nonbank public and bank reserves affect the volume of bank deposits. Multiple deposit expansion or contraction then causes fluctuations in monetary base. Economic disturbances, such as major strikes or natural disasters, also cause unexpected fluctuations in the demand for currency and bank reserves. The Fed's account manager must respond to unintended increases or decreases in the monetary base and sell or buy securities to maintain the monetary policy indicated by the FOMC's guidelines.

Open Market Operations versus Other Policy Tools

Open market operations have several benefits that other policy tools lack: control, flexibility, and ease of implementation.

Control. Because the Fed initiates open market purchases and sales, it completely controls their volume. Discount loans also increase or decrease the monetary base, but discount loans enable the Fed to influence the direction of the change in the monetary base rather than to control the volume of reserves added to or taken from the monetary base.

CONSIDER THIS . . .

A Day's Work at the Open Market Trading Desk

9:00 a.m.

The account manager begins informal discussions with market participants to assess conditions in the government securities market. From these discussions and from data supplied by the staff of the FOMC, the account manager estimates how the prices of government securities will change during the trading day.

10:00 a.m.

The account manager's staff compares forecasts on Treasury deposits and information on the timing of future Treasury sales of securities with the staff of the Office of Government Finance in the Treasury Department.

10:15 a.m.

The account manager reads staff reports on forecasted shifts in the monetary base arising from temporary portfolio shifts, fluctuations in financial markets or the economy, or weather-related disturbances (for example, events that might extend the time for checks to clear).

11:15 a.m.

After reviewing the information from the various staffs, the account manager studies the FOMC's directive. This directive identifies the ranges for growth rates of the monetary aggregates and the level of the federal funds rate desired. The account manager must design *dynamic* open market operations to implement changes requested by the FOMC and *defensive* open market operations to offset temporary disturbances in the monetary base predicted by the staff. The account manager places the daily conference call to at least two members of the FOMC to discuss trading strategy.

11:30 a.m.

On approval of the trading strategy, the traders at the Federal Reserve Bank of New York notify the primary dealers in the government securities market of the Fed's desired transactions. If traders plan to make open market purchases, they request quotations for asked prices. If traders plan to make open market sales, they request quotations for bid prices. (Recall that government securities are traded over the counter.) The traders select the lowest prices offered when making purchases and accept the highest bids when making sales.

12:30 p.m.

Soliciting quotes and trading take about 45 minutes, so by about 12:30 p.m., the trading room at the Federal Reserve Bank of New York is less hectic. No three-martini lunch for the account manager and staff, though; they spend the afternoon monitoring conditions in the federal funds market and the level of bank reserves to get ready for the next day of trading.

Flexibility. The Fed can make both large and small open market operations. Often, dynamic transactions require large purchases or sales, whereas defensive transactions call for small securities purchases or sales. Other policy tools lack this flexibility. Reversing open market operations is simple for the Fed. For example, if it decides that its open market sales have made the money supply grow too slowly, it can quickly authorize open market purchases. Discount loans and reserve requirement changes are more difficult to reverse quickly.

Ease of implementation. The Fed can implement its securities transactions rapidly, with no administrative delays. All that is required is for the trading desk to place buy and sell orders with dealers in the government securities markets. Changing the discount rate or reserve requirements requires lengthier deliberation.

Fed Watching and FOMC Directives

Merely observing the Fed's trading activity doesn't necessarily provide reliable information regarding the Fed's *intentions* for monetary policy. For example, the Fed could acquire securities one day and dispose of securities the next day while pursuing the same overall monetary policy.

To discern the Fed's intentions, Fed watchers read carefully the directives issued by the Fed. They do this to try to discern the Fed's policy goals. As of February 1994, the Fed began announcing policy changes made by the FOMC at the time they are made;

CONSIDER THIS . . .

How Do You Decode FOMC Statements?

Since February 2000, the essence of the FOMC's policy decisions has been expressed in its statement issued at the end of each meeting. Prior to this time, substantive statements were released only in the event of a policy action or to clarify the FOMC's view about prospective developments in the economy. Under the earlier procedures, the Fed's statements and its domestic policy directive described a "policy bias" toward increasing or decreasing the federal funds rate. The new procedures are designed to make more transparent the Fed's communication with the public.

Under these procedures, the statement will point out the FOMC's view of the "balance of risks," described in the context of the Fed's goals as follows:

> Against the background of its long-run goals of price stability and sustainable economic growth and of the information currently available, the Committee believes that the risks are [balanced with respect to prospects for both goals] [weighted mainly toward conditions that may generate heightened inflation pressures] [weighted mainly toward conditions that may generate economic weakness] in the foreseeable future.

In 2002 and 2003 the FOMC struggled with the balance of risks, as the U.S. economy's recovery from the 2001 recession came in fits and starts. The Iraq conflict and the Fed's concern over the chance of deflation (a falling price level) further complicated the assessment of the balance of risks. For example, in its statement on January 29, 2003, the FOMC argued that "the risks are balanced with respect to the prospects for both goals [low inflation and maximum sustainable economic growth] for the foreseeable future." Yet, on March 18, the Committee opined that geopolitical uncertainties surrounding the conflict in Iraq made a risk assessment too difficult: "[T]he Committee does not believe it can usefully characterize the current balance of risks with respect to the prospects for its long-term goals of price stability and economic growth."

By May 6 (and similarly on June 25), the FOMC actually split its balance of risk assessment for output growth and inflation: "[T]he Committee perceives that over the next few quarters the upside and downside risks to the attainment of sustainable growth are roughly equal. In contrast, over the same period, the probability of an unwelcome substantial fall in inflation, though minor, exceeds that of a pickup in inflation from its already low level. The Committee believes that, taken together, the balance of risks to achieving its goals is weighted toward weakness over the foreseeable future."

While over the five-month period, the FOMC left the federal funds rate unchanged at 1.25 percent, it sent increasingly strong signals that it was prepared to cut the federal funds rate in the face of deflationary pressures. Response to the Fed's statements was mixed; some analysts praised the FOMC's emphasis on deflation, while others argued that the statements gave too few clues about the direction of monetary policy.

analysts still read directives carefully for clues about the likely future course of monetary policy. In February 2000, the Fed began to discuss the future "balance of risks" in its FOMC statement, giving its opinion about the relative risk toward economic weakness or higher inflation.

Open Market Operations in Other Countries

Although the Fed relies most heavily on open market operations to change the money supply, central banks in some other countries favor different policy tools. Often, the choice of policy tools depends on the organization of a country's financial markets and institutions. The Fed uses open market operations because the markets for U.S. government securities are highly liquid.

In contrast, historically, the Bank of Japan did not rely on open market operations because a market for government securities didn't exist until the mid-1980s. Japan issued its first six-month treasury bills in 1986 and its first three-month treasury bills in 1989. Until then, the Japanese central bank had used interest rate controls and direct discount lending to banks to influence the money supply in the *Gensaki* market. The Bank of Japan conducts transactions for repurchase agreements in that market; the market is open to financial institutions and nonfinancial corporations and has been free of interest rate regulations since its inception in 1949. Nevertheless, the government treasury bill market in Japan is smaller than that in the United States. Economists studying the Japanese financial system predict that the market for short-term government securities will continue to grow in the new century, providing a better environment for open market operations by the Bank of Japan.

While the European Central Bank commenced operation only in January 1999, it has continued to conduct open market operations principally through fixed-term, fixed-frequency securities repurchase operations, the regular money market tenders through which European central banks have injected liquidity into the financial system. Outright transactions and foreign-exchange repurchase agreements are also used.

Discount Policy

Discount policy, which includes setting the discount rate and terms of discount lending, is the oldest of the Federal Reserve's principal tools for regulating the money supply. Discount policy affects the money supply by influencing the volume of discount loans, which are part of the monetary base. An increase in the volume of discount loans raises the monetary base and the money supply, whereas a decrease in the volume of discount loans reduces the monetary base and the money supply. The discount rate at which the Fed lends funds to depository institutions and its general attitude toward discount lending depend on the effects it wants to have on the money supply. The **discount window** is the means by which the Fed makes discount loans to banks, serving as a channel to meet the liquidity needs of banks.

Before 1980 (except for a brief period during 1966), the Fed made discount loans only to banks that were members of the Federal Reserve System. Indeed, banks perceived the ability to borrow from the Fed through the discount window as an advantage of membership that partially offset the cost of maintaining reserve requirements. Since 1980, all depository institutions have had access to the discount window. Each Federal Reserve bank maintains its own discount window.

Using the Discount Window

The Fed influences the volume of discount loans in two ways: It sets the price of loans (the discount rate) and the terms of its loans.

We can describe the *price effect* on discount loans of a change in the discount rate as follows. Suppose that the Fed increases the discount rate. Banks react to the higher discount rate by reducing their borrowing at the discount window. Hence an increase in the discount rate decreases the volume of discount loans, reducing the monetary base and the money supply. The higher discount rate also exerts upward pressure on other short-term interest rates. As a result, banks find it more expensive to raise funds from other sources, such as by borrowing in the federal funds market or by issuing certificates of deposit. A decrease in the discount rate has the opposite effect: The volume of discount loans rises, increasing the monetary base and the money supply. However, the Fed cannot be sure that banks will borrow from the discount window when the discount rate declines. If profitable lending and investment opportunities aren't available, banks might not increase their discount borrowing.†

Web Site Suggestions:
http://www.frbdiscountwindow.org
Provides details about the Fed's discount lending programs.

Since 2003, the Federal Reserve has reformed its discount lending programs to accomplish better its objectives of ensuring adequate liquidity in the banking system and serving as a backup source of short-term funding for banks. The Fed's discount loans to banks now fall in one of three categories: (1) primary credit, (2) secondary credit, and (3) seasonal credit.

Primary credit is available to healthy banks (generally those with adequate capital and supervisory ratings for safety and soundness). Banks may use primary credit for any purpose and do not have to seek funds from other sources before requesting a discount window loan from the primary credit facility, or *standing lending facility*. The primary credit interest rate is set above the primary credit rate (usually by 1 percentage point). Hence primary credit is only a backup source of funds, as healthy banks choose to borrow less expensively in the federal funds market or from other sources. With few restrictions on its use, primary credit should minimize banks' reluctance to borrow from the discount window, and funds will be available in the event of a temporary shortage in liquidity in the banking system.

Secondary credit is intended for banks that are not eligible for primary credit, and may not be used to fund an expansion of a bank's assets. The secondary credit interest rate is set above the primary credit rate (by 0.5 percentage point), at a penalty rate, because these borrowers are less financially healthy.

Seasonal credit consists of temporary, short-term loans to satisfy seasonal requirements of smaller depository institutions in geographical areas where agriculture or tourism is important. These loans reduce banks' costs of maintaining excess cash or seasonally liquidating loans and investments. The seasonal credit interest rate is tied to the average of rates on certificates of deposit and the federal funds rate. Because of improvements in credit markets, the case that a seasonal credit facility is needed is increasingly difficult to make.

Benefits of Discount Policy

Discount policy offers the Fed certain advantages that the other policy tools do not have. We describe two of these next: (1) contributing to the Fed's role as lender of last resort and (2) signaling the Fed's policy intentions. We then discuss drawbacks of discount policy as a monetary policy tool.

Averting financial crises: lender of last resort. The discount window provides the most direct way for the Fed to act as a lender of last resort to the banking system. Open market operations can change the level of bank reserves and affect short-term interest rates (such as the federal funds rate), but they can't address well the

†Historically, in addition to setting the discount rate, the Fed set the conditions for the availability of loans. One category of loans was made to financial institutions under exceptional circumstances to alleviate severe liquidity problems and restore the bank to financial health. An example is the more than $5 billion in discount loans that was extended to Continental Illinois Bank before its takeover by the FDIC. On January 9, 2003, the Federal Reserve replaced its previous programs, "adjustment" and "extended" credit, with "primary" and "secondary" credit programs. (The "seasonal" credit program was not changed.) In the new regime banks face few, if any, restrictions on their use of primary credit, and interest rates charged are now set above, rather than below, the prevailing rate for federal funds.

illiquidity problems of individual banks. Hence the Fed relies more on discount lending in its role as lender of last resort. The Fed's successes in handling the Penn Central crisis in the commercial paper market in 1970 and the stock market crash of 1987 suggest that decisive discount policy can reduce the costs of financial disturbances to the economy.

The Fed historically extended discount loans at its discretion, and an overly generous discount policy during financial crises may have encouraged too much risk taking by banks and the nonfinancial corporations that borrow from them. The reason is that banks, knowing that the Fed provided discount loans at favorable terms during business downturns, enforced credit standards less strictly, as happened during the 1980s.

But many analysts praise the Fed's discount window interventions, such as those that took place during the Penn Central crisis of 1970, the Franklin National Bank crisis of 1974, the Hunt brothers' silver manipulation efforts in 1980, the Continental Illinois Bank collapse in 1984, the stock market crash of October 1987, and the aftermath of the September 11 terrorist attacks. They conclude that these cases demonstrate the need for the Fed to continue its use of the discount window to extend credit, case by case, as a lender of last resort during financial crises.

Drawbacks of Discount Policy as a Monetary Policy Tool

Few economists advocate the use of discount policy as a tool of *monetary control.* Fluctuations in the spread between the federal funds rate and the discount rate set by the Fed can cause unintended increases or decreases in the monetary base and the money supply. Moreover, the Fed doesn't control discount policy as completely as it controls open market operations, and changing discount policy is much more difficult than changing open market operations (because banks must decide whether to accept discount loans). Hence the Fed doesn't use discount policy as its principal tool for influencing the money supply.

Discount Policy in Other Countries

Outside the United States, central banks generally use discount lending as a monetary policy tool and as a means of mitigating financial crises. In Japan, for example, the Bank of Japan quotes the *official discount rate* as the cost of its loans to private financial institutions that have accounts at the bank. Changes in the official discount rate are interpreted by financial market participants as reflecting changes in the Bank's basic stance on monetary policy. The European Central Bank uses standing discount facilities to provide and absorb overnight liquidity and signal the stance of monetary policy. As is the case in the United States (where discount loans are made by regional Federal Reserve Banks), the standing facilities are administered in a decentralized manner by national central banks.

CHECKPOINT

When reading *The Wall Street Journal*, you notice that short-term market interest rates (such as the federal funds rate or the yields on three-month Treasury bills) have been declining but that the Fed hasn't reduced its discount rate. Are the Fed's intentions for monetary policy expansionary or contractionary? The Fed may be trying to signal to financial markets that it wants short-term rates to rise. In that case, the Fed would be signaling a contractionary policy. ♦

Reserve Requirements

The Fed mandates that banks hold a certain fraction of their deposits in cash or deposits with the Fed. These **reserve requirements** are the last of the Fed's three principal monetary tools that we examine. In Chapter 17, we showed that the required reserve ratio is a determinant of the money multiplier in the money supply process. Recall that an increase in the required reserve ratio reduces the money multiplier and the money supply, whereas a reduction in the required reserve ratio increases the money multiplier and the money supply. Reserves can be stored as vault cash in banks or as deposits with the Federal Reserve. About 90% of banks meet their reserve requirements with vault cash. The other 10% comprise larger banks whose deposits at Federal Reserve banks account for most of those deposits.

The Board of Governors sets reserve requirements within congressional limits, an authority that was granted by Congress in the Banking Act of 1935. Historically, reserve requirements varied geographically, with member banks in large cities being required to hold more reserves relative to deposits than were banks in smaller cities and towns. This difference dates back to 1864, following the passage of the National Banking Act of 1863, and is another instance of the political compromises between rural and urban interests. Representatives of agricultural states feared abuse by large Eastern banks. To garner these representatives' support for the National Banking Act (1863) and later the Federal Reserve Act (1913), Congress authorized low reserve requirements for rural banks. Between 1966 and 1972, the Fed altered reserve requirements to reflect the size as well as location of depository institutions. In 1980, the Depository Institutions Deregulation and Monetary Control Act established uniform reserve requirements for all depository institutions, regardless of location.

Changes in Reserve Requirements

The Fed changes reserve requirements much more rarely than it conducts open market operations or changes the discount rate. Therefore Fed watchers view the announcement of a change in reserve requirements as a major shift in monetary policy. Because changes in reserve requirements require significant alterations in banks' portfolios, frequent changes would be disruptive. As a result, in the 30 years between 1950 and 1980, the Fed adjusted required reserve ratios gradually (about once a year) and followed changes by open market operations or discount lending to help banks adjust.

During the 1980s, the only changes in reserve requirements were shifts that were mandated by the Depository Institutions Deregulation and Monetary Control Act. Examples were a reduction (from November 1980 through October 1983) in the maturity of nonpersonal time deposits subject to a 3% reserve requirement (from four years to 18 months) and the automatic adjustment of the level of checkable deposits subject to the 3% requirement. In 1990, the Fed lowered reserve requirements on certain other time deposits to zero. In 1992, it reduced the reserve requirement on checkable deposits to 3% on the first $46.8 million and 10% on those in excess of $46.8 million. In 2003, the reserve requirement on checkable deposits was 0% on the first $6 million, then 3% up to $42.1 million, and 10% on those in excess of $42.1 million. Eurocurrency liabilities and nonpersonal time deposits currently have no reserve requirement. Over the past several years, lower reserve requirements and the introduction of sweep accounts at banks (which move customer deposits each day from liabilities against which reserves are required to liabilities with no reserve requirement) have reduced required reserve balances.

Measurement and Compliance

Every two weeks, the Fed monitors compliance with its reserve requirements by checking a bank's daily deposits. These two-week *maintenance periods* begin on a Thursday and end on a Wednesday. For each period, the Fed measures the bank's daily deposits with Federal Reserve banks. It calculates the average daily balances in the bank's transactions accounts over a two-week period ending the previous Monday. The Fed also checks the bank's vault cash over a two-week period ending the Monday three days before the maintenance period begins. These built-in accounting lags give the Fed time to analyze the reserve–deposit ratio and give the bank time to adjust its portfolio.

If a bank can't meet its reserve requirements, it can carry up to 4% or $50,000, whichever is greater, of its required reserves to the next two-week maintenance period. If this carryover proves inadequate and the bank still is deficient, the Fed charges interest on the deficit at a rate 2% above the discount rate. This higher rate gives banks an incentive to satisfy reserve requirements. (Similarly, a bank can carry forward up to 4% surplus of required reserves in anticipation of future deficits.) A bank that has inadequate reserves also may borrow funds in the federal funds market or from the Fed through the discount window. The federal funds market can be very active on Wednesdays, when maintenance periods end, as banks try to meet their reserve requirements.

Criticism of Reserve Requirements

Economists and policymakers continue to debate what the Fed's role in setting reserve requirements should be. In the following discussion, we present arguments for and against reserve requirements as a monetary policy tool.

Reserve requirements are costly as a monetary policy tool. Reserves earn no interest, so the use of reserve requirements to control the money supply process effectively places a tax on bank intermediation. In other words, by not being able to lend reserves, banks face a higher cost on funds that they obtain from depositors. For example, suppose that banks pay depositors 5% on deposits and that the required reserve ratio is 10%. On a deposit of $100, the bank must keep $10 in reserves and may loan the remaining $90. It must pay depositors $5 in interest, so its cost of funds to lend $90 is ($5/$90)(100) = 5.6%, rather than 5%.

Large increases in reserve requirements can adversely affect the economy. Increasing the tax on bank intermediation reduces bank lending, which decreases credit availability and the money supply.

Because reserve requirements are a tax on bank deposits and because unwise changes in reserve requirements may have bad economic consequences, economists and policymakers often debate whether the Fed *should* set reserve requirements. Over the years, they have offered two arguments in support of reserve requirements: the liquidity argument and the monetary control argument. To analyze whether the Fed should set reserve requirements, we need to find out how well each argument stands up to close scrutiny.

Liquidity argument. When banks convert liquid deposits to illiquid loans, they incur liquidity risk. As a result, some analysts argue that reserve requirements create a liquid pool of funds to assist illiquid, but solvent, banks during a banking panic. One problem with this view is that, although reserve requirements do produce a pool of liquid funds for the banking system as a whole, they have a limited effect on the liquidity of an individual bank. The decision to hold liquid assets is a portfolio allocation decision

OTHER TIMES, OTHER PLACES ...

An Early Mistake in Setting Reserve Requirements

During the banking crisis of the early 1930s, commercial banks cut back on lending and accumulated excess reserves of about $800 million by the end of 1933. Excess reserves were greater than 40% of required reserves, compared to less than 1% today. By the end of 1935, the level of excess reserves reached more than $3 billion, or about 115% of required reserves. The newly created Federal Open Market Committee worried that significant levels of excess reserves would eliminate its ability to dominate the money supply process. For example, an economic upturn could lead banks to reduce their excess reserves, thereby expanding the money supply.

The Fed needed to find a way to reduce the level of reserves. Large-scale open market sales of securities weren't possible; at about $2.5 billion, the Fed's portfolio of government securities wasn't large enough to eliminate banks' excess reserves. As a result, after it obtained control over the setting of reserve requirements in 1935, the Fed's first significant change was a series of increases in required reserve ratios between August 1936 and May 1937. These effectively doubled the level of required reserves relative to deposits. This strategy was unsuccessful because bank holdings of excess reserves reflected deliberate portfolio allocation decisions. Hence when the Fed increased reserve requirements, banks maintained their high excess reserves by cutting back on loans. This decline in bank lending made credit unavailable for many borrowers. Many economists blame the large reduction in the growth of the money supply and in the supply of bank credit as important causes of the business recession in 1937 and 1938. As bank lending declined, the Fed was pressured to reduce reserve requirements, which it did.

that is made by a bank. Reserve requirements limit the funds that a bank has available to invest in loans or securities, but they don't eliminate the need to maintain some portion of these funds in liquid assets. Individual banks still need to hold some of their portfolios in marketable securities as a cushion against unexpected deposit outflows.

Another problem with the liquidity argument is that the likelihood of a liquidity crisis depends not only on the volatility of withdrawals from banks, but also on the volatility of the value of bank assets and the availability to banks of funds from nondeposit sources. However, improvements in markets for loan sales and the growing number of nondeposit sources of funds make liquidity crises less likely, regardless of the volatility of depositors' withdrawals. Moreover, the Fed's ability to intervene directly in a liquidity crisis by making discount loans lessens the danger of such a crisis.

Monetary control argument. A second argument for reserve requirements is that they increase the central bank's control over the money supply process. Recall that the percentage of deposits that are held as reserves is one determinant of the money multiplier and hence of the responsiveness of the money supply to a change in the monetary base. Fed control of the reserve–deposit ratio through reserve requirements makes the money multiplier more stable and the money supply more controllable.

There are two problems with this argument. First, banks would hold reserves even if there were no reserve requirements. Hence reserve requirements need not greatly increase monetary control. Second, there is little evidence that reserve requirements actually improve the stability of the money multiplier.

Nobel laureate Milton Friedman proposed an extreme example of the monetary control argument: Banks should hold 100% reserves. Under such a system, bank reserves would equal deposits, and the monetary base (the sum of bank reserves and currency in the hands of the nonbank public) would equal the sum of currency and bank deposits, or the *M1* money supply. With 100% reserves, multiple deposit expansion would cease, giving the Fed complete control over currency plus deposits but not over the composition of deposits.

Would complete control of currency and bank deposits translate into control of the *effective* money supply? Probably not. Under a 100% reserve system, banks could not originate or hold loans. Alternative financial intermediaries would emerge to fill this lending vacuum. Because banks have special information advantages in certain types of lending, this shift in financial intermediation could be costly for the economy. Therefore high reserve requirements are not likely to improve monetary control or promote financial intermediaries' role in matching savers and borrowers.

Coping with reserve requirements. One incentive to form bank holding companies (BHCs) was the exemption of such companies' debt from reserve requirements. The Fed responded in 1970 to the growth in this alternative source of funds by imposing a 5% reserve requirement on commercial paper issued by BHCs. In October 1979, in an attempt to increase its control over the money supply, the Fed announced reserve requirements of 8% for several nondeposit sources of bank funds, including repurchase agreements, federal funds borrowing, and asset sales to foreign banks. Since passage of the Depository Institutions Deregulation and Monetary Control Act of 1980, the Fed has applied reserve requirements only to checkable deposits, Eurocurrency accounts, and nonpersonal time deposits with a maturity of less than 18 months. (And since 1992, reserve requirements apply only to checkable deposits.) Hence banks (particularly large banks) can effectively avoid the tax on intermediation as they acquire funds.

Reserve Requirements in Other Countries

Although the reserve requirements imposed by the Bank of Japan do not allow for the payment of interest (consistent with U.S. practice), not all countries follow this practice. In late 1998, for example, the European Central Bank (ECB) inaugurated a system of interest-bearing minimum reserves as a monetary policy tool for the members of European economic and monetary union. The ECB's required reserve ratio varies between 1.5% and 2.5%, and reserve balances are credited with interest at the prevailing repo rate, the ECB's key short-term interest rate. In August 2003, China raised reserve requirements to curb what was deemed to be excessive growth in bank lending.

Around the world there has been a general trend toward lower reserve requirements. Such requirements were eliminated entirely in the 1990s in Canada, Australia, New Zealand, and Switzerland, for example. One reason for this trend is the acknowledgment of central banks that reserve requirements effectively tax banking and financial intermediation. Such a tax raises the cost of funds and can make banks less competitive in the global financial marketplace. When the Fed announced lower reserve requirements in the United States in 1992, it specifically cited the "tax cut" argument to justify its action.

Because reserve requirements are now very low, some central bankers have worried that at very low levels of required reserves, the central bank has little control over short-term interest rates. Some countries (including Australia, Canada, and New Zealand) have responded to this concern by setting up a *channel* or *corridor system* for conducting monetary policy. Under this system, the central bank establishes a standing lending facility (like that used in the United States) ready to lend any amount to banks at a fixed *lombard rate*, i_l. The central bank then establishes another standing facility that pays a set interest rate i_r on any reserves that banks wish to deposit with the central bank. Hence as the demand curve for reserves shifts, the overnight interest rate always lies between i_r and i_l.

CHECKPOINT

Suppose the Fed reduces the reserve requirement on checkable deposits. How does your bank benefit? Do you and other depositors benefit? In the short run, your bank's profits increase; it can invest the freed funds and earn additional income from loans and investments (reserves pay no interest). In the long run, returns to depositors increase, as the bank becomes willing to pay more to attract deposits. ♦

Fed Watching: Analyzing the Policy Tools

All three of the Fed's principal monetary policy tools influence the monetary base primarily through changes in the demand for or supply of reserves. Hence to develop your skills as a Fed watcher, you need to study carefully the market for reserves, also known as the federal funds market. This section demonstrates how you can predict the outcome of changes in Fed policy on the level of bank reserves, *R*, and the federal funds rate, i_{ff}. The change in the federal funds rate will be mirrored by other short-term interest rates. Thus being able to predict how the fed funds rate will change will help you to make more informed investment decisions.

The Federal Funds Market

To analyze the determinants of the federal funds rate, we need to examine the banking system's demand for and the Fed's supply of reserves. We use a graphical analysis of the demand for and supply of reserves to see how the Fed uses its policy tools to influence the federal funds rate and the money supply.

Demand. Reserve demand reflects banks' demand for required and excess reserves. The demand function for federal funds, *D*, shown in Fig. 20.1, includes both required reserves, *RR*, and excess reserves, *ER*, for constant reserve requirements and market interest rates other than the federal funds rate. As the federal funds rate, i_{ff}, increases, banks prefer to hold a lower level of reserves; a higher federal funds rate increases the "reserve tax," so required reserves are negatively related to market interest rates. Banks' demand for excess reserves is also sensitive to interest rate changes; at a lower federal funds rate, the opportunity cost of holding excess reserves falls and the quantity of excess reserves demanded rises. Hence the total quantity demanded of reserves is negatively related to the federal funds rate.

Supply. The supply function for reserves, *S*, also shown in Fig. 20.1, represents the supply by the Fed of borrowed reserves (discount loans) and nonborrowed reserves (supplied by open market operations). Note that the supply curve is not a straight line: The vertical portion represents nonborrowed reserves, *NBR*, supplied by the Fed; that is, regardless of the federal funds rate, reserves equal to *NBR* are available. The change in the slope of the supply curve occurs at the discount rate, i_d: At a federal funds rate below the discount rate, borrowing from the Fed is zero because banks can borrow more cheaply from other banks. Hence, in this case, reserves equal nonborrowed reserves. When there is demand pressure for the federal funds rate to move above the discount rate, borrowing increases. Specifically, if i_{ff} were greater than i_d, banks would want to borrow as much as they could from the Fed at rate i_d and lend the funds out at the higher rate i_{ff}. Hence the supply curve becomes flat (that is, perfectly elastic), as shown in Fig. 20.1.

Web Site Suggestions: http://www.federalreserve.gov/fomc/fundsrate.htm Discusses federal funds rate targets.

Equilibrium. The equilibrium federal funds rate and level of reserves occur at the intersection of the demand and supply curves in Fig. 20.1. Equilibrium reserves equal R^*, the equilibrium federal funds rate equals i^*_{ff}, and the discount rate is i_d.

Open Market Operations

Suppose that the Fed decides to purchase $1 billion of Treasury securities. If nothing else changes, an open market purchase of securities by the Fed shifts the reserve supply curve to the right, from S_0 to S_1, as in Fig. 20.2(a), increasing bank reserves and decreasing the federal funds rate. As a result of the open market purchase, the volume of bank reserves increases from R^*_0 to R^*_1, and the federal funds rate declines from i^*_{ff0} to i^*_{ff1}. Similarly, an open market sale of securities by the Fed shifts the reserve supply curve to the left, from S_0 to S_1, in Fig. 20.2(b), decreasing the level of bank reserves from R^*_0 to R^*_1 and increasing the federal funds rate from i^*_{ff0} to i^*_{ff1}. An open market purchase of securities by the Fed decreases the federal funds rate. An open market sale of securities increases the federal funds rate.

Changes in the Discount Rate

Now let's examine the effects of a change in the discount rate on the level of reserves and the federal funds rate. Suppose that the Fed decides to raise the discount rate. An increase in the discount rate means that banks will find borrowing to be less attractive at any federal funds rate. (Assume, as in the figure, that some discount lending is occurring.) Figure 20.3(a) shows that an increase in the discount rate from i_{d0} to i_{d1} shifts the horizontal portion of the supply schedule upward from S_0 to S_1. The equilibrium level of reserves falls from R^*_0 to R^*_1, and the federal funds rate rises from i^*_{ff0} to i^*_{ff1}.

Suppose that the Fed decided to cut the discount rate. In this case, banks now find borrowing more attractive at any federal funds rate. Figure 20.3(b) shows that a decrease in the discount rate from i_{d0} to i_{d1} shifts the horizontal portion of the supply

FIGURE 20.1

Equilibrium in the Federal Funds Market

Equilibrium in the market for reserves is at the intersection of the demand (D) and supply (S) curves. Given nonborrowed reserves, NBR, and the discount rate, i_d, equilibrium reserves equal R^*, and the equilibrium federal funds rate is i^*_{ff}.

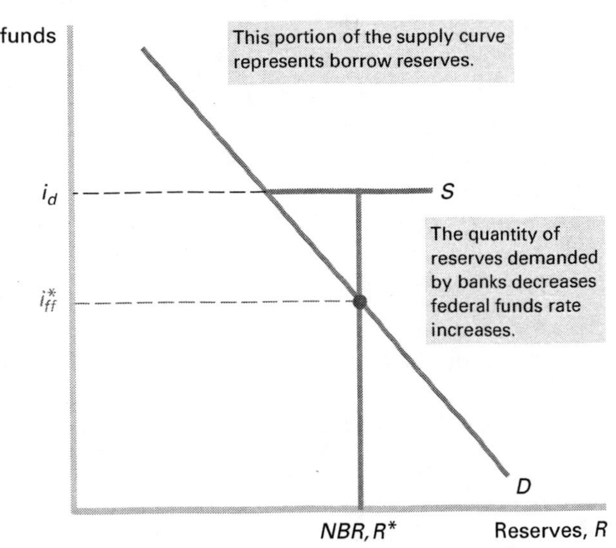

FIGURE 20.2 Effects of Open Market Operations on the Federal Funds Market

As shown in (a):

1. An open market purchase of securities by the Fed increases nonborrowed reserves, shifting the supply curve to the right from S_0 to S_1.
2. Reserves increase from R_0^* to R_1^*, while the federal funds rate falls from i_{ff0}^* to i_{ff1}^*.

As shown in (b):

1. An open market sale of securities by the Fed reduces nonborrowed reserves, shifting the supply curve to the left from S_0 to S_1.
2. Reserves decrease from R_0^* to R_1^*, while the federal funds rate rises from i_{ff0}^* to i_{ff1}^*.

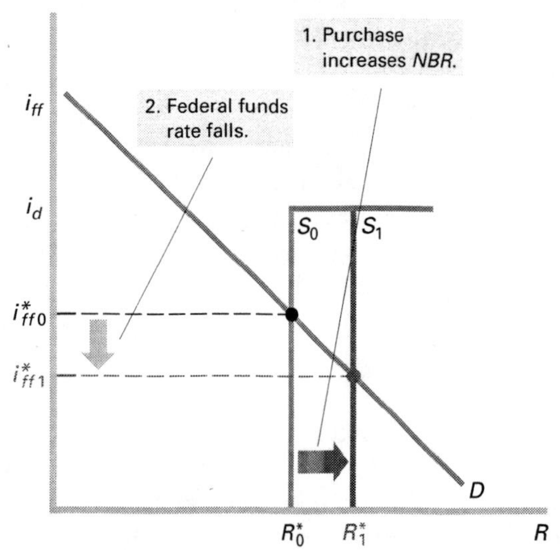

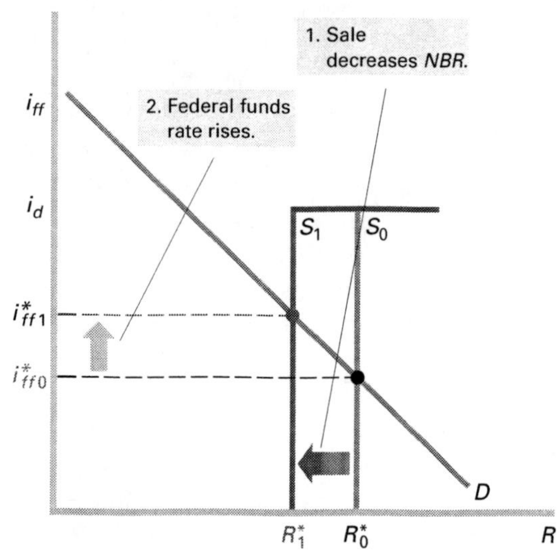

curve downward from S_0 to S_1. The equilibrium level of reserves rises from R_0^* to R_1^*, and the federal funds rate falls from i_{ff0}^* to i_{ff1}^*.

Changes in Reserve Requirements

Finally, suppose that the Fed decides to raise the required reserve ratio. If the other factors underlying the demand and supply curves for reserves are held constant, an increase in the required reserve ratio shifts the demand curve to the right (from D_0 to D_1) because banks have to hold more reserves, as in Fig. 20.4(a). As a result, the federal funds rate increases (from i_{ff0}^* to i_{ff1}^*). However, a reduction in the required reserve ratio, as shown in Fig. 20.4(b), shifts the demand curve to the left (from D_0 to D_1) because banks demand a smaller amount of reserves, decreasing the federal funds rate (from i_{ff0}^* to i_{ff1}^*). If nothing else changes, an increase in reserve requirements increases the federal funds rate. A decrease in reserve requirements decreases the federal funds rate. Generally, however, the Fed does not use changes in reserve requirements to affect the federal funds rate; instead, the Fed uses changes in nonborrowed reserves to offset effects on the federal funds rate of a change in reserve requirements.

Other Disturbances of the Monetary Base

You can use graphs to analyze other disturbances of the monetary base that might lead the Fed to conduct defensive open market operations. For example, an increase in Federal Reserve float increases nonborrowed reserves (Chapter 18). Hence the supply

FIGURE 20.3 **Effects of Changes in the Discount Rate on the Federal Funds Market**

As shown in (a):

1. The Fed raises the discount rate from i_{d0} to i_{d1}.
2. The new supply curve is S_1.
3. The level of reserves falls from R_0^* to R_1^*, and the federal funds rate rises from i_{ff0}^* to i_{ff1}^*.

As shown in (b):

1. The Fed cuts the discount rate from i_{d0} to i_{d1}.
2. The new supply curve is S_1.
3. The level of reserves rises from R_0^* to R_1^*, and the federal funds rate falls from i_{ff0}^* to i_{ff1}^*.

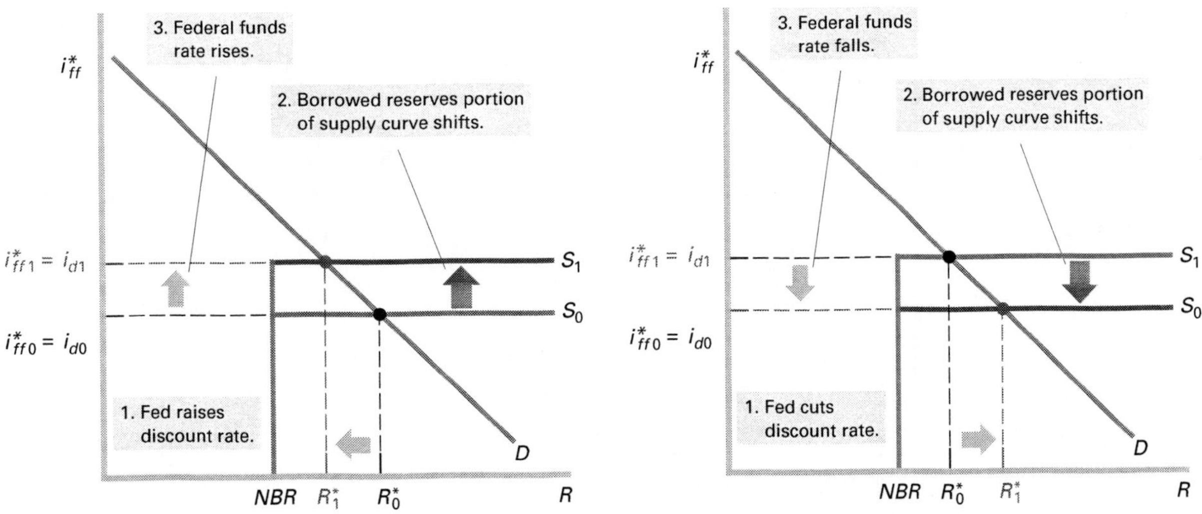

curve for reserves shifts to the right, leading to higher reserves and a lower federal funds rate than otherwise would occur. As we noted in discussing defensive transactions earlier in this chapter, the Fed can shift the supply curve for reserves back to the left (by reducing nonborrowed reserves) with an open market sale of securities.

As another example, a large increase in U.S. Treasury deposits with the Fed causes bank deposits to fall. As a result, reserves fall, the supply curve for reserves shifts to the left, and the federal funds rate rises. The Open Market Trading Desk, being in contact with the Treasury, knows about the Treasury action and therefore offsets it with another defensive open market purchase of securities. This action shifts the supply curve back to the right and restores the level of reserves and the federal funds rate to their initial levels.

The Federal Funds Rate and Monetary Policy

Many economists and financial market analysts use changes in the federal funds rate as a summary measure of the Fed's intentions for monetary policy. The reason is that the Fed's substantial control of the level of bank reserves gives it great influence over the level of the federal funds rate. An increase in the federal funds rate relative to other interest rates is interpreted as contractionary, signaling the Fed's intention to raise interest rates and discourage spending in the economy. Conversely, a decrease in the federal funds rate relative to other interest rates is interpreted as expansionary, signaling the

FIGURE 20.4 **Effects of Changes in Required Reserves on the Federal Funds Market**

As shown in (a):

1. An increase in reserve requirements by the Fed increases required reserves, shifting the demand curve from D_0 to D_1.
2. The federal funds rate rises from i^*_{ff0} to i^*_{ff1}.

As shown in (b):

1. A decrease in reserve requirements by the Fed decreases required reserves, shifting the demand curve from D_0 to D_1.
2. The federal funds rate falls from i^*_{ff0} to i^*_{ff1}.

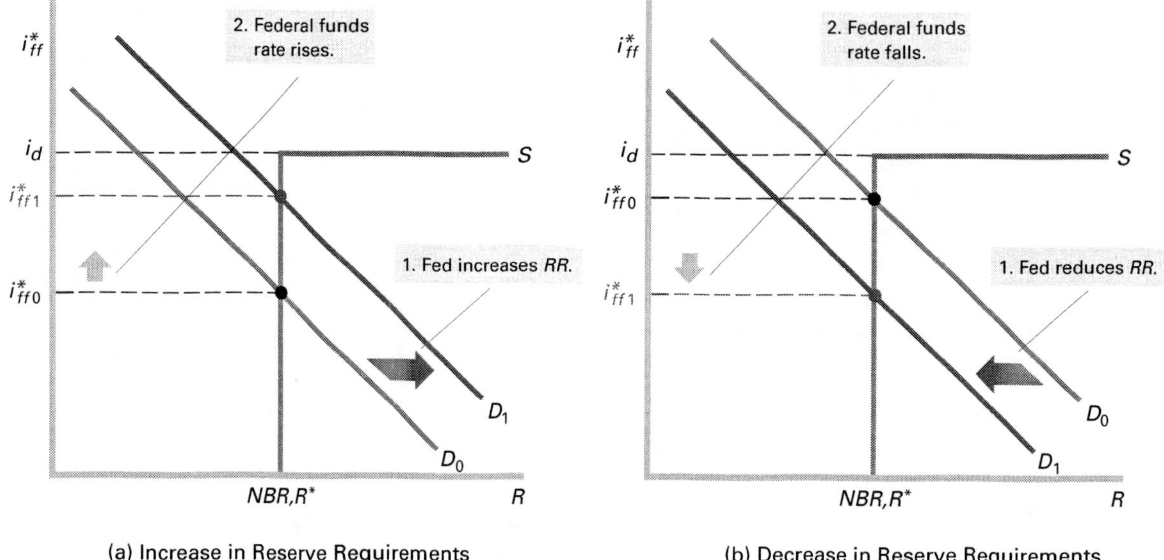

Fed's intention to reduce interest rates and encourage spending. The use of short-term interest rates to signal shifts in monetary policy is also common in countries in the European Monetary Union, the United Kingdom, and Japan.

Our graphical analysis confirms this view and shows how analysts can predict consequences of the Fed's actions for the level of reserves and the federal funds rate. Thus, if nothing else changes, an open market purchase of securities by the Fed reduces the federal funds rate. Purchases are expansionary because they increase the supply of reserves that banks use either to purchase securities or to make loans. As a result, the larger reserves in the banking system lead to lower short-term interest rates. Sales are contractionary because they reduce reserves and increase short-term interest rates. An increase in the discount rate is contractionary when it signals that the Fed wants to raise short-term interest rates. A reduction in the discount rate is expansionary when it signals that the Fed wants to reduce short-term interest rates. If nothing else changes, an increase in reserve requirements with no offsetting changes in the supply of reserves is contractionary and raises the federal funds rate. A decrease in reserve requirements is expansionary and lowers the federal funds rate.

Predicting the outcome of a change in the Fed funds rate. On November 6, 2002, the Federal Open Market Committee voted to lower its federal funds rate target from 1.75% to 1.25%, its first change in 2002, but after 11 cuts in 2001. How does this action affect the federal funds rate? It is a market-determined interest rate, not literally set by the Fed. We can illustrate what happens using the reserves market diagram.

As in Fig. 20.2(a), the Fed fulfills its intention to reduce the federal funds rate by increasing the supply of reserves. It conducts open market purchases to increase nonborrowed reserves. This action shifts the supply curve from S_0 to S_1, increasing reserves from R_0^* to R_1^* and lowering the federal funds rate from i_{ff0}^* to i_{ff1}^*.

The falling cost of funds to lenders leads to lower interest rates charged to private borrowers, as indicated by the decrease in loan rates to household and business borrowers. This decrease in loan rates increases demand for business investment and consumer durables.

Concluding Remarks

Fed watchers try to predict the Fed's actions regarding open market operations, discount policy, and reserve requirements so as to forecast changes in the federal funds rate. (Recently, analysts have also begun to consider the role played by uncertainty in bank reserve balances in determining the federal funds rate; for example, on busier days, banks may desire to hold a larger cushion of reserves to protect against penalties for overnight overdrafts.) Predicting Fed changes is the first step toward predicting the effects of monetary policy on other interest rates. However, the Fed's significant control over the federal funds rate does not imply that it can control other interest rates. Recall, for example, that the expectations theory of the term structure of interest rates states that longer-term interest rates reflect, in part, expectations of *future* short-term rates. Therefore *expected future Fed actions*, not just current Fed policy, are important.

CHECKPOINT

Suppose that you read in *The Wall Street Journal* that the Fed raised its target for the federal funds rate by one-half of a percentage point. How would you expect the Fed to achieve its objective? Using the graphical analysis of the federal funds market, you would expect the Fed to use open market sales to reduce nonborrowed reserves, shifting the *NBR* curve to the left and raising the federal funds rate. ♦

KEY TERMS AND CONCEPTS

- Discount policy
  - Discount window
  - Primary credit
  - Seasonal credit
  - Secondary credit
- Open market operations
  - Defensive transactions
  - Dynamic transactions
  - Federal Reserve repurchase agreements
  - General directive
  - Matched sale-purchase transactions
  - Open Market Trading Desk
  - Outright purchases and sales
- Reserve requirements

SUMMARY

1. Open market operations (purchases and sales of securities in financial markets) are the most widely used of the Fed's principal monetary policy tools. The Federal Open Market Committee (FOMC) issues guidelines for open market operations as general directives. Some transactions are dynamic—that is, designed to implement changes in the monetary base suggested by the FOMC. Most transactions are defensive—that is, designed to offset unintended disturbances in the monetary base.
2. The Fed's discount policy sets the discount rate and the terms of discount lending. The Fed fulfills its role as the lender of last resort by providing primary, secondary, and seasonal credit.

MOVING FROM THEORY TO PRACTICE . . .

FINANCIAL TIMES JUNE 26, 2003

Fed Rate Cut Combats Deflation

The Federal Reserve cut interest rates by a quarter-point yesterday and
a signaled continued determination to counter the danger that the U.S. would slide towards deflation.

Although the cut took the Fed funds rate to 1 percent, the lowest for four decades, it was smaller than the average market expectation and was accompanied by a muted statement that largely reiterated the Fed's existing stance.

As in May, the Fed's open market committee said the risks were tilted towards a further unwelcome fall in inflation from its already low level. It added: "On balance the Committee believes that the latter concern is likely to predominate for the foreseeable future."

Although this statement was more explicit than that issued after the May meeting, many investors had expected an even clearer promise to keep rates low and stamp out the risk of deflation.

Bond yields and expec-
b tations of future short-term interest rates rose sharply after the decision, while stock prices fell.

Explaining its decision, the Fed statement said the committee thought "a slightly more expansive monetary policy would add further support for an economy which it expects to improve over time."

The Fed continued to sound an optimistic note about the prospects of the U.S. economic recovery gathering speed. Although it noted the economy had "yet to exhibit sustainable growth"—often defined as 3–3.5 percent—it said
c the risks were balanced around the prospect of achieving such growth in the next few quarters.

"Recent signs point to a firming in spending, markedly improved financial conditions, and labour and product markets that are stabilising," the Fed said. . . .

Yesterday's announcement is the latest stage in a campaign to prevent deflationary psychology taking hold in the U.S. which has taken the Fed beyond its traditional strategy of changing short-term interest rates. Fed officials have emphasised the need to act pre-emptively against deflation, while continuing to argue that the prospect of a sustained fall in prices in the U.S. remains remote.

Longer-term interest rates have fallen sharply over the past two months as investors inferred a commitment to keep its official short-term rate low over the medium term.

Before the Fed's decision yesterday, data were released showing business investment, the missing piece of the faltering US economic recovery, continuing to disappoint. Official figures on durable goods for May showed new orders for non-defence capital goods—often used as a proxy for investment—falling by 0.9 per cent. Overall, durable goods orders fell by 0.3 per cent, against economists' average expectations of a 0.8 per cent rise.

But separate figures suggested that the housing market was still responding strongly to low mortgage interest rates, with sales of new homes in May reaching a record high.

ANALYZING THE NEWS ...

Analysts first look for effects of the Fed's use of open market operations and discount policy in the federal funds market, the market through which banks lend to each other overnight. Actions by the Federal Reserve to push the federal funds rate down are interpreted as expansionary monetary policy, since interest rates that are charged to households and businesses will also fall, encouraging spending.

a On June 25, 2003, the Federal Open Market Committee voted to lower its federal funds rate target from 1.25% to 1%, the lowest rate in nearly four decades. How does this action affect the federal funds rate? It is a market-determined interest rate, not literally set by the Fed. We can illustrate what happens using the reserves market diagram. In the figure, the Fed fulfills its intention to reduce the federal funds rate by increasing the supply of reserves. It conducts open market purchases to increase nonborrowed reserves. This action shifts the supply curve from S_0 to S_1, increasing reserves from R_0^* to R_1^* and reducing the federal funds rate from i_{ff0}^* to i_{ff1}^*. As a consequence of the Fed's action, the discount rate (the rate charged on primary credit) also declined from i_{d0} to i_{d1} (in this case, from 2.25% to 2%).

b Short-term interest rates are closely linked to the federal funds rate. The falling cost of funds to lenders leads to lower interest rates charged to private borrowers, as indicated by the decrease in loan rates to household and business borrowers. This decrease in loan rates raises demand for business investment and consumer durables, lessening the likelihood of an economic downturn.

Because many market participants expected the Fed to reduce the funds rate by more than 0.25%, market expectations of expected future short-term rates rose. As a consequence, interest rates on longer-term bonds, which reflect in large part those expected future short-term interest rates, rose as well.

c The Federal Reserve's statement revealed both the FOMC's commitment to support the emerging economic recovery in the United States and its view that risks of achieving sustainable growth were balanced. Market participants interpreted this statement as indicating that, barring future adverse developments in the U.S. economy, further reductions in the federal funds rate were unlikely.

For further thought...

Given the FOMC's concern about deflation, or a falling price level in the United States, what effect would news that deflationary pressures were receding (or nonexistent) have on the federal funds rate target? On longer-term interest rates? Explain.

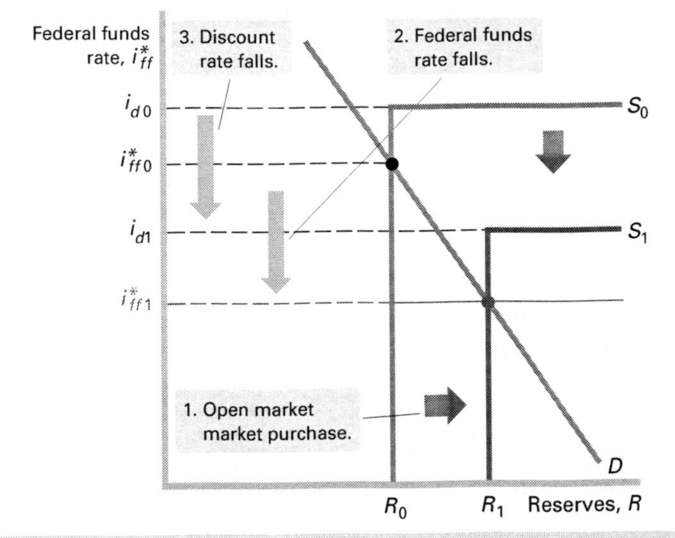

3. Reserve requirements are a potent but drastic way to control the monetary base. Increases in reserve requirements decrease the money multiplier; decreases in reserve requirements increase the money multiplier. Because large changes in reserve requirements can cause costly reallocations of banks' portfolios, the Fed generally avoids them.

4. The federal funds rate is one indicator of monetary policy. A decrease in the federal funds rate relative to other market interest rates is usually associated with an expansionary monetary policy. An increase in the federal funds rate relative to other market interest rates is usually associated with a contractionary monetary policy.

REVIEW QUESTIONS

1. If open market operations are considered the Fed's most important monetary policy tool, why were they not mentioned in the original Federal Reserve Act?
2. Since the 1930s, what has been the Fed's most important tool for monetary policy? What part of the Federal Reserve System determines how this tool is used?
3. What advantages do open market operations have over the other monetary policy tools available to the Fed?
4. *Evaluate*: The Fed was originally established to use discount loans to help put an end to banking panics. Deposit insurance has effectively put an end to banking panics; therefore, we no longer need the Fed. If we allow the Fed to continue to operate we ought, at the very least, to eliminate its ability to grant discount loans.
5. What causes changes in the rate charged on discount loans?
6. *Evaluate*: The Fed changes the reserve requirement frequently because it is such a powerful tool.
7. What is the maintenance period for bank reserves? How does the Fed calculate a bank's required reserves?
8. If a bank is required to hold reserves of $150 million but held only $149 million of reserves over the maintenance period, will the Fed penalize it? Why or why not?
9. What is wrong with the liquidity argument for reserve requirements?
10. How does the Fed police the discount window?
11. *Evaluate*: Because deposit insurance can eliminate the chance of bank lending, discount lending is unnecessary.
12. What type of credit (primary, secondary, or seasonal) does each of the following discount loans represent?
    a. Well-capitalized Bigbank borrows from the Fed because of liquidity problems when one of its major depositors suddenly switches its accounts to another bank.
    b. Weaker Megabank has seen large depositors to withdraw their funds, forcing Megabank to borrow from the Fed.
    c. First Bank borrows $5 million so that it can make loans to farmers for planting, as it does every April.
13. What is a Fed watcher?
14. In daily trading by the Open Market Trading Desk at the Federal Reserve Bank of New York, why does the account manager consult with market participants? With the Treasury Department? With two or more members of the FOMC?
15. What are the differences between dynamic and defensive open market operations?

ANALYTICAL PROBLEMS

16. What interest rate is most directly affected by open market operations? What happens to this interest rate and the money supply when the Fed engages in open market purchases? When the Fed engages in open market sales?
17. If the money multiplier is 8, how large a change in the money supply will result from the sale of $1 billion of bonds by the Fed on the open market? Will the money supply increase or decrease?
18. How could the Fed use its three principal monetary policy tools to decrease the money supply by $100 million if the money multiplier is 10 and the monetary base is $500 million?
19. What is the Fed likely to do near the Christmas holiday season, when the public uses more currency?
20. Which of the following open market operations are defensive and which are dynamic?

a. The Treasury makes a large payment, which the Fed offsets with an open market purchase.

b. The economy strengthens unexpectedly, to which the Fed responds with open market sales.

c. Bad weather prevents checks from being cleared as quickly as usual, allowing float to increase in the banking system; the Fed responds with open market sales.

d. The dollar's foreign exchange value declines, prompting the Fed to respond with open market sales.

21. The following list contains parts of two different directives to the Open Market Trading Desk from the FOMC. Which is expansionary and which is contractionary?

a. . . . risks are weighted mainly toward conditions that may generate economic weakness in the foreseeable future . . .

b. . . . risks are weighted mainly toward conditions that may generate inflationary pressures in the near future . . .

22. Suppose that the Fed were no longer allowed to grant discount loans. Show the effects on the reserves market diagram. Under these circumstances would an open market purchase have a smaller or a larger effect on the equilibrium federal funds rate? Use a reserves market diagram to illustrate your answer.

23. On the reserves market diagram, show how the Fed can use open market operations to offset an increased demand for reserves by holding the federal funds rate constant.

24. For (a)–(d), use the graphical analysis of equilibrium in the reserves market to predict changes in nonborrowed reserves, borrowed reserves, and the federal funds rate.

a. The Fed conducts open market sales of securities.

b. The Fed more strongly discourages banks' use of the discount window.

c. Banks and the nonbank public become concerned that a banking crisis is imminent and that depositors will prefer to invest in securities in financial markets.

d. The Fed lowers the discount rate and conducts open market purchases of securities.

DATA QUESTIONS

25. Banks complain that reserve requirements hurt their profits because they pay interest to depositors but don't earn anything on their reserves. In the latest *Federal Reserve Bulletin*, find the table that lists reserve requirements. Suppose that a bank has $1 billion in transaction accounts. Calculate the bank's required reserves. In the same publication, look at the average federal funds rate for the past year. Multiply the federal funds rate times the amount of required reserves to determine the cost to the bank of complying with reserve requirements. However, the bank would have held reserves for transaction purposes, even if no reserves were required. Suppose that the bank would hold 5% of its deposits in reserve even if reserves were not required. How much does this holding of nonrequired reserves reduce the bank's profits? What, then, is the true cost of reserve requirements?

26. In carrying out open market operations, the open market desk buys and sells U.S. government securities on a daily basis. What type of securities—short term, intermediate, or long term—do you think it buys and sells the most? Locate the third chapter of the Federal Reserve publication "The Federal Reserve System: Purposes and Functions" at http://www.federalreserve.gov/pf/pf.htm to find out. In terms of liquidity, why does the choice of this security type make sense with respect to the conduct of open market operations?

27. The Federal Reserve's Discount Window Web site (http://www.frbdiscountwindow.org/) maintains information that would be of interest to banks that use the discount market. Consider the historical data listed for the seasonal credit. Does it seem to follow changes in the effective federal funds rate (which can be found at http://research.stlouisfed.org/fred2/data/DFF.txt)? Explain the likely outcome if the Fed kept this rate consistently higher than the federal funds rate. What would happen if it kept this rate consistently lower? Answer verbally and graphically, using a supply and demand diagram for the federal funds market.

28. During a recession, the Federal Reserve's Open Market Committee can be expected to lower its target for the federal funds rate. Consider the federal funds rate targets that existed since 1990 (at http://www.federalreserve.gov/fomc/fundsrate.htm#basis). During the most recent recession, it lowered this rate to 1 percent (the lowest rate in 45 years). How does this rate compare with the lowest target that resulted in response to the recession of the early 1990s? Compare the length of time that each rate was maintained during each recession. Why do you suppose there is a difference?

Glossary

Accommodating policy Actions to stimulate aggregate demand to restore output and jobs, but at the cost of greater inflation. (28)

Adverse selection The problem of distinguishing good-risk applicants from bad-risk applicants before making a loan or providing insurance. (11, 12)

Agency office A foreign bank office in the United States that cannot take deposits from U.S. residents, although it can transfer funds from abroad to the United States and make loans in the United States. (16)

Agents Managers who control (but do not own) the assets of a firm or organization. (11)

Aggregate demand The sum of demands for an economy's goods and services for consumption, investment, government purchases (not including transfer payments), and net exports. (25)

Aggregate demand (*AD*) curve The graph of the relationship between the aggregate demand for goods and services and the aggregate price level. (25)

Aggregate supply The total amount of output that producers in the economy are willing to supply and sell at a given price level. (25)

Aggregate supply (*AS*) curve The graph of the relationship between the aggregate output that firms in the economy are willing to supply and the aggregate price level. (25)

Appreciation An increase in the value of a currency against another currency. (8, 22)

Asset A thing of value that can be owned; a use of funds and a claim on a borrower's income. (2, 3)

Asymmetric information A condition that occurs when borrowers have some information about their opportunities or activities that they do not disclose to lenders, creditors, or insurers. (3, 11)

Auction market A secondary financial market in which prices are set by competitive bidding by a large number of traders acting on behalf of individual buyers and sellers. (3)

Automated teller machines Electronic devices for performing banking transactions. (2, 13)

Balance-of-payments accounts An accounting device for measuring private and government flows of funds between a country and foreign countries. (22)

Balance sheet A statement showing an individual's or firm's financial position at a point in time. It lists assets, liabilities, and net worth. (13)

Balance sheet channel A description of ways in which interest rate changes from monetary policy affect borrowers' net worth and spending decisions. (27)

Bank A financial institution that accepts deposits from savers and makes loans to borrowers. (12, 13)

Bank assets Cash items and funds used in securities investments, loans, and other asset holdings by the bank. (13)

Bank failure A situation in which a bank cannot pay its depositors in full and still have enough reserves to meet its reserve requirements. (13)

Bank holding company A large firm that holds many different banks as subsidiaries. It was originally used by banks to get around branching restrictions. (14)

Bank lending channel A description of ways in which monetary policy influences spending decisions of bank-dependent borrowers. (27)

Bank liabilities Funds acquired by the bank from savers. (13)

Bank net worth The excess of the value of bank assets over the value of bank liabilities. (13)

Bank reserves The sum of an institution's vault cash and deposits with the central bank. (13)

Bank run A sequence of events in which depositors lose confidence in a bank, for real or imagined reasons, and make withdrawals, exhausting the bank's liquid funds. (14)

Bankers' acceptances Time drafts that establish credit between parties who do not know each other, facilitating international trade. (3, 16)

Banking panics Waves of severe bank runs that cause contractions in credit availability, often culminating in business recessions. (14)

Barter The exchange of goods and services by trading output directly with one another. (2)

Basel I Accord Initial framework for capital regulation of banks, put forth under the Bank for International Settlements. (14, 15)

Basel II Accord Updated and extended framework for bank capital regulation, reflecting improved techniques for measuring and managing risks. (14, 15)

Basis risk The imperfect correlation of changes in the price of a hedged instrument and changes in the price of the instrument actually traded in the futures market. (9)

Beta A measure of the response of a security's expected return to changes in the value of the market portfolio. (5)

Board of Governors The Board of the Federal Reserve System, made up of seven members, appointed by the President, who administer monetary policy and set the discount rate. (19)

Bond rating A single statistic summarizing the assessment of a firm's net worth, cash flow, and prospects—in short, its likely ability to meet its debt obligations. (7)

Borrowed reserves (*BR*, discount loans) A component of the monetary base consisting of reserves borrowed from the central bank. (17)

Borrowers Demanders of funds for consumer durables, houses, and business plant and equipment. (3)

Borrowings Nondeposit liabilities of a bank, including short-term loans in the federal funds market, loans from the bank's affiliates, and discount loans. (13)

Branches Individual banking offices in different locations owned by the same banking firm. (13, 14)

Branching restrictions Geographical limitations on banking firms' ability to open more than one office, or branch. (14)

Bretton Woods system A fixed exchange rate system that permitted smoother short-term economic adjustments than were possible under the gold standard, based on the convertibility of U.S. dollars into gold at a price of $35.00 per ounce. (22)

Brokered deposits A financial innovation in which a depositor with an amount to invest over the deposit insurance limit goes to a broker who buys certificates of deposit in different banks, giving the depositor insurance on the entire amount. (15)

Brokers Individuals who earn commissions by matching buyers and sellers in a particular market. (12)

Bubble A situation in which the price of an asset is more than its fundamental value. (10)

Budget deficit The excess of government spending over tax revenue. (5, 18)

Business cycle The periodic fluctuations in aggregate output, consisting of expansion (a boom) followed by contraction (a recession). (1, 26)

Call option The right to buy an underlying asset, which is obtained by the buyer of the call option. Sellers have an obligation to sell. (10)

Call report Periodic report filed by a U.S. bank with regulatory authorities, describing its earnings, assets and liabilities, and operations. (14)

CAMELS rating system Bank examination grade in the United States in the form of C (capital adequacy), A (asset quality), M (management), E (earnings), L (liquidity), and S (sensitivity to market risk). (14)

Capital account The balance-of-payments account that measures trade in existing assets among countries. (22)

Capital account balance A country's capital inflows minus its capital outflows. (22)

Capital controls Government-imposed barriers to foreign savers' investing in domestic assets or to domestic savers' investing in foreign assets. (22)

Capital inflow The flow of funds into a country to buy domestic assets. (22)

Capital markets Financial markets for trading debt instruments with a maturity greater than one year and equity instruments. (3)

Capital outflow The flow of funds from a country to buy foreign assets. (22)

Cash markets Markets in which actual claims are bought and sold with immediate settlement. (3)

Central bank A special governmental or quasi-governmental institution within the financial system that regulates the medium of exchange. (2)

Central bank credibility The belief by the public that central bank announcements reflect its true policy intentions. (28)

Certificate of deposit (CD) A fixed-maturity instrument, sold by a bank to depositors, that pays principal and interest at maturity, with a penalty for early withdrawal. (3)

Channel or corridor system System for conducting monetary policy that keeps short-term interest rates within the range between the interest rate paid on reserves and the discount rate. (20)

Checkable deposits Accounts that grant a depositor the right to write checks to individuals, firms, or the government. (13)

Checks Promises to pay definitive money on demand; checks are drawn on funds deposited with a financial institution. (2)

Circuit breakers Interventions that are designed to restore orderly securities markets. (10)

Closed economy An economy of a country that neither borrows from nor lends to foreign countries. (5)

Closed-end mutual fund A fund that sells a fixed number of nonredeemable shares, which are then traded over-the-counter like common stock. The price fluctuates with the value of the underlying assets. (12)

Coinsurance An insurance option that requires the policyholder to pay a certain fraction of the costs of a claim, in addition to the deductible. (12)

Cold turkey Reducing inflation all at once, rather than gradually. (28)

Collateral Assets that are pledged to pay for a loan in the event of default on the loan. (11, 13)

Commercial bank(s) The largest group of depository institutions, which offer risk-sharing, liquidity (checking accounts), and information services that benefit savers and borrowers. (3, 12, 13)

Commercial bank loan A loan to businesses or consumers that is made by banks and financial companies. (3)

Commercial paper A liquid, short-term investment for savers that is used by high-quality, well-known firms and financial institutions to raise funds. (3, 13)

Commodity money Physical goods (particularly precious metals) that are used as the medium of exchange. (2)

Compensating balance A required minimum amount in a checking account that is used as a form of collateral in commercial loans. (13)

Compounding Earning interest on interest as savings are accumulated over a period of time. (4)

Consol A (perpetual) coupon bond with an infinite maturity; its price is based on the present value of the coupon payments. (4)

Consumer price index (CPI) An index of prices of a marketbasket of goods purchased by urban consumers. It is a commonly used measure of inflation. (2, 28)

Contagion The spreading of bad news about one bank to other banks. (14)

Contractual saving institutions Financial institutions (insurance companies and pension funds) that allow individuals to transfer risk of financial hardship and accumulate funds for retirement. (12)

Corporate bonds Intermediate and long-term obligations issued by large, high-quality corporations to finance plant and equipment spending. (3, 7)

Corporate control A contest for ownership and control of a firm that pits shareholders against managers in an effort to direct the firm's resources to their highest-valued use. (11)

Corporate governance The system of checks and balances that guides decisions of corporate managers. (12)

Corporate restructuring firms Investors that raise equity capital to acquire shares in other firms to reduce free-rider problems and moral hazard. (11)

Cost-push inflation Price increases resulting from workers' pressure for higher wages. (28)

Coupon bond A credit market instrument that requires multiple payments of interest on a regular basis, such as semiannually or annually, and a payment of the face value at maturity. (4)

Coupon rate An interest rate equal to the yearly coupon payment divided by the face value. (4)

Credit controls Regulatory restrictions on bank lending. (27)

Credit crunch A decline in either the ability or the willingness of banks to lend at any given interest rate. (14, 26, 27)

Credit derivative Swap contract allowing the user to exchange credit risk without having to exchange the underlying asset. (9)

Credit market instruments Methods of financing debt, including simple loans, discount bonds, coupon bonds, and fixed payment loans. (4)

Credit rationing The restricting of credit by lenders such that borrowers cannot obtain the funds they desire at the given interest rate. (11, 13)

Credit risk (default risk) The probability that a borrower will not pay in full promised interest, principal, or both. This characteristic of a credit market instrument influences its interest rate. (7, 13)

Credit-risk analysis The examination of a borrower's likelihood of repayment and general business conditions that might influence the borrower's ability to repay the loan. (13)

Credit union A financial intermediary that takes deposits from and makes loans to individuals who work at the same firm or in the same industry. (12)

Crowding out The reduction in private consumption and investment that accompanies an increase in government purchases in a closed economy. (24)

Currency A type of money, such as dollar bills and coins. (2)

Currency in circulation Federal Reserve Notes (official currency) held by the nonbank public. (17)

Currency–deposit ratio The relationship of currency, C, held by the nonbank public to checkable deposits, D. (17)

Currency premium A number that indicates investors' collective preference for financial instruments denominated in one currency relative to those denominated in another. (8, 22)

Currency swap An exchange of expected future returns on debt instruments denominated in different currencies. (16)

Current account A balance-of-payment account that summarizes transactions among countries for purchases and sales of currently produced goods and services. (22)

Current account balance The sum for a country of the trade balance, services balance, net investment income, and unilateral transfers. (22)

Current output The output of goods and services produced in the economy in the immediate period. (24)

Current yield The coupon payment divided by the current price of a bond. (4)

Day traders Individuals trading stocks on-line. (12)

Dealers Individuals who hold inventories of securities and sell them for a price higher than they paid for them, earning the spread between the bid and the asked price. (12)

Debt A claim that requires a borrower to repay the amount borrowed (the principal) plus a rental fee (interest). (3)

Debt deflation A decrease in prices that raises the real value of households' and firms' outstanding debt, reducing their net worth and their ability to finance desired spending. (11, 27)

Deductible A specified amount to be subtracted from a policyholder's loss when a claim is paid by the insurance company. (12)

Default The inability to repay all or part of an obligation. (3)

Default risk (credit risk) The probability that a borrower will not pay in full promised interest, principal, or both. This characteristic of a credit market instrument influences its interest rate. (7)

Default-risk-free instruments Securities that guarantee that principal and interest will be repaid in nominal terms. For example, U.S. Treasury securities are default-risk-free. (7)

Default swap Bilateral contract in which the hedger pays a periodic fee in return for a contingent payment by a speculator following a credit event, which could be triggered by a bankruptcy or default by a reference entity. (9)

Defensive transactions Open market transactions used by the Fed to offset fluctuations in the monetary base arising from disturbances in portfolio preferences of banks and the nonbank public, financial markets, and the economy. (20)

Defined benefit pension plan A common pension plan in which the employee is promised an assigned benefit based on earnings and years of service, and payments may or may not be indexed for inflation. (12)

Defined contribution pension plan A pension plan in which contributions are invested for employees, who own the value of the funds in the plan. (12)

Definitive money Money that does not have to be converted into a more basic medium of exchange, such as gold or silver. (2)

Deflation A condition in which falling prices cause a given amount of money to purchase more goods and services. (2, 28)

Demand deposit An account against which checks convertible to currency can be written. (13)

Demand for money A decision by the public concerning how much of its wealth to hold in money balances, which is affected by current and anticipated future changes in output. (23, 26)

Demand-pull inflation Price increases resulting from policymakers' attempts to increase aggregate demand for current output above the full employment level. (28)

Depository institutions Commercial banks, savings and loan institutions, mutual savings banks, and credit unions that accept deposits and make loans, acting as intermediaries in the saving-investment process. (3, 12)

Depository Institutions Deregulation and Monetary Control Act of 1980 (DIDMCA) Regulatory reform eliminating interest rate ceilings, providing for uniform reserve requirements, and broadening the scope of permissible activities by S&Ls. (15)

Depreciation A decrease in a currency's value against another currency. (8, 22)

Derivative instrument An asset, such as a futures or option contract, that derives its economic value from an underlying asset such as a stock or bond. (9)

Derivative market Markets in which such claims as futures or option contracts—that derive their economic value from an underlying asset such as a stock or bond—are traded. (9)

Determinants of portfolio choice The key factors affecting a saver's portfolio allocation of assets. They are a saver's wealth, expectations of return on assets, degree of risk of assets, liquidity of assets, and the cost of acquiring information about assets. (5)

Devaluation The lowering of the official value of a country's currency relative to other currencies, thereby resetting the exchange rate. (22)

Direct finance A form of financing wherein an individual saver holds financial claims issued directly by an individual borrower. (3)

Discount bond A credit market instrument in which the borrower repays the amount of the loan in a single payment at maturity but receives less than the face value initially. (4)

Discount loan A loan made by the Federal Reserve System (central bank) to a member bank. (14, 17)

Discount policy The oldest of the Federal Reserve's principal tools for regulating the money supply. It includes setting the discount rate and terms of discount lending. (20)

Discount rate The interest rate specified by the Fed for loans to depository institutions. (17)

Discount window The means by which the Fed makes discount loans to banks, serving as a channel for meeting the liquidity needs of banks. (20)

Discretion strategy An attempt by the central bank to adjust monetary policy as it sees fit to achieve its goals. (28)

Disinflation A policy-induced decline in long-run inflation. (28)

Disintermediation An exit of savers and borrowers from banks to financial markets. (15)

Diversification Splitting wealth among many different assets to reduce risk. (3, 5)

Dividends Periodic payments (usually once each quarter) that owners of equities generally receive from the firm. (3)

Dual banking system The system in the United States in which banks are chartered by either the federal government or a state government. (14)

Duration For an asset or liability, the responsiveness of the percentage change in the asset's or liability's market value to a percentage change in the market interest rate. (13)

Duration gap A bank's exposure to fluctuations in interest rates, measured as the difference between the average duration for bank assets and the average duration for bank liabilities. (13)

Dynamic transactions Open market operations aimed at achieving desired changes in monetary policy indicated by the Federal Open Market Committee. (20)

Economic growth A goal of monetary policy, seeking increases in the economy's output of goods and services over time. (21)

Economies of scale A fall in the transactions costs per dollar of investment as the size of the transactions increases. (11)

Edge Act corporations Special subsidiaries of U.S. banks that conduct only international banking services, as provided in the Edge Act of 1919. (16)

Efficient financial market A market in which all information that is available to market participants is reflected in market prices. (10)

Efficient markets hypothesis A proposition that applies rational expectations to the pricing of assets. It says that when traders and investors use all available information in forming expectations of future rates of return and the cost of trading is low, the equilibrium price of the security is equal to the optimal forecast of fundamental value based on the available information. (10)

Electronic cash (e-cash) Digital cash employed to buy goods and services on the Internet. (2)

Electronic communications network (ECN) An automated trading system that disseminates orders to third parties and dealers and can execute such orders within the network itself. (12)

Electronic funds transfer systems Computerized payment clearing devices, such as debit cards and automated teller machines. (2)

Electronic money (e-money) Money stored electronically on cards or computer accounts. (2)

Equation of exchange An equation stating that the quantity of money times the velocity of money equals nominal spending in the economy. (23)

Equilibrium real interest rate The interest rate at which desired lending and desired borrowing are equal. It is determined by the intersection of the demand curve and the supply curve for loanable funds in a closed economy. (6)

Equity A claim to a share in the profits and assets of a firm. (3)

E-trading Trading financial instruments via computerized systems as opposed to using the floor of an exchange. (12)

Eurobonds Obligations that are denominated in a currency other than that of the country where they are sold, usually in U.S. dollars. (3)

Eurocurrency deposits Time deposits that are denominated in a currency other than that of the issuing domestic financial center (for instance, dollar deposits at a French bank). (16)

Eurodollars A deposit denominated in dollars in a bank or bank branch outside the United States. (3, 16)

Euromarkets Relatively unregulated banking centers in which funds are raised in a currency other than that of the issuing domestic financial center. (16)

European Central Bank A European-wide monetary institution that has been proposed to conduct monetary policy and control a single currency. (22)

European Monetary System A monetary agreement by a number of EC nations to limit exchange rate fluctuations. (22)

European monetary union A plan drafted as part of the 1992 single European market initiative, in which exchange rates are fixed (as of 1999), ultimately by using a common currency. (22)

Excess reserves Reserves that depository institutions elect to hold that are greater than the reserves required by the Fed. (13, 17)

Exchange rate The price of one country's currency in terms of another, such as yen per dollar or francs per pound. (1, 8)

Exchange rate mechanism A device used by a group of EU nations to limit fluctuations in the values of their currencies relative to one another. (22)

Exchange rate regime A system of adjusting currency values and flows of goods and capital among countries. (22)

Exchange rate risk The potential fluctuations in an asset's value because of increases or decreases in exchange rates. (16)

Exchanges Auction markets at which buyers and sellers of securities trade, such as the New York and American Stock Exchanges. (3, 12)

Expectations-augmented Phillips curve An expanded Phillips curve relationship in which the Phillips curve shifts with changes in expected inflation. (28)

Expectations theory of the term structure of interest rates The proposition that investors view assets of all maturities as perfect substitutes, given the same levels of default risk, liquidity, information costs, and taxation. (7)

Expected real interest rate The nominal interest rate minus the expected rate of inflation. (4)

Fads Overreaction to good or bad news about an issue or a class of assets. (10)

Federal deposit insurance A federal government guarantee of certain types of bank deposits for account balances of up to $100,000. (13, 14, 15)

Federal Deposit Insurance Corporation Improvement Act of 1991 (FDICIA) Regulatory reform in which the bank supervisory framework connected enforcement actions to the bank's level of capital. (14)

Federal funds instruments ("Fed funds") Overnight loans between banks of their deposits with the Fed. (3)

Federal funds rate The interest rate charged on the overnight loans among banks. (3, 13, 20)

Federal Open Market Committee (FOMC) The Federal Reserve System committee, with 12 members, that gives directions for open market operations. Members include the Board of Governors, the president of the Federal Reserve Bank in New York, and the presidents of four other Federal Reserve banks. (19)

Federal Reserve bank A district bank of the Federal Reserve System that, among other things, conducts discount lending. (19)

Federal Reserve float The difference between cash items in the process of collection and deferred availability cash items reported in the Fed's balance sheet. (18)

Federal Reserve System (the Fed) The central bank in the United States, which promotes price stability in the banking industry and issues currency. (1, 14, 17, 19, 20, 21)

Fiat money Money authorized by central banks as the definitive money, which does not have to be exchanged by the central bank for gold or some other commodity money. (2)

Finance company Intermediaries that raise funds in large amounts through the sale of commercial paper and securities to make (generally smaller) loans to households and businesses. (12)

Financial distress A situation in which households or firms must sell illiquid assets, possibly at a loss, to meet current obligations. (27)

Financial futures (contracts) Claims that imply settlement of a purchase of a financial instrument at a specified future date, though price is determined at the outset. (3, 9)

Financial innovation Alterations in the operation of financial markets and institutions caused by changes in costs of providing risk-sharing, liquidity, or information services, or changes in demand for these services. (3, 15)

Financial institutions Go-betweens for savers and borrowers, such as banks or insurance companies. (1, 3, 12)

Financial Institutions Reform, Recovery, and Enforcement Act of 1989 (FIRREA) The regulatory reform that eliminated the FSLIC and formed the Resolution Trust Corporation to clean up the thrift crisis. (15)

Financial instruments IOU notes created by financial institutions, which are assets for savers and liabilities for (claims on) borrowers. (1, 3)

Financial integration The way in which financial markets are tied together geographically—domestically and internationally. (3)

Financial intermediaries Institutions such as commercial banks, credit unions, savings and loan associations, mutual savings banks, mutual funds, finance companies, insurance companies, and pension funds that borrow funds from savers and lend them to borrowers. (1, 3)

Financial intermediation Indirect finance through institutions that raise funds from savers and invest in debt or equity claims of borrowers. (3)

Financial markets Places or channels for buying and selling newly issued or existing bonds, stocks, foreign exchange contracts, and other financial instruments. (1, 3)

Financial panics Periods characterized by violent fluctuations in financial markets, bank runs, and bankruptcies of many firms. (14, 27)

Financial structure The mix of finance between equity and debt, as well as the source of funds (direct finance through financial markets or indirect finance through financial intermediaries). (11)

Financial system A network of markets and institutions to transfer funds from individuals and groups who have saved money to individuals and groups who want to borrow money. (1, 3)

Fisher hypothesis A proposition stating that the nominal interest rate rises or falls point-for-point with expected inflation. (4)

Fixed exchange rate system A system in which exchange rates are set at levels determined and maintained by governments. (22)

Fixed payment loan A credit market instrument that requires the borrower to make a regular periodic payment (monthly, quarterly, or annually) of principal and interest to the lender. (4)

Flexible exchange rate system An agreement among nations in which currency values are allowed to fluctuate freely. (22)

Floating-rate debt Loans whose interest payments vary with market interest rates. (13)

Foreign bank branch A full-service affiliate of a foreign financial institution, bearing its name, accepting deposits, and making loans. (16)

Foreign-exchange market intervention Deliberate action by the central bank to influence the exchange rate. (22)

Foreign-exchange market stability A goal of monetary policy to limit fluctuations in the foreign-exchange value of the currency. (21)

Forward transactions Agreements to exchange currencies, bank deposits, or securities at a set date in the future. They provide savers and borrowers the ability to conduct a transaction now and settle it in the future. (8, 9)

Free cash flow Funds that represent the difference between the firm's cash receipts and cash disbursements, including payments to equityholders and debtholders. (11)

Free reserves The difference between excess reserves and borrowed reserves (discount loans) in the banking system. (21)

Free-rider problem A situation in which individuals obtain and use information that others have paid for. (11)

Frictional unemployment Unemployment caused by searches by workers and firms for suitable matches of workers to jobs. (28)

Full employment (*FE*) line A vertical line depicting the economy's production level achieved by the use of all available production factors, regardless of the real rate of interest. (24)

Full employment output The production level achieved by using all available factors of production in place in the economy in the current period, irrespective of the real rate of interest. (24, 25, 28)

Fully funded pension plan A pension plan in which the contributions, together with the projected future earnings, are sufficient to pay the projected assigned benefits. (12)

Fundamental value The present value of an asset's expected future returns, which equals the market price of the asset in an efficient financial market. (10)

Futures contract An agreement that specifies the delivery of a specific underlying commodity or financial instrument at a given future date at a currently agreed-upon price. (10)

Garn-St. Germain Act of 1982 Regulatory reform authorizing banks to issue money market deposit accounts and broadening the permissible activities of S&Ls. (15)

GDP deflator An index of prices of all goods and services included in the gross domestic product, which is the final value of all goods and services produced in the economy. (2)

General Account The U.S. Treasury's deposit account with the Federal Reserve. (18)

General directive A summary of the Federal Open Market Committee's overall objectives for monetary aggregates and/or interest rates. (20)

General equilibrium Outcome in which all markets in the economy are in equilibrium at the same time. (24)

Gold standard A fixed exchange rate system in which the currencies of participating countries are convertible into an agreed-upon amount of gold. (22)

Goods market The market for trade in all goods and services that the economy produces at a particular point in time. (24)

Government allocation Distribution of goods and services by which a central authority collects the output of producers and distributes it to others according to some plan. (2)

Government budget constraint An equation depicting the relationships among federal spending and tax decisions, sales of securities by the Treasury, and changes in the monetary base. (18)

Gradualism A policy, recommended by new Keynesian economists, in which the rate of growth of the money supply is slowly reduced so that the inflation rate can adjust slowly, with smaller losses of output and jobs. (28)

Gramm-Leach-Bliley Financial Services Modernization Act of 1999 U.S. regulatory change that repealed the Glass-Steagall Act and removed the separation of the banking and securities industries. (14)

Hedge fund A largely unregulated speculative investment vehicle for high-net-worth individuals and institutional investors. (12)

Hedging Reducing one's exposure to risk by receiving the right to sell or buy an asset at a known price on a specified future date. (9)

High employment A goal of monetary policy emphasizing a low rate of unemployment. (21)

Hyperinflation Rapid inflation in excess of hundreds or thousands of percentage points per year for a significant period of time. (2, 28)

Hysteresis A situation in which unemployment rates can be higher than those associated with full employment for extended periods of time. (25)

Idiosyncratic risk (unsystematic risk) A unique risk that assets carry that does not affect the market as a whole. For example, the price of an individual stock is influenced by factors affecting the company's profitability, such as a strike or the discovery of a new product. (5)

Income The flow of earnings over a period of time. (2)

Indexed bond A bond whose payments of principal and interest are adjusted for changes in the price level. (4)

Indicator A financial variable whose movements reveal information to the central bank about present or prospective conditions in financial markets or the economy. (21)

Inflation A condition in the economy in which rising prices cause a given amount of money to purchase fewer goods and services, thus decreasing the purchasing power of money. (2, 28)

Inflation target A goal for inflation announced by the central bank and pursued by using its policy tools. (21)

Information Facts about borrowers and about expectations of returns on financial assets. (3)

Information costs The costs that savers incur in finding out the creditworthiness of borrowers and monitoring how borrowers use the funds acquired. (3, 11)

Information lag A condition that makes it impossible for the Fed to observe instantaneously movements in GDP, inflation, or other goal variables. (21)

Insider information Facts that are known to a firm's management but are not available to other investors or prospective investors in the firm. (10)

Insurance company Financial intermediaries that specialize in writing contracts to protect their policyholders from the risk of financial loss associated with particular events. (12)

Interest A rental fee for using borrowed funds. (4)

Interest rate The cost of borrowing funds, usually expressed as a percentage of the amount borrowed. (1, 4)

Interest rate risk The risk that the value of financial assets and liabilities will fluctuate in response to changes in market interest rates. (13)

Interest rate stability A goal of monetary policy focusing on reducing fluctuations in interest rates. (21)

Interest rate swap An agreement to sell the expected future returns on one financial instrument for the expected future returns on another. (9, 13)

Intermediaries See *Financial intermediaries*.

Intermediate targets Objectives for financial variables—such as the money supply or short-term interest rates—that the Fed believes will directly help it to achieve its ultimate goals. (21)

Intermediate-term debt A debt instrument that has a maturity between 1 and 10 years. (3)

International banking facilities (IBFs) Institutions within the United States that cannot conduct domestic banking business but can take time deposits from and make loans to foreign households and firms. They are exempt from reserve requirements, federal restrictions on interest payments to depositors, and, in some states, state and local taxation. (16)

International banks Financial institutions that provide risk-sharing, liquidity, and information services to firms and individuals engaged in international trade and finance. (16)

International capital market The market for lending and borrowing across national boundaries. (1, 5)

International capital mobility The ability of investors to move funds among international markets. (8)

International Monetary Fund (IMF) The multinational lender of last resort, created by the Bretton Woods agreement to help countries make short-run economic adjustments to a balance-of-payments deficit or surplus while maintaining a fixed exchange rate. (22)

International reserves A central bank's assets that are denominated in a foreign currency and used in international transactions. (22)

International transactions currency The currency of choice in settling international commercial and financial transactions. (16)

Investment banks Securities market institutions that assist businesses in raising new capital and advise them on the best means of doing it (issuing shares or structuring debt instruments). (12)

Investment institutions Financial institutions (mutual funds and finance companies) that raise funds to invest in loans and securities. (12)

***IS* curve** The negative relationship between the real interest rate and the level of income, all else being equal, that arises in the market for goods and services. (24)

Junk bonds Corporate bonds issued by lower-quality and thus riskier firms. (3, 7)

Lags in policymaking and implementation process Delays in deciding upon and carrying out monetary policy. (26)

Large open economy The economy of a country whose domestic saving and investment shifts are large enough to affect the real interest rate in the international capital market. The United States, Japan, and Germany are examples of countries with large open economies. (5)

Law of one price A theory stating that if two countries produce an identical good, profit opportunities should ensure that the price of the good is the same around the world, no matter which country produces the good. This law assumes that the goods are tradeable and allows differences that reflect transportation costs. (8)

Legal tender The requirement that a particular currency be acceptable in the settlement of commercial and financial transactions. (2)

Lemons problem An adverse selection problem in which individuals do not know the quality of asset choices (for example, of used cars), so they average quality, overvaluing some assets and undervaluing others. At the average price, owners of the undervalued assets are less likely to sell, but owners of the overvalued assets are more likely to sell. (11)

Lender of last resort The ultimate source of credit to which banks can turn during a panic. (14)

Leveraged buyout (LBO) A type of restructuring in which external equity is replaced by debt. (11)

Liabilities Sources of funds and claims on future income of borrowers. (3)

Life insurance company A firm that sells policies to protect households against a loss of earnings from disability, retirement, or death of the insured person. (12)

Liquidity The ease with which one can exchange assets for cash, other assets, or goods and services. (1, 3, 7)

Liquidity of balance sheet positions The quantity of liquid assets that households and firms hold relative to their liabilities, which is a determinant of spending on business investment, housing, and consumer durables. (27)

Liquidity preference theory A proposition, developed by John Maynard Keynes, that emphasizes the sensitivity of money demand to changes in interest rates. (23)

Liquidity risk The possibility that depositors may collectively decide to withdraw more funds than the bank has on hand. (13)

***LM* curve** The positive relationship between the real interest rate and the level of income, all else being equal, that arises in the market for real money balances. (24)

Load fund A mutual fund that charges commissions for purchases and/or sales. (12)

Loan A transaction in which the borrower receives funds from a lender and the borrower agrees to repay funds with interest. (4)

Loan commitment An agreement by a bank to provide a borrower with a stated amount of funds during some specified period of time. (13)

Loan sale A financial contract in which a bank agrees to sell the expected future returns from an underlying bank loan to a third party. (13)

Loan syndicate An arrangement in which a loan is arranged and managed by a lead bank; other banks hold fractions of the loan. (16)

Long-run aggregate supply curve (*LRAS*) The graph of the relationship of firms' output to price level in the long run. It is vertical at the full employment output. (25)

Long-term debt A debt instrument that has a maturity of 10 years or more. (3)

Luxury asset An asset for which the wealth elasticity of demand exceeds unity. (6)

M1 The narrowest monetary aggregate, which measures money as the traditional medium of exchange, including currency, traveler's checks, and checkable deposits. (2)

M2 A monetary aggregate that includes the components of *M1* plus short-term investment accounts that could be converted to definitive money, but not as easily as the components of *M1*. *M2* now includes money market deposit accounts, noninstitutional money market mutual fund shares, and other very liquid assets of firms such as overnight repurchase agreements and overnight Eurodollars. (2)

M3 A monetary aggregate that includes *M2* plus some less liquid assets, including large-denomination time deposits, institutional money market mutual fund balances, term repurchase agreements, and term Eurodollars. (2)

Main bank In Japan, a large bank within a finance group that owns some equity in member firms, is a major source of credit for group firms, and monitors activities of member firms. (14)

Managed float regime Exchange rate regime in which central banks intervene to affect foreign exchange values from time to time. (22)

Management buyout (MBO) A form of restructuring in which a firm's managers acquire a greater stake in the firm by buying back shares from other shareholders. (11)

Market risk (systematic risk) A risk that is common to all assets of a certain type, such as potential general fluctuations in economic conditions that can increase or decrease returns on stocks collectively. (5)

Marketable securities Liquid assets that banks hold and can trade in secondary markets. (13)

Matched sale-purchase transactions (reverse repos) Agreements that are often used by the Fed Trading Desk for open market sales, in which the Fed sells securities to dealers in the government securities market and the dealers agree to sell them back to the Fed in the very near future. (20)

Maturity The length of time before a debt instrument expires. The maturity can be a very short period of time (30 days or even overnight) or a long period of time (30 years or more). (3)

Medium of exchange A term that economists use to describe money. (2)

Member banks Banks that are members of the Federal Reserve System. (19)

Menu costs Costs to firms that are caused by changing prices because of inflation (reprinting price lists, informing customers, and so on). (28)

Misperception theory Propositions about the effects of imperfect information on the part of firms on aggregate supply. (See also *New classical view*.) (25)

Monetary aggregates Measures of the quantity of money that are broader than currency. They include *M1*, *M2*, and *M3*. (2, 23)

Monetary base All reserves held by banks as well as all currency in circulation. (17)

Monetary neutrality The proposition that money has no effect on output in the long run because an increase (decrease) in the nominal money supply raises (lowers) the price level in the long run but does not change equilibrium output. (25)

Monetary policy The management of the money supply and its links to prices, interest rates, and other economic variables. (1, 21, 26)

Monetary policy goals Objectives set by the central bank in carrying out monetary and regulatory policy. (21)

Monetary theory The area of study concerning the relationships linking changes in the money supply to changes in economic activity and prices in the economy. (1)

Monetizing the debt The Fed's purchasing of Treasury securities to finance budget deficits. (18)

Money Anything that is generally accepted as payment for goods and services or in the settlement of debts. Money acts as a medium of exchange, is a unit of account and a store of value, and offers a standard of deferred payment. (1, 2)

Money center banks Large, established national banks. (14)

Money channel The path through which monetary policy affects output through effects on interest-sensitive spending. (27)

Money demand function A function relating the demand for real money balances to its underlying determinants. (23)

Money market deposit account (MMDA) Federally insured bank deposit accounts that provide services similar to those of money market mutual funds. (15)

Money market mutual funds Funds that issue shares to savers backed by holdings of high-quality short-term assets. (12)

Money markets Financial markets that trade assets used as the medium of exchange, such as currency or shorter-term instruments with a maturity of less than one year. (3, 12)

Money multiplier The number that indicates how much the money supply changes in response to a given change in the monetary base. (17)

Money supply The stock of the medium of exchange supplied by the central bank. (17)

Money supply process The means by which actions of the central bank, the banking system, and the nonbank public determine the money supply. (17)

Moral hazard The lender's difficulty in monitoring borrowers' activities once the loan is made. (11)

Mortgages Loans, usually long-term, to households or firms to purchase buildings or land. The underlying asset—house or factory or piece of land—serves as collateral. (3)

Multiple deposit contraction The process by which a decrease in bank reserves reduces the volume of checkable deposits in the banking system. (17)

Multiple deposit expansion Part of the money supply process in which funds are deposited and redeposited in banks. Banks serve as a link between the central bank and the nonbank public, taking increases in reserves from the central bank and funneling them to the nonbank public by making loans. (17)

Municipal bonds Obligations of state and local governments that are exempt from federal, state, and local income taxes. (7)

Mutual funds Financial intermediaries that raise funds by selling shares to individual savers and investing them in diversified portfolios of stocks, bonds, mortgages, and money market instruments. (3, 12)

Narrow banking Deposit insurance reform in which only deposits in safe assets would be insured. (15)

National banks Federally chartered banks supervised by the Office of the Comptroller of the Currency, a department of the U.S. Treasury. Originally, national banks were allowed to issue bank notes as currency. (14)

Natural rate of unemployment The rate of unemployment that exists when the economy produces the full employment level of output. (28)

Negotiable certificate of deposit A large-denomination fixed-maturity instrument that is sold by a bank to investors and can be traded in a secondary market. (3, 13)

Negotiated Order of Withdrawal (NOW) Effectively, a bank checking account that pays interest. (15)

Net worth (equity capital) The difference between a firm's current and expected future holdings (assets) and its debts (liabilities). (11, 13)

Neutrality of money The absence of an effect of change in the nominal money supply on output and the real interest rate. (24, 26)

New classical view A theory stating that for short-run aggregate supply, there is a positive relation between aggregate supply and the difference between the actual and the expected price level. (25)

New Keynesian view Economic explanations for price stickiness in the short run, based on features of many real-world markets: the rigidity of long-term contracts and imperfect competition among sellers in the goods market. (25)

No-load funds Funds that earn income only from management fees (typically about 0.5% of assets), not from sales commissions. (12)

Noise traders Relatively uninformed traders who pursue trading strategies with no superior information and who may overreact. (10)

Nominal exchange rate The value of one currency in terms of another currency. (8)

Nominal interest rate An interest rate that is unadjusted for changes in purchasing power. (4)

Nominal interest rate parity condition The market equilibrium condition in which domestic and foreign assets have identical risk, liquidity, and information characteristics, so their nominal returns—measured in the same currency—also must be identical. (8)

Nonbank banks Financial institutions that take demand deposits but do not make loans. (14)

Nonbank office Affiliates of bank holding companies that do not accept demand deposits but do make loans. (14)

Nonmoney asset market A market that handles trading in assets that are stores of value, including stocks, bonds, and houses. (24)

Nontransaction deposit Claims on banks including savings deposits and time deposits. (13)

Off-balance-sheet lending Bank lending activities in which the bank does not necessarily hold as assets the loans that it makes, including standby letters of credit, loan commitments, and loan sales. (13)

Official reserve assets Assets held by central banks that can be used in making international payments to settle the balance of payments. (22)

Official settlements balance The net increase in a country's official reserve assets. (22)

Offshore markets International financial centers that are located in unregulated areas with low tax rates on banks—for example, in the Caribbean (the Bahamas and Cayman Islands) and in Hong Kong and Singapore. (16)

Okun's law A statistical relationship identified by Arthur Okun between changes in output and the unemployment rate. (28)

Open economy An economy in which borrowing and lending take place in the international capital market. (5)

Open-end mutual funds Mutual funds that issue redeemable shares at a price tied to the underlying value of the assets. (12)

Open market operations The purchase and sale of securities in financial markets by the Federal Reserve System. Open market operations are its most direct route for changing the monetary base. (17, 20)

Open market purchase The buying of government securities by the Fed, with the intent of raising the monetary base. (17)

Open market sale The sale of government securities by the Fed, with the intent of reducing the monetary base. (17)

Open Market Trading Desk A group of traders at the Federal Reserve Bank of New York who buy and sell securities for the Fed's account. (20)

Operating targets Variables directly under the Fed's control that are closely related to the intermediate targets of monetary policy. Operating targets include the federal funds rate and nonborrowed reserves. (21)

Options contract A right (option) conferred upon a trader to buy or sell a particular asset (shares of stock, a bond, or unit of foreign currency, for example) within a predetermined time and at a predetermined price. (3, 9)

Outright purchase or sale The Fed's buying securities from or selling securities to dealers. (20)

Over-the-counter (OTC) markets Secondary financial markets for broker-dealers that are organized via telephone and computer, with no centralized place for auction trading. (3, 12)

Payments system A mechanism for conducting transactions in the economy. Commercial banks play a key role in this system by clearing and settling transactions in the economy. (2, 13)

Payments system factors Substitutes for money in transactions that affect the demand for money. (23)

Pension fund A financial institution that invests contributions of workers and firms in financial assets to provide retirement benefits for workers. (12)

Phillips curve A relationship, found by A. W. Phillips, in which high unemployment was associated with a low rate of wage inflation, and vice versa. (28)

Plan funding A method by which pension assets accrue to finance retirement benefits. (12)

Political business cycle model The theory that the policymakers will urge the Fed to try to lower interest rates to stimulate credit demand and economic activity prior to an election. (19)

Portfolio A collection of assets. (3, 5)

Preferred habitat theory of the term structure of interest rates Proposition that investors care about both expected returns and maturity, viewing instruments with different maturities as substitutes, but not perfect ones. (7)

Present value (*PV*, present discounted value) A concept that is used to evaluate credit market instruments by placing all payments in terms of today's dollars so that they can be added together. (4)

Price controls Official government restrictions on price changes. (28)

Price index A summary statistic that incorporates changes in the price of a set of goods relative to the price in some base year. (2)

Price level The average price of a market basket of goods and services in the economy. (1)

Price stability A goal of monetary policy to stabilize the purchasing power of the currency. (21)

Primary credit Discount loans available to healthy banks (generally those with adequate capital and supervisory ratings for safety and soundness). (20)

Primary markets Financial markets in which newly issued debt or equity claims are sold to initial buyers by private borrowers to raise funds for durable-goods purchases or new ventures and by governments to finance budget deficits. (3)

Prime rate Traditionally, the interest rate charged on six-month loans to high-quality borrowers. (13)

Principal-agent problem The type of moral hazard that may arise when managers (agents) who control a firm's assets do not own very much of the firm's equity and therefore do not have the same incentive to maximize the firm's value as the owners (principals) do. (11)

Principal-agent view A theory of central bank decision making implying that officials maximize their personal well-being rather than that of the general public. (19)

Principals Owners (but not direct managers) of a firm or organization. (11)

Producer price index (PPI) An index of the prices that firms pay in wholesale markets for crude materials, intermediate goods, and finished goods. It is a commonly used measure to calculate inflation. (2, 28)

Productivity growth A measure of the growth of output in a country relative to the growth of inputs. (8)

Program trading Using computer-generated orders to buy or sell many stocks at the same time, causing rapid adjustments of institutional portfolios. (10)

Property and casualty insurance company A firm that sells policies to protect households and firms from risks of illness, theft, accident, or natural disasters. (12)

Public interest view A theory of central bank decision making implying that officials act in the interest of citizens' well-being. (19)

Purchasing power The ability of money to be used to acquire goods and services. (2)

Purchasing power parity (PPP) theory of exchange rate determination The proposition that changes in the nominal exchange rate between two currencies are accounted for by differences in inflation rates in the two countries. This theory assumes that real exchange rates are constant. (8)

Put option The right to sell an underlying asset, which is obtained by buying the put option. Sellers of put options have an obligation to buy the asset. (10)

Quantity theory of money demand A theory, developed by Irving Fisher and others, that states that the determinant of the demand for real balances is the real volume of transactions. (23)

Quota A common trade barrier that limits the volume of foreign goods that can be brought into the country. (8)

Rate of capital gains The percentage change in the price of a financial asset. (4)

Rational expectations The assumption in the model of an efficient market that participants will use all available information in estimating the expected price level or change in the money supply so that the market price equals the present value of expected future returns. (10, 26)

Real business cycle view The theory that changes in aggregate demand have no effect on output, even in the short run, assuming perfect information and perfectly flexible prices. Short-term changes to output are primarily temporary shocks to productivity, such as changes in the availability of raw materials. (25)

Real exchange rate The purchasing power of a currency relative to the purchasing power of other currencies. (8)

Real interest rate An interest rate that is adjusted for changes in purchasing power caused by inflation. (4)

Real money balances The value of money balances adjusted for changes in purchasing power. (23)

Recession A contraction in current output in the business cycle. (26)

Regulation Q The regulation, authorized by the Banking Act of 1933, that placed ceilings on allowable interest rates on time and savings deposits and prohibited the payment of interest on demand deposits (then the only form of checkable deposits). (15)

Repurchase agreements (repos or RPs) Very short-term loans that are used for cash management by large corporations. Maturities are typically less than two weeks and often the next day. (3, 13)

Required reserve ratio The percentage of deposits that banks must hold as reserves, as specified by the Fed. (17)

Required reserves The minimum amount that depository institutions are compelled to hold as reserves by the Federal Reserve System. (13, 17)

Reserve requirement The requirement that banks hold a fraction of checkable deposits as vault cash or deposits with the central bank. (17)

Reserves A bank asset consisting of vault cash (cash on hand in the bank) plus deposits with the Federal Reserve. (13)

Restrictive covenants Limits on the actions of a borrower or insured person made by a lender or insurer. For example, a lender may restrict risk-taking activities of the borrower, require the borrower to maintain a certain level of net worth, or require the borrower to maintain the value of collateral offered to the lender. (11, 12)

Restructuring Rearranging the financial structure of a firm to shift control over the resources of the firm and to provide incentives for managers to maximize the firm's value. (11)

Return on assets (ROA) A measure of a bank's operating performance (net after-tax profit/bank assets). (13)

Return on equity (ROE) A measure of banks' shareholders' returns (net after-tax profit/bank equity capital). (13)

Revaluation Raising the official value of a country's currency relative to other currencies, thereby resetting the exchange rate. (22)

Riegle-Neal Interstate Banking and Branching Efficiency Act of 1994 Act providing a consistent nationwide standard for interstate bank expansion, eliminating the significance of prior state branching restrictions. (14)

Risk The degree of uncertainty of an asset's return. (1)

Risk-averse Characteristic of savers who desire to minimize variability in return on savings. (5)

Risk-based premium A fee for insurance that is based on the probability of the insured individual's collecting a claim. (12)

Risk-loving Characteristic of savers who actually prefer to gamble by holding a risky asset with the possibility of maximizing returns. (5)

Risk-neutral Characteristic of savers who judge assets only on their expected returns. (5)

Risk premium The difference between the yield on a financial instrument and the yield on a default-risk-free instrument of comparable maturity. It measures the additional yield a saver requires to be willing to hold a risky instrument. (7)

Risk sharing Services provided by the financial system wherein savers and borrowers spread and transfer risk. (3)

Risk structure of interest rates The differences in risk, liquidity, information costs, and taxation that result in differences in interest rates and yields across credit market instruments of the same maturity. (7)

Rules strategy An attempt by the central bank to follow specific and publicly announced guidelines for policy. (28)

Sarbanes-Oxley Act of 2002 Recent U.S. law to promote timeliness and accuracy of financial information for investors. (11)

Savers Suppliers of funds, providing funds to borrowers in the anticipation of repayment of more funds in the future. (3)

Saving curve A graph that illustrates the relationship between aggregate saving and the expected real rate of interest. (5)

Saving-investment diagram A graph that shows the relationship between the saving and investment curves. It is used to determine the equilibrium real interest rate. (24)

Savings institution A category of banking firms including S&Ls and mutual savings banks. (12)

Seasonal credit Discount lending to satisfy geographically specific seasonal liquidity requirements. (20)

Secondary credit Discount lending intended for banks that are not eligible for primary credit, and may not be used to fund an expansion of a bank.

Secondary markets Financial markets in which claims that have already been issued are sold by one investor to another. (3)

Securities market institutions Financial institutions (investment banks, brokers and dealers, and organized exchanges) that reduce costs of matching savers and borrowers. (12)

Segmented markets theory The proposition that yields on each financial instrument are determined in a separate market, with separate market-specific demand and supply considerations. (7)

Shoe leather costs The cost to consumers and businesses of minimizing currency holdings due to inflation. (28)

Short-run aggregate supply (*SRAS*) curve A plot of the relationship between aggregate output supplied and the price level. (25)

Short-term debt A debt instrument that has a maturity of less than one year. (3)

Simple deposit multiplier The reciprocal of the required reserve ratio. (17)

Simple loan A credit transaction in which the borrower receives from the lender an amount of funds called principal and agrees to repay the lender principal plus an additional amount called interest (as a fee for using the funds) on a given date (maturity). (4)

Simple Phillips curve The statistical relationship between inflation and the difference between unemployment and the natural rate of unemployment. (28)

Small open economy An economy in which total saving is too small to affect the world real interest rate, so the economy takes the world interest rate as a given. (6)

Special Drawing Rights (SDRs) Paper substitute for gold, issued as international reserves by the International Monetary Fund in its role as lender of last resort. (22)

Specialist A broker-dealer on the floor of the exchange who makes a market in one or more stocks and matches buyers and sellers. (12)

Specialization A system in which individuals produce the goods or services for which they have relatively the best ability. (2)

Speculation The attempt to profit from disagreements among traders about future prices of a commodity or financial instrument by anticipating changes in prices. (10)

Speculative attack The sale of weak currencies or purchase of strong currencies by market participants who believe a government will be unable or unwilling to maintain the exchange rate, in an attempt to force a devaluation or revaluation of the currency. (22)

Spot transactions Transactions in which trade and settlement occur at the same time. (9)

Stabilization policies (activist policies) Public policies designed to smooth short-run fluctuations in output involving shifts of the *AD* curve by changes in government purchases or taxes or by changes in the nominal money supply. (26)

Standard of deferred payment The feature of money by which it facilitates exchange over time in credit. (2)

Standby letter of credit (SLC) A promise that a bank will lend the borrower funds to pay off its maturing commercial paper if necessary. (13)

State and local government bonds (municipal bonds) Intermediate- and long-term bonds issued by municipalities and state governments that are exempt from federal income taxation and allow governmental units to borrow the funds to build schools, roads, and other large capital projects. (3)

State banks Banks that are chartered by a state government. (14)

Statistical discrepancy An adjustment to the capital account in the balance-of-payments accounts to reflect measurement errors and omissions. (22)

Sterilized foreign-exchange intervention A transaction in which a foreign-exchange intervention is accompanied by offsetting domestic open market operations to leave the monetary base unchanged. (22)

Stock market A market in which owners of firms buy and sell their claims. (1)

Stocks Equity claims issued by corporations. They represent the largest single category of capital market assets. (3)

Store of value A function of money; the accumulation of value by holding dollars or other assets that can be used to buy goods and services in the future. (2)

Subsidiary U.S. bank Affiliate of a foreign bank that is subject to domestic banking regulations and need not bear the name of its foreign parent. (16)

Supply shocks Shifts in the price or availability of raw materials or in production technologies that affect production costs and the aggregate supply curve. (25)

Syndicate See *Loan syndicate.* (16)

T-account A simplified accounting tool that lists changes in balance sheet items as they occur. (13)

Takeover A struggle for corporate control in which a group of current or new shareholders buys a controlling interest in a firm, reshapes the board of directors, and even replaces managers. (11)

Targets Variables that a central bank can influence directly and that help to achieve monetary policy goals. (21)

Tariff A common trade barrier consisting of a tax on goods purchased from other countries. (8)

Taylor rule Monetary policy guideline for the federal funds rate target developed by economist John Taylor. (21)

Term premium The additional yield that investors require for investing in a less preferred maturity. (7)

Term structure of interest rates The variation in yields for related instruments differing in maturity. (7)

Terrorism risk insurance Special insurance in a private–government partnership against large losses from terrorist events. (12)

Theory of portfolio allocation A statement that predicts how savers allocate their assets on the basis of their consideration of their wealth, expected return on the assets, degree of risk, liquidity of the assets, and the cost of acquiring information about assets. (5)

Time deposits Accounts with a specified maturity, which could range from a few months to several years. (13)

Total rate of return The sum of the current yield of a credit market instrument and the rate of capital gain or loss on it. (4)

Total return swap Bilateral contract transferring interest rate risk and credit risk by exchanging the total economic performance of a specified asset for another cash flow. (9)

Trade balance The component of the current account that equals the difference between merchandise exports and imports. (22)

Transactions costs The cost of trade or exchange; for example, the brokerage commission charged for buying or selling a financial claim like a bond or a share of stock. (3, 11)

Treasury tax and loan accounts U.S. Treasury's deposit accounts with commercial banks. (18)

Underfunded A term used to describe a defined benefit plan when contributions, together with the projected future earnings, are not sufficient to pay off projected defined benefits. (12)

Underground economy Economic activity that is not measured in formal government statistics. (17)

Underwriting A way in which investment banks earn income; in the simplest form, they guarantee a price to an issuing firm that needs capital, sell the issue at a higher price, and keep the profit, known as the "spread." (12)

Unit of account A function of money; the provision of a way of measuring the value of goods and services in the economy in terms of money. (2)

Universal banking Allowing banks to be involved in many nonbanking activities with no geographic restrictions. (14)

Unsterilized foreign-exchange intervention A transaction in which the central bank allows the monetary base to respond to the sale or purchase of domestic currency. (22)

U.S. government agency securities Intermediate- or long-term bonds issued by the federal government or government-sponsored agencies. (3)

U.S. Treasury bills (T-bills) Debt obligations of the U.S. government that have a maturity of less than one year. (3)

U.S. Treasury bonds Securities issued by the federal government to finance budget deficits. (3)

U.S. Treasury securities Debt obligations issued by the federal government to finance budget deficits. (3)

Value-at-risk (VAR) approach Use of statistical models to estimate the maximum loss in a portfolio's value likely to be sustained over a particular time period. (13)

Vault cash The cash on hand in the bank. (13, 17)

Velocity of money The average number of times a unit of currency is spent each year on a purchase of goods and services in the economy. (23)

Venture capital firm A firm that raises equity capital from investors to invest in emerging or growing entrepreneurial business ventures. (11)

Venture capital funds (VCs) Intermediaries raising funds from institutional investors and wealthy individuals to invest in portfolio companies. (12)

Wealth The sum of the value of assets. (2)

Wealth elasticity of demand The relationship of the percentage change in quantity demanded of an asset to the percentage change in wealth. (5)

World Bank (International Bank for Reconstruction and Development) The bank created by the Bretton Woods agreement to grant long-term loans to developing countries for their economic development. (22)

World real interest rate The real interest rate determined in the international capital market. (6)

Yield curve A graph showing yields to maturity on different default-risk-free instruments as a function of maturity. (7)

Yield to maturity The interest rate measure at which the present value of an asset's returns is equal to its value today. (4)

Selected Answers to Questions and Problems

CHAPTER 1

Review Questions

1. No, the funds would not generally be allocated to most valued uses; financial markets and institutions work better.
3. The financial system provides three key services to savers and borrowers: risk sharing (people can share and transfer risk), liquidity (people can exchange their assets for other assets at low cost), and information (financial markets communicate information, and financial institutions specialize in gathering and using information about borrowers, so they can lend more efficiently).

Analytical Problems

7. The local bank provides you risk-sharing, liquidity, and information services.
9. In a global economy, their exports to the United States would decline, possibly leading to an economic downturn.

CHAPTER 2

Review Questions

1. To serve as money, they must generally be accepted as means of payment. Your acceptance of dollar bills and checks as money is based on your belief that others will accept them.
3. In a barter system, there are too many prices, and nonstandard goods complicate pricing. Trade requires a double coincidence of wants.
5. Commodity money has real uses (e.g., gold, silver); fiat money has no intrinsic value.
7. A payments system is a mechanism for conducting transactions. If the payments system became less efficient, the costs to the economy would be fewer and more costly transactions, that is, losing gains from specialization.
9. No. Houses, bonds, and stocks are also stores of value. There is an advantage to money's being a store of value, because after trading for it, it can be held; otherwise, something else is likely to become money that is also a store of value.
11. The definitions of the money supply range from narrow, *M1*, to broad, *L*. The definitions of the money supply can be used for different purposes and have varied over time in their usefulness for predicting future movements in prices and output.

Analytical Problems

13. Whether caused by inflation or deflation, changes in the purchasing power of money affect money's usefulness as a store of value and as a standard of deferred payment.
15. The reason is convenience; one avoids transactions costs of running to the bank all the time.
17. Not necessarily; if prices rose more than 10%, your real income has fallen.
19. In Friedmania, bad money drives out good; people will spend the new crowns and hoard the old crowns.
21. Liquidity indicates the ease with which an asset can be converted to definitive money. Ranking from most to least liquid: dollar bill, checking account, money market mutual fund, passbook savings account, corporate stock, gold, house.

CHAPTER 3

Review Questions

1. Savers have more resources than they want to spend currently; borrowers have fewer resources than they currently want to spend. Risk sharing allows diversification and transfer of risk; liquidity allows flexibility in asset holdings; and information is efficiently gathered by financial intermediaries who specialize in doing so. Taken together, the three services reduce the costs of financial transactions.
3. There tend to be more buyers and sellers of money market assets than there are buyers and sellers of capital market assets. Hence, money market assets tend to be more liquid than capital market assets. Because the assets of banks are primarily capital market assets, banks sometimes have difficulty converting their assets into cash.
5. "Integration" represents the extent to which financial markets are tied together geographically. Increased integration tends to equalize returns across geographic boundaries (raising costs and returns for some and lowering them for others), likely reducing borrowing costs by allowing for geographical diversification.

7. The transaction (a) takes place through a financial intermediary, (b) is in a primary market, and (c) is in a capital market.
9. The transaction (a) takes place in a financial market, (b) is in a primary market, and (c) is in a capital market.
11. The transaction (a) takes place through a financial intermediary, (b) is in a primary market, and (c) is in a money market.

Analytical Problems

13. Asset A yields 6% after taxes; asset B yields 6%; asset C offers the highest return, yielding 6.5%.
15. *Insider trading* refers to trading by managers who own large amounts of a firm's stock or by others who have privileged information. Legalizing insider trading might reduce the confidence of investors in the fairness of financial markets, thereby reducing their participation in them.
17. Investors want to eliminate unnecessary risk in their returns; they may trade off additional risk for additional return.
19. Leading candidates include government regulation and economic and financial stability; it is unlikely that financial technology varies greatly across industrialized countries.

CHAPTER 4

Review Questions

1. In a discount bond, the borrower repays face value at maturity; in a simple loan, the borrower repays the stated principal plus interest at maturity.
3. The yield to maturity is the interest rate that equates value of asset today with present value of future payments. It can be derived from present-value formulas.
5. The total rate of return includes current interest payment plus capital gain; it equals current yield plus percentage change in price.
7. According to the Fisher hypothesis, the nominal interest rate moves one-for-one with expected inflation. While there is broad support for the proposition that nominal interest rates move in response to changes in expected inflation, the Fisher effect, narrowly defined, is not supported exactly by U.S. data.

Analytical Problems

9. With a discount rate of 10%, the present value of the Yankees' offer is: $3,000,000 + ($6,000,000/1.1) + ($7,000,000/1.1^2) + ($8,000,000/1.1^3) = $20,250,188. The present value of the Giants' offer is: $6,000,000 + ($5,500,000/1.1) + ($6,000,000/1.1^2) + ($6,000,000/1.1^3) = $20,466,566. So, based on the present value criterion, the Giants are making the more valuable offer. With a discount rate of 5%, the present value of the Yankees' offer is: $3,000,000 + ($6,000,000/1.05) + ($7,000,000/1.05^2) + ($8,000,000/1.05^3) = $21,974,193. The present value of the Giants' offer is: $6,000,000 + ($5,500,000/1.05) + ($6,000,000/1.05^2) + ($6,000,000/1.05^3) = $21,863,298. So, the Yankees' offer is more valuable.
11. The present value is $857.
13. Option (a) has the highest present value.
15. At an initial interest rate of 7%, the bond's value is $700/1.07 + 700/(1.07)^2 + 700/(1.07)^3 + 700/(1.07)^4 + 10{,}000/(1.07)^4 = 654.21 + 611.41 + 571.41 + 549.43 + 7849.02 =$ $10,235.48. At an interest rate of 5%, the bond's value is $700/1.05 + 700/1.05^2 + 700/1.05^3 + 700/1.05^4 + 10{,}000/1.05^4 = 666.67 + 634.92 + 604.69 + 575.89 + 8227.02 =$ $10,709.19. Hence the bond's value rises as the yield falls.
17. The present value of two one-year subscriptions is $60 + $60/1.10 = $114.55. The present value of a two-year subscription is $115. Hence you prefer the one-year subscription today. There is a complication, however—the price next year is unknown.
19. The current yield is 2/55, or 3.6%. The capital gain is 5/55, or 9.1%. The total rate of return is 12.7%.
21. Because of higher inflation in the mid 1970s, stock prices declined in real terms.
23. The actual real interest rate will differ from the expected real interest rate if the actual inflation rate differs from the expected inflation rate. The longer the term of a loan, the greater the concern of the lender that the actual real interest rate might differ from the expected real interest rate.
25. In the first institution's case, there should be little effect because of short maturities of the assets. In the second institution's case, however, there will be a major loss of net worth on account of capital loss on long maturities.

CHAPTER 5

Review Questions

1. The five key determinants of portfolio choice are wealth, relative return, relative risk, relative liquidity, and relative cost of acquiring information.
3. The difference lies in the attitude toward risk relative to return. A risk-loving individual is more likely to hold stocks and options. A risk-averse individual is more likely to hold bonds and cash. A risk-neutral individual cares only about an asset's expected return and not its risk.
5. The saying states the benefit of diversification. It means that one can reduce portfolio risk by owning many different assets.
7. Mutual funds provide small investors with diversification, which lowers their risk from investing in equities.
9. Market risk refers to the risk in the returns on assets generally, whereas idiosyncratic risk relates to the risk in an individual asset. Idiosyncratic risk can be reduced through diversification.
11. The variability of the return on an individual stock should be greater than that for the market portfolio. The reason is that individual returns are imperfectly correlated.

Analytical Problems

13. Asset 1 yields 6% after taxes; asset 2 yields 6%; asset 3 offers the highest return, yielding 6.5%.
15. The interest rate is lower because investors do not like the call provision (the government calls the bond only if the current market interest rate is below the rate on the bond). Hence investors prefer noncallable bonds and will pay more for them, so the interest rate is lower.
17. They offer greater liquidity. Some people (who wanted to invest for the long term) did not like having to reinvest coupon payments with unknown interest rates; they preferred the second part. Others preferred the steady income stream but did not want to have to reinvest the principal; they preferred the first part.
19. a. Your rates of return are 20%, −10%, 35%, −15%, 27.5%, and −12.5%, respectively.
    b. Your rates of return are now 15%, −15%, 30%, −20%, 22.5%, and −17.5%, respectively. You are now less likely to hold both stocks and may be more likely to hold riskier Lowrunner stock.
21. a. You are more willing (higher wealth).
    b. You are less willing (higher risk).
    c. You are more willing (higher return).
    d. You are less willing (alternative asset has increased liquidity).

CHAPTER 6

Review Questions

1. a. The bond demand curve shifts to the right in response to a fall in current income or a rise in expected future income.
   b. The bond demand curve shifts to the right in response to a rise in current income or a fall in expected future income.
   c. The loanable funds demand curve shifts to the left in response to a fall in expected future profitability or a rise in corporate taxes.
   d. The loanable funds supply curve shifts to the right in response to a rise in bonds' liquidity or to an increase in the expected return on bonds.
3. You would not expect the real interest rate to be the same in all small open economies because of transactions costs and because some countries impose barriers to international borrowing and lending.
5. In a small open economy and a large open economy, domestic lending and borrowing need not be equal. The difference between domestic lending and borrowing is international lending—if desired domestic lending exceeds desired domestic borrowing—or international borrowing—if desired domestic borrowing exceeds desired domestic lending.
7. Shifts in domestic lending and borrowing in a small open economy have no effect on the world real interest rate, while such shifts in a large open economy can affect the world real interest rate.

Analytical Problems

9. The shift in the bond supply curve is greater than the shift in the bond demand curve, so the price of bonds falls, and the interest rate rises. In a small open economy, there is no such effect, as the world real interest rate is given.
11. In a small open economy, the real interest rate is unaffected in each case.
    a. Domestic borrowing rises.
    b. Domestic borrowing falls.
    c. Domestic borrowing does not change.
    d. Domestic borrowing does not change.
13. a. Aggregate wealth rises.
    b. Aggregate wealth rises.
    c. The increase in the real interest rate increases saving and wealth.
15. a. Net expected profitability falls, so the demand for loanable funds falls.
    b. Expected profitability rises, so the demand for loanable funds rises.

c. The increase in the expected after-tax real interest rate reduces the demand for loanable funds.
17. The country with social insurance should have lower levels of saving and, all else being equal, lower wealth.
19. The bond supply curve shifts to the right in response to the increase in stock prices. In a closed or large open economy (assuming no shift in the bond demand curve), the interest rate will rise.
21. Not necessarily; the *expected* real interest rate likely was positive, but actual inflation exceeded expected inflation.

CHAPTER 7

Review Questions

1. The bonds have different times to maturity.
3. Long-term yields fall below current short-term yields.
5. In the preferred habitat theory, term premiums account for the upward bias in the slope.
7. U.S. Treasury bonds have no default risk.
9. The taxable bond pays a higher before-tax interest rate.
11. A recession raises default risk. The phenomenon is known as a flight to quality.
13. Factors include default risk, liquidity, and taxability. In the latter case, information cost is an additional factor.
15. If more investors were willing to purchase these bonds as a result of Milken's arguments, then their liquidity would have increased.

Analytical Problems

17. The current two-year rate is 4%. The current three-year rate is 5%.
19. a. $1000(1.06⁴) = $1262.48;
    b. $1000(1.055³)(1.09) = $1279.92;
    c. $1000(1.05²)(1.07)(1.09) = $1285.85;
    d. $1000(1.04)(1.065)(1.07)(1.09) = $1291.79.
    You should choose option (d).
21. In 1981, investors expected short-term yields to decline. In 1984, investors expected short-term yields to rise.
23. The analyst must be arguing that either an increase in expected inflation or an increase in borrowing will increase the yield on long-term bonds relative to the yield on short-term bonds.
25. The coupon on the state bond will not be subject to tax, so its pre-tax yield will also be 8%. The $75 coupon on the federal perpetuity will be subject to a tax of $29.70. If its after-tax yield is 8%, its price must be $45.30/.08 = $566.25. Therefore, its pre-tax yield must be $75/$566.25 = 13.25%.
27. Federal income tax rates were lower in the 1980s than in the 1970s.
29. Liquidity is an important consideration; as a young firm, Fred's may have only a thin market for its assets.
31. According to expectations theory, it should not; but according to preferred habitat theory or segmented markets theory, it should, because the Fed is unlikely to have any reason to prefer a particular maturity (at least for its long-run portfolio).
33. The expected future short-term rate is higher, so the borrower gets the same rate over the two-year period.

CHAPTER 8

Review Questions

1. This idea is the nominal interest rate parity condition.
3. A fall in the value of the yen lowers the foreign currency price of Japanese exports and raises the yen price of foreign imports to Japan. This would increase demand for Japanese businesses that export or that compete domestically with foreign imports. Japanese consumers would be hurt by higher prices of foreign imports.
5. The euro has appreciated; the Japanese yen and British pound have depreciated.
7. The yen/dollar rate is 300 yen/dollar. The euro/dollar rate is 550/500 = 1.1 euros/dollar.
9. The dollar should appreciate, as demand for U.S.-produced goods rises.
11. The dollar should appreciate, as funds flow into the United States.
13. The new common European currency is the euro. England is not participating in the move to a common currency. When a country gives up its domestic currency it loses control over its domestic money supply (and monetary policy). Some persons may also be reluctant to give up a domestic currency for political reasons.

Analytical Problems

15. Both appreciate relative to the dollar.
17. It is not a sure thing. A depreciation in the value of the dollar versus the yen could wipe out the apparent gain from higher U.S. interest rates.
19. You should invest at home.

21. The United States should benefit from greater investment flow from Japan.
23. a. $EX_r = EX(P)/P_f$ = (200 yen/\$)(\$16/CD)/(3500 yen/CD) = 8/9.
    b. $EX_r = EX(P)/P_f$ = (2 pounds/\$)(\$16/CD)/(6 pounds/CD) = 4/3.
25. $\Delta EX^e/EX = -1\%$, so EX^e = 247.5 yen/dollar.
27. In this case, the difference is maturity (preferred habitat) versus country (currency premium) for assets that are otherwise perfect substitutes. The preference arises because of differences in risk, liquidity, or information across countries versus across maturities. A "segmented markets" analogue is inconsistent with large observed capital flows.
29. Portfolio investors would prefer to invest in Japanese bonds if inflation were lower in Japan (so that the total return is higher) or if the pound were expected to depreciate.

CHAPTER 9

Review Questions

1. The difference is trade today (spot transaction) versus trade in future (forward transaction). A futures contract offers greater liquidity and lower information costs.
3. A hedge transaction reduces risk for the hedger; in speculation, a trader accepts increased risk to try to profit.
5. Options work like life insurance; by paying a small premium, you can hedge against changes in your asset's value.
7. The exchanges guarantee all contracts, so information and search costs are reduced, thereby permitting anonymous trading.
9. At a price of 60, the put is in the money; at a price of 70, neither is in the money; at a price of 80, the call is in the money.
11. You might well disagree, as these markets provide useful risk-sharing benefits, promoting liquidity and the transmission of information.
13. You could buy a put option, which gives the option of selling the underlying security. If the market price of the stock drops below the strike price of the option, you would be able to profit by buying the stock in the market and reselling it at the higher strike price.

Analytical Problems

15. Investors who bought put options would benefit by being able to purchase stock at prices below the strike price in their options contracts. Investors who sold put options would be hurt by having to buy stock at prices above their current market values.
17. Because Tropicana is purchasing oranges, they would be better off if orange prices were low. They could hedge the risk of an increase in orange prices by buying futures contracts.
19. You could buy put options. If interest rates rise, your Treasury bonds lose value, but you make money on the put option; if interest rates fall, your Treasury bonds rise in value, and your puts are worthless.
21. You could buy Treasury put options.

CHAPTER 10

Review Questions

1. Rational expectations make use of all available information. In a market in which investors and traders have rational expectations the market price of an asset equals its fundamental value.
3. When traders and investors use all available information in forming expectations of future rates of return and the cost of trading is low, the equilibrium price of a financial instrument is equal to the optimal forecast based on the available information.
5. There is a bubble. In the future, the bubble is likely to burst. Yes, bubbles have burst many times; the latest prominent examples occurred in 1987 in the United States and in 1991–1992 in Japan.
7. Not always. Usually, an informed trader can profit from noise traders, but only if they do not make the equilibrium price deviate from fundamental value.
9. Fads are characterized by overreaction to good or bad news, so prices do not reflect fundamental value. Someone could profit by investing when there is bad news and selling when there is good news.

Analytical Problems

11. Active portfolio management raises trading costs and provides a lower total return.
13. No; this seasonality in returns is not consistent with efficient markets. An investor could profit by buying at the end of December, and selling at the end of January.
15. Darts are cheaper (but don't balance risk).
17. At a 4% discount rate, you would be willing to pay $D(1 + g)/(i - g) = 1.04 \times \$7/(0.04 - 0.02)$ = \$364. At a 3% discount rate, you would be

willing to pay 1.03 × \$7/(0.03 − 0.02) = \$721. If Bigbuck's dividends grow at only 1% per year you would be willing to pay 1.04 × \$7/(0.04 − 0.01) = \$242.67.

19. In this case, you could adopt a contrarian strategy: Buy after bad news, sell after good news.

CHAPTER 11

Review Questions

1. Financial intermediaries are able to take advantage of economies of scale to reduce transactions costs.
3. Moral hazard occurs when borrowers make different use of borrowed funds than they would have made with their own; adverse selection occurs when bad risks are more likely to accept a financial contract than are good risks. Each makes information asymmetric: the lender may not know what the borrower will do with the funds because of moral hazard, and the lender may not know the riskiness of the borrower because of adverse selection.
5. The "lemons problem" refers to the adverse selection problem that arises from asymmetric information. Because potential investors have difficulty in distinguishing good borrowers from bad borrowers, they offer good borrowers terms they are reluctant to accept. Because banks specialize in gathering information, they are able to overcome this problem.
7. Such provisions are restrictive covenants; banks use them in order to reduce moral hazard problems.
9. A large firm with many shares is more likely to suffer principal-agent problems because organizing challenges to management is more costly.

Analytical Problems

11. The problem is adverse selection. It is likely that only a lemon would be sold so fast. A buyer could circumvent the problem by having a mechanic inspect the car or by getting a guarantee from the dealer (or trusting the dealer's reputation).
13. Moral hazard is less likely to be a problem in (b). Note that you can use this question to explain why large companies often provide stock options as part of executives' compensation packages.
15. Asymmetric information owing to moral hazard and adverse selection makes information costs for external funds higher than for internal funds. No; it depends upon the extent to which problems are solved by debt finance, takeover or threat of takeover, high internal net worth, or greater shareholder control.
17. You would not be happy in the first case because higher default risk reduces the bond's price. In the second case, you would be happy because lower default risk raises the bond's price.
19. No, because business cycles are less pronounced in Japan than in the United States.

CHAPTER 12

Review Questions

1. The five main groups of financial institutions are securities market institutions (investment banks, brokers and dealers, and organized exchanges); investment institutions (mutual funds and finance companies); contractual savings institutions (insurance companies and pension funds); government financial institutions; and depository institutions (commercial banks, savings institutions, and credit unions).
3. No, the NYSE is a secondary market. You are buying the shares of stock from someone else, not from IBM.
5. E-trading is on-line trading conducted over the Internet. Combined with the competition from electronic trading, the effect of e-trading has been to reduce the value of seats on the major stock exchanges.
7. Moral hazard describes the situation where those with insurance take on greater risks than they would have in the absence of insurance. Insurance companies use a variety of methods to reduce moral hazard problems, including deductibles, coinsurance, restrictive covenants, limits on individual claims paid, reserving the right to cancel policies, and the hiring of claims adjustors to investigate claims.
9. Predicting property and casualty losses is more difficult than predicting deaths.
11. Banks address adverse selection by specializing in gathering information about the credit risk of borrowers and by custom-tailoring loans (e.g., including collateral and covenants).
13. Mutual funds pool resources to invest in a diversified portfolio (allowing risk sharing). They also lower transactions costs of investing, increasing liquidity. Mutual funds do not make commercial loans; they pass funds through to existing direct instruments. There is less need for regulation because they just pass funds through, as long as information is made available to

investors.

Analytical Problems

15. These institutions pool risk of death and investment risk that individuals may not be able to do. Self-insurance would be more costly for individuals.
17. Such a country is more likely to develop significant markets in mutual funds. The funds would help savers more than borrowers because mutual funds just buy well-known assets, they do not make commercial loans.
19. If the stock market is efficient, an actively managed fund is unlikely to generate high enough returns to offset its additional costs, so the index fund would be preferred.
21. Yes, past performance is not necessarily a guide to future returns; risk levels may be different; transactions costs may be different; sales loads may be different; liquidity may be different; and taxability may be different.

CHAPTER 13

Review Questions

1. A bank's liabilities, principally deposits and borrowings, are its sources of funds. Its assets, principally loans and securities, are its uses of those funds.
3. Banks are able to offer small savers deposit insurance. This gives them an advantage over other intermediaries in acquiring funds from small savers.
5. Banks borrow (unsecured) from each other at the federal funds rate; repos are secured by underlying securities.
7. The three types of risk faced by banks are credit risk (the risk of default); liquidity risk (the risk of running out of cash when needed); and interest rate risk (the risk that changes in interest rates affect the value of the bank's portfolio).
9. The interest rate charged depends on the default risk of the loans, the opportunity cost of funds, and the cost of funds.
11. Banks manage assets and liabilities to reduce liquidity risk. To meet these goals they mix lending through the federal funds market and repurchase agreements (RPs), and keep enough cash to meet needs without sacrificing too much return by using CDs, RPs, Eurodollars, and federal funds.
13. Off-balance-sheet banking activities include trading in derivative assets, selling liquidity and information services, and securitizing loans. Banks have participated in these activities to capitalize on the transactions-cost and information-cost advantages to augment income.

Analytical Problems

15. Yes, there would still need to be transactions services and a payments system even if there were no need for commercial lending by banks.
17. If depositors had full information on borrowers, there would not be a bank run started by the unfounded fear that bad loans had been made; this would be possible if bankers had private information. However, a run could start for other reasons, such as bad economic times.
19. Banks welcome it because the action reduces the implicit tax on reserves (because reserves pay no interest); banks can then lend the freed reserves at a positive interest rate. In the second case, no, since they would not reduce their level of reserves.
21. First: assets: −$1000 in reserves, liabilities: −$1000 in checkable deposits; Melon: assets: +$1000 in reserves, liabilities: +$1000 in checkable deposits.
23. No, because with such a large proportion of assets in the form of loans—and no securities—it has no defense against a liquidity crisis; also, with no equity cushion, a small bad event could cause the bank to fail.
25. $5 million excess reserves; reserves $10 million, securities $40 million, loans $140 million, deposits $140 million, capital $50 million; −$4 million excess reserves, so borrow $4 million; same as before but reserves $14 million, borrowings from banks $2 million, borrowings from Fed $2 million.
27. $MV = \bullet PV_t = \$1100/1.1 + \$1210/1.1^2 + \$1331/1.1^3 = \$3000$. Duration $= d = \bullet\, t(PV_t/MV) = 1(\$1000/\$3000) + 2(\$1000/\$3000) + 3(\$1000/\$3000) = 1/3 + 2/3 + 3/3 = 2$. $(MV/MV = -d\,[i/(1 + i)] = -2(0.02/1.1) = -0.036$, so the market value falls 3.6%.
29. $GAP = d^A - d^L(L/A) = 13 - 7(93/100) = 6.49$.

CHAPTER 14

Review Questions

1. Under the dual banking system, some banks have national charters, while others have state charters. There are different sets of regulations for

national versus state banks that allow specialization by different types of banks.

3. Historically, political concerns over large banks have been fueled by the public's fear of large banks. These concerns led to the creation of the Federal Reserve System, federal deposit insurance, and branching restrictions.
5. No, it would be efficient. Bank runs may cause contagion, which could lead to the failure of solvent banks.
7. Under the payoff method, the bank's goodwill is lost, but the purchase and assumption method maintains goodwill; purchase and assumption may be attractive to other banks wanting to diversify; the payoff method often costs less because only insured depositors are covered, whereas under the purchase and assumption method uninsured depositors do not lose anything.
9. *Branching Restrictions:* The McFadden Act kept national banks from expanding into other states—owing to fear of the monopoly power of large banks. *Activities Restrictions:* The Glass-Steagall Act kept banks from engaging in nonbank activities (investment banking and brokerage)—to restrict risks taken by banks. Neither regulation seems likely to survive in the future.
11. Banks tried to use bank holding companies (regulated by the Bank Holding Company Act of 1956), nonbank banks (regulated by the Competitive Equality Banking Act of 1987), and ATMs to expand geographically. Most states have allowed at least regional banking.
13. The Glass-Steagall Act of 1933 forced the separation of commercial and investment banking. It was enacted to prevent conflicts of interest in banks. Its restrictions, whittled away in various ways over the years, were repealed by the Gramm-Leach-Bliley Financial Act of 1999.
15. Banks can (1) finance growth opportunities in sectors in which information problems are important; (2) make sure that managers of large-scale enterprises are working to maximize the long-run value of those firms; and (3) reduce costs of financial distress for firms having difficulty meeting their current obligations to banks and other creditors.

Analytical Problems

17. Bankers attempted to deal with the problem of bank runs by operating clearing houses, the members of which agreed to lend funds to banks threatened by a run. A clearing house could deal effectively with localized runs, but could not deal effectively with a common shock, such as a financial panic, that affected most members simultaneously.
19. The Fed was concerned about a contagion effect that might have arisen from the failure of Long-Term Capital Management. Because the Fed helped to arrange for the creditors of Long-Term Capital Management to keep the company in operation, it may have increased the moral hazard problem.
21. You do not care, because you are fully insured. You pull at least $100,000 out of the bank. No, because runs can occur, as they did at Continental Illinois Bank in 1984.
23. Possibly. Before the introduction of federal deposit insurance, depositor discipline forced banks to have a lot of capital; with deposit insurance, depositors are no longer concerned about the banks' level of capital.

CHAPTER 15

Review Questions

1. A lender of last resort should (a) lend to solvent banks that are threatened by a run and (b) have a large source of funds to handle large, common shocks.
3. a. The Penn Central default caused a temporary shock to the supply of funds to commercial paper issuers, as lenders questioned the default risk on commercial paper. This could have disrupted the supply of funds to firms (and thus caused reduced output) if the Fed had not stepped in to accelerate bank lending to firms.
   b. The stock market crash of 1987 could have caused markets to shut down owing to illiquidity of market makers. This would have reduced the flow of information about firms that had issued stock, making it difficult for them to raise funds for investment. The Fed's action prevented a loss of information and allowed smooth working of the system.
5. Innovations to circumvent deposit-rate ceilings included the use of negotiable CDs, repos or overnight Eurodollars, and ATS and NOW accounts.
7. The sudden rise in interest rates in the late 1970s and early 1980s led to big capital losses at S&Ls, which had loaned long-term and borrowed short-term. The problems were magnified owing to the interaction of deregulation, undiscovered fraud, lax supervision, and failure to close insolvent institutions (which assumed additional risks) made losses greater.

9. FIRREA was passed to end the S&L crisis. The act replaced the FSLIC with a new deposit insurance fund, the Savings Association Insurance Fund, organized by the FDIC; it formed the Resolution Trust Corporation to handle thrift insolvencies; it authorized the Office of Thrift Supervision to supervise and examine S&Ls; it raised the deposit insurance premiums of S&Ls; and it reregulated investment activities of S&Ls.
11. A "narrow bank" is one that takes deposits and invests them in safe assets. There is no default risk (except for possible fraud), so there is no need for deposit insurance in a narrow banking system.
13. If a firm goes bankrupt with an underfunded plan, retirees may lose all their income, and the PBGC is by itself inadequate to cover all possibly underfunded plans. This issue is significant because, in the event that many firms fail at the same time (as in a major recession), the bailout of pension plans could be perhaps as large as the S&L crisis.

Analytical Problems

15. Although the Fed had been established as a lender of last resort to help stabilize the banking system, it also felt obliged to maintain a fixed exchange rate under the gold standard. After England left the gold standard in 1931, the Fed took actions (including raising the discount rate) that increased interest rates in order to attract foreign investors and, thereby, maintain the fixed exchange rate. The higher discount rate made it difficult for banks to borrow from the Fed. Hence, the Fed appears to have put its responsibility to maintain the gold standard ahead of its responsibility to maintain the stability of the banking system.
17. You could pay U.S. depositors to move their money to accounts outside the United States so that you could avoid reserve requirements.
19. You would follow strategy (b), as you will surely be closed if you follow strategy (a). Strategy (b) loses money, on average, but its losses are covered by the insurance fund. If you get lucky, the S&L will make money and survive. The consequence of this moral hazard situation is that a socially bad decision is made—one that is inefficient, as it channels funds inappropriately. A regulator could prevent this occurrence by shutting down the S&L before it reaches this point.
21. Here is one possibility: If it is solvent, you could lend to the big bank to get it to cover its securitized mortgages and end the crisis; if it is not solvent, the bank must be shut down, however. In this case, you could organize other banks together to convince them to cover the large banks' losses, paving the way for this by offering discount loans at below-market interest rates.

CHAPTER 16

Review Questions

1. The international banking market exists to satisfy the demand for banking services (risk sharing, liquidity, and information) with lower transactions costs than could be provided by domestic banks, especially with regard to international trade.
3. The leading financial centers are located in the United Kingdom, Japan, the United States, and Switzerland.
5. IBFs are subsidiaries of U.S. banks that do not conduct banking operations in the United States, but cater to customers who trade internationally. They can branch across state lines, do not have to hold required reserves, and are not subject to interest rate ceilings; hence they can be more competitive with foreign banks.
7. A currency swap is the exchange of debt instruments denominated in different currencies. Using currency swaps allows firms to borrow in their own countries so that borrowing costs are lower (because information about the company is more available) and then swap the payments to obtain foreign currency.
9. There is an information problem because trading partners are in a foreign country, so there is limited information about their credit worthiness. Banks and their customers use the bankers' acceptance, in which a bank guarantees repayment by the borrowing firm, earning a fee for its investment in information collecting and monitoring.
11. In a loan syndication individual banks hold fractions of a loan. Loan syndication is often used with Euroloans because they are quite large and would result in a lack of diversification for a single commercial bank.
13. The problem of interest rate risk is reflected in a mismatch of the duration of assets and liabilities. The problem of exchange rate risk is reflected in the mismatch in the value of currencies of assets and liabilities. Possible risk management strategies include hedging with futures or options and using currency swaps.
15. U.K. regulations that banks could not use pounds for overseas loans led to use of the U.S.

dollar. Binding Regulation Q interest rate ceilings in the United States led to U.S. banks acquiring dollar deposits overseas. The role of the lender of last resort becomes complicated in Eurocurrency markets—large multinational banks have deposits and loans in many countries, so which country should be the lender of last resort for these banks is not clear.

Analytical Problems

17. No; bankers' acceptances are negotiable and often sold in the market, just like any other financial asset.
19. Ichi-ball's bank writes a letter of credit and sends it to Big Ball to pay for the balls. When Big Ball ships the baseballs from the United States to Japan, it presents the letter of credit to its own bank in the United States, which pays it in dollars. Big Ball's bank issues a time draft and sends it to Ichi-ball's bank. Ichi-ball's bank pays Big Ball's bank. All that remains is for Ichi-ball to pay off its bank at some point in the future; in the meantime, the bankers' acceptance, which is a liability of Ichi-ball's bank, exists and can be traded in the market.

CHAPTER 17

Review Questions

1. Principal assets include (1) U.S. government securities, held to earn interest, and (2) discount loans to banks, usually due to banks' short-run financing needs. Principal liabilities include (1) currency, held by the nonbank public for transactions purposes, and (2) reserves, held by banks as vault cash or as deposits with the Fed.
3. Currency in circulation = Currency outstanding − Vault cash. Currency in circulation is part of the monetary base.
5. To increase the money supply, the Fed can conduct open market purchase or increase the volume of discount loans. To decrease the money supply, the Fed can conduct open market sales or reduce the volume of discount loans.
7. A single bank has to take into account that funds it loans out may leave the bank, reducing its reserves. For the system as a whole, funds that are loaned out only reduce the total reserves in the system if those funds are converted into currency.
9. (C/D) would have declined steadily.
11. The Fed should increase the monetary base by 10% − 2% = 8%.

Analytical Problems

13. Assets: Δ Loans = +\$100,000; Liabilities: Δ Deposits = +\$100,000; Assets: Δ Reserves = −\$100,000; Liabilities: Δ Deposits = − \$100,000; Δ Assets = 0; Δ Loans = +\$100,000; Δ Reserves = −\$100,000; Δ Liabilities = 0.
15. Required reserves: $(0.14 \times 300) + (0.03 \times 200) = 42 + 6 = 48$; $0.16 \times 300 = 48$. Excess reserves are 0 in both cases.
17. If the elimination of deposit insurance made depositors more concerned about the safety of bank deposits, then we might see a return to larger fluctuations in the currency-deposit ratio, C/D, destabilizing the money multiplier and reducing the Fed's control over the money supply.
19. a. $RR = (0.03 \times 30) + (0.12 \times 150) = 18.9$. $ER = 0$.
    b. Assets: Reserves = 23.9, Securities = 26.1; everything else the same. Total reserves are now 23.9; since RR still equal 18.9, $ER = 5$.
    c. Assets: Loans = 155; Liabilities: Checkable deposits = 185; everything else the same as in (b). $RR = 19.5$, $R = 23.9$, $ER = 4.4$.
    d. Assets: Reserves = 18.9; Liabilities: Checkable deposits = 180; everything else the same as in (c). $RR = 18.9 = R$, so $ER = 0$.
21. $(1 + 100/800)/(100/800 + 0.20 + 40/800) = 3$.
23. No, the demand for U.S. dollars rises, as the United States is a safe haven for wealth.
25. The money multiplier is 1; the Fed cannot affect the money supply beyond the change in the monetary base.
27. a. $B = C + R = [(0.06 + 0.14) \times 2000] + (0.2 \times 2000) = 400 + 400 = 800$; $M1 = C + D = 2400$; $M2 = M1 + N + MM = 2400 + (1.5 \times 2000) + (0.5 \times 2000) = 6400$. Bank A required reserves are \$300 million × 0.14 = \$42 million; total reserves are \$48 million; excess reserves are \$6 million. Economy required reserves are \$2000 billion × 0.14 = \$280 billion; total reserves are \$400 billion; excess reserves are \$120 billion.
    b. Using multiplier formulas: $M1$ multiplier $= (1 + C/D)/[(C/D) + (R/D) + (ER/D)] = 1.2/(0.2 + 0.14 + 0.06) = 3$; $M2$ multiplier $= [(1 + C/D) + (N/D) + (MM/D)]/[(C/D) + (R/D) + (ER/D)] = (1 + 0.2 + 1.5 + 0.5)/(0.2 + 0.14 + 0.06) = 3.2/0.4 = 8$.
    c. Bank A's balance sheet is unchanged; required reserves = \$300 million, so excess reserves = 0. $M1$ multiplier $= (1 + C/D)/[(C/D + (R/D) + ER/D)] = 1.2/(0.2$

+ 0.16) = 3 1/3; $M2$ multiplier = [1 + (C/D) + (N/D) + (MM/D)]/[(C/D) + (R/D) + (ER/D)] = 3.2/0.36 = 8 8/9. (Notice that other variables can be calculated, given the same ratios defined above: Since B = 800, and given the multipliers, we can derive $M1$ = \$2666 2/3 billion, $M2$ = \$7111 1/9 billion; N + MM = $M2$ − $M1$ = \$4444 4/9 billion; N/D + MM/D = 2 implies that D = \$2222 = 2/9 billion; C/D = 0.2 implies that C = \$444 4/9 billion; B = R + C implies that R = \$355 5/9 billion, since B is unchanged at \$800 billion.)

d. Bank A loses \$1.5 million in securities and gains \$1.5 million in reserves. Required reserves are \$42 million, as in part (a). Total reserves are \$49.5 million, so Bank A has \$7.5 million in excess reserves. The new monetary base is \$888 8/9 billion. (*Additional effects:* Multipliers for $M1$ and $M2$ are 3 and 6, as in (b), so with B = \$888 8/9 billion, $M1$ = \$2666 2/3 billion, $M2$ = \$7111 1/9 billion; so $M1$, $M2$, N, MM, D, and C are all the same as in (c), but now reserves are higher (888 − 8/9) − 444 4/9 = \$444 4/9 billion) than in part (c).)

CHAPTER 18

Review Questions

1. Sources of the monetary base are enumerated in Eq. (18.3). Uses of the monetary base are enumerated in Eq. (18.1).
3. Items (a), (c), and (e) are assets of the Fed. Items (b), (d), (f), (g), and (h) are liabilities of the Fed.
5. The Fed's largest asset is its security holdings; its largest liability is Federal Reserve Notes outstanding.
7. If the central bank is not independent, it is likely to monetize the debt, causing inflation. If the central bank is independent, it will not monetize the debt, and inflation may be low even if deficits are high.
9. The start of the Korean War substantially increased government spending and borrowing. The Fed was obliged to buy large quantities of Treasury securities in order to peg the interest rate on them. The Fed was afraid that the consequent increases in the monetary base would cause an acceleration in the inflation rate.

Analytical Problems

11. The Federal Reserve float rises \$1 billion; the monetary base rises \$1.75 billion. (Just add up sources of the base and subtract uses of the base in Eq. (18.3).)
13. Deposit withdrawals need not cause the monetary base to change. An increase in the currency-deposit ratio, C/D, would cause the money multiplier and, therefore, the money supply to fall. The Fed could make discount loans to help banks deal with the withdrawals. An increase in discount loans would increase the monetary base. The Fed might not want to take action to offset this increase in the base if the increase in the base were offsetting the decline in the money multiplier.
15. The monetary base will not necessarily grow by less than it would without the deal (if the Fed has not let the size of the deficit affect monetary policy).
17. Federal Reserve float equals \$2 billion. The Fed loses interest on float. Accordingly, if Federal Reserve float were reduced, the Fed would hold more securities, earning more interest.
19. There is no change in the monetary base (this is called a "sterilized intervention")—the Fed has \$100 million more of foreign-exchange reserves and \$100 million less of securities.
21. The rise in the deficit tends to raise interest rates. To stabilize interest rates, the Fed must increase the monetary base, thereby monetizing the debt.

CHAPTER 19

Review Questions

1. Congress passed the Federal Reserve Act in order to deal with recurring financial panics. The Panic of 1907 had a particular impact on Congressional thinking.
3. The FOMC consists of members of the Board of Governors, the president of the Federal Reserve Bank of New York, and presidents of four other Federal Reserve Banks.
5. The Fed's independence is enhanced by long, overlapping, nonrenewable terms of office and independent financing. The Constitution does not protect the Fed.
7. The Federal Open Market Committee guides the Fed's open market operations.
9. No; stock in Federal Reserve Banks pays only a flat 6% dividend, so there is no opportunity for high profits; in any event, only member banks can own the stock.

11. This observation does apply to the Federal Reserve System. Although in some respects power within the system appears to be decentralized, in fact, power within the system is highly centralized.
13. This is not necessarily true; monetary policy is a type of public policy and so should be the responsibility of elected officials. Also, the Fed's independence may make it more difficult to coordinate monetary and fiscal policy.

Analytical Problems

15. Less developed countries often have more trouble marketing governmental debt than do industrial countries. As a result it is often difficult for a central bank to act independently in a less developed country. Research has shown that the more independent a central bank is, the lower the inflation will be. So, on these grounds we would expect the average inflation rate in less developed countries to be higher than in industrial countries.
17. The Fed is operating a political business cycle to get incumbents reelected. The conclusion would change, as the weakening economy justifies the monetary easing; doubts remain, however, that the Fed would have eased monetary policy as much if an election were not coming up.
19. This might appear to contradict the public-interest view, but it could be that Fed policymakers really were pursuing what they believed were correct policies. As discussed in later chapters, in the early 1970s, policymakers and staff at the Fed (like most macroeconomists at that time) did not understand the difference between short-run and long-run trade-offs between inflation and unemployment. Having never before faced large supply shocks such as those caused by OPEC in the 1970s, the Fed's response didn't give enough attention to reducing inflation. In other words, the Fed tried to pursue socially beneficial policies but lacked the knowledge to do so successfully.
21. Reduce independence: The President of the United States would have much more control over the FOMC; it would be more accountable, as all members of the FOMC would be political appointees, whereas the Federal Reserve bank presidents are not; would lose information about regional concerns, except as they are communicated through political channels (currently at each FOMC meeting there is a "go around" at which each Federal Reserve bank president discusses conditions in each district).
23. Because the European Central Bank is newly created it may feel that it is particularly important to demonstrate its independence from European politicians. It may be particularly inclined to demonstrate its independence of political pressure from Germany, the most economically powerful state in Europe.
25. This is not true. The Fed may feel that its independence is necessary to carry out the public interest, so it mobilizes groups that support it to help guarantee its independence.

CHAPTER 20

Review Questions

1. When the Fed was set up its main purpose was to use discount loans to stop bank panics. It only began using open market operations during the 1920s.
3. The Fed has greater control over open market operations, considers them to be more flexible, and considers them to be easier to implement than its other monetary policy tools.
5. Under the new system for the United States, healthy banks may borrow at the federal funds rate; weaker banks pay a premium.
7. Maintenance periods are two weeks.
9. Reserve requirements have a limited effect on the liquidity of an individual bank. In addition, improvements in markets for loan sales and the growing number of nondeposit sources of funds make liquidity crises less likely, regardless of the volatility of depositors' withdrawals.
11. Discount lending can still offer a buffer for banks to obtain funds, particularly during a crisis (such as September 11, 2001).
13. A *Fed watcher* is someone who interprets what the Fed is doing and possibly predicts what the Fed is likely to do in the future.
15. Dynamic operations are for implementing monetary policy. Defensive operations are for offsetting minor disturbances to the economy that are unrelated to the business cycle.

Analytical Problems

17. The money supply decreases by 8 × $1 billion, or $8 billion.
19. The Fed will use defensive open market operations to increase money supply, offsetting the seasonal demand without a change in interest rates.
21. a. Expansionary
    b. Contractionary
23. The Fed's supply of reserves would become a vertical line. An open market purchase would have a larger effect on the equilibrium exchange rate.